GREATER MESOAMERICA

GREATER MESOAMERICA

The Archaeology of West and Northwest Mexico

EDITED BY
MICHAEL S. FOSTER AND SHIRLEY GORENSTEIN

The University of Utah Press
Salt Lake City

© 2000 by The University of Utah Press. All rights reserved.

First paperback printing 2010

Partial funding for this volume provided by
the Center for Indigenous Studies in the Americas (CISA), Phoenix, Arizona

14 13 12 11 10   1 2 3 4 5

 The Defiance House Man colophon is a registered trademark
of the University of Utah Press. It is based upon a four-foot-tall,
Ancient Puebloan pictograph (late PIII) near Glen Canyon, Utah

LIBRARY OF CONGRESS CATALOGING-IN-PUBLICATION DATA

Greater Mesoamerican : the archaeology of West and Northwest Mexico
/ edited by Michael S. Foster and Shirley Gorenstein
p. cm.
Includes bibliographical references and index.
ISBN 978-0-87480-950-3
1. Indians of Mexico—Antiquities. 2. Indians of Mexico—Mexico,
North—Antiquities. 3. Mexico—Antiquities I. Foster, Michael S., 1947–.
II. Gorenstein, Shirley.
F1219. G738 2000
972'.01—DC21   00-012315

In memory of J. Charles Kelley,
student, teacher, and friend

CONTENTS

Figures and Tables   ix
Foreword   xiii
Preface   xv

ONE
West and Northwest Mexico: The Ins and Outs of Mesoamerica
Shirley Gorenstein and Michael S. Foster   3

TWO
The Late and Terminal Preclassic in Southeastern Guanajuato:
Heartland or Periphery?
Charles A. Florance   21

THREE
A Summary of the Archaeology of North-Central Mesoamerica:
Guanajuato, Querétaro, and San Luis Potosí
Beatriz Braniff C.   35

FOUR
The Evolution and Decline of a Core of Civilization:
The Teuchitlán Tradition and the Archaeology of Jalisco
Phil C. Weigand   43

FIVE
Tarascans and Their Ancestors: Prehistory of Michoacán
Helen Perlstein Pollard   59

CONTENTS

SIX
Tarascan External Relationships
Helen Perlstein Pollard 71

SEVEN
Prehispanic Cultural Development along the Southern Coast of West Mexico
Joseph B. Mountjoy 81

EIGHT
The Prehistory of Mexico's Northwest Coast:
A View from the Marismas Nacionales of Sinaloa and Nayarit
Stuart D. Scott and Michael S. Foster 107

NINE
The Aztatlán Mercantile System: Mobile Traders and the Northwestward
Expansion of Mesoamerican Civilization
J. Charles Kelley 137

TEN
Archaeology of Southern Zacatecas:
The Malpaso, Juchipila, and Valparaiso-Bolaños Valleys
Peter F. Jiménez Betts and J. Andrew Darling 155

ELEVEN
The Archaeoastronomical System in the Río Colorado Chalchihuites Polity,
Zacatecas: An Interpretation of the Chapín 1 Pecked Cross-Circle
J. Charles Kelley and Ellen Abbott Kelley 181

TWELVE
The Archaeology of Durango
Michael S. Foster 197

THIRTEEN
Recent Advances in Chihuahuan Archaeology
Ronna Jane Bradley 221

FOURTEEN
The Archaeological Traditions of Sonora
María Elisa Villalpando 241

FIFTEEN
From Tzintzuntzan to Paquimé: Peers or Peripheries in Greater Mesoamerica?
Michael W. Spence 255

References 263
Contributors 297
Index 301

FIGURES AND TABLES

FIGURES

1.1. The northern frontier of Mesoamerica as variously defined 5
1.2. Major sites and areas in west and northwest Mexico 9
1.3. Natural regions of central and northern Mexico 10
1.4. Climatic types of central and northern Mexico 11
1.5. Mean annual precipitation in central and northern Mexico 12
2.1. Chupícuaro and neighboring sites 22
2.2. Chupícuaro vessel forms 23
2.3. A Chupícuaro slant-eyed, thin figurine 23
2.4. The location of the El Rayo cemetery near the original Chupícuaro village 25
2.5. Distribution of pottery in pit 1, near the original Chupícuaro village 26
2.6. Red-on-brown and black and red-on-brown rim sherds 26
2.7. Early Chupícuaro, Chupícuaro, and Mixtlán settlement patterns in the Puroaguita survey area 27
2.8. Chimalhuacán Type I figurines and distinctive rim sherd 30
2.9. Chronologies from the Basin of Mexico, southern Guanajuato, and the highland lake district of Jalisco 33
3.1. North-central Mesoamerica 36
3.2. Preclassic period chronological sequences of the north-central mesoamerican frontier and central Mexico 37
3.3. Morales Red-on-buff ceramics 38
3.4. Morales Polychrome (black and white-on-red) 39
3.5. Chronological sequences of the north-central mesoamerican frontier and central Mexico 40
3.6. Type I figurine, El Cóporo, Guanajuato 41
3.7. Type I figurine head, El Cóporo, Guanajuato 41
4.1. Teuchitlán tradition and other west Mexican sites 44
4.2. Chronology for the Teuchitlán region 46
4.3. El Opeño style shaft tomb near Citala in the Ahualulco-Sayula Basin 47
4.4. Huitzilapa (Cerro de las Navajas precinct) 48
4.5. Cerro de los Monos shaft tomb 48
4.6. Temporal correlation of artifact types, ceramic types, architecture, and phases for the Teuchitlán tradition 49
4.7. The Guachimonton Complex, Teuchitlán, Jalisco 51

5.1. Major archaeological sites in Michoacán 60
5.2. General cultural sequences for Michoacán and neighboring areas 61
5.3. General chronology for Michoacán 61
5.4. A *yácata* at the main platform at Tzintzuntzan 67
5.5. Features and areas recorded at and in the vicinity of Tzintzuntzan 68
5.6. A chacmool from Ihuatzio 69
5.7. A Tarascan polychrome vessel 69
6.1. The Protohistoric Tarascan empire 72
6.2. Towns and limits of the Tarascan empire 73
6.3. How enemy towns are conquered (*Relacíon de Michoacán*) 77
7.1. Archaeological sites along the coast of west Mexico 82
7.2. The Matanchén site 83
7.3. San Blas Complex ceramics 85
7.4. Ceramic figurine head from Ixtapa 87
7.5. Hollow rattle figurine 89
7.6. Shaft Tomb tradition hollow figurine 91
7.7. Shaft Tomb tradition burial offering 91
7.8. Site map of El Palmar de Santo Domingo 93
7.9. Aztatlán Incised jar placed as an offering at Las Vegas 95
7.10. Aztatlán Red-on-buff Incised bowl recovered from La Pedrera 98
7.11. Aztatlán cylindrical spiked incense burner 98
7.12. Mazapan-style figurines recovered from the vicinity of Ixtapa 99
7.13. Site map of Arias 101
7.14. Stone figurine from El Ranchito in the Banderas Valley 105
8.1. Archaeological sites along the coast of west Mexico 108
8.2. Coastal progradation in the area of the Marismas Nacionales 109
8.3. Phase schemes for major sites along the coast of west Mexico 110
8.4. Black-banded ware 113
8.5. Early Chametla Polychrome bowls 114
8.6. Middle Chametla Polychrome, Plain and Engraved 115
8.7. Chametla ceramic types 116
8.8. Aztatlán Polychrome pottery 117
8.9. Cerro Isabel Engraved pottery 118
8.10. Guasave ceramic types 119
8.11. Guasave ceramic types 120
8.12. Guasave Polychrome bowls 121
8.13. Early Culiacán Polychrome 123
8.14. Middle Culiacán Polychrome 124
8.15. Late Culiacán Polychrome 124
8.16. Culiacán incised wares 125
8.17. Amapa ceramic types 126
8.18. Amapa ceramic types 127
8.19. Amapa ceramic types 128
8.20. Shell mound in the Marismas Nacionales 129
8.21. The Marismas Nacionales 130
8.22. Figurine fragments from El Calón 133
9.1. Trading trips of Tarascan mobile traders 138
9.2. Late Classic period expansion of West Coast mobile traders 143
9.3. Early Aztatlán trade system in west and northwest Mexico 145
9.4. Late Aztatlán trade system in west and northwest Mexico 148
10.1. Archaeological traditions and cultures of northwest Mexico 156
10.2. La Quemada prehistoric road system 158
10.3. Site of La Quemada 161
10.4. La Quemada 162
10.5. Votive pyramid at La Quemada 162
10.6. Lower terraces at La Quemada with the ball court and Hall of Columns 163
10.7. Early Chalchihuites and Malpaso ceramics 164
10.8. Tepozan negative paint wares of the La Quemada complex 165
10.9. Suchil Red-on-brown jar (Chalchihuites culture) 165
10.10. Soyate Red-on-cream and red-on-brown ceramics of the La Quemada complex 166
10.11. Vista Paint Cloisonné, Alta Vista, Chalchihuites 167
10.12. Type I figurine of the La Quemada complex 167
10.13. Interaction spheres of north-central and northwestern Mesoamerica 168
10.14. Negative polychrome plate, Apozol, Juchipila Valley 169
10.15. Negative polychrome tripod bowl, Apozol, Juchipila Valley 169
10.16. Horned-style figurines, Cerro Encantado, Jalisco 170
10.17. Negative polychrome tripod bowl, Apozol, Juchipila Valley 170
10.18. Negative polychrome tripod molcajete, Juchipila Valley 171
10.19. Juchipila Valley ceramics 172
10.20. Negative paint polychrome annular base bowl, Juchipila Valley 173

10.21. Obsidian raw material distribution networks in the north-central frontier of Mesoamerica 176
10.22. Distribution of prismatic blades from raw material sources in the north-central mesoamerican frontier 177
11.1. Ceremonial center of Alta Vista, Chalchihuites, Zacatecas 182
11.2. Labyrinth Observatory at Alta Vista 183
11.3. Chalchihuites astronomical array 184
11.4. Chapín 1 pecked cross petroglyph 185
11.5. Basic numerology of the Chapín 1 pecked cross 186
11.6. Representations of caiman-like figures 187
11.7. Suchil Red-on-brown bowl from the site of Potrero del Calichal with a possible representation of a robed priest 187
11.8. Chapín 1 petroglyph with Solar Year 1, Veintena 1 represented 190
11.9. Chapín 1 petroglyph with Solar Year 1, Veintena 2 represented 192
11.10. Chapín 1 petroglyph, 360 days plus 5 days *nemontemi*; end of Solar Year 1, Veintena 18 192
11.11. Chapín 1 petroglyph, end of Solar Year 1, beginning of Solar Year 2 193
11.12. Chapín 1 petroglyph, end of Solar Year 4, Veintena 18 193
12.1. Archaeological sites and areas of Durango 198
12.2. Fluted point from Durango 199
12.3. Chalchihuites phase sequences 204
12.4. Ayala phase ceramics 206
12.5. Neveria Red-on-brown (Las Joyas phase) 207
12.6. Otinapa Red-on-white (Río Tunal phase) 208
12.7. Calera phase ceramics 209
12.8. Molino Red-on-cream (Molino phase) 210
12.9. Weicker site compounds 212
12.10. Possible tumpline headbands from Cueva de San Pablo 213
12.11. Examples of tabular erect cranial deformation 214
12.12. Petroglyphs from the Zape observatory 216
12.13. Loma San Gabriel site 217
13.1. Major sites in Chihuahua 222
13.2. Site map of Paquimé 227
13.3. View from the House of the Well to the main plaza at Paquimé 228
13.4. Macaw nesting boxes at Paquimé 229
14.1. Archaeological sites, traditions, and ecological boundaries of Sonora 242
14.2. A corral site in the Altar Valley 244
14.3. La Playa 245
14.4. Cerro de Trincheras 246
14.5. Figurines from Huatabampo 247
14.6. Seri Tiburón Plain tecomates 249

TABLES

Table 5.1. Genealogy of the Tarascan kings 66
Table 6.1. Tarascan-Aztec military engagements 77
Table 6.2. Pátzcuaro Basin obsidian sources 78

FOREWORD

THIS BOOK REPRESENTS the culmination of nearly seven years' hard work by the two editors, Michael S. Foster and Shirley Gorenstein, and the many authors who have contributed chapters on the archaeology of west and northwest Mexico. The project was partially supported by the Center for Indigenous Studies in the Americas (CISA), an organization based in Phoenix, Arizona, established to promote archaeological and anthropological research in the indigenous peoples and natural history of the Americas. CISA seeks to contribute to a fuller knowledge of the archaeology, cultural diversity, ethnology, and arts of Native Americans. It is the nonprofit arm of Soil Systems, Inc. (SSI), a cultural resource management firm in Phoenix. CISA was founded in 1990 by the senior staff at SSI as a means of conducting archaeological research in the Americas outside compliance-based contract and academic settings. Since 1990, CISA has completed a number of research projects, provided funding for publications, and awarded grants for travel, conference registration, and analysis for scholars working in the New World. CISA has conducted projects in Mexico, has provided a mechanism for grant-sponsored round tables such as the one published here, and in 1998 began a long-term excavation project and archaeological field school on the north coast of Peru. Results of CISA-sponsored research are disseminated to the scientific and public communities through symposia, lectures, and publication in scholarly journals and other related publications. One of CISA's programs is a Round Table Series on New World Prehistory, which brings scholars together to discuss current methodological, cultural historical, and theoretical problems in New World prehistory. The series is designed to be a working conference with published proceedings. This volume represents the publication of the first CISA round table, Cultural Dynamics of Precolumbian West and Northwest Mexico, which was held in Phoenix in February 1992.

The conference was supported by the Wenner-Gren Foundation for Anthropological Research Conference Grant Number 48-81, administered by Laurie Obbink, the conference program associate at Wenner-Gren. The conference grant paid for the travel and subsistence of the participants and some local support and materials. The number of conference participants was larger than the number of authors contributing chapters to this book. Several conference participants were unable to prepare a chapter because of other commitments or were simply observers at the conference. It was held at the historic Hotel San Carlos in downtown Phoenix. The intimate setting allowed the participants to concentrate for three days on discussions of the state of archaeological knowledge in west and northwest Mesoamerica and to agree, or disagree, in informal but active debates about how our current understanding of this understudied region articulates with other regions of Mesoamerica and the southwestern United States. At the end of each day discussions continued over dinner at various venues around town.

At the conclusion of the conference a schedule for completion of publishable chapters by the participants was agreed on. Although some time has passed since the conference was held, the volume has now come together and will be a lasting contribution to our knowledge of the archaeology of west and northwest Mexico. CISA is proud to contribute to the cost of the publication of this book and to support the efforts and hard work of Foster, Gorenstein, the authors, and the University of Utah Press. This volume fills a significant void of underpublished information on an important area of Mesoamerica and begins to provide the links to other cultures in Mesoamerica and cultures in the southwestern United States. I hope this CISA Conference publication will continue to spark interest and debate for some time to come.

A number of CISA staff and volunteers helped behind the scenes to make the inaugural round table a success. Adrian S. White, vice president, Christine K. Robinson, and Douglas R. Mitchell all helped with logistics, registration, travel and local arrangements and still found time to attend most of the conference. Neil McCallum, long-time CISA supporter and conference volunteer, was the real reason the local arrangements and evening dinners went so smoothly. Neil has also maintained a strong interest in seeing this book completed and has provided financial support toward this effort.

Cory Dale Breternitz
President
Center for Indigenous Studies in the Americas
Phoenix, Arizona
August 1999

PREFACE

THE LAST FIFTEEN years have seen a relative explosion of interest in the Precolumbian archaeology of west and northwest Mexico. Both Mexican and foreign archaeologists are recognizing the research potential of the region's vast unexplored archaeological record. Scholarship is being greatly aided by the support and archaeologists of the various Instituto Nacional de Antropología e Historia Centro Regionals across the area. Their commitment to the study of their nation's unique and varied prehistory is exemplary. The role and importance of ancient west and northwest Mexico in the development of Mesoamerica as a whole can be ignored no longer.

For the most part, the last seventy years of anthropological and archaeological research in this area was carried out by a handful of dedicated individuals, including Donald Brand, Carl Sauer, Isabel Kelly, J. Charles Kelley, Charles Di Peso, Campbell Pennington, Carroll Riley, Pedro Armillas, Beatriz Braniff, Gordon Ekholm, Wigberto Jiménez Moreno, J. Alden Mason, Roman Piña Chan, Walter Taylor, Robert Lister, and Clement Meighan. These individuals, most of whom are no longer with us, were and are truly pioneers in the archaeology of west and northwest Mexico. Their work laid the foundations on which the research of today and the foreseeable future is built. They dedicated their lives to their work. It will be many years before their contributions are matched or overshadowed.

What follows in this book are the first major syntheses of the archaeology of west and northwest Mexico since the publication of the *Handbook of Middle American Indians* by the University of Texas Press in the late 1960s and early 1970s. As with any such effort, however, topics, areas, and alternate views are shorted or overlooked in favor of the authors' perspectives and space limitations. Nevertheless, this work is presented as a broad-ranging introduction to the archaeology of some of the least studied areas in ancient Mexico. It is hoped that it will serve not only as a valuable reference but as a point of genesis for future research as well.

In the early 1990s, the Center for Indigenous Studies in the Americas (CISA) initiated a Round Table Series on New World Prehistory, designed to bring together scholars who were working in the same region or on similar issues in the interpretation of prehistory or archaeological and historical methods and theory. The inaugural round table was entitled Cultural Dynamics of Precolumbian West and Northwest Mexico.

The conference was held in Phoenix, Arizona, as a three-day seminar. The participants were scholars from the United States and Mexico who had done primary fieldwork in west and northwest Mexico, who had written the fundamental interpretations of the data, and who had thoughtfully offered explanations for the dynamics of cultural change and connection. It was an intense experience. There were formal presentations, critiques, debates, and long and searching discussions. After we parted, the discussion continued through the writing and editing of the chapters. All but one of the chapters in this volume were presented, in one form or another, as part of the conference, and some of the papers presented there were not included because of the direction the final publication took. The editors appreciate the time and effort put in by the chapter authors. The editors would also like to thank two of the discussants, Jeffrey Dean and E. Charles Adams. Jeff and Chuck provided a southwestern perspective on the issues that arose. Because of the final content of the volume, however, they were not asked to provide any written commentary.

Funding for the round table was provided by the Wenner-Gren Foundation for Anthropological Research and CISA. We very much appreciate the vision of Sydel Silverman, president of Wenner-Gren, who supported this conference as a contribution to the program of fostering anthropological knowledge. We also appreciate the valuable assistance of Laurie Obbink, the conference program associate, who provided us much useful guidance.

The publication of this book is, in part, supported by a grant from CISA. The editors thank Cory Dale Breternitz, president of CISA, for his support. We also thank Neil McCallum for his support of the publication of this volume through a gift to CISA. In addition, Neil provided varied and generous assistance during the conference which was greatly appreciated by the participants and guests.

The editors also thank Peter Jiménez Betts and J. Andrew Darling for varied editorial and other assistance. We are grateful in addition to Jeff Grathwohl, director of the University of Utah Press, and his staff for their professionalism, assistance, and support of this project.

Finally, the editors, speaking on behalf of the non-Mexican authors, would like to thank the nation of Mexico and its generous people for allowing us the privilege to work in their country.

Michael S. Foster
Shirley Gorenstein

My first fieldwork in west Mexico started in early 1970 at the site of Cerro Encantado under the direction of the late Betty Bell and her husband, William Winnie. I will always be grateful to Betty and Bill for introducing me to the wonders and glories of Mexico. The memories of that adventure thirty years ago are still vivid. La Quemada was the first mesoamerican site I saw. Several years later, working at the site of El Grillo on the outskirts of Guadalajara, I had the opportunity to meet J. Charles and Ellen Kelley, Stuart Scott, Phil Weigand, and Joe Mountjoy at an end-of-the-field-season get-together in Ajijic. These people formed the core of investigators working in west Mexico beginning in the late 1960s, and their numerous and varied contributions continue three decades later. The Kelleys and Stuart Scott were to provide me with many opportunities and play significant roles in my career in Mexican archaeology. Their friendship and guidance are appreciated.

Regardless of all the help and effort cited above, this book could never have been completed without the support and extraordinary patience of my wife, Ann, and my daughter, Megan. I would also like to thank Megan for compiling and formatting several of the tables that appear in this volume.

Michael S. Foster

I began my fieldwork in Mexico in 1966, and since then I have become indebted not only to many Mexican and North American colleagues but also to institutions, particularly the Instituto Nacional de Antropología e Historia and Rensselaer Polytechnic Institute, for permitting and supporting my research. I am especially indebted to Sydel Silverman, who has understood both anthropologically and philosophically the nature and effect that gatherings of researchers have in facilitating and enhancing scholarship.

Shirley Gorenstein

GREATER MESOAMERICA

CHAPTER ONE

WEST AND NORTHWEST MEXICO

The Ins and Outs of Mesoamerica

SHIRLEY GORENSTEIN AND MICHAEL S. FOSTER

IN THE HISTORY of New World archaeology, one of the most successful knowledge-producing fields is mesoamerican studies. It is an area in which many archaeologists have worked, it has captured a big slice of the funding pie, and it has generated large numbers of articles, so large that it has propagated its own specialized journals. And there is, of course, its ubiquitous presence in popular culture worlds such as museums, film, television, and novels.

There are many ways of understanding why this happened. Certainly, an easy and ready answer is that beginning in the sixteenth century, Europeans appreciated in Mexico what was most like their own culture. The native cultures, for example, had a materiality, displayed in monumental architecture, sculpture, and portable art, that was accessible and familiar though, paradoxically, not altogether comprehensible. Although there was a change in emphasis, it was this materiality that guided Europeans in succeeding centuries. The pursuit of these objects became less equated with their ability to be converted immediately and literally into European wealth and more connected to their place in the economy and aesthetics of the European art world. So, whereas sixteenth-century Europeans melted gold portable art into ingots, later Europeans collected art objects because they had been declared valuable in their original form.

Another, more complex answer to the question of the Europeans' intense interest in Mesoamerica lies not directly in art but in history and archaeology, disciplines that were sometimes connected and sometimes disconnected to art. Because the materiality of Mesoamerica related to what Europeans studied in their own history and archaeology—namely, cities or centers and the artifacts of wars, kingdoms, and royalty—scholars began to investigate these cultural dimensions in the parts of the New World where they appeared to have existed. In this endeavor, they relied on observations of those who lived in the sixteenth century and actually saw the viable Prehispanic cultures or their ruins.

These observers, however, were caught in their own historical circumstances. Would archaeology and ethnohistory be different, for example, if the Spaniards had first landed on the west rather than the east coast; if they had encountered the Tarascans before they encountered the Maya, Tlaxcalans, and Aztecs; if they had not become enmeshed in central Mexican politics at the outset? But that is not what happened. The Spaniards focused first on central Mexico, and it became their administrative base for three hundred years. Acknowledging that historical circumstance allows us to consider that the course of archaeology and ethnohistory in the area may be more about the history of knowledge than the knowledge itself. If scholars are aware that they may be buffeted by the winds of the history of their own disciplines, it is more likely that they will be able to critique concepts and rubrics in the discipline that are commonly accepted without questioning.

Considerable effort has been put into the details of the spatial and conceptual definitions of "Mesoamerica." But the bases for the definitions have been taken for granted. Archaeologists working in Mexico and parts of Central America are often unsure if they are indeed working in "Mesoamerica." Part of the purpose of this book is to answer this question by examining critically the meaning of the term itself. The term, its meaning and usage, has been largely unexamined for more than fifty years.

It is widely acknowledged that the baseline essay for the discussion of "Mesoamerica" as space and as a concept is by Paul Kirchhoff, written in 1943 and titled "Mesoamerica." In defining Mesoamerica, Kirchhoff accepted the organizing principle of taxonomy, which had been a powerful intellectual tool in the nineteenth century and the first part of the twentieth century. In this he followed ethnologists and archaeologists such as Otis Mason, Clark Wissler, and William H. Holmes, who were in the throes of sorting out the knowledge accumulated by those who had preceded them. They applied taxonomy to space. Cultural traits were selected and then plotted geographically, and boundaries (forming the taxa) were drawn depending on where these traits waned and waxed. In 1914, Holmes suggested five divisions for the space between North and South America: Northern Mexico, Middle Mexico, Southern Mexico, Maya Province, and Central America. Quite consciously, Kirchhoff began with his predecessors' work when, in his first sentence, he referred to "geographic classifications of native culture of America." But his concern was that political geography had superseded anthropology in setting the boundaries for the continents and subcontinents of the New World. There is North and South America, of course, but what lies between is not so clearly agreed on, he said. Is it "Mexico and Central America" (all of Mexico to the eastern border of Panama)? Is it "Middle America" (an area that sometimes excludes the north of Mexico and sometimes includes the Antilles)? What Kirchhoff argued is that this confusion could be ameliorated if anthropological perspectives were more strongly put to the task of defining the space between North and South America.

Anthropologists had plotted cultures over the whole of the New World on the basis of subsistence patterns. The result was the creation of "large areas," namely (1) food gatherers, hunters, and fishers, (2) interior cultivators, (3) superior cultivators, and (4) inferior cultivators. Yet culture was not entirely homogeneous in these "large areas." Smaller areas had greater cultural homogeneity, noted Kirchhoff. Within the "large area," then, there were "superareas" and "subareas" with differing degrees of homogeneity. He declared Mesoamerica a "superarea" where cultures were fundamentally alike. How were they alike? He began with a nineteenth-century notion of "Tribe" and defined mesoamerican tribes on the basis of the languages they spoke at the time of the Conquest and on the affiliation of the tribes' languages with one another. Moving back and forth between a tentative notion of the geographic limits of Mesoamerica and the distribution of tribes that would define Mesoamerica, he noted that three linguistic groups (Zoque-Maya, Maya-Otomangue, and the Nahua family) reach both the northern and southern limits of what would be called Mesoamerica. The Tarascans, he said, stand alone as speakers of a language not yet classified. Unexpectedly, he viewed the disconnection of Tarascan from other languages as an indicator of Tarascan speakers' ancient occupation of Mesoamerica. He set the northern boundary "more or less from the Río Panuco [East Coast] to the [Río] Sinaloa [West Coast], passing along the [Río] Lerma" (Figure 1.1). Having defined the geographical extent of Mesoamerica through these means, Kirchhoff went on to list "traits exclusively . . . or typically Mesoamerican," "traits common to Mesoamerica and to other American superareas," and "traits significant for their absence in Mesoamerica" (1943:107).

Despite his disquisition on method and the pains he took to define his categories, Kirchhoff did not critique them. In the end, the exclusive mesoamerican traits are essentially Aztec with a recognition of Mayan-based cultural antecedents.

In the decades following Kirchhoff's essay, parallel and peculiarly separated discussions of Mesoamerica were carried on. One concentrated on the geography of Mesoamerica, trying to determine boundaries. The other focused on the form and content of society and culture and the dynamic of change and was bound up with concepts of the nature and evolution of society, civilization, and urbanization. Initially, it seemed that these two discussions hardly had the same intellectual weight: the former was considered far less important than the latter. But, as boundary studies have shown, the struggle about where to draw boundaries is a struggle about their deepest meaning. Disputes about placing a region (or

Figure 1.1. The northern frontier of Mesoamerica as variously defined.

object or person) inside or outside the boundary reflect in a powerful way the basic meaning of what the boundary is meant to enclose and define.

Eric Wolf, in *Sons of the Shaking Earth* (1959), provided a diachronic and ecological perspective to the matter of boundary. In his definition of "Middle America," he focused on the central highlands and from there moved north and south. For the north, he wrote, "No major barrier of land and sea marks the boundary between the central highlands and the north. It is increasing aridity and decreasing rainfall that divide the two regions" (Wolf 1959:8).

In 1964, Pedro Armillas (1964a) forthrightly defined Mesoamerica. His opening sentence interpreted the Kirchhoff article: "The term 'Mesoamerica' has been defined by Kirchhoff . . . to refer to the culture area comprising the Mexican and Mayan civilizations." He also tried to give a precise northern boundary for Mesoamerica. The boundary he drew was essentially the same as Kirchhoff's, but he described it more exactly. It began at the mouth of the Río Sinaloa on the Pacific, crossed over the Sierra Madre Occidental, and continued south along the edge of its piedmont to the plateau of the Río Lerma middle valley (Bajío). It proceeded northeast following the Río Moctezuma across the eastern escarpment of the uplands, along the drainages of the Ríos Tamuin and Tamesi to the mouth of the Río Soto la Marina on the Gulf Coast. The Kirchhoff-Armillas boundary descended from about 25° north latitude to about 20° north latitude, just to the outskirts of Wolf's central highlands, and then rose north again to its eastern terminus at about 22° north latitude.

In 1969, Armillas focused his attention on the northern boundary again. He expanded on Wolf's notion of boundary flexibility. Climate underlies subsistence, which is connected to cultural configurations. But over time, especially over long periods, climate changes. Aridity and annual rainfall vary. If climate and its cultural consequences changed, the northern boundary would vary as well. He referred to the changing boundary as a soft frontier, differentiating it from a hard frontier. Depending on cultural configuration, northwest Mexico could be inside or outside Mesoamerica. For the Postclassic, Armillas put the central part of the northern frontier inside Mesoamerica at between the 22° and 23° parallels, two to three degrees farther north than he had put it previously. Although the underpinnings were well reasoned, the conclusion that west and northwest Mexico was on the one hand inside Mesoamerica and on the other hand outside Mesoamerica gave west and northwest Mexico an ambiguous position. Most mesoamericanists accepted this inside/outside concept, and it was clearly expressed, although in different ways, in subsequent scholarly literature.

In 1966, Gordon Willey, in his influential textbook, acknowledged Kirchhoff's view of the northern boundary, but he drew his northern boundary with a simple, barely sloping line that connected his Pacific and Gulf termini (Figure 1.1). It started at the Río Fuerte in Sinaloa at about 26° north latitude and ended just south of 24° north latitude at the mouth of the Río Sota la Marina in Tamaulipas. Although that line appears to provide the most inclusive boundary for Mesoamerica, counting in most of northern and all of western Mexico, it is subverted by the use of "subareas." Willey defines and sets the boundaries for ten subareas. His tenth and last subarea is "the West and Northern Frontier." This vast space is, he noted, "of relatively lower cultural contour than the [other nine subareas] . . . and it appears as definitely derivative of the main developments in the south and east" (Willey 1966:89). Although different from Armillas's climate-change view, Willey's solution to what to do with northwest and west Mexico was to continue its ambiguous inside/outside position.

The editors of the *Handbook of Middle American Indians*, published in the 1960s and 1970s, recognized both "Middle America" and "Mesoamerica" without explicitly launching a discussion about the meaning of these terms. Nevertheless, the inside/outside position of west and northwest Mexico was reiterated and thereby strengthened. Several volumes in the series identified two areas: a "Northern Mesoamerica" and a "Southern Mesoamerica." On the one hand, central Mexico and northwest and west Mexico were discussed in the Northern Mesoamerica volumes. On the other hand, the map of Mesoamerica in the theoretical article in Volume 1 of the *Handbook of Middle American Indians* (Willey et al. 1964:Figure 22) has a northern boundary dipping deeply south to meet the Río Lerma, and the prose describes the regional subdivision of "Western Mexico and the Northern Frontier" as "a region containing a number of distinctive cultural expressions, all somewhat less highly developed and seemingly peripheral to the major centers of civilization in regions farther to the east" (Willey et al. 1964:475).

In 1972, Muriel Porter Weaver, in *The Aztecs, Maya, and Their Predecessors* (1972, 1981, 1993), braced the inside/outside concept by refining the northern Mesoamerica boundary's chronological and spatial dimensions. She regarded pre-Postclassic Michoacán, Jalisco, Nayarit, Colima, and Sinaloa as outside Mesoamerica (Weaver 1972:7, 37). Recognizing the cultural and societal changes that took place in the north and west beginning around A.D. 1000, she included some previously categorized "outside" regions inside Mesoamerica. Her Postclassic Mesoamerica, then, included Michoacán, Jalisco, Nayarit, Colima, Sinaloa, and parts of Durango and Zacatecas (Figure 1.1).

The baseline essay for discussions of the form and content of society was written by Julian Steward in 1949 and called "Cultural Causality and Law: A Trial Formulation of the Development of Early Civilizations." The essay found a wider readership when it was republished in *Theory of Culture Change* (Steward 1955). In his discussion of five "early civilizations," Steward noted that "Meso-America" meant "Mexico and the Maya area" (Steward 1955:185). His description of "eras" gave a more detailed account of what he meant by "Mexico." For the source of data of the "Formative era of basic technologies and folk culture," Steward (1955:192) named Zacatenco and Ticomán in highland Mexico; for the "era of regional development and florescence," he referred to Teotihuacán and Monte Albán in central Mexico (Steward 1955:194). For the last era before the Spanish Conquest, which he called "cyclical conquest," he recognized Toltec, Aztec, and Monte Albán and what he called "Tzintzuntzan Tarascan." But the last-mentioned was not used again in the essay or book. He referred to the "inroads of the [northern] Chichimecs into the Valley of Mexico," apparently in relation to the origins of the Toltec or Aztec or both.

Certainly this essay was a bold theoretical step for mesoamerican archaeology in setting its sights on the goal of identifying cultural types such as early civilizations and determining the cause-and-effect relationships that produced the types. What is remarkable in retrospect is that Steward launched that program with so little appropriate archaeological data. The combination of strong theory and weak data had at least two important consequences for subsequent archaeology. First, because it melded model and findings, what was called mesoamerican early civilization, stratified and state society, was simply an abstraction of the culture of the Aztecs (and their predecessors) or the culture of the Maya (and their predecessors) or both. Second, with mesoamerican studies thus implicitly defined, funding agencies found the research projects that most successfully met their criteria were big (later smaller) projects in the central Mexico and the Maya areas. Expectedly, there was a corollary diminution of support for research projects elsewhere, such as west and northwest Mexico.

So, by the third quarter of the twentieth century, the archaeological community for the most part shared an idea of Mesoamerica that made data from regions other than central Mexico and the Maya area irrelevant to the central thrust of future theory development. Old and new knowledge about west and northwest Mexico was difficult to use because these regions had not been an integrated part of the theoretical frame of mesoamerican studies. Even when the regions were included as part of Mesoamerica geographically, they were given no role in the conceptual definition of Mesoamerica. And there was no metatheory that demanded a critique of "Mesoamerica." Operationally, it would have meant revamping the basic concepts not only about mesoamerican early civilization but also about mesoamerican states and stratified societies—a formidable task that would have disrupted the trajectory of research. And so research in west and northwest Mexico was not considered part of the dynamic of knowledge production for mesoamerican studies. To hold on to their conceptual framework, mesoamericanists simply chose not to know the knowledge of west and northwest Mexico. It went largely unacknowledged and unreferenced and certainly did not influence even the later increasingly refined and thoughtful conceptions of Mesoamerica.

Of course, the mesoamericanists of northwest and west Mexico knew this. Their emphasis was on collecting data from this little-known region. Their baseline compendium was *El occidente de México* (Sociedad Mexicana de Antropología 1947). For the next twenty-five years, new discoveries were published for the most part as monographs or articles in journals. In more recent years, compendia not only have published the results of archaeological investigations in the region but also have begun to raise the question of west and northwest Mexico as Mesoamerica: *The Archaeology of West Mexico* (Bell, ed. 1974), *The Archaeology of West and Northwest Mexico* (Foster and Weigand 1985), *Origen y desarrollo en el occidente de México* (Boehm de Lameiras and Weigand 1992).

By the 1990s, this state of mesoamerican affairs led to a conference supported by the Wenner-Gren Foundation: Cultural Dynamics of Precolumbian West and Northwest Mesoamerica. The application for this conference pointed out that before the 1970s, west and northwest Mexico had been among the least archaeologically studied regions in the history of mesoamerican studies. In addition to the lack of funding support, there was a lack of scholarly community interchange among the archaeologists working in these regions, not only because they came from diverse parts of the globe but also because they worked in a vast geographical expanse that forced an isolation even when they were in the field during the same season. Despite these drawbacks, between the 1970s and the 1990s, new and notable research had been carried out.

This book not only presents this research but also engages the argument concerning Mesoamerica as a paradigm. Clifford Geertz has said that "the locus of study is not the object of study" (Geertz 1973:22). In that sense, the editors do not present this volume as a study of mesoamerican civilization. More than that, neither do they accept the monographs of archaeological work in central Mexico and the Maya area as studies of mesoamerican civilization. We are all doing archaeology in geographically close regions. What we want is information about what is contemporary, later, and earlier; about how people distribute themselves across the landscape; about daily life in different parts of the community; about the meaning of things and of behavior (when it can be inferred); about how culture changes; and on and on. This is not to say that the study of mesoamerican civilization is not the goal here. It is. But it cannot be reached by fiat. Reaching the goal begins with a loose understanding of early civilization, which then acts as an unconfining guide in the description and interpretation of archaeological data. The process continues with small generalizations that are tested against larger generalizations, leading to evaluations and perhaps reformulations, which can take place on any conceptual level.

It is in this spirit that this research about west and northwest Mexico is presented. In some cases, new cultural configurations are discovered or new connections are found, new cultural complexities are revealed or new meanings are seen. The authors have all done archaeological survey and excavation in their regions and present primary data, for the most part their own, as well as syntheses. They have avoided initially any consideration of connections to central and southern Mesoamerica in order to present field results in their most immediately meaningful context, namely, local development. Generalizations are layered above these descriptive and interpretive presentations.

The authors have used several chronological systems. Their intent is to use a periodization that immediately points to what is contemporary in other places. Following general New World archaeological practice, early periods are called Paleoindian or Lithic and Archaic. For later periods, authors follow the basic periodization of mesoamerican studies (built on historical events in central and southern Mesoamerica): Preclassic or Formative, Classic, and Postclassic. In this volume, these latter designations do not have the meaning that is inherently implied. The development of culture in west and northwest Mexico has a different momentum from that of the areas for which the period labels were designed. The use of the same periodization should be understood to be a tool to provide chronological coherence for the whole of Mesoamerica. It does not signify and is not meant to imply a parallel pattern of development. Indeed, such inferences, which have been made occasionally, have distorted west and northwest Mexican prehistory, preventing the discernment of its own trajectory and reducing it to an unaccountable peculiarity in central Mexican prehistory.

When available, the authors use calendar dates largely based on radiocarbon dating. Although these dates are not exact, they can form the basis of a chronological scaffolding independent of central and southern mesoamerican periodization, and the authors are aware of that possibility somewhere down the road.

Before proceeding, however, it is important to understand something about the history and scale of archaeological research in west and northwest Mexico. Historically and currently, work in this vast region is and has been undertaken by a handful of researchers. This region has not seen the broad-scale systematic surveys and excavations that have been common in places such as the Valley of Mexico, Oaxaca, the Maya region, or even the neighboring American Southwest. In some areas more work was done before 1950 than has been done since, and only a handful of sites have seen some excavation. For example, the reconstruction of the Teuchitlán tradition of highland Jalisco is based almost solely on reconnaissance survey and the examination of looters' pits in sites. In Durango, there has not been a major excavation of a site since the initial excavations of the Schroeder site in the 1950s. Even the recent work at sites such as La Quemada and the Trincheras site was limited in scope. There are, however, some exceptions. Casas Grandes (Paquimé) in Chihuahua, in the Tarascan area of Michoacán, and the southwestern coast of Jalisco are places where considerable time and effort have been profitably expended to produce quantities of data that have allowed more detailed interpretations of the local prehistory. Despite the variability and limitations of site-specific and regional data from most of west and northwest Mexico, the chapters that follow provide current and, as far as existing data will allow, comprehensive summaries of the region's Precolumbian past.

Geographically, west Mexico includes the southwestern Pacific coast from the Río Santiago in central Nayarit in the north to the Río Balsas between Michoacán and Guerrero in the south. Inland it includes the current Mexican states of Jalisco, Michoacán, and Guanajuato (Figure 1.2). Physiographically, the area is quite varied. Features range from the desert and subtropical coastal plains along the Pacific Ocean, to the highlands of the Sierra Madre Occidental and the Transverse Volcanic Axis, to the interior basin and range country of the Mesa del Norte, to the highland lake country of western Mexico (Figure 1.3). Local topography often affects climatic conditions, which vary from one of the hottest and driest places on earth, the Sonoran Desert, to the cool wet pine forests of southern Jalisco and Michoacán (Figures 1.4 and 1.5).

As noted, there are several regions in west Mexico in which a fair amount of research has been done: Michoacán, the Jalisco highlands, and Guanajuato. Guanajuato stands in a crucial position between the highland lake districts of Jalisco and the Basin of Mexico. Charles Florance is acutely aware of this in his work on the Chupícuaro culture of southeastern Guanajuato, dated to the Late and Terminal Preclassic period, described in Chapter 2. It is for this reason that he subtitles his chapter "Heartland or Periphery?" In his chapter he puzzles out the relationship between Chupícuaro and the contemporary Teuchitlán tradition of highland Jalisco and the Cuicuilco culture of the Basin of Mexico. There has been a historical proclivity in mesoamerican archaeology to find the roots of structurally complex or stylistic elaborate cultures, such as Chupícuaro, in the Basin of Mexico. Yet other investigators have proposed an autochthonous origin for Chupícuaro and evaluated its influence elsewhere in Mesoamerica.

Figure 1.2. Major sites and areas in west and northwest Mexico.

Florance recorded 45 sites in his survey of the Puroaguita area. Using more than seven thousand sherds, he refined the existing chronology for Chupícuaro and interpreted relationships among contemporary Late and Terminal Preclassic cultures based on stylistic connections. Using all research data, he differentiated among an Early Chupícuaro, a Chupícuaro, and a Mixtlán phase.

With this more sensitive chronology, Florance is able to deal with contemporaneity with a surer hand. Nevertheless, he recognizes that "cultural systems . . . [can be] dynamic, interactive, and in some respects synchronically continuous," and, therefore, even with contemporaneity established, proposals about connection require interpretation. He suggests that in the Early Chupícuaro phase a population moving in from the west of Mexico along the Río Lerma began to establish settlements. He sees surface features at the Puroaguita sites as similar to those described by Weigand (this volume) for the contemporary phase in the Jalisco highlands. Florance interprets

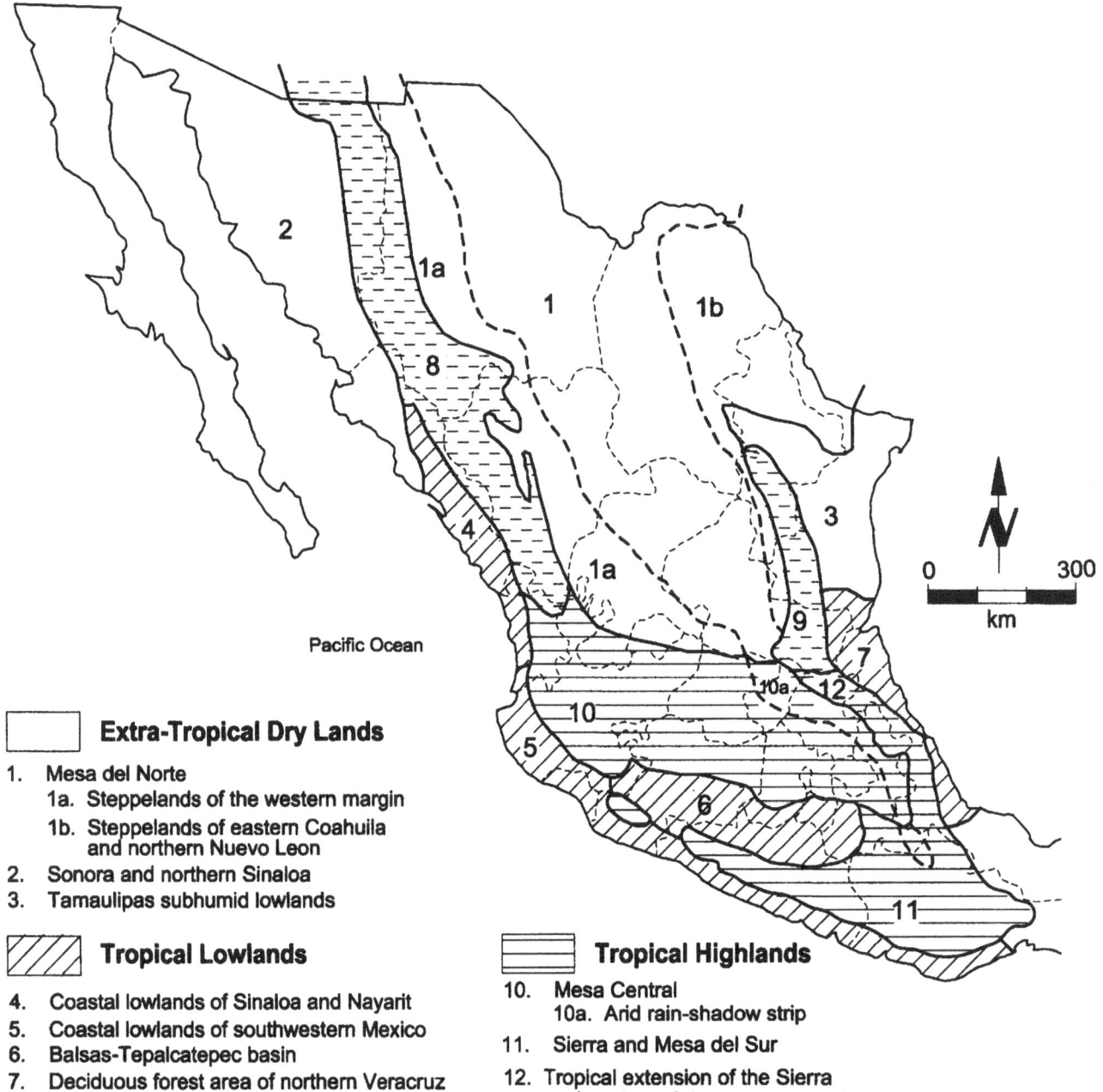

Figure 1.3. Natural regions of central and northern Mexico (West 1964). By permission of the University of Texas Press.

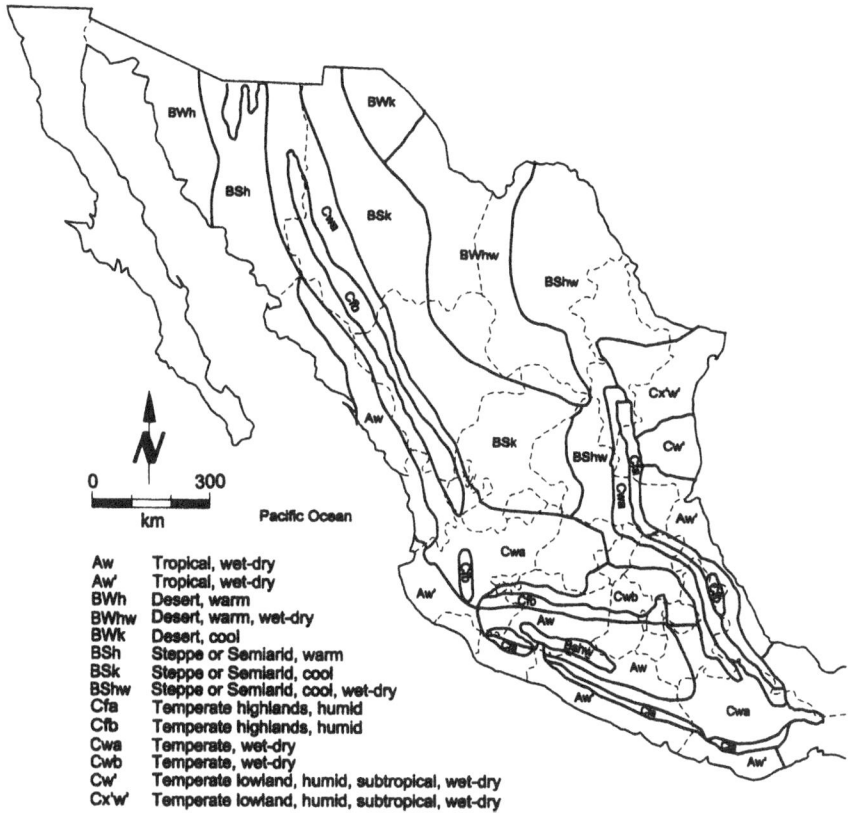

Figure 1.4. Climatic types of central and northern Mexico (Vivó Escoto 1964). By permission of the University of Texas Press.

this as indicating that Chupícuaro was peripheral to the more established Jalisco highland lake district in Early Chupícuaro times.

In the subsequent Chupícuaro phase, there is evidence of a connection with the Basin of Mexico. Florance views that connection as the manifestation of a broad interregional trade system fostered by Cuicuilco, which was at the center of a stable pan-basin market system that it had created and controlled. The Chupícuaro phase settlements' role in the trade system, Florance argues, makes them part of the heartland. In this conception, Florance has "gone outside the box" by being able to see geographical expanses, identified as discrete cultural regions (i.e., the Basin of Mexico and southeastern Guanajuato) in later times, as joined in earlier times. That association, however, is not pervasive. A certain autochthonous distinctive element exists in the Chupícuaro phase, as testified by the stylistically singular figurine and pottery forms.

Not all the parameters of the relationships within the Cuicuilco trade system are known. Compounding the difficulties in identifying them is recognizing simultaneously the changes that took place over the several hundred years of Cuicuilco's existence. The one definitive event of Cuicuilco's history is the volcanic eruption of Xitli, which diminished its agricultural base and led to the loss of its prominence in the basin. As a consequence, the Río Lerma was no longer a transportation corridor between Cuicuilco as a major market center and its economic partners. Southeastern Guanajuato lost its previous role. Other regions came to the fore in central and western Mexico by the Terminal Preclassic. Florance notes the developmental parallels between Teotihuacán in the northeast sector of the Basin of Mexico and the Jalisco highland lake districts, notably, massive population aggregations and the consequent cultural and societal patterns. In asking the question heartland or periphery, Florance has tried to shake off the unexamined assumptions of predecessor archaeolo-

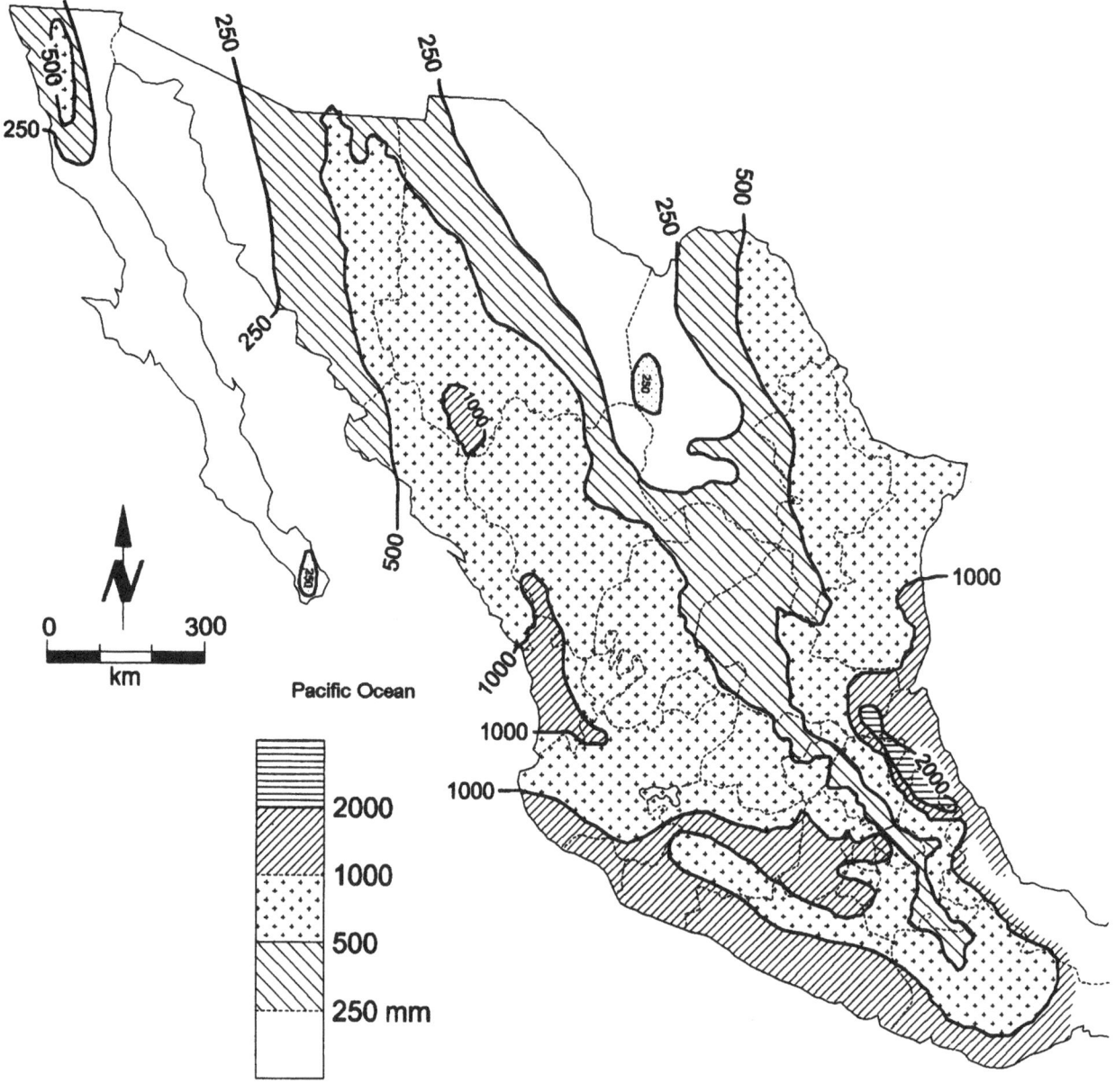

Figure 1.5. Mean annual precipitation in central and northern Mexico (Vivó Escoto 1964). By permission of the University of Texas Press.

gists and to seek an answer based on local developments and interrelationships.

In Chapter 3, Beatriz Braniff discusses the "north-central" region, which she defines as north of the Río Lerma in the central highlands. She concentrates on two localities: the Bajío and the Tunal Grande. Cultural development in the central highlands south of the Río Lerma, expressed by the designations Formative (Preclassic), Classic, and Postclassic, she notes, does not find a parallel in these northern regions, where the pace of cultural change was different. Indeed, it is a region best seen as connected not only to the south but also to the west and north.

Beginning with an internal analysis, Braniff raises questions about the Chupícuaro phase and subsequent Mixtlán phase chronology. What can be plotted are early Chupícuaro components, notably complex architecture, in northern Michoacán, Querétaro, southern Guanajuato, and even Tlaxcala. Late Chupícuaro/Mixtlán attributes can be located in parts of Guanajuato, Zacatecas, Michoacán, Querétaro, and the highlands of Jalisco. With a clearer local chronology, Braniff is able to do a finer reconciliation of phases across regions, which is needed for an understanding of the relationship between Chupícuaro and other regions, particularly central Mexico.

What Braniff sees in the "north-central" region by about A.D. 1 is a flowering of complex culture that expands what has been called the mesoamerican tradition, both in its components and in its distribution over the landscape. By A.D. 250, the Bajío region is the site of towns and cities with satellite settlements. There is evidence of connection with Teotihuacán to the south as well as to highland Jalisco's Teuchitlán tradition. Between A.D. 600 and A.D. 850, the Bajío exhibits material traits that define the later Toltec tradition in the northern Valley of Mexico. Around A.D. 900, the indigenous "north-central" tradition begins to lose its agricultural base, and the structure of society changes. Later in this second millennium, there is some indication of a Toltec revival that lasted until the Toltec collapse.

In Chapter 4, Phil Weigand describes the highland lake districts of western Jalisco as rich environments for agriculture and with abundant rare and strategic resources. There are no internal natural barriers between the lake basins or any external natural barriers between the region and that of the Lerma Valley to the south, and the topography eased communication both internally and externally. This observation is part of the basis of Weigand's view that the lake districts were not isolated from one another or from other parts of Mesoamerica. Weigand has developed a chronology that begins with the recognition of Paleoindian and early Archaic cultural activity. The distinctive shaft tombs found in Michoacán and the connection to Colima through Capacha ceramics mark the Formative in the region. Weigand suggests that a multicultural, multiethnic ambience was established by this time. In addition and more important, he proposes that the shaft tombs and associated architecture are indicators of a nucleus of complex sociocultural activities that was beginning to evolve in parts of the lake districts. This differential sociocultural development among localities became the core/hinterland relationship of the important Teuchitlán tradition, continuing for a thousand years. One of the characteristics of the cultural tradition is the concept of circularity in the production of architecture and architectural features.

In the Classic period, there is what Weigand describes as a process of societal intensification and of demographic implosion. What emerges is a stratified social order, perhaps organized in a state structure, combined with a cultural differential between what can be called the core and the hinterland. As the process continued, fortified sites were built in the core, and population pressure there began to strain natural resources. Agricultural production was intensified by the construction of an integrated system of terraces and chinampas in what Weigand suggests was a state-involved project. Whether the huge habitation zone of Teuchitlán can be classified as a city depends, expectedly, on the indicators used. Weigand suggests that it is more like the Lowland Maya than the central Mexican centers. In this discussion, he reflects on the definition of city that illuminates the problems of the Mesoamerica controversy. The cultural symbolism of circularity continues to be manifested in architecture despite the difficulty of carrying out the concept in more elaborate constructions. Indeed, the material expression of circularity seems to be a west Mexican idea, and many hundred circular buildings can be found throughout the region in this and later times.

At the end of the Classic period, the Teuchitlán tradition began to wane. The great habitation zone was beginning to break up. There were very few new architectural undertakings, although there was a fair amount of remodeling. New precincts were built outside, but not within, the former habitation zone, and these did not follow the hallmark circular architectural model. In the larger Jalisco region, new architectural concepts such as the open "U" patio/pyramid complexes and the double pyramid on a joint platform were manifested. These forms are found earlier and later in other parts of Mesoamerica, including west Mexico. Since chronology and directionality cannot be securely traced at this early stage of research, it would be prudent to say only that populations were in contact and ideas about abstract forms and architecture moved about among neighboring complex societies.

In Chapter 5, writing on Michoacán, Helen Perlstein Pollard traces the early periods but focuses on the last centuries before the Conquest, when the Tarascan culture flourished. Little is known of the Paleoindian and Archaic periods, but recent work has revealed some things about life in the Preclassic. Maize was domesticated about 1500 B.C. The results of this stable food supply can be seen in the flourishing Chupícuaro culture of the Río Lerma Valley and in its extension to the south and west; in the Chumbícuaro culture of the

13

Tepalcatepec Basin; and in the Balsas/Mezcala culture. At one time in the history of mesoamerican studies, these autonomous village societies were thought to characterize the full development of west Mexican society. Another distinguishing feature of the Preclassic is the construction of shaft tombs, which had a distinctive architecture and indications of an elaborate grave ritual.

In the Classic, the population of villages grew rapidly. But the most distinctive development was the construction of ceremonial centers and the emergence of elites. In addition, these centers exhibited architecture and artifacts known from Teotihuacán in central Mexico. Pollard discusses what can be inferred from this, evaluating the kinds of relationships that may have existed between the two regions.

In the Postclassic, Pollard notes there are indications of population nucleation at defensible locations in several lake basins. For this period in Michoacán, not only ceramics but also metallurgy can provide clues to the cultural exchange and population movement that took place. Postclassic Michoacán and environs was characterized by the development of regional culture. During these developments, there appears to have been little direct interaction with central Mexico. In the late Postclassic, there is a developmental change with the emergence of the Tarascan culture and the Tarascan state. In what is called the Protohistoric period, the Tarascan state expanded its territory outside its Pátzcuaro Basin heartland into the rest of Michoacán and beyond. The extent of the northern expansion was marked by the Río Lerma (commonly considered the northern border of Mesoamerica, as noted), and the southern expansion by the Río Balsas. In the west, the Tarascan empire reached into the current states of Jalisco and Guerrero. In the east, it shared a continually disputed frontier with the Aztecs.

In Chapter 6, her second chapter in this volume on Tarascan external relationships, Pollard points out that from the perspective of the history of the west Mexico cultural region, the Tarascan state not only went head to head with the Aztec empire, its counterpart to the east, but also dealt with the legacy of the highland lake district complex culture of Jalisco to the west. She traces the Tarascan-Aztec relations in intertwined military, political, economic, and social matters. They were both enemies and associates, a relationship less paradoxical than it first appears. The Tarascan expansion in west Mexico had a different military, political, economic, and social nature. For one thing, the Tarascans encountered a variety of small states, and for another, they located attractive raw materials. The ramifications of these interrelationships were not trivial in the development of Tarascan institutions.

Joseph Mountjoy, in Chapter 7, describes a unique region of west Mexico, namely, the southern coast. It is a region with shallow and deep bays that attract many varieties of shellfish, fish, and birds in large numbers. In addition, there is good access to inland mineral and stone and resources to support agriculture. Mountjoy begins by noting briefly the evidence of the earliest habitation in the area, dated to the late third to early second millennium B.C. In his discussion of later periods, Mountjoy devotes a section to "external relations," in which he places the cultures of this region in a larger context. An early characteristic culture of this region is the Capacha tradition, based on horticulture and dated to the Preclassic. The tradition is related to El Opeño in Michoacán and Tlatilco in the Valley of Mexico as well as to San Blas in Nayarit. Its origin is unclear. It may have come from northwest South America by sea or from eastern and central Mexico through Michoacán to the coast. Having reached Colima and Jalisco, the horticulturalists of the Capacha tradition may have moved up the coast of west Mexico.

Mountjoy identifies two traditions after about 300 B.C.: the Shaft Tomb and the Tuxcacuesco, with an almost but not quite discrete distribution. In both traditions, there is an increase in population based on slash-and-burn garden farming and coastal resources. There is evidence of ranked settlement hierarchy and craft specialization in the Tuxcacuesco tradition. Funerary offerings of both traditions reveal a connection with the west Mexican highlands. Coastal shell appears to have been exchanged for highland obsidian. A stylistic link with the central Mexican highlands is exhibited through the types and styles of hollow and solid figurines.

Following the Red-on-buff tradition, the important Aztatlán tradition of the Late Classic/Postclassic emerges. Mountjoy describes it as constituting the "highest development of mesoamerican culture ever achieved in some areas of west Mexico." He points out that there was at least one Aztatlán ceremonial/civic center in every large river valley along the coast from the Río Tomatlán in Jalisco to the northern border of Sinaloa, as well as in the highlands along routes of communication and commerce. Mountjoy notes that the origin and early development of metalworking in this region are associated with the Aztatlán tradition. He describes a distribution system of high-quality worked obsidian, centers of pottery production, and a shell jewelry industry at Amapa. Mountjoy suggests that these pan-Aztatlán commercial activities and their associated traits are indicators not only of economic connections but also of political and religious ties. Elite burials and residences speak to social ranking.

Aztatlán ceramics have been found well beyond this area into Durango, Chihuahua, and New Mexico. On the other hand, Toltec Plumbate pottery and Mazapan figurines have been found associated with Aztatlán pottery and at Aztatlán sites. In addition, Aztatlán pottery iconography is similar to Mixteca-Puebla and early Aztec iconography. This distribution indicates considerable movement and interaction among various neighboring and distant populations at this time.

Post-Aztatlán times are characterized by local cultural developments but are still rooted in the Aztatlán tradition. There was a population expansion, and marginal lands were vitalized by irrigation. Each valley was an independent political unit under the leadership of a local chief, although there is an indication that in huge valleys there were several local chiefs and a paramount chief. The cultural hegemony of the Aztatlán tradition disappeared, replaced by fragmentation and diversification.

In Chapter 8, Stuart Scott and Michael Foster summarize the archaeology of Mexico's northwest coast from the perspective of the Marismas Nacionales (Marismas). Scott directed a ten-year, multidisciplinary project in the Marismas, a vast estuary and lagoon system on the Sinaloa and Nayarit border. He organizes his discussion of Marismas prehistory around the geologic and developmental record of the area's coastal plain. The growth and tectonic history of this portion of the coastal plain clearly affected the nature and extent of the prehistoric human occupation of the area. Specifically, the archaeology of the Marismas is notable for its extensive shell middens and a unique shell mound, El Calón. El Calón is a temple-like mound made from the articulated shells of a large ribbed clam. A series of radiocarbon dates suggests the mound was constructed about 3700 B.P.

Scott divides the ceramic period in the Marismas into two broad phases dating from about A.D. 400 to Spanish contact. It is during this time that numerous villages and hamlets appear throughout the Marismas as the coastal plain expands. Nevertheless, there is evidence to suggest a hiatus of two hundred to three hundred years in the occupation of the area between ca. A.D. 900 and 1200. This may be associated with the subsidence of the coastal plain. More than five hundred shell middens, many found at villages and hamlets, were recorded. Most of the decorated ceramics found in these sites are types associated with the Amapa and Chametla area.

Foster places the Marismas in a regional context by summarizing early and recent work along the northwest coast. Early research on the West Coast resulted in the definition of the Aztatlán culture, and work at Chametla, Culiacán, and Guasave in Sinaloa produced three partially overlapping sequences that cover the period from A.D. 250/300 to Spanish contact. More recent work in northern Nayarit, in the Amapa region, expanded the understanding of the area's prehistory. Other than the work in the Marismas, recent investigations have been limited to either archaeological salvage projects or reassessments of existing data. Also of note is interaction between the Chalchihuites culture of Durango and the cultures of the West Coast, interaction associated with the Aztatlán Mercantile System.

J. Charles Kelley's contribution on the Aztatlán Mercantile System, Chapter 9, is the culmination of a series of evolving discussions of the subject. This version of his model of long-distant trade and traders uses new data to support his arguments for the role of trade in the spread of mesoamerican influence in west and northwest Mexico. Kelley begins his discussion by identifying the theoretical framework he employs and then considers examples of the activities of mobile traders in Mexico from the ethnohistoric literature. He provides background on the origin of the "Aztatlán" concept and on the origin and spread of mesoamerican traits and culture into west and northwest Mexico, specifically his own work at the Schroeder site in Durango; that of Ekholm at Guasave, Sinaloa; and, more recently, that of Ganot and Peschard at Cañón del Molino, Durango. Kelley summarizes the evidence for the distribution of Aztatlán materials in west and northwest Mexico and their link to the Mixteca-Puebla complex of central Mexico.

Kelley explicitly states several hypotheses regarding the nature and workings of the Aztatlán Mercantile System. He turns to the archaeological record to document the evidence for the existence of the Aztatlán tradition and the development of trade and trade routes. The Aztatlán Mercantile System is seen as a Postclassic phenomenon with the Early Aztatlán system dating between ca. A.D. 900/950 and 1150 and the Late Aztatlán system dating between ca. A.D. 1150 and 1350/1400+.

Kelley argues further that the expansion of the Aztatlán Mercantile System resulted in the development of Paquimé into a central place and a mesoamerican gateway community. Although he acknowledges the likely Mogollon roots of Paquimé, Kelley notes that the town was transformed into something unlike anything else Mogollon or anything else in the American Southwest. He goes on to summarize the evidence he sees for mesoamerican influence or presence while noting that Paquimé was the center of a large interaction sphere that dominated the international Four Corners area and west Texas.

Kelley concludes his discussion by asserting his belief in the existence of the Aztatlán Mercantile System and in his model of its functioning. He notes that the system probably collapsed with the expansion of the Tarascan empire into the Chapala Basin around A.D. 1450 to 1500.

In Chapter 10, Peter Jiménez Betts and J. Andrew Darling focus on the archaeology of the Malpaso, Juchipila, and Valparaiso valleys of southern Zacatecas. They present a summary of previous research and show how it led to current views of the area's prehistoric cultural configurations. During the initial stages of investigation, researchers held the notion that there was a single dominant cultural pattern, the La Quemada–Chalchihuites. As work progressed, however, researchers recognized significant local variation. Jiménez and Darling also discuss the views of the occupational histories of the various areas, noting that there are many clear parallels between the early occupations of the La Quemada and Chalchihuites areas. These cultural traditions diverge significantly as time passes, however. They conclude the introductory discussion by lamenting a recent return to the idea of a pan-Chalchihuites cultural tradition that consumes the La Quemada (Malpaso), Chalchihuites, and Juchipila cultures of the region, a view that ignores or homogenizes the area's local archaeological sequences.

Jiménez and Darling open their discussion of current research in three valleys with a description of the Malpaso Valley and the site and culture of La Quemada. The site, truly the most extensive and impressive in northern Mexico, is a massive complex with a ball court, hall of columns, and numerous plaza complexes situated on a series of masonry terraces that cover the south face of a mountain. The site dominated the lesser towns and villages in the valley and was connected to them by a network of roads. A tentative cultural chronology for the area is summarized by focusing on the ceramics of each phase. The dominant ceramic types, their distribution, and affinities with neighboring areas are described.

The Juchipila Valley, the second valley, is a geographical corridor that linked southern Zacatecas to west Mexico. Jiménez and Darling further state that the Juchipila Valley is key to our understanding the earliest sedentary occupations of the area and subsequent Classic and Postclassic period development. Again focusing on ceramic sequences and distributions, Jiménez and Darling describe the archaeology of the area. In evaluating investigations in the Valparaiso Valley, they cite in particular work at the site of La Florida that resulted in definition of the Bolaños culture. The economy of the Bolaños culture appears to have been directly tied to those of the Chalchihuites, Malpaso, and Magdalena Lake Basin areas. Also of importance is the site of Totoate, for which Jiménez and Darling incorporate a recent assessment of previous research. They offer a resolution to several perplexing questions about discrepancies between the work of Hrdlicka and the subsequent work by J. Charles Kelley. They go on to suggest that the Bolaños Valley culture was an important economic intermediary for the cultures of the Pacific Coast and those of the northern upland regions. This discussion is supported with a summary of recent research by Darling on obsidian procurement and distribution in the region.

Jiménez and Darling conclude by noting that a great deal of work is yet to be done. Recent work at La Quemada has provided a somewhat better understanding of the site's chronology and therefore has allowed a better assessment of its place in local and regional prehistory. They further argue that La Quemada was one of several regional developments in northwest Mexico. Jiménez and Darling suggest that one of the unique characteristics of the cultures of northwest Mexico was the rapid and complex formative stage through which they passed and that these cultures (i.e., La Quemada, Chalchihuites, etc.) all appear to peak between A.D. 650 and 800. Questions of major concern are, What were the stimuli for early developments? What are the larger sites in the area, and how were these developments related to one another? Finally, the authors suggest that intense peer-polity interaction in the northwest frontier during the Epi-Classic was the mechanism for the spread of various traits across the region.

In Chapter 11, J. Charles Kelley and Ellen Kelley offer a provocative interpretation of archaeoastronomical features at the sites of Alta Vista and Cerro Chapín. Their discussion focuses on a pecked cross-circle at the site of Cerro Chapín. Alta Vista was the principal ceremonial site of the Chalchihuites culture of western Zacatecas. It is unique in many ways, and one of its more intriguing aspects is the fact that it is located nearly on top of the Tropic of Cancer. The site is clearly ceremonial in nature and is thought to have been occupied between

A.D. 400/450 and 950/1000. The Kelleys believe there is strong evidence to suggest that an astronomically oriented group from the mesoamerican core, probably Teotihuacán, established Alta Vista. They believe these ancient astronomer-priests founded Alta Vista as a result of discovering the place where there was only one zenith passage of the sun, the Tropic of Cancer.

Early in their work at Alta Vista, the Kelleys discovered the importance of the Cerro de Chalchihuites, to the east of Alta Vista, as a horizon calendar. In a subsequent discovery, they excavated a structure at Alta Vista that they called the Labyrinth. This zigzag feature extends eastward from the southeast corner of the main plaza, paralleling the Hall of Columns. At its eastern end stands a gnomon that was clearly used with Picacho Pelón, the most prominent peak in the Cerro de Chalchihuites, to mark equinox sunrises.

In collaboration with Anthony Aveni, observations were made for the previously recorded pecked crosscircles on Cerro Chapín, located south-southwest of Alta Vista. From the pecked cross-circle petroglyphs on Cerro Chapín, the alignment with Picacho Pelón marked the summer solstice sunrise. It was also determined that from Cerro Pedroegosa, northeast of Alta Vista, the alignment of Picacho Pelón marked the winter solstice sunrise. The astronomical significance of Alta Vista and the area was clearly established with these observations.

The Kelleys set the stage for their detailed analysis of the Cerro Chapín, Chapín 1, pecked cross-circle petroglyph by summarizing calendrical and related iconographic data from elsewhere in Mesoamerica. The petroglyph itself consists of two concentric circles made up of a series of small circles pecked into the rock. The Kelleys take the reader through a step-by-step interpretation of the Chapín 1 petroglyph, arguing that it appears to be based on the observation of the summer solstice. They conclude that although, when compared with those found in central Mexico and other parts of Mesoamerica, it appears that the Chapín 1 device was adapted to local use and circumstances, its complexity suggests that it was not of local invention.

In his review of Durango archaeology in Chapter 12, Michael Foster begins with a brief summary of previous research, noting that archaeological remains were described in some of the first accounts of Spanish exploration of the area. Although Durango was investigated in the early 1900s, it was not until the 1950s that there was any systematic effort invested in the study of the region's archaeology. That work, conducted by J. Charles Kelley, led to the definition of two ceramic period cultural traditions along the eastern foothills of the Sierra Madre Occidental: the Loma San Gabriel and the Guadiana branch of the Chalchihuites culture. This work also resulted in the identification of scattered Paleoindian remains and a substantial Archaic period occupation. The Archaic period remains, assigned to the Los Caracoles complex, appear related to Archaic period materials in Chihuahua, western Coahuila, and the southern portion of the American Southwest. Based on the continuation of tool types, it appears that the Loma San Gabriel tradition developed out of the Archaic population of the area as agricultural and ceramic technology moved north.

The Loma San Gabriel (Loma) is a nonmesoamerican culture that occupied western Zacatecas and eastern Durango, probably from about 300 B.C. to the mid A.D. 1400s. It appears to be a component of a larger plainware/brownware tradition that was widespread over much of northwestern Mexico and the American Southwest before A.D. 1000. Plain and brown wares with some red-on-brown, textured, red, and white wares dominated the Loma ceramic assemblage. Many Loma lithic tool types carry over from the Archaic period. Settlements generally appear as hamlets and small villages with communal structures and rock pile altars. Sites are most commonly located on elevated points of land above water and agricultural lands. Because of the lack of systematic, stratigraphic excavations in Loma sites, no chronometrically based phase scheme has been proposed for Loma and a full understanding of its temporal and spatial variability has not been obtained.

In western Zacatecas, segments of Loma may have given rise to the Canutillo phase while others were marginalized with the florescence of the mesoamerican Suchil branch ceremonial center of Alta Vista. In Durango, Loma seems to have been pushed out of the way as the Chalchihuites culture expanded up the eastern foothills of the Sierra Madre. Interaction between the two groups appears to have been intense in some areas, however, and during the A.D. 1300s and early 1400s an amalgamation of the two cultures may have given rise to the historic Tepehuan of the area.

The Chalchihuites expansion into Durango appears to be associated with the collapse of the Suchil Chalchihuites of western Zacatecas. The Ayala and Las Joyas phases of the Durango (Guadiana) Chalchihuites are thought to parallel the Calichal and Retoño phases of western Zacatecas, beginning at A.D. 600 to 650. Late in the Ayala phase, there appears to be a significant penetration of the Durango highlands by the Aztatlán cultures of the West Coast. West Coast ceramics, copper items, smoking pipes, and spindle whorls appear widespread as the area is incorporated into the Aztatlán Mercantile System. The Chalchihuites sequence in Durango is based almost solely on the excavations at the Schroeder site south of the city of Durango. By the Río Tunal and Calera phases, A.D. 950 to 1400, the Chalchihuites culture had undergone considerable change as a result of its contact with West Coast societies. One of the best examples of this interaction is found at the site of Cañón del Molino, where a fifth phase (the Molino phase) was added to the Chalchihuites sequence.

In Chapter 13, Ronna Jane Bradley reviews Chihuahuan prehistory in terms of past archaeological research in the region and major research trends, summarizing the work of individuals such as Hewett, Kidder, Noguera, Sauer, Brand, and Sayles. These works provided detailed descriptions of the area's archaeology and offered some of the first interpretations of Chihuahuan prehistory. Lister's survey of Cave Valley represents the culmination of early research in Chihuahua. Bradley notes that these works laid the foundation for modern archaeological research in the area. Specific issues raised included the origin of the Casas Grandes population, the nature and extent of the Casas Grandes system, and the role of Mesoamerica in the development of the American Southwest.

The modern era of archaeological investigation is said to begin with Charles C. Di Peso's Joint Casas Grandes Expedition at Paquimé. Limited excavations were also carried out at four other sites. The project resulted in the accumulation of a wealth of information, much of which has been subsequently used to evaluate Di Peso's assessment of the Casas Grandes culture. The work resulted in the definition of six periods for the Chihuahua culture: the Preceramic, Plainware, Viejo, Medio, Tardío, and Españoles. Di Peso, using a pochteca model, argued that Paquimé was a mesoamerican trading outpost and craft production center. Bradley goes on to summarize various arguments for indigenous development of the Chihuahua culture by reviewing the archaeological data and cultural historical reconstructions presented as supporting evidence.

One of the most contentious issues presented by Di Peso was the dating of the Casas Grandes sequence, especially the Medio period. Bradley cites various criticisms of Di Peso's dating and briefly reviews a recent reanalysis of the tree-ring dates from Paquimé. She concludes her discussion of Chihuahuan prehistory by examining the extent, social complexity, and nature of production of the Casas Grandes system as well as the varied and extensive use of water control (canals, check dams, trincheras) to maximize agricultural production. In her summary of the extent of the Casas Grandes system, Bradley reviews the presence of Casas Grandes remains and influence in southern New Mexico, west Texas, and beyond the limits of the Casas Grandes Valley in Chihuahua. She concludes her chapter by discussing the role of Casas Grandes as a trade center, the integration of Paquimé into the Aztatlán Mercantile System, Paquimé and the mesoamerican world system, peer-polity interaction, and prestige exchange.

In Chapter 14, María Elisa Villalpando focuses on the ceramic period culture history of Sonora. She begins her discussion by pondering the question why the area seems not to have been extensively occupied by the Spanish. Was there a cultural or ecological boundary that deterred Spanish colonization? To address this issue, Villalpando turns to the archaeological record. She organizes her discussion by dividing Sonora into two geophysical and environmental provinces, the lowland desert and plains of western Sonora and the upland basin-range country of eastern Sonora.

Three cultural traditions occupied the lowlands: the Trincheras tradition, the Huatabampo tradition, and the Central Coast tradition. The Trincheras tradition, thought to date between A.D. 750 and 1450, is best known from sites concentrated in the Altar, Magdalena, and Concepción valleys. Trincheras sites extend to the Gulf of California in northern Sonora, however. The Trincheras tradition is also known for the cerros de trincheras, the best-known of which is the site of Cerro de Trincheras.

The second major cultural tradition of the lowlands is the Huatabampo. The Huatabampo area is south of the Trincheras region. Sites occur along extinct lagoons and estuaries as well as in the river valleys of the area. Huatabampo pottery—a hard, unpainted redware with complex vessel forms—is distinctive. Like their Trincheras neighbors to the north, members of Huatabampo society valued the manufacturing of shell jewelry. Some aspects of Huatabampo material culture show traits reminiscent of Chametla to the south and the Hohokam to the north. Villalpando suggests that the Huatabampo tradition disappeared around A.D. 1000.

The Central Coast tradition, the third major cultural manifestation of the lowlands of Sonora, is generally seen as the prehistoric Seri. The central coast of Sonora is an arid place lacking the resources suitable, prehistorically, for agriculture and sedentary life. The Central Coast tradition was a hunting-gathering tradition.

It appears that strong links, based on shell exchange, existed between the Central Coast and Trincheras traditions.

Two cultural traditions, the Río Sonora culture and the Casas Grandes tradition of central Chihuahua and eastern Sonora, dominated the Sonoran uplands. The Casas Grandes polity was centered at Paquimé in north-central Chihuahua. Viejo and Medio period settlements and material culture are common in eastern Sonora. The influence of Casas Grandes extended all the way to the Trincheras culture of the lowlands.

Río Sonora culture sites are found throughout central Sonora, extending from the international border to northern Sinaloa. Sites in the Río Sonora Valley are the best-documented. The Río Sonora occupation of north and central Sonora is broken into three phases: Early, Middle, and Late. A precise beginning date for this sequence has not been determined, but it ends by the early A.D. 1300s. A pithouse occupation eventually gives way to the use of surface dwellings. Shell and copper bells are also found in Río Sonora contexts.

Villalpando concludes by noting the differences in social, political, and economic complexity between the cultural traditions of the uplands and those of the lowlands. She also notes that significant desertization of Sonora had occurred by the mid A.D. 1400s. By the time the Spanish arrived, there was little left of the cultures that had once occupied the region. The lack of any coherent cultural systems to monopolize and build on prevented the Spanish from quickly spreading through the area. It was not until the Spanish mission system was established that a European foothold was established.

Michael Spence, one of the few central Mexicanists who is cognizant of west and northwest Mexican archaeology, concludes the volume in Chapter 15. After discussing some of the salient points of the book, Spence goes on to argue that Mesoamerica has been defined so narrowly that it excludes the west and northwest of Mexico. He notes that these areas are too often seen as peripheries that only benefited from, rather than contributed to, the development of civilization. Finally, he offers some directions future research might take.

CHAPTER TWO

THE LATE AND TERMINAL PRECLASSIC IN SOUTHEASTERN GUANAJUATO

Heartland or Periphery?

CHARLES A. FLORANCE

A CRUCIAL PART of the interpretation of the connection between west Mexico and the Basin of Mexico in the Late and Terminal Preclassic hinges on the body of material culture found in an archaeological zone in southern Guanajuato known as Chupícuaro, named after the modern village. The Chupícuaro zone is located in the easternmost part of west Mexico, near its border with central Mexico (Figure 2.1). It was drawn even closer to central Mexico by its location on the bank of the Río Lerma, which flows between west Mexico and central Mexico and provided an easy means of transport between the two regions throughout prehistoric times. Chupícuaro has occupied a special position in west Mexican chronology. It provides anchoring information for the west Mexican Preclassic, a period that is still being defined. Moreover, there are thousands of extant Chupícuaro artifacts that provide the basis for comparative studies (e.g., Frierman 1969) both within west Mexico and between west Mexico and other regions. They are also a source for understanding the content of the culture that produced them.

Some of the difficulties of interpreting Chupícuaro have to do with the peculiar archaeological history of the type-site itself. In the early 1920s, a previously unknown group of ceramic objects appeared on the art market. They were identified as coming from Chupícuaro, Guanajuato, which had not yet been the subject of archaeological investigation and so did not appear in archaeological schematics of Mexican prehistory. In 1926, the Dirección de Arqueología of the Instituto Nacional de Historia e Antropología (INAH) sent Enrique Juan Palacios on a reconnaissance of Chupícuaro, and in 1927, Ramón Mena and Porfirio Aguirre undertook a small investigation of this "new archaeological zone." They described pottery and figurines (which were so elaborate they thought they must be Tarascan) and a circular-based mound (see Weigand, this volume). Archaeological investigation did not continue in the next years, but the collection of artifacts from Chupícuaro did. A local doctor, Don Camarino Espino of Acambaro, stimulated the search for Chupícuaro artifacts and amassed a collection of several thousand items. In addition, there were several thousand Chupícuaro artifacts in the Museo Nacional in Mexico City, in the Morelia regional museum, and in various museums in the United States. Thus, Chupícuaro artifacts were well known in the art market before any extensive archaeological excavation had been launched.

More extensive archaeological work began when, in the 1940s, the government of Mexico was preparing for the construction of the Solis Dam, which would flood the village of Chupícuaro and the locality of the archaeological remains. INAH sponsored salvage excavations at

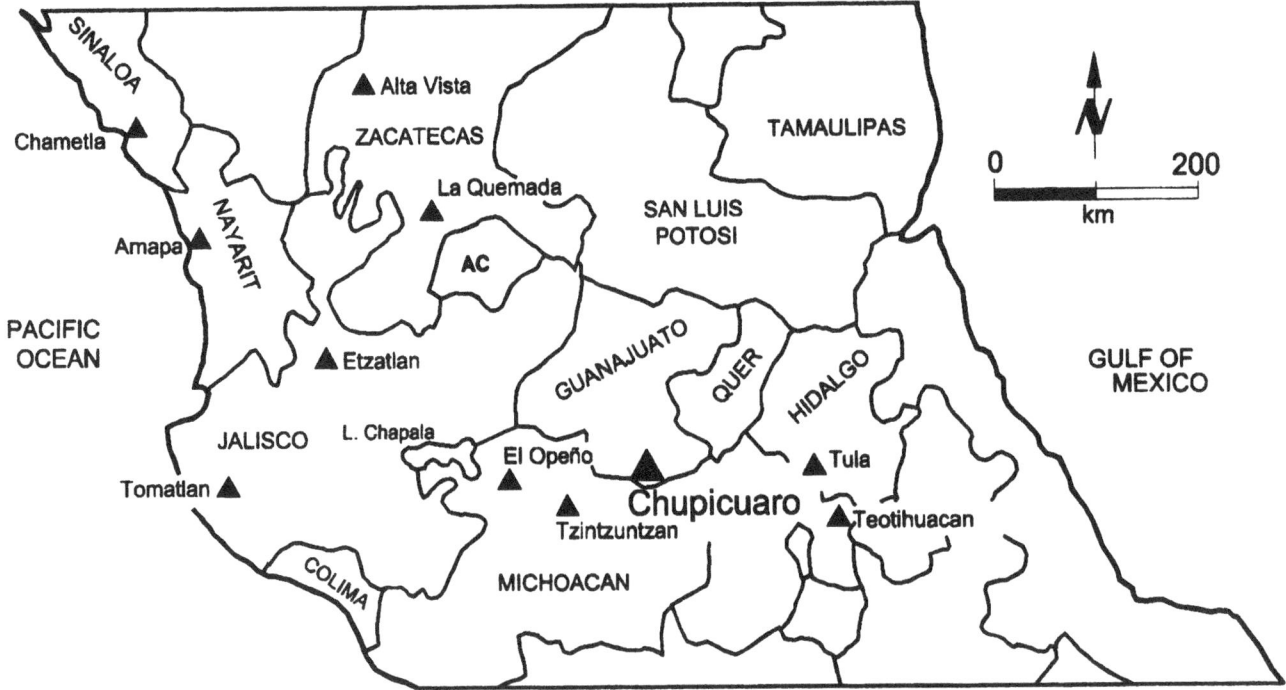

Figure 2.1. Chupícuaro and neighboring sites.

Chupícuaro under the direction of Daniel F. Rubin de la Borbolla. The excavations took place during 1946 and into the first weeks of 1947 and resulted in the seminal monograph *Excavations at Chupícuaro, Guanajuato, Mexico,* by Muriel Noé Porter (1956). The previous excavations that had yielded blackware types similar to blackware types in the Valley of Mexico led Porter (Porter de Moedano 1945) and Estrada Balmori (1945) to hypothesize a Preclassic or "Archaic" date for the site. Using survey data, Porter blocked out a Chupícuaro archaeological zone that extended over a large region of southern Guanajuato.

With these temporal and spatial touchstones, excavations were launched in several places in the vicinity of the village of Chupícuaro. The result was the uncovering of 390 burials, 46 dog skeletons, an ossuary, fragmentary stone alignments, 44 *tlecuiles* (depressions in the soil, lined with clay, where fires were built), and around 1,300 complete or nearly complete ceramic vessels, about two-thirds of which were associated with graves. About 1,000 figurines, approximately one-fifth associated with graves, were also recovered. In addition, there were other ceramic objects such as beads, stamps, pipes, earplugs, and musical instruments (commonly interred with children); stone artifacts, some of obsidian; and shell and bone objects.

The defining ceramic collection exhibits an extensive diversity of design choices in form, decoration, and motifs. There are blackware and painted wares, including red-rimmed, redware, black and red, brown-on-red, red-on-buff, black polychrome, and brown polychrome. The forms include ollas, tecomates, cylinders, and bowls of various shapes (Figure 2.2). Some vessels have additional features such as stirrup spouts, pedestals, tripods, and tetrapods. There are also effigy vessels with human, animal, and bird forms.

The many kinds of figurines of men, women, and babies, and women with elaborate hairstyles clad in headdresses and neckpieces, required systemization in order to set the groundwork for interpretation, initially and primarily spatial and temporal readings. Categories that have been devised are slant-eye (Figure 2.3), choker, crude, prognathic, and round-eye.

In the 1956 publication, Porter laid out a Chupícuaro sequence of phases, connected to the chronology established in the Valley of Mexico, and described them largely in terms of changes in material culture. In her segment on exterior relations, she speculated briefly on Chupícuaro connections with west Mexico and with north-central Mexico. Almost presciently aware that interpreting and placing Chupícuaro would plague archaeologists, including Porter herself, for some time, she suggested

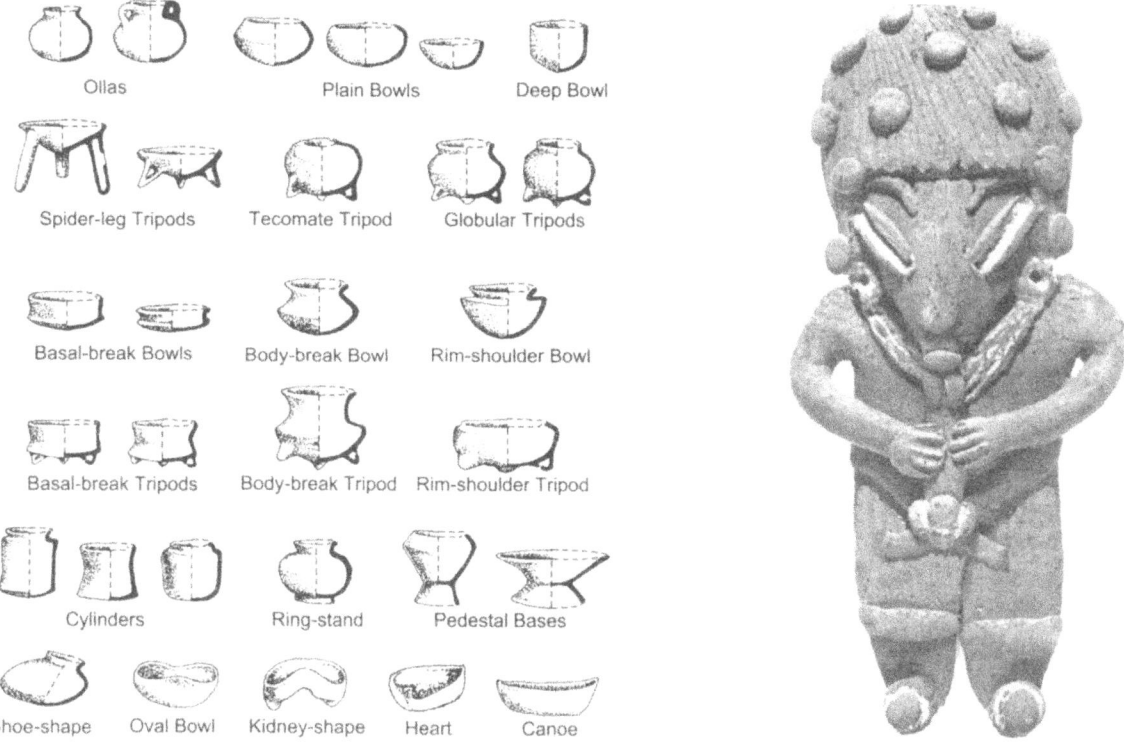

Figure 2.2. Chupícuaro vessel forms (Frierman 1969).

Figure 2.3. A Chupícuaro slant-eyed, thin figurine (height 11.5 cm).

that future archaeologists continue investigating Chupícuaro not only in the vicinity of Chupícuaro and to the north of it but also in the boundary area between it and central Mexico, particularly the Valley of Mexico. Beneath this apparently simple statement lay the recognition of basic questions about the Chupícuaro remains. What was the nature of the cultural configuration that authored these remains, what were its spatial and temporal dimensions, and what was the character of its connections within the mesoamerican world?

As early as 1945, resemblances between the Preclassic material culture in southeastern Guanajuato and that in the Basin of Mexico and adjacent regions were noted (Estrada Balmori 1945:110; Porter de Moedano 1945:100) and prompted speculation on the nature of the relationship between the two regions during this early period. In the 1960s, additional archaeological survey and excavation both in Guanajuato and in the Basin of Mexico generated new speculation about the relationship between the two areas. This speculation fell into two schools. One school, represented by Muriel Porter (Weaver) and Beatriz Braniff, viewed the Preclassic culture history of southeastern Guanajuato as linked to what were considered the largely similar traditions in the Basin of Mexico. In her 1969 reappraisal of the Chupícuaro tradition, done in the context of the research advances in the Basin of Mexico during the 1960s, Muriel Weaver made the following observations: "Although considerable work has been done in the far north and to the west, my prognostication that 'more Chupícuaro-like material will be forthcoming from north-central Mexico' (Porter 1956:574) has not proved to be the case. On the other hand, ties between Chupícuaro and the Basin of Mexico have been strengthened" (Weaver 1969:9–11).

Braniff's early 1960s archaeological survey and excavation in areas of Guanajuato and San Luis Potosi identified other sites with Chupícuaro-like material culture (Braniff 1965, 1974). Based on this research, Braniff concluded: "Chupícuaro is not, then, an isolated example of the Late Preclassic. The significance that this place has culturally, as well as Morales, León, Cóporo, and an infinity of other sites that ought to exist in Guanajuato, increases considerably since it seems to constitute the oldest village element in these areas, and it ought to be, as a consequence, the vanguard of the mesoamerican push into these northern zones" (Braniff 1965:15, my translation).

In contrast to the first school, James Bennyhoff and H. W. McBride viewed the Preclassic culture history of southeastern Guanajuato as an autochthonous one. The new understanding of cultural sequence in the Basin of Mexico in 1966 and the material culture defining it led Bennyhoff to conclude: "The emergence of the Teotihuacán tradition lay in a reformulation of the Cuicuilco tradition due to its partial collapse under extreme pressure from the north or northwest by a culture of the 'Chupícuaro' tradition and simultaneous pressure from the south by members of the 'Cholula' tradition" (Bennyhoff 1966:20).

McBride also viewed the Chupícuaro Preclassic manifestation as an autochthonous one. Whereas Porter, in 1969, believed that the research accomplished in north-central Mexico had not supported her earlier prediction that more Chupícuaro-like material would be found, McBride disagreed: "She [Weaver] correctly predicted that 'more Chupícuaro-like material will be forthcoming from north-central Mexico.' Sufficient ceramic and figurine evidence now exists for us to postulate an extensive Chupícuaro cultural tradition that influenced much of central and north-central Mexico from about 500 B.C. to 0 A.D." (McBride 1969:33).

According to McBride (1969:46), this cultural tradition had its best-known development in the Chupícuaro heartland on the Río Lerma. His concluding assessment is that "the Chupícuaro cultural tradition should take its place as a major component of the greater Mesoamerican cultural sphere. It can thus be employed in the same way that we use the greater Olmec tradition in the early and middle Preclassic and the Teotihuacán, Toltec, and Mixteca-Puebla traditions in the Classic and Postclassic periods for creating historical reconstructions from archaeological evidence" (McBride 1969:47).

Thus by the end of the 1960s, a dichotomy had emerged in the interpretation of the significance of the Preclassic manifestation found in southeastern Guanajuato. Was it a periphery to the Preclassic tradition in the Basin of Mexico, or was it a cultural heartland during the Preclassic, significantly influencing its neighbors, including those in the Basin of Mexico?

Archaeological investigation in southeastern Guanajuato during the 1970s had, as one of its goals, clarification of the heartland/periphery question. Until the 1970s, such research had failed to define a chronologically ordered sequence of cultural stratigraphy for the region. This deficiency was corrected by an important research project carried out in the early 1970s near Acambaro, Guanajuato. The Acambaro Project, initiated in 1971 to investigate the nature of fortified sites on the eastern frontier of the Late Postclassic and Protohistoric Tarascan polity, was directed by Shirley Gorenstein (1985:1). Stratified archaeological deposits excavated on Cerro el Chivo, near Acambaro, provided a sequence of occupational history from Preclassic to Postclassic times. Two ^{14}C dates helped anchor the sequence. Although the phases of the Cerro el Chivo sequence are in need of refinement, they present a general framework for the temporal assignment of cultural material, particularly pottery, in southeastern Guanajuato. My own research in this region has benefited greatly from the Cerro el Chivo sequence.

In 1975 and 1976, I carried out a reconnaissance survey near Puroaguita, Guanajuato (Florance 1985, 1989) and identified dense Late and Terminal Preclassic settlement in the 3.5 km^2 surveyed. A large sample of rim sherds (7,282) collected from 45 surface sites was analyzed in an attempt to refine the archaeological phasing of the Late and Terminal Preclassic in this region. Also, I was able to study the Late and Terminal Preclassic settlement history there.

In the Puroaguita study, arguments were presented to support three archaeological phases: the Early Chupícuaro, the Chupícuaro, and the Mixtlán. The arguments derive from three sources: (1) the published analyses resulting from the excavations at Chupícuaro in the 1940s; (2) the pottery analysis on which the Cerro el Chivo sequence is based; and (3) the differential distribution of chronologically sensitive rim sherd attribute aggregates among the 45 sites identified in the Puroaguita survey (Florance 1989). The argument for the Early Chupícuaro phase in the survey area was supported by the analyses from the 1940s excavations at Chupícuaro. These excavations documented the presence of two types of polychrome pottery in the region, brown and black. Stratigraphic evidence suggested the black polychrome pottery persisted for a longer period than the brown polychrome. Therefore, the presence of brown polychrome at a site denoted an Early Chupícuaro phase settlement. The disappearance of brown polychrome pottery was used to mark the commencement of the Chupícuaro phase. At all sites studied, settlement histories were continuous between the Early Chupícuaro and Chupícuaro phases. In other words, the disappearance of brown polychrome pottery was not accompanied by any disruption of the existing settlement pattern. Here I review the argument for the Early Chupícuaro phase in order to strengthen the credibility of the Early Chupícuaro phase and to better integrate the 1940s excavation data into current efforts to understand the Late and Terminal Preclassic culture history of southeastern Guanajuato.

THE EARLY CHUPÍCUARO AND CHUPÍCUARO PHASES

The village of Chupícuaro is located near the confluence of the Ríos Coroneo (Tigre) and Lerma (Figure 2.4). In 1945, four test pits were excavated on a hill south of the Hernandez corral (Porter de Moedano 1945:94). In pit 1, a 2-x-2-m unit, excavation through a meter of cobble fill exposed Preclassic deposits. More important, pit 1 penetrated an intact architectural feature. Deposits above, between, and below two stucco floors were excavated. Figure 2.5 is a composite schematic showing the result of the excavation in pit 1. The figure is adapted from figures in the original report (Porter de Moedano 1945:Gráfica no. 1 and Figura 4). The unit is laid on its side to facilitate comparison of the pottery found there. The amounts of the various pottery types identified above, between, and below the floors are shown in relative terms, as in the original graph. Brown polychrome (red, brown/buff) and black polychrome (red, black/buff) occur in abundance below the deeper of the two floors (Figure 2.6). Between the floors, brown polychrome is absent, and black polychrome occurs in moderate amounts. Above the shallower floor, both polychrome types are absent. Two other pits excavated to a depth of 1.2 m near pit 1 did not encounter floors. These pits contained black polychrome pottery, but brown polychrome was absent. This stratigraphic evidence suggested that brown polychrome pottery could be used to identify an early group of Chupícuaro settlements.

In the Puroaguita survey, eight of the 45 sites had brown polychrome rim sherds in the samples collected. Therefore, these eight sites were assigned to the Early Chupícuaro phase (Figure 2.7). Half these sites (1, 2, 3, and 5) are located adjacent to the Río Lerma channel. Three of the other four sites (23, 24, and 42) lie close to springs, and site 15 lies adjacent to a thermal spring. The distribution of these settlements suggests a colonial population that placed some settlements near the principal avenue of transportation and a source of food and water, the Río Lerma. These colonists placed other settlements near areas that had good soils and topography for cultivation, springs, and streams adaptable to simple irrigation techniques. During the Chupícuaro phase, the early settlements continued to be occupied, but there

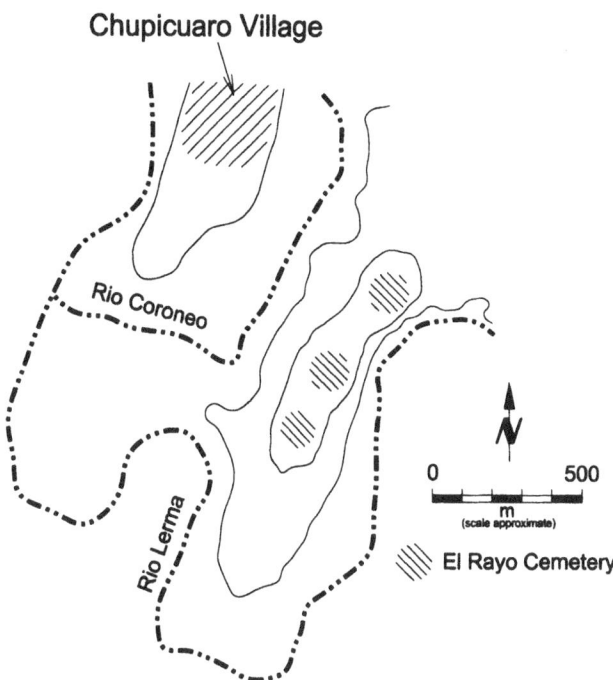

Figure 2.4. The location of the El Rayo cemetery near the original Chupícuaro village.

was an expansion of settlement into areas less favorable for cultivation and not as near water.

I have reanalyzed the 1940s data on the Chupícuaro burials that originally suggested a temporal difference in the two types of polychrome pottery. Data on the burials were published as an appendix to the volume edited by Frierman (1969). Most of the burials excavated in the 1940s were found at the El Rayo cemetery (see Figure 2.4). Therefore, this analysis concerns itself only with those burials at El Rayo.

One goal of the analysis was to investigate the distribution of the burials with associated polychrome pottery in the area excavated at El Rayo. To this end, the pits and trenches at El Rayo were abstracted for graphic display. In the southern and central cluster of units, there is no obvious pattern of differences in the distribution of burials with the three possible combinations of polychrome pottery—brown alone, brown and black together, or black alone. The northern cluster of units is distinctive in this regard, however. Two units, pits 146 and 147, yielded one individual each with brown polychrome pottery alone associated with it. A third unit, trench 10, yielded one individual with brown polychrome alone and another individual with brown and black polychrome pottery together associated with it.

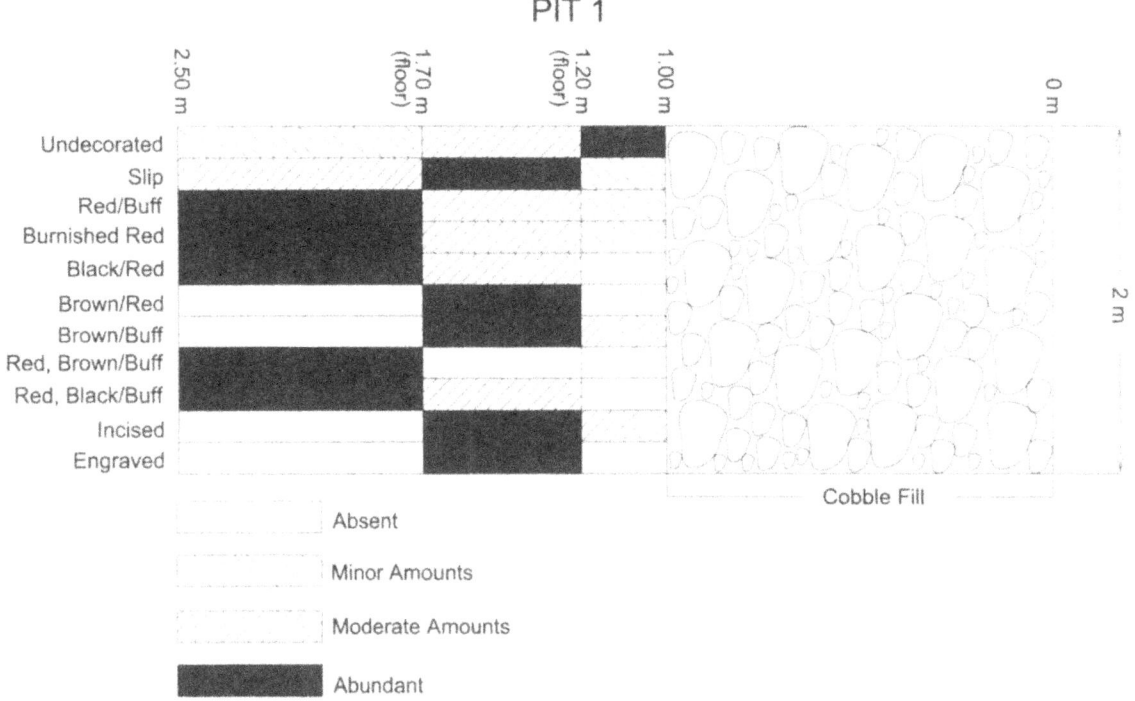

Figure 2.5. Distribution of pottery in pit 1 excavated near the original Chupícuaro village.

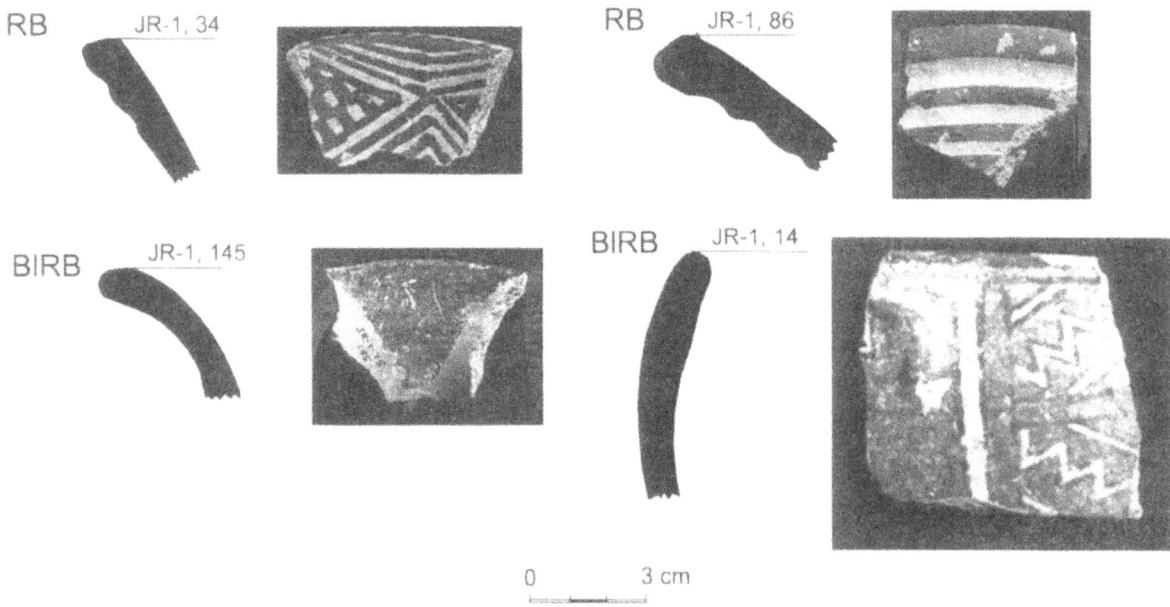

Figure 2.6. Selected red-on-brown and black and red-on-brown rim sherds.

pottery was being produced. Both the southern and central clusters of units had burials associated with only black polychrome pottery. Thus, it would appear that the southern and central sections of the El Rayo ridge became the focus of burial activity in the cemetery during the later phase of Preclassic settlement at Chupícuaro.

Having considered distributions within the cemetery itself, I then looked at the distribution of offerings accompanying those burials with polychrome pottery. Mammiform supports, ring-bases, and ringstands are absent from the brown polychrome burials. Distributional differences suggest that these features appear only in the Chupícuaro phase and not in the Early Chupícuaro phase. Distributional differences also suggest that pedestal bases are rare in the Early Chupícuaro phase, becoming more common in the Chupícuaro phase.

The distribution of figurines between the two groups of burials reveals that there are no slant-eye figurines associated with burials with brown polychrome. This distribution suggests that the slant-eye figurine is not present in the Early Chupícuaro phase but is associated with the Chupícuaro phase only and, therefore, would be a diagnostic of that phase. Seventy of the 78 figurines associated with burials with brown polychrome are of the choker type, whereas only one of the 55 figurines associated with burials with only black polychrome is of this type. This distribution suggests that the choker figurine style is primarily associated with the Early Chupícuaro phase, and, although it appears in the Chupícuaro phase, it is rare in this later phase.

There are distributional differences between the two groups of burials for three other categories of pottery in the El Rayo burials, namely, body-break, basal-break, and cylindrical vessels. In all cases, these categories occur with greater percentages in burials with only black polychrome.

The preceding analysis has revealed a whole series of differences between the two groups of burials—those with brown polychrome and those with only black polychrome. These differences support the argument that the presence of brown polychrome in association with a burial, or with a surface scatter, can be used to place that burial or scatter in the Early Chupícuaro phase.

THE MIXTLÁN PHASE

The Mixtlán phase is the third and latest phase defined in the Puroaguita survey. The Mixtlán phase was initially defined at Acambaro (Gorenstein 1985). The analysis of rim sherds from the Puroaguita survey identified

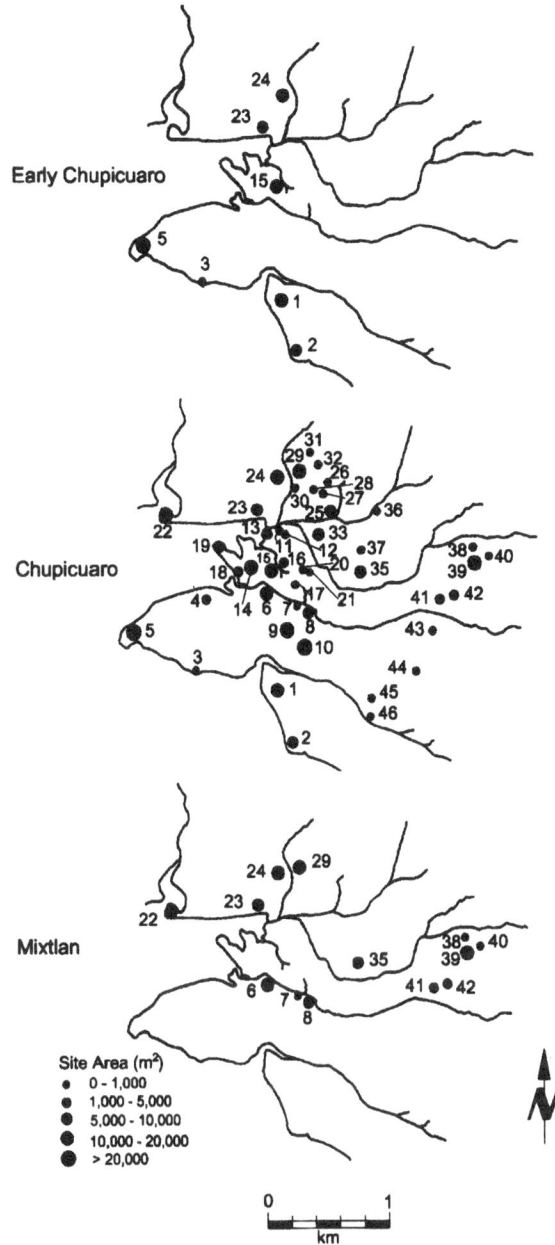

Figure 2.7. Early Chupícuaro, Chupícuaro, and Mixtlán settlement patterns in the Puroaguita survey area.

Based on the implications of the polychrome pottery found in the unit with the two stucco floors described above (pit 1), it can be suggested that the northern section of the cemetery at El Rayo was used during the early phase of Preclassic settlement at Chupícuaro. The absence of burials associated with black polychrome alone in the units of the northern section suggests that this section was not used in the later phase of Preclassic settlement at Chupícuaro, when only black polychrome new rim sherd attribute aggregates associated with the Mixtlán pottery complex—that complex defining the phase. A summary of the analysis is presented elsewhere (Florance 1989:455–456) and is not addressed here since the Mixtlán complex and phase lie outside the principal focus of this discussion. Recent discussions with Beatriz Braniff, however, indicate that the Mixtlán complex corresponds with the pottery defining her Morales phase.

Furthermore, Joseph Mountjoy (personal communication 1992) indicates that elements of the Mixtlán complex appear in the deepest cultural deposits he has excavated at the site of Ixtapa in the Banderas Valley of Jalisco. Based on this new information, a future reconsideration of the Mixtlán phase may be warranted.

HEARTLAND OR PERIPHERY?

The preceding archaeological data provide a basis for evaluating the dichotomy of opinion described at the beginning of this chapter. Were the Preclassic settlements in southeastern Guanajuato a periphery to the Preclassic tradition in the Basin of Mexico, or were they a cultural heartland that had a significant impact on its neighbors, including those in the Basin of Mexico? The question is one of culture history and, as such, must be considered in spatial and temporal terms. Cultures are dynamic, interactive, and, in some respects, synchronically continuous. On the other hand, geographic and systemic boundaries are arbitrary, and using them may falsely divide spatial and temporal continua. Nevertheless, boundaries are needed to create heuristic units that facilitate analysis. That said, I would argue that the Late and Terminal Preclassic settlements in southeastern Guanajuato could be viewed as both heartland and periphery as spatial and temporal scales change.

The analysis of the El Rayo burial data together with the results of the Puroaguita survey provide a basis for new insights into the culture history of the Late and Terminal Preclassic in southeastern Guanajuato. The results of the Puroaguita survey suggest the arrival of a colonial population within the survey area in the Early Chupícuaro phase. These settlements lie along the Río Lerma channel and near thermal and nonthermal springs found within the survey zone. Both at the confluence of the Río Coroneo and Río Lerma and in the Puroaguita area, the settlements seem to indicate that the Río Lerma itself provided the corridor along which these colonial populations moved and along which they communicated with one another. Population densities were low.

Though previously unsure, I am now convinced that the colonial populations moving along the Río Lerma were coming from the west rather than from the Basin of Mexico. In my earlier work (Florance 1989), I presented models of colonization that allowed both a Basin of Mexico origin and a west Mexico origin. Beginning my work with a basin bias, I concluded my study by admitting, "I am no longer so sure that the Preclassic cultural history of southeastern Guanajuato can be completely explained by events in the Basin of Mexico" (Florance 1989:684). I left that possibility open, however. The analysis of the El Rayo burials provided the evidence needed to resolve my previous ambivalence, as I detail below.

Phil Weigand (1977a, 1985, also this volume) has developed a sequence of archaeological phases for the highland lake district of Jalisco. A 1989 comparison of chronology between the Basin of Mexico and the highland lake district of Jalisco showed conflicting period terminology between the Basin of Mexico sequence and that for Jalisco (Florance 1989:671, Figure 7.2). As defined by Weigand, the date range for the Middle Formative in Jalisco encompassed the Late Preclassic in the Basin of Mexico. His Late Formative spanned the basin's Terminal Preclassic. What this suggested to me was that Weigand might have overextended the temporal range of the El Arenal phase. I proposed an alternative chronology. I began the El Arenal phase at 300 B.C., following Weigand's scheme. In the Basin of Mexico, this aligns the El Arenal phase with the earlier portion of the basin's Terminal Preclassic or the Patlachique-Chimalhuacán phase. Furthermore, I suggested moving the subsequent Ahualulco phase into alignment with the Tzacualli phase of the basin's Terminal Preclassic. Thus, I began the Ahualulco phase at 100 B.C. rather than at A.D. 200, where Weigand began it. This compressed the El Arenal phase to a two-hundred-year span between 300 B.C. and 100 B.C. The San Felipe phase, preceding the El Arenal phase, was left in alignment with the Early Chupícuaro phase in the Late Preclassic. In 1989, I suggested that my own assessment of the temporal span of the Early Chupícuaro phase in southeastern Guanajuato was too compressed. Following Weigand, I allowed for the possibility that the Early Chupícuaro phase might extend as far back as 1000 B.C.

Although the dating of the Early Chupícuaro phase remains uncertain, Weigand's studies in the highland lake district of Jalisco have begun to define some of the settlement characteristics of the phase. These characteristics are seen in Weigand's San Felipe phase settlements. Constructions associated with the San Felipe phase consist of "circular or oval burial mounds and platforms" (Weigand 1985:63). The platforms "are often built into hillsides," whereas the mounds are "usually located at the very top of the beach zone, or, as frequently, on the first terraces above the beach" (Weigand 1985:63).

The Puroaguita survey identified surface features at sites that are similar to the constructions described by Weigand for the San Felipe phase. Circular mound features were found at sites 14 and 18, and, based on the amount of looting observed at the feature, it is highly probable that those mounds contained burials. They appear to be similar to the San Felipe stand-alone, circular, and oval burial mounds. The terrace at site 29 definitely had burials, and it is highly probable that burials were present in the terrace at site 2. The San Felipe burial platforms that are built into hillsides may be similar to the terrace found at site 2.

To my knowledge, detailed descriptions of San Felipe phase pottery have not been published. It is possible that the rim sherd collection from the Puroaguita survey contains rims that are similar to those found in the San Felipe phase pottery complex and that these rims are currently not recognized as such.

Weigand (1985:63) has conceded that the San Felipe phase is only poorly understood. Recognition of the San Felipe phase components at most of the major San Felipe phase sites is complicated by overlays of later occupations. Weigand has explained the problem this creates: "If that overlay is Postclassic, there are no problems since the Classic/Postclassic time boundary (despite the disputes of exactly when, how, and why) is the only clear one to emerge for this region. But a Classic hamlet on a Formative center is close to impossible to isolate" (Weigand 1985:63).

Given the current data, little more can be said about the Early Chupícuaro phase in southeastern Guanajuato. Although this phase appears to share characteristics with the San Felipe phase, more definitive data are necessary to better support such an argument. Nevertheless, it seems reasonable to conclude that the Early Chupícuaro phase settlements in southeastern Guanajuato are a colonization from the west along the Río Lerma corridor. As such, these settlements can be characterized as peripheral to their source areas.

The first significant contact between Preclassic settlers in southeastern Guanajuato and their contemporaries in the Basin of Mexico marked the onset of the Chupícuaro phase in southeastern Guanajuato. The El Rayo burials reveal the nature and extent of that contact. New pottery forms appear for the first time: mammiform supports, ring-bases and ring-stands, pedestal bases, body-break and basal-break vessels, and cylinders. The burials also suggest that slant-eye figurines, one of the hallmarks of the "Chupícuaro tradition," were one of the new ceramic elements appearing in southeastern Guanajuato at this time. In addition, the Puroaguita survey identified rim sherds from utilitarian vessels that are diagnostic of the Late Preclassic period in the Basin of Mexico (Florance 1989:566–570).

In 1989, I aligned the Chupícuaro phase with the basin phase associated with the early portion of the Terminal Preclassic period, the Patlachique-Chimalhuacán phase. In light of the evidence from the El Rayo burials and from the above-mentioned rim sherds identified in the Puroaguita survey, I would now shift the beginning of the Chupícuaro phase into the Late Preclassic period. Adding a century to the Chupícuaro phase in this manner would shift the Early Chupícuaro phase into an earlier portion of the Late Preclassic. The beginning of the Late Preclassic in the Basin of Mexico is placed at 650 B.C. by Sanders et al. (1979:Table 5.1). Thus, the Early Chupícuaro phase in southeastern Guanajuato would fall within a 250-year span between 650 B.C. and 400 B.C. The Chupícuaro phase would span another 250-year period between 400 B.C. and 150 B.C. That the Chupícuaro phase falls within the earlier part of the Terminal Preclassic period is predicated on a utilitarian olla with an outflaring rim and two figurine heads collected during the Puroaguita survey. The olla rim carries a series of indentations or punctations along the upper surface of the rim (Florance 1985:Figure 14a). The figurine heads were collected at site 9 (Figure 2.8a) and 10 (Figure 2.8b) in the Puroaguita survey. I believe these figurine heads to be of the Chimalhuacán Type I type. A more detailed discussion of material correlates between the basin's Terminal Preclassic and the Puroaguita survey can be found in Florance (1989:570–577).

Of particular interest for the Late and Terminal Preclassic of western and central Mexico is the site of Cuicuilco and the Tezoyuca phase (for a detailed discussion, see Florance 1989:636–654). In summary, researchers in the Basin of Mexico have argued that the final phase of the Late Preclassic is followed by a period of dramatic change in the distribution of settlements and population there. Heizer and Bennyhoff (1972) argue that the initiation of these changes can be attributed to influences external to the basin, that is, Chupícuaro and Cholula. M. S. West (1964, 1965) and later Sanders and Parsons (Sanders et al. 1979) initiate the Terminal

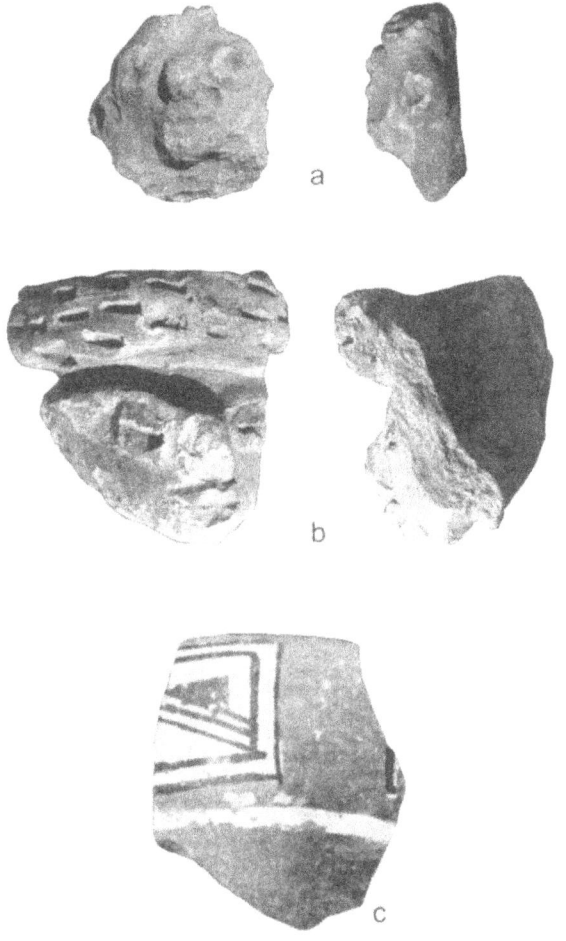

Figure 2.8. Exotic materials from sites 9 and 10: (*a* and *b*) Chimalhuacán Type I figurines; (*a*) from site 10; (*b*) from site 9; (c) distinctive rim sherd from site 10.

Preclassic with the Tezoyuca phase. This phase is characterized as a period of great instability in the basin with many polities in conflict with one another. What was happening at Cuicuilco during this period is a crucial issue that remains unresolved. West's (1965) work attributed the Tezoyuca phase conflict in the Teotihuacán Valley to a migration of Chimalhuacán people there when volcanism reduced Cuicuilco. This argument suggests a contemporaneity between the Tezoyuca and Chimalhuacán (Patlachique) phases, however, and advances the major volcanic reduction of Cuicuilco to a time that is now seen as too early. Heizer and Bennyhoff (1972) speak of a disruption in the Cuicuilco tradition, but they do not speculate about what is happening at the settlement of Cuicuilco itself. If Cuicuilco were the largest and most complex settlement in the basin during the Late Preclassic, it is difficult to accept the argument that a short period of time (50 years, according to Sanders et al. 1979) existed at the beginning of the Terminal Preclassic when Cuicuilco lost its cultural dominance and basin settlement unraveled.

Having reviewed the various arguments concerning Cuicuilco in the Late and Terminal Preclassic and the disagreement over the Tezoyuca phase, I am now convinced that Cuicuilco was the preeminent polity in the Basin of Mexico by the end of the Late Preclassic (300 B.C.). Cuicuilco continued in this position to its zenith in the Terminal Preclassic Chimalhuacán-Patlachique phase, when a volcanic eruption from Xitli adversely affected its agricultural base. Furthermore, I believe the Tezoyuca hilltop centers and Tezoyuca pottery do not represent a phase that is chronologically earlier than the Patlachique-Chimalhuacán phase. Rather, the Tezoyuca hilltop settlements, found in the Texcoco and Tenayuca regions as well as in the Teotihuacán Valley, are administrative settlements established by Cuicuilco to better integrate and control the more distant portions of its domain in the Basin of Mexico. The appearance of foreign ceramics from southeastern Guanajuato and Cholula in the Basin of Mexico, which Bennyhoff interpreted as intrusive and as indicative of disruption, was the result of broad interregional trade fostered by a stable, pan-basin market system created by and controlled through Cuicuilco.

The changes in settlement that occurred in the southern Basin of Mexico between the Late Preclassic Cuicuilco III phase and Terminal Preclassic Patlachique-Chimalhuacán times are the result of urbanization at Cuicuilco and overpopulation in the most productive areas of the southern basin. One focus of these settlement changes involved the largely unsettled, undeveloped alluvial plain in the Teotihuacán Valley. This plain was recognized for its potential to relieve population pressure in the southern basin. The expertise that had produced the agrarian revolution in the southern Basin of Mexico and had created the Cuicuilco urban center was put to work in the Teotihuacán Valley to develop the full agricultural potential of the Río San Juan and the springs that fed it. A sister metropolis to Cuicuilco was laid out to accommodate population that was relocating to the Teotihuacán Valley. The work in the Teotihuacán Valley may have been pursued with urgency in late Patlachique-Chimalhuacán times when volcanic activity in the southwestern basin began to manifest itself. When subsequent volcanic activity severely curtailed the agricultural capacity of the Cuicuilco zone, relocation to the Teotihuacán Valley followed and the Tzacualli phase of basin prehistory began.

The question of heartland versus periphery can now be addressed in the southeastern Guanajuato region during the Chupícuaro phase. At a regional scale encompassing southeastern Guanajuato, the Chupícuaro phase settlements may be thought of as a heartland development. The Chupícuaro phase settlement pattern defined in the Puroaguita survey area may provide an example of what a regional center is during this phase. No one settlement is continuous over a large area. Rather, many discontinuous settlements are aggregated together in a particularly favorable zone. In the case of the Puroaguita survey area, the focus of aggregated settlement is a small alluvial basin formed by the confluence of three arroyos—Salao, La Estancia, and La Huertita. Most of the surface scatters identified during the Puroaguita survey were located within or around the margin of this basin.

The Puroaguita survey area is favorably located in terms of both its local environment and its strategic position along the Río Lerma, a major route of intra- and interregional communication. During the Chupícuaro phase, local leaders were in a position to enhance their prestige among their followers by gaining access to the Basin of Mexico economy and its political system elite. I believe that this is what we are seeing in the Puroaguita survey area during the Late Preclassic portion of the Chupícuaro phase. Basin pottery and figurines became the symbols manipulated by local leaders to enhance their status. Satellite settlements within the basin itself were established to facilitate the movement of goods and symbols between the basin and southeastern Guanajuato. Successful leadership attracted followers to a locale. Thus, during the Chupícuaro phase, there is a significant population ingathering, as witnessed in the Puroaguita survey area.

A still unresolved question in my mind is whether or not the Puroaguita heartland became a periphery to the Cuicuilco polity in the Basin of Mexico at some point in Patlachique-Chimalhuacán times. I raise this question because of the location of two settlements (sites 9 and 10) within the Puroaguita survey area. These two surface scatters were defined based on concentrated artifactual material at two separate but adjacent spots. However, the two scatter concentrations were joined across a zone of reduced concentration. Sites 9 and 10 combined make the largest area of surface scatter in the Puroaguita survey zone (4.2 hectares) and lie on what can be characterized as a hilltop or ridge crest between the arroyos of El Ocote and Salao (Florance 1989:604).

It will be recalled that sites 9 and 10 are where the Chimalhuacán-like figurine heads were found. Also, a distinctive rim sherd was collected at site 10 (Figure 2.8c). This relatively thin-walled, incurved bowl had surface colors of orange, red, and white. Part of a distinctive motif appears on the bowl exterior. These exotic materials may result from the presence of unique functional activities at sites 9 and 10. I have suggested that these sites are a frontier version of the Tezoyuca hilltop center (Florance 1989:659). As such, the Chimalhuacán-like figurines and exotic pottery may be evidence of the presence of Cuicuilco officialdom. On the other hand, the presence of these materials may simply indicate the residential locus of a local leader who enjoyed access to these symbols of power and prestige from the Basin of Mexico.

The substantial material evidence of Basin of Mexico presence in southeastern Guanajuato during the Chupícuaro phase begs the question whether or not that presence can be found in other regions of west Mexico. An answer may be found in the El Arenal phase of the highland lake district of Jalisco. During this phase, a unique and exotic architectural form appears. As for the uniqueness of this architecture, Weigand makes the following observation: "One possible exception to the Western Mexico uniqueness of the five-element circular complex may exist: Cuicuilco, in the southern sector of the Central Valley of Mexico" (Weigand 1985:70).

Weigand's cultural sequence has the five-element architectural form appearing in the highland lake district of Jalisco at the same time Cuicuilco is approaching its maximum size and greatest hegemony during the Patlachique-Chimalhuacán phase. Also at this same time, southeastern Guanajuato may have been directly subjugated by the Cuicuilco polity. I am not suggesting that the highland lake district of Jalisco is directly controlled by Cuicuilco in this period. Rather, it is more likely that the elite within the highland lake district societies were manipulating the symbols of Cuicuilco's power to enhance their own power and prestige. One preeminent symbol of Cuicuilco's power was its architecture. Adapting elements of this architecture to an existing funerary cult architecture, the circular platforms and hillside terraces, would serve to bolster the legitimacy of the elite within the indigenous tradition.

The Ahualulco phase in the highland lake district of Jalisco witnessed "an intensification of the processes" begun in the El Arenal phase (Weigand 1985:72). The architectural manifestations of the intensification include monumental ball courts, usually appended to the circular complexes; larger and taller platforms and pyramids in larger circles; and the appearance of multiple circles at a settlement.

Associated with the Ahualulco phase were important changes in settlement. This suggested that "neighboring districts are being unified into larger polities" (Weigand 1985:72). On a regional basis, "the center of gravity within the northern lake zone begins to shift more conclusively to the Ahualulco-Teuchitlán-Tala valley, corresponding to a drop in the number of sites in nearby valleys" (Weigand 1985:72). What this settlement change suggested to Weigand was a population implosion.

Elsewhere, and in this chapter, I have suggested aligning the Ahualulco phase with the Tzacualli phase in the Basin of Mexico. This would also make the Ahualulco phase contemporary with the Mixtlán phase in southeastern Guanajuato. The alignment would correlate a number of major changes in all three regions. In the Basin of Mexico, Teotihuacán becomes the preeminent urban center, superseding the crippled Cuicuilco. Thus, population and commerce within the basin is shifted to the northeastern sector. This shift necessitated the development of new transportation routes to neighboring regions. The Río Lerma with its course through southeastern Guanajuato lost its importance as a transportation corridor. Another process affecting southeastern Guanajuato during Mixtlán times was population implosion. Weigand sees this process beginning in the Ahualulco phase in the highland lake district of Jalisco. In the Teotihuacán Valley, this implosive process begins in the Tzacualli phase. In southeastern Guanajuato, there is a significant loss of population during the Mixtlán phase. If the Puroaguita survey area was a regional center during the Chupícuaro phase, it certainly lost that position by Mixtlán phase times.

It is of interest to note that the Mixtlán phase settlement pattern in the Puroaguita survey area had no settlement along the Río Lerma channel per se (see Figure 2.7). Site 5, the second largest single surface scatter identified in the survey (2.1 hectares), was not occupied during Mixtlán phase times. Site 5 was strategically positioned at the confluence of the Lerma and the stream formed by the combined flows of the arroyos in the northern portion of the survey area. This stream crossed the alluvial basin within and around which the majority of Preclassic settlement occurred. Thus, site 5 was situated at the entrance to the alluvial basin and can be viewed as a point of entry into the vicinity when transportation was principally focused on the Río Lerma. Site 5 may have been functionally distinctive as a site where commodities were gathered for transport from the area or for distribution to the hinterland settlements in the zone. If site 5 was not occupied during the Mixtlán phase, it may be that the Río Lerma, or at least that portion in southeastern Guanajuato, had lost its significance as a major transportation corridor in Mixtlán phase times. Thus, in the Mixtlán phase, southeastern Guanajuato became a peripheral region to heartland areas focused elsewhere.

SUMMARY AND CONCLUSIONS

A reanalysis of the El Rayo cemetery burials with associated polychrome pottery has presented data that have led to a reformulation of the Preclassic archaeological chronology in southeastern Guanajuato developed in an earlier work (Florance 1989). Figure 2.9 summarizes the chronological arguments made in this chapter. The controlling sequence is that for the Basin of Mexico as presented in Sanders et al. (1979:Table 5.1). My review of arguments for a disruptive Tezoyuca phase that marks the commencement of the Terminal Preclassic period in the basin has led me to conclude that the phase is nonexistent, however, and that the purported disruption does not offer a plausible explanation of existing data. Therefore, the Tezoyuca phase appears in the same time span as the Patlachique and Chimalhuacán phases.

For southeastern Guanajuato, Figure 2.9 illustrates the placement of the Early Chupícuaro phase in the earlier portion of the Basin of Mexico's Late Preclassic period. The commencement of the Chupícuaro phase in southeastern Guanajuato is aligned with the later portion of the Late Preclassic in the Basin of Mexico. The first significant contacts with the Basin of Mexico mark the onset of this phase. Also, the Chupícuaro phase in southeastern Guanajuato is aligned with the Patlachique-Chimalhuacán phase. A frontier version of a Cuicuilco administrative settlement may appear in southeastern Guanajuato at this time.

Weigand's archaeological sequence for the highland lake district of Jalisco has had a considerable influence on the chronological arguments presented here. His San Felipe phase, together with the El Rayo burial reanalysis, suggests that the Early Chupícuaro phase could be moved back in time. His El Arenal phase, with its innovative five-element architectural style and its alignment with the Patlachique-Chimalhuacán phase in the Basin of Mexico, raises the specter of Cuicuilco in that distant region. The impact of the Cuicuilco polity in southeastern Guanajuato during the early Terminal Preclassic in-

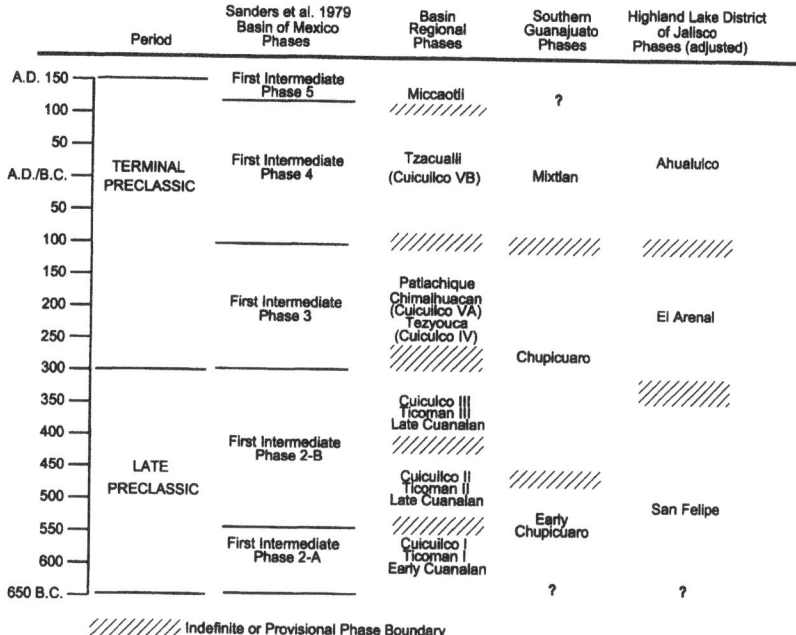

Figure 2.9. Chronologies from the Basin of Mexico, southern Guanajuato, and the highland lake district of Jalisco.

creases the plausibility of its having had some effect on the more distant highland lake district of Jalisco. The nature of that effect requires further study, but it may, in part, be architectural.

Finally, Figure 2.9 locates the Ahualulco phase in the later portion of the Terminal Preclassic. Thus, the process of massive population aggregation seen in the Teotihuacán Valley during the Tzacualli phase has a parallel in the highland lake district of Jalisco. This implosive process, together with the shift of population and economic activity to the northeastern sector of the Basin of Mexico, changed the strategic position that southeastern Guanajuato and the Lerma corridor had enjoyed during Cuicuilco's hegemony in the basin.

The question posed by the title of this chapter was answered earlier. The Late and Terminal Preclassic settlements in southeastern Guanajuato can be viewed as both heartland and periphery as spatial and temporal scales change. Only with an interregional perspective can the complexity of culture history and process in the Late and Terminal Preclassic of the central highlands be fully understood. Studies in one region can lead to new insights into the events of adjacent regions and vice versa. Interregional studies are essential to breaking down parochial perspectives. Regional entrenchment will only hinder our broader understanding of the mesoamerican cultural system during this or any time period.

CHAPTER THREE

A SUMMARY OF THE ARCHAEOLOGY OF NORTH-CENTRAL MESOAMERICA

Guanajuato, Querétaro, and San Luis Potosí

BEATRIZ BRANIFF C.

THE REGION DISCUSSED in this chapter is located in portions of Guanajuato, Querétaro, and San Luis Potosí in north-central Mexico; specifically, it is north of the Río Lerma in the Mesa Central and along the southern tip of the Mesa del Norte surrounding the extinct Lago Gran Salado. Within this region there are two areas of particular interest to this discussion: the large lacustrine and alluvial basin known as the Bajío, and the Tunal Grande in the highlands of San Luis Potosí and neighboring portions of Zacatecas and Jalisco (Figure 3.1). For detailed discussions of the archaeological characteristics of these two areas, see Crespo and Brambila 1991; Braniff 1972, 1974, 1975a, 1975b, 1991a, 1992a; Brown 1985; Castañeda and others 1988; and Saint-Charles 1990.

This north-central region of Mesoamerica occupies a xerophytic and grassland biotic zone (Rzedowski 1978). Precipitation in the area ranges from 400 to 800 mm annually, and it becomes more arid as one moves northward. Rainfall is generally sufficient to allow temporal farming, which is, nevertheless, a risky endeavor (Braniff 1989a). Although temporal farming was undoubtedly the main farming technique employed prehistorically, it is likely that the precolonial inhabitants occupying areas north of the Tropic of Cancer used some form of water control to help maintain their sedentary lifestyles.

From a general perspective, it is important to distinguish "traditional" mesoamerican cultural development, as seen to the south, from the cultural development that occurred along the northern frontier of Mesoamerica. Cultural development in the mesoamerican core is seen as progressing in a continuous evolutionary process from the Preclassic period to the Classic period, to the Postclassic period and Spanish conquest. Cultural developments along the northern frontier of Mesoamerica did not follow this path. The Formative period along the northern mesoamerican frontier has been characterized as "retarded" (Braniff 1989b; Kelley 1989a) because it is said to represent the expansion of, or possibly colonization by, the Late Preclassic period proto-urban hearths located to the south.

The cultures within the study area seem to have achieved their greatest development and complexity during the first millennium A.D. A general cultural collapse of the area began ca. A.D. 900 to 1000, and after A.D. 1000 to 1200 the occupants of the region returned progressively to or were replaced by inhabitants with a semisedentary or nomadic way of life. It is interesting to note that the general collapse of this area coincides with the historical myths associated with the arrival of the northern hero Mixcoatl and his four hundred archers and the beginnings of the Toltec state.

Despite the general collapse along this section of the

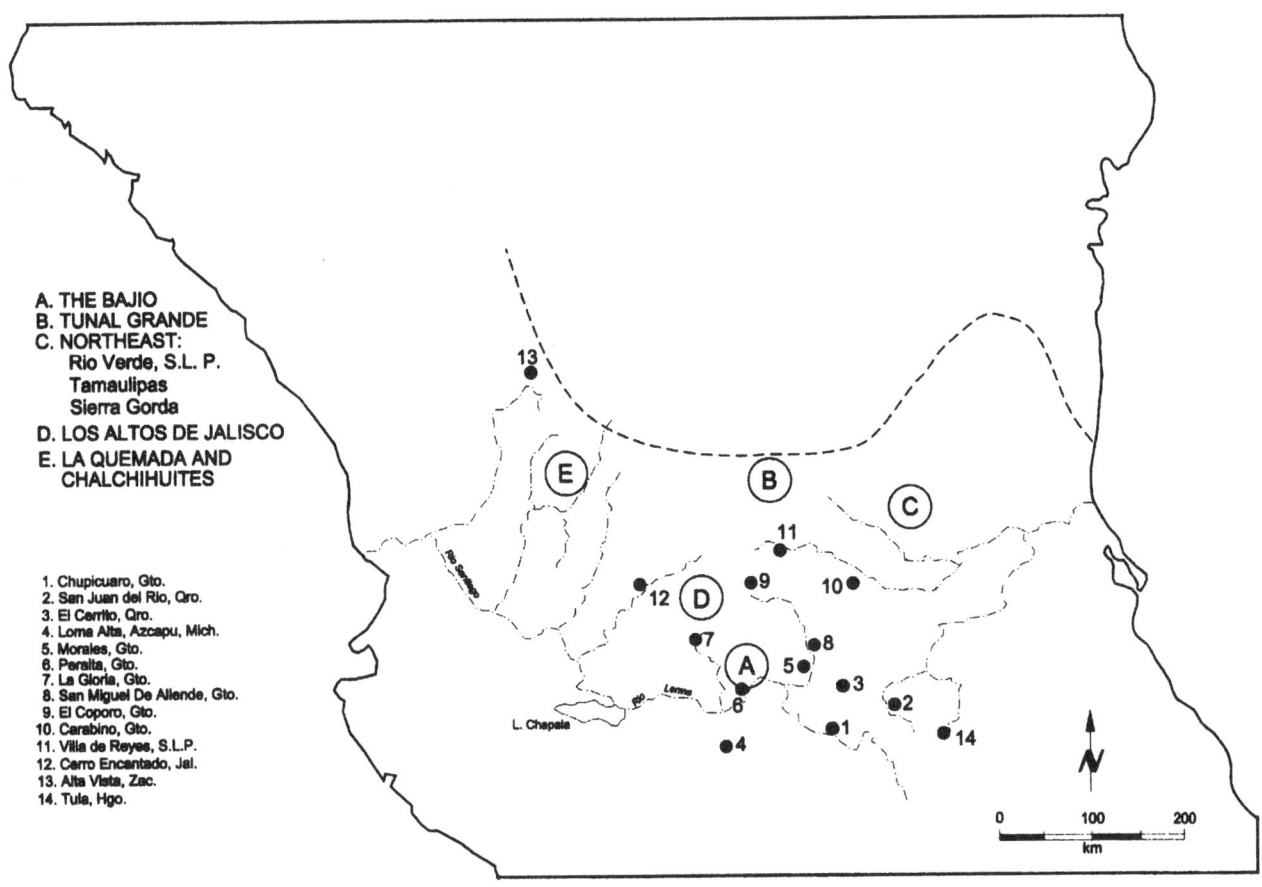

Figure 3.1. North-central Mesoamerica.

northern frontier, a clear Toltec (Tollán phase, A.D. 950–1150) intrusion is evident along a line from the site of El Cerrito in the Valley of Querétaro, through Carabino (northeast of Guanajuato), to Villa de Reyes in the San Luis Potosí highlands (Braniff 1975b, 1992a; Castañeda et al. 1988:328). The end of a mesoamerican presence in this region corresponds to the end of Tula itself. Armillas (1964b, 1969) has suggested that this was the result of increased aridity in the region. The Spanish conquest of this area was a prolonged and difficult process, one that continued beyond the sixteenth century.

EXTERNAL CONNECTIONS

Peoples of the Bajío and Tunal Grande were in contact with and influenced by peoples from surrounding regions, including the nomadic hunter-gatherers of the desert to the north. Cultures to the west seem to have had the greatest influences on these areas. A clear cultural boundary separates the Bajío and Tunal Grande areas and peoples from the other cultures of northeastern Mesoamerica, those that lie in the Sierra Gorda of Querétaro, the Río Verde Valley in San Luis Potosí, and the Sierra de Tamaulipas (Figure 3.1). These latter cultures exhibit affinities to cultures along the Gulf Coast and Teotihuacán (Braniff 1975b; MacNeish 1958; Michelet 1986; Velasco 1990).

Some efforts have been made to identify and describe remains associated with the nomadic groups who lived in this part of Mesoamerica before and after the mesoamerican intrusion into the region (Rodríguez 1983, 1985). The identification of cultural remains associated with these groups has been problematic, however. Most of the work in the area has focused on pottery-producing sedentary peoples. Nevertheless, evidence suggests that there was considerable interaction between the sedentary peoples of the area and their nomadic counterparts living in the deserts to the north (Braniff 1975a; Cervantes et al. 1981). Understanding the scale and nature of that interaction is problematic. It has been suggested that such a relationship was an antagonistic one,

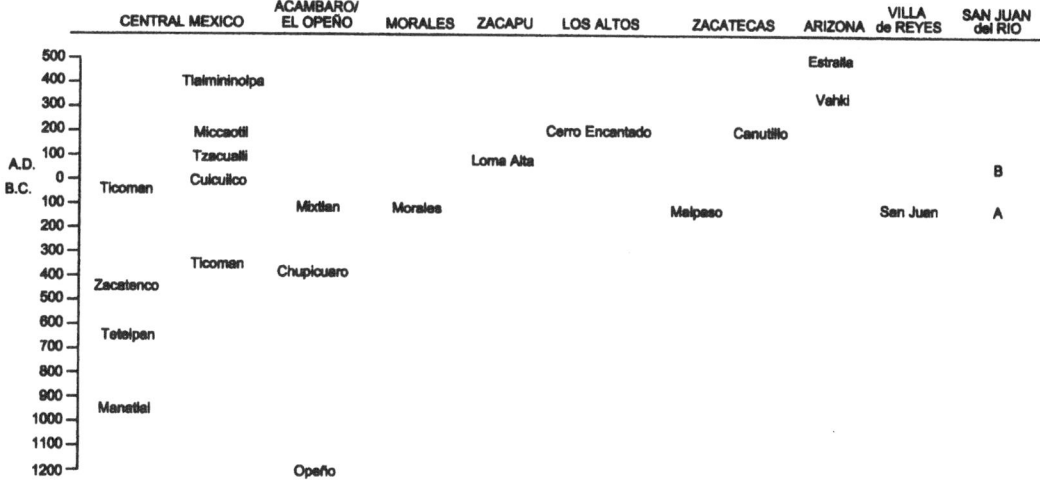

Figure 3.2. Preclassic period chronological sequences of the north-central mesoamerican frontier and central Mexico.

but this assumption is in need of reevaluation. Perhaps a new model should be developed and evaluated, one that explores the possibility of a symbiotic relationship between the hunter-gatherers of the northern deserts and their sedentary mesoamerican neighbors.

As previously stated, most of the work in the Bajío and Tunal Grande has focused on mesoamerican ceramic traditions. The following discussion summarizes what is currently known of these areas from the Preclassic period through the collapse of this portion of the north-central mesoamerican frontier.

THE FIRST SETTLEMENTS, 650 B.C.–A.D. 200

The best known of the early ceramic period developments in the Bajío and Tunal Grande areas, especially in the Bajío, is Chupícuaro. It is important to note, however, that the Chupícuaro culture as reported by Porter (1956) exhibits many elements that originate in the earlier El Opeño and Capacha complexes of west Mexico (Braniff 1975a, 1991a:Figure 80). West Mexican elements, along with Olmec and Zacatenco traits, are also manifested in the Manantial phase (1000–800 B.C.) at the site of Tlatilco (Neiderberger 1987; Figure 3.2).

The Chupícuaro phase at Acambaro, Guanajuato, has been suggested to begin at ca. 650 B.C. (Gorenstein 1985). Based on the presence of El Opeño and Capacha elements in the Chupícuaro culture, this date seems generally acceptable. If it is correct, Florance's (1985:45, see also this volume) suggestion that Chupícuaro was a "component in an expanding state system focused in Cuicuilco" is problematic in that Cuicuilco did not become a political or economic force until a later time. The following Mixtlán phase, A.D. 100–450 (Gorenstein 1985), is clearly a manifestation of the Chupícuaro ceramic tradition. One of its hallmarks was the use of distinctive white linear decorations on the ceramics (Florance 1985:26, 39).

Many authors, including myself (Braniff 1972), have not differentiated between these two phases. Bennyhoff (1966:24) indicates that "the Tezoyuca phase (200–100 B.C.), of the Terminal Preclassic sequence in the Valley of Mexico, features a distinctive local ceramic complex that may be derived from the Chupícuaro tradition. It includes various vessel forms and a distinctive white-on-red style." Although these decorative elements are suggested to be associated with the Chupícuaro tradition (Florance 1985), Porter (1956) does not report any white-on-red vessels at Chupícuaro. But white-on-red design elements are characteristic of Mixtlán polychromes (Florance 1985). Muller (1990:61) also identified a white and red-on-buff ware, a Chupícuaro polychrome, at Cuicuilco. This polychrome is assigned to the Cuicuilco 6 (Tezoyuca) phase, dating 200–150 B.C. This suggests a much earlier date for Mixtlán phase than that proposed by Gorenstein (1985).

Clearly, a reconsideration of the place of Chupícuaro materials in the Preclassic period sequence in the Valley of Mexico is needed. This is especially important when the regional impact of Chupícuaro is considered. Chupícuaro's influence can be seen in the Cuicuilco-

Ticoman I phase dated by Millon (1981; see also Mastache and Cobean 1989) to 600–500 B.C. and the later Cuicuilco III (300 B.C.) phase. During Cuicuilco III times, Cuicuilco came under extreme pressure from the Chupícuaro region (Bennyhoff 1966:20–21; see also McBride 1974).

Both the early Chupícuaro phase and variation of the Mixtlán phase are recognized in northern Michoacán and in the Bajío. A site near San Juan del Río, Querétaro (Saint-Charles 1991; Saint-Charles and Arguelles 1991), and several large centers (with platforms, pyramids, and sunken patios) in southern Guanajuato (Castañeda et al. 1988:322–324, Figures 2–4) are or have components of the early Chupícuaro phase. A large fortress site near Tlaxcala also has an early Chupícuaro phase component (García Cook and Rodríguez 1975). Thus, it appears that complex architecture may also be a trait of the early Chupícuaro phase.

As the Chupícuaro phase developed into the Mixtlán phase at Acambaro, it also evolved into several related but poorly understood complexes in other areas of the north-central frontier. A number of early Chupícuaro phase traits (design elements, ceramic traits, and figurines) appear randomly scattered in these subsequent developments. Many of these traits and design elements may have had symbolic significance since they also appear in later contexts. These include the division of the interiors of bowls into four quarters, as seen very early in the Manantial phase at Tlatilco; an element in the form of a stepped pyramid which occasionally contains a small, centrally located rectangle or triangle, as often seen in Chupícuaro; a triangular element with one stepped edge; the *ojo de dios* element; and so-called frog legs, which also are frequently expressed in Chupícuaro.

Late Chupícuaro-Mixtlán phase materials in the north-central frontier area are associated with the Morales complex as identified at the Morales site near San Miguel de Allende, Guanajuato (Figures 3.3 and 3.4). At the Morales site these materials are tentatively dated 300–200 B.C. (Braniff 1972, 1991a). Morales traits and related materials also occur elsewhere in Guanajuato (Braniff 1974); in the Juchipila Valley in Zacatecas (Jiménez 1989, 1995; Jiménez and Darling this volume); at Loma Alta and Zacapu, Michoacán, where they are dated 11 ± 99 B.C. (Carot 1990, 1992); in Phase A and possibly Phase B in the San Juan del Río, Querétaro, region, where they are dated 500–1 B.C. and A.D. 1–400, respectively (Nalda 1975:99–105); in the earliest phase at Cerro de la Cruz, San Juan del Río, dating 500 B.C.–A.D. 200 (Saint-Charles and Arguelles 1991); and in the

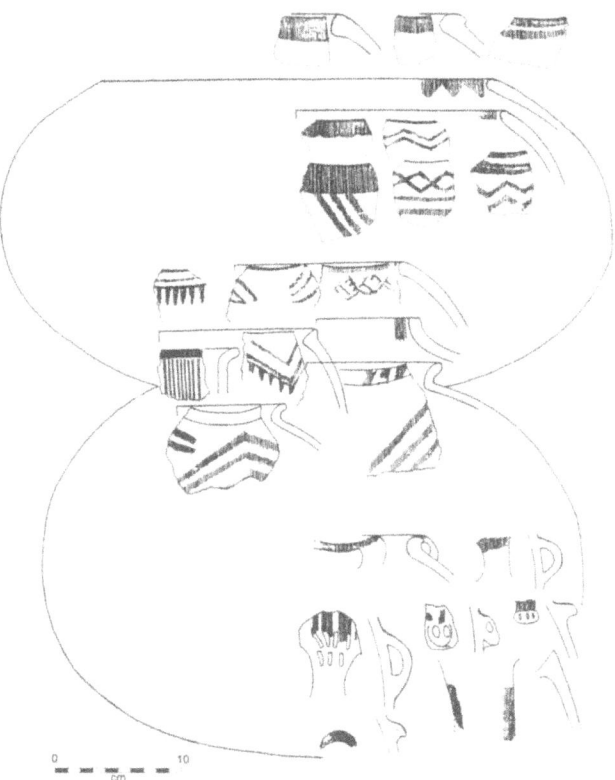

Figure 3.3. Morales Red-on-buff ceramics.

San Juan phase of the Tunal Grande area, where they are dated 70 B.C. ± 200 (Braniff 1975b, 1992a).

To the northwest in the Altos de Jalisco, the Cerro Encantado complex, A.D. 100–250 (Bell 1974), certainly belongs to the late Chupícuaro tradition, as may the Canutillo phase of western Zacatecas. Formative period elements such as the quartered designs and knee-foot supports on legged vessels carry over to post-Canutillo times in western Zacatecas (Kelley and Kelley 1971).

The above suggests that a mesoamerican colonization of the north-central mesoamerican frontier by west Mexican and Chupícuaro-related peoples had occurred by at least A.D. 1. This expansion coincides with the mesoamerican urban revolution. As the cultural traditions of central Mexico expanded and their demands for more and new resources and lands grew, new territories, some in the environmentally marginal zones of the north-central frontier, were settled. These subsequent cultural traditions were not identical to their Chupícuaro forebears. Rather, they manifested many new traits that, in part, were derived from contact with adjacent peoples. The Morales complex, for example, used design elements

Figure 3.4. Morales Polychrome (black and white-on-red).

that included frogs, birds with wings spread, a squirrel-like figure, and lizards. Nevertheless, many design elements derived from the Chupícuaro tradition carried over, including the stepped pyramid, the stepped-triangle, and the H4 figurine. Similar elements and traits are present in the related Loma Alta complex. Other Loma Alta design elements include ducks, an alligator monster, a serpent outlined in dots, and the stepped fret (*greque*).

The Morales complex also contains design elements that may be derived from central Mexico, including engraved linear frets on the interior of vessels, scalloped rims, and ollas decorated with a hand element. The quartered design, white linear decoration, and the stepped triangle are also present at Cerro Encantado (Bell 1974). Some of the above-mentioned zoomorphs are associated with the stepped fret and the four-quarter division that appear at the end of the Canutillo phase and are especially numerous in the Alta Vista and later phases of western Zacatecas (Kelley and Kelley 1971).

Many of these design elements also appear in the Hohokam sequence of Arizona. The stepped fret and quartered designs are found in the Estrella phase, and zoomorphs, which appear first in the Snaketown phase, are common in the Gila Butte and Santa Cruz phases. By the Sacaton phase, A.D. 900–1100 (Haury 1976), these generally disappear. It is of note that this date coincides with the general collapse of the mesoamerican frontier at ca. A.D. 900.

URBAN DEVELOPMENTS, A.D. 250–850/900

After the initial colonization and spread of Chupícuaro-related cultures, the north-central frontier region saw the evolution of more complex societies. This is particularly true in the Bajío region, where towns and cities with monumental and ceremonial architecture dominated lesser towns and villages (Castañeda et al. 1988; Crespo 1991; Martínez and Nieto 1987; Zepeda 1986). Bajío sites are associated with three ceramic traditions that exhibit local variation. The most widespread is the Blanco Levantado tradition. This ceramic type may be derived from a shadow-stripped ware that dates as early as 200 B.C. in Colima and Jalisco (e.g., Kelly 1949; Kelly and Braniff 1966; Meighan 1972:45–46). Based on radiocarbon dates from El Cerrito, Querétaro, however, it appears Blanco Levantado is best dated between A.D. 400 and 600 (Crespo 1986a).

The second ceramic tradition of the area is a red-on-buff or orange-on-buff tradition that is sometimes called "Cantinas," following Snarskis's (1985) description of a similar ceramic tradition at Acambaro, where it is associated with the Lerma phase, A.D. 450–1450 (Gorenstein 1985:97). Many investigators see these red-on-buff types as a development out of earlier Chupícuaro types (Castañeda et al. 1988:325; Snarskis 1985:239). Others see their origins in the Coyotlatelco wares that appear in the Valley of Mexico at A.D. 600–700, close to the collapse of Teotihuacán (Braniff 1972; Cobean 1978, 1990; Mastache and Cobean 1989).

The third ceramic tradition is a fine gray-black ware with exterior engraving. At Acambaro such engraving is represented in a ceramic type called Garita (Castañeda et al. 1988:326). Engraved types are found in many areas of the north-central frontier, including Zaquil Black, Garita related types in Guanajuato, the incised-engraved blackwares of the Malpaso Valley, and Michilia Engraved of western Zacatecas (Kelley and Kelley 1971). Black engraved wares also occur in Colima, Jalisco, and Sinaloa and are often found in association with red-on-buff types similar to Cantinas and Coyotlatelco Red-on-buff (Kelly 1938; Meighan 1972).

A Teotihuacán presence, suggested by the presence of Thin Orange sherds, is evident at El Cóporo and other sites near Querétaro: Celaya and Cuitzeo south of the

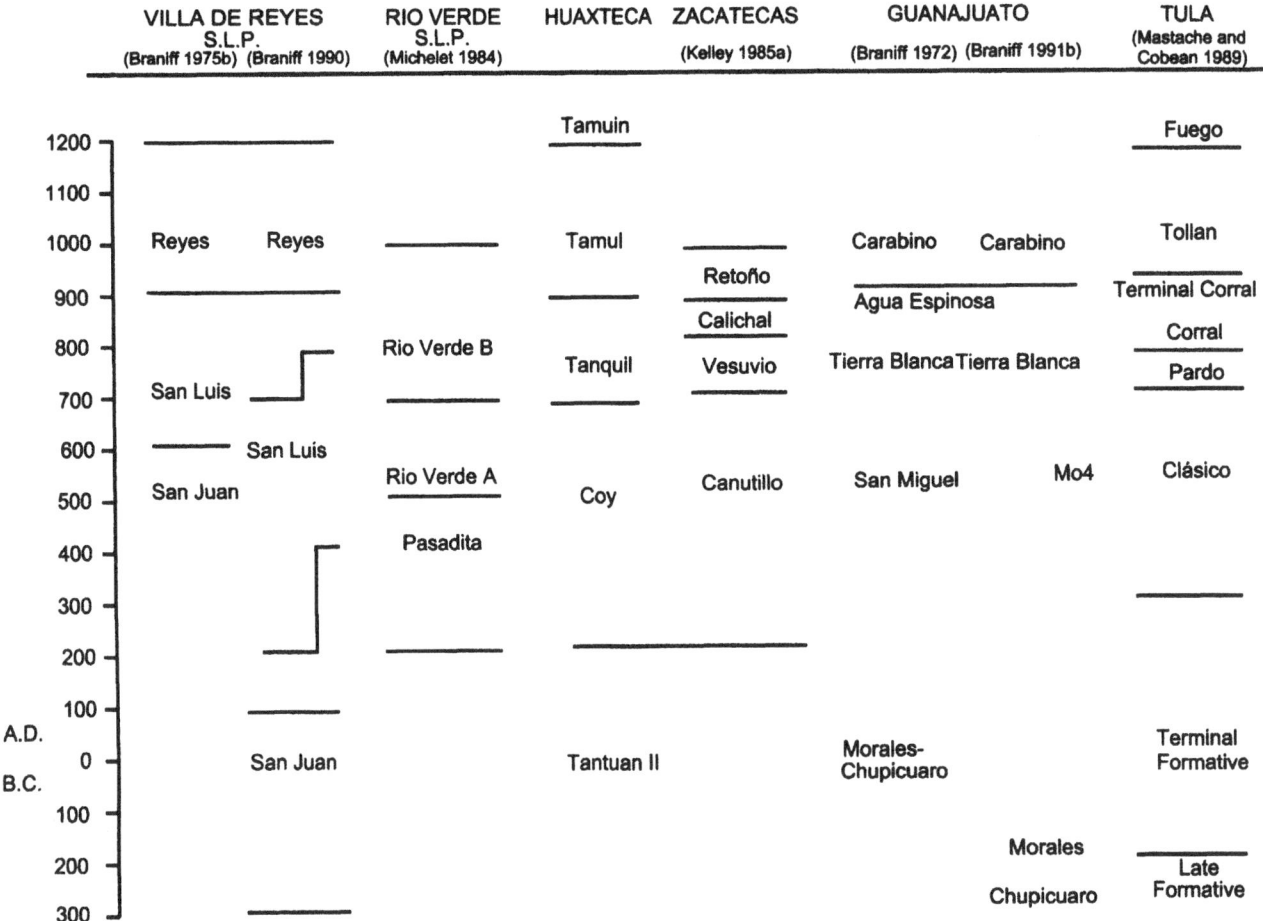

Figure 3.5. Chronological sequences of the north-central mesoamerican frontier and central Mexico, Preclassic through Postclassic periods.

Río Lerma. This may be evidence of a corridor to or link with the lake region of Michoacán (Castañeda et al. 1988:327, Figure 14).

West Mexican influence may also be seen in the architecture of the area. Two circular structures of the Teuchitlán tradition (see Weigand this volume) have been reported in western Guanajuato at La Gloria on the Río Turbio (Sánchez and Marmolejo 1990) and at Peralta A on the Río Lerma near Abasolo (Zepeda 1986). Also, El Cóporo, Guanajuato, and Cuarenta, Jalisco, both near or in the Altos region, have halls of columns.

Another time of particular interest is the period between ca. A.D. 600 and 850 (Figure 3.5). A looted collection from a large and complex site near San Miguel de Allende contained a variety of ceramic vessels, including elaborate red-on-buff plates, pseudocloisonné vessels, pipes, anthropomorphic urns, pot covers, incense burners, and a special variety of Blanco Levantado. The Blanco Levantado specimen was an olla with a modeled braid around its lip (Malo Zozaya 1972). This type of olla appears only in the most recent level of the Morales sequence (Braniff 1991a). At Tula this type of Blanco Levantado appears as an intrusive type in the Terminal Corral (A.D. 900–950) and Tollán (A.D. 950–1150) phases (Cobean 1990:449–457). Along with the above-mentioned items and a series of other traits, including Tezcatlipoca, the chacmool, the eagle eating a serpent, and halls of columns, Blanco Levantado is thought to represent a second wave of people who influenced the inhabitants of the northern Valley of Mexico, initiating the Toltec tradition (Braniff 1972, 1991a; Hers 1989a; Mastache and Cobean 1989; Odena 1990).

Another interesting association is noted at El Cóporo, Guanajuato, near the Altos area of Jalisco. Here Blanco Levantado is associated with a few sherds of Thin Orange ware typical of Teotihuacán II and III, A.D. 100–

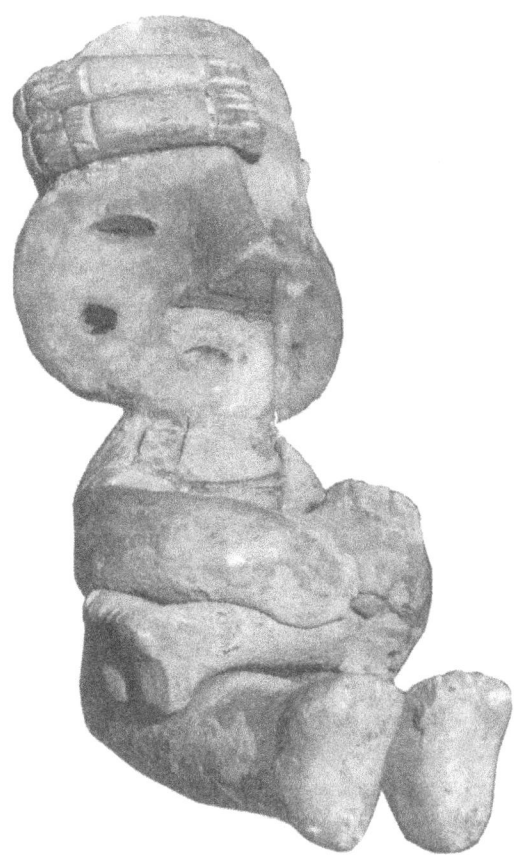

Figure 3.6. Type I figurine, El Cóporo, Guanajuato (height 5.4 cm).

Figure 3.7. Type I figurine head, El Cóporo, Guanajuato (height 4.7 cm).

500 (Millon 1981). Also found in association were a few sherds of pseudocloisonné (A.D. 600–850; Kelley 1985a); a few sherds of San Luis Valley Polychrome from the Tunal Grande area (A.D. 340 ± 70–714 ± 44; Braniff 1992a), and three Type I figurines (Jiménez 1989; see Jiménez and Darling this volume; Figure 3.6). One of the figurines (Figure 3.7) has multiple earrings and a noseplug and is quite similar to a hollow figurine from El Vergel, Zacatecas (Jiménez 1988:46). This type of figurine was also present at Cerro Encantado (Bell 1974) and is thought to date to a later occupation in the site (ca. A.D. 600–850).

The distribution of this figurine type may be a marker of widespread culture contact and interaction. Jiménez (1989) documents this figurine type from the Alta Vista phase in western Zacatecas extending through a number of continuous regions.

In the Tunal Grande area, the San Juan phase is followed by the Valle de San Luis phase (A.D. 350–850).

This phase is manifested at one large and numerous smaller villages throughout the San Luis Potosí and Zacatecas highlands around the southern shores of the Gran Salado Lake. Adobe construction is common. The site of Villa de Reyes, the only large, complex site with the only pyramid in the area, produced an interesting set of materials. Several of the ceramic types recovered are reminiscent of Early Chametla Polychrome from Sinaloa (Kelly 1938). Figurines have coffee-bean eyes and protruding noses and are again similar to figurines from the West Coast (Kelly 1945a). The figurines are also similar to types from Huatabampo, Sonora (Alvarez Palma 1991a), and Santa Cruz phase types from Snaketown (Gladwin et al. 1938:Plate CXCVII I, k; Haury 1976:Figure 13.19). Surely strong connections between the peoples of the highlands of San Luis Potosí and Zacatecas and those of the West Coast cultures must have existed during these times.

The lithic assemblage associated with these sites is mostly rhyolite, like that found in Guanajuato. Small end scrapers and projectile points are typically made from chert, however. Many of the small, notched-end scrapers are similar to specimens from La Paila Cave (Aveleyra et al. 1956:Plates III, VII, and IX). Small-handled scrapers are also found and are quite similar to specimens from late preceramic and early ceramic period contexts of western Zacatecas and Durango (e.g., Spence 1971:31, Plate V*j*). Stone and pottery pipes from this time appear similar to specimens from the Caddoan area (MacNeish 1948).

COLLAPSE OF THE NORTH-CENTRAL MESOAMERICAN FRONTIER AND THE TOLTEC INTRUSION

Much of the northern frontier began to be abandoned by mesoamerican agriculturists about A.D. 900. In many areas, people apparently returned to a hunting and gathering lifestyle or were replaced by hunters and gatherers. This time marks the transition between the Classic and Postclassic periods throughout Mesoamerica. With the exception of Durango and the West Coast areas (see Foster, and Scott and Foster this volume), the northern frontier was never again occupied by complex societies. One interesting exception is noted, however. An apparent, but poorly understood, Toltec intrusion into the north-central frontier has been tentatively identified. This Toltec complex is recognized at a number of sites, from El Cerrito near the city of Querétaro, to Carabino near San Luis de la Paz, Guanajuato, to Villa de Reyes in the Tunal Grande. The Toltec intrusion is defined by the presence of new architectural patterns and ceramic traits associated with the Terminal Corral (A.D. 900–950) and Tollán (A.D. 950–1150) phases. These include Plumbate, Mazapa figurines, Blanco Levantado (the Tula Water Colored version), and Naranja a Brochazos. At El Cerrito, the Toltec complex is dated to A.D. 950–1150 (Braniff 1972, 1975a, 1992a; Castañeda et al. 1988; Crespo 1976, 1986b, 1991). The general belief is that these Toltecs were living in the midst of a declining frontier setting and that the frontier had collapsed by the end of the Toltec era, A.D. 1150–1200.

Finally, in the southern region of Guanajuato above the Río Lerma, a Tarascan or Otomi (or both) presence dating between A.D. 1350 and 1500 has been identified archaeologically. During the early A.D. 1500s, the frontier continued its retreat southward to an agricultural zone below the Río Lerma. During this time, the north-central frontier extended along a line from Maravatio and Acambaro to Uriria, Penjamillo, and Jacona (Castañeda et al. 1988).

CHAPTER FOUR

THE EVOLUTION AND DECLINE OF A CORE OF CIVILIZATION

The Teuchitlán Tradition and the Archaeology of Jalisco

PHIL C. WEIGAND

IT HAS LONG been recognized that the western sections of Mexico contained rich archaeological cultures. The ceramic figurines from this zone have constituted a mainstay of museum and private collections for a century. Researchers have viewed these collections in isolation—separated and decontextualized from their physical and cultural settings. An anthropological tradition developed conclusions about the nature of the sociocultural systems of the ancient societies of Jalisco, Colima, and Nayarit, conclusions that now appear incorrect. The historiographical arguments about these earlier reconstructions are not repeated here (see Weigand 1985, 1990a, 1993a). Suffice it to say that recent field projects have demonstrated the existence of a unique expression of monumental architecture, large settlement and irrigation systems, high demographic profiles, a possible ideographic glyphic system, and other markers of civilization in these parts of western Mexico long before the beginning of the Postclassic. It is my purpose here to outline these developments, emphasizing the evolution of a Key Economic Area (cf. Chi 1963) in the highland lake districts of western Jalisco during the Formative and Classic periods, and its decline, collapse, and rebuilding during the Postclassic period.

THE SETTING

The lake regions of western Jalisco are very rich natural environments (Figure 4.1). Excellent soils abound, and the rare resource profile is superior to those of most other areas of early civilization in Mesoamerica. High-quality obsidians, blue-green stones, various types of crystals, and salt are among the minerals that are easily obtained in this region. The semitropical climate meant that two crops per year were possible if irrigation was employed during the dry season. Rainfall varies from 900 to 1,600 mm per year throughout the region, with around 1,000 mm as an average and with about 85 to 90 percent falling during the months of June through October. Though it contains rugged mountains, the area is not disadvantageously divided into small and isolated pocket valleys. There are no natural barriers between the middle and lower Lerma Valley and the lake districts, nor are there any barriers whatsoever between the lake valleys themselves, from Sayula in the south, Chapala in the east, and Etzatlán in the northwest. This enormous valley system is indeed surrounded by mountains and canyons, but they do not break up its natural continuity. Rather, the mountains and canyons dramati-

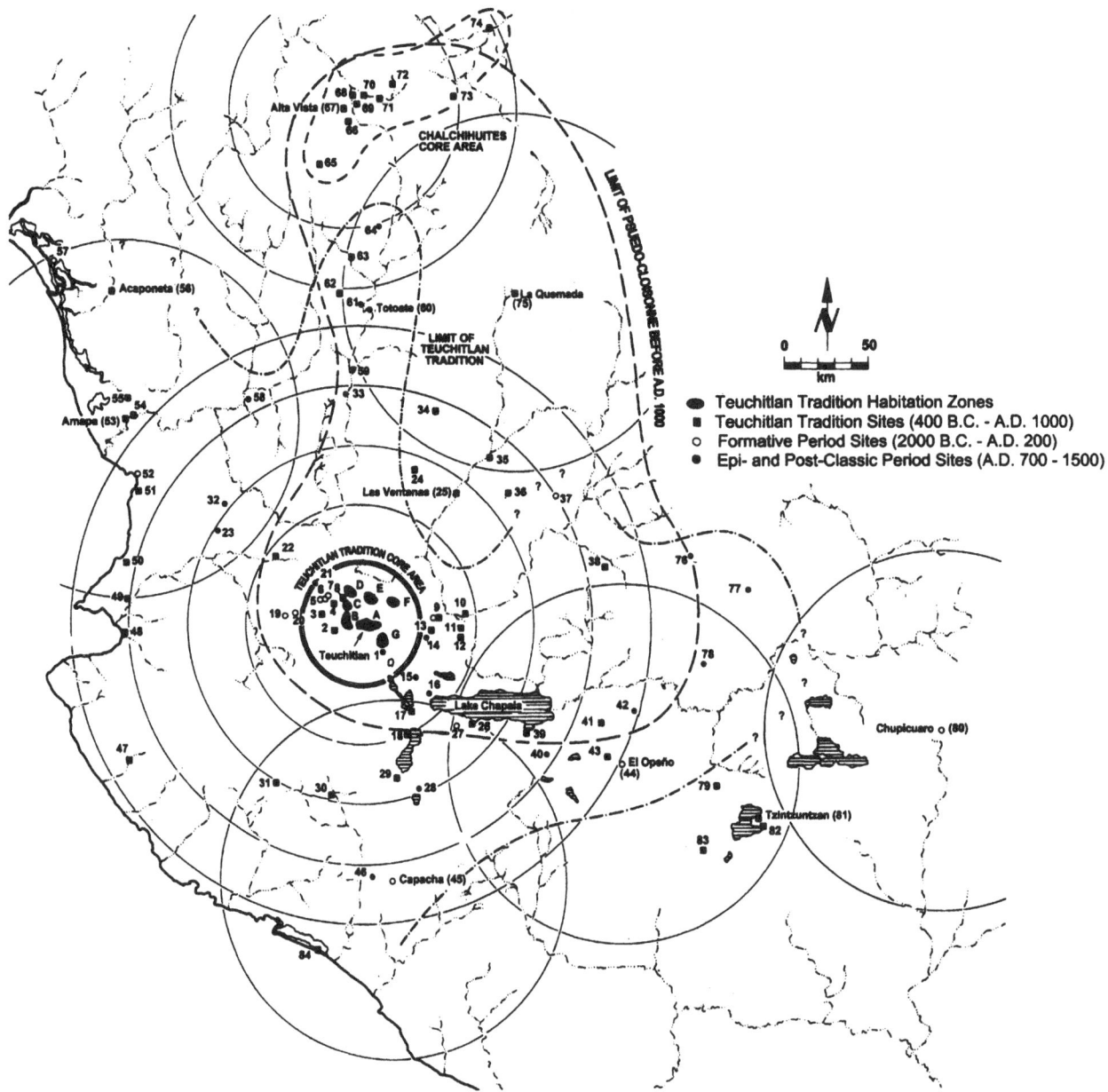

Figure 4.1. Teuchitlán tradition and other west Mexican sites. a. Teuchitlán/El Refugio; b. Ahualulco; c. La Providencia; d. Huitzilapa; e. Las Pilas; f. Santa Quiteria; g. San Juan de los Arcos; 1. Santa María de las Navajas; 2. Santa Cruz de Barcenas; 3. Etzatlán; 4. Las Cuevas; 5. El Arenal; 6. Santa Rosalia; 7. San Pedro; 8. La Joya; 9. Tabachines/El Grillo; 10. Matatlán; 11. Coyula; 12. Tonala; 13. Ixtepete; 14. Bugambilias; 15. El Molino; 16. Jocotepec; 17. Zacoalco; 18. Techaluta; 19. Pipiole; 20. San Felipe; 21. Llano Grande; 22. Ixtlán del Río; 23. San Pedro Lagunillas; 24. Teul; 25. Juchipila/Las Ventanas; 26. Tizapan; 27. Citala; 28. Gomez Farias; 29. Sayula; 30. Tuxcacuezco; 31. Autlán; 32. Santa María del Oro; 33. Cerro Cototlán; 34. Tlaltenango; 35. Jalpa; 36. Nochistlán; 37. Teocaltiche; 38. San Miguel el Alto; 39. Cojumatlán; 40. Jiquilpan; 41. Ixtlán/El Salitre; 42. Ecuandureo; 43. Jacona; 44. El Opeño; 45. Capacha; 46. Comala; 47. Tomatlán; 48. Ixtapa; 49. San Juan de Abajo; 50. La Penita; 51. Santa Cruz; 52. Matanchén; 53. Amapa; 54. Ixcuintla; 55. Coamiles; 56. Acaponeta; 57. El Calón; 58. Guaynamota; 59. Las Juntas; 60. Totoate; 61. Cerro Prieto; 62. Tenzompan; 63. Huejuguilla; 64. La Florida; 65. San Andres de Teul; 66. El Chapín; 67. Alta Vista; 68. Pedragoso; 69. Calichal; 70. Gualterio; 71. Moctezuma; 72. Cruz de la Boca; 73. Sain Alto; 74. Río Grande; 75. La Quemada; 76. San Francisco del Rincon; 77. La Gloria; 78. El Cobre; 79. Zacapu; 80. Chupícuaro; 81. Tzintzuntzan; 82. Ihuatzio; 83. Tingambato; 84. Cuyutlán.

cally amplify the resource profile by offering very different assets nearby. In this region, a huge zone of relatively flat valley floors ideally suited to agricultural exploitation does not preclude ecological variability. The combination of high-quality profiles for both rare and strategic resources offered an excellent backdrop for the development of complex societies.

THE FORMATIVE PERIOD DEVELOPMENTS

Figure 4.2 outlines the suggested chronological sequence for the core area of the emergent civilization of western Mexico. Aside from some isolated finds of late Pleistocene and early Holocene fauna, there are little reliable data concerning Paleoindian or Archaic period cultural activity for this zone. This is most certainly an artifact of the lack of systematic work oriented toward these periods. By far, the best summary for these periods is that of Solórzano (1980). Only a few fluted point finds have been recovered from this area, though isolated points of the general Lerma-Angostura variety are fairly frequent. Evidence of Archaic cultures, also defined almost exclusively from projectile points, is found with more frequency though still is quite rare. We have called the material of the Teuchitlán-Ahualulco-Etzatlán region the San Pedro Archaic, after the site with the most extensive scatter of points, scrapers, and debris.

Better defined, though still poorly understood from an anthropological perspective, are the cultures of the early Formative period. At El Opeño, Michoacán, Oliveros (1974, 1989, 1992; Noguera 1931, 1940) has defined the best evidence for early Formative cultures in the lake districts of western Mexico. Oliveros's work at this highly important site continues, and some of the observations concerning El Opeño that follow are from the more recent work. As yet, with one possible exception, no habitation area or any archaeological features that are not tombs have been found. The tombs, however, show that the social system in this great valley system was already beginning a process of ranking. The tombs are entered through shafts and stairways carved out of the consolidated *jal* (volcanic ash). The chambers themselves are oval, each lobe of which constitutes a burial room for multiple interments. These burials occurred and recurred over a long period of time, each new burial accompanied by lavish offerings of figurines, elaborate ceramic vessels, semiprecious stones, and obsidian artifacts. During the 1992 field season, Oliveros found a shaft tomb of the same overall style but far larger than the others. It appears, then, that there were status differentials even within the elite who were buried at this elegant cemetery. Small quantities of both turquoise and jade were also recovered. Oliveros's ^{14}C dates from these tombs, though not numerous, average around 1500 B.C.

Our survey elsewhere in the lake district zone has produced three additional sites with El Opeño style shaft tombs, though they are all looted and barren of most of their original contents. These sites are located at San Juanito (the Etzatlán area), near Teuchitlán (in the Ahualulco-Teuchitlán-Tala Basin), and near Citala (in the Ahualulco-Sayula Basin; see Figure 4.3), thus indicating a very wide distribution for this tomb type in the lake district. This may mean that the culture(s) that participated in the El Opeño type burial ceremonialism were the basic cultural strata for the entire lake district. These observations should be tempered by the following information. Capacha ceramics, especially the stirrup-handled vessels, composite vessels, and polychrome pumpkin/gourd-shaped vessels, very similar to those illustrated in Isabel Kelly's (1980) report for Colima, have been found at sites in our survey area. Capacha ceramics have also turned up at three sites: near Mazata, at San Juanito, and at San Pedro, all in the Etzatlán Valley. The site at San Pedro had an altar with a floor pit that contained human leg bones. This altar was within a middle Formative San Felipe phase platform and may represent our earliest example of surface architecture from the lake districts of western Mexico. Regrettably, it has been heavily damaged by the construction of the Magdalena-Etzatlán all-weather road.

Given the side-by-side occurrences of sites that have Capacha and El Opeño traits, it may be that the highland lake districts were already multicultural and multiethnic as early as the beginning of the Formative sequence. With Harbottle's (1975) study, we know that there are technological differences between the ceramics of the El Opeño (Michoacán) and Capacha (Colima) sites. The problematic interrelationships between these two cultures, if that is indeed what they are, cannot be resolved with the data set at hand, nor can either of these cultures' relationships with the coastal materials examined by Mountjoy and by Scott and Foster (see this volume).

The middle Formative San Felipe phase materials are very poorly understood also. By about 1000 B.C., however, it seems that the idea of constructing surface burial mounds was becoming widespread within the lake districts, though the only ones documented to date are

CHRONOLOGY OF THE TEUCHITLÁN REGION

Date	Phase	Reference
A.D. 1250-Spanish Contact Late Postclassic	Etzatlán	Weigand 1990b, 1991
A.D. 900-1250 Early Postclassic	Santa Cruz de Barcenas	Glassow 1967; Galván 1991; Weigand 1990b
A.D. 700-900 Epi-Classic	Teuchitlán II	Galván 1991; Weigand 1985
A.D. 400-700 Middle Classic	Teuchitlán I	Galván 1991; Weigand 1985;
A.D. 200-400 Early Classic	Ahualulco*	Weigand 1985
300 B.C.-A.D. 200 Late Formative	El Arenal*	Long 1966
1000-300 B.C. Middle Formative	San Felipe	Weigand 1985
1500-1000 B.C. Early Formative	El Opeño	Oliveros 1974

*Florance (personal communication 1992) suggested a downward revision of the El Arenal and Ahualulco phases.

Figure 4.2. A chronology for the Teuchitlán region.

within the San Marcos, Etzatlán, and Teuchitlán-Ahualulco-Tala valleys. Although many are in extremely poor condition because of looting and agricultural activities, a few are preserved well enough to map. They were round to oval, averaging 28–30 m in diameter and 2 m high. The best-preserved one is located at San Felipe and shows indications of terracing. Each platform has at least two shaft tombs. These tombs are occasionally deep, up to 8–10 m, but most are shallower. All have one boot-shaped chamber, with a step at the base of the shaft. Flat or slab figurines abound as offerings. These also occur as offerings in later burials, in which case they are accompanied by hollow figurines. Stylistically, they can be easily separated. Research currently under way by Jane Day (Denver Museum of Natural History) should help us evaluate this flat figurine tradition more fully. It should be noted that most burials at the San Felipe phase platforms are simple pit interments. They too have offerings, but these are far less elaborate. As indicated with the prior El Opeño phase, the social system appears to have had at least two ranks. The appearance of two elegant tombs per platform may indicate a principle of dualism in operation in the social organization of the society or societies of this phase. No burials from this phase have been scientifically excavated, however, nor have such platforms been reported as yet from other areas within western Mexico. At best, this archaeological phase is only superficially understood.

The figurines from the late Formative cultures of west Mexico have been the mainstays of art historians and the illicit art market for the entire history of archaeology of this region. With recent fieldwork within the lake districts, these figurines can now be contextualized by an anthropological discussion of their cultural role within the societies of the El Arenal phase (about 300 B.C. to A.D. 100/200). The research involving the concepts of

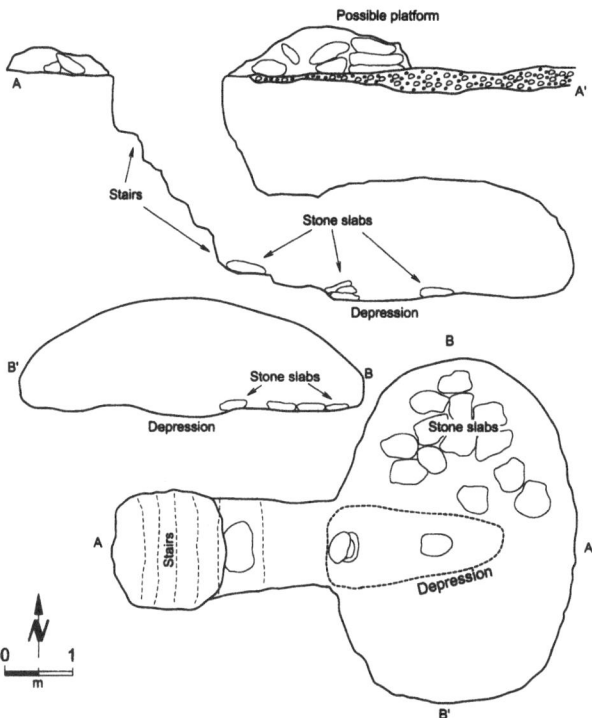

Figure 4.3. El Opeño style shaft tomb near Citala in the Ahualulco-Sayula Basin.

"ceramic ecology" (see Matson 1965), concerning the figurines and burial ceramics from the region, is just now starting to get under way (Aronson 1993, 1996; Butterwick 1993). These studies will certainly supplement the more analytical tradition established by such art historians as von Winning and Hammer (1972) and Graham (1989). The studies by Graham, Aronson, and Butterwick have had the advantage of the results of more recent field programs within the area where the development of shaft tombs achieved its most monumental expression. Their studies show that the figurines and burial ceramics have complex social meanings far beyond the ideas expressed in normative art history and archaeology concerning the area (see Díaz 1987).

The shaft tombs per se, as well as the associated architecture, show that a nucleus of complex sociocultural activities was beginning to evolve within certain parts of the lake districts. This area was beginning to outstrip its cultural neighbors in the pace of change and complexity. In other words, a process of differential development was beginning to occur, thus marking the origins of a core/hinterland relationship that remained in place, though it grew far more complex, for the next one thousand years. We have termed this period of growing "differential development," including its culmination in the Classic period, the Teuchitlán tradition.

During the El Arenal phase, the figurines depicting groups of individuals and architecture offer insights into the ceremonial building of the time period because the figurines are almost photographic in their detail and ethnographic quality. They often show house platforms around a circular patio, which in turn surrounds a circular altar. The altars are occasionally the focal point for *volador* poles and for the accompanying ceremonialism (Weigand 1996, 1999). It is important to note that the architecture represented in these figurines can be located in the field and often looks quite the same. In the field, though, the circular compounds are frequently far more complex, with up to eight platforms surrounding the inner concentric elements (Figure 4.4). Some of these architectural circles are found in clusters, up to three in number, and these precincts moreover are the ones that usually have more than one ball court (also up to three in number). In the cases of multiple circles and ball courts, however, one compound always is more elaborate and larger. Since most sites from this period do not have multiple circles and ball courts, it seems that the emergence of a regional site hierarchy within the Etzatlán-Teuchitlán zone was under way. More detailed descriptions of this unique architectural configuration can be found in Weigand 1985, 1990a, 1990b, 1992a, 1992b, 1993a, 1999. At this point, suffice it to say that the architectural circles are unique to this section of ancient Mesoamerica, and they mark membership in or affiliation with the earliest periods of the Teuchitlán tradition.

The habitation zones were still quite small. The one at El Arenal is just over one kilometer in radius and includes 18 compounds or compound clusters. Another one that could be measured and counted was found at Cerro de los Monos. Its radius, too, is nearly one kilometer, and it has 20 compounds or compound clusters within it. Our population estimates for these late Formative habitation zones range from 500 to 1,000 individuals. These precincts are found an average of 7 to 10 km apart and are located on the uppermost fossil beaches of the lakes.

The tombs within and near these precincts have been the focal point for some of the most methodical looting efforts in Mexico and so cannot now yield much archaeological data. Only the relatively unelaborated tombs at Tabachines in the Atemejac Valley (Galván 1991) have been systematically studied. The tomb at Cerro Encantado (Bell 1972, 1974), located at a consid-

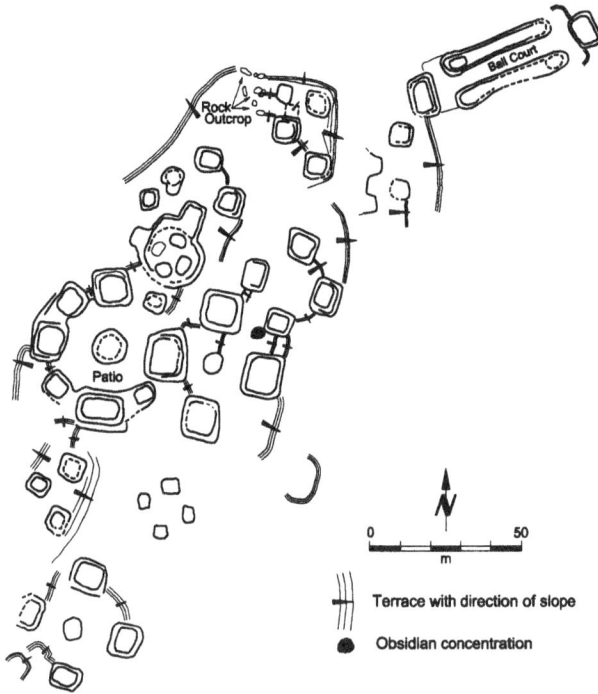

Figure 4.4. Huitzilapa (Cerro de las Navajas precinct).

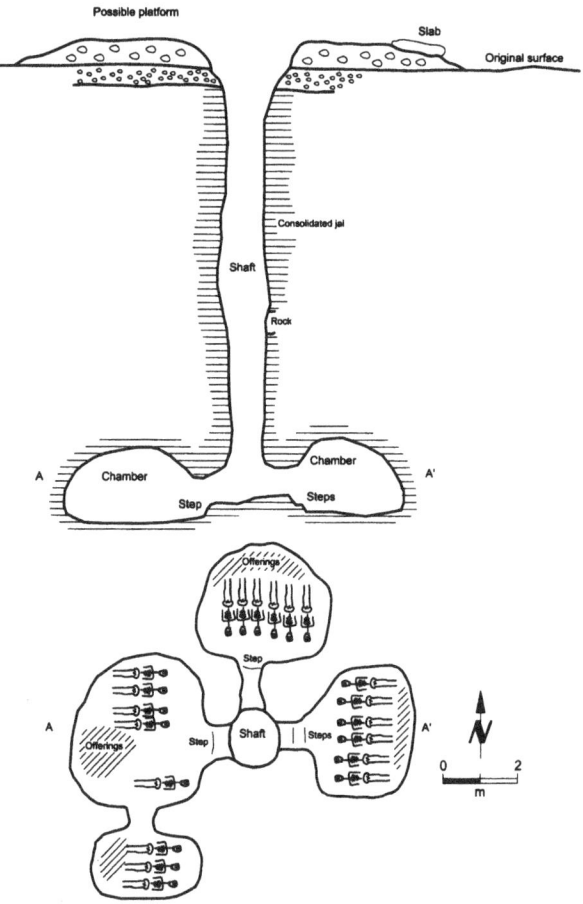

Figure 4.5. Cerro de los Monos shaft tomb.

erable distance from the emerging core, was also scientifically studied but never fully reported. The salvage excavations at the Cerro de las Navajas precinct, in the Huitzilapa habitation zone (Figure 4.4), have encountered a shaft tomb 8 m deep, with two chambers, multiple burials, and a treasure trove of artifacts, many of them perishable (Ramos de la Vega and López Mestas 1996). This is the only scientifically excavated tomb yet explored within the emerging core region. Long's (1966) study, which was actually an observation of looters in the process of emptying a tomb at El Arenal, is the best up to this point.

Like the circular architecture and associated ball courts, the tombs express the idea of social hierarchy. The truly monumental ones, more than 12 m deep, are extremely rare and located only in or near the largest precincts. The best-known one is the 18-m tomb reported by Corona Núñez (1955) at the site of El Arenal, but others exist at San Juan de los Arcos (22 m) and other places, such as San Andrés and Cerro de los Monos (Figure 4.5). Medium-sized shaft tombs, such as those explored by Ramos at Huitzilapa, are more frequent. These two types of deep tombs, however, are found only within the emerging core area. The shallower shaft tombs, such as those at Tabachines, are far more frequent both within the core and throughout the neighboring valleys.

Artifacts from the El Arenal phase, aside from the figurines, are complex. A ceramic ware, Oconahua Red-on-white (with fugitive Black, at times), is an example. This is predominantly a burial ware but is also found within the elite habitation areas and the circular precincts. It is eggshell thin and rings like a bell when tapped. The clays have a high kaolin content, and the vessels were fired in well-controlled circumstances at high temperatures. The painted designs are carefully executed and, though polished, are not smeared as often as one sees with the later Teuchitlán Red-on-cream wares. Ceramics, especially decorated pieces, in the habitation areas are quite rare. Cooking and storage wares are the most frequent but occur in fairly small quantities. It can be posited that the paucity of sherds in habitation areas may be due to the reliance on gourds for many functions that pottery had assumed elsewhere in Mesoamerica. Habitation areas, thus, are often hard to define and date. For the relationships of ceramic and figurine types with tombs and other architectural features, see Figure 4.6.

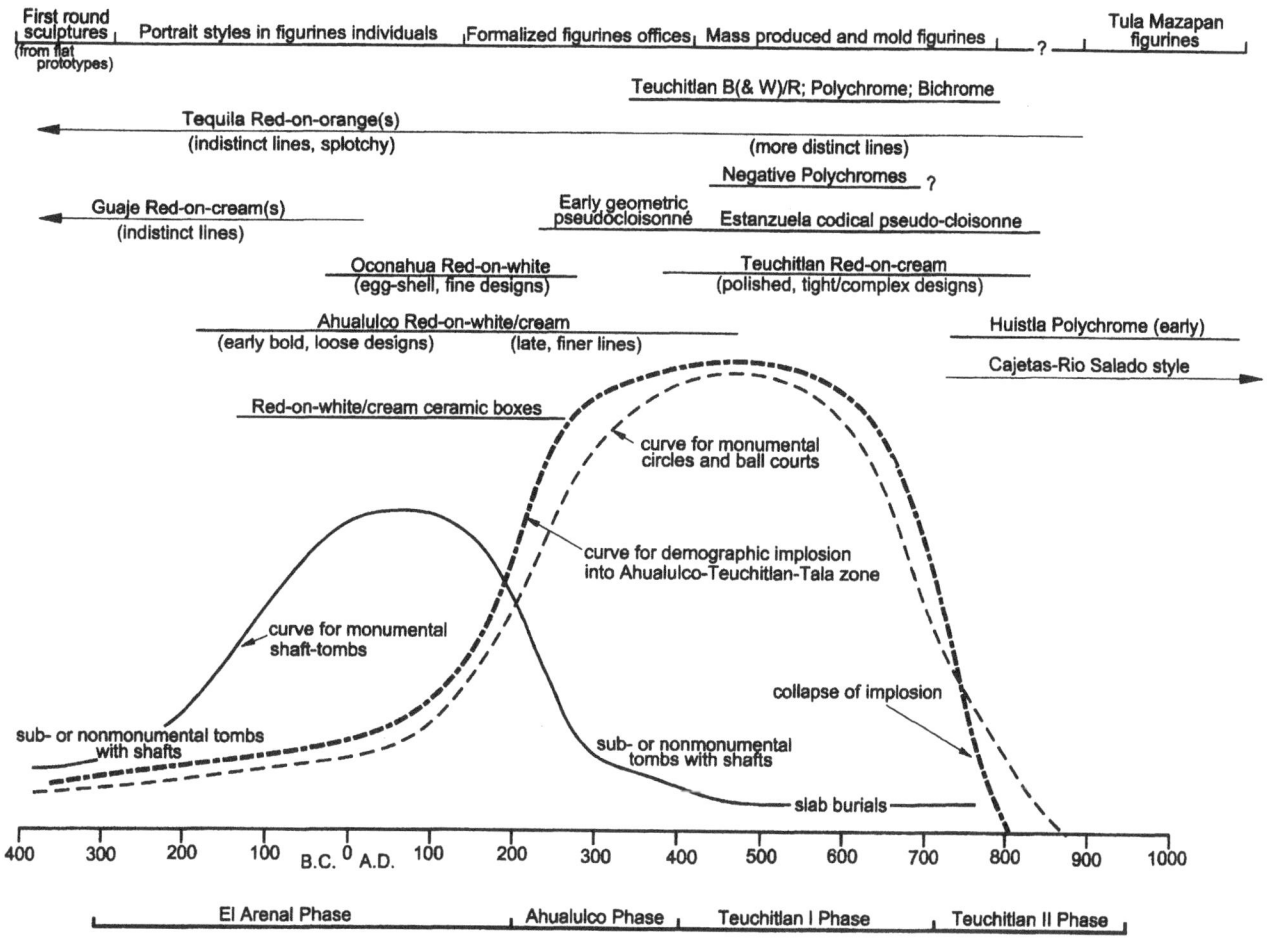

Figure 4.6. Temporal correlation of artifact types, ceramic types, architecture, and phases for the Teuchitlán tradition.

Obsidian artifacts are more numerous than sherds within the habitation areas and precincts. In the tombs, these artifacts are often elaborate: cruciforms, lunates, thin circles, long pendants, massive but carefully made double-pointed knives, probable mirror backs (Schöndube, personal communication 1993), beads, ear spools, and so on. These items were popular during the Classic period, too, but their origins are in the El Arenal phase. This careful obsidian work, along with the presence of prismatic blades, indicates that procurement of high-quality materials was an important economic activity and that some degree of specialization was in place to produce such a varied and finely made array of artifacts. Blue-green stone jewelry (including small amounts of turquoise and jade), quartz crystals, an occasional opal, seashells (especially the fine conch trumpets), and other rare and exotic materials are abundant. The high quality of the portrait-style figurines, the shell trumpets, the Oconahua Red-on-white wares, and the obsidian work constitutes strong evidence for some degree of craft specialization.

During this period, the buildings were beginning to acquire the characteristics of formal architecture (Weigand 1999). This implies, as Graham (1989) noted from another perspective, the emergence of highly organized symbol sets and the social specialists to manage them. Far from being a backwater, western Mexico was keeping pace socioculturally with many of the other emerging cores of complex civilization within Mesoamerica.

THE CLASSIC PERIOD

We view the transition from the late Formative to the Classic as a process of intensification. Although it resulted in the emergence of a society(ies) different in kind from its Formative forerunners, it nonetheless retained a continuity of expression within the same cultural heritage. Hence, we have chosen the term "tradition," instead of "culture," to characterize the continuity and at the same time to emphasize the dramatic differences in social character between the Formative and Classic periods. The reasons for this intensification are still unclear. Scenarios have been offered (e.g., Weigand 1992c, 1993a) wherein Teotihuacán provided just enough socioeconomic pressure on the zone to stimulate a response through intensification. Though historical cases of response state formation are well known, in truth we still have little idea about the processes at work during this intensification. Aronson (1993, 1996) has provided a critical evaluation of these hypotheses but has arrived at no firm conclusions either.

Chronology poses yet another problem, particularly the line between the Late Formative El Arenal phase and the Early Classic Ahualulco phase, the latter dated at around A.D. 200 to 400. The Ahualulco phase, which culminated during the Teuchitlán I phase around A.D. 400 to 700, is thought to be a period of great intensification and implosion. It remains very poorly defined, however, because of the later rebuilding of almost all Ahualulco phase precincts. Nevertheless, several excellent profiles exist that help resolve the issue of the transition from El Arenal to Ahualulco. The best is within the Ahualulco "A" pyramid, where the first major rebuilding of the Formative phase architecture is visible and datable through the occurrence of a small number of Thin Orange sherds identified as "Teotihuacán III" materials, hence dating to around A.D. 300.

Florance (1993, see also this volume), however, has suggested a downward revision of the beginning date of this phase to around A.D. 100 in order to bring it in line better with the sequence as understood from Chupícuaro. Given the excavations in the Zacapu area of Michoacán by Carot (1990, 1992) and by Michelet (1990), it is now possible to see more clearly the continuities between the Chupícuaro region and the lake districts farther west. This may help us answer some questions about dating, but it does little to resolve the controversies about the concept of "Chupícuaro culture," about the nature of "Chupícuaro culture," and the about the importance of "Chupícuaro culture" in the western regions. In the lake districts of western Jalisco, there existed a complex and signal variety of architecture and shaft tombs, which were becoming monumental during this period. But neither complex tombs nor complex architecture exists in the Chupícuaro area.

The "Chupícuaro culture" has been defined almost exclusively on the basis of figurine types and ceramics (see Florance 1985, 1993, this volume). Can this slender cultural reed alone support a postulation of a center of diffusion or influence? Just because an elegant ceramic association was first defined from a cemetery in southeastern Guanajuato, it does not mean that this area should be viewed as the center for a complex that culturally affected a large area of western Mexico. The center that presumably would include an architectural complex may well exist elsewhere, probably closer to the Zacapu, a region where complex tombs have been found. As with much of western Mexico, a ceramocentric view of archaeology appears to have distorted our view of ancient civilization. Ceramic provinces have become "cultures," and then they have been manipulated as if they were comparable to cultures that have been constructed from a rich array of information about many aspects of life. To this author, the entire question of the nature of "Chupícuaro influences" throughout the Lerma and lake valleys of Jalisco should be reevaluated, avoiding the pitfalls of viewing ceramic provinces as cultures. Further critiques of this ceramocentrism in western Mexico can be seen in Rousseau 1990 and Weigand 1992b.

However the chronological problem of the beginning of the Ahualulco phase is resolved, what happened during its two or three hundred years seems fairly clear. An enormous population implosion began and for all practical purposes culminated by between A.D. 300 and 400. Monumental surface architecture replaced the monumental shaft tombs as the symbol of sociopolitical power within the region. Many of the most elegant shaft tombs belong to the early Ahualulco phase, but by the phase's conclusion, tombs were architecturally quite simple (though still richly furnished and at times painted with murals). Taken with the demographic implosion, the shift from monumental mortuary to monumental surface architecture probably signifies the attainment of a stratified social order, perhaps organized as a state or states within the core. The figurines changed, too. They became much more formalized, losing their portraiture characteristics. This shift in figurine styles probably connotes the importance of offices rather than personalities within the sociopolitical order.

As the intensification and implosion proceeded, a large percentage of the near hinterland population appears to have dissipated. Nothing like the monumental structures of the Classic period in the core area (Figure 4.7) existed in this sector of the hinterland, although relatively

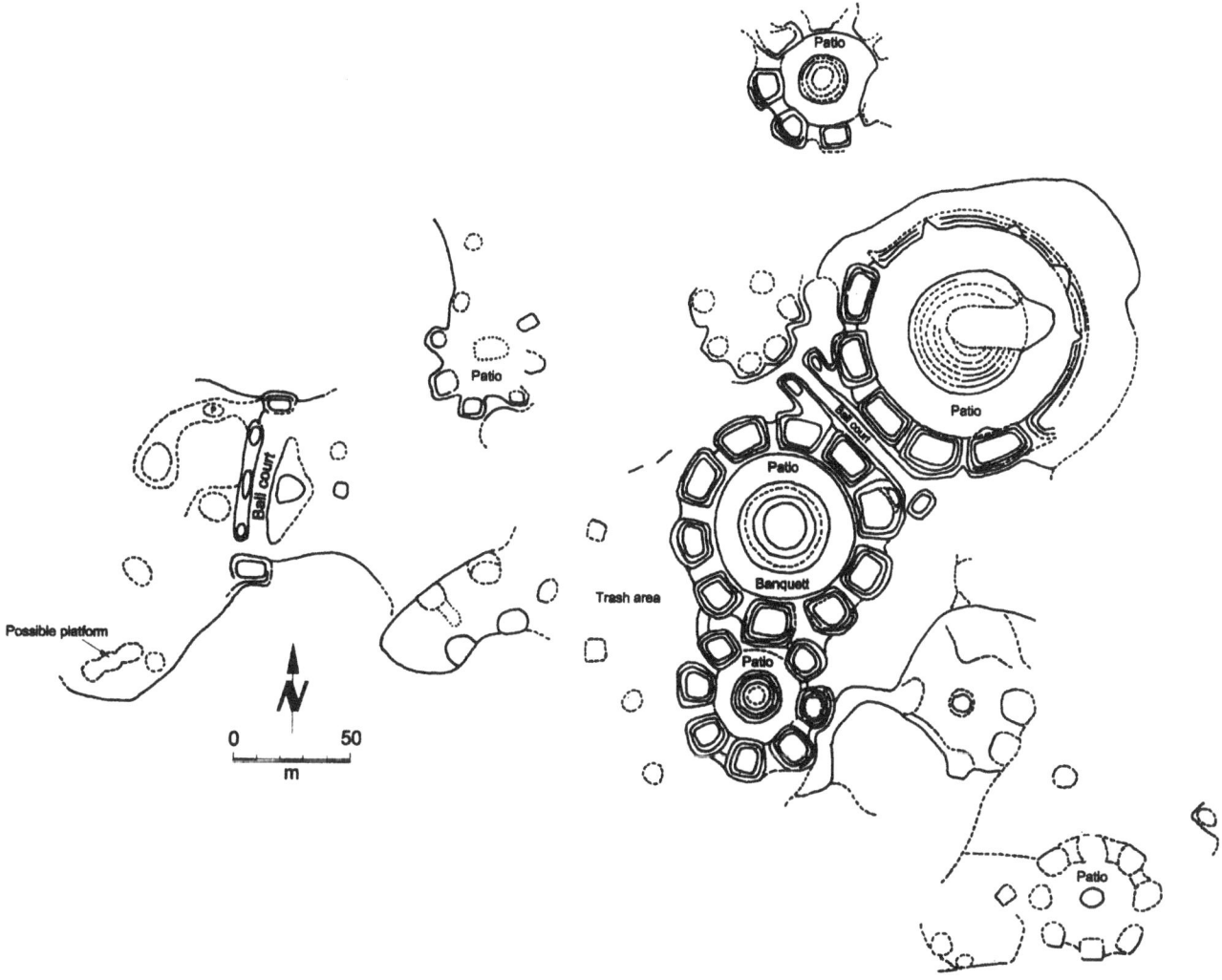

Figure 4.7. The Guachimonton Complex, Teuchitlán, Jalisco.

small precincts, featuring circular architecture (but with very few ball courts), were constructed. Settlement numbers fall off dramatically from the El Arenal phase, and those settlements that persisted were located at strategic localities for rare resource procurement or as fortifications to guard access into the core. By around A.D. 400, the core area was surrounded by fortified sites. At the northeast, where access is easy, is the La Venta site, guarding the pass to the Atemejac Valley (Beekman 1996a, 1996b). At the southeast are two fortified complexes—El Molino, guarding the access from the Chapala Basin, and Sta. María de las Navajas, which sits above the access from the Tlajomulco Basin. At the southwestern corner of the core is the Pipiole fortification, high above the access from the Río de Abajo and the Valle de las Banderas. At the northwestern corner is Llano Grande, guarding the mountain trail to the Ahuacatlan–Ixtlán del Río areas.

The construction of core-fortified sites accompanied the intensification of the core. Perhaps the depopulation of the surrounding valleys created a vacuum, with densities too low to give some areas the needed demographic mass to act as buffers for the core or to maintain themselves in the face of migrations. This may have been the case for the Atemejac Valley, where the transition from the Tabachines to the Ixtepete phase was abrupt (about A.D. 300 to 400), the latter representing an entirely alien element in burial ceremonialism, architecture, and ceramic production (Aronson 1993; Galván 1991). Although these same trends are visible within the core area during the Teuchitlán I and II phases, they appear to be far more gradual than the abrupt and earlier transition in the Atemejac area. For example, the box burial tradition, an obvious marker of these outside influences, was slowly adopted within the core and for a long period of time coexisted with the more traditional burial formats. It should be noted that the ceramic miniatures, which frequently accompany the box burial ceremonialism, were made in entirely local styles; especially notable were the Teuchitlán Red-on-cream wares (Figure 4.6). Certainly the Teuchitlán area was populous enough to have been multiethnic and multicultural, and it was flexible enough to have responded to changed circumstances over time, too. But the transition in the Atemejac Valley is of a different order and seems to represent the middle Classic arrival of peoples influenced from central Mexico and/or the Bajio long before the same process was initiated in the Teuchitlán zone. The inclusion of the Atemejac Valley in the interaction sphere postulated by Jiménez (1992a) would date from this time period because in prior times it was a periphery to the lake basins just to its west (Galván 1991).

The depopulations (and perhaps vacuums) created in the near periphery (Figure 4.1, 2nd circle), however, do not reflect what was occurring in the far hinterland (Figure 4.1, 3rd circle and beyond). Beginning about A.D. 200, small circular complexes were being constructed at strategic locations (for both rare resource procurement and communications) within this zone. The best-understood example is the Bolaños salient (Cabrero 1989, 1992; Jaramillo 1984; Kelley 1971; Weigand 1977, 1985, 1993a). The ^{14}C dates acquired by Kelley at Totoate span the period from A.D. 200 to 700, thus marking not only the origin but also the long life of this salient. The architectural design of the circular buildings in the Bolaños Valley shows without doubt that the inspiration came from the Teuchitlán region. Another fact to note is the directionality that the salient assumed. Its northernmost outpost at La Florida is literally in the backyard of the Chalchihuites culture of Zacatecas (Jaramillo 1984).

Given this directionality, plus the strong presence of pseudocloisonné vessels in the Chalchihuites region, a marker of the high culture of the core (see below), it seems unlikely that diffusion or unstructured relationships characterized the Bolaños settlements, and hence the contacts between the core and the Chalchihuites system. Since the Chalchihuites area is noted for one of the most massive mining operations yet described for the New World (Hers 1989a; Kelley 1971; Weigand 1968, 1982), producing far more mineral products than it could have conceivably consumed, it must have had systematic relationships with the outside world. Because of the poorly understood chronologies, this same argument could be made, albeit with less force, for the Comala region of Colima. Angeles Olay of the Centro Regional de Colima surveyed several circles in Colima, and Catarina Serat surveyed others near Guainmota, Nayarit. In the Bajio, Sánchez C. and Marmolejo M. (1990) have found five sites with circular architecture of the Teuchitlán variety. An additional 17 have been located by Cárdenas (personal communication 1995). Most of these circles are embedded in the rectangular architecture more traditional to the Bajio, but at Mesa de la Gloria, near León, a monumental circle was found without accompanying rectangular courts.

Mesa de la Gloria is in a fortified position. So are most of the Bolaños circles. But they are also near points essential for either the direct control over rare resources or the movement of such resources across the landscape. They seem to be strategically located "outposts in the surrounding periphery," in Algaze's (1993:310) phrase. He wrote that such outposts are common occurrences in the early life histories of civilizations, reflecting the ability both to project their cultural power and to serve their expansionary economies. Direct control by the core polity or polities over these outposts is not requisite. They are defined by their cultural affiliation and their service to a long-distance trade/exchange economy (Algaze 1993). These faraway circles do not make any sense unless interpreted in such a fashion. Although those circles in the Bolaños salient and in the Colima region have a continuous distribution with the architecture of the near hinterland and the core, the Bajio structures do not. The cultures of the Atemejac and lower Lerma valleys intercede. Whatever the role of the circles, the picture we now have for their distribution outside the core and near hinterland is surely highly complex and multifaceted.

As the demographic implosion progressed in the Teuchitlán-Ahualulco-Tala area, the zone began to strain its resources. A very preliminary paleopalynological study by Glenn Stuart (1992) has shown the distinct possibility of a period of massive deforestation associated with the demographic implosion, which culminated during the Teuchitlán I phase (A.D. 400 to 700). In addition, the climate became a bit warmer, perhaps reflected by lowered water levels in the lakes and marches within the core. The botanical differences between the upper shore and piedmont plant communities disappeared as the closed canopy of pine and oak was replaced by an open canopy community of huisache, mesquite, and acacia. This botanical process is obviously related to the sociocultural intensification within the same area. The human impact on the natural environment within the core was severe.

The implosion and resultant ecological transformation required a strategy in order to increase food production in an environment undergoing such changes. The response was to intensify agricultural production by constructing what appears to be an integrated system of terraces and chinampas. The chinampas were highly geometric, thus suggesting that they were planned and executed with the participation of the state. The engineering linked sub-basins, diverted streams into other drainages, and altogether built over 30 km² of marsh gardens. This figure is most probably only a percentage of what was actually constructed, as land leveling for sugarcane fields has obliterated all but the most ephemeral traces in many areas (Weigand 1993b).

The cultural symbolism of the architectural circles must have been unlike anything else in the mesoamerican world during the Classic period. There is no doubt that this architecture is formal (Weigand 1999). Although circular buildings in general are difficult to design and construct, within western Mexico there are many hundreds of them. They may have served as the focal points for the worship of an Ehecatl-like deity (among others), which has been identified using the *volador* style figurines as well as the codical style pseudocloisonné vessels. In discussing this issue, we should keep in mind that the definition of monumentality is not simply a measure of volume but also a measure of design complexity. From a design perspective, the concentric circles were certainly complex. Some of the circles are masonry buildings, as well. Stone was set into cement made from caliche and fine clays. These masonry structures were able to obtain very steep construction angles. The Guachimontones at Teuchitlán are such buildings (Figure 4.7). When viewed from the perspective of complex design and masonry construction, this precinct's approximately 80,000 m³ of fill is even more impressive.

Aside from the massive obsidian workshops, such as the one explored by Soto de Arechavaleta (1982) near Teuchitlán and others near San Juan de los Arcos and Huitzilapa, evidence for specialization can be found in salt production. Salt from the Atoyac-Sayula Valley seems to be another rare resource that was exploited on a massive scale during the Teuchitlán I phase and possibly before. The salt-working tells in this valley are truly impressive, as are the great number of salt evaporation pits and pans set into the Playa de Atoyac's upper shores. A current project headed by Francisco Valdez (1993a) has finally dated this industry. It had always been assumed that it had been coeval with the Epi-Classic and Postclassic monumental architectural complexes, such as that at Techaluta. In fact, the salt industry dates primarily to the Classic period. There are no major architectural complexes for the Classic period, however, and the level of salt production firmly indicates that the zone was not just producing for itself. The only well-organized, intensified polity nearby capable of consuming such vast quantities of salt was the neighboring Teuchitlán Valley. Indeed, it appears as if the Atoyac region had become part of the near periphery, first depopulated (to judge from the paucity of architectural remains), then reoriented in service of the core at Teuchitlán. "Monopolies" (implying preferred access in procurement for regional use and exchange) over high-quality obsidian and salt may have helped form the economic underpinnings of the political system(s) evident in the core. Specialization in procurement and production of these two resources (from mining and evaporation to processing and distribution) is strongly implied, too. Competition may have indeed occurred within the core for the procurement and distribution of these basic resources, but certainly there were no competitors outside the core.

The inspiration for the pseudocloisonné vessels that were widely distributed throughout western Mexico before A.D. 1000 (Figure 4.1) certainly came from the general Teuchitlán zone, though many examples of manufacture outside the core exist (Aronson 1993; Holien 1977). The codical style seems to have originated around A.D. 500 in the Teuchitlán region and spread quickly from that point to other areas, including the Chalchihuites zone (Holien 1977; Holien and Pickering 1978) and the Atemejac Valley (Aronson 1993; Galván 1991), thus marking some sort of ideological participation within the Teuchitlán tradition. It should be noted that the pseudocloisonné technique might have been used to decorate gourds, which provide a highly suitable background, many centuries before it was used on ceramics.

Just to the east of the Teuchitlán area is another zone, using negative polychromes, that is obviously integrated in a like manner. Jiménez (1992a) and Carot (1992) have examined different aspects of this interaction sphere, but no center or social mechanisms, beyond peer-polity exchange, have been suggested for its wide distribution and obvious cultural significance. Negative polychrome wares are rare within the Teuchitlán core region, but they do occur. During the 1890s, Lumholtz collected a number of negative polychromes at the Estanzuela burial area (within the Teuchitlán habitation zone). His collection is housed in the American Museum of Natural History. Galván (1991; Aronson 1993) found them in the Atemejac Valley, and they have turned up in surveys elsewhere in the lake districts. It is possible that the middle and lower Lerma Valley was the focal point for this wide system of exotic exchange, which in many ways equaled or rivaled the system that the pseudocloisonné ware emulated. Neither the pseudocloisonné nor the negative polychrome wares have singular centers of production. Rather, these two kinds of wares appear to mark an idea set and thus participation within a system during the Classic period.

THE CLASSIC PERIOD LANDSCAPE IN THE CORE REGION

The creation of the Teuchitlán tradition's landscape within the core region was an impressive accomplishment. Landscapes, defined as large-scale organizations of human-made spaces, designed and created as elements of a society, can be vernacular or political (see Jackson 1984). A political landscape is constituted as "spaces and structures designed to impose or preserve a unity and order on the land, or in keeping with a long-range, large-scale plan," whereas the vernacular landscape is constituted as spaces that are "usually small, irregular in shape, subject to rapid change in use, in ownership [and] in dimensions" (Jackson 1984:150–151). During the Classic period, the core region of the Jalisco highland lake districts appears to be a political landscape. It was obvious early in our field studies that the size of the habitation zones within the core was immense. In 1985, I offered a guess as to the overall scale of the habitation systems in the entire Teuchitlán system: 30,000 ha. The subsequent work by Ohnersorgen and Varien (1996), using the settlement and habitation system map generated by our field research in 1992, has considerably refined this prior work. Since the habitation compounds are so difficult to date, it seems reasonable to offer a conservative percentage of coevality at this stage of study. Fifty percent coevality yields an estimate of 50,000 to 60,000 people within the great settlement arc that extends from San Juan de los Arcos in the southeast, to Ahualulco in the southwest, the San Juanito area in the northwest, and the Refugio zone in the northeast. This arc covers about 240 km^2. Keeping in mind the production estimates for the chinampa fields, this suggested population number seems reasonable.

Some of the estimates of compound populations were arrived at statistically: in the areas where sugarcane agriculture has completely destroyed all but the deepest archaeological features (usually burials or canals), residential architecture simply could not be located. For these areas, constituting about 30 percent of the area represented, we multiplied a constant of 10 compounds per major cemetery (defined as having 100 or more successful lootings) to arrive at estimates for that area's settlement density. In areas where we can actually count the numbers of compounds associated with a major cemetery, the number is closer to 18 compounds or compound clusters, so the statistical construct is conservatively stated. Otherwise, the density contours were established by actual counts. Ohnersorgen and Varien were able to demonstrate a high degree of correlation between the diameters of selected circles and their volumes. These calculations were used in the critical evaluation of the tier structure within the overall habitation zone.

In 1985, it was postulated that four tiers of ceremonial buildings with aspects of formal architecture were within the habitation zone. The Ohnersorgen and Varien study strongly suggests that three tiers are represented. Given the regional hierarchy (see the discussion above on the hinterlands), this is still quite sufficient to posit a state level of social and political organization for the core. Their plot (see Ohnersorgen and Varien 1996:Figure 9) of volume against the size of the associated high-density habitation areas shows several remarkable trends: for Tier II and III habitation areas, the volume and density match fairly closely, though Tier II habitation areas are beginning to diverge from the volumetric line. With the Tier I areas, however, there is a complete divergence. This divergence means that the monumental architecture of these areas had to be supported by a far wider community than just those habitations nearby. In other words, Ohnersorgen and Varien (1996) have demonstrated statistically what we strongly suspected more impressionistically: the presence of a hierarchy of ceremonial architecture and associated residential zones within the overall habitation zone and the likely organization of the habitation zones into wards. Concerning this latter point, Ohnersorgen and Varien also characterized the core with diagrams using gravity models for calculating the interaction for areas with formal architecture. The first plot (see Ohnersorgen and Varien 1996:Figure 5), which emphasizes volume and area as variables, shows that the Guachimonton compound is clearly the premier precinct within all the settlement systems. The second plot, which emphasizes distance as variables (Ohnersorgen and Varien 1996:Figure 6), shows the possible ward organization within the overall settlement system. These two plots are not incompatible with each other. The first shows society within the core operating at the regional level and represents a view of the system from above and from the outside. The second shows it operating from a neighborhood perspective, that is, within the habitation zone, and is a view of the system as seen from below and from the inside. The work of Ohnersorgen and Varien, for the first time, draws on solid quantification methods to help explain the dynamics and characteristics of this huge habitation zone.

It is apparent that not only the ceremonialism involving the circular compounds but also the ball-court hierarchy provided the social mechanisms that held the core together. The monumental ball courts are found only in direct association with the most monumental circles. Those of lesser elaboration are found with Tier II and III precincts. Very few ball courts of the lesser varieties are found outside the core, and no monumental zones are so situated. This distributional pattern strongly implies that the ball game played a highly important integrative role within the core, but not necessarily between the core and its hinterlands (Weigand 1991). These structures are open "I" courts and very frequently actually append the circular buildings. Examples of free-standing ball courts also exist.

The question of the extent of urbanization that was achieved in the Teuchitlán area is still open. It seems clear that the processes of urbanization were under way, though less clear as to whether or not an actual urbanized society resulted. Of course, most of this discussion depends on how cities are defined in the first place. Impressionistically, the huge Teuchitlán habitation zone (about 240 km^2 of precincts and residential compounds, 30+ km^2 of chinampas, 300+ km^2 of open terraced fields) looks like the polynucleated "new cities" spreading across the North American landscape. In ancient Mesoamerica, the settlement system represented in the Teuchitlán zone resembles far more the Classic period Lowland Maya pattern (see Ashmore 1981; Culbert 1977; Culbert and Rice 1990; Folan et al. 1983) than the mononucleated city sites such as Teotihuacán (Millon et al. 1973; Sanders et al. 1979), Cantona, and, perhaps, Cholula. As urban historians Lewis Mumford (1938, 1961), Handlin and Burchard (1963), and Wheatley (1971) have noted, however, the highly centralized, mononucleated format is not the only one available. Just as old, and probably more widespread in ancient Mesoamerica, were the "green" cities. These open cities were semidispersed, or seminucleated, probably having demographic densities of about 800 to 900 per km^2. To use the exceptional type of urban form, for example that of Teotihuacán and Tenochtitlán (with densities of about 2,000 per km^2), to characterize the entire mesoamerican experiment in urbanization is faulty logic.

A graphic way to depict the centralized mononucleated cities is a to use a hub-and-spoke model. A way to conceptualize the decentralized, multinucleated urban form is to visualize a grid wherein the lattices of production, consumption, and administration only partially overlap. Grid/lattice urban configurations stress juxtaposition and repetition in the economic and sociopolitical structure. Production is often highly decentralized, though luxury consumption is less so. If we view the huge Teuchitlán habitation area as a zone undergoing the processes of urbanization, then it was apparently evolving toward a multinucleated and grid/lattice type of city, rather than the mononucleated, hub-and-spoke format. As Gottman (1964) observed, cities of all types should be conceptualized as economic regions, rather than just sites. The site is but the small, nucleated or seminucleated section of a city-region. The cultural landscape within and around a city, of whatever type, is part of its construction (Cattaneo 1956). Arensberg (1968) noted that cities in history must be defined empirically, not by using a priori, or derivative, assumptions. Possibly the worst variety of assumptions concerns centralization: "Enshrined in the scale . . . is the notion that the city is a large and dense population aggregate" (Arensberg 1968:39). Arensberg (1968:43) also pointed out: "What seems to obscure the social science perception of the variable forms of the city, and of the varieties of settlement pattern common to city and rural community alike, is not merely the unfamiliarity of the cities of diverse civilizations to anthropologists and the unfamiliarity of tribal and peasant villages to urban sociologists. Equally obscuring is the hold (perhaps unconscious) of unilinear concepts of social and cultural evolution." More recently, Fischer (1976) has also noted the hold that unilinear concepts of urbanization have in the social sciences, the result of deterministic theories about urbanization and urbanism. The seminucleated type of urban experiment was very widespread in ancient

Mesoamerica, and it should be evaluated on its own terms rather than pigeonholed within unilinear concepts.

THE CLASSIC PERIOD COLLAPSE AND THE POSTCLASSIC PERIOD REORGANIZATION

By the Epi-Classic period, or Teuchitlán II phase (A.D. 700–900), the great habitation zone in the Ahualulco-Teuchitlán-Tala Valley was beginning to break up. Very few new circular precincts were being constructed during this phase, though many were moderately remodeled. Some variations on the circular architectural theme are in evidence: crowding of the platforms atop the banquette often altered the symmetry and balance of the older circles; setting back platforms from the inner banquette (or patio) edge emphasized their monumentality. Other such variations are common to the Teuchitlán II phase. But more than anything else, it is the building of new precincts near the habitation zone (but never within it), which had no circular architecture and featured only different types of rectangular and square buildings, that shows dramatic sociocultural changes were occurring within the core. Box burials were quickly becoming the rule, though burials in bell-shaped pits and very modest boot-shaped tombs still occurred.

Changes in ceramic types were also important. The Huistla series of bichrome and polychrome molcajetes, with mold-made tripod feet, increased rapidly in popularity. The pseudocloisonné style changed. In addition, the ollas became quite large, and the copas, formerly an independent element in the set, were attached, upside-down, to the olla rim in order to form a single vessel. The codical styles continued, but they included motif elements in their iconography from outside the western basins. In general, some elements of Mixteca-Puebla iconography were introduced (Bell 1971). The artistic leadership the Teuchitlán tradition had enjoyed was now replaced by the southern pseudocloisonné style (presumably focused in Michoacán after around A.D. 900 to 1000) and the elegant Iguanas-Roblitos polychrome tradition from the general Amapa zone of Nayarit (Meighan 1976; Bell 1971). Both the aforementioned ceramic types began to turn up within the lake districts of Jalisco by around A.D. 900, if not a little earlier. Ceramic spindle whorls became popular, and these were often mold stamped. Mold-made figurines of the Tula-Mazapan style appear at the end of the Teuchitlán phase.

The newer settlements appear to be more nucleated though still fairly spread out. None is anywhere near as large as the Teuchitlán habitation zone had been. Open "U" patio/pyramid complexes are seen at El Grillo in the Atemejac Valley, Tepehuaje in the Chapala Basin, La Venta between the Teuchitlán and Atemejac valleys (Beekman 1996a), Santa Cruz de Barcenas in the Teuchitlán Valley, and other localities. This is an architectural format that is documented for the Hidalgo area near Tulancingo as well (Muller and Lizardi Ramos 1959). I postulate that the arrival of this architectural format in the lake districts of western Mexico signifies, in part, both the directionality from which the changes originated (i.e., the Bajio and northern central Mexico) and the types of new cultures that were being established in the area. At Santa Cruz de Barcenas, the open U-shaped building is but one complex within a moderately sized habitation zone. Two pyramid complexes, featuring rectangular and square structures, also exist. All the square pyramids at Santa Cruz de Barcenas are 40 m^2 and about 8 to 10 m high. One of the square pyramids had carved stone stelae atop its highest terrace. The only fragments of the stelae we were able to examine looked similar to the "Atlantean" carvings at Tula, which were also originally located on top of a similar type of pyramid. Galván (personal communication 1993) identified sherds from the Santa Cruz de Barcenas site as belonging to both the Epi-Classic and the early Postclassic. The site apparently reached its maximum development around A.D. 1000 to 1100. Before its decline around A.D. 1250 to 1300, its settlement area covered about 450 ha. Its decline is mirrored by the rise of the protohistorical states of Etzatlán and Tala (Weigand 1993a).

The northernmost complex at Tepehuaje (Chapala Basin) has a possible double pyramid, that is, two pyramids, side-by-side, atop a common platform. This complex dates to the Epi-Classic and early Postclassic period. It is interesting to note that this same type of structure is seen at Ihuatzio (see Caso 1930; Noguera 1931), in the Pátzcuaro Basin of Michoacán. The double pyramid at Ihuatzio is certainly not in the definitive *yácata* style that marked so much of the Tarascan-sponsored building activity. The *yácatas* formed the signature for that architectural tradition in the same fashion that the concentric circular buildings were the fingerprints of the Teuchitlán tradition in earlier times. It is possible that the double pyramid at Ihuatzio is earlier than the spread of the *yácata* style and therefore related to the Tepehuaje structure in some fashion. It appears from these highly preliminary observations that the idea of a double/dual pyramid is not unique to central Mexico and might actually be earlier in western Mexico.

The large sites of the Atemejac Valley, such as Ixtepete (Castro-Leal and Ochoa 1975; Galván 1976), Coyula (Weigand 1986), and El Grillo, were remodeled and expanded during the Epi-Classic and early Postclassic. The characteristic building style for this valley during this time period is the very large, but relatively low, rectangular platform. Ixtepete has one of these great platforms. Coyula (also Coyutla) had at least four of them, along with the only cruciform-shaped platform yet reported from the west. It was situated on a natural salient into the Río Grande de Santiago canyon and had a commanding view of that entire sector of the barranca. The citadel covered around 55 ha. The habitation zone has never been surveyed. The site was destroyed by the building of a garbage dump for the city of Guadalajara.

In addition, the Techaluta site in the Atoyac-Sayula Valley appears to have flowered during these periods (Valdez et al. 1996; Weigand and Neal 1989). The major pyramids in the precincts characteristically face west across sunken square *plazuelas*. On the west side of the precincts are smaller platforms that face east. The tabular masonry is very fine. One of the predominant ceramic types is an orange and black-on-cream ware, on which the design elements were boldly executed. To the west, much of the building activity seen at Ixtlán del Río also belongs to these periods (Bell 1971). In the coastal areas of Nayarit, as represented by the Cerritos phase (around A.D. 700 or 800 to 1200 [Meighan 1976]), dynamic and expanding societies prospered. The complexes to the south of the collapsing core, too, were expanding; the Autlán and Tuxcacuesco (Kelly 1945a, 1949) area is the best documented.

All this cultural activity in what had been the relatively underpopulated near hinterland (with the exception of the Nayarit coastal area) of the Teuchitlán core is in stark contrast to prior periods. It appears that when the core collapsed, the former near hinterlands came back into their own. But the cultural models that were chosen for this resurgence were non-Teuchitlán tradition models. They were patterned on either the regional rectangular/square architectural traditions that had survived the implosions or, just as likely, architectural traditions that were brought in from the east.

Of course, the changes that occurred within the lake districts of western Mexico were not unique. Change swept the mesoamerican ecumenes, from the collapse of Maya Classic civilization to the sociocultural intensifications among the Hohokam and Anasazi, and all points in between. The changes were thorough and often revolutionary (see Weaver 1993 for an overview). Nevertheless, the fact of pan-mesoamerican changes within the approximate same time frame does not explain the particulars of collapse and reorganization in any one area, such as western Mexico.

The collapse of the Teuchitlán tradition might be explained in three ways, none of which is mutually exclusive (Weigand 1993a):

1. *vis inertiae*: This hypothesis stresses the period of decline represented by the Teuchitlán II phase. It appears that the polity(ies) lost its momentum, and perhaps even its raison d'être, with the decline and collapse of Teotihuacán, which thereby lessened the cultural, political, and/or economic pressures placed on it, either directly or indirectly, from the east. This argument has a premise: the Teuchitlán tradition coalesced, in part, as a response to the growth of Teotihuacán. In decline, the system weakened and became susceptible to major structural changes, including those introduced from the outside.

2. *vi et armis*: This hypothesis stresses the definitive collapse of the Teuchitlán tradition as an event or series of events that would include migrations and/or invasions into the core region from the outside, presumably the east. Since the legends of the Tolteca-Chichimeca migrations seem probable enough, we know that peoples were often migrating and leaving sociocultural changes in their wakes. Newcomers in the western lake districts may not have been favorably disposed to the exotic traditions there before them and therefore effected the thoroughgoing changes that are clearly in evidence.

3. Changing procurement and exchange relationships: This hypothesis stresses the economic role the Teuchitlán tradition had played before its collapse, with its possible "monopolies" in high-quality obsidian and salt (along with, possibly, blue-green stones, crystals, and other products) and its strong cultural role as reflected by the pseudocloisonné materials. We know that metallurgy was beginning to emerge in the Epi-Classic period (Hosler 1988a), though it was neither widely popular nor widespread until after about A.D. 900 to 1000. Very small amounts of copper have been found by looters in burials belonging to the Teuchitlán II phase. But the emergence of metallurgy per se without doubt introduced completely new demands on the procurement systems for rare resources, as well as on the distribution network to include these new commodities. With metals entering into the procurement and distribution equation, the Teuchitlán tradition may not have been equipped to adapt to the new circumstances. Therefore,

it may have been eclipsed by societies more flexible and better placed to exploit the changing procurement and trade/exchange situation made necessary by the increasing popularity of metal artifacts.

Whatever actually happened, the core of western mesoamerican civilization moved definitively out of the western lake districts, not to return until the flowering of Guadalajara in the Colonial and modern periods. The activities that characterize a core (such as the construction of a Key Economic Area, demographic implosion, rare resource "monopolies," etc.) conclusively collapsed in the Ahualulco-Teuchitlán-Tala region. Eventually, a core reemerged in the eastern lake districts of western Mesoamerica during the late Postclassic. The history of the Tarascan empire (Pollard 1987, 1993, this volume) expresses this transformation. That expansive state played a major role in the culture histories and social developments that took place in the trans-Tarascan zone (Weigand 1993a).

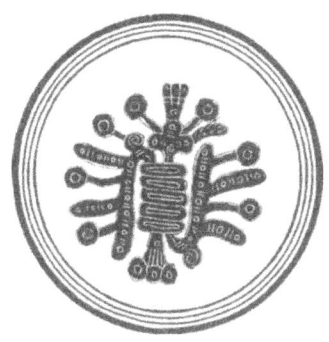

CHAPTER FIVE

TARASCANS AND THEIR ANCESTORS

Prehistory of Michoacán

HELEN PERLSTEIN POLLARD

IN 1948, EDUARDO NOGUERA attempted the first regional synthesis of the prehistory of the Tarascan zone (Figure 5.1). Working without the benefit of radiocarbon dating, he based his chronology on barely a decade of modern archaeological work and included a comparison with central Mexico:

Tzintzuntzan	Azteca III–IV
Zacapu–Los Gatos	Matlatzinca-Tula-Mazapan
Jiquilpan	Teotihuacán
Chupícuaro	Ticoman III
Curutaran	Zacatenco II–III
El Opeño	Zacatenco I

More than forty years later, the prehistory of central Mexico is understood in great detail and serves as primary evidence for the testing of major theories of cultural dynamics. By comparison, archaeological research in the territory once controlled by the Tarascan kingdom, the modern state of Michoacán and adjacent parts of Guanajuato, Jalisco, and Guerrero, was sporadic and site-oriented (see Schöndube 1987). Moreover, much of this work has been directed to sites occupied during the florescence of Tarascan culture. In the last decade, however, major new projects have been undertaken, some of which have been regional in scope and pre-Tarascan in focus. The Salvage Archaeology division of the Instituto Nacional de Antropología e Historia has launched several large regional surveys in Guanajuato, Michoacán, and Jalisco and has recorded many new sites. The large Centre d'Etudes Mexicaines et Centramericaines (CEMCA) Proyecto Zacapu was located in north-central Michoacán, including the Zacapu Basin, the Zinaparo obsidian mines, and the zone between Zacapu and the Río Lerma (Arnauld et al. 1988; Michelet 1989, 1992; Michelet et al. 1989, 1995). The Proyecto los Señorios Urichu, Xarácuaro y Pareo (Pollard 1992, 1995, 1996), the Proyecto Zinapécuaro (Healan 1992), and the Proyecto Cuitzeo (Macías Goytia 1989, 1990, 1992; Macías Goytia and Vackimes Serret 1990) are also in Michoacán.

Because of the status of scholarship in Michoacán, the summary of cultural development and the chronologies (Figures 5.2 and 5.3) presented here are highly abstracted from limited information and therefore quite tentative. In many important respects, not only have the major substantive and theoretical questions posed in 1948 not been resolved; many have not even been tested by archaeological field research.

THE TARASCAN ZONE

The Tarascan empire spanned the lands between two of Mexico's greatest rivers, the Lerma-Santiago to the north

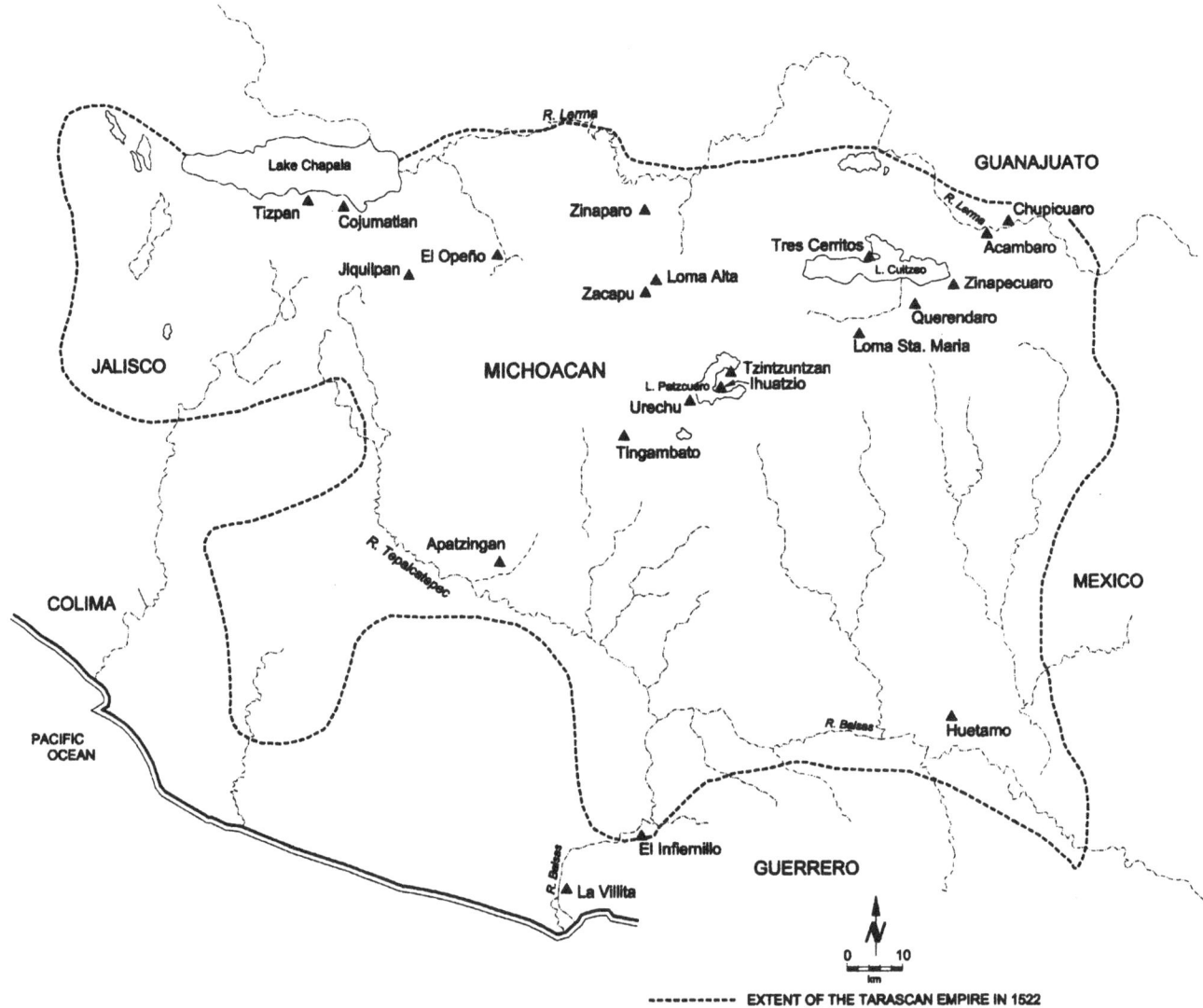

Figure 5.1. Major archaeological sites in Michoacán.

and the Balsas to the south. In this domain the Tarascans controlled four major geographic regions and an enormous variety of resources (INEGI 1985; Gorenstein and Pollard 1983). The Tarascan Central Plateau is a high volcanic region that constitutes the western extension of the Mexican *mesa central*. It is dominated by Cenozoic volcanic mountains and small lake basins above 2,000 m. Human occupation of this region has been focused on the lake basins, such as Pátzcuaro, and the marshes, such as Zacapu. The absence of large surface streams and rivers has led to a dispersal of settlements adjacent to springs in the remainder of the region. Nevertheless, the central plateau offers abundant forest resources and temperate agriculture with few recorded droughts.

The semitropical rims of the central plateau contain volcanic mountains and plains decreasing in elevation from 2,000 m to 1,200 m, occurring to the north and south of the central plateau. The northern rim includes the Río Lerma Basin, Lake Chapala, Lake Cuitzeo, and Lake Yuriria. In the northeast and northwest are thermal springs, obsidian flows (Zinapécuaro-Ucareo in the northeast and Zinaparo in the northwest), and, in the northeast, small deposits of silver and gold. The southern rim, often referred to as the southern escarpment, is characterized by fertile, black vertisols that have attracted human settlement, and mountain andosols that support pine-oak forests. A large variety of subtropical domesticated plants, including fruits, vegetables, and cotton, can be grown here.

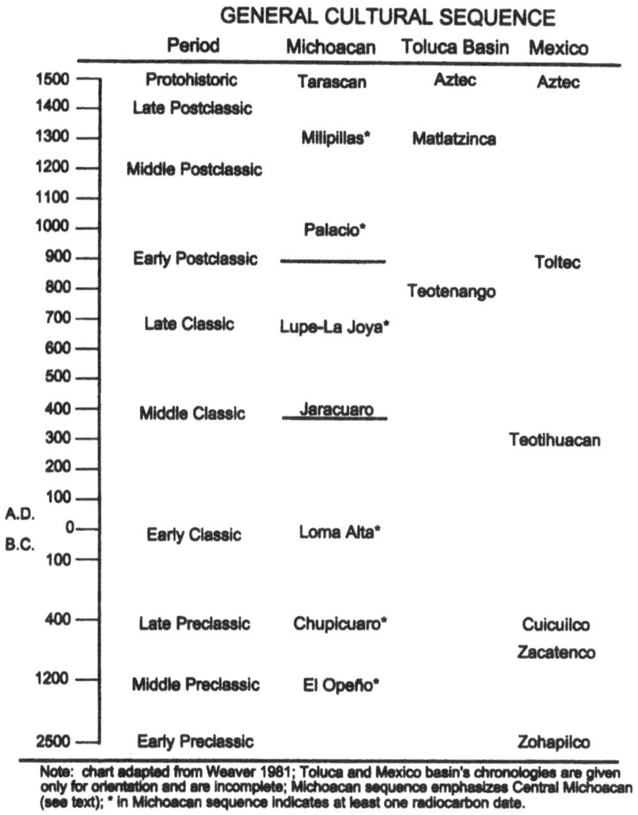

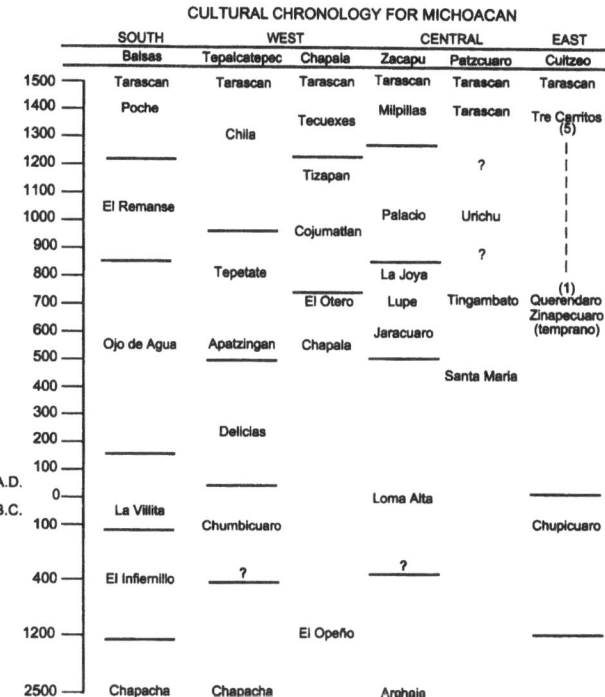

Figure 5.2. General cultural sequences for Michoacán and neighboring areas.

Figure 5.3. General chronology for Michoacán.

South of the escarpment lie the two remaining regions, the Balsas Depression and the Southern Sierra Madre, often treated as one. Directly south of the central plateau is the Balsas Depression, including the middle and lower Balsas Basin and the tributary Tepalcatepec Basin, both below 500 m. The complex geomorphology includes a number of resources of particular value to human occupation, among them marble deposits in the southwest Tepalcatepec Basin and copper, gold, silver, iron pyrites, and lead deposits in the eastern and central Balsas Basin. The final major region of the Tarascan domain is the Southern Sierra Madre, largely located southwest of the Tepalcatepec Basin. It is composed of volcanic mountains and small intermontane valleys, mixed with metamorphic and sedimentary deposits. Mineral deposits of copper, gold, and silver are found in the southeast portion of this region near Huetamo and the southwest portion near Coalcoman. Human settlement has always been dispersed and primarily focused on the mineral resources.

LITHIC PERIOD

The earliest occupation of Michoacán took place during the Paleoindian, or Lithic, period (before 2500 B.C.) by small groups of hunter-gatherers (Schöndube 1987). The evidence for these earliest inhabitants is limited to fluted projectile points and other stone implements found in association with Pleistocene mammoths and bison (Oliveros 1975). Though the best documentation comes from the Lake Chapala Basin, it is reasonable to suggest that similar occupations were taking place along other late Pleistocene lakes, such as Cuitzeo, Zacapu, and possibly Pátzcuaro.

ARCHAIC PERIOD

The Archaic period is virtually unknown in Michoacán. During the Zacapu Project, preceramic deposits dating to 2500–2200 B.C. were located in Los Portales Cave

(Michelet et al. 1989). The associated artifacts included waste flakes of basalt and obsidian, one projectile point, and one mano. The obsidian is believed to have come from the Zinaparo and Prieto flows located some 10 km from the site.

PRECLASSIC PERIOD

By the Early Preclassic, populations were located in agriculturally based villages, known from El Opeño in the west and the Balsas Basin on the south. From the remains of these earliest-known ceramic-producing societies it is clear that the region was occupied by many localized cultures, each with distinct histories, patterns of interaction with adjacent zones, and patterns of interaction with one another. This diversity remains characteristic of Michoacán until the emergence of the Tarascan state. El Opeño, one of the best documented of Formative cultures, is known from 11 excavated shaft tombs dating from 1500 to 800 B.C. (Noguera 1931; Oliveros 1975, 1989; Oliveros and de los Ríos Paredes 1993; Schöndube 1987; Weaver 1981). The burial cult revealed by these tombs, including ceramic vessels, figurines, and the shafts themselves, suggests cultural interaction along the Santiago-Lerma river system with cultures to the west in Jalisco and Nayarit, as well as linkages to the east. Farther south, in the middle and lower Balsas Basin, El Infiernillo small village sites containing ceramics suggest ties to the Capacha culture of Colima and the Pacific coast from Nayarit to Guerrero (Cabrera Castro 1986; Chadwick 1971; González Crespo 1979; Maldonado 1980; Muller 1979). Pollen cores from the Pátzcuaro Basin reveal domesticated maize pollen from approximately 1500 B.C. (Hutchinson et al. 1956; O'Hara et al. 1993; Watts and Bradbury 1982). The botanical data suggest that human settlement was far more widespread in the Early and Middle Preclassic than the current archaeological evidence reveals.

By the late Preclassic, there were at least three regional cultures found in Michoacán: the Chupícuaro culture of the northern and central zones, the Chumbícuaro culture of the Tepalcatepec Basin in the southwest, and the Balsas/Mezcala culture (El Infiernillo and La Villita phases) of the central Balsas to the south. Each zone was characterized by small village societies, and each has been identified primarily by variation in burial-associated ceramics. The best known is the Chupícuaro culture, found along the middle Lerma drainage in southern Guanajuato, the Cuitzeo Basin, and, with localized variants, near Morelia (Santa María) and in the Zacapu and Pátzcuaro basins (Arnauld et al. 1993; Carot et al. 1998; Chadwick 1971; Gorenstein 1985; Macías Goytia 1988; Michelet 1986, 1988a, 1988b; Michelet et al. 1989; Moedano 1946; Moguel Cos 1987; Oliveros 1975; Pollard 1993; Weaver 1981; see also Braniff this volume and Florance this volume). Chupícuaro communities appear to have been primarily adapted to lacustrine ecosystems, locating their villages either on islands within marshes or along lakeshores or rivers (e.g., Chupícuaro, Acambaro, Zacapu–Loma Alta, Lake Pátzcuaro, and the many Lake Cuitzeo sites along the southern shore of the lake).

CLASSIC PERIOD

During the Late Preclassic/Early Classic period, local changes in ceramic style and more elaborate public architecture, including sunken patios and platforms, are found at the site of Santa María, near Morelia (Manzanilla 1988; Piña Chan 1977); Loma Alta, in the Zacapu Basin (Carot et al. 1998); and Chehuayo, in the Cuitzeo Basin (Macías Goytia 1989). The Loma Alta occupation includes some Thin Orange sherds, cloisonné, and an unusual necropolis. There is evidence for the repeated use of the necropolis and four different types of burial (Arnauld et al. 1993; Carot et al. 1998; Pereira 1996). This evidence plus more widely known variations in burial artifacts suggest that by the first centuries A.D. social ranking may have existed at the larger settlements (see Pollard 1996; Schöndube 1987). Nevertheless, the location of settlements on the floor of lake basins, and the general absence of settlements in defensible positions, indicates minimal local aggression and/or movements of peoples. Chupícuaro artifacts or stylistically similar artifacts are found along the upper Río Lerma in the Toluca Basin and farther east into the Basin of Mexico and Tlaxcala, indicating significant, if indirect, social interaction between northern Michoacán and central Mexico at this time. The Chumbícuaro culture is known primarily from the plain of Apatzingán (Kelly 1947) and is dated from 100 B.C. to A.D. 100; the Balsas/Mezcala culture is located along the central Balsas (Cabrera Castro 1986; Maldonado 1980; Muller 1979). Though regionally distinct, each appears to be related to adjacent zones to the south and west (Schöndube 1987).

A major cultural transformation took place between

A.D. 400 and 900. After centuries of autonomous village societies, distinguishable by stylistic variation in artifacts and local economic adaptations, a new form of settlement, the ceremonial center, appeared in Michoacán. Those ceremonial centers known from this period, including El Otero (near Jiquilpan), Tres Cerritos (near Cuitzeo, C-53 in Gasoducto survey), with possibly minor centers at Querendaro or Zinapécuaro in the Cuitzeo Basin or both, and Tingambato (near the Pátzcuaro Basin), are widely dispersed in central Michoacán. They are separated by lands occupied by populations essentially continuing regional traditions although in interaction with these new centers. In the Zacapu Basin, this is a time of rapid population growth. There is a doubling of the number of sites in the Jaracuaro phase (from 13 to 22) and another doubling in the Lupe phase (from 22 to 42 in the early part, A.D. 600–700, and to 43 in the latter part, A.D. 700–850). By the end of the Late Classic (La Joya phase, A.D. 850–900), there are 58 sites. Moreover, settlements are now also located away from the lakeshore, especially in the zone between Zacapu and the Río Lerma, and include pyramids, plazas, and ball courts (Michelet et al. 1989). In the Pátzcuaro Basin, a deeply buried irrigation canal dates to the Lupe–La Joya phase, suggesting more intensive use of agrarian resources (Fisher et al. 1998).

The major centers themselves contain architectural forms and artifacts indicating direct contact with the Teotihuacán culture of the Basin of Mexico. At El Otero, this includes a ball court, plazas and pyramids, stucco painting, and large group tombs, one of which held 42 individuals, jade, rock crystal, pyrites, and turquoise (Noguera 1944; Oliveros 1975). Tres Cerritos, a site that continued to be occupied until Spanish contact, has three large mounds and two sunken plazas. The earliest architecture at the site includes talud-tablero and at least two large tombs, one of which contained more than 30 individuals, 120 vessels, marine shell, jade, turquoise, rock crystal, and an alabaster Teotihuacán mask (Macías Goytia 1988). At Tingambato, there are a series of plazas, altars, a central pyramid, a ball court, and a large tomb containing the remains of at least 30 to 40 people (Pereira 1997; Piña Chan and Oí 1982). Among the artifacts are a cloisonné-decorated vessel, marine shell, and mosaic disks inlaid with pyrites, jadeite, jade, and turquoise. For the first time, there is evidence of dental mutilation in six of the Tingambato male burials, exhibiting A-2, A-4, and B-4 patterns (Romero Molina 1986). The talud-tablero architecture on the pyramid and plazas reveals links to central Mexico, although all but a few ceramics are local. Based on the ball-court architecture, Taladoire (1989:91) suggests a date of A.D. 800–900 for Tingambato. Outside these centers, from the Río Lerma and Cuitzeo Basin to the middle Balsas, a few sites in each zone contain Thin Orange pottery, cloisonné decoration, mosaic disks, Teotihuacán-like figurines, and occasionally talud-tablero architecture (Cabrera Castro 1986; Maldonado 1980; Oliveros 1975). In all cases the number of such artifacts is low, often a handful, and they represent only a small proportion of material goods associated with central Mexican Classic period culture. Thus, for example, although dental mutilation appears for the first time at Tingambato, it represents only a limited variety of such mutilation found at this time and includes practices known elsewhere since the Middle Preclassic; dental incrustation (Romero's [1986] types E and G) is never found in Michoacán.

The meaning of these new centers and Teotihuacán style artifacts is extremely unclear. Because of the salvage nature of most research, none of the deposits at the larger centers has been dated to anything more precise than A.D. 400–900. This means that they, and the more dispersed artifacts, may date to the Middle Classic and reflect populations interacting with the extensive Teotihuacán economic network; or they may date to the Epi-Classic (A.D. 700–900) and reflect small groups of elite/priests/artisans who migrated out of the Basin of Mexico following the collapse of Teotihuacán, bringing some aspects of their heritage with them. A third possibility is that the archaeological evidence reflects a complex mixture of both processes, plus the added impact of the independent emergence of complex societies in Jalisco during the Classic period (Weigand 1985, see also this volume). There are strong adherents to all alternatives, although the current evidence suggests Teotihuacán interaction along the Balsas during the Middle Classic and significant central Mexican interaction with central and northern Michoacán after A.D. 600 (Michelet 1988a, 1988b). Thus, Thin Orange pottery, a Teotihuacán mask, and "al fresco" decoration on a few sherds at Loma Alta in the Zacapu Basin are not associated with major changes in settlement patterns or ceramic styles during the Loma Alta and Jaracuaro phases (A.D. 0–600). When major changes are seen in settlement patterns and ceramics during the Lupe and La Joya phases (A.D. 600–900), they are associated with populations moving from lakeshore sites and occupying the zone between Zacapu and the Río Lerma. This pattern raises the possibility that central Mexican traits introduced at this time may be entering Michoacán from the north via Classic period populations in southern Guanajuato, rather than directly from the east.

The effect of these contacts was to speed up the process of social differentiation already taking place and stimulate the emergence of territorially discrete and competing polities. What they, or more precisely their elites, were competing over is unclear, but it may have included access to inter- and intraregional trade to both the east and west. The high proportion of Zinapécuaro-Ucareo obsidian used at Tula, Hidalgo, from A.D. 800 to 1000 (Diehl 1974; Healan 1989) suggests that by A.D. 800 portions of northeastern Michoacán were interacting directly with central Mexico (Healan 1992). Such long-distance exchange may have stimulated the increased production at the Zinaparo obsidian mines, which can be documented by A.D. 700 (Darras 1994; Michelet et al. 1989).

POSTCLASSIC PERIOD

By A.D. 900, the effects of these changes resulted in major shifts in settlement patterns. In the Cuitzeo and Zacapu basins, best-known areas for this time period, but also along the Lerma and Balsas rivers, there are indications of population nucleation at defensible locations. In many zones, this is the beginning of a pattern, which grows until the emergence of the Tarascan state. Along with these settlement changes comes the widespread adoption of red-on-cream ceramics, which are integrated with local ceramic traditions. Such shifts in style are known from a wide region of north and central Michoacán, including Zinapécuaro, Cuitzeo, Tiristaran, Morelia, Teremendo, Zacapu, Lake Pátzcuaro, Carapan, Zamora, and Tangamendapio. In the Pátzcuaro Basin at the site of Urichu, we can document by A.D. 400 the appearance of polychrome pottery with negative decoration that bears strong similarity to ceramics of southern Guanajuato. After A.D. 900, the polychromes become more common and clearly are ancestral to later Tarascan polychromes.

The coincident appearance of metallurgy in Michoacán, possibly earlier in Nayarit and Jalisco (Hosler 1988a; Mountjoy 1969; Mountjoy and Torres 1985) and in the lower Balsas Basin (Maldonado 1980), suggests that cultural exchange and/or population movements linked Michoacán directly to societies to the north and west. Again, the Santiago-Lerma and Balsas-Tepalcatepec rivers appear to have been the primary routes of change. Hosler (1988b, 1994) suggests that the introduction of metallurgy was made by means of merchants plying the coastal canoe trade from southern Ecuador up the west Mexican coast. Hosler's suggestion is based on technical analyses of the metal objects themselves. Oliveros (1975) has noted that at the time of Spanish contact canoe traders along that coast would put in at the port of Zacatula, at the mouth of the Río Balsas, for up to six months before their return voyage was possible. During the early Postclassic, the metal objects, known almost exclusively from burials, were made of copper and copper-silver by means of cold hammering, annealing, and lost-wax casting in styles and types of objects known earlier from coastal Ecuador.

By the Middle/Late Postclassic (A.D. 1200), societies throughout the region had little direct interaction with central Mexico but were instead participating in regional cultures, sharing traits and beliefs that later were characteristic of the Tarascans. Some of these traits appear to have diffused from farther west in Mexico, particularly along the Santiago-Lerma river system; others were products of local cultural change. Specific traditions appearing now include (1) more complex metallurgy, (2) abundant ceramic pipes, (3) polychrome pottery with negative decoration, (4) large-scale rubble-filled mounds clustered into plazas and located on hillslopes or malpaís, and (5) petroglyphs later associated with the Tarascan sun-hunting deity, Curicaueri. The Tarascans later gave sites occupied at this time sacred significance.

Hosler (1994) notes that a number of metallurgical techniques and styles were introduced at this time into west Mexico. The source of these innovations appears to be south coastal Peru trade with coastal Ecuador, and then trade from Ecuador to west Mexico. Among the new features were loop-eye needles, ax money (of sheet metal), and wirework bells, which, in addition to previously made forms, were worked hot. New alloys were produced during the Late Postclassic, including copper-arsenic, copper-tin, and copper-arsenic-tin.

The current archaeological evidence suggests that during the Early/Middle Postclassic, local elites competed for communities, marking their relative success with polychrome pottery, metal goods, and patron deities. The absence of regional authority with decision-making power in the face of what appear to have been increasing populations led to the formation of highly nucleated populations in some areas. The best-documented example is that of Zacapu, with an estimated occupation of the malpaís (known as El Palacio in the literature) of 13 sites covering 11 km^2 (5 km^2 densely occupied) and upward of 20,000 people (Arnauld and Faugere-Kalfon 1998; Michelet 1988b, 1995; Michelet et al. 1995; Michelet et al. 1989); at the same time, the lake marsh below was abandoned. The sites themselves include multiple barrios, each with public centers dominated by *yácatas*, with one plaza complex larger than all others. Michelet (1995) interprets this as reflecting relatively rapid movement of individual communities onto the malpaís, clustering together for defensive purposes and shortly thereafter (A.D. 1250) each reorganizing under the control of a single authority.

According to the *Relación de Michoacán*, during the Late Postclassic there was a series of migrations of peoples into central Michoacán. These included groups referred to as *Chichimecs, Nahuas,* and the ancestors of the Tarascan royal dynasty known as *Uacúsecha* (eagles). They are said to have been hunters and gatherers, especially deer hunters, who migrated from the north and settled in discrete communities within and adjacent to the Pátzcuaro Basin, joining the already existing Tarascan-speaking population. Current evidence indicates that either the numbers of migrants were very small or they had assimilated local cultural traditions before actually entering central Michoacán. Although there are clear ties between some Late Postclassic traits and the Río Lerma Basin, there is no evidence of movement of Chichimecs, in the sense of hunter-gatherer Uto-Aztecans from north of the mesoamerican frontier. To what extent this origin legend is myth or history will probably always be uncertain, but unlike the Postclassic period in the Basin of Mexico, which saw the spread of the Nahuatl language associated with population movements from the north, Tarascan remained the language of the Michoacán central plateau.

Nevertheless, even if their numbers were relatively small, in the context of the Late Postclassic their effects may have been great. There were several different language-ethnic groups in the Pátzcuaro Basin by A.D. 1200, but their relative sizes must have varied greatly. For example, the Nahuatl speakers of Xaraquaro (Jaracuaro) indicated in the *Relación de Michoacán* (1980), "We are many more than they, for there are not many Chichimecs," in referring to the *Uacúsecha* of Pátzcuaro. The subsequent competition between their elites for access to basic resources is given as the cause for a succession of wars in which political and economic power was concentrated in the *Uacúsecha* elite. According to official Tarascan history (*Relación de Michoacán* 1980), the warrior-leader Taríacuri united the several independent polities of the Pátzcuaro Basin into a unified state during the first half of the fourteenth century (Table 5.1). Following his death, his son and nephews extended the state beyond the Pátzcuaro Basin and began the political and economic changes that saw the emergence of a new mesoamerican civilization. Current archaeological research in the southwestern zone of the Pátzcuaro Basin is targeted to these centuries of transformation in order to understand the process by which the Protohistoric (A.D. 1450–1530) kingdom came into being (Pollard 1992, 1995, 1996). In the Middle Postclassic, the number of sites increased and the area of occupation doubled (McCosh et al. 1997). A large proportion of the new sites were located on the newly exposed islands and on fertile lacustrine soil exposed by an episode of lake regression (and exposed again only after lake levels dropped since 1990). During the Postclassic, these low-lying sites were flooded, and settlement shifted to the new lakeshore and to areas of high agricultural fertility back from the lakeshore. The number of sites and area occupied again doubled, including the maximum expansion of Urichu (> 90 ha), Pareo (> 45 ha), the entire exposed island of Xarácuaro, and densely occupied towns with public architecture at Tocuaro, Arocutin, Charahuen, and Ajuno (Axuni).

The data from all surveyed regions in Michoacán suggest that population density reached its highest point during the Late Postclassic. Moreover, the data also suggest that the largest and most populous settlements within any single region, whether ceremonial centers or cities, also date to the Late Postclassic.

PROTOHISTORIC PERIOD

As I have already indicated, although archaeological research in Michoacán has been limited and sporadic, much of what has been done relates to the Tarascan state. The greatest amount of research has been carried out at the Tarascan capital, primarily under the auspices of the Instituto Nacional de Antropología e Historia, Mexico. In 1930, when modern archaeological research began, Alfonso Caso and Eduardo Noguera placed test pit excavations in two of the ethnohistorically known Tarascan centers (Tzintzuntzan and Ihuatzio) in an effort to provide collections for the National Museum (Caso 1930; Noguera 1931). Caso returned in 1937 and 1938 to begin mapping and excavations on the Great Platform at Tzintzuntzan (Acosta 1939); in 1940, 1942–44, and 1946, this work was continued under Rubín de la Borbolla, along with reconstruction of several pyramid

Table 5.1. Genealogy of the Tarascan Kings.

	Date	Seat of Power
Colonial Period		
Don Antonio Huitziméngari	1545–62	Governor of Michoacán
Don Francisco Tariacuri	1543–45	Governor of Michoacán
Don Pedro de Arellano assumes control as corregidor of Michoacán following the execution of Tangáxuan II and acts as regent for the king's sons.	1530–43	
Protohistoric Period		
Trangáxuan II (Tzintzicha Don Francisco)	1520–30	Tzintzuntzan
Zuangua	1479–1520	Tzintzuntzan
Tzitzispandáquare	1454–79	Tzintzuntzan
Late Postclassic Period		
Tangáxuan I	?–1454	Tzintzuntzan
Hirepan		Tzintzuntzan
Hiquingaje (younger son)	ca. 1350–	Pátzcuaro
Taríacuri (rule interrupted by brief rule by Curatame II, his older son.)	ca. 1300–1350	Pátzcuaro
Pauacume II		Pátzcuaro
Early Postclassic Period		
Uapeani II		Uayameo
Curatame I		Uayameo
Uapeani I		Uayameo
Pauacume I		Uayameo
Sicuirancha		Uayameo
Thicatame (Hireti-ticatame)		Zacapu, then Zichaxuquaro

Note: Adapted from the *Relación de Michoacán* (1980:Figure 139), with paleography by Francisco Miranda; the *Relación de Michoacán* (1956:XXXIII), introductory essay by Paul Kirchhoff; and data in *The Conquest of Michoacan* (Warren 1985) and *Historia sucinta de Michoacán* (Bravo Ugarte 1962). All Postclassic period dates are estimates, given for general orientation only. Protohistoric period dates are derived from either Postconquest Spanish documents or correlation with Mexica events (primarily battles).

bases (Acosta 1939; Gali 1946; Moedano 1941, 1946; Rubín de la Borbolla 1939, 1941, 1944); in 1956, under Orellana, limited excavations were continued; in 1962, 1964, and 1968, Román Piña Chan resumed this work on the Great Platform at Tzintzuntzan (Figure 5.4; Castro Leal 1986). The tenth season of work by the INAH at the ceremonial core of Tzintzuntzan was carried out by Ruben Cabrera Castro in 1978–79 (Cabrera Castro 1987), and Efraín Cárdenas completed restoration and test excavations in 1992–94. In 1970, I conducted an intensive surface survey of the urban extent of Tzintzuntzan (Figure 5.5; Pollard 1972, 1977).

On the regional level, a study of the Protohistoric period political system of the Pátzcuaro Basin by Gorenstein and Pollard (1976–80) led to the identification of 91 settlements occupied during the apex of the Tarascan state (Gorenstein and Pollard 1983; Pollard 1980). In 1981–82, 83 sites were recorded in the eastern half of the Pátzcuaro Basin as part of the Proyecto Arqueológico Gasoducto (Tramo Yuriria-Uruapan), under the direction of Carlos Silva Rhoads, INAH Salvamento Arqueológico (Moguel Cos 1987), of which more than 30 were tentatively assigned to the Protohistoric. The following year (1983), a surface survey of the western half of the lake basin added 60 sites to the basin total, 44 of which were assigned to the Protohistoric. More recent work within the Pátzcuaro Basin has been done by Cabrera Castro (1987), Mogul Cos (1987), and Pollard (1992, 1995, 1996). Surveys in the Balsas Basin undertaken before the construction of dams in the zones of Infiernillo (1963) and La Villita-Palos Altos (1967–68) provide archaeological documentation of Tarascan presence in this important southern zone of the empire (Cabrera Castro 1986; González Crespo 1979; Maldonado Cárdenas 1980).

Outside the Pátzcuaro Basin, two projects have focused on the period of Tarascan domination. The first, carried out from 1971 to 1974 under the direction of

Figure 5.4. A *yácata* at the main platform at Tzintzuntzan.

Shirley Gorenstein, was a study of the Tarascan-Aztec military frontier. Several of the Tarascan fortified sites were located and surveyed, with major excavations focused on Cerro del Chivo, Acambaro (Gorenstein 1985). The second, carried out from 1983 to 1987 (with analyses still under way) by the Centre d'Etudes Mexicaines et Centramericaines (CEMCA), under the direction of Dominique Michelet, entailed excavations and mapping at the Tarascan center of Zacapu, a regional survey of the Zacapu Basin, and study of the obsidian quarries in the region of Zinaparo (Arnauld 1987; Michelet 1986, 1988a, 1988b, 1995).

In addition to the research within the Pátzcuaro Basin, the regional surveys, and targeted study of Tarascan archaeology, many other archaeological projects carried out within the territory once held by the Tarascan state have provided some information. These have been summarized by Chadwick (1971) for the period through 1970 and appear as salvage reports, rarely published, for the period since 1970 (Pollard 1993; Michelet 1995).

The Cuitzeo Basin project, under the direction of Macías Goytia, INAH, has included excavations at Huandacareo, an administrative center founded after Tarascan conquest of the basin, and Tres Cerritos (Cuitzeo), an earlier center that continued in use under the Tarascans (Macías Goytia 1988, 1989, 1990). The Sayula Basin project has documented Tarascan occupation at major centers, following incorporation into the empire (Valdez 1993a, 1993b; Valdez and Liot 1993). Technical analyses of Tarascan artifacts (Figures 5.6 and 5.7) from museum collections provide information about raw materials, technology, style, and economic interaction (Bray 1989; Castro-Leal 1986; Flores de Aguirrezabal and Quijada López 1980; Grinberg 1988; Hosler 1988a, 1988b, 1994; Pollard and Vogel 1994a, 1994b). Finally, paleoecological studies in the Pátzcuaro and Zacapu basins have determined resource distribution and human impact under the Tarascan state (Fisher et al. 1998; Metcalfe and Harrison 1983; Metcalfe et al. 1987; O'Hara et al. 1993; Pétrequin 1994; Pollard 1979,

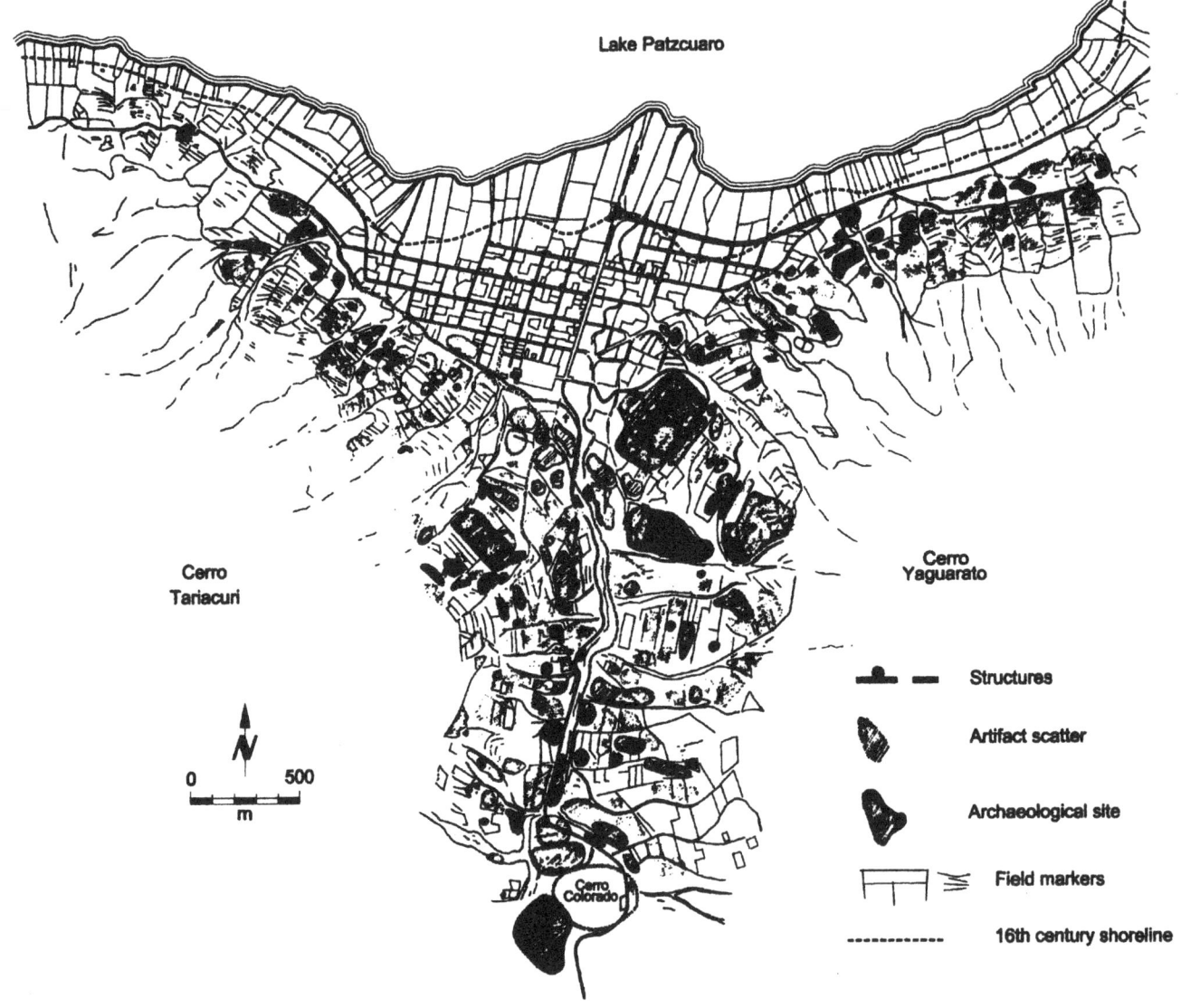

Figure 5.5. Features and areas recorded at and in the vicinity of Tzintzuntzan.

1982a, 1983; Pollard and Gorenstein 1980; Street-Perrott et al. 1989; Watts and Bradbury 1982).

Despite all this archaeological research, the only chronology for the Late Postclassic/Protohistoric periods comes from sixteenth-century ethnohistoric and historic documents, especially the *Relación de Michoacán*. Based on these documents, it has been possible to map the geographical expansion of the empire (Herrejon Peredo 1978; Pollard 1988), analyze the imperial political economy (Beltrán 1982, 1986; Carrasco 1986; Paredes 1976, 1979; Pollard 1982b, 1987; Roskamp 1998), detail the social structure and incorporation of subject peoples (García Alcaraz 1976; Pollard 1994a), and even describe Tarascan religious and political ideology (Caso 1943, 1967; Corona Núñez 1957; Freddolino 1973; Hurtado Mendoza 1986; Lopez Austin 1975; Pollard 1991; Sepúlveda y H. 1988). But few of these analyses have been tested with archaeological data, and major gaps exist in our understanding of Tarascan culture.

MICHOACÁN PREHISTORY AND MESOAMERICA

In the prehistory of western Mesoamerica, Michoacán occupies a key position between central Mexico and the highland lakes of Jalisco to the west. Since the turn of

Figure 5.6. A chacmool from Ihuatzio. INAH Regional Museum in Morelia.

Figure 5.7. A Tarascan polychrome vessel. INAH Regional Museum in Morelia.

this century, the monumental architecture of the Tarascan *yácatas* and the epic legends of the *Relación de Michoacán* have been incorporated into the understanding of Mesoamerica's past (León 1888a, 1888b, 1979; Lumholtz 1902; Lumholtz and Hrdlicka 1898; Seler 1908). At least two versions of this past have dominated the interpretation of regional prehistory. The first version describes a powerful, centralized Tarascan empire that emerged from culturally homogeneous societies as a small-scale replica of the same evolutionary sequence as in the Basin of Mexico, albeit "delayed" in its unfolding. This focus on Tarascan evolution as an example of secondary state development carries with it the implicit notions that (1) only the Tarascan period is worthy of study and (2) the regional prehistory is redundant to an understanding of Mesoamerica as a whole.

A second version of the past sees the Tarascan state as a barbarian, quasi-mesoamerican polity that emerged following the conquest of culturally isolated Chupícuaro-like villages by Chichimecs, who then ruled by "copying" their Aztec relatives. In this version, Michoacán prehistory is not only marginal to Mesoamerica, it is only partly mesoamerican.

This a priori marginalizing of the region has impeded

research without reflecting the culture-historic dynamics revealed by the limited evidence we have. The assumption that the ethnic, linguistic, political, and economic patterns of the Protohistoric period reflect a "culmination" or apex of cultural evolution in the region misinterprets the reality of patterns of interaction in the long prehistory of Mesoamerica. Until there are more regionally focused, long-term archaeological projects in the state that are able to produce chronometrically dated cultural sequences, however, the questions raised in 1948 will remain unanswered and Michoacán will continue to be ignored in the construction of Mexico's past.

CHAPTER SIX

TARASCAN EXTERNAL RELATIONSHIPS

HELEN PERLSTEIN POLLARD

WITH THE EMERGENCE of the Tarascan state (Figure 6.1) in the last two centuries before European contact, the Pátzcuaro Basin became a demographic, political, and economic core region in western Mexico (Figure 6.2). Large quantities of food, cloth, metals, tropical goods, and manufactured products were sent into central Michoacán through the tribute system (Pollard 1982a). In addition, the labor of large numbers of people was under the direct control of the royal dynasty resident at Tzintzuntzan, in the form of military service, household servants, corvée labor, and agricultural workers on state lands. Although the precise means by which Michoacán was transformed from a mesoamerican periphery into a mesoamerican core have yet to be understood, it is possible to indicate some of the significant ways in which this core related to other parts of the region.

TARASCAN-AZTEC RELATIONS

Despite their contemporaneity and proximity, the interaction between the Aztec and Tarascan states was dominated by military hostility that restricted the flow of individuals (including members of the elite), altered economic exchange, and allowed the creation of ethnic stereotypes that persist to the present.

Military and Political Engagement

The Tarascans are generally considered to have been the foremost enemy of the Aztecs (Davies 1987:291). From the 1450s until the Spanish conquest, these two powers were continually engaged in offensive or defensive military actions. The sequence of interaction is summarized in Table 6.1, based on material reported in Brand 1943a; Contreras Ramírez 1987; Hassig 1988; Herrejón Peredo 1978; Warren 1985; the *Relación de Michoacán* 1956, 1980; and the *Relaciones Geográficas* 1985, 1987.

It is clear that both the Tarascans and the Aztecs had economic interests in portions of the disputed territory. The middle Balsas is a zone of metamorphic rock with copper, tin, silver, and gold deposits; greenstone; and localized salt production. Smith (1996:183–184) points out the role of Alahuistlán (Ajuchitlán) in salt production, seeing the Aztec effort to protect that region as part of the mission of the fortifications of Oztoman. The northern border region was of great value to the Tarascans because it had major obsidian deposits and sacred thermal springs.

In a larger framework, the most active sections of the border controlled access to the Lerma and Balsas river systems, with the Tarascans preventing Aztec penetration of either. That effectively forestalled further Aztec penetration to the west and northwest along major trade routes.

Figure 6.1. The Protohistoric Tarascan empire.

Over time, Aztec actions were both defensive, preventing Tarascan movement into the Toluca Basin, and offensive, finding alternative means of reaching the trade center at Zacatula. Hassig (1985) sees these actions as a policy of encirclement by the Aztecs. If that is so, it was clearly only a partial success, as only one of the Tarascan borders was effectively closed to further expansion by the Aztec actions. Other parts of the Tarascan border remained fixed, owing to the inability of the Tarascan central government to field armies and retain tight control of distant populations to the north, west, and south.

The Tarascan frontier with the Aztecs was clearly a closed border. Although it was only 160 km from the border settlement of Taximaroa to Tenochtitlán, and messengers could move between the two capitals (Tzintzuntlán and Tenochtitlán) in four days of travel (Gorenstein and Pollard 1991), movement was strongly restricted. Aztec messengers had to present themselves at the official "ports of entry" and await permission to pass into the Tarascan domain, under Tarascan escort. Safety was obviously the enforcing principle, and the continuing hostilities along the border bred distrust of spies, who might precede raids or major campaigns. The movement of Tarascans within Aztec territory was probably also difficult since Tarascan culture and language was clearly distinct from the Aztec. On both sides, one solution was to use Otomí or Matlatzinca messengers and spies, but this meant that communication between the elites of these states was indirect and intermittent.

Economic Exchange: State Merchants

The available ethnohistoric and archaeological data indicate only two classes of economic interaction between the Tarascan and Aztec domains. The first, and primary, class includes goods acquired by Tarascan and Aztec long-distance traders. Tarascan long-distance merchants traveled to the borders of the Tarascan state, including

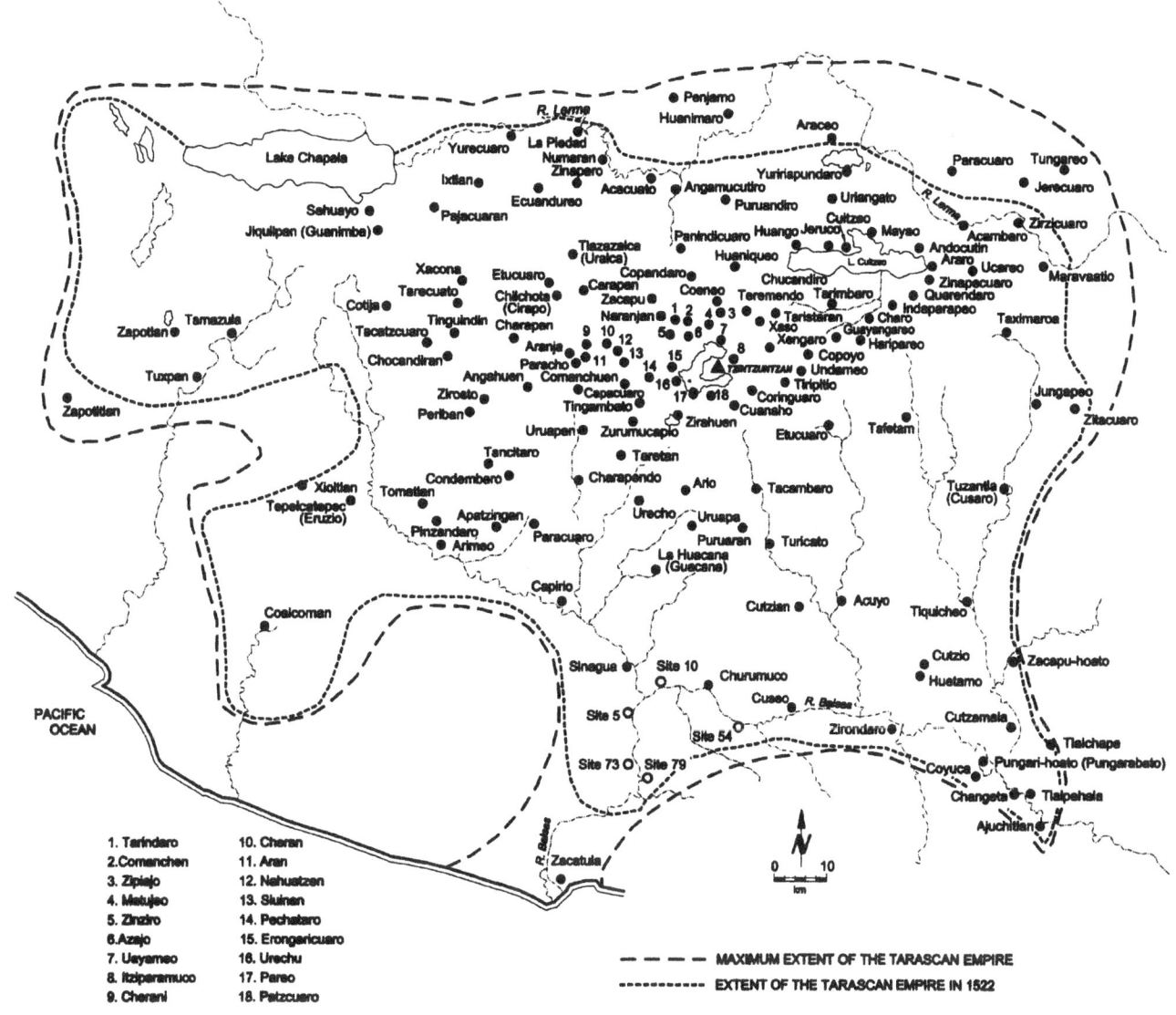

Figure 6.2. Towns and limits of the Tarascan empire.

Zacatula on the Pacific coast and Taximaroa on the frontier with the Aztecs, to acquire materials used by the elites of Tzintzuntzan: green obsidian from central Mexico and a range of raw materials that would have come from central and southern Mexico, including jade, onyx, serpentine, pyrites, and copal. There is, however, no indication that Tarascan long-distance merchants went beyond the borders of the Tarascan domain, nor that Aztec merchants (*pochteca*) entered Tarascan territory. Exchanges at frontier settlements, such as Taximaroa, may have been made directly between Tarascan and Aztec merchants, or Tarascan merchants may have dealt with Matlatzinca or Otomí traders at these places. At the present time, only two types of commodities can be documented as having been exported to the rest of Mesoamerica: foodstuffs and manufactured metal objects, especially those of bronze and bronze alloys (Hosler and Macfarlane 1996). The familiarity of the Aztec nobility with the fish, featherwork, and wood products of Michoacán (Hosler and Macfarlane 1996:41) might be due to the movement of these products across the eastern military frontier, but there is no independent evidence of such exchange. Ucareo obsidian, which was widely distributed within Mesoamerica before the Late Postclassic (Healan 1997), appears to have been "captured" by the state and redirected within Michoacán.

Metals found outside the Tarascan empire include

Table 6.1. Summary of Tarascan-Aztec Military Engagement.

Date	Event
1430s	Aztecs under Itzcoatl begin conquests in the Toluca Basin.
1440s	Aztecs under Moctezuma I (Motecuczomah Ilhuicamina) conquer south and west of the Toluca Basin, including Oztoman.
1455–62	Tarascan conquests, under Tzitzipandaquare, into Toluca Basin as far east as Xiquipilco, previously conquered by Itzcoatl.
1472	Aztecs under Axayacatl retake areas of Toluca Basin and defend area from future Tarascan attempts to take region. Hassig (1988:185) places this as part of the 1477–78 campaign.
1475–77	Aztecs under Axayacatl conquer central and western portion of Toluca Basin and move south to Oztoman and its neighbors.
1479–80	Aztecs' third major western campaign under Axayacatl moves against Tarascan territory after Toluca Basin is placed under military rule. The army masses at Toluca (Tollocan), including Tezcuanos, Tepanecas, Chalcas, Xochimilcas, Chinampanecas, Otomies. It takes Taximaroa and marches toward Querendaro up to Charo-Undameo. Aztecs are defeated here by combined Tarascan-Matlatzinca forces, and all communities are retaken by the Tarascans up to the frontier at Taximaroa. A small force harasses the Aztec force back to the Toluca Basin. This is a major defeat involving up to 32,000 Aztec and 50,000 Tarascan soldiers, of whom up to 30,000 Aztecs are said to have died.
1486	Ahuitzotl crowned tlatoani in Tenochtitlán. The Tarascans refuse to attend. There is an Aztec military campaign to Xiquilpa and Toluca Basin.
1488	Cazonci (Irecha) attends dedication of Great Temple in Tenochtitlán. No sacrificial victims are Tarascan.
1489	Ahuitzotl attacks Oztoman after this border settlement refuses to acknowledge tributary status to the Aztecs. The entire population of Oztoman and several neighboring communities are killed or dispersed; the settlements are repopulated with settlers from the Triple Alliance capitals.
	Tarascans establish a series of fortifications at strategic points from the Lerma to the Balsas basins. Tarascans are settled at some, and all are under direct control of the Tarascan capital.
1490–91	Aztecs expand into Guerrero, to the Pacific coast, and move north along the coast. Hassig sees this as attempt to encircle the Tarascans (1988:211).
1499	Tarascans attack fortified Oztoman, and Aztecs respond with additional buildup of population and fortifications in the region.
1502	Moteuczomah Xocoyotl (Moctezuma II) is crowned tlatoani in Tenochtitlán. Durán indicates that the cazonci attended but was brought in secret.
1515	Aztecs attack from the Toluca Basin under Moctezuma II, with great Tlaxcalan general Tlahuicole in command. This is the first direct attack on Tarascans since Axayacatl's defeat. The Aztecs fail to take any sites but attack along a line including Taximaroa, Maravatio, Acambaro, Ucareo, and Zinapécuaro. A major Aztec defeat takes place between Maravatio and Zitácuaro (La Rea insisted that even in 1639 the bones from the battles were still visible, in Beaumont 1932).
1519–20	Continued harassment by Tarascans along southern border, with repeated attacks against Oztoman.
1519–21	Aztecs request Tarascan help against the Spaniards in a series of embassies to Tzintzuntzan. At least two embassies are ignored, and the Aztec ambassadors are killed and sacrificed. In all cases, the embassy traveled to the Tarascan frontier settlement of Taximaroa, where it was detained until a messenger was sent to Tzintzuntzan and permission was received from the cazonci allowing safe passage, under escort, to the Tarascan capital. A Tarascan party did go to Tenochtitlán in 1520 at Moctezuma II's request. The cazonci Zuangua was suspicious either that the Aztecs would use a Tarascan alliance to defeat the Spaniards and then turn on them or that Moctezuma would sell the Tarascan soldiers to the Spaniards as sacrificial victims. Zuangua blames the Aztec misfortunes on the fact that "they merely sang songs to their gods, instead of carrying wood to their temples to keep the fires burning" (Warren 1985:28; *Relación de Michoacán* 1956:243–244, 1980).
Summer 1521	When Tenochtitlán is surrounded by the Spaniards, another embassy is sent to the Tarascans. The Tarascans send the Aztecs back, agreeing to consider the request for help. As soon as the Aztecs leave, messengers are dispatched to capture three Otomies, who are then questioned about the truth of the Spanish siege.
1521	Late August to November of this year, following the fall of the Aztec capital to Cortés, some Tarascans and Matlatzincas from the Taximaroa-Charo region are brought to Tenochtitlán. Cortés sends them to Tzintzuntzan with gifts and messages to the cazonci. An offer of an Aztec escort is rejected in favor of an escort of Tlaxcalans (Warren 1985:30), indicating again the distrust of Aztec intentions as well as Tarascan knowledge of central Mexican politics.

large numbers of copper and bronze alloyed objects of Tarascan design and production (Hosler 1994). Sourcing of the ores of well-provenienced artifacts indicates that many metal objects, including bells, needles, tweezers, and ax monies were mined and produced within the Tarascan empire and then exported throughout Mesoamerica (Hosler and Macfarlane 1996). The export zone includes examples from Aztec sites in Morelos, from southern Oaxaca and Soconusco, from the Huasteca, and from the Maya site of Lamanai. In most of these samples, some of the objects were made from ores coming from the Tarascan western frontier (or beyond the western frontier) in Jalisco. It is not clear whether these objects were both mined and fabricated into objects in Jalisco or whether ores and/or ingots were imported (by trade or tribute) and then fabricated into objects within the empire. The mechanism by which they were exported is also unclear. The Tarascan long-distance merchants, working directly on behalf of the royal dynasty, traveled to the borders of the state to exchange goods with other, similar merchants. The *Relación de Michoacán* (1956, 1980) records what the merchants were obtaining from outside the empire but is silent on what was exchanged in return. Finely crafted metal objects are likely commodities to have been used in these exchanges. As Hosler and Macfarlane (1996) point out, the evidence from Soconusco suggests one avenue of export—canoe traffic from the port of Zacatula at the mouth of the Balsas—for distribution to southern Mesoamerica. The fortress of Taximaroa is documented to have been a primary port-of-exchange between Tarascan and Aztec merchants (Gorenstein 1985; Pollard 1994b).

Economic Exchange: Markets

Sahagún (1950–69, Book 10:66–67) indicates that maize and chili from Michoacán were sold in the large Aztec market at Tlatelolco. Given the need for these products in central Michoacán and the distances involved in their transport, the only region of Michoacán from which such exports would have come is the frontier, especially the eastern portion of the Cuitzeo Basin. This region, in the northeast of the Tarascan domain, was both productive enough to export basic commodities and close enough to the Aztec-controlled upper reaches of the Río Lerma. Exchange across the frontier was probably carried out by the non-Tarascan groups occupying both sides of the border, especially Otomí and Matlatzinca communities.

PROTOHISTORIC ETHNIC STEREOTYPES

One result of the restriction in communication across the military borders was the ease with which each government could develop negative stereotypes of its enemies. Much of what Sahagún was told about the Tarascans probably falls into this category, but because of the detail and authority with which his informants spoke, his words have entered the mesoamerican literature as "truth" about the Tarascans.

Aztec views of the Tarascans include the following: They are called Michoaque (singular *Michoa*), from the fact that fish in plenty come from there. They are called Quaochpanme (singular *Quaochpa*) because they shave their heads—all men, women, even old women. Their land has all manner of food: maize, amaranth, beans, chia, gourds, fruit. Their clothing for men includes sleeveless jackets, bows, woven reed quivers, animal skin clothing (ocelot, wolf, lynx, fox, deer), yellow fan-shaped things, squirrel-skin headgear, and *ayoquan* feather capes (heron?). Their houses are good but made of straw. They are artisans (tolteca), feather workers, carpenters, cutters, woodworkers, painters, and lapidaries. The women work well with cotton thread, are good embroiderers, and make cross-weave capes. The men make wonderful sandals. They prepare food all at once for several days, or up to a week.

Their faults included the following: They wear no breech clouts—only a *cicuilli*, or long sleeveless shirt. Their lip plugs are very big, as well as the holes in their ears and lips for them. The women wear only a shirt, reaching only to above the knees. The people are unskilled with food.

The name of their god is Taras, and they are now called Tarascos. This god is Michoacatl in Nahuatl, in Chichimeca is called Coatl, and birds and rabbits are sacrificed to him. They do not sacrifice people but keep captives as slaves. The Tarascan ruler is shown obedience and sent tribute by his subjects. "He was the equal of him who was the ruler of Mexico" (Sahagún 1950–69:Book 10:188–189).

A number of patterns are suggested by the views Sahagún recorded. First, most of the characteristics of dress and adornment relate to battle dress, reinforcing the view that the primary contact between these peoples was in battle. Many of the faults fall in the traditional category of complaints about "foreigners" where there is limited contact (the food is bad, their houses are different, their lip plugs are too big). The informants reveal that they are totally unfamiliar with Tarascan religion, or they would not confuse the word *taras* (term for a statue or figurine) with the major deities. Some of these inaccuracies, such as the statement concerning the lack of human sacrifice, suggest second- or thirdhand sources of information (or wishful thinking?) and are simply wrong. Of interest is that the centrality and power of the Tarascan king was clearly recognized, although the informants omit any reference to Tarascan warriors or the inability of the Mexica to penetrate Tarascan territory. Although the king may have been seen as "equal" to the Aztec ruler, and the artisans are praised, politically the Tarascans were considered "barbarians." Perhaps to rationalize the difficulty of obtaining Tarascan prisoners, Tlacaelel is said to have reminded the Tlatoani of the limit of the gods, including Quetzalcoatl, to accept barbarian offerings (Durán in Davies 1987:232). The "barbarian" offerings included sacrificial victims from the Yopis, Huaxtecs, and Tarascans.

For the Tarascan view of the Aztecs, there is less specific information. The cazonci had several Nahuatl interpreters (*Relación de Michoacán* 1980:239, 296, lamina XLIII). At one time, he sent four to Tenochtitlán. They were used as both messengers (*uaxanoti*) and spies and were housed in the cazonci's court. The Tarascans acknowledged the Aztec as the only other kingdom they viewed as politically significant, expressing this as, "It is a long time since these two kingdoms, Mexico and Mechuacán, were appointed" (*Relación de Michoacán* 1980:297–299). They knew the Aztecs referred to them as fellow Chichimecs, although unlike the Aztecs they did not refer to the Aztecs in their origin legends or histories. Perhaps most pervasive was the belief that the Mexica wanted to conquer them (*Relación de Michoacán* 1980:297).

The continual military hostilities between these two powers resulted in the emergence of a territorial frontier marked by the restricted flow of people and information. Communication was dominated by military or diplomatic information and was often (if not usually) passed through neutral parties (e.g., Otomí or Matlatzinca) living in the frontier zone. This limited interaction fostered the creation of ethnic stereotypes, which would have served both to rally support for military action and to further decrease social interaction. One result can be seen in the material record, in which the Tarascan sphere is marked by distinctive forms of architecture, art, religion, artifact types, and manufacturing processes that abruptly stopped at the eastern border. Even more dramatic is the total absence of Tarascan material among the many artifacts unearthed in the Templo Mayor excavations at the Aztec capital.

TARASCAN-WEST MEXICAN RELATIONS

Military and Political Engagement

Unlike the unified empire encountered on their eastern border, on the north and west the Tarascans faced a variety of small states. This seems to have made conquest easier (Figure 6.3) but incorporation into the empire more difficult. By 1440, the northern Tarascan border included the Jacona-Zamora region taken from the Tecos (Tecuexes; Brand 1943a). During the 1460s, major campaigns were launched into the Chapala Basin and to the southwest to Zacatula (Zacatollan; Brand 1943a, 1980). In the following two decades, much of the territory gained from what are now Jalisco and Colima was lost. Major defeats were suffered in battles at Zacoalco, Acatlán, and Tlajomulco, and the western frontier was consolidated in the zone of Tamazula-Zapotlán and Coalcoman (Brand 1943a; *Relación de Michoacán* 1980:214; Tello [1968:120–121], quoted in Weigand 1992c). These defeats and the consolidation of the western and northwest borders occurred at the same time that the Tarascans were retreating from positions north of the Río Lerma on their eastern border, building up the fortified border against the Aztecs in the east, and facing repeated attacks along their Aztec frontier in the Balsas Basin. The inability of the Tarascans to hold territory west or north of Lake Chapala was probably due to (1) the politically factioned nature of this region, where rebellion was a constant threat, (2) the diversion of Tarascan military strength to the eastern portions of the empire, and (3) the general difficulties Prehispanic states experienced trying to hold hostile territory beyond five to six days' distance from political capitals (Gorenstein and Pollard 1991).

The Tarascan sources indicate that at Spanish contact their empire included Tamazula, Zapotlán, and the "pueblos de Avalos," which had been conquered by both the father and the grandfather of the ruling king (*Relación de Michoacán* 1980:214). The "pueblos de Avalos" included the towns of Sayula, Atoyac, Teocuitatlán, Techaluta, Zacoalco, and Cocula (Ortega 1528 in Warren 1977:411–425). This border region was clearly very unstable, however, and military service on the frontiers was part of the tribute of many communities throughout the empire. Thus we know that the northern and western borders were manned by soldiers from the northeast (Acambaro and Cuitzeo), the east (Tuzantla), the Balsas (Zirondaro), and the west (Chilchota, Jiquilpan, Periban, Tarecuato, Tinguindan, Tamazula, and Zapotlán) (*Relaciones Geográficas* 1985, 1987).

Economic Exchange: State and Market Interaction

The Tarascan military expansion to the west was clearly motivated by the desire of the royal dynasty to control specific raw materials. Once conquered, the western region supplied silver, gold, copper, and salt through the state tribute system (Pollard 1987). A number of other scarce raw materials found in Jalisco and Nayarit were

Figure 6.3. How enemy towns are conquered (*Relación de Michoacán* 1956, folio 15 verso; lamina XXXII).

used by the Tarascan elite, including tin, marine shell, chrysocolla, malachite, azurite, hematite, cinnabar, pyrites, lead, specular iron, opal, quartz crystals, and gourds (Weigand 1992c). In addition, the presence of the term *peyote* in the great *Diccionario grande* of the Tarascan language (Warren 1990), without a Tarascan name, suggests that it was imported from Nahuat-speaking peoples. The most likely sources would have been populations to the west and north of the empire. Finally, it is likely that Tarascans obtained turquoise through trade networks operating beyond their northwestern border. Within the Tarascan empire there were several channels through which goods circulated (Pollard 1982a). Those under the direct control of the state included the state long-distance merchants, the tribute system, and various categories of land/water resources allocated by the royal dynasty. In addition, there were regional and local markets, which appear to have had overlapping territories and which crossed the borders of the state itself. Because of the small amount of archaeological research in most of the territory under Tarascan control and the absence of studies assigning specific artifacts to source locations, it is not possible to determine which scarce materials were actually imported from the west and the mechanisms by which goods were acquired by Tarascans. The one exception is obsidian, whose pattern of acquisition and distribution is described below. This preliminary analysis of obsidian suggests that economic relations between Tarascans and the populations to the west were both varied and complex. Those goods exchanged through local and regional markets were probably only marginally affected by the military hostilities along this border, whereas the long-distance networks, which depended on safe passage and the needs of distant elites, may have fluctuated repeatedly throughout the Postclassic.

Economic Exchange: Obsidian

In the absence of a large historical record documenting Tarascan interactions to the west and north, it is necessary to turn to the available archaeological sources. One basic resource for which there is scant documentary evidence but ample archaeological evidence is obsidian. Apart from the mention of "precious stones" obtained for the cazonci by long-distance merchants (*Relación de Michoacán* 1956:178), obsidian is absent from any list of tributary goods or state gift exchange. Clearly, Tarascan settlements were obtaining obsidian, and the logical conclusion is that this occurred through the regional marketing networks. Since obsidian is a nonperishable basic resource, the study of how it was obtained by Tarascan communities provides an excellent model for "tracing" the Protohistoric market system.

In 1987, almost four hundred obsidian artifacts from the Late Postclassic Tarascan capital of Tzintzuntzan were analyzed by XRF (Table 6.2). That analysis found that more than 94 percent of the gray-black obsidian artifacts came from the Zinapécuaro-Ucareo source zone, that the closer Zinaparo source zone was used selectively for red and clear obsidians, and that small numbers of obsidians, primarily green prismatic blades, were imported from outside the borders of the Tarascan empire (Pollard and Vogel 1994b). Based on the intrasite distribution of obsidian artifacts and debitage at Tzintzuntzan and ethnohistoric data, it was suggested that obsidian from within the Tarascan empire was distributed through regional marketing systems and that material from outside the imperial borders was acquired by long-distance merchants under the direct control of the royal dynasty.

In 1997, 198 artifacts from the Pátzcuaro Basin, Michoacán, were analyzed by instrumental neutron activation (INAA) at the University of Missouri Nuclear Reactor for the purpose of determining their sources (Pollard et al. 1999). These artifacts were selected from the sites of Urichu and Xarácuaro and surface survey collections from the sites of Urichu, Xarácuaro, and

Table 6.2. Pázcuaro Basin Obsidian Sources (Pollard and Vogel 1994a, 1994b; Pollard et al. 1999).

ARTIFACT COUNT

Phase	Site	PENJAMO-1	ZINAPARO	VARAL	PRIETO	UCAREO	CRUZ NEGRA	ZINAPEC	PACHUCA-1	ZACUALTIPAN	PIZARRIN	PUEBLA	ND	TOTAL
TARIACURI	XARACUARO	1		15		1	1	1						19
	COPUJO(P38)			4		1								5
	PAREO(78,79)			5		1		4						10
	URICHU-1		1	11		4		1	2					19
	URICHU-2	2		2		7			2					13
	URICHU-5		1	3	1	9							2	16
	TZINTZUNTZAN-XRF		8	13		290		24	20		1	5	20	381
L. URICHU	URICHU-2		1	8		1								10
	XARACUARO-4		1	3		1								5
E. URICHU	URICHU-5			1				1						2
	URICHU-5 B.13								2	1				3
	URICHU-9		1	8										9
	XARACUARO-3			2			1	2						5
LUPE-LA JOYA	URICHU-5		6	15		7	1		2	2				33
JARACUARO	URICHU-1			4		1			1					6
	URICHU-5		9	27		6			1					43
	Total	3	28	121	1	329	2	34	30	3	1	5	22	579

PERCENTAGE

Phase	Site	PENJAMO-1	ZINAPARO	VARAL	PRIETO	UCAREO	CRUZ NEGRA	ZINAPEC	PACHUCA-1	ZACUALTIPAN	PIZARRIN	PUEBLA	ND	TOTAL
TARIACURI	XARACUARO	5		80		5	5	5						100
	COPUJO(P38)			80		20								100
	PAREO(78,79)			50		10		40						100
	URICHU-1		5	58		21		5	10					99
	URICHU-2	15		15		54			15					99
	URICHU-5		6	19	6	56							13	100
	TZINTZUNTZAN-XRF		2	3		76		6	6		<1	1	5	99
L. URICHU	URICHU-2		10	80		10								100
	XARACUARO-4		20	60		20								100
E. URICHU	URICHU-5			50				50						100
	URICHU-5 B.13								67	33				100
	URICHU-9		11	89										100
	XARACUARO-3			40			20	40						100
LUPE-LA JOYA	URICHU-5		18	46		21			6	6				100
JARACUARO	URICHU-1			67		16			16					99
	URICHU-5		21	63		14			2					100
	Percent of Total	<1	5	21	<1	57	<1	6	5	<1	<1	<1	4	100

Pareo obtained during the course of a research project entitled "Emergence of the Tarascan State: The Urichu, Xarácuaro, and Pareo Polities" (1990–1997), with a collection of 8,512 artifacts.

The artifacts from the site of Urichu date to Classic, Epi-Classic, and Postclassic periods. Those from the Xarácuaro polity include the Postclassic site of Xarácuaro (X–10) and two Early (X–3-field 11) and Middle (X–4-field 12) Postclassic sites. Those from the Pareo polity include the Late Postclassic sites of Pareo (P–78, 79) and Copujo (P–38). This second analysis of artifacts from the Pátzcuaro Basin was designed to determine (1) whether the dominance of Ucareo obsidian observed at Tzintzuntzan during the Late Postclassic under the centralized state was also true at other basin centers under the state, (2) whether there was a shift in obsidian sources associated with the emergence of the state, (3) whether the specialized role of Zinaparo obsidians found at Tzintzuntzan characterized other settlements, and (4) whether non-Michoacán obsidians are from similar quarries and in similar proportions outside the capital during the Late Postclassic and for periods before the emergence of the centralized state, when they were acquired by state-sponsored long-distance merchants.

Unlike the results from the Tzintzuntzan collection, in all phases the primary source of obsidian is Cerro Varal (50 to 90 percent). The remainder of the obsidian is from Cerro Zinaparo, Ucareo, and Zinapécuaro, with small quantities of Pachuca–1, Zacualtipan, Cruz Negra, Cerro Prieto, and Penjamo–1, and one unknown source (Table 6.2). In two of the three areas of the site of Urichu, during the Late Postclassic, Ucareo obsidian is the primary source of obsidian. Yet even when compared with only the gray-black obsidian, Ucareo is not as dominant and Cerro Varal is the second most important source. The samples from the Early Postclassic (Early Urichu phase) contain no Ucareo obsidian, although they include Cruz Negra and Zinapécuaro obsidian from the same flow area. This is the period when Ucareo obsidian is dominating other markets, including the urban center of Tula. There is a marked increase in prismatic blades (including prismatic blade cores) in the Late Postclassic, following the emergence of the Tarascan state, but it is not universal, even for the elite centers sampled. The increase in the proportion of prismatic blades to flakes (the only measure that can be tracked with sampled material) is noted at all excavated areas of Urichu, at Pareo, but not at the island polity of Xarácuaro (also sampled from excavated collections).

In all phases except the Early Urichu, the majority of prismatic blades are from Ucareo, with the second most common source being Pachuca–1.

The preliminary analysis of INAA-source obsidian artifacts suggests that the pattern of obsidian procurement observed in the Tarascan capital of Tzintzuntzan was not characteristic of the Pátzcuaro Basin as a whole, even during the Late Postclassic period. Ucareo obsidian, dominant at the capital, is a prominent source at only one of the three elite centers sampled and is never prominent in periods before the emergence of the centralized state. This suggests that the differential distribution of Ucareo obsidian at the capital, and its significance at Urichu, associated in both cases with prismatic blade technology, may be due less to market exchange than to direct intervention by the state. Thus, in contrast to what has been written (Pollard 1994b), there is good evidence to suspect that indeed the Tarascan central dynasty directly controlled either the Ucareo obsidian mines or the distribution of prismatic blades from the mines.

The pattern of distribution of the Zinaparo obsidians, including Cerro Varal and Cerro Zinaparo (and, in one case, Cerro Prieto), is also distinct from that of the capital. Not only are these obsidians the dominant ones for all phases before the Late Postclassic, and dominant at the Late Postclassic center at Xarácuaro, but their use is not specialized at any time or place outside the capital. In all phases the opaque dark gray-colored obsidian from Cerro Varal is more common, with reddish and clear-colored obsidians coming from a variety of sources. Since Cerro Varal is the source area closest to the Pátzcuaro Basin, this pattern is the expected result of market exchange.

Finally, in all phases there are small quantities of obsidian from sources outside Michoacán. All the yellow-green obsidian was from Pachuca–1, primarily in the form of prismatic blades, with dark green obsidian from Penjamo–1. All, however, were from the central plateau of central and western Mexico and were probably obtained through long-distance merchants. These nonlocal sources appear to have been fewer in number and closer in distance to the Pátzcuaro Basin than those from Tzintzuntzan. Thus, the emergence of state-sponsored long-distance merchants may have led to the representation of a larger number of sources, but the greater variety was distributed primarily in the capital. As the context of many of these "exotic" obsidians is in elite burials of all time periods, it is likely that the Tarascan state merchants of the Late Postclassic replaced non-Tarascan merchants who had been supplying local elites either directly or through local markets in earlier phases.

Thus, obsidian procurement under the Tarascan empire was a complex combination of market exchange, state control of provisioning elites and the capital, and state long-distance merchants' exchange with foreign merchants at the borders of their territory.

EXTERNAL RELATIONS IN MICHOACÁN PREHISTORY

Although the prehistory of western Mexico is still poorly understood, it is clear that during the Classic period parts of Michoacán were incorporated into the economic and/or political periphery of Teotihuacán. By the late Classic, central Michoacán was located between the economic centers of Teuchitlán to the west in Jalisco and the Matlatzinca centers to the east in the Toluca Basin. During the Epi-Classic period (A.D. 700–900), some portions of Michoacán were still part of the economic periphery of central Mexico. Indeed, during this time the northeast (especially Ucareo), including the Cuitzeo Basin, may have become more directly tied to Toltec economic networks. Sometime between A.D. 1000 and 1200, the Teuchitlán polity to the west, and then the Toltec polity to the east, lost its political centrality, triggering population movements and political instability. It is probable that for the first time since the late Preclassic period, large portions of Michoacán were not part of the hinterlands of empires to the east or west. In order to understand these processes, and those that produced the Protohistoric patterns of interaction only sketched in this chapter, it is necessary to undertake the regional analyses that will allow us to link the many isolated sequences of cultural change into macroregional spheres of development.

CHAPTER SEVEN

PREHISPANIC CULTURAL DEVELOPMENT ALONG THE SOUTHERN COAST OF WEST MEXICO

JOSEPH B. MOUNTJOY

THIS CHAPTER focuses on Prehispanic cultures in the coastal area of southern Nayarit and Jalisco, an area that includes the coastal plain and adjacent foothills from the Río Santiago in central Nayarit on the north, to the Río Balsas on the south, at the border of Michoacán and Guerrero (Figure 7.1). This area is topographically different from the relatively broad and flat coastal plain farther north. A short distance south of the Río Santiago, the coastal plain is cut by the Central Mexican Volcanic Axis. Thus, from San Blas, Nayarit, south, the coastline varies from rugged mountain fringe with sharp embayments, to coastal piedmonts and even some alluvial flats formed by rivers that empty into the Pacific Ocean.

The topography of the southern coast had important implications for the development of Prehispanic culture there. Mountain and foothill resources such as stone and metal ores are more easily exploited near the southern coast than in coastal areas farther north. On the other hand, compared with the northern coast, the southern coast has fewer and smaller estuaries and lagoons, although bays (shallow or deep) are more common. This has potentially important consequences for the type and abundance of coastal resources (shellfish, fish, and birds) available to the Prehispanic inhabitants, as well as for the ease or difficulty of coastal travel.

Movement along the southern coast by land or water was probably more difficult than travel along the northern coast. Travel by foot along the coast would have been made difficult because of the rugged mountains. Canoe travel along the southern coast would have required navigating long stretches of rough open sea, whereas travel by canoe along the northern coast could take advantage of extensive estuaries and lagoons. Travel between the interior highlands and the southern coast would have been relatively easier, however, because the path to the highland valleys from the coast is shorter and less rugged than in the north.

In this chapter, I rely heavily on the results of my own research in the area, much of it new, previously unpublished information. I have included the site of Amapa, located on the north side of the Río Santiago, in this discussion. Although it is technically on the northern coast as defined here, data obtained from archaeological investigations at Amapa (Meighan 1976) are essential for understanding the archaeology of the southern coast. For similar reasons, information from sites on the south bank of the Río Balsas is also included.

INITIAL SETTLEMENT: THE COASTAL ARCHAIC SHELLFISHING TRADITION

At present, there is no evidence of an early hunting and gathering occupation of the area, as there is for the inte-

Figure 7.1. Archaeological sites along the coast of west Mexico.

Figure 7.2. The Matanchén site, an Archaic period shell midden exposed by road construction.

rior highlands of the Zacoalco-San Marcos-Chapala Lake Basin before 7000 B.C. and possibly as early as 16,000 to 13,000 B.C. (Solórzano 1980). Likewise, there is no archaeological evidence on the southern coast of the kind of Archaic period occupation involving intensive plant collecting and small animal hunting that is so well documented in some of the highland basins of central Mexico. There are probably good ecological reasons for this, including a scarcity of such natural plant resources as nopal cactus, grasslands, and oak forests that could sustain large populations of deer, squirrels, rabbits, and other game (Mountjoy 1998a).

Distribution and Date

The earliest evidence for human use of the southern coast is a campsite at the base of a volcanic hill at the northern end of Matanchén Bay just to the south of San Blas, Nayarit (Figures 7.1 and 7.2; Mountjoy et al. 1972). Three overlapping radiocarbon determinations date shell from the site within a range of 2200 B.C. to 1730 B.C.

Despite extensive survey of portions of the southern coast, no other Archaic period sites have yet been located there (Mountjoy 1970a, 1982a, 1995a, 1998a; Nicholson and Smith 1962).

Subsistence and Economy

The Matanchén site consists of the remains left by a people who appear to have subsisted almost entirely by harvesting mollusks, mostly clams, which were probably dredged with nets from the bottom of Matanchén Bay. The scarcity of bone in the shell midden is surprising, and it suggests that such coastal resources as sea turtle, pelican, and fish were extremely minor components of the diet.

The lack of Archaic shellfishing sites in the region is probably due in great part to the rarity of localities that, like Matanchén Bay, are rich enough in molluscan resources to have supported humans dependent on exploiting shellfish for survival. Not all west coast bays are so richly endowed. For example, Banderas Bay, the largest on the west Mexico coast, is precipitously deep, and shellfish are found in abundance only along a shallow stretch of ocean along its northern shoreline.

Another factor to consider in Archaic site distribution is the instability of the coastline. For instance, there is an impressive sequence of fossil beaches around the northern end of Matanchén Bay and San Blas, indicating that the coastline has been rising for a long time. In the southern part of Matanchén Bay, however, the Los Cocos beach area south of the town of Aticama appears to have been eroding away coincident with the growth of beach lines to the north. Thus, there are areas along the coast where Archaic deposits may have been either eroded away or submerged.

Sociopolitical Organization and Relations

It seems likely that society at this time consisted of small bands of individuals living in basically unranked, egalitarian social groups. The origin of the Archaic occupants of the Matanchén site is unclear. These people would likely have interacted with peoples with similar adaptations who had settled for a time to exploit other areas of the coastline. The nearest shell middens of roughly comparable date have been found at Acapulco, Guerrero (Brush 1965), to the south, and at El Calón, Sinaloa (Connally 1974; see Scott and Foster this volume), to the north. There are, however, other Archaic period shell middens far to the north, on both sides of the Baja California peninsula, and extending up the coast of California (Hubbs and Roden 1964:145). Furthermore, there is no known relationship between the Archaic coastal mollusk collectors of Matanchén Bay and any contemporary peoples who might have been living in the interior highlands of west Mexico.

INITIAL HORTICULTURAL EXPANSION: THE CAPACHA TRADITION

Distribution and Date

The term *Capacha,* as used here, incorporates the remains of three somewhat different, but I believe culturally related, developments that probably had the same origin and that represent somewhat different aspects of the initial expansion of garden farmers into west Mexico. These three developments are Capacha in Colima (Kelly [1974, 1980] related these to El Opeño and Tlatilco); El Opeño, Michoacán (Noguera 1942; Oliveros 1974); and San Blas in Nayarit (Mountjoy 1970a, 1970b, 1974a, and related to Capacha in Colima by Mountjoy 1983a, 1989a, 1993c).

The Capacha tradition in Colima is known primarily from pottery offerings associated with human burials. No habitation sites of the Capacha tradition have yet been found in Colima. It is possible, however, that the characteristic Capacha funerary pottery is not present at the habitation sites, thus making it difficult to identify Capacha sites. The favored location for settlements dating to this period appears to have been the hilly interior of Colima and northward into the uplands of western Jalisco (Greengo and Meighan 1976; Kelly 1980; Weigand 1988).

Four radiocarbon dates for Capacha or Capacha-related material in Colima range from 1650 B.C. to 880 B.C. The eight obsidian-hydration dates available range from 806 B.C. to 520 B.C. A review of all the information available on the problem of chronological placement of this Capacha material suggests the most acceptable range is 1200 B.C. to 800 B.C. (Mountjoy 1989a, 1993a).

Characteristic zoned incised and punctated pottery of the Capacha tradition has been found on the coast of Jalisco in the Tomatlán and Banderas valleys. In the Tomatlán Valley, a few sherds of Capacha pottery have been recovered in excavations or surface collections at two sites on opposite sides of the river (Mountjoy 1982a, 1989a, 1995c). Excavations in one of these settlements also yielded several sherds of what appear to be jar rims that are decorated on their flattened tops with incised and punctate designs similar to some on incised vessel rims from El Opeño (Mountjoy 1995c; Oliveros 1974). One sherd of San Blas zoned decorated pottery was also found (Mountjoy 1995c). Other sherds of a type similar to El Opeño incised have been found on the surface of two other sites in the central part of this coastal valley (Mountjoy 1978). The excavated sherds of these types come from a context radiocarbon dated between 110 B.C. and A.D. 300 (Mountjoy 1989a, 1995c). These appear to be from a context containing refuse from a later habitation. Dates of a few obsidian items from that same context are much earlier than the radiocarbon dates.

In the Banderas Valley, a sherd of Capacha type zoned, incised, and painted pottery was recovered at the site of Ixtapa. It was associated with monochrome painted and plain sherds of types radiocarbon dated in the range of 380 B.C. to 220 B.C. (300 B.C. ± 80 years) at another location in the Ixtapa site (Mountjoy 1989a). Similar monochrome painted and plain sherds have been dated in the range of 740 B.C. to 390 B.C. (440 B.C. ± 50 years

Figure 7.3. San Blas Complex ceramics: zone-decorated sherds (painted, incised, brushed, corncob impressed, and punctated).

and 570 B.C. ± 170 years) at the La Pedrera site near Puerto Vallarta (Mountjoy 1995a). Sherds of San Blas rose or purple painted pottery have also been found in the same early context at Ixtapa and La Pedrera.

Abundant remains that appear to be Capacha-related, including purple or red painted pottery with incisions or punctations in the unpainted zones (Figure 7.3), have been found at San Blas (Mountjoy 1970a, 1970b, 1974a, 1983a). Eight shell samples associated with the San Blas materials have been radiocarbon dated in the range of 890 B.C. to 335 B.C. (Mountjoy and Claassen 1989).

In addition, a few sherds of rare zoned-decorated Capacha-like pottery have been found at Amapa, Nayarit. These appear to have been mixed into later deposits (Meighan 1976:478, Plate 172, h–t). The decoration on these sherds is virtually identical to that on pottery found in the Río Balsas drainage, which the discoverers attribute to the Middle Preclassic (Chadwick 1971).

In 1966–67, excavations at site 42 near the mouth of the Río Balsas uncovered a Middle Preclassic cemetery beneath a Postclassic house mound (Litvak 1968). Dating was based on the style of decoration on some of the mortuary vessels. The designs consist of zoned geometric patterns outlined with grooves and filled in with hyphen-like incisions or punctations, executed on redware or brownware jars (Chadwick 1971). These designs are basically the same as those found on the Zoned Punctate ware of Amapa (Meighan 1976). The same design patterns and design fill elements are found on Capacha vessels (Kelly 1980; Mountjoy 1993a). Furthermore, the plainware or monochrome jars from the burials of site 42 were of an uncinctured bule form, a form also present, along with some cinctured bule forms, in the San Blas deposits. None of the vessels from site 42 appears to have been of the unusual trifid form associated with Capacha in Colima. Just to the east of site 42, along the Río Balsas, pottery decorated with zoned punctation and zoned cross-hatching similar to Capacha style has been found and attributed to the Middle Preclassic (Muller 1979).

It is also important to note that poorly fired black-brown, undecorated, sand-tempered potsherds were found at depths below the Middle Preclassic burials at site 42. These are thought to have been from tecomates (Chadwick 1971:665) and may represent an Early Preclassic occupation.

Subsistence and Economy

Given the absence of domestic trash at Capacha mortuary sites in Colima, it is difficult to assess related subsistence patterns. There is no evidence for the use of marine resources. On the other hand, much of the pottery appears as imitation of gourds, and there are grinding stones that may have been used for processing the seeds of plants such as maize. Stone molcajetes for mashing and grinding plants and seeds were also found, as were stones for smashing nuts. This evidence suggests that small-scale horticulture was practiced as part of a subsistence pattern that was probably dependent on the collecting and hunting of undomesticated inland plant and animal resources.

Habitation of the Jalisco coast during the Capacha tradition appears to have been by small exploratory populations that settled in the central part of the coastal river valleys where they could plant their gardens and still be well positioned to take advantage of the plant and animal resources found in the coastal valley, the foothills, and the seacoast. One exception to this generalization is La Pedrera (Mountjoy 1998a). This site is situated on a foothill peninsula overlooking Banderas Bay to the west and extensive wetlands, where the inhabitants could exploit lagoon resources, to the north. Excavations at the site recovered several long and slender obsidian points that might have been effective for spear fishing. Their firm assignment to the earliest deposit at the site (740 B.C. to 390 B.C.), however, must await hydration analysis. Shell and bone are not preserved in this deposit.

The coastal settlement at San Blas in Nayarit is also unusual in the heavy dependence on seacoast resources represented. The site may have been a seasonally occupied settlement (late spring–early summer dry season) used for the exploitation of the rich local coastal resources. Its occupants may have lived during the rest of the year by garden farming in a riverine setting such as that found at Amapa (Mountjoy and Claassen 1989). On the other hand, the Middle Preclassic occupation at San Blas was not a mere transitory camping one. The people who lived there terraced the hillside with impressive walls made of large boulders, and on the artificially flattened areas behind the terrace walls, they raised mounds of rock on which to build their houses (Mountjoy 1983a).

San Blas peoples exploited several species of clams, large conches, and some oysters, as well as sea urchins, marine catfish, dolphins, sea turtles, river turtles, crabs, pelicans, and boobies. They also used pottery vessels in the form of gourds and squash and many grinding stones, both of which suggest some dependence on domesticated plants. Some grinding stones, however, are very small and may have been used to prepare seafood (Mountjoy 1974a, 1983a; Mountjoy and Claassen 1989).

At San Blas, the economy seems best characterized as self-sufficient. Apart from acquiring their foodstuffs locally, there is evidence that the inhabitants made some of their own grinding stones, pottery, net weights, nets, basketry, and jewelry (Mountjoy 1974a, 1983a). Although it is not abundant in the archaeological deposits, obsidian may have been the only material that was imported; on the other hand, it may have been available nearby as nodules in river gravels.

At site 42 on the Río Balsas, numerous projectile points were found with Middle Preclassic burials, suggesting hunting was an important activity there. Given the location of the site, the excavators noted what they thought was a curious near absence of fishbones. Since the Middle Preclassic remains recovered are from mortuary contexts, however, the scarcity of domestic refuse is not unexpected (Chadwick 1971:666).

Sociopolitical Organization and Ritual

Interpreting sociopolitical organization and belief systems for this period of time is difficult. What can be said comes from a limited amount of data, most of it from a limited number of burials. Burials at site 42 were simply laid on the beach surface and then covered with sand (Chadwick 1971). They are similar to the Capacha burials studied by Kelly (1980) in Colima that were deposited in shallow subsoil pits (Mountjoy 1993a). One of the Middle Preclassic burials found at site 42 was of a female accompanied by abundant offerings, including jewelry and two males (buried on each side of her and without offerings). She also exhibited dental mutilation and perhaps intentional cranial deformation. Associated burial offerings included a small greenstone metate; a shell trumpet; shell bracelets incised with parrots with turquoise eyes; a necklace of jade, shell, and turquoise beads; and plaques along with small ducks carved from bone. A belt of shell ornaments was found on her stomach (Chadwick 1971:665). The two males, one on each side, have been viewed as retainers or servants who were buried to serve the woman in the afterworld. It has been suggested that she was a female cacique in a matrilineal society (see Chadwick 1971:665).

Northward along the coast, the near absence of burials dating to this period makes mortuary-based inferences about social organization and ritual difficult. The size of the habitation sites and the remains found there suggest the populations lived in isolated hamlets or widely dispersed small villages that lacked internal social or economic differentiation.

Other items that provide some insight include a sherd from the Tomatlán Valley that has part of what may have been a "sunburst" motif on it. It is like that found on some of the funerary vessels in Colima and may possibly be connected to sun-related ritualism (Mountjoy 1989a, 1993a).

Some pottery figurines are also attributed to the Capacha tradition in Colima (Kelly 1980). A figurine head of a similar style was excavated from a site in the Tomatlán Valley (Mountjoy 1982a). One figurine with strong similarities to Capacha and El Opeño figurines was recovered from a burial (#177) at a Middle Preclassic site in the lower Río Balsas drainage (Maldonado 1980:163 and 219, Figure A.41).

The earliest dated pottery figurines (740 B.C. to 220 B.C.) at Ixtapa (Figure 7.4) have several facial features and a head shape similar to the tomb #3 figurines from El Opeño (Oliveros 1974:Figure 16). The upper half of a head of a similar figurine type was found on the surface at San Blas–17 and attributed to the San Blas complex there (Mountjoy 1974a:Figure 5). No pottery figurines were recovered from San Blas complex deposits, but part of an anthropomorphic flute was found during the 1983 excavations there (Mountjoy 1983a). Some figurine bodies (Mountjoy 1970a:Figure 28a and b) from both the San Blas (Mountjoy 1970a:Figure 28a and b) and Banderas Valley (Mountjoy 1992:Figure 4, line 4, no. 2) areas associated with heads of this type have large hips and wasp-like waists. In the San Blas area, this figurine type appears to just postdate the San Blas complex. Figurines of this type are common at sites on the southern side of the Banderas Valley, especially at Ixtapa, where they are found in a stratum dating to 300 B.C. ± 80 years.

Several small crude stone figurines were found in the San Blas complex deposits. Some of them may have served as the core of clay figurines with a modeled and unfired exterior (Mountjoy 1974a).

External Relations

There are two possible explanations for the origin and expansion of the Capacha tradition. One is that it originated in northwestern South America and was introduced to Mexico via the western coast through sea travel (Kelly 1980). The second possibility is that the Capacha tradition is at least partially related to the Tlatilco or Olmec tradition. Middle Preclassic garden farmers may have expanded northwestward out of the central interior highlands of Mexico (around Morelos and the Valley of Mexico), moving along the southern edge of the Central Mexican Volcanic Axis through Michoacán to Colima and Jalisco (Kelly 1980; Mountjoy 1989a, 1993a, 1998a).

Apart from the question of its origin, there is an important question of how far this early garden farming adaptation spread up the coast of west Mexico, and perhaps beyond (Baus de Czitrom 1989), where the diagnostic Capacha ceramic traits are rarely found. They may have become even rarer or dropped out altogether as people of this tradition spread northward, leaving only relatively vague traits such as rose-red, squash-form vessels to indicate Capacha affiliations.

Although the people associated with the expansion of Capacha-affiliated culture up the northern coast seem to have been rather self-sufficient, it is notable that several of the obsidian flakes associated with the earliest (740 B.C. to 400 B.C.) deposits there came from a high-

Figure 7.4. Ceramic figurine head from a stratum dated 300 B.C. ± 80 at the site of Ixtapa (height 4.2 cm).

land source at Teuchitlán, about 150 km to the east (Glaascock et al. 1997).

THE SPREAD OF ADVANCED GARDEN-FARMING SOCIETIES: THE SHAFT TOMB AND TUXCACUESCO TRADITIONS

Site Distribution and Date

Following the Capacha tradition, after about 300 B.C., there appears to have been a considerable increase in population in the southern coastal area. Two major related cultural traditions in distinct geographical areas develop. One is the Shaft Tomb tradition. It was distributed in an arc extending from near the southern coast of Colima through the highlands of west-central Jalisco and down to the south-central coast of Nayarit. It also included parts of western Michoacán, southern Zacatecas, and perhaps southern Sinaloa. Burials, found in *sotano* tombs dug into the tepetate subsoil at a site in the Balsas area (Chadwick 1971), may be a local variant of shaft-and-chamber burial.

The Shaft Tomb tradition in Colima is thought to begin sometime between 300 B.C. and possibly as late as A.D. 500 (Kelly 1980:5–6). In the central highlands of Jalisco, radiocarbon dates on shaft tombs at San Sebastian suggest they were used within the range of 367 B.C. to A.D. 334 (Furst 1966). Radiocarbon dates from the recent double-chambered shaft tomb at Huitzilapa in the Jalisco highlands west of Guadalajara indicate its use in the first couple of centuries A.D. (Ramos et al. 1996; López and Ramos 1998). Obsidian-hydration dates from shaft tombs at Tabachines fall in a range of 222 B.C. to A.D. 478 (Galván 1991; Schöndube and Galván 1978), and one shaft tomb at Teocaltiche has been dated to between A.D. 94 and A.D. 309 and between A.D. 92 and A.D. 325 through hydration analysis of two artifacts (Delgado 1969).

In Nayarit, obsidian-hydration dates for Shaft Tomb remains at El Alacrán in the foothills east of San Blas range from A.D. 185 to A.D. 640 (Mountjoy 1989a). Ceramic crossties with radiocarbon-dated shaft tomb offerings in the Bolaños Valley to the east indicate a placement in the early part of that range (López and Cabrero 1995; Pickering and Cabrero 1998). There is also a radiocarbon date of A.D. 340 ± 60 years available from a cremated burial placed in front of a shaft tomb door at the site of El Reparito, in the foothills of the Banderas Valley east of Puerto Vallarta (Mountjoy 1993b).

The second tradition, the Tuxcacuesco, was spread throughout the highlands and the coast of Colima and Jalisco to the west of the Shaft Tomb arc. Although it appears to lack shaft tombs on the northern, southern, and perhaps eastern borders, there is some blending of Tuxcacuesco style pottery and mortuary customs with pottery and burial customs of the Shaft Tomb tradition. This is especially apparent at some sites in the southern half of the Banderas Valley, notably in the Late Preclassic burial offerings placed in the Middle Preclassic deposit at La Pedrera (Mountjoy 1998b).

There are no radiocarbon dates for the Tuxcacuesco tradition for the western highlands of Jalisco, where it was first defined (Kelly 1949). However, the lowest levels of the Morett site on the northwest coast of Colima contain artifact types that seem related to the Tuxcacuesco tradition of the highlands. The earliest materials date (uncorrected) in a range from 440 B.C. to A.D. 140 (Meighan 1972:99, 109). Obsidian-hydration dates for these deposits range from 300 B.C. to A.D. 100. Some Tuxcacuesco tradition decorated pottery types appear to continue at Morett until at least A.D. 500, and Tuxcacuesco type figurines are most common in the deposits dated between 300 B.C. and A.D. 100 (Meighan 1972:18). In the Río Tomatlán Valley, material of the Tuxcacuesco tradition has been radiocarbon dated to between 190 B.C. and A.D. 300 (Mountjoy 1989a).

At the site of Ixtapa there is an early stratum, dated in the range of 380 B.C. to 220 B.C., in which have been found remains of red or orange painted vessels combining features of the Capacha gourd-form vessels and the Shaft Tomb squash-form vessels. Also found were a solid dog figurine, a seated hollow figurine of a person holding a bowl (Figure 7.5; both possible forerunners to more elaborate Shaft Tomb figurines), and the head of a solid human figurine of a style found at San Blas and attributed to post–San Blas complex deposits there (Mountjoy 1974a, 1989b, 1991a).

Subsistence and Economy

The subsistence pattern probably included widespread slash-and-burn clearing of the land for garden farming. Twenty-one of the 47 sites studied in the area of San Blas had remains of the Shaft Tomb tradition (Mountjoy 1970a, 1970b, 1987a), indicating a sizable and widely dispersed population. The majority of the Shaft Tomb sites in the San Blas area were located in the foothills bordering the coastal plain, three sites were found on the coastal plain associated with estuaries, and two oth-

Figure 7.5. Hollow rattle figurine found in association with Capacha-like vessels (300 B.C. ± 80). Early Ixtapa phase, Mound 1, Ixtapa (height 10 cm).

ers were found on the coast, all suggestive of the use of coastal resources.

The stratum of Shaft Tomb tradition material overlying earlier Capacha-affiliated material at San Blas is black with wood charcoal. Shaft tomb looters report that a similar stratum is frequently found at shaft tomb burial sites. It seems probable that this layer of carbon resulted from the widespread slash-and-burn clearing of large tracts of virgin forest. Many of the plants that the Shaft Tomb tradition people either grew or collected in the wild are illustrated in the modeled pottery deposited as offerings in the tombs, especially in Colima (Schöndube 1998). Squash-form vessels are extremely common and widespread (Mountjoy 1970a), and wild fruit is commonly depicted in Colima vessels (Schöndube 1998). The lack of depictions of certain plants, especially maize, is curious. Food residues found in pottery vessels left as offerings at Huitzilapa are currently being analyzed and promise to expand considerably our knowledge of plant food resources used by the people who buried their dead in such tombs (López and Ramos 1998).

A similar increase in population and dispersal of settlement is associated with the Tuxcacuesco tradition in the Tomatlán Valley. La Pintada was the predominant center and contained an estimated 38 percent of the total population of the area. There were at least 35 hamlets spread throughout the coastal portion of the valley and at least one in the foothills (Mountjoy 1996a).

The importance of domesticated plants in the Shaft Tomb and the Tuxcacuesco traditions is reflected by the number of manos and metates found in deposits of domestic trash and in tombs (Galván 1991; Meighan 1972; Mountjoy 1970a, 1982a, 1993a, 1995c). Typically, metates are four-footed, in contrast to the nonfooted metates of some later traditions. As in the Shaft Tomb tradition, Tuxcacuesco remains include pottery modeled in the form of squash (Mountjoy 1982a). Nonetheless, the analysis of faunal remains from Tuxcacuesco trash deposits at La Pintada indicates an important if not essential broad-spectrum use of natural resources found in the foothills, central valley, and coast (Mountjoy 1983b; Polaco and Alvarez 1978). A similar broad-spectrum utilization of natural resources is reported for Tuxcacuesco deposits at Morett (Meighan 1972).

Some of the sites found on the southern side of the hills overlooking the Banderas Valley are littered with grooved mauls. These are sometimes found in association with large boulder mortars with depressions about a meter in diameter and 10 to 20 cm deep. Farther back into the hills, in the small valley of Soyatan, which has severely limited potential for bottomland agriculture, there are at least 57 of these boulder mortars associated with one habitation area, and 152 more at another site, along both sides of an arroyo. I believe the primary function of these mauls and mortars was to crush and grind seeds of the ramón tree. The meal produced from ramón seeds is high in protein (the ramón tree appears to have played an important role in subsistence of the Maya). The mortars at Soyatan are of unknown date, but some of the Banderas Valley sites where these mauls are found have significant quantities of Shaft Tomb and/or Tuxcacuesco pottery, and there are some unconfirmed reports of such mauls being found in shaft tombs. One site (PV-58) where 32 mauls were found on the surface yielded only pottery of Late Preclassic and Early Classic periods. Thus, there is an indication that this subsistence activity became important as early as the Shaft Tomb and Tuxcacuesco traditions, and other evidence from the Banderas Valley suggests it continued to be significant in some areas, perhaps until the arrival of the Spaniards.

Spindle whorls are reported from Shaft Tomb contexts in the central highlands of Jalisco (Long 1966:276) but appear to be rare. One spindle whorl of the type attributed to the Amapa phase at Amapa (Meighan 1976) was found at El Reparito (Banderas Valley) in front of the door of a shaft tomb chamber as part of an offering. Charcoal from a human cremation associated with it dates in the range of A.D. 280 to 400 (Mountjoy 1993b). Also, one of the pottery vessels associated with the spindle whorl is an Amapa phase polychrome type (Meighan 1976).

At La Pintada, there was a Tuxcacuesco tradition jewelry-making industry that focused on shell but also included exotic materials such as rock crystal, serpentine, and chrysocolla (Mountjoy 1978). It may be that some of the shell jewelry was being exported to the interior highlands, where it was worn by people of the Tuxcacuesco tradition or sometimes ended up deposited in the graves of people of the Shaft Tomb tradition.

One intriguing aspect of the mortuary customs of the Shaft Tomb tradition is the production of the large numbers of pottery vessels and figurines that were left as offerings in the tomb chambers (López and Ramos 1998). Some vessels appear to have had prior domestic use as containers for food or drink. The figurines, however, as well as perhaps many of the vessels, may have been produced and fired in kilns at the cemetery site as part of burial rituals.

Sociopolitical Organization and Ritual

There was a ranked settlement hierarchy of the Tuxcacuesco tradition in the Tomatlán Valley (noted previously) that seems related to craft specialization at the La Pintada site, by far the largest site in the valley at this time. The craft specialization includes the manufacture and use of ear spools of pottery, shell, and stone, presumably indicating the development of sociopolitical ranking at that settlement. No ear spools have been found at other contemporary sites in the valley.

There may have been a ranked social system in the Banderas Valley at this time as well. Evidence for this can be seen in the differential treatment of the deceased, in regard to the use of the shaft and chamber tomb as a burial option, and in the varying elaborateness of tombs as well as the richness and kind of burial offerings. There is little evidence of architectural hierarchy at Shaft Tomb or Tuxcacuesco tradition sites on the southern side of the Banderas Valley. One site, however, which appears to date to late in this phase, has the type of circular mound and plaza ceremonial architecture associated with the Teuchitlán tradition centered in the western highlands of Jalisco (Mountjoy 1993b; Weigand 1985; Weigand and Beekman 1998; see Weigand this volume). In the San Blas area, there is a system of ceremonial centers with associated hamlets that may indicate some hierarchical sociopolitical organization associated with the Shaft Tomb tradition there (Mountjoy 1970a).

Shaft tomb sites in the San Blas area have ceremonial centers that contain mounds and plazas (Mountjoy 1970a, 1970b). It has been proposed (Mountjoy 1989a, 1998a) that many aspects of the remains found in these and other shaft tombs in Nayarit can be explained by assuming that there was an annual ceremony near the end of the dry season, in which the members of each community buried those who had died during the year in a communal shaft-and-chamber tomb. This would help explain why many burials share a single tomb and why some of the skeletons are articulated while others are disarticulated or represented only by a skull. It would also help explain why sometimes it was necessary to excavate more than one chamber at the base of a shaft (to accommodate a high number of deaths during a given year) and why there are offerings of so many different types and styles accompanying the burials (they may be donated by different families). Furthermore, this hypothesis would account for the fact that some tombs appear never to have held burials or offerings (if the shaft and tomb were dug in preparation for anticipated deaths but no member of the community died during that year).

This idea has gained some support from recent shaft tomb excavations near the coast in the southern half of the Banderas Valley and from the Huitzilapa site in the highlands of Jalisco. In both cases human remains appear to have been curated for some time before burial in the tombs (Mountjoy and Sandford 1995; Pickering and Cabrero 1998). On the other hand, the burials at Huitzilapa may have been only of the deceased of a relatively high stratum of a community or of a lineage, rather than the deceased from a whole community.

Funerary offerings provide some insight into sociopolitical organization and ritual activities. Many explanations have been offered for the meaning or function of the hollow figurines deposited in shaft tombs (Furst 1966, 1974; von Winning 1974). In the San Blas area, there is found a hollow figurine style suggestive of females in mourning (Mountjoy 1970a:205–207, 1970b). Another example is a plate decorated on the interior with arrows oriented toward a group of embers (Mountjoy 1970a:215). This may represent a ceremony that has been recorded among the Huichol in the mountains to the east (Weigand, personal communication 1969). Also, one of the tombs yielded a necklace of 64 cream-colored rhyolite beads (Mountjoy 1970a), and other tombs have contained several small solid figurines (Mountjoy 1970a).

Figure 7.6. A Shaft Tomb tradition hollow figurine recovered from a burial at La Pedrera.

The Banderas Valley appears to have been a soft frontier between the Shaft Tomb and Tuxcacuesco traditions. At one site in particular, La Pedrera, there appears to be a mixing of mortuary offerings and burial customs characteristic of the two traditions, including shaft tombs, urn burials, and direct pit inhumation all in the same cemetery (Mountjoy 1996b, 1998b). One very simple shaft-and-chamber tomb, perhaps for the burial of an infant, was found to contain a single small jar as an offering. Some other burials were in simple pits whose location was marked with a smooth, white, river rock. Several of these burials contained pottery decorated with incisions or red-on-cream painting clearly in the Tuxcacuesco tradition, but one burial had an offering of a cream-slipped bowl and a hollow figurine typical of the Shaft Tomb tradition (Figure 7.6). Another burial contained the offering of a Shaft Tomb type figurine in a style typical of the Nayarit area, with its head resting on a plate with Tuxcacuesco incised decoration typical of the Jalisco coast (Figure 7.7).

To the south, several human burials with associated grave offerings were excavated at a Tuxcacuesco tradition cemetery at La Pintada. The burials were in shallow pits on top of a low hill or laid on top of the hill and covered with earth (Mountjoy 1982a, 1983b). They appear to have been placed in a communal cemetery,

Figure 7.7. A Shaft Tomb tradition burial offering with a Nayarit style figurine and a Tuxcacuesco tradition (Jalisco) incised plate from La Pedrera.

and judging from some large postholes, burial may have been inside a mortuary building. The bodies were directionally oriented according to sex, and a few offerings were left with each adult body, mainly small jars that may have held offerings of food or drink. One of the burials, however, consisted of a single skull accompanied by shell bracelets, a necklace of tubular shell beads, and two vessels, one polychrome squash-form vessel and one miniature tripod modeled in the semblance of a badger covering its eyes with its paws (Mountjoy 1982a, 1983b).

In the domestic refuse deposited over these burials and around the habitation areas in general are a tremendous number of small solid figurines and a few hollow ones that appear to have been broken intentionally and discarded in the trash (Mountjoy 1991b, 1995c). These may represent shamanistic curers and have functioned to ward off ill health (Mountjoy 1991b). One of the small hollow figurines appears to indicate a heart extraction sacrifice (Mountjoy 1991b, 1995c). Also, an incised design on the interior bottom of one plate combines serpent bodies with the heads of birds in a Quetzalcoatl-like representation. In addition, pottery whistles in the form of birds or dogs are abundant, as are fragments of flutes in the later levels. Both may have had important ritual functions.

Several extended skeletons were excavated from a communal grave of the Tuxcacuesco tradition at Morett (Meighan 1972:22–25). They were accompanied by a few offerings such as stone beads, pottery vessels, and both hollow and solid figurines. One of the burials was of a solitary skull. Meighan (1972:25) suggests that these burials and their offerings may represent the common people's version of the kind of communal burial found in shaft and chamber tombs in other areas.

One other ritual practiced by this time was the pecking of petroglyphs, mainly of the pit variety. There are simple pit petroglyphs associated with Shaft Tomb tradition remains in the area of San Blas (Mountjoy 1987a), and they are also abundant at the site of La Pintada (Mountjoy 1987b). Meighan (1972:142) found a large flat-topped boulder at Morett with pits in the surface. Many of these were so large and deep he called them bedrock mortars, but the photograph of the boulder appears to show many small pits as well. The argument has been presented (Mountjoy 1987b) that in the Tomatlán Valley, these pits, of whatever size and age, represent the eye or face of the sun god and were related to ceremonies held to bring rain near the end of the dry season. A door slab from a relatively late shaft tomb at El Reparito in the Banderas Valley (where one of the shaft tombs is radiocarbon dated to A.D. 340 ± 60 years) had a petroglyph design that combines a sun symbol with what appears to be the outline of an animal, perhaps a dog.

External Relations

There is some evidence that the southern coast of west Mexico was linked at this time with some areas of the west Mexican highlands. This is best seen in the offerings associated with funerary rituals. One of the most important items of exchange at this time appears to have been marine shell used for jewelry and other funerary offerings (Villanueva et al. 1996). Shell may have been exchanged for obsidian from yet-to-be-identified highland sources. Two prismatic blades of rare red obsidian were recovered from Tuxcacuesco deposits at La Pintada. Items of serpentine, rock crystal, and what appears to be chrysocolla, all of unknown origin, are also present in these deposits.

Farther afield, a developmental link appears to continue between the Shaft Tomb and Tuxcacuesco traditions and more ancient traditions in the central Mexican highlands. There is a persistence of similar types and styles of hollow and solid figurines. There is also evidence of contact between shaft tomb societies in the west Mexican highlands and peoples living in the Gulf and Caribbean coastal areas from whence came the conch shells commonly used in west Mexico as trumpets, as well as the jade items left as offerings in some of the shaft tombs (Furst 1966; López and Ramos 1998; Villanueva et al. 1996).

CONTINUITY AND CHANGE: THE RED-ON-BUFF TRADITION

Distribution and Date

The Red-on-Buff cultural tradition is the hardest of any along the southern coast of west Mexico to define and date. It is only loosely definable as a major cultural tradition. In some areas it could be characterized as "all that stuff between the Shaft Tomb or Tuxcacuesco tradition and the Aztatlán horizon." On the early end, there seems to be continuity from previous traditions of some polychrome pottery styles and the use of simple shaft tombs. On the late end, the Red-on-Buff tradition may provide the roots for the common unslipped red-on-buff pottery of the succeeding Aztatlán tradition. At this time, there does not seem to be any overriding appropriate name to apply to this development. In its various local manifestations and subphases, it includes the Amapa phase at Amapa (Meighan 1976); the Los Cocos complex at San Blas (Mountjoy 1969, 1970a, 1970b, 1987a); the Late Classic Llañitos phase in the Banderas Valley (Mountjoy 1989b, 1991a); the Guayacan phase in the Tomatlán Valley (Mountjoy 1982a); the Late Period at Morett (Meighan 1972); the Tesoro phase at Playa del Tesoro, Colima (Beltrán 1991); and possibly some of the early Armeria phase material from the Río Armeria Valley of Colima (Kelly 1980). There is little evidence of habitation around the mouth of the Río Balsas at this time (Chadwick 1971:676), but red-on-buff pottery similar to that from the Jalisco coast is found at several sites inland in the Balsas-Tepalcatepec drainage (Muller 1979:56–57) and at the highland site of Apatzingán, where it is attributed to the Delicias phase (Kelly 1947).

There appears to be considerable local variation in material culture of the Red-on-Buff tradition. A major common trait is use of pottery decorated with simple red designs on a buff, brown, or orange slipped background. During the early part of this tradition, other types of decoration, including solid white painting or slipping, incising, and even some polychromes, are also common and widespread. There are some pottery molcajetes and "stools," also. In the latter part of this tradition, pottery figurines tend to be slab-like and sometimes have appliqué features (Mountjoy 1970a). In some areas, spindle whorls appear in abundance for the first time (Mountjoy 1995b).

Material of the Red-on-Buff tradition is known from stratigraphic deposits at Amapa and Morett, and settlement pattern and site pattern data are available from the San Blas and the Banderas and Tomatlán valleys. In the San Blas area, material of the Red-on-Buff tradition has been found at 31 of the 47 sites recorded. The sites are relatively small, averaging 4,818 m² and 2.2 mounds per site, are often on the top or side of low hills overlooking the coastal plain, and are associated with some terracing. Some deposits are found on the coastal plain, however, buried under later occupations (Mountjoy 1970a:88–101, 1987a). The mounds on these sites are, as a rule, relatively small and probably served as house platforms. At least some mounds are square or rectangular, and there are many rectangular cobble foundations of houses at one of the sites (Mountjoy 1987a).

In the Banderas Valley, many Red-on-Buff sites occur in the foothills overlooking the Río Mascota. Some of them, probably those late in the phase, are architecturally complex. They have walls nearly a meter high, large and small rooms with baked clay floors, sunken courtyards, large artificial platform extensions, and pyramidal mounds up to 4 m high (Figure 7.8; Mountjoy 1991a). Some fairly large mounds at sites closer to the river appear to have been constructed during this phase. At Ixtapa, one platform mound measuring 25 m long and 3.5 m high was constructed between A.D. 720 and 830. It was later buried under a much larger Postclassic platform mound (Mountjoy 1990).

In the Tomatlán Valley, Red-on-Buff tradition pottery has been found at 71 of the 165 sites recorded, double the number of hamlets occupied during the previous Tuxcacuesco phase. This seems to indicate a significant

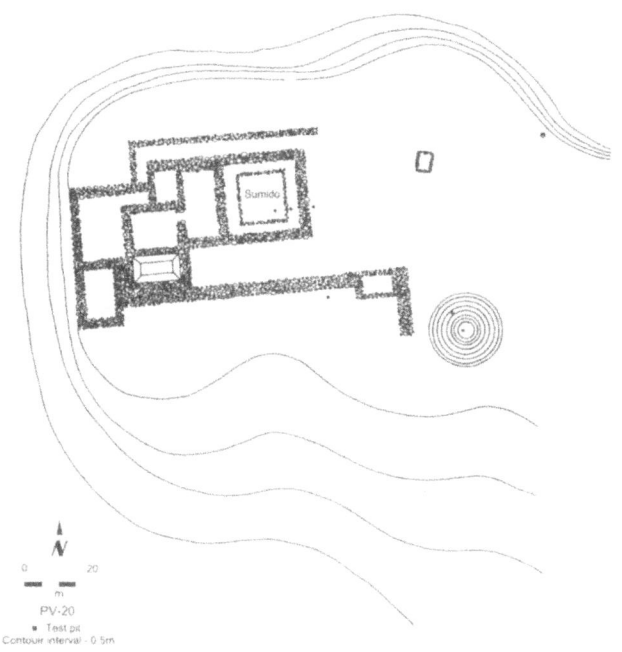

Figure 7.8. Site map of El Palmar de Santo Domingo, believed to date to the local Llanitos phase of the Red-on-Buff tradition.

increase in settlement dispersal and population (Mountjoy 1996a). There is also evidence that one site was significantly larger than all the others (see below).

At Amapa, obsidian-hydration dates indicate that Amapa phase material dates from A.D. 143 to 417 (Meighan 1976:57). At Morett, obsidian-hydration dates place Late Period materials between A.D. 150 and 750 (Meighan 1972:21). At Playa del Tesoro, radiocarbon dates from carbon directly associated with grave goods range from A.D. 280 to 725 within 1 sigma of deviation (Beltrán 1991:411), and a radiocarbon date from shell from the Armería phase ranges from A.D. 560 to 820 (Kelly 1980:4). In the Tomatlán Valley, the early end of the Red-on-Buff tradition appears to postdate A.D. 300 (Mountjoy 1989a). And, as previously mentioned, in the Banderas Valley, a radiocarbon date of A.D. 770 ± 50 years from a ceremonial platform mound suggests that the late end of this tradition falls after A.D. 720 to 830 (Mountjoy 1990).

Subsistence and Economy

Maize subsistence is probably reflected in the large number of manos and metates found at many Red-on-Buff tradition sites. In the San Blas area, there are also many mortars and pestles, mauls, and pitted stones that may have been used for cracking nuts of the *coyul* oil nut palm (Mountjoy 1970a, 1970b), and there was continuing dependence on the ramón seed at some sites in the mountains. At Playa del Tesoro, in addition to a large number of grinding stones that may indicate the use of maize, there is ample evidence of the use of many coastal resources such as shellfish, fish, birds, and sea turtles, and perhaps domesticated dog as well (Beltrán 1991).

An important new item is added to the material culture in some areas along the southern coast. Pottery molcajetes that may have been used for grinding plant foods such as chili (Beltrán 1991; Meighan 1972) are found. Pottery griddles for cooking maize tortillas may also make their first appearance in Jalisco and Nayarit near the end of the Red-on-Buff tradition (Meighan 1976; Mountjoy 1991a). Spindle whorls appear to become more common (Beltrán 1991; Mountjoy 1987a). One salt extraction site located at the head of a coastal estuary in the Tomatlán area has been tentatively assigned to this tradition (Mountjoy 1982a, 1995b). At Playa del Tesoro, there is evidence of a local industry for processing shells into fishhooks, beads, pendants, bracelets, and trumpets, as well as an industry for converting shell to lime, apparently for the production of pottery (Beltrán 1991).

Sociopolitical Organization and Ritual

The size and distribution of sites in the San Blas and Tomatlán areas suggest scattered farmsteads. The evidence for centralized organization in the Tomatlán Valley consists of one site that is significantly larger than the others, having perhaps as much as 12 percent of the population of the valley at this time (Mountjoy 1996a). In the foothills south of Ixtapa, there is some evidence for political centrality in the Banderas Valley in a group of sites with domestic and ceremonial architecture (Figure 7.8), and there are medium-sized ceremonial mounds at Ixtapa (Mountjoy 1991a).

Pottery figurines continue to be abundant in the Red-on-Buff tradition. They are usually solid and of locally distinctive styles. Some of the anthropomorphic ones, probably the earliest ones, are similar to solid figurines modeled in the round that are sometimes found in shaft tombs, refuse, or burials of the Tuxcacuesco tradition. Others, probably the later ones, have flat slab-like bodies and appliquéd features such as eyes, hair, and breasts (Beltrán 1991; Meighan 1972, 1976; Mountjoy 1970a, 1987a). The great majority of these figurines at Playa del Tesoro and Morett appear to be females, and some of the Morett ones seem to indicate pregnancy. Also common at Playa del Tesoro and Morett are figurines of dogs and birds. Some human figurines of the flatter type give the impression of being imitations of slab-shaped mold-made figurines (Meighan 1972; Mountjoy 1991a). Pottery whistles, ocarinas, and flutes are also found at some Red-on-Buff tradition sites.

The best evidence of burial customs during the Red-on-Buff tradition comes from Playa del Tesoro, where the remains of at least 31 persons were found in what appears to have been a cemetery. Most of these burials were primary in extended, supine positions in shallow graves dug in the sand and covered by hard-packed clay (Beltrán 1991:315). They were accompanied by a great variety of grave offerings: pottery vessels, figurines, whistles, spindle whorls, ear spools, bells, and stamps; obsidian projectile points, scrapers, and prismatic blades; stone axes; necklaces, bracelets, and pendants of carved shell; and beads and other items of exotic stone. Associated with some of the burials were considerable quantities of unmodified animal bones and shells.

The disarticulated bones of a child, an isolated adult skull, and a dog burial were found at Morett (Meighan 1972), and a few tightly flexed primary human burials at Barra de Navidad (Long and Wire 1966) are likely associated with this tradition as well. In the Banderas Valley, a large red-on-buff bowl containing cremated human bone was found in the vicinity of the town of Tebelchia.

In portions of Jalisco, the use of shaft tombs appears to persist into the Red-on-Buff tradition. A number of vessels with Mazapan-like parallel wavy line red-on-buff decoration were recovered from shaft tombs at Tabachines in the central highlands of Jalisco on the outskirts of Guadalajara (Galván 1991; Schöndube and Galván 1978). In the Banderas Valley, a radiocarbon date of A.D. 340 ± 60 years was obtained from a shaft tomb with polychrome vessels of the type attributed to the Amapa phase at Amapa and the Los Cocos phase in the San Blas area—phases also characterized by quantities of red-on-orange or red-on-buff pottery (Meighan 1976; Mountjoy 1970, 1987a).

There is also the continuation of the pecking of petroglyphs. The simple pit types common earlier continue, with what seems to be an added emphasis on spiral designs (Mountjoy 1987a, 1987b). In the Tomatlán area, spiral designs appear to represent the eye or face of the sun god. Near San Blas there is a petroglyph with a ladder and sun glyph representing the sun's passage through the sky (Mountjoy 1987a). Wherever these petroglyphs were pecked, the majority seem to symbolize the sun god and were associated with rainmaking ceremonies (Mountjoy 1987a, 1987b).

External Relations

Red-on-Buff tradition pottery shows close ties between the southern coast and the interior highlands of west Mexico. Wares like those of the coast have been found in the Chapala Basin, the southeastern highlands of Jalisco, and the highlands of Michoacán (Kelly 1947, 1949; Meighan and Foote 1968). Also, there appears to be some connection between red-on-buff pottery wares of the southern coast and the early red-on-buff ceramic tradition of northern Mexico, as represented at some sites in Guanajuato (Braniff 1972; see Braniff this volume). Remains from sites around the mouth of the Río Balsas suggest contacts between that area and the highlands of western Jalisco and Colima at this time, as well as with the Teotihuacán area of central Mexico (Maldonado 1980).

TEMPLE TOWN CENTERS, AGRICULTURE, AND COMMERCE: THE AZTATLÁN TRADITION

Distribution and Date

The Aztatlán tradition was a widespread and relatively uniform cultural expansion over a considerable part of the west Mexican coast and up into the northwestern part of the central Mexican plateau, at least into the Durango area (Ganot and Peschard 1995; see Kelley this volume). It constitutes the highest development of mesoamerican culture ever achieved in some areas of west Mexico (Mountjoy 1990; Sauer and Brand 1932). It is likely that at least one ceremonial/civic center of the Aztatlán tradition was established near the center of every large coastal river valley between Tomatlán, Jalisco, and the northern border of Sinaloa, as well as in strategic locations along routes of communication and commerce in many highland areas, such as at Ixtlán del Río, Nayarit.

Aztatlán sites occur along the southern coast of west Mexico for at least 200 km from the Río Santiago to the Río Tomatlán, and sherds of Aztatlán pottery have been found as far south as the coast of Michoacán (Novela and Moguel Cos 1998:123). Several of the settlements are known major centers: Chacalilla, Nayarit, north of

Figure 7.9. An Aztatlán Incised jar placed as an offering in the top of a ceremonial mound at the site of Las Vegas.

San Blas near the Río Sauta (Guevara 1981; Mountjoy 1970a); Ixtapa, Jalisco, in the Banderas Valley on the Río Mascota (Mountjoy 1988, 1989b, 1991a); and Nahuapa, Jalisco, in the Río Tomatlán Valley (Mountjoy 1982a). All these centers are accessible by canoe up the rivers from the seacoast.

In the San Blas area, Aztatlán tradition materials are scarce at sites other than Chacalilla, but in the Banderas Valley 33 sites apart from the primary ceremonial center at Ixtapa have Aztatlán pottery. Aztatlán sherds from these sites are uniformly similar in decoration and are of principally five types: red-on-buff (natural color of the paste), black-on-buff incised (Figure 7.9), red-on-buff incised, and red-and-white-on-buff incised. The distribution of this material suggests a rapid spread and relatively short duration for the Aztatlán tradition, at least in the Banderas Valley. Some Aztatlán sites are even located in relatively remote areas of the foothills overlooking the valley. They range in size and complexity from hamlets, to sites that contain one or more small ceremonial mounds and platforms, to a site (at Arroyo Seco) with several large platform mounds and a ball court (Mountjoy 1993b, 1995a). In the Tomatlán Valley, Aztatlán material has been found at 48 hamlet-sized sites apart from the major center constituted by the Nahuapa I and II sites (Mountjoy 1982a, 1983b).

Thus far, no major Aztatlán centers have been reported south of the Tomatlán Valley, although the Mazapan figurines that are sometimes associated with Aztatlán vessels in the Banderas Valley have been found at Playa del Tesoro and a few other sites on the coast of Colima. Figurines reported to be similar to Mazapan have been found at sites at the mouth of the Río Balsas (Chadwick 1971:680). The decorated pottery at many of these sites does not appear similar to characteristic Aztatlán tradition vessels, however. Therefore, the extent of the expansion of the Aztatlán tradition southward along the coast of west Mexico, as well as its possible impact on Prehispanic development along the coasts of Colima and Michoacán, is yet to be fully investigated and resolved.

More than 24 radiocarbon dates are available for Aztatlán deposits on the west coast, and 17 of them have been corrected for the Seuss Effect. They range from A.D. 883 to A.D. 1400 (Mountjoy 1990:541–542). There are 280 obsidian-hydration determinations associated with Aztatlán ceramic material that range from A.D. 520 to A.D. 1664 (Mountjoy 1990:542).

Five recent radiocarbon dates associated with Aztatlán remains from the Banderas Valley average A.D. 1147 ± 75 years. These dates are associated with a context that has the same characteristic types of decorated pottery, figurines, and stone implements found consistently at Aztatlán sites throughout the southern half of the Banderas Valley. One date, A.D. 1145 ± 60 years, was obtained from charcoal that may have resulted from the burning of a wooden structure that presumably sat atop the "stela mound" at Ixtapa. Post-Aztatlán offerings placed into the top of the mound included pieces of two, presumably Aztatlán, stelae that were reused in the construction of an altar. The entrance of Aztatlán colonists into the Banderas Valley appears rather late and rather short-lived. During the Late Classic, the valley was occupied by a comparatively large and well-organized Red-on-Buff tradition population that probably resisted the intrusion of the Aztatlán outsiders and eventually forced them out.

Based on recently calibrated hydration dates from Aztatlán prismatic obsidian blades, it appears the Aztatlán tradition flourished in the Tomatlán Valley around A.D. 900. An uncorrected radiocarbon date from a post-Aztatlán deposit indicates that the Aztatlán tradition had been replaced in the Tomatlán Valley by a local tradition probably derived in part from the Aztatlán by around A.D. 1130 ± 120 (Mountjoy 1990:547). Interestingly, the apparently earlier Aztatlán material of the Tomatlán Valley includes not only large quantities of red-on-buff pottery but also large quantities of red-on-buff incised, and red and white-on-buff incised with codex-type designs (fancier than most of the Aztatlán pottery from Ixtapa), as well as the fancy multicolored Iguanas Polychrome pottery found at Amapa. Iguanas Polychrome is absent in Aztatlán deposits in sites on the southern side of the Banderas Valley, however. Also, Mazapan style mold-made figurines are common in the Banderas Valley Aztatlán deposits, but they are nearly absent in the apparently earlier Aztatlán deposits in the Tomatlán Valley. Recent analysis of radiocarbon dates and obsidian-hydration measurements suggest that Aztatlán remains date about A.D. 800 at Amapa, about A.D. 900 in the Tomatlán Valley, and about A.D. 1100, the latest date, in the geographically intermediate Banderas Valley.

Subsistence and Economy

The location of many Aztatlán temple-town centers dominating large areas of fertile and humid river alluvium at Amapa on the Río Santiago, Ixtapa on the Río Mascota, and Nahuapa in the Tomatlán Valley suggests more extensive, and possibly more intensive, floodplain agriculture along the southern coast at this time.

Judging from the relative abundance of spindle whorls in Aztatlán deposits at Amapa and other sites to the north in Sinaloa, cotton was probably grown in many of the coastal valleys in these areas. Cotton was probably spun locally into yarn for weaving cloth most likely used by the elites. Aztatlán spindle whorls are rarely found at sites along the coast to the south of Amapa, however. Nevertheless, it is also possible that cotton was produced in valleys along the southern coast but exported in raw form to other areas, where it was spun, woven into cloth, and perhaps worn. On the other hand, it is possible that by this time cacao had become a major "cash crop" in coastal valleys such as the Banderas, as was the case at the time of the Conquest. Also, in contrast to the northern coast, where many Aztatlán pipes are found and may indicate the cultivation of tobacco, no pipes of certain Aztatlán affiliation have been found on the southern coast.

The large quantities of grinding stones, pottery (tortilla) griddles, and molcajetes seem to indicate the continued use and perhaps increased importance of food crops such as maize, squash, beans, and chili peppers along the southern coast in Aztatlán times. It is known that mollusks, especially oysters, were extremely important in the subsistence of Aztatlán people along the northern coast, and perhaps the oyster meat was an important Aztatlán export item (Shenkel 1974). This seems not to have been the case along the southern coast, where oyster shells are rare or absent at Aztatlán deposits in the southern part of the Banderas Valley (Mountjoy 1988, 1991a). A large quantity of Aztatlán domestic trash was excavated from the interior of a large urn found at La Pedrera, which overlooks Banderas Bay, yet there were no shells in the trash (Mountjoy 1992). However, the lack of shell at sites of the Aztatlán and other traditions in the southern Banderas Valley may be due to high acidity or some other corrosive factor in the soils.

In the Tomatlán Valley, almost all the shell excavated from Aztatlán deposits at Nahuapa II was of very small clams that inhabit brackish water coastal sand- and mudflats around the mouth of the Río Tomatlán (Polaco and Alvarez 1978; Villanueva 1979). These clams are so tiny that their contribution to the total diet must have been slight. There is a curious lack of evidence for the consumption of fish by the people living at this site (Villanueva 1979).

Another important aspect of the economy of the Aztatlán tradition of the southern coast is its participation in an apparently pan-Aztatlán distribution system of high-quality obsidian in the form of either finished prismatic blades or cores. Most of this obsidian is clear golden brown in color, with gray and green obsidians less abundant. The main source for the golden brown obsidian and the gray obsidian was La Joya, Jalisco, in the highlands west of Guadalajara (Glaascock et al. 1997; Weigand and Spence 1982), which probably provided obsidian for many Aztatlán settlements along the Pacific coast.

The origin and early development of metalworking on the west Mexican coast appears intimately related to the Aztatlán tradition. Aztatlán metallurgy focused on the production of copper ornaments such as bells and plaques and small utilitarian items such as needles (Mountjoy 1969; Mountjoy and Torres 1985; Pendergast 1962a). A large collection of Aztatlán metal artifacts was recovered from Amapa, and there was evidence that metal ore was smelted there as well (Meighan 1976). Metal artifacts have also been found in Aztatlán deposits at Nahuapa II in the Tomatlán Valley and include strips of copper foil, a cast bell, tweezers, buttons, and what may be parts of a needle and a chisel (Mountjoy and Torres 1985).

Some metal, including at least one copper fishhook, was found in contexts with Mazapan-like figurines in sites around the mouth of the Río Balsas (Chadwick 1971). Inland, metal artifacts were recovered from 10 of the 18 sites excavated in the Infiernillo dam salvage project (Maldonado 1980). Some of the metal objects were found in contexts that are thought to date to the Early Postclassic, and indeed some of the associated band-decorated pottery is vaguely similar to Aztatlán red-on-buff or incised ware. Most of the metal items came from 3 of the 10 sites. One of the sites (11), believed related to Tarascan culture (see Pollard this volume), is thought to date to the Late Postclassic, based in part on obsidian-hydration dates that range from A.D. 1464 to 1664 ± 190 years. The other two sites have similar metal assemblages that appear to date earlier than site 11. One of these sites, site 68, may be responsible for the oft-mentioned possible early date of about A.D. 700 for metallurgy in the Balsas drainage. The date of A.D. 754 ± 530 is derived from a hydration measurement of an obsidian artifact from a burial that had no metal offerings, however, making it useless for resolving the question of when metallurgy first appears in the Balsas drainage. Another obsidian artifact from another burial in this same site, likewise with no metal offerings, yielded a hydration date of A.D. 1464 ± 180 years (Maldonado 1980:224). On the other hand, in many cases the presence of metal artifacts was used to assign a post–A.D. 900 (Early Postclassic) date to associated burial offerings, even when associated pottery might suggest an earlier date (Maldonado 1980).

Unfortunately, work in the Banderas Valley (1986–94) has turned up only one metal artifact from excavated contexts. It appears to be the basal part of a small copper celt or chisel, and it was found in a cistern or storage pit in an area of abundant Aztatlán pottery. This near absence of metal artifacts from the 107 sites recorded in the southern part of the Banderas Valley is, to put it mildly, surprising and may possibly be attributed to high concentrations of carbonic acid in the soils.

Major Aztatlán pottery production centers appear to have supplied large areas of the coast with vessels of a consistently fine, hard paste, commonly decorated with red painted or incised geometric designs in a band circling the exterior or interior of the vessel (Figure 7.9). Some Aztatlán vessels are decorated with complex codex-like designs that indicate a similarity of ritual iconography, tying together sites over considerable distances (see Kelley this volume). For example, an Aztatlán Red-on-buff incised bowl from La Pedrera (Figure 7.10; Mountjoy 1992) has three iconographic motifs virtually identical to those of Aztatlán pottery found at Guasave, Sinaloa (Ekholm 1942), some 670 km to the north.

Amapa (Meighan 1976) was an important Aztatlán center for shell jewelry manufacture. No comparable Aztatlán shell-working industry has been discovered

Figure 7.10. An Aztatlán Red-on-buff Incised bowl recovered from the interior of an urn at La Pedrera.

along the coast to the south of Amapa. At Amapa, there was some carving of exotic stone (possibly serpentine, apparently brought from the mountains immediately to the east [Meighan 1976]) into beads and spindle whorls in Aztatlán times. Ixtapa also appears to have been involved in the manufacturing of jewelry from serpentine of different colors. In the Banderas Valley, this industry may have had its inception in the Aztatlán tradition, but its firmest associations are in post-Aztatlán contexts.

Sociopolitical Organization and Ritual

The presence of a major Aztatlán center in many large coastal valleys, at which there was an extensive village with monumental architecture that includes large platform mounds and a ball court, seems to indicate strong centralized political control of at least some individual valleys. The widespread distribution of pottery of uniform shape, decorative style, and composition; prismatic blades of high-quality obsidian; and copper metallurgy all support the idea that there was some rather uniform system of political, economic, and religious organization that linked these coastal valleys, probably through some sort of political alliance mechanism, such as elite marriage. Burials at Amapa and some sites farther north indicate that a degree of sociopolitical or economic ranking existed within local societies. Elite burials and residences are known from Ixtapa, and there is evidence of a resident elite group of the Aztatlán tradition at Nahuapa.

Ball courts that appear to be of the Aztatlán tradition have been found at Amapa (Meighan 1976), south along the coast at Chacalilla, Nayarit (Guevara 1981; Mountjoy 1970a), and on the southern (Jalisco) side of the Banderas Valley at Ixtapa and Arroyo Seco (Mountjoy 1989b;

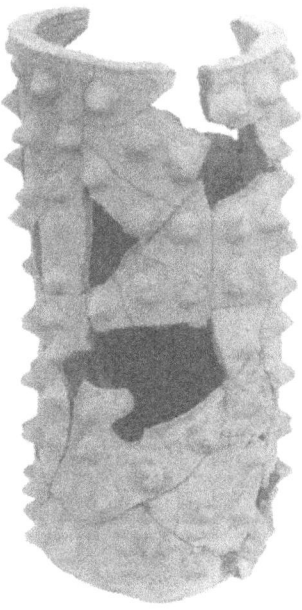

Figure 7.11. An Aztatlán cylindrical spiked incense burner recovered from an elite cemetery at Ixtapa.

1993b). These occur in association with monumental platforms of earth and cobbles on which major civic and/or religious structures appear to have been built.

Cemeteries are common in the Aztatlán ceremonial centers. The dead were buried as extended or flexed inhumations, disarticulated in a bundle, or placed in a large pottery jar or urn, and some were accompanied by decorated pottery. The most elaborate Aztatlán pottery on the southern coast is decorated with iconography of such mesoamerican codex-like designs as the feathered serpent, a long-nosed earth monster, stone knives, and feathered headdresses (Meighan 1976; Mountjoy 1990, 1991a, 1992). There is also evidence of the use of frying pan and spiked cylindrical incense burners in the mortuary rituals at some centers such as Ixtapa (Figure 7.11; Mountjoy 1991a).

Most of the figurines found in Aztatlán deposits at Amapa were mold-made in the Mazapan style (Meighan 1976:155). Mazapan-style figurines are also found at Chacalilla and in Aztatlán context at Ixtapa and some other sites in the Banderas Valley (Figure 7.12; Mountjoy 1990, 1991a, 1992), but they are nearly lacking at sites in the Tomatlán Valley (Mountjoy 1982a:279). There is a good possibility that some of these figurines represent a goddess of human fecundity and earth fertility and may have been involved in household rituals, whereas others may represent warriors.

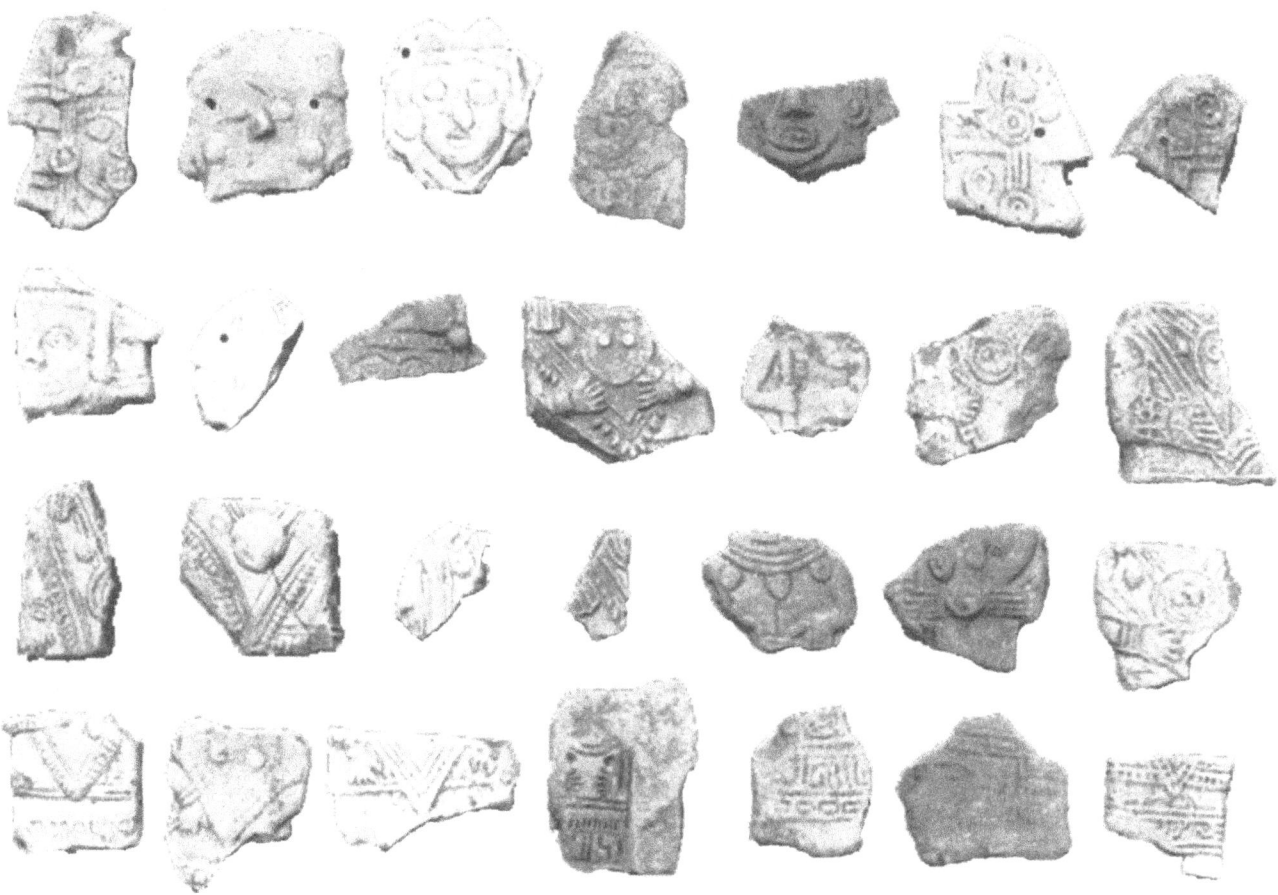

Figure 7.12. Mazapan-style figurines reportedly recovered from the vicinity of the Ixtapa site. The middle item on the bottom row is a figurine mold.

It appears the long-standing rainmaking-related custom of petroglyph pecking continues unabated during the Aztatlán tradition in many areas of the southern coast (Mountjoy 1987b), although the general rarity of petroglyphs in the Banderas Valley throughout Prehispanic times is very curious. I suspect this may have been due, at least from Aztatlán times to the European contact period, to a more extensive reliance on irrigation agriculture in the Banderas Valley as opposed to some areas along the coast, such as the Tomatlán Valley, where dry farming based on rainfall may have been much more important. Certainly, in the southern half of the Banderas Valley, petroglyphs are usually found up in the foothills in areas where the opportunities for irrigation farming are severely limited if not nonexistent.

Among petroglyphs in the Tomatlán Valley is one stone in an Aztatlán context at Nahuapa II which appears to have been an altar (Mountjoy 1982b, 1983b). In the Banderas Valley, some stone stelae can be assigned to the Aztatlán tradition. As previously noted, at Ixtapa, fragments of two stelae presumed to be from the original Aztatlán construction were reused in a post-Aztatlán altar on top of the mound. Six other stelae that also may have been associated with the Aztatlán tradition were found in front of this platform mound (Mountjoy 1991c, 1993a).

External Relations

The pottery typical of the Aztatlán tradition covers an impressive area of west and northwest Mexico. It has been found as far north as Mochicahui in the Río Fuerte Valley near the northern border of Sinaloa (Manzanilla and Talavera 1988) and in abundance in Durango (Ganot and Peschard 1995; Kelley and Winters 1960; see Foster this volume). Aztatlán pottery is also common on sites in the Chapala Basin (Koll 1982; Lister 1949; Meighan and Foote 1968). Some possible Aztatlán sherds have been reported from Casas Grandes, Chihuahua (Di Peso 1974), and Wind Mountain, New Mexico (Kelley 1993).

A heavy concentration of Plumbate pottery was found associated with Aztatlán pottery at Amapa, and rare sherds of Plumbate have been found at El Canton in the Banderas Valley and at Nahuapa II (Mountjoy 1990). Plumbate pottery is commonly linked to the expansion of Toltec culture of the central Mexican highlands and is known to have been manufactured at sites in southeast Mexico in the Mexican/Guatemalan Pacific coast border.

Mazapan figurines are also associated with Toltec culture. Mazapan-type figurines have been found at many sites on the southern coast, including Amapa and Ixtapa, as well as at other sites in the southern half of the Banderas Valley. They are rare in the Tomatlán Valley but have been found farther south at the Playa del Tesoro. Mazapan figurines have also been found at so many west Mexican sites it has been suggested that they have originated in west Mexico (Stocker 1983).

The codex-type iconography on some of the most elaborate Aztatlán pottery has been linked to iconography of the Mixteca-Puebla or early Aztec cultures (Ekholm 1942; Fahmel 1981; see Kelley this volume). Some Mixtec codices begin with histories of Toltec events, and had the Aztecs not destroyed the Toltec codices, I suspect we would have found that their iconography was quite similar to Aztatlán iconography.

POPULATION GROWTH AND CULTURAL DIVERSIFICATION: THE POST-AZTATLÁN TRADITIONS

Distribution and Date

At Amapa, the San Blas area, and in the Banderas and Tomatlán valleys, there is ample evidence of local cultural developments that appear clearly rooted in the earlier Aztatlán tradition. Although people practiced certain Aztatlán crafts such as metallurgy, their metal items and pottery took on local characteristics. Also, other Aztatlán traits such as stone stelae and pecked petroglyphs became more widespread and elaborate during post-Aztatlán times, referred to here as the Post-Aztatlán traditions (Mountjoy 1991c). Whether this model of Aztatlán and Post-Aztatlán localized traditions is an accurate representation of the situation also along the coast from the Tomatlán Valley south to the Río Balsas is as yet unknown.

Associated with the Post-Aztatlán traditions in the area of the coast from the Río Santiago to the Tomatlán Valley is an apparent growth in population and, in some cases, a corresponding dispersal of that population into areas that are agriculturally much more marginal. In the San Blas area, 28 sites have been located that have material of the local Post-Aztatlán (Santa Cruz) tradition. The sites average 35,696 m^2 in area and 14.8 mounds. In the immediate area of Santa Cruz, Nayarit, along the banks of the Río Santa Cruz, six sites have a combined area of 585,000 m^2 and contain more than 246 mounds, including both house mounds and temple mounds (Mountjoy 1970a:102). One of these six is the Arias (SB–3; Figure 7.13). In several instances, these sites have groups of four platforms that form a rectangular or square pattern surrounding an open plaza. This is probably a reflection of kin-associated settlement groups within the village or town. There are also some small, hamlet-sized settlements of this tradition, located in areas that are relatively marginal for farming.

In the Banderas Valley, there is evidence of some continuity of habitation and culture at Ixtapa from Aztatlán times to Spanish contact. During this time, the site covers some 60 hectares, a result of the expansion of the settlement during the local Post-Aztatlán (Banderas) tradition (Mountjoy 1990, 1991a). Furthermore, data from site survey in the Banderas Valley suggest an increase in and widespread dispersal of settlements in the local Post-Aztatlán (Banderas) tradition, especially into some remote areas of mountainous terrain overlooking the valley, as well as along the coast on the north-ern side of Banderas Bay (Mountjoy 1991a, 1993b, 1995a).

Likewise, in the Tomatlán Valley there is apparent continuity from the Aztatlán tradition to the localized Post-Aztatlán (Nahuapa) tradition, especially at the site of Nahuapa, which appears to have been the principal center of the valley throughout this phase (Mountjoy 1982a). Of 148 habitation sites recorded in the valley, 132 appear to have remains of the local Aztatlán Derived tradition (Mountjoy 1982a:329, 1996a). During this time, population appears to have grown significantly and was dispersed more widely throughout the coastal valley as well as into the far upper mountainous reaches of the Río Tomatlán drainage. In the mountains, the people settled on hilltops or hillsides along the Río Tomatlán or a branch thereof, near a stable water supply and a small patch of river valley alluvium that could be farmed with simple gravity irrigation. The hamlets consist of one or more round houses located on the edge

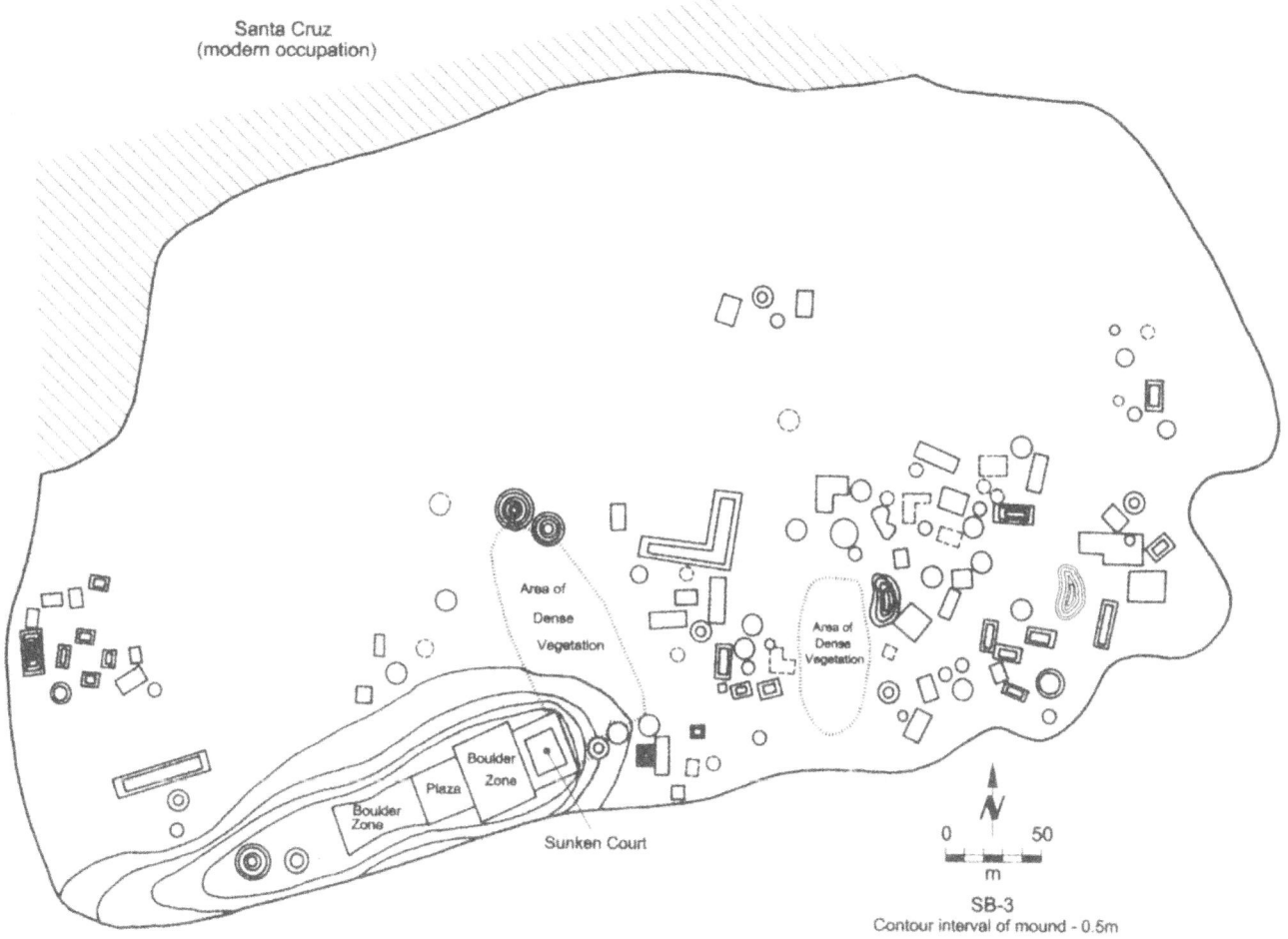

Figure 7.13. Site map of Arias (near Santa Cruz, Nayarit).

of or, rarely, completely encircling a plaza. This arrangement probably reflects kin-based settlement for the plaza, and likely for each hamlet as well (Mountjoy 1982a, 1996a).

There is also a localized Post-Aztatlán site at Barra de Navidad, Colima (Long and Wire 1966). In the Tomatlán Valley, the Post-Aztatlán Nahuapa tradition is identified throughout the coastal area by the presence of grooved redware jars (Mountjoy et al. 1983).

Because of the derived nature of the Post-Aztatlán local traditions, it is difficult to determine exactly when they became significantly different from the Aztatlán tradition. This may have occurred during or certainly by the end of the Ixcuintla phase at Amapa. Radiocarbon dates for the Ixcuintla phase fall somewhere in the range of A.D. 1190 to 1385. Obsidian-hydration dates place it between A.D. 1014 and 1274 (Meighan 1976:50–53). There is one radiocarbon date from the Tomatlán area that indicates that the Post-Aztatlán local (Nahuapa) tradition was fully developed there by sometime between A.D. 1010 and 1250 (Mountjoy 1990), and in the Banderas Valley area this tradition must begin after A.D. 1070 and perhaps as late as 1230 (Mountjoy 1990).

The Post-Aztatlán traditions of the southern coast came to an end during the early period of Spanish contact. This probably occurred much later than the initial contact period of A.D. 1522 to 1531, based on a radiocarbon date from the Tomatlán Valley of about A.D. 1620 ± 130 years (Mountjoy 1982a:99, 1983b). Another radiocarbon date, A.D. 1550 ± 60, from the Banderas Valley is associated with the destruction of indigenous stone "idols." Ethnohistorical data suggest that the local indigenous tradition of the Banderas Valley was defunct by A.D. 1621 (Lázaro de Arregui 1946) and that it had been eliminated along the entire coast of Jalisco by A.D. 1653 (Tello 1968).

Subsistence and Economy

The population expansion and the use of both large and small patches of fertile river alluvium and more marginal lands seem to indicate continued agricultural intensification at this time, probably with widespread use of irrigation. There are ethnohistorical data on Contact period irrigation in the west Mexican highlands and on the coast in the Banderas Valley (Beals 1932:158). Some of these lands appear to have been devoted to crops such as maize, beans, squash, and chili. At least the maize and chili cultivation seems attested to by the many large and deeply worn trough metates and the abundance of pottery molcajetes at many sites.

One site in the Banderas Valley is especially intriguing because it appears to reflect the transition from the indigenous Prehispanic economy to the Colonial tributary one. This is the Mesa del Temascal site that has been identified as the village of Quilitlán on the *Relación de Compostela* map of 1584 (Mountjoy 1993b). This site covers an area of 6 hectares and has the remains of at least 8 house foundations and one small ceremonial mound. Forty-eight metates, 40 manos, and 21 fragments of tortilla griddles were recorded on the surface of the site, and it has been suggested that they reflect the tribute payment of corn dough or tortillas to the encomendero (Mountjoy 1993b, 1993c).

Other important crops grown on the coast include cotton and cacao. According to Contact period ethnohistorical accounts, cotton was widely grown and woven by indigenous peoples all along the coastal plain of west Mexico. In 1518, a group of 12 towns near the mouth of the Río Balsas was required to send Moctezuma II a yearly tribute of 800 bales of raw cotton, 3,200 colored cotton cloths, and 4,800 large white cotton cloths (Peñafiel 1890:81–98). Along the coast of Colima, cotton was probably the most important negotiable crop, and in the form of cloth, shirts, small awnings, and painted bedding, it was the most important tribute item (Sauer 1948:65). Cotton was abundant in the San Blas area in 1530 (López-Portillo and Weber 1935:234–235), and spindle whorls are found there at sites of the local Santa Cruz tradition. At Amapa, perhaps 120 of the 164 spindle whorls recovered there are of the Post-Aztatlán local tradition. Spindle whorls are also closely associated with remains of the Nahuapa tradition in the Tomatlán Valley, both at the primary center at Nahuapa and in remote hamlets, and they are also present in the Navidad tradition at Barra de Navidad.

Although the abundance of spindle whorls seems to attest to the importance of cotton at many locations along the southern coast (Mountjoy 1995b), one curious exception is the Banderas Valley. Investigations of 107 sites on the southern side of the valley have yielded no spindle whorls in Post-Aztatlán Banderas tradition contexts. Nevertheless, it is certainly possible that cotton was grown there but exported in raw form to be spun into yarn elsewhere.

There is ethnohistorical evidence of the cultivation of cacao in the Banderas Valley as early as A.D. 1530 (Mariano de Torres 1965:57), probably with irrigation. By A.D. 1605, cacao is mentioned for the San Blas area (Mota y Escobar 1940:82), although it is not reported by the first Spaniards to visit that area. They noted cotton and an abundance of fish, oysters, and honey (López-Portillo and Weber 1935:234).

On the southern side of the Banderas Valley, many stone-lined pits have been found. They are over a meter deep, approximately 2 m in diameter, and sometimes have a rock-paved floor (Mountjoy 1993b; 1995a). They may be cisterns or food storage pits. The earliest of the three excavated seems associated with the Aztatlán tradition. One at Tebelchia, however, was filled with Post-Aztatlán trash of the Banderas tradition (Mountjoy 1995a).

There is abundant archaeological evidence of the harvesting of oysters in the Post-Aztatlán traditions, especially along the Nayarit coastline south of San Blas, as well as along the northern coast of Banderas Bay (Mountjoy 1995b). At Barra de Navidad, there are significant quantities of oyster shells from this period, but by far the most abundant are clamshells that come from intertidal sand beaches and sandflats (Long and Wire 1966:39). In striking contrast, archaeological data do not indicate that fish were important along the coast at this time, although some of the ethnohistoric accounts document their importance (Visitación 1937).

Ethnohistorical data also indicate that the exploitation or production of salt was a very important activity for indigenous people along the southern coast (Mountjoy 1995b). There are Contact period records of numerous saltworks all along the southern coast (Othón de Menhdizábal 1946). Linked archaeologically to the Post-Aztatlán local tradition just north of San Blas is the Zapotillo saltworks. More than 150 earthen mounds appear to be the remains of salt-extraction locations, and these can be seen on a pre–1967 aerial photo of that area. One sizable habitation site of the Post-Aztatlán Santa Cruz phase local tradition has been found associated with these salt-making mounds (Mountjoy

1970a:253–254, 1995b). A Banderas phase local tradition saltworks that may have been functioning during this time has been recorded near the mouth of the El Salado estuary, just north of Puerto Vallarta (Mountjoy 1993b, 1993c), and, oddly, three earthen mounds of the kind associated with salt working along the coast have been found at a site near El Colorado in the Banderas Valley, some 17 km inland from the coast (Mountjoy 1995a).

It appears the obsidian prismatic core and blade distribution system between the highlands and the coast broke down in Post-Aztatlán times. There are many fewer prismatic obsidian blades in Post-Aztatlán contexts. On the other hand, some household craft industries are evident at some Post-Aztatlán sites. At four sites on the southern side of the Banderas Valley, there is evidence of the manufacture of jewelry from different colored serpentine stone. This soft serpentine, most commonly cream-colored, but some bluish-gray or reddish, was chipped, cut, drilled, ground, and polished into such items as short cylinders (possibly hair ornaments), beads, pendants, and lip ornaments (Mountjoy 1991a, 1995a, 1995b). At the same time, in the Tomatlán Valley there is evidence of a flourishing household industry in copper metalworking (Mountjoy and Torres 1985).

Pottery specialization appears to continue in the Post-Aztatlán local traditions, with definite centers of production and definable areas of distribution. Fine paste pottery with red-and-black painted designs appears to have been made in the Tomatlán Valley at Nahuapa (then named Tetitlán) and probably distributed to hamlets throughout the area through its function as the major market center (Mountjoy et al. 1983). Associated with this kind of painted pottery in the Tomatlán Valley is a type of grooved/incised red painted or nonpainted jar that appears to have been manufactured outside the area and to have been distributed through coastal commerce to certain centers between Barra de Navidad and Banderas Bay. These jars may have been exported primarily for what they contained (perhaps salt), making the vessels themselves secondary exports that could be used for other household purposes once emptied of their original contents (Mountjoy et al. 1983). In the Banderas Valley, an orange and black-on-buff (natural color) decorated ware with geometric designs was the typical fancy pottery of the Banderas tradition, whereas more common domestic wares were orange painted bowls and jars with parallel horizontal grooved lines on the neck and shoulder.

Similar well-defined distributions of pottery types can be traced for other wares. For example, abundant black-on-buff (natural color) decorated bowls found at Santa Cruz, Nayarit, which may have been the center of their manufacture, appear in significant quantities as far south as the Banderas Valley but do not appear to reach as far south as the Tomatlán Valley. One small bowl of this type was left as an offering in the top of a ceremonial mound in the remains of a settlement at La Mesa del Temascal (village of Quilitlán [see above]). In the Santa Cruz area, this black-on-buff decorated pottery is found along with great quantities of incised pottery bowls of a type that is abundant at Amapa but does not appear to reach the Banderas Valley along with the black-on-buff pottery.

Sociopolitical Organization and Ritual

Both ethnohistorical and archaeological data indicate that some valleys on the southern coast were independent political units under the leadership of a local chief. This is especially true for relatively small valleys in the coastal area between Tomatlán and Cihuatlán (Tello 1968:72–73). In the relatively huge Banderas Valley, however, it is reported that there was one paramount chief who ruled over some 80 major towns each with its own local chief (Tello 1968:57). South of the Banderas Valley was a distinctive political province centered in the Tuito Mountains that seems to have reached as far south as the Tomatlán Valley (Tello 1968:63–68). Ethnohistorical data indicate that in southern Nayarit there were conflicts between coastal people and those who lived in the mountains immediately to the east (Tello 1968).

Archaeologically, it appears that the huge Prehispanic town near the mouth of the Río Santa Cruz on the coast of south-central Nayarit dominated that river valley and the area northward to San Blas, including another large settlement of the same local tradition at Aticama, between San Blas and Santa Cruz (Mountjoy 1970a). A large site on the top of the volcanic Ceboruco Hill on the northern end of Matanchén Bay is probably the town visited by Spaniards in 1530—a town Nuño de Guzmán described as having 60 houses and a population of more than two hundred people (López-Portillo and Weber 1935; Mountjoy 1970a:117).

Archaeological survey on the south side of the Banderas Valley has located only a few large sites with pottery of the Post-Aztatlán Banderas tradition even though 80 major towns were reported in the area at Spanish contact. Perhaps agricultural development and the growth of Colonial and modern settlements destroyed many of these sites. Nonetheless, there are only about 15 settlements of appreciable size in the valley today, so the figure of 80 major towns at Spanish contact may be too high, unless they included other towns located in the mountainous part of the Río Ameca Valley.

In the Tomatlán Valley during post-Aztatlán times, there was only one major town, probably Tetitlán, located at the site of the present-day village of Nahuapa (Mountjoy 1982a). This settlement appears to have been the political and economic center of the valley. The Spanish probably arrived there in 1525, and it is said that they were welcomed by a large crowd of people, some of whom were dancers dressed in feathered finery (Tello 1968:67–68). All other sites in the area at this time appear to have been hamlets or small villages.

Ritualistic activity for the southern coast in post-Aztatlán times included the burial of human remains in large jars or urns (Crabtree 1961; Kelly 1939). This practice of burying cremated human remains in jars or urns is first found in the Banderas Valley during the Shaft Tomb tradition and continues to Contact times. At Ixtapa, cremated remains of infants were placed in small jars or bowls and buried around a platform-like structure built on top of a mound, originally constructed during the Aztatlán tradition. Under this altar-like structure, a small rustic stela was buried in an upright position, and fragments of Aztatlán stelae were used to build a small altar in front of the platform (Mountjoy 1989b, 1991a, 1993b).

At Ixtapa, Post-Aztatlán (Banderas phase) people built small, low, clay mounds like those described as cenotaphs at Amapa (Meighan 1976). Partial excavation of one of these did not reveal any burials in or under the mound. Nevertheless, fragments of crude incense burners and small, orange-painted offertory bowls found on top of these mounds indicate the performance of rituals there (Mountjoy 1989b).

A Postclassic multiple burial, similar to the one found in a mound at Ixtapa, was found at a site near the mouth of the Río Balsas. At this site, 18 urn burials were found placed around what appeared to be an altar situated in front of a pyramidal mound (Chadwick 1971).

Two possible Post-Aztatlán tradition burials of high-status individuals interred with rich grave offerings, including jewelry of metal and precious stones, have been reported on the southern coast. One is from the north side of Banderas Valley at San Juan de Abajo (Corona Núñez 1950), and the other is from Lo Arado, Jalisco, near the border of Jalisco and Colima (Covarrubias 1961). Unfortunately, there is no report of associated diagnostic pottery that would aid in placing the finds in a temporal context. I have inspected a collection of sherds reported obtained from the surface of Lo Arado. Most probably the sherds are post-Aztatlán; no characteristic Aztatlán sherds were noted.

In the Tomatlán Valley, the only burials known from post-Aztatlán contexts are in pits dug in the floors of circular houses, near the center of the house (Mountjoy 1982a, 1983b). Many of these burials had groups of copper rings that may have been strung on a thong or cord and worn around the neck (Mountjoy and Torres 1985).

In the San Blas area, there are large mounds that presumably supported structures dedicated to ritual activities. These mounds are located within the habitation areas. At Arias (Figure 7.13) is a hilltop ceremonial center with a large mound, sunken plazas, and many petroglyphs that were pecked on boulders around the plazas or down the slope (Mountjoy 1970a, 1974b). At Ixtapa, it appears that the Post-Aztatlán Banderas tradition people continued to use, and may have enlarged, some of the large and medium-sized platform mounds that appear to have been built at the beginning of the Aztatlán tradition. An earlier, pre-Aztatlán ceremonial mound was also covered. One of these mounds was approximately 8 m high and 75 m long on one side.

A similar use of Aztatlán monuments by post-Aztatlán people has been reported at Amapa (Meighan 1976). As at Amapa, Banderas tradition people seem to have mainly built small cenotaph-type mounds on the top of which they performed ritual activities (Mountjoy 1989b, 1991a). Some of these rituals may have involved the burning of paper decorated with designs of religious significance. Several flat pottery stamps that could have been used to imprint such designs were found at Amapa (Meighan 1976). Some of them may be attributable to the Aztatlán tradition there, but others seem to be Post-Aztatlán. One remarkable pottery stamp was found at Tebelchia in a rock-lined (storage?) pit associated with Post-Aztatlán (Banderas phase) trash.

Petroglyphs appear to have been pecked all along the southern coast during post-Aztatlán times and on into the Contact period (Mountjoy 1984). They appear to have been especially widespread and abundant in the San Blas and Tomatlán areas in the Post-Aztatlán traditions (Mountjoy 1974b, 1987b). The petroglyphs are sometimes found on rocks associated with ceremonial structures and at other times on rocks that are part of house foundations in rural hamlets. Many petroglyphs are associated with habitation sites; others may be isolated from such remains, often in areas associated with water (Mountjoy 1974b, 1987b). There are six known instances of petroglyphs on stone stelae (Mountjoy 1991c, 1993b). One large rock with more than two hundred painted (pictograph) designs that probably belongs to the Post-Aztatlán Nahuapa local tradition has been recorded in the upper Tomatlán Valley (Mountjoy 1982b).

Analysis of the pecked and painted rock art that appears to have been produced at this time indicates that in addition to the earlier pits and spirals, there are many more complex designs. Most of them appear to be elaborations of the same early theme of representing the eye or face of the sun, which was also conceived as a rain-giving god. In fact, it has been argued (Mountjoy 1987b) that the act of painting or pecking these symbols was a way of giving physical expression to a prayer for rain and, further, that rock art was in a place that could be easily seen by the sun god. The "smoke" produced by pecking glyphs into rock such as granite may have had a magical sympathetic relation to the production of rain clouds. There are some other pictographs and petroglyphs that appear to depict the central mesoamerican rain god Tlaloc, as well as such natural forms as coiled serpents, dogs, turtles, birds, and human footprints, many of which can also be interpreted in the context of rainmaking ceremonialism (Mountjoy 1974b, 1987b, 1991a). There is also one petroglyph of a patolli game board that has been found in the Tomatlán Valley, and what were probably the pottery dice and position markers for playing the game have also been found at sites in the same valley (Mountjoy and Smith 1985). A similar petroglyph is found on a rock stored at a museum at Compostela in southern Nayarit.

To date, more than 53 stone stelae have been found in sites along the southern coast. The earliest known stelae appear to date to the Aztatlán occupation of Ixtapa. Several of the stelae were found in one Aztatlán mound in the Ixtapa ceremonial complex. As noted previously, the mound was reused in post-Aztatlán times and included the burial of one crude post-Aztatlán stela in upright position under a low platform built on the top of the mound (Mountjoy 1991a, 1991c, 1993a). In the Banderas Valley, similar crude stelae were used on top of mounds in which Banderas tradition human burials are interred. It has been proposed that many stelae are related to sun worship, but it is also possible that in the Banderas Valley some post-Aztatlán stelae are related to a revival of a Shaft Tomb and Tuxcacuesco tradition mortuary custom of using cobbles or short stone shafts to mark the location of burials (Mountjoy 1993a).

Pottery figurines are not commonly found in the Post-Aztatlán local traditions in the southern coastal areas of San Blas, Tomatlán, and Barra de Navidad. They are

Figure 7.14. A stone figurine from El Ranchito (PV-33) in the Banderas Valley found in post-Aztatlán contexts (Banderas phase) dating A.D. 1550 ± 60 years (height 16 cm).

more frequently found in the Banderas Valley, sometimes in house mound refuse. Some of these figurines have mold-made bodies with appliqué noses, eyes, and mouth. These Banderas figurines have the same reddish-orange slip commonly found on vessels, and they resemble some of the slab figurines associated with the Santiago phase at Amapa (Meighan 1976:337–38).

In the Banderas Valley at this time, there is evidence of a curious tradition of columnar stone sculpture. These sculptures, averaging about 60 cm in height, range from about 30 cm to about a meter high. At least some of them are carved from an unusual, probably foreign, volcanic stone that contains tiny green peridot crystals. The columns, some of which are phallic, are carved with a single anthropomorphic figure on the upper portion. Some of these figures seem to be hermaphroditic, and as a group they are mainly distinguishable by variation in headdress (Alcaraz 1991; Mountjoy 1991a, 1993b, 1995a; Regino 1991). Pieces of several of these sculptures (Figure 7.14) were found broken, burned by intense heat, and left in a pit containing other burned rocks and a few sherds of the Banderas local tradition, along with charcoal dating to A.D. 1550 ± 60. The destruction of these sculptures may have been instigated by Colonial period Spanish priests (Mountjoy 1993b).

External Relations

The overall impression of cultural development along the southern coast during Post-Aztatlán times is one of fragmentation and diversification. There are some cultural traits such as the erection of stone stelae and certain decorative types of pottery that link the valleys along the coast, but there appears to have been a definite breakdown in the cultural hegemony of the Aztatlán tradition. Certain river valleys or sections of the coast appear to develop their own local pottery styles and probably specialized in certain kinds of subsistence or other economic activities. There also seems to be an increase in population density and dispersal, with population exerting considerable pressure on the local resources of some coastal river valley systems and the stress on nonsubsistence crops occasionally causing severe adverse consequences for the nutrition of the general populace.

There is some indication of continued interaction between the coast and some highland centers such as Ixtlán del Río, Nayarit, at this time. Based on archaeological and ethnohistorical data, it appears that coastal products such as salt, fish, and mollusk meat were exported into highland valleys to the east.

Despite the fact that the Tarascans pushed westward during Post-Aztatlán times, there are only hints of contact between the Tarascans and the cultures of the southern coast (for further discussion of the Tarascans, see Pollard this volume). One Tarascan style cast copper bell was found in the excavation of a Nahuapa phase house floor at El Ciruelo in the Tomatlán Valley (Mountjoy and Torres 1985), and a patolli petroglyph from the same area could have been played following rules recorded ethnographically among the Tarascans (Mountjoy and Smith 1985).

Coastal Michoacán near the mouth of the Río Balsas was in close contact with the Tarascans (Maldonado 1980:132), and contact between Late Postclassic peoples of that general area and the Aztecs of the central Mexican highlands is recorded in the *Mendocino Codex*. It is recorded that in 1518 a group of 12 towns on the coast of Guerrero and Michoacán were being required to send a yearly tribute, consisting of 1,600 shells (apparently *Spondylus princeps*), 160 loads (about 960 bushels) of cacao, 800 bales of cotton, 3,200 colored cotton cloths, and 4,800 large white cotton cloths, to Moctezuma II (Peñafiel 1890:81–98).

Although there is ample evidence in Postclassic times of contact between northwestern South America and the southern coast of west Mexico, possibly in search of *Spondylus* shells to satisfy ritual demands by Andean cultures (Anawalt 1998; Chadwick 1971; Hosler 1994; Meighan 1969; Mountjoy 1969), there is also new intriguing evidence suggesting long-distance Late Postclassic contact between indigenous peoples of the Jalisco-Nayarit coast and indigenous peoples of southern Central America, possibly specifically Costa Rica. This can be seen primarily in peg base anthropomorphic stone statues (Figure 7.14), carved greenstone slab-shaped pendants, and large stone spheres (Mountjoy 1997).

CLOSING

The information I have presented regarding the evolution of Prehispanic culture in the southern coastal area of west Mexico from the earliest human inhabitants up into the Contact period has allowed me to provide the reader with some idea (and considerable details in some instances) regarding the sequential development of certain widespread cultural traditions. Within this framework, I have also attempted to convey some sense of site distribution and date, subsistence and economy, sociopolitical organization and ritual, and external relations concerning these cultural traditions. Nevertheless, many questions of what, when, how, and why along this coast and in other areas of west Mexico remain to be answered (Mountjoy 1998c).

CHAPTER EIGHT

THE PREHISTORY OF MEXICO'S NORTHWEST COAST

A View from the Marismas Nacionales of Sinaloa and Nayarit

STUART D. SCOTT AND MICHAEL S. FOSTER

FROM 1968 TO 1978 the State University of New York conducted a multidisciplinary research program in the Marismas Nacionales of coastal Sinaloa and Nayarit (Figure 8.1). Project headquarters were established in Teacapán, Sinaloa, a rural commercial and agricultural village of about 2,500 inhabitants. Using data from soil stratigraphy, mangrove ecology, pollen and faunal analysis, archaeology, ethnohistory, human osteology, and burial practices, the researchers aimed to provide an objective view of the natural world of the Marismas Nacionales, to examine the record of human occupation there, and, to the extent that the data might support them, to examine the implications for human social organization in this specific environmental setting (Scott 1974, 1985). The west Mexican coastal plain is a distinct physiographic province (Connally 1977) about 200 km long and 4 to 35 km wide. The rugged Sierra Madre Occidental, which reaches altitudes of 3,000 m or more, forms the eastern border and backdrop for the coastal plain. Most of the arable land lies on emergent beach ridges between Mazatlán and Teacapán or on the alluvial plain between San Blas and the Río San Pedro. The rest of the coastal plain comprises the Marismas Nacionales (Marismas), a complex of interlacing waterways, salt pans, and mangrove forests. The Marismas is one of Mexico's larger compound deltaic estuaries.

The scope of the present chapter, however, is restricted to (a) summary descriptions of the basic chronology and natural and cultural structure of the Marismas setting and (b) the possible implications of research findings for comparison with other maritime cultures of the Americas.

THE ACCRETIONAL COASTAL PLAIN

The larger chronological framework for the Marismas is based on an understanding of the origin and development of the regional coastal plain during the late Quaternary and Holocene (Allen and Connally 1977). Our data indicate that from several thousand years ago to about 7,000 years ago, the area that was to become the Marismas and adjacent coastal zone was yet to develop. The area surrounding the archaeological site of El Calón and the present location of Teacapán were out to sea (Figure 8.2).

After several thousand years ago, the first phase of coastal construction began. Sediments consisting of sand, silt, and clay were dumped seaward on the adjacent shallow continental shelf. Clearly, this process was dynamic, and the configuration of the growing coastal plain was affected by the interplay of longshore currents and fluctuations in the supply of sediments available. Large and small rivers dumped sediment into the sea, forming small deltas, floodplains, swamps, and lagoons. Longshore currents are thought to have been flowing northward,

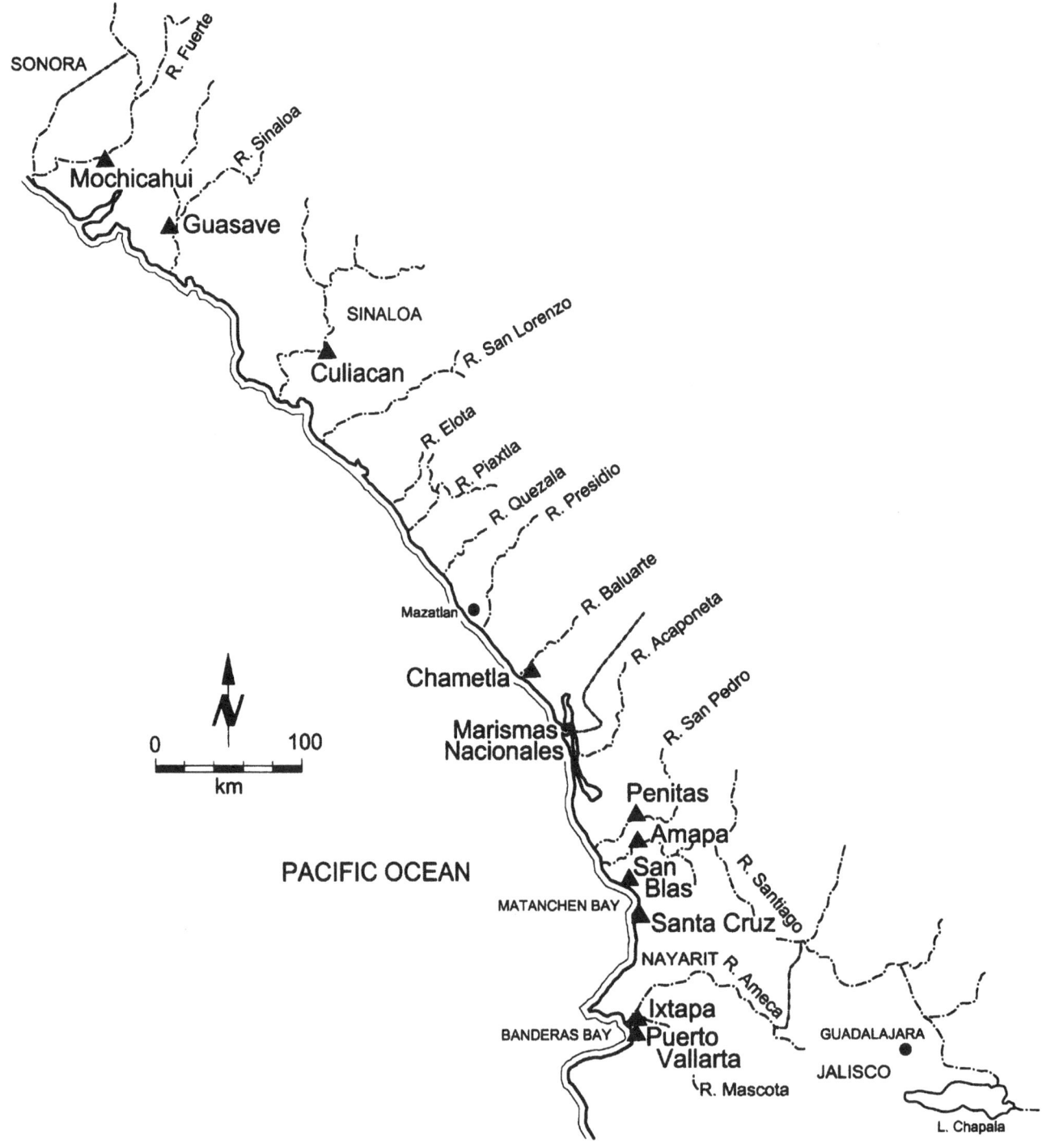

Figure 8.1. Archaeological sites along the coast of west Mexico.

perhaps moderating the climate and making the area more suitable for human occupation. In any case, we estimate the El Calón mound to have been constructed at ca. 2000 B.C., at or close to the existing shoreline.

Some five hundred years later, the construction of the Teacapán coastal plain was the result of marine processes rather than fluvial processes. Longshore currents shifted to south-flowing, resulting in rapid progradation as a recessive phase. The coastal plain extended seaward through the formation of a series of subparallel beach

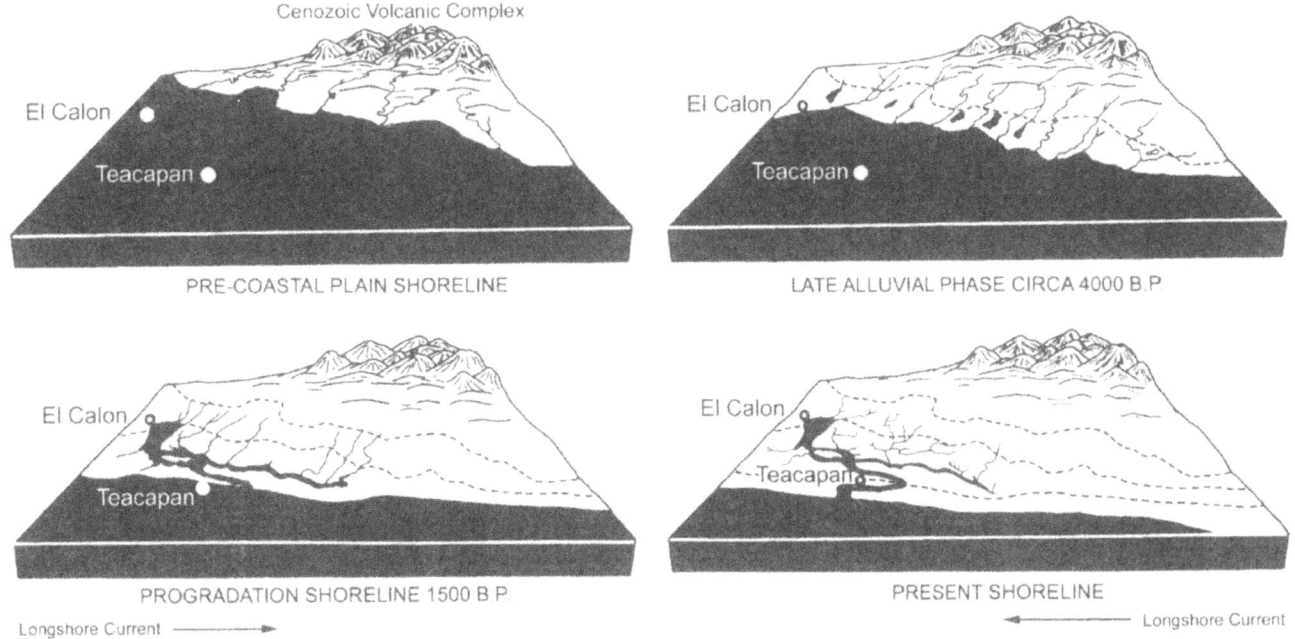

Figure 8.2. Schematic view of coastal progradation in the area of the Marismas Nacionales.

ridges. Rivers pushed through the beach ridges, building floodplains but being forced to adopt sinuous passages through the beach ridges. This time, 1,500 years ago, coincides with the appearance of new settlements on the then partly constructed Teacapán peninsula.

Today, the longshore current has reversed again, bringing about the construction of the new peninsula that encloses the estuary of Teacapán. El Calón is well inland, and the village of Teacapán, with time and continued growth of the coastal plain, will also be well inland.

Additionally, the sequential growth of this alluvial plain was punctuated by periods of submergence, one of which occurred during Middle Beach progradation. This accounts for the gap in which no evidence of human occupation was found. It appears that other than the El Calón mound and possibly two other nearby low *Anadara* mounds, archaeological data for the earliest occupations of the Marismas area are either buried or submerged and are not readily available for investigation.

Based on evidence from both local geologic processes and the local ceramic sequence, there is another indication of how the area's culture history coincided with landform development. It appears there is another hiatus of about two hundred to three hundred years (ca.

A.D. 900 to 1200) in the occupation of the Marismas. A similar pattern was found at Amapa, where there is also physical and cultural evidence of a break in occupation (Grosscup 1964, 1976). In the original Amapa sequence, the hypothetical Tuxpan phase was proposed to account for missing connections between earlier and later phases. Meighan (1976) also recognizes the interruption but places it earlier, based on obsidian-hydration dating (Figure 8.3).

REGIONAL CULTURAL SETTING

The Sites

It is not difficult to mine the published literature on the archaeology of the northwest Mexican seaboard. Archaeological investigations of the northwest Mexican coast began with Sauer and Brand's (1932) survey of Sinaloa. Based on their observations, the Aztatlán culture was defined. Sauer and Brand's contributions were many, but of particular note is their recognition that the West Coast was an important center of Prehispanic cultural development. Despite this early recognition of the region's importance, archaeological research along the

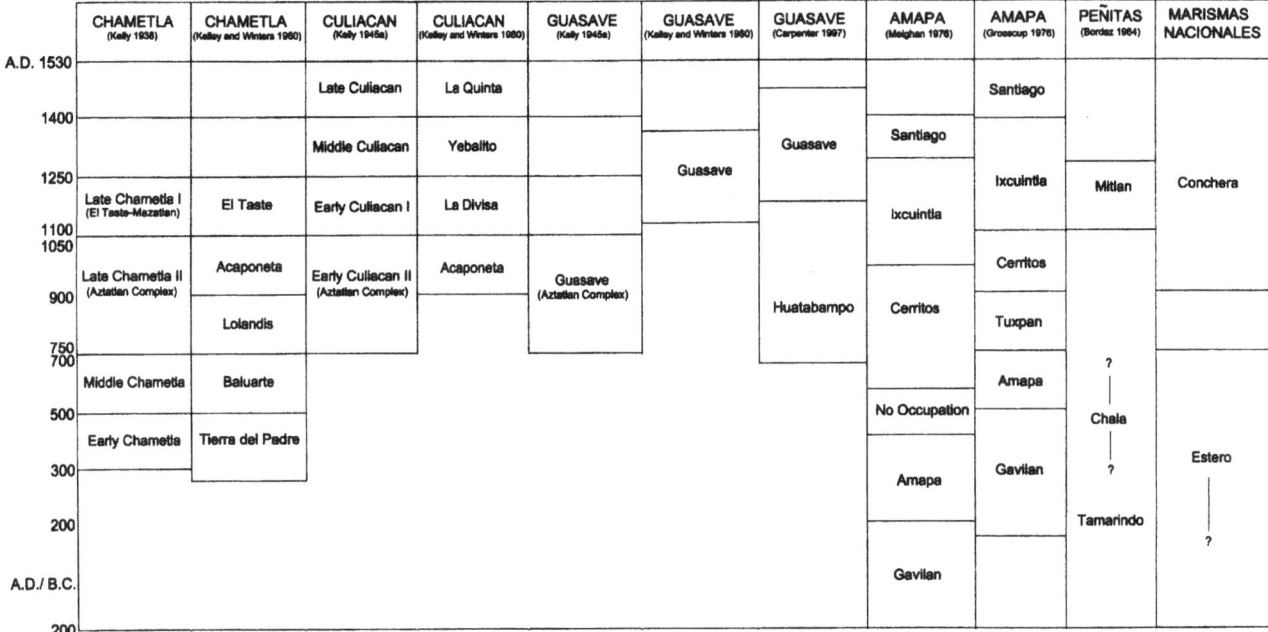

Figure 8.3. Various phase schemes for major sites along the coast of west Mexico.

northwest coast has been limited. It is largely restricted to several major sites, including Chametla (Kelly 1938), Guasave (Ekholm 1942), Culiacán (Kelly 1945a), and Amapa (Meighan 1976). The work at Amapa was part of a larger undertaking, Project A (Nicholson and Meighan 1974), that included survey and testing along the coast and in the highlands. It is important to note that the Chametla and Amapa areas seem to have had extensive influence in the Marismas.

Guasave is known essentially from the excavation of a single burial mound on a remnant channel of the Río Sinaloa. Ekholm (1942) described this as a mound of unstratified silty sand, with a rudely circular form. He guessed, probably correctly, that the periodic silting and changes in the drainage channels have obscured other burial sites and living surfaces along the alluvial floodplain of the Sinaloa. At Culiacán, Kelly (1945a) found the same kind of settlement evidence up and down the length of the Culiacán Valley. Sites consist of low irregular earth mounds, poorly defined for the most part, usually no more than a barely perceptible rise above the floodplain surface. Moving south to the Baluarte Valley, we find some qualitatively different circumstances regarding surface evidence of settlement. What are basically refuse or house platform mounds or both, constructed of silty sand, flecked with ash and charcoal, without much visible stratification, continue to be the rule. At Chametla (Kelly 1938), however, there are larger mounds located on terraces of the present river channel with twice the depth of debris of any of the mounds excavated at Culiacán. Also, in their 1930 reconnaissance, Sauer and Brand (1932) mention seeing rectangular stone foundations of more substantial structures. Kelly, however, makes no mention of masonry construction at Chametla.

South of the Río Baluarte where the plain widens, the mountains recede from the coast and the coastal plain drainage becomes sluggish and discharges into a maze of lagoons and tidal channels that are the Marismas Nacionales. The Marismas straddle the boundary of Sinaloa with Nayarit. In terms of natural history, this area is distinct from the rest of the coastal floodplain. Guasave, Culiacán, and Chametla are situated on alluvial soils deposited on elevated marine terraces. In southern Sinaloa and northern Nayarit, the coastline is subsiding, producing a large drowned area of lagoon marshes and swamps. As unattractive as that might sound, this broad tract of marshy strand plain, fed by the Ríos Cañas, San Pedro, and Acaponeta, was a very extensive human habitat. Here hundreds of visible archaeological sites are dispersed across peninsulas and beach dune ridges and along tide channels and large lagoons.

Just as elsewhere, the Marismas has its own large share of relatively low and irregular "lomitas" that seem to have served as multipurpose refuse, burial, and house mounds. The signature sites in the Marismas, though, are the linear shell middens and earth mounds that were overlaid with massive deposits of oyster shell.

Farther south, Amapa, Nayarit (see Mountjoy in this volume), on the delta plain of the Río Santiago, offers some even more distinguishing site characteristics. This site consists of a concentrated areal center with mound groupings in patterned arrangements. This is not to suggest that Amapa's more apparent formal community patterning is unique on the coastal plain. Kelly (1945b) remarked that several of the Culiacán sites exhibit more complicated settlement plans, with mounds arranged in parallel rows or, more frequently, about a hollow square (plaza). She further suggests this central plaza may have served as a market, which according to historical accounts was enclosed by the village. There is a strong presumption that Amapa is a site that is more complex than those to the north, however. Amapa is characterized by well-executed, elongated, and steep-sided mounds in the familiar mesoamerican mound-and-plaza arrangement, aligned to the cardinal points; a ball court; the use of stone masonry in stairways; and a separate cemetery area.

If we look at the coastal lowland, then, only in terms of the sites themselves as artifacts, how do they compare? Though it may not have always been the case, the far north looks less complex in the amount of visible surface residue of Prehispanic occupation as compared with the density and visibility of mounds south of the Río Baluarte. The Guasave site was the only thing vaguely recognizable as an artificial mound that Ekholm had seen working from north to south, and Sauer and Brand spoke of their failure to find evidence of what they called the local culture north beyond the valley of Culiacán. In contrast, Meighan describes the mound group at Amapa as only one of many aboriginal communities that can be seen thickly scattered in the delta plain merging one into another, all the way to the ocean. Based on the published archaeology of Sinaloa, the pattern of occupance of the coastal plain is one of site development on the middle-reach floodplain zones of the so-called master streams, with apparently an increasing prevalence or intensity of Prehispanic settlement locations from north to south. Could the heavier density of house clusters in the south be related to the wetter climate and a more dependable seaward growth of the coastline over time? The exploitation of shellfish in the Marismas, far in excess of anything mentioned at the other sites, suggests that the productivity of marine and estuarine resources should be seen as one of the reasons for the rather rich record of settlement there.

Phase Sequences and Material Culture

Sauer and Brand (1932:31–41) found an array of material culture associated with their Aztatlán remains. The pottery they observed was well made from a fine paste, hard, and very well polished. Vessel form and decoration varied widely. The utility ware was painted with a broad red rim and bands of various widths across the body of the vessel. Other design elements included dotted circles and motifs thought to represent feather headdresses, stylized figures and designs, and geometric and nongeometric patterns. Engraving was also common on both monochrome and polychrome vessels.

Figurines, pipes, incised spindle whorls, cylindrical clay stamps, and urn burials also appeared to be characteristic traits of the Aztatlán culture. Sauer and Brand observed that stone carving was not particularly well developed and that the chipped stone assemblage conspicuously lacked projectile points, although many of the points recovered were well made from obsidian. Obsidian blades and debitage were common, and a light gray obsidian was particularly notable. Sauer and Brand suggested the gray obsidian, and obsidian in general, was likely imported, since they had not discovered or heard of any local sources.

Sauer and Brand (1932:37–41) also noted significant local variation in Aztatlán materials along the coast. Culiacán produced none or few of the red-rimmed and red decorated types found elsewhere. Culiacán Polychrome was the most striking ceramic type noted for the area. A fluted ware and a polished black or black-brown type, both apparently restricted to the Culiacán area, occurred along with Culiacán Polychrome. Also of note was a "walnut or mahogany colored" type with incising on the upper half of bowl exteriors. Bowls with incised interiors were also common, as were tripod vessels with ball feet, many of which functioned as rattles. Many of these served as molcajetes, or chili grinders.

Farther south, in the Chametla area, Sauer and Brand (1932:38–39) noted that the only ceramic type that seemed to tie Chametla to Culiacán was Mazatlán Polychrome. Aztatlán ware, the red-rimmed red-on-buff incised type sometimes decorated with white paint, was fairly common along with a local version with black painting. Chametla Polychrome was defined and occurred with a well-polished blackware and "full-fashioned" terra cotta figurines.

To the north, Sauer and Brand (1932:40–41) defined a third subregion of the Aztatlán culture, the Tacuichamona. Sites were smaller and ceramics were crudely decorated as compared with those to the south. Overall, the Tacuichamona culture seemed less well developed, and although influenced by the Aztatlán phenomenon, it does not seem to be part of it.

Later Kelly (1938) excavated in the Chametla area. She divided its occupation into four complexes (Kelly 1938:34–44): Early Chametla, Middle Chametla, Late Chametla II (Aztatlán Complex), and Late Chametla I (El Taste–Mazatlán). The Early and Middle Chametla complexes predate Aztatlán remains in the area. Associated ceramic types consist of red-rimmed utility and black-banded wares, and although they were found throughout the ceramic sequences at the sites investigated, their frequencies from site to site varied, as did their distribution through time. The same can be said for the red and black wares present as well. A variety of polychromes were also identified, and engraving was common on many of the Chametla pottery types (Figures 8.4, 8.5, 8.6, and 8.7).

The latest two complexes, the Aztatlán and El Taste–Mazatlán, are associated with the Aztatlán period. Aztatlán complex ceramics include Aztatlán Polychrome, Cocoyolitos Polychrome, a red-rim decorated ware, and a black-on-buff ware. Kelly noted the red-rim decorated ware was a basic element of the Aztatlán complex ceramic assemblage. Although the Chametla data were inconclusive regarding the Aztatlán association of Cocoyolitos Polychrome, Kelly believed it was a major trait of the Aztatlán complex. El Taste–Mazatlán complex ceramics were dominated by El Taste Red-bordered, El Taste Polychrome, Mazatlán Polychrome, El Taste Satin, and El Taste Rough. Also associated with these two late complexes were smoking pipes, large incised spindle whorls, and late, El Taste slab figurines.

After Kelly's work at Chametla, Ekholm (1942) excavated at Guasave, where he recovered a variety of ceramic, shell, metal, ground, chipped, and carved stone. He believed the Guasave materials postdated the early complexes at Chametla and were clearly associated with the Aztatlán complex (Ekholm 1942:123–124). He also believed that the Guasave remains reflected a single temporal and cultural component.

Guasave ceramics included a variety of elaborate polychromes, incised and engraved types, polished red-on-buff, red and plain wares, and grooved wares that came in various forms including a variety of bowls, tripods, and jars (Figures 8.8, 8.9, 8.10, 8.11, and 8.12). Ceramic spindle whorls, smoking pipes, and masks were also found, along with clay plaques, animal and human figurines, whistles, beads, earplugs, and a cylinder stamp. Various other artifacts—stone bowls, a pipe, manos, metates, pestles, axes, shell beads, pendants, bracelets, turquoise, and copper items including bells, an ear spool(?), a finger ring, a flat plate, and a necklace—were also recovered. There was also evidence of paint cloisonné on gourd fragments.

The richness and elaborate nature of the Guasave assemblage clearly reflects the fact that it was a burial assemblage. Nevertheless, the Guasave materials demonstrated that the Aztatlán phenomenon was more complex and elaborate than described by Sauer and Brand or reported at Chametla (Kelly 1938). Also of importance was Ekholm's (1942:125–132) recognition of similarities between the Guasave materials and central Mexican cultures. Ekholm (1942:127) listed 44 traits he believed originated in central Mexican culture, several of which appeared to be directly derived from the Mixteca-Puebla culture. Ekholm felt these similarities were so strong that he suggested a migration of Mixteca-Puebla people must have occurred.

More recently, the Guasave mound and its materials have been the subject of restudy (Carpenter 1996). Carpenter believes the burial mound was associated with a Huatabampo occupation of the area dating between approximately A.D. 700 and 1400. He indicates that two components are represented, the Huatabampo period, dating between A.D. 650/700 and 1050/1100, and the Guasave period, between A.D. 1050/1100 and 1400/1450. Carpenter also conducted an analysis of the burials and concluded that the data support evidence of ranked social organization at Guasave. There appears to have been unequal access to goods, based primarily on age distinctions, with both males and females included in the highest ranks of society.

Carpenter rejects the notion that the Guasave mortuary assemblage represents a migration of central Mexican peoples (Ekholm 1942) into the area or that Guasave was some kind of node in a macroregional exchange system (Kelley 1986a; see Kelley this volume). He argues that the exotic goods in the burials are associated with the ideological realm of the society and do not represent any strong participation or integration, politically or economically, into any mesoamerican political or economic sphere. Carpenter also suggests that the assemblage of nonlocal items more closely resembles a pres-

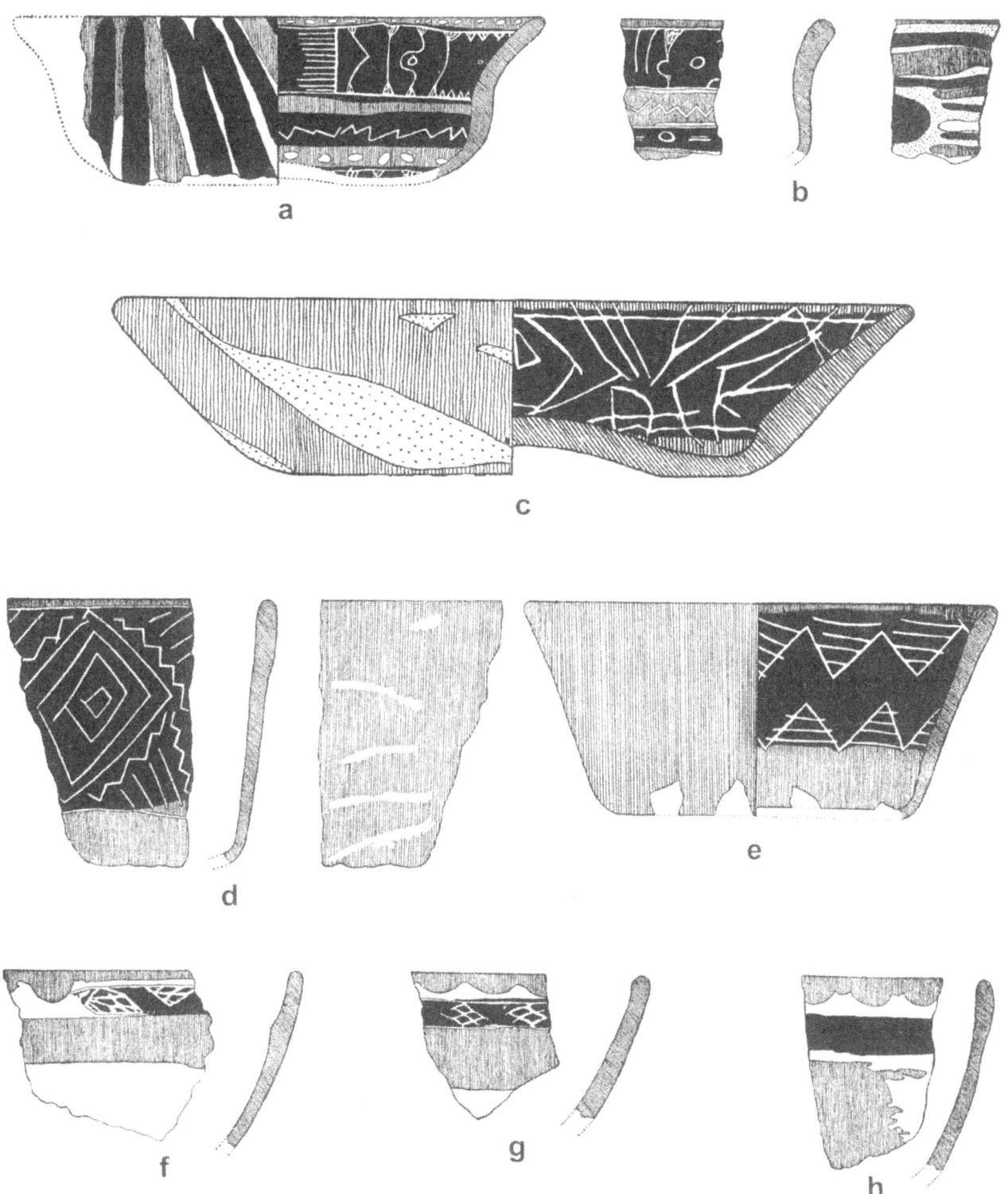

Figure 8.4. Black-banded ware: *a–c,* Early engraved with polychrome exterior; *d–g,* Late engraved with red exterior; *h,* Nonengraved (Kelly 1938:Figure 4). Courtesy of the University of California Press.

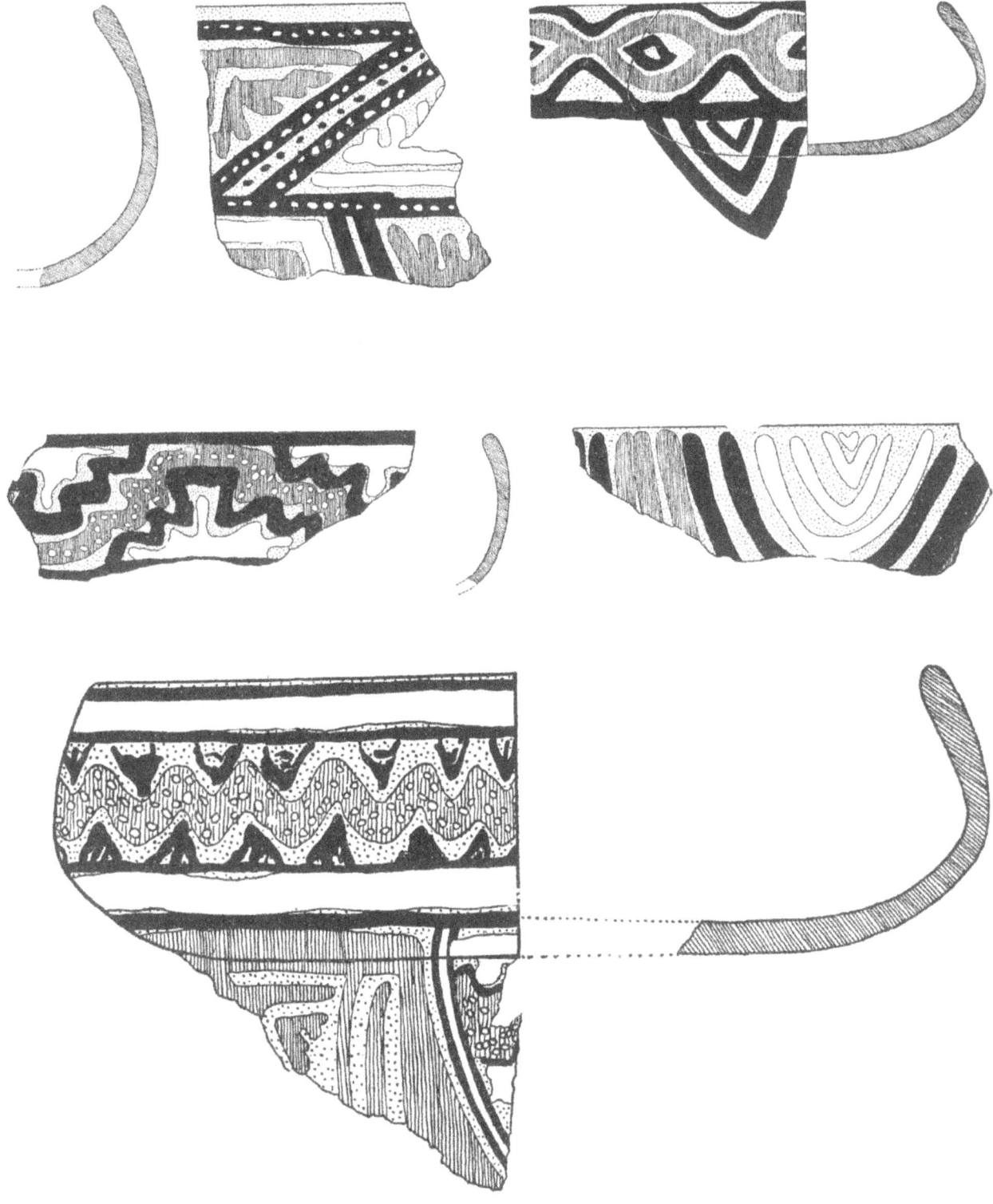

Figure 8.5. Early Chametla Polychrome bowls (Kelly 1938:Figure 1). Courtesy of the University of California Press.

Figure 8.6. Middle Chametla Polychrome, Plain and Engraved (Kelly 1938:Plate 5). Courtesy of the University of California Press.

Figure 8.7. Chametla ceramic types. *a,* El Taste Red-bordered; *b–e,* El Taste Polychrome; *f,* Mazatlán Polychrome (Kelly 1938:Plate 8). Courtesy of the University of California Press.

Figure 8.8. Aztatlán Polychrome pottery (Ekholm 1942:Figure 4). Courtesy of the American Museum of Natural History.

Figure 8.9. Cerro Isabel Engraved pottery (Ekholm 1942:Figure 6). Courtesy of the American Museum of Natural History.

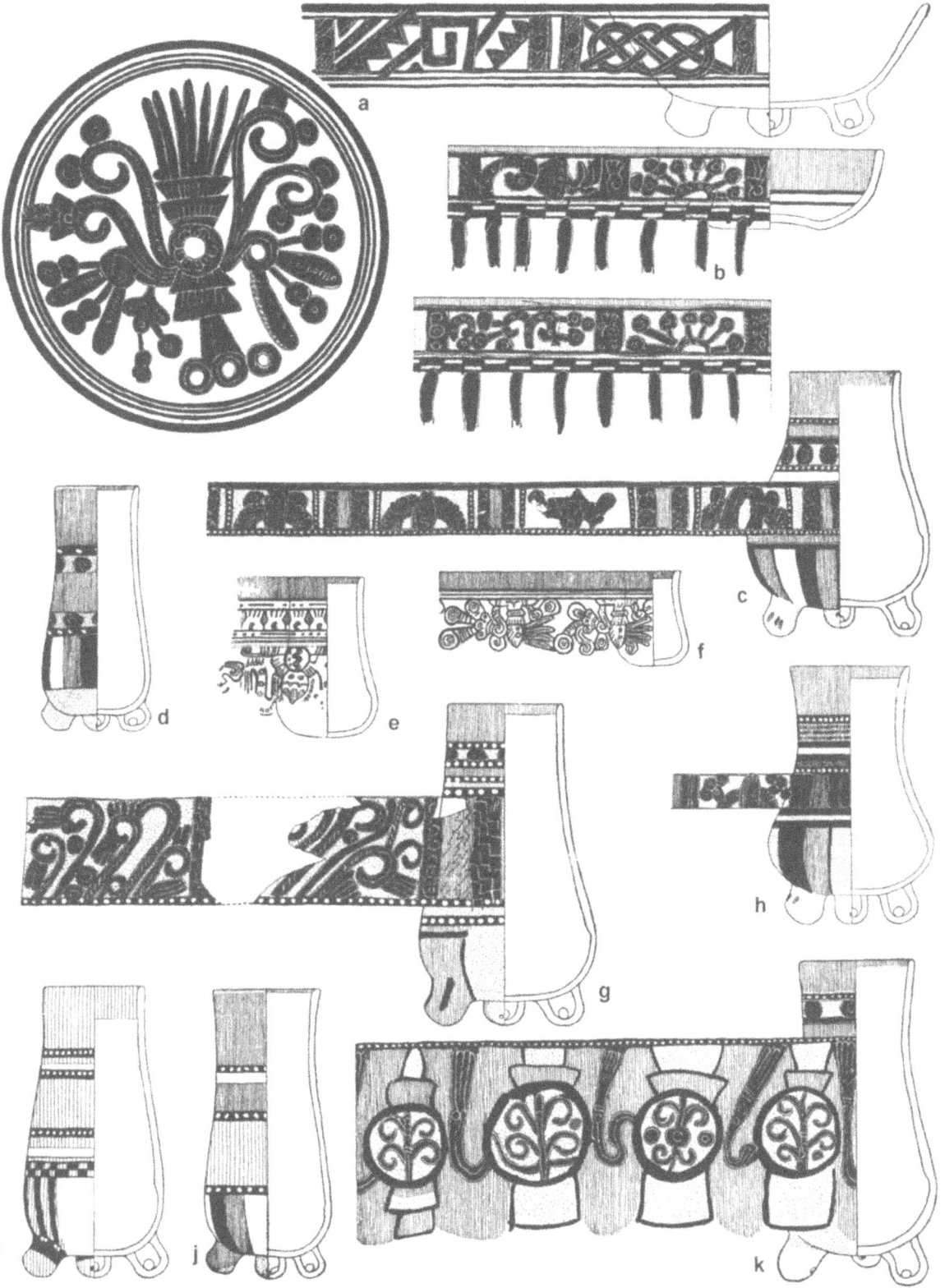

Figure 8.10. Guasave ceramic types. *a–b*, Cerro Isabel Engraved bowls; *c, d, g–k*, Sinaloa Polychrome jars; *e–f*, small legless jars (Ekholm 1942:Figure 7). Courtesy of the American Museum of Natural History.

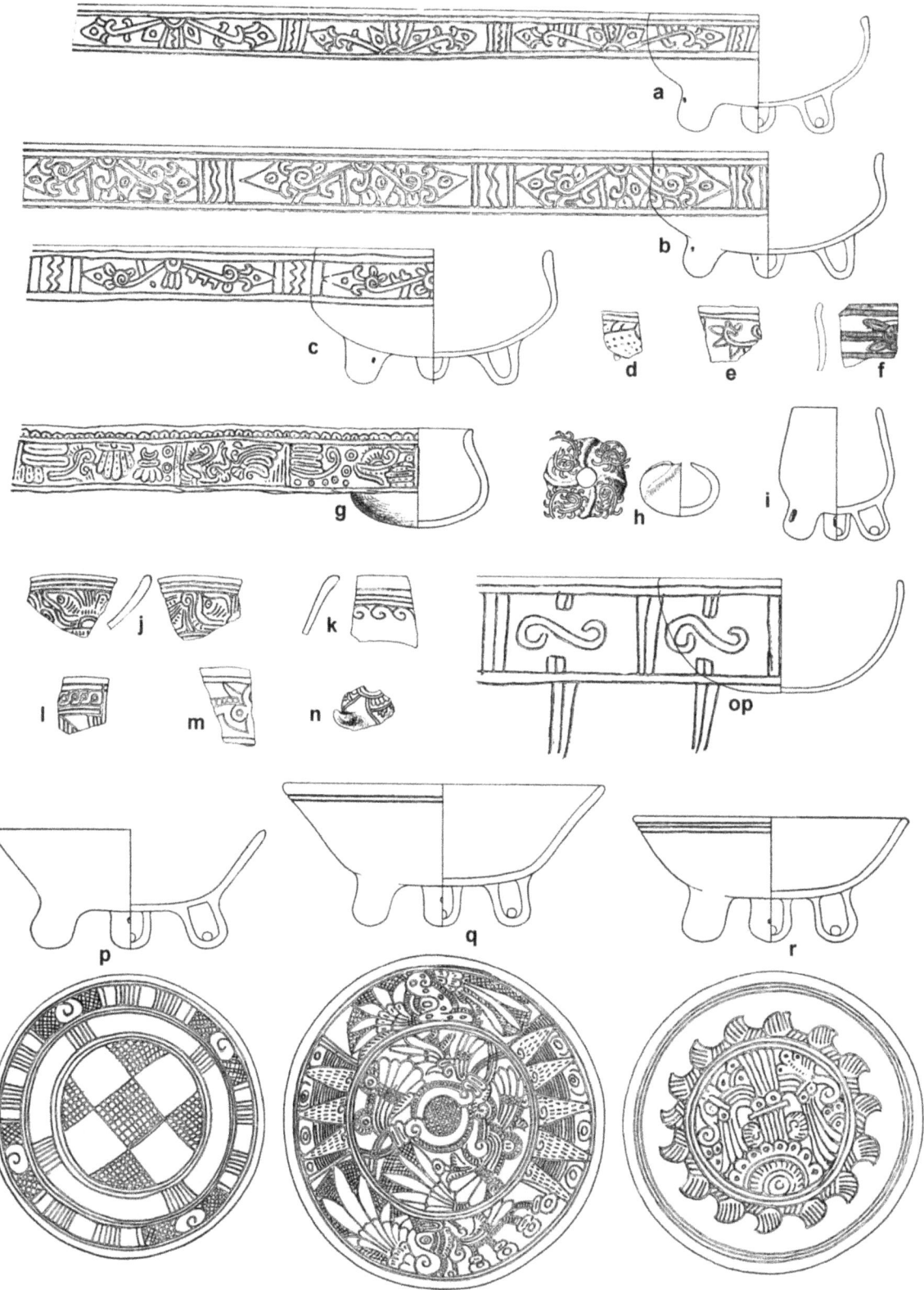

Figure 8.11. Guasave ceramic types. *a–f*, El Dorado Incised pottery; *g–r*, Aguaruto Incised and other Black-Smudged wares (Ekholm 1942:Figure 8). Courtesy of the American Museum of Natural History.

Figure 8.12. Guasave Polychrome bowls (Ekholm 1942:Figure 9). Courtesy of the American Museum of Natural History.

tige-goods economy and therefore it is likely their acquisition and presence is a consequence of local social intensification rather than a manifestation of some form of foreign dominance. Nearly sixty years ago, Ekholm (1940) had suggested that what Carpenter calls the Guasave period was an amalgamation of Huatabampo and influences from the south. Although Carpenter has rejected an actual migration of mesoamerican peoples or imposition of a mesoamerican presence at Guasave, he has not considered that the integration of the northern Sinaloa area into the Aztatlán Mercantile System may have provided local elites with a mechanism that allowed them to establish alliances (e.g., elite exchange, marriage) with individuals or polities to the south. Such alliances may have resulted in their strengthening and maintaining their status in local societies. The nature and quantity of mesoamerican items present in the Guasave burial mound indicate that a mechanism other than just their possession and use in the local ideological realm may have been at work.

Kelly's (1945a) excavations at Culiacán resulted in the identification of four complexes, all of which post-date the Early and Middle Chametla complexes. The Culiacán sequence includes the Early Culiacán II (Aztatlán Complex), Early Culiacán I, Middle Culiacán, and Late Culiacán complexes. A substantial quantity of material was recovered. Ceramics (Figures 8.13, 8.14, 8.15, and 8.16) included the Aztatlán types Early Culiacán, Navolato, and Aguaruto polychromes, Aguaruto Incised, and Cerro Izabal and Alamitos Engraved wares. The Red-rimmed and Aztatlán wares found elsewhere along the Sinaloa coast occurred in limited numbers. Ceramic cylindrical stamps, human figurines, rattles, smoking pipes, spindle whorls (incised); horn and bone tools; shell bracelets, beads, and pendants; copper bells, pendants, and wire; and chipped and ground stone implements and effigies were also recovered.

Despite the abundance of materials recovered from Culiacán, items related to the Aztatlán phenomenon were not well represented (Kelly 1945a:118–121). Nevertheless, Kelly found evidence of a "pure" Aztatlán component in the area, and Aztatlán materials were found in association with Early Culiacán I materials. Based on these findings, she concluded that an Aztatlán manifestation preceded and was partly contemporaneous with the Early Culiacán I complex.

Thus, during the 1930s the work on Mexico's northwestern coast resulted in the identification of three major cultural provinces, Guasave, Culiacán, and Chametla.

The occupational sequences developed for these three areas overlapped in part. Based on the archaeological evidence, it appears the sequences manifested at these sites fell within the Classic and Postclassic periods.

Although Kelly's Culiacán report was published in 1945, archaeological research along the northern west Mexican coast came to a standstill beginning in the 1940s and languished for more than 15 years. In the mid to late 1950s, a series of projects conducted by archaeologists from the University of California at Los Angeles (UCLA) was initiated (Nicholson and Meighan 1974). These projects included work on the coastal lowland of Nayarit as well as excavations and survey in the highlands of Jalisco. It was not until 1960, however, that the issues and questions raised by Kelly and Ekholm received renewed interest as a result of research in the highlands of Durango by J. Charles Kelley and his associates.

Excavations at the Schroeder site, a Guadiana branch Chalchihuites site near the city of Durango (Kelley 1971, 1990a; Kelley and Winters 1960; see Foster this volume), led to the recovery of a number of intrusive West Coast artifacts. Kelley and Winters (1960:559–561) undertook a detailed reassessment of the coastal data as well as an evaluation of contextual and chronological placement of the intrusive coastal assemblage at the Schroeder site. As a result, they offered revision of the coastal sequences, substituting phase names in place of general chronological designations. Although the temporal designations presented by Kelley and Winters were seen as tentative, subsequent work in the region has generally used and supported their scheme (e.g., Foster 1995a; Grosscup 1976:248–254). Kelley and Winters's work also provided independent verification of the relative sequences established by Kelly and Ekholm, and they provided the first critical review of the nature and extent of the Aztatlán phenomenon on the West Coast.

UCLA excavated in the Peñitas area (Bordaz 1964) and at Amapa (Meighan 1976) in northern Nayarit. Peñitas appears to have been occupied between ca. A.D. 400 and 1300. Three phases, the Tamarindo, Chala, and Mitlán, were defined. The report (Bordaz 1964) focuses on ceramic production. Most of the ceramics recovered exhibited strong affinities to Amapa, although some of the Chala and Mitlán phase materials showed ties to the Chametla area. Chala phase ceramics included Early Chametla Polychrome, red-rimmed utility ware, and black banded ware. The Mitlán phase is apparently early Postclassic in date, and the ceramics were similar to Lolandis, Acaponeta, and El Taste phase materials at Chametla and to Acaponeta and La Divisa phase mate-

Figure 8.13. Early Culiacán Polychrome (Kelly 1945a:Figures 20 and 25). Courtesy of the University of California Press.

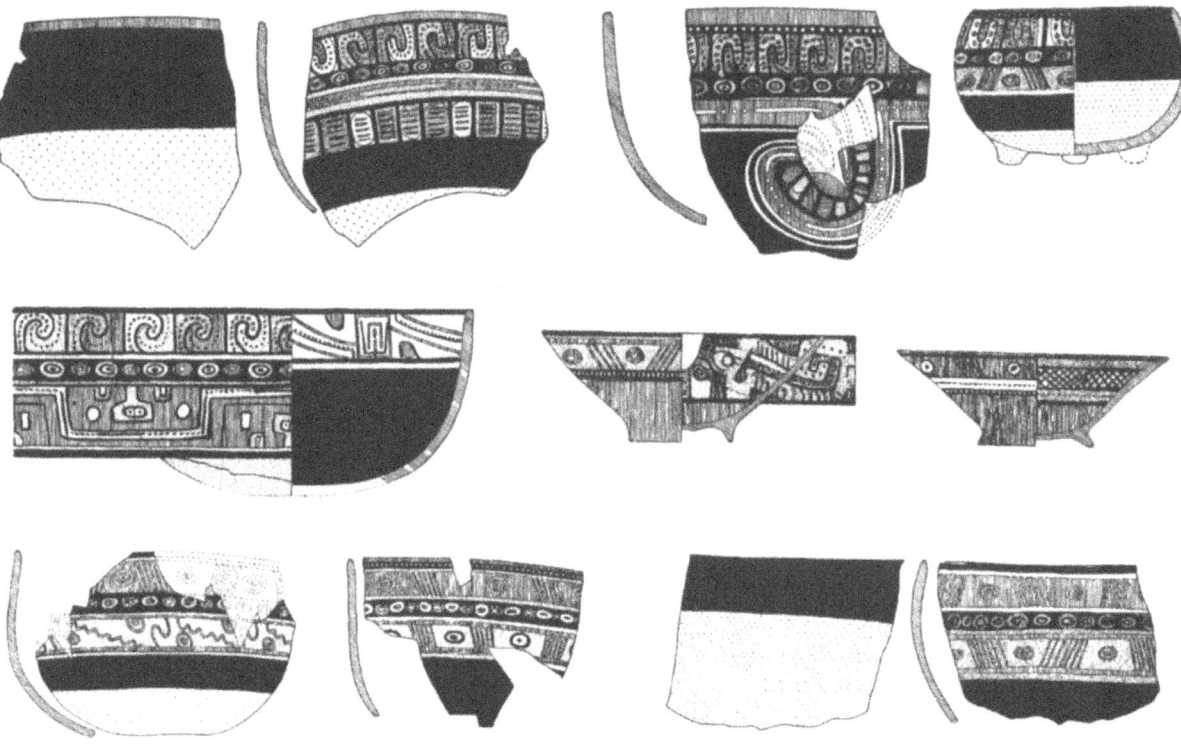

Figure 8.14. Middle Culiacán Polychrome (Kelly 1945a:Figures 32 and 34). Courtesy of the University of California Press.

Figure 8.15. Late Culiacán Polychrome (Kelly 1945a:Figures 43 and 53). Courtesy of the University of California Press.

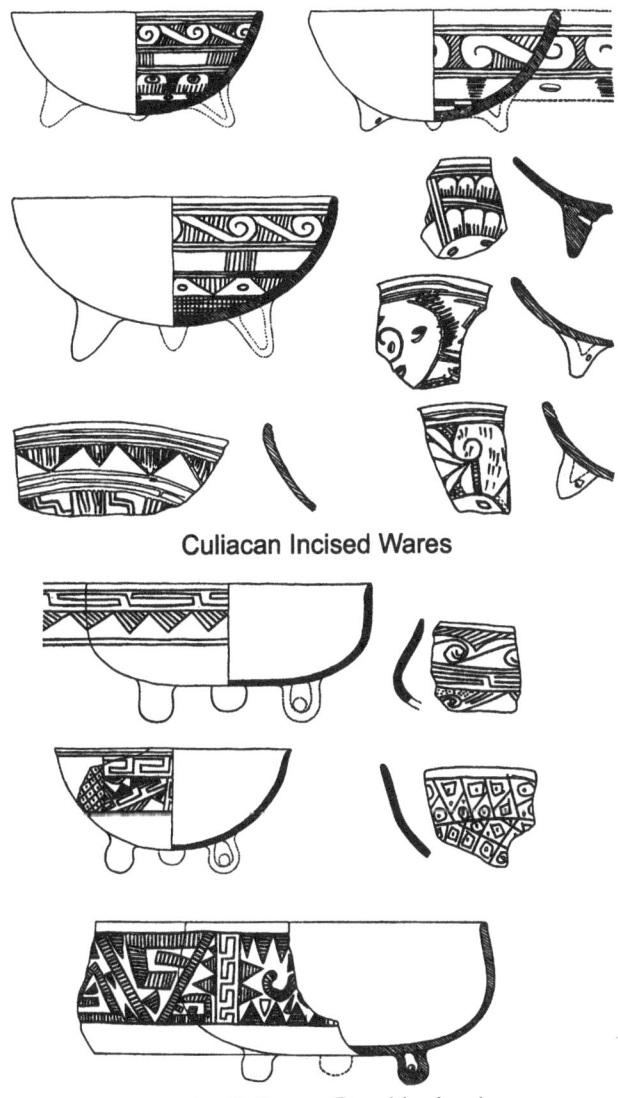

Figure 8.16. Culiacán incised wares (Kelly 1945a:Figures 20 and 25). Courtesy of the University of California Press.

rials at Culiacán. Bordaz also noted many elemental and design pattern similarities between the Peñitas materials and those of central Mexico, especially Cholula. A collection thought to have been looted from Peñitas reportedly included copper bells, an alabaster effigy jar painted with blue and gold, and several ceramic conch shells similar to some found at Teotihuacán (Bell 1971; von Winning 1956). Ceramics associated with the earlier Tamarindo phase, radiocarbon dated to A.D. 180, appear to be related to shaft tomb materials from Preclassic Nayarit.

The most extensive excavation of a single site on the West Coast was undertaken in 1959 at Amapa (Meighan 1976). The Amapa occupation generally parallels that of Chametla (Grosscup 1976). Meighan (1976), however, has offered an alternative sequence for Amapa that varies somewhat from the Chametla sequence (see Figure 8.3). The hypothetical Tuxpan and the Cerritos and Ixcuintla phases of Amapa are associated with the Aztatlán tradition.

Amapa's Aztatlán materials are abundant, varied, and elaborate. Grosscup (1976:254–264) noted many specific resemblances between the Amapa ceramic assemblage (Figures 8.17, 8.18, and 8.19) and the Aztatlán ceramics from Chametla, Guasave, and Culiacán. Also of note is the wealth of copper artifacts (Meighan 1976; Pendergast 1962b). The Amapa, Culiacán, and Guasave Aztatlán assemblages clearly indicate that the late Aztatlán tradition was quite elaborate, and when all late Aztatlán assemblages from the west coast are considered, Guasave looks less unique.

The reader is directed to Kelley's chapter in this volume for a detailed discussion of the Aztatlán tradition and to Mountjoy's chapter for an additional discussion of Amapa and developments along the central portion of the west Mexican coast. Since the Amapa excavations, the only systematic and extensive excavations to occur on the west coast north of Amapa are those undertaken in the Marismas Nacionales.

THE MARISMAS NACIONALES

The Marismas sequence comprises at least three distinct occupational phases, separated by periods of abandonment due to marine intrusion of the landscape. The latest phase, the Conchera, is Postclassic and is dated ca. A.D. 1000 to Spanish contact. It correlates stylistically and temporally with the Ixcuintla and Santiago phases at Amapa (Meighan 1976) and the El Taste phase of Chametla (Kelley and Winters 1960). As the name suggests, Conchera marks a phase of oyster midden accumulation. The oyster middens are the most numerous among several shell mound types. In the course of our survey, more than five hundred discrete shell middens (Figure 8.20) were located and measured (Shenkel 1971). They range in size from surface lenses of about 3 m in diameter to rather symmetrical mounds up to 60 m in length and 6 m high. They are generally distributed through most of the final meanders of the Teacapán Estuary (Figure 8.21) and contain abundant artifactual materials, potsherds, obsidian, and ground stone tools.

Figure 8.17. Amapa ceramic types. *a*, Tuxpan Red-on-orange; *b*, Tuxpan Engraved; *c*, Botadero Black-on-buff; *d*, Cerritos Engraved; *e–f*, Cerritos Polychrome (Meighan 1976:Plates 168, 175, 128, 130, and 131). Courtesy of the UCLA Institute of Archaeology.

Figure 8.18. Amapa ceramic types. *a,* Iguanas Polychrome; *b–d,* Ixcuintla Polychrome (Meighan 1976:Plates 133, 137, 139, and 148). Courtesy of the UCLA Institute of Archaeology.

Figure 8.19. Amapa ceramic types. *a*, Mangos Engraved; *b*, Mangos Polychrome; *c*, Santiago Engraved; *d*, Sentispac Buff; *e*, Peñitas Engraved (Meighan 1976:Plates 156, 157, 161, 165, and 169). Courtesy of the UCLA Institute of Archaeology.

Figure 8.20. A shell mound in the Marismas Nacionales.

The Estero phase is the cultural occupation of the Los Angeles Soil that developed on Middle Beach ridges between 1,500 and 1,100 years ago. This pre–oyster midden horizon, Classic in time period, produces pottery that correlates with the Amapa phase at Amapa and the Baluarte phase at Chametla. A corpus of nearly two dozen radiocarbon dates supports the assignment of Estero and Conchera phase earth and shell mounds to the Classic and Postclassic periods (Foster 1995a), respectively.

With regard to issues in the sociocultural evolution of Marismas coastal societies, during the Classic and Postclassic periods, there is little reason to doubt Meighan's (1971:755) characterization of this region as one with no dominating capital but rather a series of small city-states, each with its own political center, tributary towns, and villages such as are described in the earliest historic documents. This kind of political organization explains a feature of the region's archaeology—the fact that in delta, estuary, and floodplain regions, the sites appear to go on for kilometers. In very general terms of total subsistence economy, the presence of metates and manos, carbonized maize kernels, and cultigens in the pollen record points to agriculture as a common if not the dominant method of food procurement for both Estero and Conchera peoples. In spite of the considerable amount of shell refuse, we suspect that the oysters were probably no more than a dietary supplement to what would otherwise be a typical Precolumbian agrarian subsistence.

Earliest in the Marismas record of occupation is the El Calón phase, which takes its name from the presence of a single large shell mound, one of the three sites located near or adjacent to the northernmost meander of the Teacapán Estuary, where it broadens into the Laguna de Agua Grande (see Figure 8.21). The El Calón mound is a unique archaeological feature, remarkable for its size, height, and apparent articulated shells of the large marine pelecypod *Anadara grandis,* and is situated 13 km inland. From auger probes surrounding the site, Cottrell (1973:100) concluded that "El Calón rests upon an older alluvial surface." Subsequently, Connally

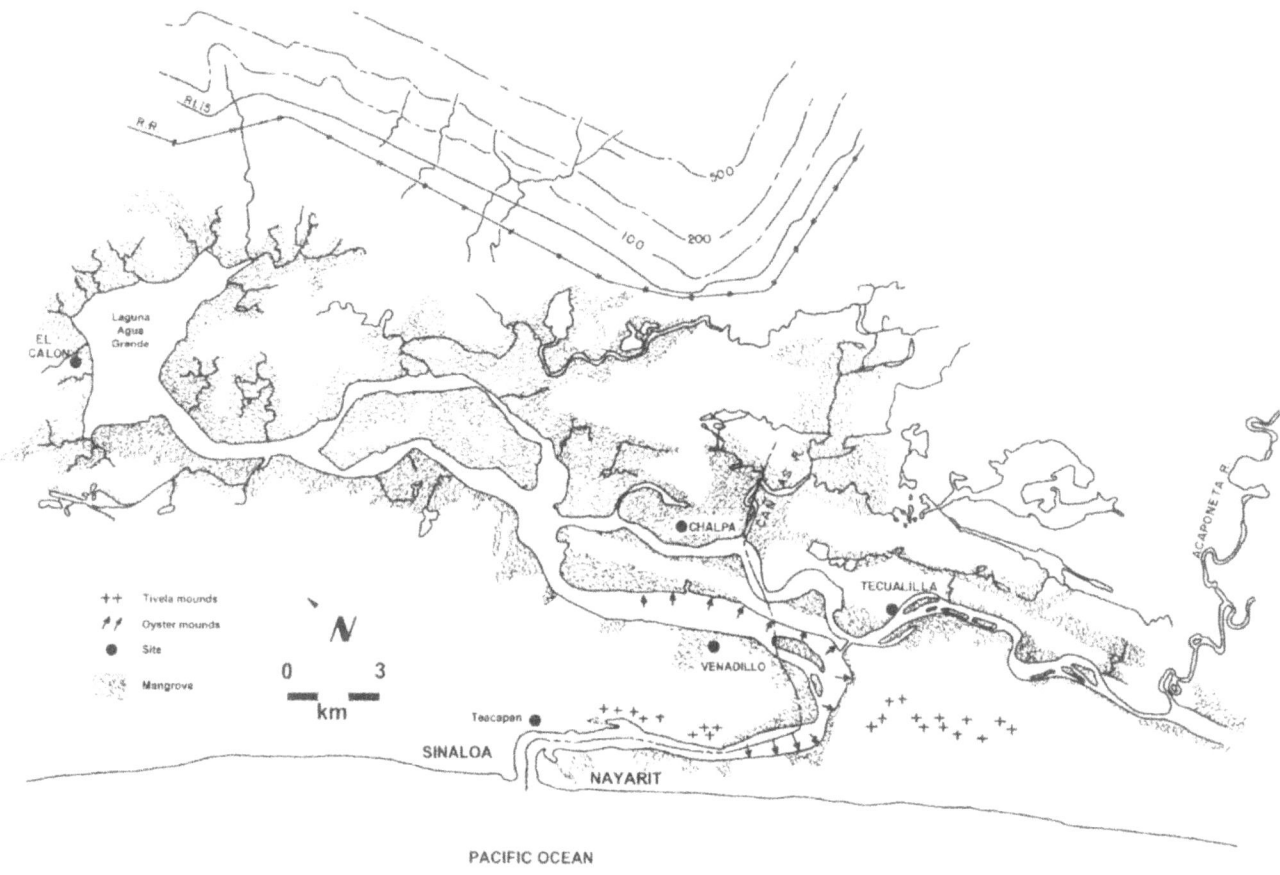

Figure 8.21. The Marismas Nacionales.

(1984a) probed the entire vicinity to reach the same conclusion, namely, that a compact shell layer at 1 to 1.25 m below the present surface, appearing in all cores, served to identify the surface on which El Calón was constructed.

No excavations have been undertaken at El Calón, but extensive observations and surface collections on the mound were made during each of four succeeding field seasons following its discovery. Hundreds of other shell mounds recorded in the Marismas were formed more or less amorphously by the discards of shellfish harvesting, though many were probably used as living surfaces. In contrast, El Calón was built by the purposeful raising of a steep-sided, semipyramidal platform mound, using live mollusks as a construction medium. Its summit was finished as a semisquared and leveled plateau that measures approximately 7 m by 10 m.

Shell samples for radiocarbon dating were taken from cleaned profiles within erosional sloughs on the mound's sloping surfaces (Connally 1984b). In all such gully walls the deposition of shell appeared to be very clean without the soil or organic accumulation that would be expected in a midden. Although there are thus no apparent mound strata, suggesting therefore a single construction period, some future penetrative excavation might well discriminate different occupations or construction phases and identify them as cultural components of a longer occupation span.

As for when construction may have occurred, we have six radiocarbon dates on three different materials from two different laboratories. The first was an organic carbon date of about 4600 B.P. from a segment of a pollen core. The sample came from a depth of about 1 m in the substrate and within 10 m of the base of the mound. Although such an early date could be thought of as setting an outside limit, we would eliminate the pollen core from consideration in the age of El Calón since it was not in direct association with the mound. That leaves us with five shell dates that average out to about 3,700 radiocarbon years, or about 1750 B.C.

Can we consider this a secure chronological placement for El Calón, in view of the problem of variations in marine shell ^{14}C values (Berger et al. 1966; Taylor 1987)? In a regime influxed by fresh water, shells are known to incorporate quantities of older dissolved carbonates—the sort of contamination that increases the radiocarbon age. Although contamination is a serious problem with shell, the problem can be circumvented by choosing only well-preserved shell samples and pretreating them by careful leaching with dilute acid to remove the outer surfaces of the shell. All such precautions were observed for the El Calón series.

One possible explanation for the early average age would be the prehistoric use of fossil shell beds for the source material. This would be an attractive explanation for those who feel that a temple-like, public works structure in the Marismas at such an early time is unlikely. In view of the number of whole, closed shells, however, we suggest that fresh shells were used. When a pelecypod mollusk dies, its valves quickly become separated as it is scavenged or wave-washed (though some of the shells of certain mudflat species may stay closed when buried in the mud).

Species diversity and habitat are other factors in the emerging environmental picture of El Calón. *Anadara grandis* appears to be the primary constituent, but other shells used in construction were obtained from a variety of ecological regimes (Shenkel 1978). The *Anadara* ribbed clam is a mangrove swamp and sandbar species, and it is only one of the molluscan species found at present in the Laguna de Agua Grande (Wing 1968:97), although its population densities are low (Snedaker 1971:16). *A. subrucosa* is a saline mudflat inhabitant; *M. niaritus* is a carnivorous conch that lives on reefs and sandy beaches. The oyster is a mangrove species, but it requires a greater salinity than present in the Laguna de Agua Grande. *C. gnidia* is found in bays and offshore to depths of 18 fathoms (Keen 1958:144). *A. tuberculosa* is a low-salinity mangrove-flat dweller. *M. patula* and *H. brassica* both inhabit intertidal beaches and sandflats to 10 m. *T. byronesis* is an intertidal sand- and mudflat species. In summary, the environments represented by the shells of El Calón include mangrove swamp, intertidal sand- and mudflats, reefs, and saline bays as well as offshore habitats. As shown (see Figure 8.2), the present topography places the Gulf of California 13 km distant overland; 5 km of this is mangrove forest. The closest oyster habitat is 28 km downstream, nearer the mouth of the estuary. Besides the lack of shells in the immediate environment to provide the raw materials for construction, Snedaker (1971:15–18) points to the inhospitable character of the mangrove environment and the buried or subsided lower portion of the mound itself, arguing that a far different microenvironmental regime existed at the time of mound construction. The suggested dating for El Calón, though not entirely useful for understanding the use dates of the mound, nevertheless allows for the very considerable time required for a change in the hydrostatic head of the estuary and the formation of barrier land between the site and the gulf shoreline.

Sirkin (1978) analyzed and described fossil pollen spectra from depositional basins, miscellaneous soils, and archaeological samples and undertook the analysis of the expected taxa from various coastal plant associations (e.g., thornforest, croplands, savanna, marshland). From Sirkin's interpretive summary, the following data are pertinent to the developing picture of El Calón.

Systematic probes found the thickest accumulation of estuarine sediments along the western and southwestern margins of the mangrove within 10 m of the El Calón shell mound. Core thicknesses ranged from 6.0 m to approximately 7.5 m, a depth attributed to a buried channel that follows the general curve of the mound before turning westward toward the ocean. All the El Calón cores (four) penetrate basal clastics (clay and sandy alluvium), above which the sediments are dominantly lagoonal silts with scattered shell fragments, very finely macerated organic debris, microfossil tests (of which Foraminifera are common), and occasional thin (1–3 cm) bands of brown peat.

Analysis of the cores at both 25-cm and 10-cm intervals revealed microfossils that vary in taxa and in pollen sums. Pollen first occurred at 6.25–6.50 m, where Gramineae (grass) and Compositae (composites) comprise 15 out of 22 specimens, along with three of *Rhizopora* (red mangrove) and one each of *Alnus* (alder) and *Urtica*. Sirkin (1978) speculates that the counts reflect low pollen influx, owing possibly to the oxidation of organics in an arid, terrestrial environment at that time. Higher in the El Calón pollen profile, mangrove becomes more abundant. At 6 m, they total 55 percent of the sum that includes red mangrove (11 percent), *Avicenna* (white mangrove—25 percent) with the *Terminalia*-type pollen included, and *Laguncularia* (black mangrove—3 percent), as well as Verbenaceae taxa (16 percent). Pollen of species associated with the lowland forests (e.g., *Caesalpina*, Sapotaceae, Myrtaceae [cf. *Eucalyptus*], and Palmae) are common, but upland and marsh species are rare.

The assemblages in higher stratigraphic zones show increases in upland species, *Pinus* (pine) and *Quercus* (oak), with red, black, and white mangrove in changing orders of dominance. Sirkin (1978) notes that the first probable specimen of a cultigen, melon (?), appears at 2.25 m and *Cucurbita* (squash) and agave occur at 1.75 m. Squash and melon reappear at 0.50 m, and in the surface sample *Zea* (maize) and the Solanaceae are abundant. The floral history suggests a fluctuating coastal plain with advances and retreats of several mangrove species, pine, oak, grasses, sedges, and so on. It seems probable that the builders of El Calón were agriculturists, but this is by no means confirmed.

El Calón is set off as a unique feature of the coast as much by its natural as by its cultural attributes. Earlier in this chapter the El Calón mound is proposed as the main referent for a phase of the same name. Realistically, the evidence from El Calón may be too fragmentary for a phase designation. The only other sites found in that region of the northernmost meander of the estuary are two broad, flat accumulations of *Anadara* valves (disarticulated), one at 0.5 km northwest of El Calón and the other at the entrance to the Laguna de Agua Grande. No artifacts were found at either location, and no radiocarbon samples were collected. If only as an occupation "marker," then, rather than a phase, El Calón nevertheless incorporates some cultural distinctions.

First and most obviously, El Calón calls attention to itself by its size and appearance—features that offer little toward an understanding of the mound's history and function but serve at least to point up the peculiarity of a temple-like mound with a summit plateau. There can be little doubt that a 25-m-high platform mound using unopened *Anadara grandis* as a construction medium was not just a heap of shell but rather an artifact of some localized sociopolitical-religious(?) behavior pattern. Unfortunately, by the time documentary evidence becomes available, particularly several enticing references to places sacred in the worship of the Totorame pantheon (Scott 1978), El Calón had been subject to nearly three thousand years of changing physical landscape. Thus, by the beginning of Europeanization, El Calón was no longer on or near the seaboard but instead was sequestered by forest and alluvium many kilometers from the coastline. Of course, the inshore position of El Calón would not preclude its later reuse as a focal point for religious associations, for example as a repository for offerings.

As if to further the idea that perhaps El Calón served, figuratively, as a place of worship, at least at some period, only a single artifact class—clay figurines—was found in association with the mound. The total figurine collection consists of 17 pieces with torso and limb fragments predominating, with one head and one almost-whole figure (Figure 8.22). Although no excavation of El Calón was attempted, the figurines were found buried in shell at the summit of the mound as a result of an inadvertent discovery from a workman's casual turning up of shells while resting at the top of the mound. The most diagnostic pieces were found at a depth of 8 to 10 cm at the southern edge of the crown of the mound. During a revisit the following year, the remaining fragments were found in the erosional scree down the south-facing slope of the mound. No sherds or other artifacts were seen.

Apart from the occurrence of a solitary artifact class in the general context of a cache, little can be said about such a small and fragmented sample. The pieces are solid and appear to be hand molded. The paste is heavily granular, giving the figurines the initial appearance of stone. Owing possibly to excessive leaching or weathering, there is little detail in the modeling beyond gross shape and size. The two pieces with faces have similar bulbous noses, and the head fragment has elongated blobs for ears and engraved slashes for eyes and mouth.

The extremely grainy paste is uncharacteristic of other figurine assemblages described for neighboring areas of west Mexico, all of which date to the Classic and Postclassic periods (e.g., Grosscup 1964, 1976; Kelly 1938; Meighan 1971, 1976). From his examination of the El Calón figurines, Warren Barbour (personal communication 1984) notes that the granular paste, the proportions, and the technique for making the eye all point to the figurines having been made in the Middle to Late Formative periods. Formative figurines from Guerrero and Oaxaca exhibit similar coarseness. The beige-gray paste color is reminiscent of the Middle and Late Formative figurines from the highland sites. The eye treatment is a common technique on the south coast and in the highlands during this period. Barbour suggests that the figurines are not comparable to those of the Gulf Coast Olmec because of differences in style and paste characteristics. He also notes that the treatment of the noses of the El Calón figurines is distinctive; these features appear as large projecting noses rather than represent prognathic faces.

Malcomb Webb (personal communication 1984) concurs in the probability of a Formative period date for these figurines. He notes that crude, solid clay figurines are dated as early as 2300 B.C. at Zohapilco and Tlapacoya in the Mexican basin (Neiderberger 1976) and figurines, in general, become relatively common

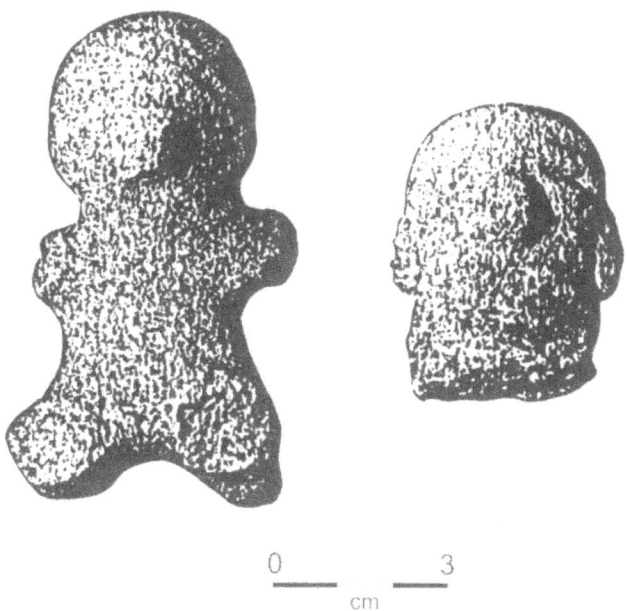

Figure 8.22. Figurine fragments from El Calón.

throughout southern Mesoamerica by 1500 B.C. (cf. Ford 1969).

Although the general resemblance of the figurines to early types would help vindicate the suggested Formative age of El Calón, they can also be seen to bear some resemblance to the figurine styles from the early part of the Chametla sequence. Kelly's solid "Bullethead" figurines (1938:Plate 15, I-l) of rough granular clay, without polish, have cylindrical heads; eyes and mouth are marked by horizontal grooves, and ears are represented in relief but never in detail (Kelly 1938:54–57).

There are, therefore, demonstrable trait affinities with both Formative figurines and those of Chametla styles that are found as concomitants of the early Classic period. No chronological significance can be assigned with confidence since such artifacts could have been deposited long after mound construction. On the other hand, the pieces found on the summit were buried at a depth of up to 10 cm, which might indicate contemporaneity of artifact and mound construction.

There is a third possibility. Kelly (1938:53–54) describes the Chametla figurine inventory in terms of several discrete stylistic groupings. Naturally, there are numbers of straggling oddments, small fragments, which cannot be placed anywhere, but her Red-face crested, Bullethead, and other distinctive figurines that are restricted to the Tierra Del Padre phase could be carryover types from an as yet undefined west Mexican Formative figurine horizon style. If so, there would be no contradiction between a Formative figurine complex at El Calón that bears considerable similarity to early Classic types from Chametla. The El Calón sample is small and the dating context tenuous, but it may yet be important in some future regionalization of early styles. This is one of many specific empirical problems in west Mexican prehistory—one that calls for a major critical review and catalog of west Mexican figurine typology. Though too small as a sample to bear reliable comparison, the occurrence of figurines is nonetheless interesting in that by the uniqueness of their appearance as an exclusive artifact class, they give the site a cultural "separateness." As we've seen, the same could be said for the mound itself, which in its height and configuration can be interpreted as an isolated case of public civic or religious architecture.

CONCLUSION

Clearly, there is much to be learned about the development of hunting-fishing-gathering societies on the west Mexican coast. Mountjoy (1990; see Mountjoy this volume) has characterized the Formative period along the West Coast as a time of adaptation to the region by people who lived in permanent settlements and depended to a significant extent on the cultivation of domestic plants. Today the area from Guaymas to Guatemala, the low, wide coastal plains of Nayarit, Sinaloa, Sonora, and the Gulf of Tehuantepec, form the major inshore fisheries of Pacific Mexico. The tidal marshes and estuaries of these areas undoubtedly offered one of the most eutrophic of coastal habitation zones in the past as well. In the intermediate area of Jalisco, Colima, and Michoacán, however, the coastal strip is more narrow and mountainous without the large tracts of marshes, estuaries, and adjoining wetlands. Thus, we might expect adaptive strategies among archaeological populations in this zone to have been different from those among peoples of other kinds of shoreline locations. The close proximity of higher ground fringing the coastal zone would have influenced mobility and subsistence as well as other social and economic strategies. Transportation would have followed the mountain river courses. This observation is not new: Kelly (1980:3), in discussing Colima's prehistory, noted that archaeological zones coincide with the major drainage systems whereas "the coastal strip of Colima seems, during certain phases, a thing apart."

The Matanchén complex, the earliest of five major archaeological complexes on the south-central coast of Nayarit and some 140 km to the south (Mountjoy 1970a; Mountjoy et al. 1972; see Mountjoy this volume), is of comparable age to that of the earliest components (El Calón) in the Marismas. The Matanchén peoples would have had access to the same general usable biomass of plants and animals as El Calonists. Present evidence, however, suggests the archaeological pattern of coastal land use is different. The Matanchén complex is known from a 3-m-thick shell deposit near the foot of a volcanic hill. At about 5 to 10 m above sea level, it is close to estuaries, a freshwater drainage channel, and the sea front. The midden contained the remains of shellfish exploited for food as well as other items, including fish, turtle and bird bones, stone flakes, and cobble implements. No pottery was recovered, however. The fact that the Matanchén site is located on high ground would account for the continued accessibility, whereas it appears that El Calón was subject to flooding and alluviation. As discussed, these processes may have submerged the occupational debris associated with El Calón and may indeed account for the eventual abandonment of El Calón itself.

Mountjoy (1970a) characterizes the Matanchén complex as the product of a "decidedly one-dimensional adaptive orientation," as an Early Formative preceramic population was attracted, perhaps through seasonal movement, to the west Mexican coast, at least partially for the abundance of its aquatic resources. Mountjoy and others (1972:1243) note that the Matanchén site is yet another link in a chain of Early Formative, preceramic shell mound deposits from California to Panama. They go on to ask to what extent these early shell midden deposits represent parallel, independent adaptations to similar ecological settings or, alternatively, a unified and specialized coastal adaptation by historically related peoples. Obviously, the answer or answers to these two postulates require far more baseline data on human use of west Mexico's coastal zones. In the context of this discussion, the question that arises is, Can we expect the Marismas research to contribute to such an inquiry?

The evidence, although limited, for developing maritime societies along the west Mexican coast suggests a number of individual evolutionary forms that responded to their biophysical and perhaps their social environment. For the Early Formative period within the Marismas, we find a low-density *Anadara* mound group, dominated by the El Calón mound. However, until more basic issues are resolved, ones of stratigraphy and context, and more information is available, the reconstitution of Early Formative life in the Marismas can only be guessed at. Were the builders of El Calón transient visitors to the coast? If not, and if instead they were permanent settlers, as the finding of cultigen grains suggests, would the community pattern be substantially different from that of other Formative period shoreline dwellers or later coastal occupants?

As with other areas along the coast, the best evidence for a Formative period occupation may lie buried by a mix of fluvial-marine deposits of the Marismas. The history of the Marismas alluvial plain was clearly punctuated by periods of submergence, one of which, Middle Beach progradation, accounts for a gap in the human occupation of the area. Furthermore, after the building of the El Calón shell mound, it became the victim of a protracted interval of environmental instability, the consequence of which was the truncation of whatever coastal tradition the El Calonists had evolved.

Because of the presence of the ceramic figurine fragments from El Calón, it cannot be said with absolute certainty that the mound was constructed during preceramic times. But if the figurines were cached long after its construction, El Calón, like Matanchén, may also be an artifact of a preceramic horizon. Thus, it is possible that the archaeological record of the Marismas may someday reveal a similar maintenance strategy as well as other common factors in coastal adaptation between El Calón and Matanchén.

El Calón appears to be at least somewhat unique on the west Mexican coast in that it seems to represent the consumptive use of shell that is not in any way comparable to the exploitation and disposition of shellfish elsewhere on the coast. Nor does it appear to bear any relationship, in cultural terms, to other sites even within the Marismas itself. And what of its associative and symbolic importance? Assigning ritualistic behavior or inferring sociopolitical organization is risky, even on the basis of more complete archaeological information. A long-held point of view is that the natural beneficence of certain coastline environments was recognized very early by aboriginal populations—people who adapted themselves, either as permanent strand loopers or as seasonal tenants only, with restricted maritime-lagoonal economies. It is also assumed that they were more or less culturally homogeneous, with unstructured, egalitarian access to the vast array of aquatic resources of coastal Mexico. Could the appearance and practice of a horticultural economy on the northwest coast of Mexico coincide with any new order change, visible in the archaeological record? In that connection, one assumption that might underlie continuing investigations of El Calón is the notion that public structures are not common in egalitarian society. If El Calón did function as an important Formative ceremonial center, we can only point to its size and special circumstances as implying an "institutionalized" expression not yet reported elsewhere on the west Mexican littoral.

CHAPTER NINE

THE AZTATLÁN MERCANTILE SYSTEM

Mobile Traders and the Northwestward Expansion of Mesoamerican Civilization

J. CHARLES KELLEY

IT IS GENERALLY agreed that mesoamerican civilization expanded from its nuclear area toward west and northern Mexico, but precisely when, by what means, and how far this movement extended remain controversial points. Cultural expansion during the Preclassic and Classic periods certainly brought the mesoamerican cultural tradition into western Mexico, to the area of the Tropic of Cancer in north-central Mexico, and to coastal Jalisco, Nayarit, and probably Sinaloa. This discussion, however, is concerned with the cultural or ethnic movements that took place primarily during the Postclassic and largely by the West Coast and highland Durango routes. The central interest lies not only in tracing the development of the Aztatlán Mercantile System (Kelley 1986a) and clarifying the part it played in this expansion but also in exploring the cultural processes involved.[1]

Various theoretical concepts are used here, including the gateway community (Hirth 1978), ecocultural interfaces (where two ecological zones or two identifiable cultures meet), geographic corridors (Sauer 1932), interaction spheres (Friedel 1979; Jiménez Betts 1992a; Kelley 1974), and especially the concept of mobile traders (Kelley 1986a). Other concepts and hypotheses regarding long-distance trade have been examined and used to the extent that they apply to the specific problems involved here.

This discussion is essentially hypothetical in nature, based on known archaeological data with support from ethnohistorical sources. The illustrations, for the most part, are to be regarded as diagrams. The trade connections shown approximate known geographic corridors and are depicted only as direct lines. Chronology is based on available dates, which are relatively few and often in conflict. These are also regarded, at best, as approximations.

Notably, what is known of the activities of mobile traders in Mexico comes primarily from the ethnohistorical sources and involves their activities in relation to trade between established mesoamerican communities. Their activities can be inferred from the archaeological record as well, however; an example is the probable co-occupation of the Cañón del Molino site in Durango by potters of both the Chalchihuites and West Coast schools (Ganot R. and Peschard F. 1990, 1995; Ganot R. et al. 1983; Kelley 1986a).

Some of the best ethnohistorical data on mobile traders comes from Lumholtz's (1902:2:367–370) description of Tarascan mobile traders (*huacaleros*) who, as late as 1895, were still carrying on extensive short- and long-distance trade on foot (Figure 9.1). In 1895, Lumholtz questioned at length two of these traders and actually weighed one trader and his load (pottery). This trader weighed 70 kilos; his load weighed 63 kilos; and

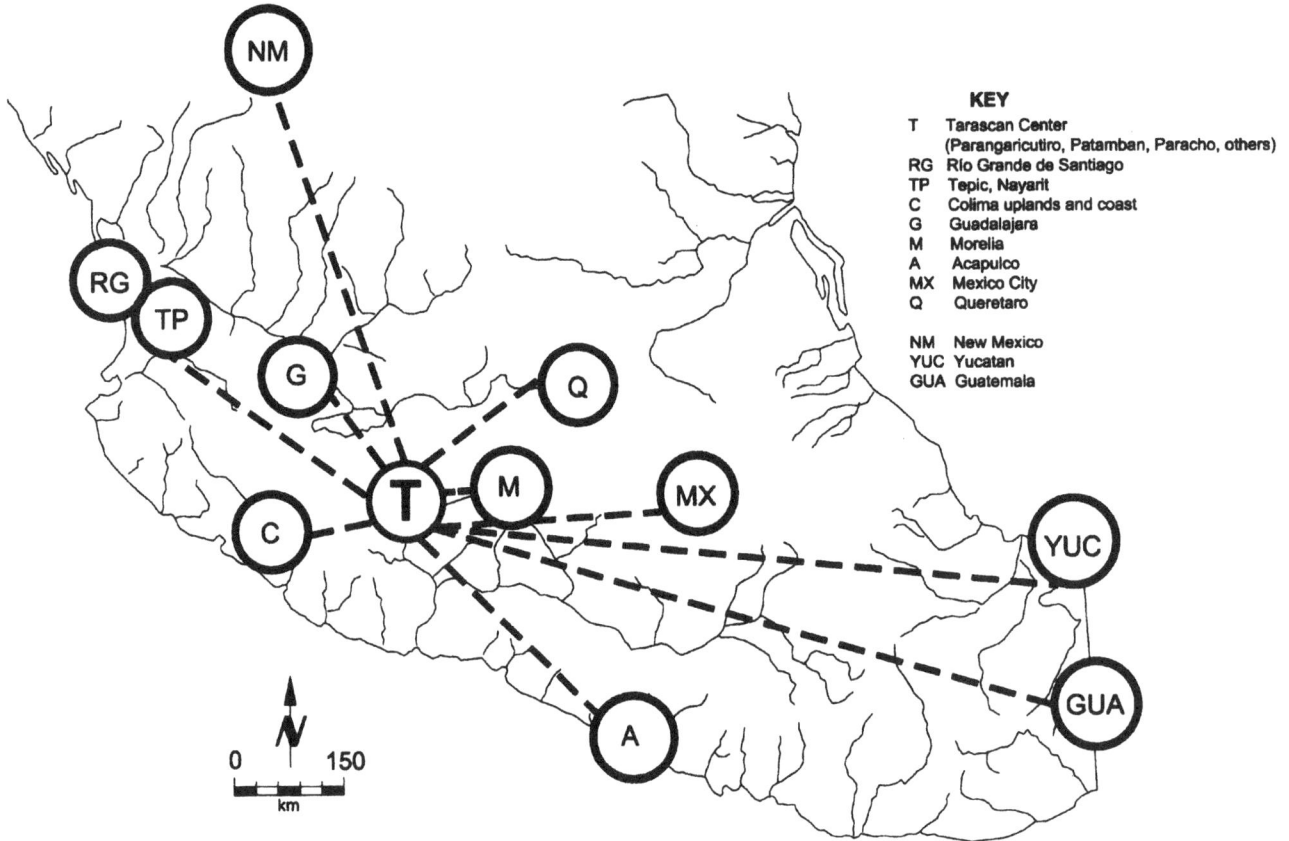

Figure 9.1. Trading trips of Tarascan mobile traders recorded in 1895.

he had been a *huacalero* for 35 years. He was able to compete with pack mules by walking twice as far each day, 30 or 40 miles, as a loaded mule. This, of course, is internal travel between established towns, not trade into the hinterland. Nevertheless, the example provides valuable data regarding the load and days' travel of mobile traders—much larger and farther than the speculations of some archaeologists would have us believe (see Drennan 1984a, 1984b). Notably, the *huacaleros* did not "consume" the commodities (in this instance, pottery) they carried; instead, they lived off the land and local hospitality.[2]

The Lumholtz observations are reinforced by data regarding the *tlamemes* (cargo carriers) in the historic period: "Thus, tlamemes, less hindered by terrain and less dependent on roads, served [such remote] areas" (Hassig 1985:265). Furthermore, Bunzel (1959:30) notes: "If Europeans hire bearers through special channels, they set 80 pounds as a limit, but Indians on their own business sometimes carry as much as 150 pounds, or more. A day's journey on mountain trails with burdens is reckoned at 6–7 leagues" (see Hassig 1985:288 n. 42). Tlamemes, who had been used by the pochteca as porters in pre-Spanish times, continued to work in the historic period even with competition from pack-mule drivers (*arrieros*) and wagon drivers (*carreteros*). Such data indicate that long-distance travel by mobile traders, using porters, in Postclassic times was entirely feasible. Indeed, archaeological data indicate the existence of many such long-distance trade routes in the Classic period. Classic period trade between Teotihuacán and Kaminaljuyu (Kidder et al. 1977) is well documented, as is that between Tula and Central America in the Postclassic (Diehl et al. 1974).

As Mesoamerica expanded in population and area, frontier settlements developed on the ecological/cultural interfaces between "civilized" and "Chichimec" peoples.[3] Essentially, such settlements represent the "gateway communities" of Hirth (1978). Mobile traders seem to have been most effective in working out of these peripheral mesoamerican settlements into the unknown lands beyond the frontier, forming a dendritic market network, or "trade diaspora" (Curtin 1986:2 n. 2), and locating areas of surplus commodities and other valuable goods for exploitation to meet the ever-growing needs of the populations of nuclear areas. These mobile traders were, in many ways, analogous to the "vanguard merchants" of the Aztec, about whom Sahagún wrote (Bandelier 1932; Coon 1950:443): "These merchants traveled over the whole land, bartering, trading, buying in some places and selling in another.... They also travel through towns, along the seashore, and in the interior. There isn't a place they do not pry into and visit, here buying, there selling."

BACKGROUND

In 1932, Carl Sauer commented on the existence of a significant cultural and geographic corridor that had both historical depth and an environmental basis: "The land passage through northwestern New Spain was mostly one great arterial highway.... From the densely peopled lands of central Mexico a road led by way of the coastal lowlands of the Mexican Northwest to the northern land of the Pueblo Indian ... here called the Road to Cibola." Sauer's (1932:3) map shows this road extending from the vicinity of Guadalajara through western Jalisco to the coastal area and continuing along the Nayarit-Sinaloa coastal strip into Sonora and beyond; significantly, the main railway line and highway today follow this same route. Sauer and Brand (1932:1), in that same year, published the results of their archaeological survey of the coastal strip, showing that there was archaeological depth to the route and that, in fact, one archaeological culture, which they called "Aztatlán," extended along the entire coastal strip.

Subsequently, such archaeologists as Isabel Kelly, Gordon Ekholm, Clement Meighan, Joseph Mountjoy, and Stuart Scott excavated a series of coastal sites in Sinaloa, Nayarit, and Jalisco, confirming the existence of the Aztatlán culture. Kelley and Winters (1960) revised the coastal sequence based on the presence of West Coast ceramics in stratified contexts at the Schroeder site in Durango. They argued for the division of the Aztatlán culture into Early and Late periods; this usage is followed in the present discussion. At the time of Spanish contact, the Jalisco-Nayarit-Sinaloa coastal strip was heavily populated, and large towns such as Aztatlán and Culhuacán (Culiacán) controlled many smaller towns. There were markets in all the towns, and the Culhuacán market was especially large. Significantly, cotton was reported to have been grown, and cotton textiles (*mantas* for men and *camisas* for women) were sold in the markets, providing clothing for the population (Sauer and Brand 1932:51–54).

Archaeologically, the presence of pottery spindle whorls in numbers in both Early and Late Aztatlán culture sites verifies the importance of weaving. Throughout Mesoamerica, clothing, especially cotton clothing, was in high demand. Hence, the region of coastal Jalisco-Nayarit-Sinaloa was a rich source for a commodity in great demand in the trade structure. Smoking pipes possibly appeared late in Early Aztatlán sites and were numerous in Late Aztatlán sites. That they were used for smoking tobacco seems virtually certain, but there are no conclusive data to support this statement. Pipes themselves became a new item in mesoamerican trade, and their use spread rapidly in the Postclassic; tobacco may have become a new product in high demand. At about A.D. 800–900, or perhaps as early as A.D. 650 according to Hosler and Mcfarlane (1996), metallurgy (copper, bronze, and gold) appeared in west Mexico and the Jalisco-Nayarit-Sinaloa strip (Hosler 1988a, 1988b; Meighan 1969; Mountjoy 1969). Metal artifacts of this complex, principally copper bells, needles, and earplugs, have been found along the south shore of Lake Chapala at Tizapan el Alto, Jalisco (Meighan and Foote 1968), at Cojumatlán, Michoacán (Lister 1949), and at other sites.

Such artifacts were well distributed along the West Coast at Amapa, Nayarit (Meighan 1976; Pendergast 1962a, 1962b), Culiacán in Sinaloa (Kelly 1945b), and Guasave in Sinaloa (Ekholm 1942), among other sites. Metal artifacts appeared in several Durango highland sites, including the Schroeder site (Kelley 1971:790), Navacoyan (Lazalde 1987), Cañón del Molino (Ganot R. and Peschard F. 1995), Cerro Hervideros, and El Zape. Metallurgy was present also at the great city of Paquimé (Casas Grandes) in Chihuahua (Di Peso et al. 1974) and at related sites. The distribution of metallurgy in western and northern Mexico appears to have corresponded approximately to the distribution of Aztatlán Mercantile System sites (and to Tarascan sites). Metallurgy quickly spread throughout west Mexico and most of Postclassic Mesoamerica, however, and as trade or trader insignia into the American Southwest as well (Hosler and Macfarlane 1996; Kelley 1995).

Turquoise also continued to be a luxury item involved in trade from the American Southwest into Mesoamerica. Cacao may have been available on the Jalisco coast. The

West Coast area was accordingly a rich procurement zone; clearly, there was ample reason for the cultures of the area to become involved in a major mercantile system extending into nuclear Mesoamerica.

THE MIXTECA-PUEBLA CONNECTION

The Mixteca-Puebla Complex is a Postclassic association of specific pottery styles, iconography, religion, and codex illustrations known to have originated in the Mixteca-Puebla areas in core Mesoamerica. Nicholson (1960, 1982), Nicholson and Keber (1994), Lind (1994), and McCafferty (1994) provide excellent descriptions and discussions of the concept and the history of its origin, characteristics, and distribution in time and space. Lind (1994:92–98, see esp. Tables 4, 5, 6 and Figures 23–26) provides a detailed breakdown of the design motifs characteristic of Mixteca-Puebla art in Oaxaca and Cholula.

Like other such broad cultural concepts, that of Mixteca-Puebla has had many supporters and some critics (Smith and Heath-Smith 1980). But the concept appears to be well founded in both Early and Late Postclassic periods. Because a variant of the artistic style and iconography spread from Cholula to Culhuacán and associated localities in the Valley of Mexico as Aztec I, the Mixteca-Puebla concept is of special value in this study. Nicholson and Keber note, regarding its widespread dispersal in Late Postclassic Mesoamerica (1994:xiv): "Long-range commercial activity is one of the most frequently invoked [causes]. The importance of extensive trading networks in Mesoamerica is evidenced by abundant ethnohistorical and archaeological data. The cultural ramifications of the contacts between diverse groups resulting from these commercial exchanges could well have included some degree of stylistic transmission and adoption."

In his excavations at Guasave, located on the northern Sinaloa coast, Ekholm (1942:125–132) identified, as part of the Aztatlán culture, a large number of traits that, taken together, represent a more or less cohesive assemblage, which he attributed to an origin in the Mixteca-Puebla culture of nuclear Mesoamerica. So close was the similarity that Ekholm believed that an actual migration of Mixteca-Puebla people must have occurred. However, Ekholm's list also included a number of traits from various places in nuclear Mesoamerica that usually are not considered specifically Mixteca-Puebla. On the other hand, Fahmel Beyer (1988:148) verifies the Mixteca-Puebla (and Aztec I–II) identification of the ceramics but points out that some ceramic vessel forms in the complex were derived from Tohil Plumbate and Fine Orange, widely traded types that are rare or not known to occur in Sinaloa north of the Marismas Nacionales.

At the Schroeder site (Structure 1, Río Tunal phase), I found a footed cylindrical Sinaloa Polychrome (Guasave) jar decorated on the exterior with three circular medallions, each containing a clear codex-style depiction of a god.[4] J. Eric Thompson identified the gods represented (Kelley 1986a). Significantly, one of the gods illustrated was Xochipilli; the "Xochipilli" theme is thought to be of Mixtec origin and later borrowed by the Aztecs (Nicholson 1982:240). The god illustrated in the two other panels was identified as Nanautzin (Nanahuatl), who also belonged to the Xochipilli complex (Nicholson 1971:Table 3). Both the codex style representations and the depiction of the gods support Ekholm's Mixteca-Puebla identification of the Guasave complex.

The age of the Mixteca-Puebla complex has also been the subject of much controversy. Mountjoy and Peterson (1973:30) have published a corrected radiocarbon date of A.D. 1250 ± 95 from a Late Postclassic deposit at Cholula that contained a high percentage of various Cholula polychrome sherds, which should be part of the Mixteca-Puebla complex (Mountjoy 1990:541–542). Other radiocarbon dates from Cholula suggest that the early Postclassic Mixteca-Puebla ceramics there should date from ca. A.D. 950–1150, and others suggest an A.D. 1150–1450, or later, date for the Late Postclassic (Lind 1994:Table 1, 81 n. 1). Meighan (1971:767) obtained a corrected radiocarbon date of A.D. 1220 ± 130 years for a specimen from the original Guasave excavations. In the Marismas Nacionales, on the Nayarit-Sinaloa border, Scott obtained uncorrected radiocarbon dates of A.D. 965 (Panales), A.D. 1132 (Tecualilla), and A.D. 1273 (Rincón de Panal) (Gill 1985:195). Although the use of such isolated radiocarbon dates is tenuous, they nevertheless fall into what appears to be the appropriate range. Thus, it appears that dates of A.D. 950–1150, perhaps even A.D. 900, for early Postclassic Mixteca-Puebla (and Early Aztatlán) and A.D. 1150–1350, or as late as A.D. 1400 or 1500, for the fully developed Mixteca-Puebla complex (and Late Aztatlán) would be generally acceptable (see Nicholson 1982:243–244).

Subsequent archaeological research has identified complexes of traits similar to those from Guasave at Amapa (Meighan 1976), Culiacán (Kelly 1945b), and other West Coast sites and at highland sites along the lower Río Lerma and the south shore of Lake Chapala, at Etzatlán, at Tomatlán, and along the Jalisco-Nayarit coast. At a number of these sites, the Mixteca-Puebla complex is represented only by Aztec I (Culhuacán Black-on-orange, Cocoyotla Black-on-natural, and Culhuacán Polychrome) ceramic designs and iconography, usually present on local wares, and is associated with copper artifacts. Aztec I pottery is especially well represented at Culhuacán (Sejourné 1970) in the Valley of Mexico and at Cholula (Noguera 1965:104). Parsons (1976:95) notes: "Moreover several writers, ourselves included, have felt that the Aztec I assemblage was a southern Basin of Mexico tradition whose origins are closely tied with the Cholula ceramic tradition." Its iconography is clearly of Mixteca-Puebla affiliation, and its decorative style and iconography are markers along the Aztatlán Mercantile System route (Kelley 1986a:83-92). Notably, at the Spanish contact, Cholula was the center of major mesoamerican trade routes, a premier religious center, and a pilgrimage center (Lind 1994:97). Díaz del Castillo (1956:181) wrote of Cholula: "They make very good pottery in the city of red and black and white clay with various designs, and with it supply Mexico and all the neighboring provinces." (See further the discussion below.) The presence of diagnostic items, including ceramics and iconographic elements, of one cultural entity at another such entity is here considered evidence of direct contact, probably by mobile merchants.

STATEMENT OF THE HYPOTHESIS

Given a lineal distribution of related archaeological traits in diverse components along a geographic corridor (river valley, coastal strip, mountain pass, etc.), it may be inferred that a trade route is represented. The distribution may not have been strictly lineal, because local trade around each component would have given some width to the route and the geographic corridor it followed. Continued development through time tied shorter routes together into one long chain characterized by (1) the presence of similar stylistic and iconographic elements in all trade route components, (2) the presence of luxury items and other commodities in high demand in the components and at the point of origin in the core area, (3) evidence for origin of the entire route in an area of large population and a high demand market, and (4) terminus of the combined routes in one or more dendritic networks (or trade diasporas) extending from gateway communities into hinterland procurement areas. Given these criteria, it may be said that the trade routes had become organized into a mercantile system. This does not mean necessarily that a formally organized institution had been created by some central entity; instead, long use of the route may have created an operational custom that became semiformalized.

Travel along the various segments of the system may have combined land and water transport.[5] Bulky goods did not necessarily require long-distance transportation because they may have changed hands at regular points along the geographic route. Hassig (1985:145) describes the Spanish and Precolumbian situation: "Primary transport was by means of *tlamemes*, a low-status hereditary occupational group whose members engaged in lifelong portage. Based on the main town, or *cabecera*, of a political district, they carried burdens from their cabecera to the next, where other tlamemes picked up the load, thus transporting it for great distances in relay fashion." The tlamemes would do the principal portage for the merchants.

Low-value commodities may have moved between two or more points on the route where demand was great, but only luxury goods or other valuable commodities would move from point of origin to ultimate destination (Wilcox 1986a:143). Hodder (1980:152) makes the point specifically: "In the first case, exchange is of higher value and less bulky materials, often being passed on many steps as in the random walk model. In the second case, exchange is of bulky or low-value items which are moved few steps from the source." Geographically lengthy systems have a high vulnerability; failure of any of the component links would interrupt the system and cause its disintegration into the original local trade routes.

In long-established trade situations, the commercial interaction would take place between elites (prestige exchange). But in developing trade relationships between gateway communities and hinterland hamlets, the recipient contacts probably were not elites; rather, the continued commercial relations eventually produced elites in such communities.

The original trade contacts in the recipient community may have been made by wandering hunter-gatherers visiting the gateway community or, alternatively, by mobile traders spreading out to discover hinterland villages, perhaps making initial contacts with "marginal persons" (Barnett 1953:380). These marginal persons, because of their low status and dissatisfaction with their own community, may have become willing receptors in such contacts, and ironically, through their relations with the outside traders, these marginal persons may eventually have emerged as the elites in their community. Intermarriage between traders and hinterland villagers would have cemented the relationship and brought about further extension of the mesoamerican frontier.

THE AZTATLÁN MERCANTILE SYSTEM: ANTECEDENTS

If the Late Aztatlán route is divided into segments, it is clear that nearly all of them participated in earlier regional trade routes during the Classic, and some during the Preclassic period. Chupícuaro clearly had such contacts along the Río Lerma and into the Valley of Mexico during the Preclassic period. In the segment from Lake Chapala to Nayarit, Weigand and associates have demonstrated that the Teuchitlán tradition polity was the center of a widespread trade diaspora in obsidian during the late Preclassic and early Classic periods (Weigand and Spence 1982). Later, in the Terminal Classic and Early Postclassic, there is considerable evidence for the presence of a trade route extending from the Valley of Mexico along the Río Lerma through the Bajío to Nayarit, with a branch extending to the Tomatlán Valley and along the Jalisco coast northward into Nayarit (Mountjoy 1993a). This branch became incorporated quite early into the Aztatlán trade system.

This branch of the Aztatlán system presents special problems. Mountjoy (1990:541–542) noted that there were available 24 radiocarbon dates associated "principally" with Aztatlán artifacts from eight sites. These dates covered a 1-sigma range of A.D. 883–1400.[6] Recently, Mountjoy (1993a) has presented a comprehensive overview in which he divides the Aztatlán sites in a region extending from Tomatlán and along the Jalisco coast to the Río Grande de Santiago into an early Colonial Aztatlán tradition and a later (but overlapping) Derived Aztatlán tradition. Superficially, these periods should correspond to Early and Late Aztatlán periods as used in this discussion. In addition to the radiocarbon dates previously cited, which he assigns to his Colonial Aztatlán tradition deposits, he has four dates from the Banderas Valley ranging from A.D. 1070 to A.D. 1160. From the Derived Aztatlán tradition in the Tomatlán Valley there is one radiocarbon date of A.D. 1020–1250. This group of dates does not correspond well to the dates tentatively assigned to the Late Aztatlán period or to the late Mixteca-Puebla dates for the Valley of Mexico.

There Aztec I ceramics are dated to the Second Intermediate, Phase III: A.D. 1150–1350 (Sanders et al. 1979: 149–153).

Mountjoy (1982a, 1990, 1993a; see Mountjoy this volume) describes ceremonial and civic centers for this tradition located in practically every coastal river valley between Tomatlán and the Río Grande de Santiago. There was intensive agriculture, many spindle whorls (suggesting the production [?] and use of cotton), molcajetes (presence of chili?), copper metallurgy, and ball courts. Smoking pipes were not found, however. Decorated ceramics have elaborate designs normally associated with the Mixteca-Puebla complex, but Mountjoy is dubious about any relationship, suggesting instead that these were widespread mesoamerican elements, possibly of Toltec origin. Mazapan figurines and plumbate pottery were found. The general impression of the Aztatlán culture revealed in this area is indeed one of colonization rather than one of traders passing through local centers.

Mountjoy's Derived Aztatlán tradition appears to have been a development out of the preceding period with considerable expansion of population and area. The cited radiocarbon date of A.D. 1020–1250 was reported as representing a fully developed Derived Aztatlán tradition. Mountjoy believes this phase survived into the early Spanish contact period. Cotton, chili (molcajetes), and cacao were grown; there was evidence of irrigation and of salt production. The decorated pottery described does not seem to have Aztatlán or Mixteca-Puebla elements. In no way does the Derived tradition correspond to the Late Aztatlán period as discussed here. In the light of concerns raised here regarding Mountjoy's reconstruction, it is important to note that more recently (see Mountjoy this volume) Mountjoy has abandoned the terms Colonial Aztatlán and Derived Aztatlán. His Colonial Aztatlán tradition is now referred to as Aztatlán, and his Derived Aztatlán tradition is now viewed as a post-Aztatlán period. These revisions allay some of the concerns raised above.

Aside from the Tomatlán-Banderas section, incorporation of the various trade route segments, probably at Amapa (Meighan 1976), marked the development of the full Aztatlán Mercantile System. An earlier "Toltec" trade route, reported as having existed along the lower Río Lerma to Amapa segment, marked by Mazapan type figurines and plumbate ceramics (Meighan 1976:69, 160, Plate XXIII), probably was actually the early Postclassic Mixteca-Puebla route. Likewise, the segment extending through the Durango highlands followed an earlier tur-

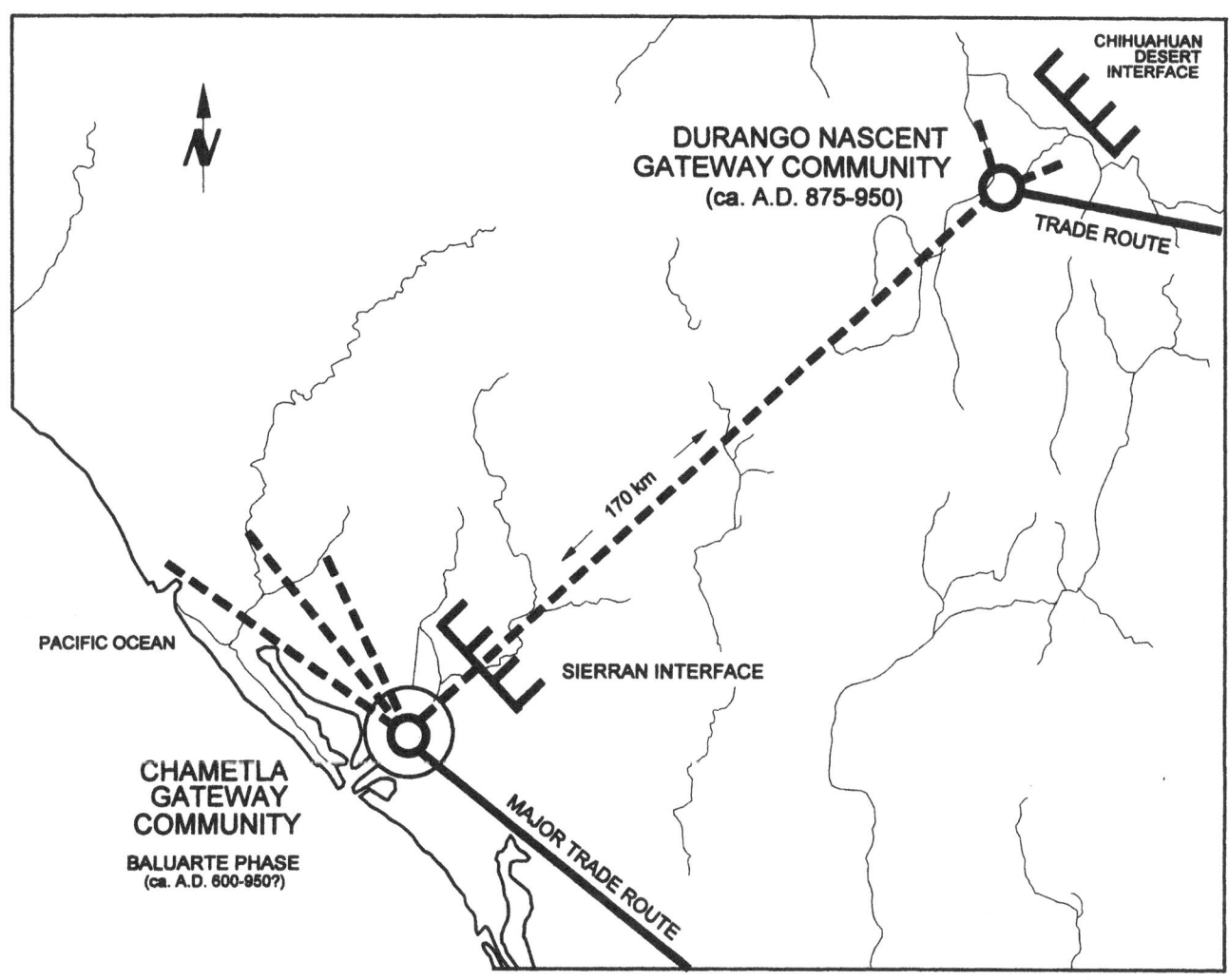

Figure 9.2. Late Classic period expansion of West Coast mobile traders into the uplands of Durango.

quoise trade route extending into the American Southwest during the Classic (and probably during the Early Postclassic).

In order to demonstrate the processes involved in the formation of the Early Aztatlán trade diaspora and the part it played in the extension of mesoamerican territory northward, I use Chametla in southern Sinaloa (Kelly 1938; Kelley and Winters 1960) as a gateway community. During the late Classic period (Tierra del Padre phase), Chametla was founded on the Río Baluarte; its origins are obscure, but there are some ties with the Gavilán phase at Amapa. The coastal area to the north formed a hinterland, as did the great Sierra Madre Occidental to the northeast.

During the succeeding Baluarte phase, Chametla traders expanded northwestward up the coast as far as Mazatlán, and, more striking, they succeeded in breaking through the Sierran Interface into the highlands of Durango (Figure 9.2).[7] There they encountered a reduced mesoamerican occupation. Toward the end of the Chalchihuites occupation of western Zacatecas, at the ceremonial center of Alta Vista and in associated villages, a reduced Calichal phase developed. There is evidence of a major emigration of Chalchihuites villagers out of the Río Suchil area into the Guadiana Valley in Durango.[8] It is possible, however, that the Calichal phase itself may have developed much earlier in the Durango area as a reduced copy of the florescent Alta Vista phase at Alta Vista.

The earliest Chalchihuites occupation at the Schroeder site in Durango was the Ayala phase, which was essentially identical to the Calichal phase. In Ayala phase deposits, a number of Baluarte phase artifacts were excavated. Sherds of seven different Chametla ceramic types, Chametla White Filleted figurines, and small engraved ceramic spindle whorls were recovered (Kelley and Winters 1960:551). At the Schroeder site, therefore, West Coast traders had made contact with Chalchihuites refugees (or neighbors) and had encountered the Chalchihuites-Chichimec interface as well.

Curiously, no Chalchihuites artifacts were found in Chametla deposits, nor have any been identified in excavations from later West Coast sites or in collections from the area. What had Baluarte phase traders brought to Durango, over more than 170 km of mountain terrain, in the pottery vessels represented? And what had the traders transported back to the West Coast in return? Here we are concerned with a well-known ecocultural situation—coastal lowlands versus highlands, each in possession of different natural and cultural resources (Foster 1993).

The pottery itself may have been the principal trade item, but the Chalchihuites people had their own well-developed ceramic tradition, so this explanation seems unlikely. Spindle whorls found suggest that West Coast cotton had been brought to Durango, together with implements to spin it. The presence of Chametla figurines may indicate the introduction of new religious ideas into Durango.

Otherwise, there can be only speculation. What were the products available to Chametla but not found in the Durango highlands? Seashells certainly, and quite possibly seawater (for use in rituals), salt, dried shrimp, smoked fish, oysters, other mollusks, pearls (?), possibly cacao and tobacco, and transportable tropical fruits. Even agricultural products may have been traded if the Durango demand was sufficient. And what went back in return? It may be suggested that minerals, *chalchihuitl* carvings, and Chichimec products from the adjacent Chihuahuan Desert, such as dried buffalo meat (jerky), animal skins, and varieties of wild plants, including peyote, cactus tunas, and agave and sotol cabbages, none of which would require ceramic vessels for their transport. Slaves, from the Chichimeca, may also have been traded. Perhaps future excavations, using developed technology for obtaining and identifying plant and fruit remains, will provide the answers.

No evidence suggests that the Baluarte phase trade was extended generally beyond the Guadiana Valley, but the Sierran interface had been pierced and later cross-Sierran trade would be more intense with the advent of the Early Aztatlán traders.

THE AZTATLÁN MERCANTILE SYSTEM: THE EARLY AZTATLÁN DEVELOPMENT (CA. A.D. 900/950–1150)

At the end of the Baluarte phase (Middle Chametla) at Chametla, there was a marked change in ceramics, but some continuity is evident. The new ceramic association there has been termed the Lolandis phase by Kelley and Winters (1960:560, Figure 8); it is the earliest of two related phases that make up the Early Aztatlán period. During this phase, component traits spread rapidly northwest up the coastal strip to approximately the Sonora border, appearing especially well developed at Culiacán and Guasave. Aztatlán elements in the Chametla and northern Sinaloa sites belonged, at least in part, to the pan-Sinaloa Acaponeta phase. This phase represents the pan-Sinaloa extension of the Early Aztatlán period occupation (Figure 9.3).

The diagnostic ceramics of the Lolandis phase included especially Lolandis Red-Rim (Red-Rim decorated); a local development of this ware from the earlier omnipresent Red-Rimmed utility ware seems likely. In higher stratigraphic levels at Chametla, "Aztatlán ware" was found in association with Lolandis Red-Rim. Kelley and Winters (1960) named this association the Acaponeta phase; it represents the pan-Sinaloa extension of the Early Aztatlán period. Wares equivalent to Lolandis have been given different names in the northern sites, especially the Red-on-buff of Guasave, Aguaruto Incised, and perhaps Aguaruto Polychrome, Cerro Izabal, Navalato Polychrome, and Black-on-buff. Essentially, however, complexes containing only Lolandis Red-Rim (and its red-on-buff equivalents) represent the Lolandis phase, whereas those containing Lolandis Red-Rim and Aztatlán Ware constitute the Acaponeta phase. Polished red and black wares and utilitarian wares appear to have been present in all West Coast phases. The presence of Aztatlán Ware in the Early Aztatlán period is significant because Aztatlán Ware decoration is essentially a "sky band" and represents the first decoration that in style and in iconography may have derived from Aztec I ceramics (Noguera 1954:107). Occasional pieces of Lolandis Red-Rim have a similar decoration—painted rather than engraved (Kelly 1938:79, Plate 7). Copper artifacts apparently were not present in either of the Early Aztatlán phases; they appeared as a major artifact type only in Late Aztatlán complexes. Another artifact type that was present and was widely traded was a spherical spindle whorl, usually decorated with an incised design of small circles (single or concentric double) connected with two or more incised lines. The intervening surface area was either plain or decorated with very small incised circles (Kelly 1938:54, Figure 24, *p, n, o*).

AZTATLÁN MERCANTILE SYSTEM

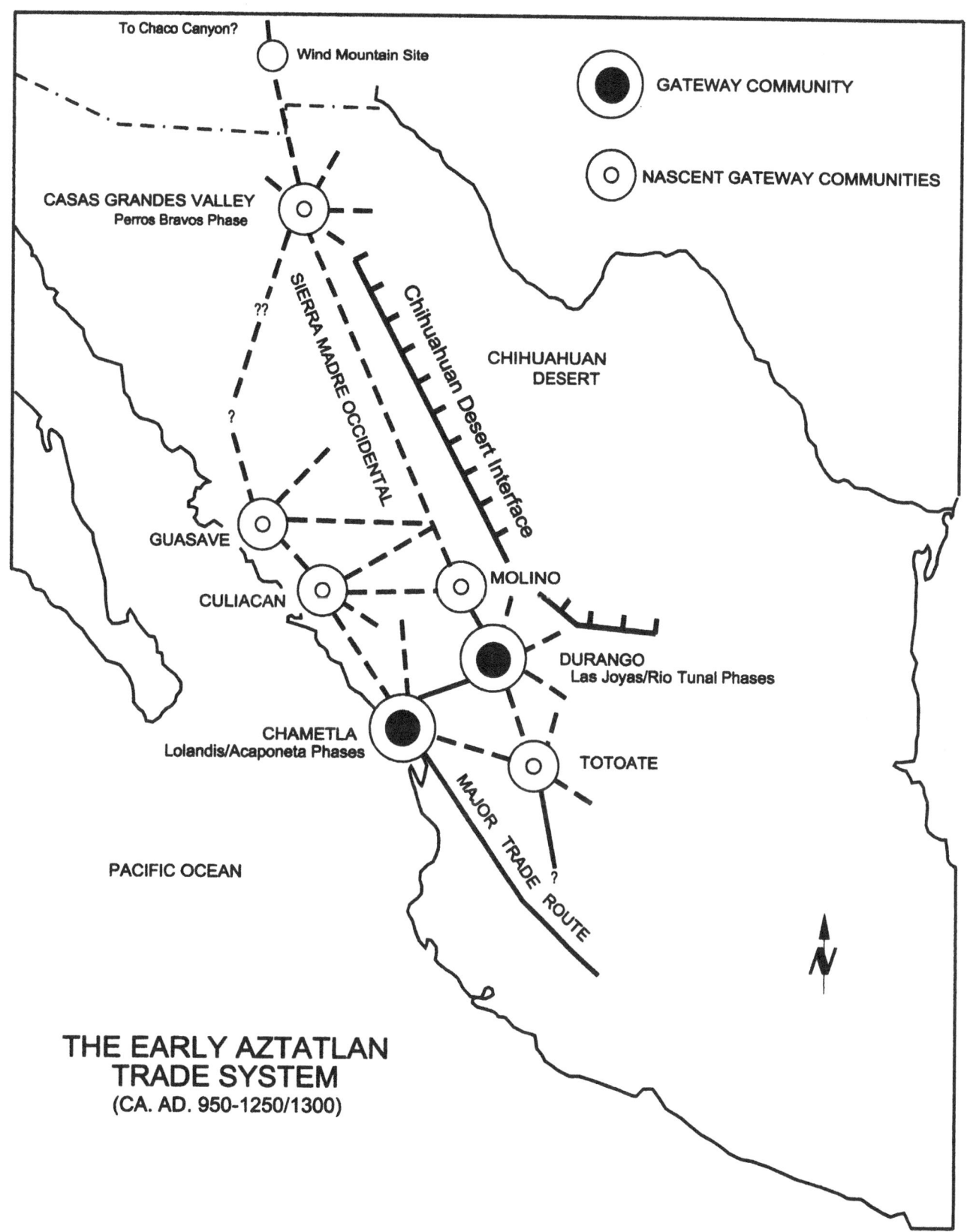

Figure 9.3. The Early Aztatlán trade system in west and northwest Mexico.

In Durango, following the Ayala phase, there was a marked change in the ceramic tradition and some indications that a similar change occurred in religion, as expressed in iconography. The diagnostic ceramic ware for the Las Joyas phase was Nevería Red-on-brown, a basket-handled high-tripod bowl whose origins can be traced back to the Suchil Branch of the Chalchihuites culture through Refugio Red-on-brown and its ancestral types in the Mercado Red-on-cream wares of the Calichal phase there (Kelley and Abbott Kelley 1971).

The simple tripod and nontripod painted bowls of the Calichal-Ayala ceramic complex were no longer made. Their place in the Las Joyas ceramic complex was taken by Lolandis Red-Rim, sherds of which were found in great numbers, not only at the Schroeder site but also at Navacoyan, Cañon del Molino, and undoubtedly in other Las Joyas sites. Actually, Lolandis sherds occurred in such numbers that they may represent not only trade items but an actual migration of Early Aztatlán peoples from Sinaloa to Durango. Also present in Durango were small numbers of Aztatlán Ware sherds, indicating that both Lolandis and Acaponeta phases of the West Coast were represented. Included among the Early Aztatlán trade sherds at the Schroeder site were examples of Aztatlán Polychrome, Aguaruto Incised, and Cerro Isabel Engraved. Also present were the spherical incised Early Aztatlán type spindle whorls (Kelley and Winters 1960:Figures 3, 4). Although most of the Early Aztatlán intrusives were found in Las Joyas phase deposits, there was some association with early Río Tunal phase materials, suggesting that Early Aztatlán trade may have overlapped the early part of that phase also.

But Early Aztatlán artifacts have been found elsewhere east of the Sierra Madre Occidental, indicating that once contact had been made with the highlands, mobile traders spread out over the area. At Totoate, located in the Río Bolaños barranca south of Mesquitic, Jalisco (Kelley 1971:771), ceramics and other artifacts were found representing trade with a number of regional centers.[9] The list of such intrusive items by region includes

1. Chalchihuites: Suchil Red-on-brown, Mercado Red-on-cream, and parts of two Refugio Red-on-brown vessels.
2. Malpaso Valley: Villanueva, Coyotes, and El Salto types (incised and red-filled black wares).
3. Tlaltenango Valley: Momax Deep Incised Red-Filled (and one sherd white-filled).
4. Amapa and West Coast: Early Aztatlán, Early Chinesco, Gavilán Polychrome, and a Lolandis type spherical spindle whorl (Amapa type 2-C).
5. Upland West and North-Central: Late-type Pseudo Paint-Cloisonné (green base coat and Mixteca-Puebla designs). Three sherds found, plus the Hrdlicka collection.
6. Local wares: Red-on-brown ware, Bolaños wide-line negative wares.
7. Figurines: One "Cerrito de Garcia" type (diagnostic of West Chapala, Sayula, and Colima coast; also, one found by Hrdlicka at Totoate).

Apparently, therefore, Totoate was indeed a focal point for diverse regional cultures. It is not clear whether it became part of the Mixteca-Puebla/Aztatlán complex by movements southward out of Durango or movements northward out of the Río Grande de Santiago region. Its situation deep in the Río Bolaños barranca does not appear to be a favorable one for a site with such extensive connections elsewhere. The associated ceramics, however, suggest that it was situated appropriately at a nexus of trade routes, completing the Mixteca-Puebla network in the south and west. Still farther away from the Durango sites, Di Peso found sherds of Aguaruto Exterior Incised in association with the Perros Bravos phase in the Casas Grandes Valley in northwestern Chihuahua (Di Peso et al. 1974:1:183, Figure 139–1). Still farther north (and on the road to Chaco Canyon) at the Wind Mountain site in southwestern New Mexico, Di Peso found (and displayed at the Protohistoric Conference in Tempe, Arizona) a sherd of Guasave Red-on-buff, identified as such by the late Gordon Ekholm, and other, similar sherds.[10]

If indeed Early Aztatlán traders were responsible for these Chihuahua and New Mexico finds, it may be asked why so few examples were found. This is certainly a matter of fall-off rate; from the Cañon del Molino site in northern Durango, where whole vessels as well as many sherds of Aztatlán ware were found, the distance to Paquimé, in the Casas Grandes Valley, by the foothill route was on the order of 500 km. According to Hodder (1980:152), "Fry notes that less portable, specialist-produced pottery has a sharp fall-off rate." Amazing indeed is the fact that even one example of the Early Aztatlán wares should have been carried such great distances over such rough terrain.

THE AZTATLÁN MERCANTILE SYSTEM: THE LATE AZTATLÁN SYSTEM (CA. A.D. 1150–1350/1400+)

By around A.D. 1200, give or take fifty years, as previously discussed, Culhuacán in the Valley of Mexico was part of the virtually pan-Mesoamerica trade structure dominated by Cholula, one linked to the cultures of west and northwest Mexico (Figure 9.4). As noted above, Cholula was a major site of the Mixteca-Puebla region, which even at the Spanish contact was known for the fine ceramics made there and widely traded. Recent studies of the Cholula/Mixteca polychrome wares, especially those by Lind (1994:79-99) and McCafferty (1994:53-77), make possible detailed comparisons with the Aztatlán wares of Jalisco, Nayarit, and Sinaloa. For example, characteristic Mixteca-Puebla bowl interior designs are illustrated by Lind (1994:Plates 2b, 3c) for the early Postclassic Aquiahuac phase (ca. 950–1150) and for the Tecama phase at Cholula (ca. 1150–1350). Similar Mixteca-Puebla designs at "Early Postclassic Cholula" are shown by McCafferty (1994:Figures 21, 22).

As previously noted, one of the connections between the two sites was the strong presence in both of the ceramic wares known variously as "Aztec" I, or Culhuacán Black-on-orange, Culhuacán Polychrome, or Cocoyotla Black-on-natural. This ware usually was decorated by elaborately painted designs incorporating feathers, highly stylized serpent heads, and other easily recognized iconography (Covarrubias 1957:324, Figure 142, I and I–II; Noguera 1954, 1965:106-107, 112-113; Sejourné 1970:48-54, Figures 50-83). McCafferty (1994:69) states: "Cocoyotla Black-on-natural [Cholula] in its basic type is the equivalent of Noguera's *negra sobre color natural del barro*, often called 'Aztec I.' . . . Subtypes include Sencillo, Incised, Banded, Elegante, and Chalco Black-on-orange."

Trade links between towns such as Culhuacán in the Valley of Mexico and those of the Toluca region, where the Río Lerma has its beginnings, long had been in existence. As previously noted, the Río Lerma had served as the geographic/cultural corridor connecting the Toluca region with the Lake Chapala and Valley of Atejemac region since the Preclassic. Mixteca-Puebla pottery, specifically Cholula ceramics, was found by Florencia Muller along the upper Río Lerma (Muller 1948:50-54, Mapa no. 1).

A collection made at the San Gregorio site on the lower Río Lerma produced ceramic vessels identified as Cojumatlán Polychrome by Meighan and Foote (1968:Figures 26 and 30.). These vessels are clearly of Mixteca-Puebla affiliation; the vessel in Figure 26 comes very close to being Aztec I, and the one shown in Figure 30 is almost as close. Cojumatlán Polychrome occurred also at the excavated sites of Cojumatlán (Lister 1949) and Tizapan el Alto, located along the south shore of Lake Chapala (Meighan and Foote 1968). Examples of vessels and sherds that show strong Mixteca-Puebla/Aztec I affinity are illustrated in Figures 4 (esp. *c*) and 6 of Lister (1949). Meighan (1976:144) states that Cojumatlán Polychrome is "a type well fixed in time at A.D. 900–1100." Such a date would place it in the Early Aztatlán period.

Also illustrated are a number of animal-headed feet. Lister (1949:20-23) notes several references to the occurrence of this foot type with the Mixteca-Puebla complex in Cholula, Puebla; in Oaxaca in Monte Albán V; and even farther to the southeast. Lister (1949:28-29) also states: "There is a resemblance between the conventionalized feathered serpent motif used on this ware . . . and the same motif employed on Aguaruto Incised at Guasave. . . . This motif is also common to Aztec I pottery from Culhuacán . . . headdress and feather motifs . . . also suggest similarities with the Aztatlán complex of Sinaloa. . . . Designs on both the Cojumatlán Polychrome and Cojumatlán Polychrome Incised . . . show similarity in motifs with Aztatlán Ware and Aguaruto Polychrome (Culiacán)." Later he adds, "These elements did not originate on the northwestern Mexican coast . . . they probably owe their origin to the Mixteca-Puebla area of the central highlands of Mexico" (Lister 1949:50-51). Objects of copper, including bells, beads, and needles, were found in association with the Cojumatlán complex. One bell (Lister 1949:Figure 32*f*) is exotic in form; an almost identical specimen was found at the Cañón del Molino site in Durango (Ganot R. and Peschard F. 1995:Figure 8.13).

Meighan and Foote (1968:Figure 26) found essentially the same situation at Tizapan el Alto. The interior decoration on a Cojumatlán Polychrome Incised bowl (Meighan and Foote 1968:Figure 26) is a variation on a common Aztec I depiction, as is the bowl shown in Plate 12, A; there are Mixteca-Puebla elements in other bowls illustrated in Plate 12 and in Plate 11, and certainly the bowl shown in Plate 14, A.

There were also copper objects (Meighan and Foote 1968:Plate 22). Meighan and Foote (1968:158) note: "At least one important cultural feature which flowed east rather than west was metallurgy. Also important is the possibility of sea contact between the Andean region and Mexico's west coast, the major river drainages [geographic corridors] serving to bring the foreign elements into Mesoamerican civilization."

Meighan and Foote (1968:159) add, "Note, however, that the site of Amapa on the west coast virtually duplicates the Tizapan assemblage, indicating that Central Mexican influences traveled all the way to the coast and

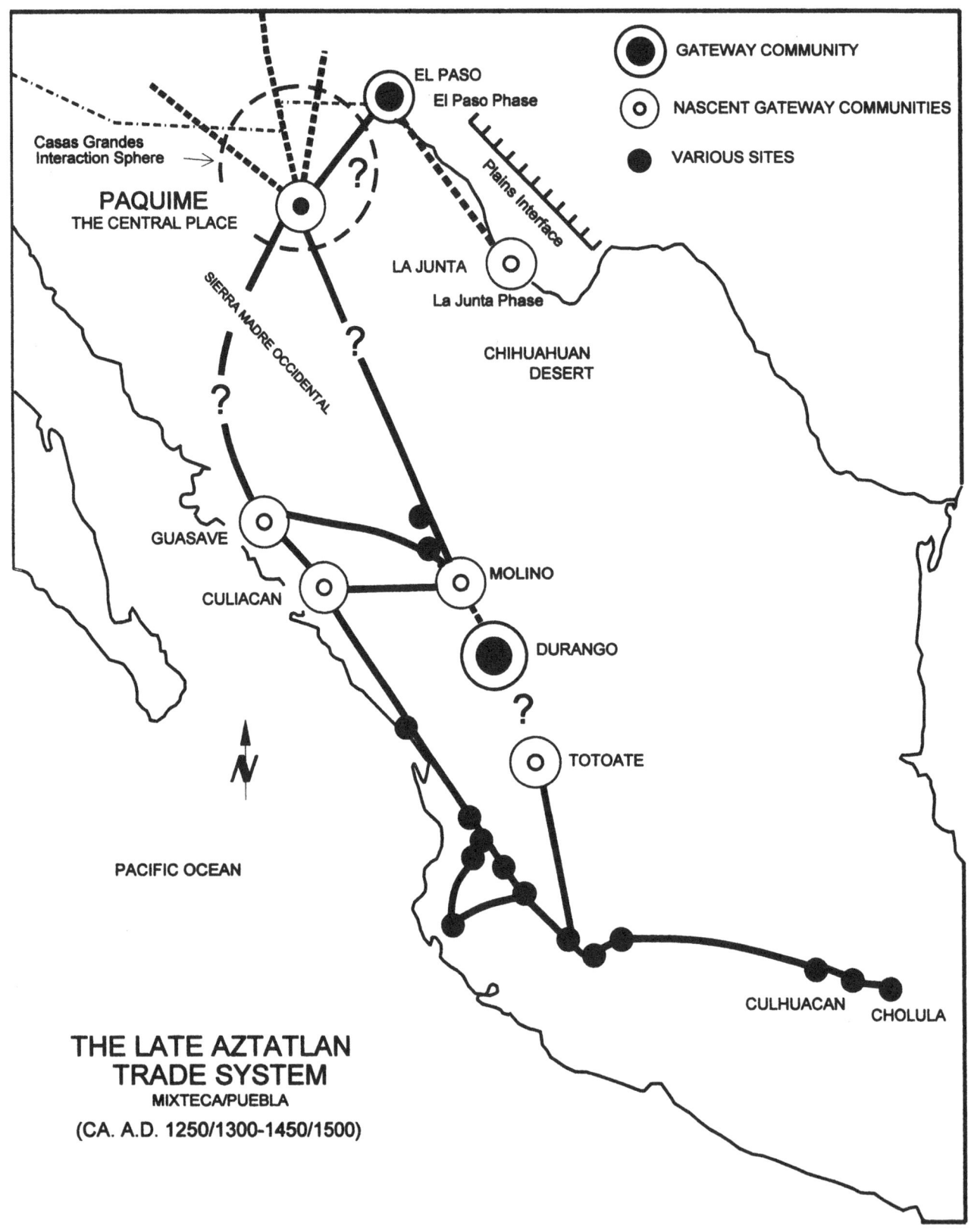

Figure 9.4. The Late Aztatlán trade system in west and northwest Mexico.

did not stop with the Chapala basin." The spacing of these sites (and others producing Aztatlán style pottery) along the south shore of Lake Chapala suggests that trade along this section was carried out by boat.

Glassow (1967) excavated a number of test pits in a site located at Huistla in the Etzatlán area of highland Jalisco. His illustrated ceramics appear to represent a transitional period between late Early Aztatlán (Acaponeta phase) and Late Aztatlán, but there are some indications that his pits may have been dug into platform fills with mixed cultural materials. Thus, the sherds depicted in Glassow's Figure 5a, included in his Huistla Polychrome, resemble Early Chametla ware of the Tierra del Padre phase at Chametla (Kelly 1938:Figure 3). The sherd at Glassow's Figure 5e in the same figure has the same design that occurs on Aztatlán Ware, whereas sherds u, v, w appear to belong with the Late Aztatlán period Mixteca-Puebla complex (as do the animal head feet at x in Figure 6). White-on-red sherds in this area should be quite late. Copper artifacts were present but in small numbers and in only one test pit (Glassow 1967:82).

A tentative conclusion would be that a mixture of sherds from several phases is represented and that the Acaponeta and Guasave phases are represented among them. Huistla is clearly another point on the Aztatlán Mercantile System route, and it is situated in a critical location.

A branch of the mercantile system extended southwest to the coast through Tomatlán and also followed up the coast through the Banderas area. In the Tomatlán area, Mountjoy (1982a:328–329, 267–269, Figures 73, 74; 1990:2:541–564) has found numerous Aztatlán sites and artifacts (see Mountjoy this volume).

In the long sequence of phases found by Meighan (1976) and associates at Amapa there was definitely a fully developed Mixteca-Puebla presence with appropriate ceramics and much copper metallurgy. But there is a conflict of interpretation between Meighan and Grosscup as to sequence of phases and chronology (Meighan 1976:206–272, Figure 6), which makes it difficult to place the Aztatlán phases there. The fully developed Late Aztatlán appears to occur in the latter part of the Cerritos phase and the following Ixcuintla phase; but Grosscup (1976) would equate the Lolandis phase with the Tuxpan phase at Amapa (the existence of which Meighan does not recognize) and the Acaponeta phase with the Cerritos phase; the full Guasave phase (Late Aztatlán–full Mixteca-Puebla) with late Cerritos and early Ixcuintla phases; Grosscup objects to the Kelley and Winters (1960) late placement of the Guasave phase.

Because copper metallurgy appears at least by the late Cerritos phase, we would agree with Meighan that Mixteca-Puebla (Late Aztatlán) equates with late Cerrillos and Ixcuintla phases.

As we move northwest up the coast, we find that Late Aztatlán apparently was missing at Chametla but was present at Culiacán (Fahmel Beyer 1988:148; Kelley and Winters 1960:555–559). The Middle, and perhaps the Late, Culiacán assemblages are characterized by a bewildering list of elaborate polychrome ceramic types; copper metallurgy was also present (Kelly 1938). Compared with the Guasave complex already discussed, the Late Aztatlán phase at Culiacán appears in many ways to be a local development with some Mixteca-Puebla elements involved.

There is some evidence from skeletal material recovered in the Marismas Nacionales for the introduction of new genetic strains appearing on the West Coast at precisely the time of appearance of the Late Aztatlán there (Gill 1971, 1985:210–213):

> Most meaningfully here [describing head deformation] is probably the fact that the paralleled variety died out in the estuary around A.D. 1250, and that this along with other possible changes . . . happened in conjunction with the first evidence of genetic change in the region. The previous population (Panales-Tecualilla) was a genetically more homogenous one. Additionally, an abrupt change in the form of primary burial happened somewhere in that short interval of time between Tecualilla and Chalpa. All adult burials at Panales and Tecualilla were extended, and all those at Chalpa (except for the deepest burial) and the other, later sites were flexed.

Later, discussing tooth mutilation, Gill (1985:214) adds: "Our Teacapan Estuary sites show the most northerly distribution of the C-4 forms of dental decoration in the Americas. These and other forms reveal a closer cultural affinity to the immediate south (at least after Tecualilla) than with the northern Sinaloa site of Guasave. This may indicate cultural diffusion from the south coincident with gene flow from the same direction." In a study of Southwest Indian dentition, Turner (1993:45, Figure 12; Schaafsma 1997:92) has indicated that the teeth of the Casas Grandes population are quite similar to those of the Sinaloa people. These data from research in physical anthropology, if they are confirmed by future research, support the hypothesis proposed in the present chapter.

We have already discussed some of the Late Aztatlán/Mixteca-Puebla traits present in the burial mound at Guasave. They are discussed thoroughly in Ekholm 1942.[11] Ceramics showing specific Mixteca-Puebla designs and iconography are illustrated in Figures 4–11 and 13 of Ekholm's report (see Scott and Foster this volume). The form of the tall, cylindrical, footed Sinaloa Polychrome vessels shown in Ekholm's Figure 7e, d, and g–k is similar to those of plumbate ware (Fahmel Beyer 1988:148), which is rare in Sinaloa; Fine Orange vessel shapes are also present. The tall cylindrical vessel decorated with god depictions found at the Schroeder site in Durango (discussed above) belongs to this type.

A large number of ceramic smoking pipes, mostly elbow pipes with flattened bottoms, were recovered, as were many spindle whorls, largely conical with rounded bottoms and some biconical types. Earplugs, pottery plaques, pseudo paint cloisonné decorated gourds, beads, pottery masks, a cylindrical pottery stamp, and a whistle were found. Stone artifacts included axes (full-grooved, three-quarter-grooved, and effigy axes), metates and manos, pipes, shaft polishers, balls, weights, an alabaster jar, and obsidian blades.

Copper metallurgy was also well represented, with a total of 134 objects, 111 of which were copper bells. Eighty-seven cast-copper bells were found tied in a row and wound around the right leg of Skeleton 29. This was an extended burial, apparently placed on an earthen platform and subsequently covered with a wooden roof (and later by the mound itself). Associated with it were 18 pottery vessels, the 87 copper bells previously noted, two large obsidian blades, two large shell plaques, 2,000 large shell beads, 19 shell bracelets, a bone dagger, and two trophy skulls. The skeleton was that of a large male wrapped in a red ochre-painted cotton blanket and, covering that, a twill mat (Ekholm 1942:43). Clearly, this was the burial of a high-status individual, and considering the number of associated copper bells, he may well have been a merchant.

One other significant find was an Amole Polychrome bowl that contained a 1-cm deposit of insect eggs, identified as a delicacy obtained from Lake Texcoco in the Valley of Mexico (Ekholm 1942:117, Figure 13d). Apparently, one individual at Guasave was of such high status that he (?) was able to obtain a favorite delicacy from distant Lake Texcoco.

The general thesis of this chapter has been that single individuals may not have traversed the entire distance from the Valley of Mexico to Guasave and Casas Grandes. But Gill's finding, previously discussed, that a new genetic strain appeared on the West Coast, coincident with the arrival of Mixteca-Puebla cultural traits, apparently indicates that at least some movement of individuals took place along most of the mercantile route. The discovery of insect eggs such as those from Lake Texcoco would also support this conclusion. Additionally, the evidence previously discussed presented by Turner (1993), that specific characteristics of the teeth of skeletons recovered at Casas Grandes equate them with human teeth recovered in West Coast sites, offers further support.

Guasave is, as far as now known, the most northwestern of the mesoamerican "colonies" on the West Coast, but there was some mesoamerican occupation extending into Sonora. It is possible that some of the Mixteca-Puebla/Aztatlán trade along the West Coast was carried out by canoe or raft travel along the coast. Day (1994) and others have pointed out the well-developed Mixteca-Puebla complexes in the Greater Nicoya region in Costa Rica and Nicaragua. Guasave, and especially Culiacán, are close to the great Topia gateway through the Sierra Madre Occidental (as well as secondary passes such as the drainage of the Río San Lorenzo). Apparently, the interest of both Culiacán (Culhuacán) and Guasave in the hinterland was centered on these passes through the Sierra and on to the Durango highlands beyond. Trade thought to be using these passes apparently survived into the Spanish contact period.

When Ibarra passed through San Juan del Río in 1563, "some natives brought information of the town of Topia ... from which they had brought and exhibited a feather shield of many colors ... ; a feather crest of silver; and cotton clothing woven of twisted thread, which the natives [Tepehuan?] had acquired by exchange from the town of Topia" (Obregon 1924).

In the Durango highlands in the northern part of the state, sites that exhibit major Late Aztatlán affiliation are Cañón del Molino and probably sites of the Zape area farther to the north. To the southeast in the Guadiana Valley, the looted site of Navacoyan produced a rich Late Aztatlán assemblage mixed with late Chalchihuites Río Tunal and Calera phase traits. From these Mixteca-Puebla colonies, converted into gateway communities, it is apparent that mobile traders may have worked southward as far as Totoate and in all probability to the northwest, following a geographic corridor through the "genial foothills" as far to the northwest as Paquimé, and beyond. The Cañón del Molino site has been discussed in some detail by Kelley (1986a:81-91) and especially by Ganot and Peschard (1995, 1997) and

Lazalde (1987). Cañón del Molino appears to have been a Mixteca-Puebla outpost, where West Coast mobile traders lived together with Chalchihuites people of the late Río Tunal and Calera phases. The rich looted material from Molino includes specific copper artifact types and pottery types from sites such as Amapa, Chametla (?), Culiacán, and Guasave and even from far distant Cojumatlán. Copper objects, spindle whorls, and smoking pipes were found in great numbers. The relationship between West Coast and Durango peoples was apparently amiable. So close was the relationship between potters of the two ceramic schools that new ceramic types appeared, blending elements of both schools.

THE PAQUIMÉ (CASAS GRANDES) INTERACTION SPHERE

The region lying to the northwest of Cañón del Molino and the Zape area is almost unknown archaeologically until the southern known boundaries of the Casas Grandes culture are reached; this is true also of the area of the Sierra Madre Occidental through which the Mixteca-Puebla mobile traders might have traveled directly from Guasave. Nevertheless, evidence has already been presented that Early Aztatlán mobile traders probably reached the Casas Grandes Valley; it seems likely that they had followed the foothill route or the eastern flanks of the Sierra and that Late Aztatlán traders did so also. That this general route continued to be followed into late historic times is indicated by Lumholtz (1902:1:430) when he was at Baborigame among the northern Tepehuan in 1883: "I was told that native traveling merchants from southern Mexico, called Aztecs and Otomies, pass through Baborigame every five years, to sell their goods. They bring articles of silk and wool, wooden spoons, needles and thread, and do nice embroidery work, and make or mend garments." Today itinerant merchants still carry on trade in the entire region, selling clothing, copper vessels, parrots, and other items, traveling by bus or pickup trucks.

That mesoamericans reached Paquimé and introduced many traits in architecture, ceramics, copper metallurgy, and city planning seems certain. In architecture it is necessary only to cite such items as a platform mound with ball court in front, a column-fronted gallery, the crossed-axis platform with circular platforms at its ends and astronomical alignments, the carefully planned interior domestic water system and its distant supply, macaw breeding pens, a major marine shell importing and crafting industry, apparently a copper-producing industry, and many others, including the extraordinary development of the city as a processing and merchandising center. Mesoamerican design iconography on ceramics (and some vessel forms) and the range of copper products are telling items. The city's early origins may have been Mogollon, but the site was remodeled into something completely different. The isolationist southwestern archaeologists who devote their professional efforts to an attempt to deny a mesoamerican presence at Paquimé would better serve the profession by attempting to prove that the full Paquimé development is indeed a Mogollon site. What Mogollon site resembles in the slightest the full Paquimé development?

The only probable mesoamerican source for the conversion of Paquimé into the center (a mesoamerican gateway community) of a major interaction sphere lies in the Mixteca-Puebla and Late Aztatlán development west and east of the Sierra Madre Occidental. Given the new dates for Paquimé of ca. A.D. 1200/1250 to 1450/1500 (Dean and Ravesloot 1993:83–103; Ravesloot et al. 1995), the timing is right, and there is indirect evidence of their presence in the finding of specifically Chalchihuites Río Tunal–Calera phase collar button spindle whorls in Paquimé Diablo phase context, as well as copper bell types that occur also at Cañón del Molino. The lack of more specific evidence in the form of diagnostic pottery vessels or sherds for the Late Aztatlán presence at Paquimé probably is due to the great distance to either the Chalchihuites sites or those on the West Coast and the resultant high fall-off rate. The question can be answered adequately only when good archaeological data are available from the area between Cañón del Molino and the Zape area and Paquimé.

That Paquimé was indeed the center of a major interaction sphere is amply demonstrated (e.g., Bradley 1993, 1996a, 1999; Schaafsma 1979, 1997). Di Peso discovered storerooms packed with trade goods, including such diverse items as shells (3,907,709 pieces [Di Peso et al. 1974]). Di Peso, Rinaldo, and Fenner (1974) also report woven mats, ceramics, turkey breeding pens to supply feathers and perhaps meat, and macaw breeding pens to supply feathers and live birds intended especially for trade into the Southwest. In addition, Paquimé ceramics are distributed over a very large area, including most of northern Chihuahua and adjacent parts of the Southwest, as well as the Río Grande Valley from the El Paso area southward to the La Junta region. Ramos Polychrome, the most diagnostic and widely traded of the Casas Grandes wares, has been the focus of study by

Woosley and Olinger (1993). They state, "We believe the production of Ramos Polychrome pottery to have been centered at Casas Grandes, rather than a situation in which smaller, more distant ceramic-producing towns and villages sent their wares to the large site" (1993:121).

It now appears that the great Paquimé Interaction Sphere extended far enough to include the El Paso phase and that the procurement area extended as far as La Junta de los Ríos at the mouth of the Río Conchos, based on the known distribution of Ramos Polychrome and other Paquimé ceramic types.

That the El Paso phase and its extension down the Río Grande to below Redford, Texas, as the La Junta phase, served as procurement groups for the Casas Grandes Interaction Sphere is demonstrated by the archaeological evidence. One specific point is the distribution of small sites along the Río Grande in the area upstream from the mouth of Capote Creek. There, at almost every arroyo mouth, sites occupy the triangular areas between the bordering hills. Only a few acres of land are represented in these triangles; the archaeological sites typically lie on the edge of the first river terrace above the river floodplain (Kelley 1952a:262 n. 26). Cultural debris is usually not great, except that in each site there is at least one large ring midden (sotol or mescal pits) present and often several in the same site. At many of these sites, the accumulated fire-cracked rock is 2–3 m high at a midden's periphery.

It seems certain that these are remains of repeatedly used large ovens whose primary function was the cooking of the "cabbages" of mescal, sotol, and agave. But the size and number of such ovens is out of all proportion to that of the small "hamlets" producing them. Associated with them are potsherds in fairly large numbers, including primarily those of El Paso phase decorated and utility wares and similar numbers of Casas Grandes polychrome and utility wares. At Casas Grandes, the El Paso wares were found in large numbers in association with baking ovens for the "cabbages," some still intact in the pits. The hypothesis presented here is that these sites were procurement and preparation loci for mescal, sotol, and agave cabbages traded by the La Junta and El Paso phase peoples to Casas Grandes. The large thin-walled El Paso Polychrome ollas would have served well for the transportation of the sticky, sugary cabbages (Kelley 1952a, 1992:136; see Mallouf 1992 for a different interpretation).

Similar large ring-midden "ovens" are found at some sites dispersed throughout much of the Trans-Pecos region. Although some of these were constructed on Archaic sites, almost universally they produce a few sherds of El Paso Polychrome (and related wares) and/or Chihuahuan polychromes and utility wares. Hines and others (1994) excavated such a site (the Wind Canyon Site, 41HZ119) in the Eagle Mountains in Hudspeth County, Texas. They concluded: "Relationships with groups south of the Río Grande are implied by Chihuahuan polychrome ceramics. . . . The ceramics establish the participation of the inhabitants of 41HZ119 in an interregional interaction sphere that was established around A.D. 1150 and was linked to the metropolis of Casas Grandes" (1994:144).

Minerals found along the Río Grande and in adjacent mountains, such as calcite (for calcite crystals), hematite, and tin, may also have been procured for trade to Casas Grandes.

This long stretch of the Río Grande also represented an interface with Plains groups in the Late Prehistoric, Protohistoric, and Historic periods. Both historical documents dating from 1581 through the eighteenth century and archaeological data indicate that Plains buffalo hunters and traders carried out intensive exchange relations in this area, especially in the La Junta villages. There the agricultural, ceramic, sedentary "Patarabues" (Amotomancos [Otoamancos] and others) hosted Plains peoples (initially the Jumano and later the Apaches) in a symbiotic relationship. Agricultural products of the villages were almost certainly exchanged for buffalo hides, jerky, buffalo bones, nuts (from the Río Nueces/Conchos of west-central Texas), and other items (Kelley 1952a, 1952b, 1953a, 1955, 1986a). During the existence of the Casas Grandes Interaction Sphere, such Plains-derived items probably were traded into Paquimé.

COMMENTS

I believe this discussion has demonstrated the existence of the Aztatlán Mercantile System and the mechanism of its functioning. Were time and space available, I could trace its entry into the core Southwest, but that must await another opportunity. If this model has merit, the expansion of the mesoamerican periphery throughout the length of Sinaloa and into southern Sonora has been demonstrated. Adduced evidence for the extension of the mesoamerican periphery into Paquimé and the Paquimé Interaction Sphere extending into western Texas and possibly into the American Southwest proper has also been presented. Finally, what can be said about the termination of the mercantile system? I have argued repeatedly (e.g., 1993) that the Aztatlán Mercantile System was destroyed when Tarascan expansionism around A.D. 1450–1500 into the Lake Chapala area cut the trade route there. Subsequently, part of the old trade route was reopened, at least as far as Culiacán, with direct interaction into the Southwest that continued into the Contact period.

GENERAL DISCUSSION

What has been presented here is the hypothesis for a specific mercantile model of entrepreneurial exchange. Stark (1986:279) has described such a model as follows: "In sum, the mercantile model is powerful, well grounded in the prevalence of ethnohistoric market institutions in Mesoamerican societies, and responsive to progressive commercialization in Mesoamerica linked to the accumulation of similar political and economic effects from earlier 'core' states and to the substantial long-term population increases in Mesoamerica, which would enlarge consumer markets."

But later Stark (1986:282) writes, surprisingly, "Note that a prestige exchange model of consecutive society links is one which can account for a spread of ritual and cognitive constructs over sizeable distances, but mercantile exchange does not." Actually, ritual constructs in the form of iconography were used as evidence in developing the present mercantile model. This model, in fact, represents a combination of Stark's prestige exchange model and her mercantile model.

Finally, Stark (1986:285) notes: "On the assumption that commodities are reasonably common in their region of origin, a shift or substitution for a good moving in a particular direction could infuse the circulation of goods with increased flow and thereby account for greater economic dependency on the chain of exchange at either terminus. Although this idea has not been proposed in the papers here it is a model which could help overcome the attritional effects of distance costs on the magnitude of exchange and hence could increase its economic impact on distant regions." This is precisely the contribution of the present model.

Some critics maintain that the Mixteca-Puebla concept is groundless and that what we have is a general diffusion of basic mesoamerican religious concepts. Others have argued that such long-distance trade systems are impossible. It has been argued that most Postclassic long-distance trade in Mesoamerica was carried out by water transport. I have already noted the possibility that, in this model, water transport was used along the south shore of Lake Chapala—as it was in historic times—and that some water transport took place along the Río Lerma and other rivers (as well as along the Sinaloa coast). But the concept that all long-distance trade in the Postclassic took place by water is patently impossible—and absurd!

Finally, I previously have identified this model as a hypothesis. For a hypothesis to be fully accepted, it must successfully provide an explanation of the known data and not be falsifiable in any way. Clearly, that is not the case with this model as presented. Archaeological hypotheses rarely can meet these two criteria; that is why there are so many different models to explain archaeological phenomena. This chapter, therefore, should be considered another attempt to explain multifaceted phenomena, subject to further detailed examination and perhaps eventual rejection. That is the common fate of archaeological hypotheses based, as archaeological models always are, on insufficient data.

NOTES

1. Since the time this work was first presented, new data have emerged from excavation and from unpublished papers. Some of these new data have been used to modify the original work, with due credit given to the sources. For previous papers on the same theme, see Kelley 1983a, 1986a.

2. Drennan (1984a:106), using maize as an example, cites a 30-kg load and 36 km per day; he calculates the bearer would consume his entire load in about 31 days. He states: "The only alternative that occurs to me is for the inhabitants of the maize importing region to eat the bearers when they arrive." Lumholtz was referring to pottery-carrying bearers, rather than those carrying maize or other bulk consumables, but it seems clear that those carrying maize and so forth would also live off the country rather than eat their cargo.

3. I am aware of the many different uses of the term "Chichimec." Here I refer to those groups, essentially hunter-gatherers, who lived outside the recognized boundaries of Mesoamerica at any given time.

4. Associated with this jar was a copper chain necklace with a turquoise mosaic pendant.

5. The spacing of sites such as San Gregorio, Cojumatlán, Tizapan el Alto, and other culturally related sites from the lower Río Lerma along the south shore of Lake Chapala suggests that they may have been canoe transshipment points on the trade route (Meighan and Foote 1968:Map 1).

6. The term "principally" used here requires explanation. Were all the dates specifically associated with Aztatlán ceramics, or were some of them associated with earlier wares?

7. The geographic route followed was probably the upper Río Baluarte into the Sierra Madre uplands and then down the Río Tunal into the Guadiana Valley. Alternatively, it may have been the Acaponeta-Mezquital-Durango route, which became the "Camino Real" between the West Coast and Durango in the late seventeenth century (Lumholtz 1902:1:486).

8. Following the abandonment of the ceremonial/astronomical center of Alta Vista, Chalchihuites, in Zacatecas, at around A.D. 875–925, occupation of associated hamlets and villages apparently continued for only a short time. The Chalchihuites hamlets that appear in the Guadiana Valley use the village plan of the hearth area, not that of the ceremonial center.

9. Identification of West Coast sherds and other ceramic artifacts at Totoate was made by Peter Jiménez Betts, Andrew Darling, and Michael S. Foster at a meeting at Blue Mountain Consultants, Fort Davis, Texas, 1996.

10. In the recently published Amerind Foundation report on the Wind Mountain site (*Mimbres Mogollon Archaeology: Charles C. Di Peso's Excavations at Wind Mountain,* by Anne I. Woosley and Allan J. McIntyre [Albuquerque: University of New Mexico Press, 1996]), I could not find a specific reference to these sherds.

11. An article by John P. Carpenter (1997) represents an attempt to rewrite West Coast prehistory as viewed from a typical southwestern viewpoint. The article is welcome in that it represents an effort by a southwestern archaeologist to go farther into Mesoamerica than Casas Grandes or Trincheras. After a review of Ekholm's research in Sinaloa and Sonora, Carpenter (1997:122) notes: "Instead of reflecting a Mesoamerican trading center, the Guasave assemblage can be interpreted largely in terms of indigenous developments. The objects of distant origin, while indicative of interaction, do not readily support mercantile expansion as a prime mover in the development of Huatabampo culture." Earlier Carpenter (1997:121) states: "Analysis of the burial data suggest that there is little, if any, indication of an actual Mesoamerican occupation. Instead, the Guasave site appears to have been continuously inhabited [by the dead of the burial mound?] by the indigenous Huatabampo population throughout its long sequence of occupation." The only necessary comment regarding Carpenter's conclusions is to repeat in part a quotation that he (1997:114) makes with approval: "Few Southwesternists know the archaeological literature of central and northern Mexico."

CHAPTER TEN

ARCHAEOLOGY OF SOUTHERN ZACATECAS

The Malpaso, Juchipila, and Valparaiso-Bolaños Valleys

PETER F. JIMÉNEZ BETTS AND J. ANDREW DARLING

With regard to the truly Mesoamerican colonization of Zacatecas-Durango, we are handicapped by a lack of knowledge of the archaeology of southern Zacatecas, and adjacent sections of Jalisco. There certainly were strong local Mesoamerican cultural developments in the Mesquitic-Bolaños region and in the Juchipila area; in these areas, at least in the south, alone in this region Mesoamerican cultures survived into historic times, as the Caxcana province. . . . Along the northern Malpaso-Juchipila drainage, near Villanueva on the Río Malpaso south of the city of Zacatecas, there was a very strong local Mesoamerican cultural development around the fortress-ceremonial center town now known as La Quemada. This cultural center was located just south of the ecological and cultural frontier with the Chichimecs; literally it plugged the Malpaso-Juchipila corridor to the south.

(Kelley 1961:6–7)

Do La Quemada and Cerro de Moctehuma to the west, both great fortress-like ruins at the very northern edge of the cultural and ecological frontier, and at opposite corners of what appears to be a shared culture, represent major garrison-strongholds erected to protect the northern frontier against penetrations of the Chichimecs down the open valleys of Zacatecas-Jalisco into Tarascan domain?

(Kelley et al. 1961:5–6)

CHALCHIHUITES AND MALPASO: INITIAL CONSIDERATIONS, EVOLVING PERSPECTIVES, AND RECURRING "DOGMAS"

UNTIL THE START of the Northern Frontier of Mesoamerica Project in 1961, there was an enormous void in the archaeology of most of the area southeast of the Chalchihuites zone (Figure 10.1) down to the Bajío, where the Chupícuaro culture had only recently been defined (Porter 1956). The concept of a generalized "La Quemada-Chalchihuites culture" (Kelley 1956; Lister and Howard 1955; Mason 1937) extending from Durango into central Zacatecas was in the process of being substantially clarified as a result of archaeological survey and excavation in Durango. A more refined definition of the Chalchihuites culture in which the Alta Vista phase was identified as the earliest and primary phase of this culture was developed. The Chalchihuites culture extended south from Durango into the Río Colorado Valley of the Chalchihuites area in western Zacatecas (Kelley and Winters 1960).

It was observed, however, that in the neighboring San Antonio Valley of the Río Suchil, there existed a cultural pattern somewhat different from that observed in the Río Colorado:

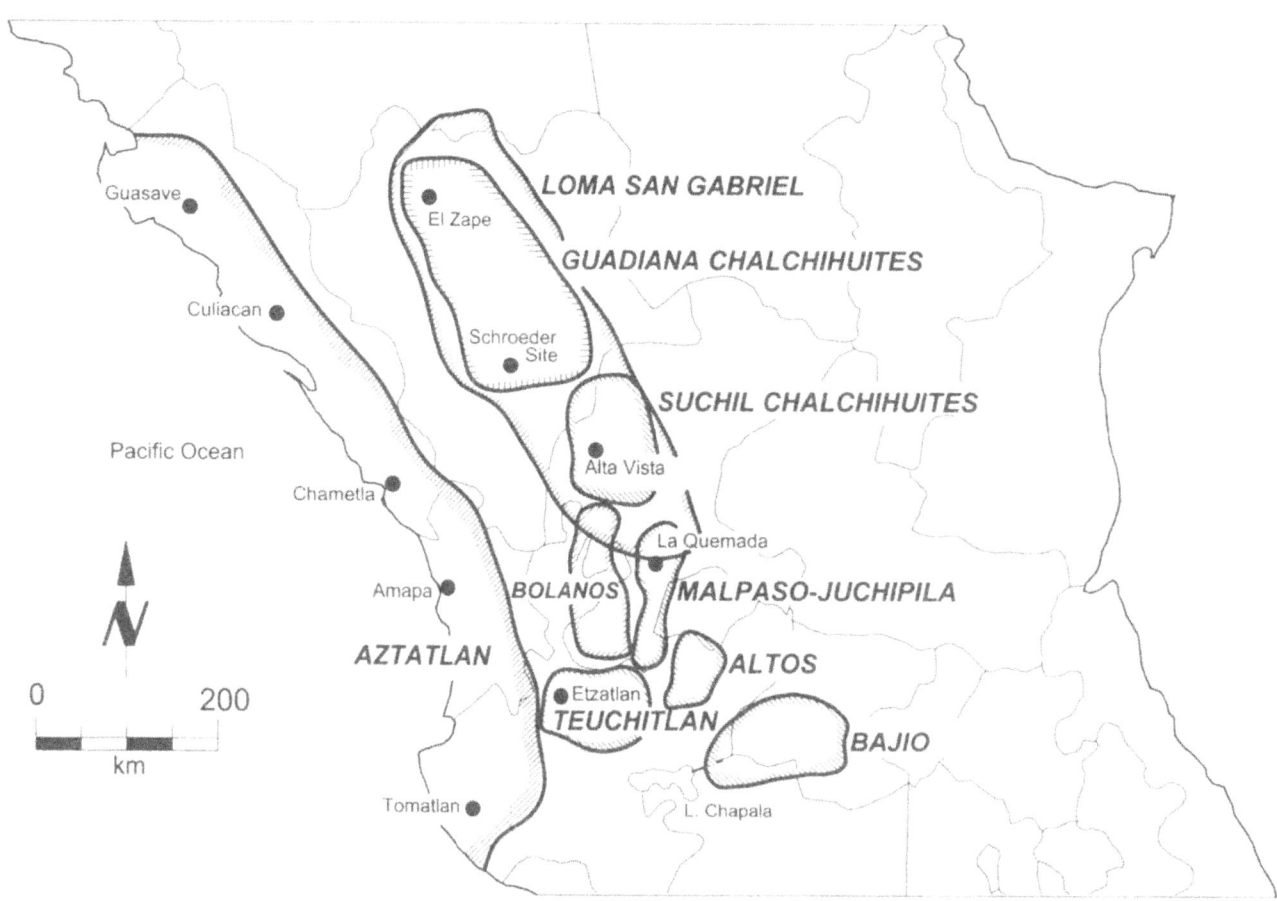

Figure 10.1. Archaeological traditions and cultures of northwest Mexico.

The pottery associated with the sites in this area, surprisingly, does not closely resemble the ceramic complex of the nearby Alta Vista phase but instead shows quite close resemblance to the ceramics of La Quemada, many miles to the southeast. This complex of ceramics and architectural forms we have tentatively named the Canutillo phase. . . . At this writing, it appears that Cerro de Moctehuma, which resembles La Quemada in situation, architecture, and pottery, is a bastion guarding the northwestern corner of the Canutillo–La Quemada territory, and it seems to mark a frontier of that culture with the Alta Vista phase of the Chalchihuites culture, assuming contemporaneity of the two phases. (Kelley et al. 1961:15–16)

Kelley's subsequent research in the San Antonio Valley between 1961 and 1965, including excavations at Cerro de Moctehuma, resulted in the definition of the Classic period Suchil branch of the Chalchihuites culture. Another significant result of this work was a better cultural and temporal definition of the Canutillo phase. This was to prove pivotal in not only differentiating the Suchil and Guadiana branches but helping define the Chalchihuites culture as one of several regional developments (Kelley 1963; Kelley and Abbott Kelley 1966). Subsequent research, including the documentation of the extensive mining activities of the Chalchihuites culture (Weigand 1968, 1982), would further establish the uniqueness of this Classic period frontier development.

In 1963, Pedro Armillas conducted a second season of fieldwork (Project B) in the Malpaso Valley, including excavations at the site of La Quemada. His 1952 excavations in the Cuartel of La Quemada produced radiocarbon dates that indicated a range of occupation between ca. A.D. 550 and 1400 (Crane and Griffin 1958a, 1958b). The terminal dates seemingly supported previous associations of La Quemada with the Tarascans (Batres 1903; Noguera 1930). These dates also raised another important issue, since the "establishment of the time of the burning of that site is of more than local significance, for it dates the retreat of sedentary farmers from that frontier territory and should be related to the general contraction of the northern marches of Mesoamerican civilization in the late pre-Columbian period" (Kelley et al. 1961:23).

Armillas's work in La Quemada explicitly focused on the hypothesis of a frontier collapse. The emphasis on the terminal occupation of La Quemada was to lead to the idea of La Quemada as a Postclassic "fortified settlement" (Armillas 1969:700; Kelley 1971:774). Thus, an initial frontier scenario, characterized by direct and permanent confrontation between sedentary populations and Chichimecs, would come to cast a large shadow over many future interpretations of La Quemada.

By the mid–1960s, the idea that Chalchihuites and La Quemada were two regions with an apparent shared culture was giving way to the concept that these two areas were separate developments. Unexpectedly, Kelley had broken the dogma of an all-encompassing Postclassic northwestern mesoamerican culture in the Chalchihuites region. The Chalchihuites culture extended back well into the early Classic period, whereas La Quemada remained the Postclassic fortress of the northwestern frontier (Armillas 1964a, 1969). Nevertheless, Kelley (1971:776) noted the similarities of the ceramic assemblages and a parallel chronology between the Malpaso Valley and the Chalchihuites cultures. This observation was based, in part, on very limited data from the early excavations of Hugo Moedano and Carlos Margain and Armillas's later work in the Malpaso Valley. The concluding pages in the monograph on the Chalchihuites ceramics probably best synthesize the Kelleys' perception of this area at the time: "From our observations the basic 'non-decorated' ceramics of the neighboring Malpaso–La Quemada and Bolaños-Juchipila cultures are similar if not identical to those of the Chalchihuites Culture, emphasizing the common Mesoamerican background of all these marginal cultures of northern Jalisco, Zacatecas, and Durango. Against this backdrop of basic ceramic unity the true decorated wares serve to distinguish regional developments and to trace artistic and craft trends over the centuries" (Kelley and Abbott Kelley 1971:175).

As a result of his work in 1963, Armillas acquired new radiocarbon dates for La Quemada. He once again insisted that the main occupation for the site occurred at around A.D. 900–1000 (J. Charles Kelley, personal communication, 1990). Armillas abruptly abandoned work on Project B, passing on both notes and materials to Phil Weigand for analysis. Weigand (1978a, 1978b) went on to propose the first archaeologically based cultural history for La Quemada. Following Armillas's idea of an early Postclassic period apogee for the site, Weigand took the presence of turquoise, together with certain architectural features found in La Quemada, as evidence for a Toltec-dominated emporium directly linked, through a northern inland route, to Chaco Canyon, New Mexico.

In direct reference to an earlier, Classic period occupation in the Malpaso Valley, Weigand (1978a:79) noted: "An earlier series of agriculturally based villages existed there. While little is known about this period, it clearly appears that the villages were Mesoamerican-influenced, and were probably similar in many aspects to the Canutillo Phase villages in the Chalchihuites area. . . . The early-period ceramics come only from surface collections, but roughly parallel the Chalchihuites sequence (Weigand 1978a, 1978b). . . . It is possible that the origins of these early sites in the Bolaños and Malpaso Valleys were part of the same cultural developments that led to the establishment of the Canutillo Phase near Chalchihuites."

Seen in retrospect, it was Armillas's ceramic materials, especially the identification of an incised-engraved series, from the Malpaso Valley that would come to break the Postclassic period dogma for La Quemada. This was the third instance since the beginning of the Northern Frontier Project that the similarities between the simple incised-engraved ceramics of Chalchihuites and Malpaso regions had been noted (Kelley 1971; Kelley et al. 1961). Kelley's brief mention of a possible parallel sequence had found an echo.

Subsequently, a survey of the Malpaso Valley by Charles Trombold (1976) in the mid–1970s resulted in a better understanding of the La Quemada road system and settlement pattern (Figure 10.2; Trombold 1991). Briefly turning his attention to the incised-engraved ceramics of the valley, Trombold (1985:254) also concluded: "The resemblance to Canutillo wares described by the Kelleys (1971:25, C–E) is striking. . . . Execution likewise seems somewhat poorer than in the Chalchihuites area. The fact that this ware is related to that of the Chalchihuites area suggests the possibility of an earlier, simple farming folk that preceded a more intense Mesoamericanization of the region."

During the past twenty-five years, of the three initially proposed mesoamerican cultures (Chalchihuites, Bolaños-Juchipila, and Malpaso; Kelley 1971), the Chalchihuites and the Bolaños regions have been the

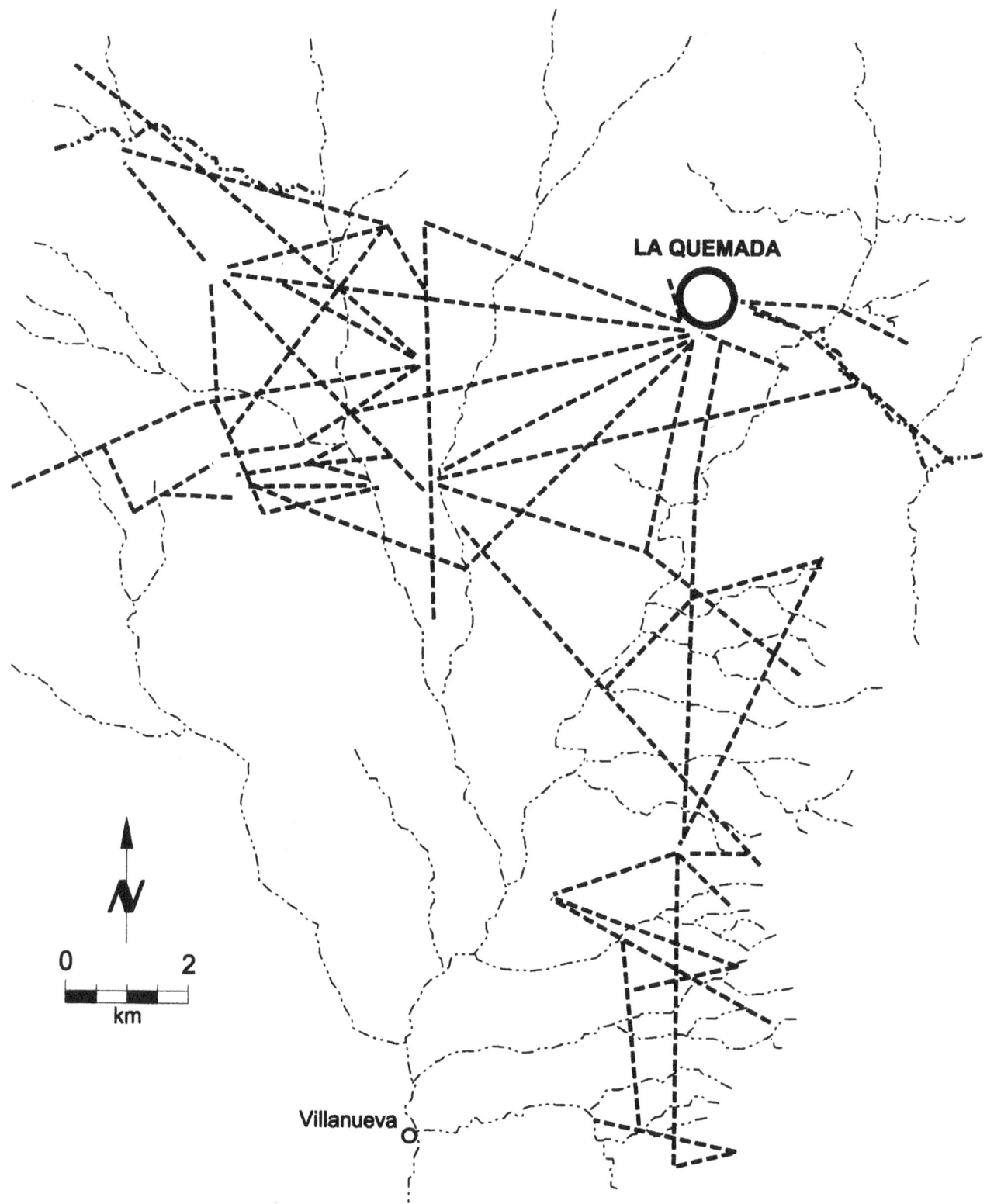

Figure 10.2. The La Quemada prehistoric road system.

subject of intense study and revision (Cabrero 1989, 1992; Cabrero and López 1998; Kelley 1985a; López 1994). Work in the Juchipila Valley is currently in progress (Mozillo 1990); archaeology in the Malpaso Valley (La Quemada) in the last decade has focused on excavations at La Quemada and Los Pilarillos (Jiménez 1988, 1989, 1990, 1992a, 1992b, 1997, 1998; Lelgemann 1992, 1997, 1999; Nelson 1990, 1993, 1997; Nelson et al. 1992).

Archaeological work by the Belgium Mission in the Nayar region of northern Jalisco in the mid-1970s is reported in a monograph oddly deficient of archaeological data (Hers 1989a). Hers, based on the presence at the site of El Huistle of Suchil branch Chalchihuites ceramics and fragments of bichrome plaques like those found in the Malpaso Valley (Lelgemann 1992:Figure 18 [La Quemada]; Trombold 1985:Figure 10.5), has advocated a return to the earlier Lister and Howard (1955) idea of an immense homogeneous Chalchihuites culture. This megaculture also included the Nayar and Malpaso regions. She further suggests that this culture be extended to include the Juchipila, Tlaltenango, and Bolaños valleys.

More recently, attempts to trace Caxcan origins to both the Malpaso and Chalchihuites regions (Weigand and García de Weigand 1995, 1996) have also reverted to this conception of a distended Chalchihuites culture. Hers's and the Weigands' interpretations of the regions in question share a basic peculiarity: their efforts to infer movements or migrations of Protohistoric and Historic groups (i.e., Tolteca-Chichimeca and Caxcans) require lumping regional developments and cultures, including Loma San Gabriel, into a common melting pot. For the needs of the historian, the lumping of the various cultural traditions of the area may seem insignificant. This superficiality appears to be a clear disregard of the archaeological data from the area, however, to say nothing of what seems to be a rather naive perception of the complexity of the northern frontier.

These new data and interpretations have rekindled a debate over an old question: Are we dealing with separate cultural traditions or a macro-Chalchihuites tradition that includes the Chalchihuites, La Quemada, and Bolaños regions? The second possibility is, in part, founded in the widespread presence of black incised-engraved wares and the intense Classic period occupation of these areas.

Kelley was among the earliest and most consistent to note the generic similarities between the Canutillo black incised-engraved ceramics of the Suchil branch of Chalchihuites and the black incised-engraved wares of the Malpaso Valley. His (Kelley 1990a) recently proposed taxonomy for the entire area restates his initial observations and what others working in the area have consistently observed. That is, the Canutillo phase in the Chalchihuites zone represents the regional expression of the basic mesoamerican cultural horizon out of which various complex regional developments later emerged. As such, the pan-regional variants of black incised-engraved wares are simply the earliest distinguishable components that form the "backdrop of basic ceramic unity" for this portion of the northwestern frontier (see Cabrero 1989; Jiménez 1989, 1995; Kelley 1989a; Strazicich 1995, 1996).

If anything can be concluded from a review of the archaeology of this area, it is that the rhetoric generated by the "lumpers" is a rather poor substitute for basic material analysis and cultural historic reconstruction. The present synthesis seeks to summarize the prehistory of the southern valleys of Zacatecas by examining the ceramic data at present available.

THE MALPASO VALLEY

Especially because of the great size and evident regional significance of La Quemada at the time of its occupation, we believe that it will be possible to work out a sequence that directly correlates with that of central Mesoamerica to the south, the basic phase of the Chalchihuites culture to the west, the adjacent Chichimec archaeological cultures to the northeast, and probably the Huasteca to the east. (Kelley et al. 1961:7)

The Río Malpaso forms the northern headwaters of the Río Juchipila. Nevertheless, these two regions are geographically and environmentally distinct. The Malpaso Valley is drier and cooler, and zones of extensive forests of nopal cactus distinguish its vegetation. The headwaters of the Río Malpaso generally lie near the town of the same name, and the valley extends to roughly El Salitre, north of the community of Tayahua in the south. The river descends from 2,200 to 1,800 m above sea level along a distance of approximately 40 km. The valley is defined by high mesas and the Sierra Fria on the east and mesas that form the northern extension of the Sierra de Morones on the west. In this sense, the Malpaso Valley is situated at the transition between the deserts of the Mesa del Norte and the northern limit of mesoamerican farming-based economies (Kelley 1971:776–777).

La Quemada stands as the most imposing site in the Malpaso Valley. Most archaeological sites in much of north-central Mexico appear as subtle prominences consisting of concentrations of stone rubble, artifacts, and vegetation. In contrast, the massive terrace walls and constructions of La Quemada (Figure 10.3) seem out of place. Most sites are buried under accumulations of sediment from deteriorating structures, but at La Quemada centuries of erosion have removed mud wall plaster and mortar only to highlight the intricate masonry that covers the escarpments on which the site is built (Figures 10.4, 10.5, and 10.6).

Apparently separated from similarly scaled archaeological vestiges of central Mexico, the imposing structures of La Quemada traditionally provoked the imagination of historians, most of whom associated the ruins with the mythical Chicomostoc through which the Mexica passed on route to Anáhuac (Clavijero 1974; Torquemada 1986). In this century, archaeologists working in the area have proposed a kaleidoscope of cultural associations and functions for La Quemada. The site has been interpreted as an enclave of Teotihuacán (Corona Núñez 1972), a Toltec emporium (Weigand 1978a, 1978b, 1982), the hub of the Chalchihuites culture (Hers 1989a), a Tarascan center (Batres 1903; Noguera 1930), a defensive bastion against Chichimec intrusions (Armillas 1964b, 1969; Kelley 1971), a fortress refuge (Hrdlicka 1903; Mason 1937; Trombold 1985), the legendary Chicomostoc of the Mexica (Hers 1989a), a pan-regional sanctuary (Hers 1993b), and a vacant ceremonial center (Nelson et al. 1992). In sum, the interpretations of La Quemada generally fall into three categories: it was a Chalchihuites site, or it was an outpost or colony of every major culture in highland Mesoamerica, or it was an empty ceremonial center or sanctuary. Fortunately, since the mid-1980s, investigators working in adjacent areas have forced researchers to consider the Malpaso Valley's history in a more regional context.[1]

As with most portions of the northwest frontier, the process or processes that resulted in the development of the basic mesoamerican way of life are still poorly understood in the Malpaso Valley. To date, Kelley's (1974) "soft diffusion" model is viewed as most coherent. Nevertheless, many questions remain: Was the Canutillo-Malpaso horizon the result of the intrusion and successive "budding off" of colonizing agriculturists from the Bajío, Altos de Jalisco, and Juchipila areas into the northern regions? Did it evolve in situ through the assimilation of mesoamerican elements by regional nomadic or seminomadic groups? Or was it a complex coalescence of both processes? In the temporal context, the events that brought about the basic mesoamericanization of this northern area appear to have occurred within the first three centuries A.D.

In terms of Kelley's initial observations cited at the start of this discussion, from a northern perspective the rise of sedentism and complexity requires an extensive study of what could be considered a prime candidate for an intermediate or transitional culture between the Archaic hunters and gatherers of the region and the mesoamerican frontier farmers (e.g., Chalchihuites, La Quemada). The Loma San Gabriel culture is thought to represent the initial sedentary, ceramic-producing culture in western Zacatecas and Durango. It appears to be part of a larger plain, brownware tradition that was widespread over much of northwest Mexico (Foster 1985, 1995b, this volume; Kelley 1971).[2]

To the south, in the northern Bajío, the Altos of Jalisco, and the Juchipila Valley, the early ceramic period is at present in process of study. The most obvious question derived from the Canutillo-Malpaso horizon concerns the origin of the basic architectural pattern of the closed-patio village. If the point of origin for the movement of this pattern could be determined, it might be possible to correlate its appearance with that of incised-engraved and red-on-buff wares. Thus it might be possible to characterize the initial wave of mesoamerican presence into the area. It is striking that fifty years after the discovery of the Chupícuaro cultural tradition, and some twenty-five years after the definition of the Morales complex (Braniff 1972), there remains a near total absence of data pertaining to architectural patterns of the Bajío and Altos areas during the late Formative and Early Classic periods.[3]

To date, the observations by Braniff (1972, 1998, this volume) and Kelley (1989a) pertaining to the Morales incised wares as possible "distant ancestors" to the northern incised-engraved ceramic tradition constitute the only insight into this problem. In view of Braniff's (1998) recent revision of the Morales chronology and the fact that only 250 km separates the Bajío and Altos areas from the Malpaso Valley, however, it can be suggested that the incised-engraved wares of these regions are probably closely related.

At present, the earliest ceramic complex that can be identified for the Malpaso Valley dates to the Middle Classic period. Diagnostic of this tentatively named Malpaso complex (ca. A.D. 350/400–600/650) are black or brown incised-engraved tripod vessels. The design

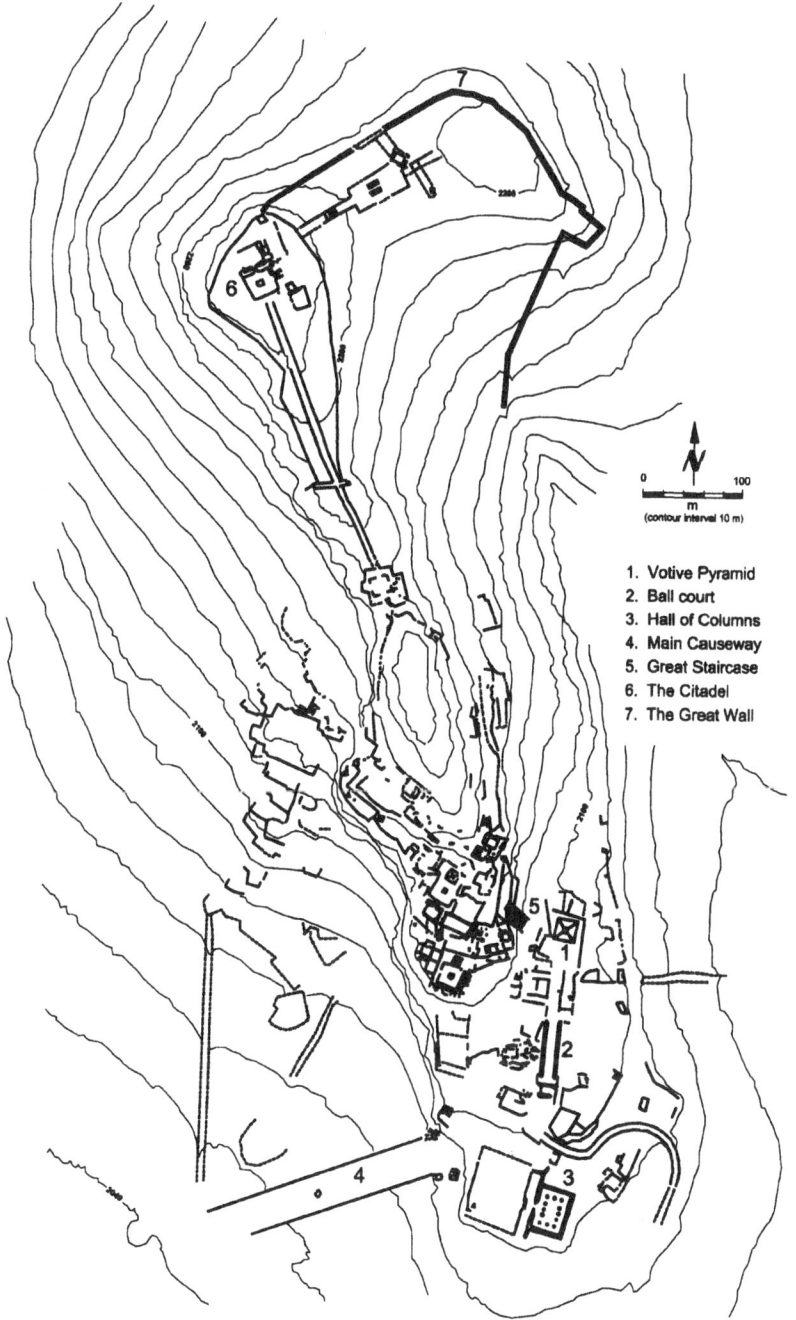

Figure 10.3. The site of La Quemada (adapted from Armillas and Weigand, courtesy of Phil Weigand).

elements of the Malpaso incised-engraved are simple and predominantly geometric (Figure 10.7). Designs are poorly executed, and the design patterns clearly define the regional character of the ware as a local manifestation and not a mere copy of the Canutillo incised-engraved wares of the Chalchihuites culture (Jiménez 1989:17–20; Nelson 1993:181; Strazicich 1995:103–107; Trombold 1985:253–255).[4]

It should be noted that beyond the Malpaso Valley, Malpaso complex incised-engraved ceramics have been found in the sites of La Florida (Villanueva Incised-engraved) in the Valparaiso Valley (Cabrero 1989; Jaramillo 1984:Lam. IV–VI) and among the materials from Kelley's excavation in Structure 1 of Totoate (Villanueva, Coyotes Incised, and El Salto Incised-engraved) in the middle Bolaños region. Ninety kilometers to the east, sites in the Villa García region (La Montesa) have yielded relatively high frequencies of Villanueva and Quisillo Incised-engraved ceramics.[5] The significance of this wide geographic distribution poses an important question for this period: Is this evidence of a simple pan-regional village horizon or could it be a manifestation of evolving social complexity within the Malpaso Valley?

(above) *Figure 10.4.* La Quemada.

Figure 10.5. The votive pyramid at La Quemada.

Figure 10.6. The lower terraces at La Quemada with the ball court and Hall of Columns.

For now, we can only speculate on the early chronology of the site of La Quemada. It is possible to infer, based on a radiocarbon date of A.D. 490 ± 80 from beneath terrace 18 (Nelson 1997), that some occupation of La Quemada occurred before the construction and occupation of the terrace. Thus, it is possible that the earliest construction and occupation of La Quemada occurred at approximately the same time as that at Alta Vista, A.D. 450–470 (Kelley 1985a). Furthermore, it appears that Chalchihuites mining activities were well established between the fifth and sixth centuries A.D. (Weigand 1968), which again leads one to ask if La Quemada would not have in some way participated or been affected by these early developments in the Chalchihuites region. If, in fact, Alta Vista and La Quemada were contemporary phenomena, we may have a case of "early" peer-polity interaction that would necessitate a reexamination of Middle Classic culture dynamics.

The Epi-Classic period was a highly important time in the Malpaso Valley. Recent work in the region has shown that the Epi-Classic marks the apogee of La Quemada as a regional system (Jiménez 1989, 1997, 1998; Lelgemann 1992, 1999; Nelson 1993, 1997; Trombold 1990). The Epi-Classic period in the Malpaso Valley is tentatively called the La Quemada complex and dates between A.D. 600/650 and 850.[6] It is during this period that the site of La Quemada reaches its maximum extent. New ceramic types, extremely elaborate negative painted wares, are introduced in this period and are thought to be derived from areas to the south (Jiménez 1988, 1995, 1998). These changes are important and seem to suggest that La Quemada was increasingly interacting southward while it maintained traditional base ties to the Chalchihuites region to the west.

The most noteworthy diagnostic ceramics of the La Quemada complex are the Tepozan negative paint wares (Figure 10.8) and the Tuitlán and Murguia incised-engraved wares. In particular, the latter represent distinctive regional types that continue to manifest similarities to the Vesuvio and Michilia types of the Chalchihuites

Figure 10.7. Early Chalchihuites and Malpaso ceramics. *a–d*, Canutillo incised-engraved wares (Chalchihuites); rows two and three are early Malpaso complex incised-engraved wares.

culture. At this time, in the Chalchihuites region, the very formalized Michilia and Suchil types mark the peak of the Chalchihuites ceramic tradition. In the Malpaso Valley, the distinct Tepozan negative wares represent the regional ceramic climax. These wares are comparable in both design layout complexity and iconography with the Suchil red-on-brown (Figure 10.9) and Michilia ceramic types.[7] The red-on-cream (e.g., Soyate Red-on-cream—Figure 10.10) and red-on-brown ceramics of the La Quemada complex in the Malpaso Valley have a very distinctive regional character, however, with the red-on-cream ollas and bowls (Ambosco type) sharing only general elements with the later Mercado ware of Chalchihuites.

Other La Quemada complex materials found in the Malpaso Valley and adjacent areas are also indicative of interregional interaction during this time. The pseudocloisonné ceramics exhibit direct parallels to the Vista Paint Cloisonné type (Figure 10.11) of the Chalchihuites culture, at the same time integrating design techniques found on southern varieties of this ware.[8] The pseudocloisonné ceramics of La Quemada were initially analyzed by Neomi Castillo (1968). Recent midden excavations associated with the "Cuartel" of the site have produced previously unknown varieties of this ware. To date, the intrusive ceramics identified in the Malpaso Valley during the La Quemada phase include Valle San Luis Polychrome from the San Luis Potosí Valley to the east (Braniff 1992a; Crespo 1976) and three types initially referred to as Sierra Brown-on-white, Jerezano White-on-red, and Morones Black-on-purple from the middle Bolaños Valley (identified from Cabrero's present work in the Epi-Classic component of the El Piñón site). Black incised and fine lined, highly stylized red-on-white ceramic plaques are also found. The black incised plaques have also been found in the Juchipila Valley to the south (Mozillo 1990) and by Kelley in Totoate, Jalisco (Kelley 1963, 1971). The dis-

tinctive red-on-white plaques (Lelgemann 1992:Figure 18; Trombold 1985:Figure 10.5) have been found in the Nayar region (Marie-Areti Hers, personal communication 1994) and in the Tlaltenango Valley as well. Both these types have been found in very high frequencies in the middle Bolaños Valley, again in the Epi-Classic contexts of the El Piñón site, which, at present, appears to be their place of origin.[9]

Also diagnostic of the La Quemada complex is the Type I figurine (Figures 10.12 and 10.19). Although it was initially defined as a type in the Altos de Jalisco region to the south (Williams 1974), this figurine type has been frequently found in the Malpaso Valley. Batres (1903) noted it in the Franco collection from La

(above) *Figure 10.8.* Tepozan negative paint wares of the La Quemada complex.

Figure 10.9. Suchil Red-on-brown jar (Chalchihuites culture).

Figure 10.10. Soyate Red-on-cream and red-on-brown ceramics of the La Quemada complex.

Quemada, and it was described in the materials from the Trombold 1985 survey of the valley, in midden deposits around terrace 18 at La Quemada (Nelson 1993), inside fire pits on the plaza of the votive pyramid, and beneath floor 2 of the Hall of Columns (Lelgemann 1992). The pan-regional distribution of the Type I figurine suggests its importance as a horizon marker (Jiménez 1989). The Type I figurine is found from the Suchil region of the Chalchihuites culture southward through the Malpaso, Juchipila, and Atemajac valleys. Recently, it has been found farther south in the Sayula Basin (Otto Schöndube, personal communication 1994; Ramírez Urrea 1997) in late Sayula phase contexts (i.e., Epi-Classic period). From here its distribution extends northeastward through the Altos of Jalisco region to sites in northwestern Guanajuato, from where it extends northwestward to the La Montesa region of Villa García, Zacatecas (east of the Malpaso Valley). This area, in which the Type I figurine is seen as a horizon marker, has been designated previously as the "northern interaction sphere" (Figure 10.13; Jiménez 1989, 1992b).[10]

At present it is still difficult to assign a definite date to the end of the occupation of La Quemada. Achim Lelgemann (1992, 1999) has been constant in pointing out the radiocarbon evidence for a late occupation of the site and has proposed a Ciudadela phase, which in our view would span the time from A.D. 850 to 1000.[11] The question of La Quemada's demise as a regional system is still open to study. The major stairway passages that connect the first four levels of the site's core were repeatedly reduced in size until they were sealed or closed off, apparently restricting access throughout much of the site. Also, both the placement and size of the northern wall seem to indicate an increase in defensive character of the site. One gets the impression that La Quemada was gradually pulling into itself, transforming itself into a defensive bastion. It should also be noted that from the Citadel at the extreme northern end of the site to the Hall of Columns at the southern edge, there is clear evidence that the site was burned. Excavation and erosion of the surface layers throughout La Quemada have exposed carbonized beams covered by large fragments of red-baked clay with the impressions of the roof matting.

Figure 10.11. Vista Paint Cloisonné, Alta Vista, Chalchihuites.

Figure 10.12. Type I figurine of the La Quemada complex.

Early-sixteenth-century historic accounts indicate the site was in ruins. They also mention that Spaniards had encountered a group of Zacatecos living in a small "ranchería" along the river to the east. As for who occupied the valley after the collapse of La Quemada, was it the semisedentary or seminomadic Zacatecos or the desert hunters and gatherers commonly known as the Chichimeca or both? The Protohistoric period in this region is poorly understood, archaeologically and culturally.

THE JUCHIPILA VALLEY

[Bolaños-Juchipila culture] is an archaeological area rather than a unitary culture, and one which is almost unknown. . . . Ceramic wares common to most of the major sites, except Banco de las Casas, are paint cloisonné, negative painted, red-on-buff or brown, red-on-white, and some white-on-red polychrome, and engraved or incised wares. There is some time depth; observed intrusives range from Chupícuaro affiliated types through very late white-on-reds, and locally there were survivals into the contact period. (Kelley 1971:769–770)

In the southern part of Area 4, along the Río Juchipila, collections demonstrate the existence of a complex of negative painted wares which should offer correlations in several directions. (Kelley et al. 1961:7)

The Río Juchipila, located in southern Zacatecas in a deep canyon, flows to the south where, after joining the Río Mezquital, it then flows into the Río Grande de Santiago. The Juchipila Valley is flanked by two mountain ranges, the Sierra de Morones, which forms a barrier between it and the Tlaltenango Valley, and the Sierra de Nochistlan on the east, which separates the Juchipila from the region known as the Altos de Jalisco. These ranges obtain maximum heights of 2,000 m above sea level in the south to more than 2,800 m above sea level in the north portion of the valley. The valley floor is roughly 900 m below the sierras, and the Río Juchipila loses approximately 700 m in elevation from its northern end above the Chique Reservoir (1,700 m above sea level) to its confluence with the Río Santiago (1,000 m above sea

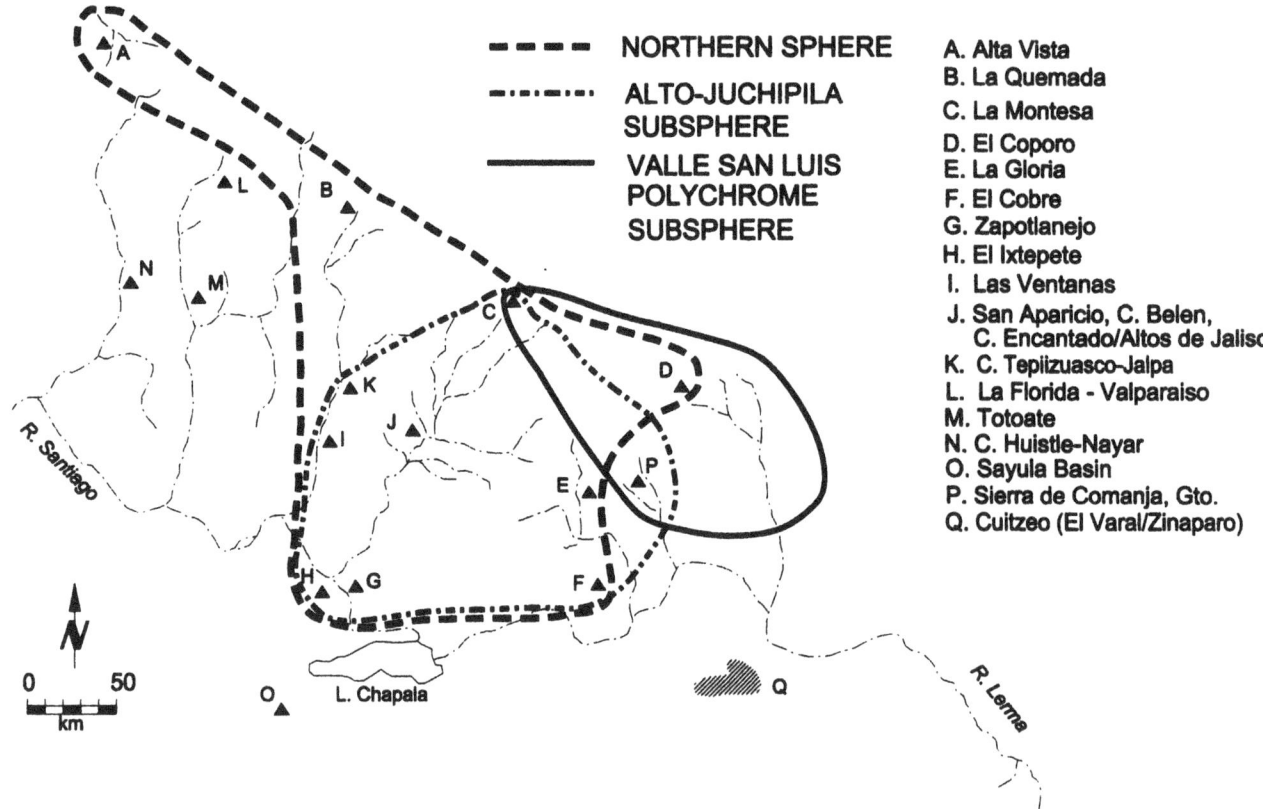

Figure 10.13. Interaction spheres of north-central and northwestern Mesoamerica.

level). The Juchipila Valley forms a geographical corridor to the Lerma-Santiago Basin and thus to west Mexico. This extremely fertile valley constitutes one of the key regions for understanding not only early sedentary occupations in Zacatecas but also the subsequent cultural dynamics of the northern frontier during the Classic period.[12]

In the design of the Northern Frontier of Mesoamerica Project, both the Juchipila Valley and the Malpaso Valley were defined as Area 4. Kelley's perception of this "archaeological area" was based on correlations observed from the detailed analysis of the Sescosse collection from the Apozol–La Purísima–La Tirisia (Juchipila) zone and other comparative collections.

Otto Schöndube (1980:173) has previously pointed out that the west Mexican shaft tomb tradition and the Chupícuaro tradition exhibited extremely little overlap except in the Altos and Juchipila regions. This Late Preclassic/Early Classic confluence is manifested in the ceramics of the Juchipila Valley. Until now the earliest ceramic wares identified for the valley were the diagnostic vessels of the Colorines group described for the Tabachines complex of the Atemajac Valley, a regional component of west Mexico's shaft tomb tradition (Galván 1991:48–50). Negative polychrome tripod bowls and plates from Apozol-Juchipila (Figures 10.14 and 10.15) are analogous to those found at Cerro Encantado in the neighboring Altos area of Jalisco (Bell 1974). They are directly related to types identified as components of the Morales complex of northwestern Guanajuato (Braniff 1972, 1998, this volume; Jiménez 1988). These are the early negative wares that Kelley defined as "Chupícuaro affiliated types." At Cerro Encantado, these diagnostic negative wares were associated with the "cornudo" style hollow figurines (Figure 10.16), an association also found in the Apozol zone. Recent salvage work in the town of Juchipila produced a series of large negative painted, dotted ollas like those found at Cerro Encantado (Bell 1974:Figure 7).

The Colorines-Tabachines/Morales nexus has likewise been defined in the Altos de Jalisco as Phase I (200 B.C.– A.D. 300; López Mestas et al. 1994; Ramos and López 1998) and seems to indicate the integration of the

Figure 10.14. Negative polychrome plate (Morales correlate), Apozol, Juchipila Valley.

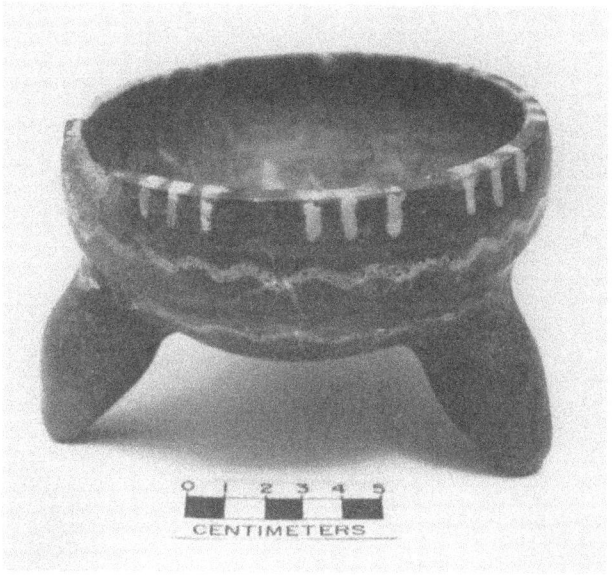

Figure 10.15. Negative polychrome tripod bowl (Morales correlate), Apozol, Juchipila Valley.

Juchipila Valley into the Altos region from an early date. Overall, the convergence is manifest in the presence of conch shell trumpets, pyrite mirrors, hollow cornudo figurines, and the geometric designed negative polychromes, a regional derivative from the Morales complex of Guanajuato.

A third component must be considered for the region at this time, one Kelley initially observed with both the Sescosse collection and artifacts from Totoate in the Bolaños Valley. The distinctive negative painted tripod bowls with claw and hollow bulbous supports (Figures 10.17 and 10.18) from the Juchipila Valley have direct analogies to specimens recently found in the sealed El Piñón shaft tomb in the Bolaños Valley, radiocarbon dated between the second and fourth centuries A.D. (Cabrero and López 1998:Figures 19, 105, 108). This Bolaños culture element suggests a confluence within the Juchipila Valley of three major west Mexican regional social systems. One cannot but suspect that the cultural dynamics resulting from the coming together of these west Mexican traditions was somehow related to the processes that produced the initial wave of mesoamerican expansion into the Malpaso Valley and the Chalchihuites regions, resulting in the Canutillo-Malpaso horizon.

Starting from at least the early Middle Classic period, the black incised red-filled bowls are the diagnostic ceramic type for the valley (Figure 10.19). One specific variety has been previously identified as a regional variant of the Atoyac incised of the Sayula Basin (Noyola 1994:Figure 5). Excavations in Cerro Tepisuazco, Jalpa, produced an extremely high frequency of these distinctive black incised bowls. Likewise, both the Sescosse collection and Muro collections from the Apozol zone include this type. The continuous distribution of this incised ware extends from the Juchipila Valley, through the Atemajac Valley (Galván 1976:lams. 11, 13; Otto Schöndube, personal communication 1994), through the Sayula Basin to the coast of Colima in what Ramírez Urrea (1997) has proposed as a ceramic marker for a major interaction sphere from ca. A.D. 500 to 750. The companion diagnostic throughout this extensive sphere, which we tentatively call the Jalisco-Colima sphere, is the Class F Cerrito de García figurine (Gómez Gastélum and de la Torre 1996:142). This Cerrito de García figurine type is present in the Juchipila Valley, in both the Jalpa and Apozol zones, and in the Bolaños Valley (Kelley and Hrdlicka found it in the excavations of Totoate). Teresa Cabrero has recently detected this figurine in the middle Bolaños in the site of El Piñón. The chronology for the Cerrito de García (F) figurine is ca. A.D. 600–900 (Otto Schöndube, personal communication 1994; Ramírez Urrea 1997).

Likewise for the Epi-Classic period, the negative painted annular based bowl (Figure 10.20) constitutes a very important horizon marker. The distribution of this diagnostic ceramic type extends from the Juchipila

Figure 10.16. Cornudo- or horned-style figurines, Cerro Encantado, Jalisco.

Figure 10.17. Negative polychrome tripod bowl, Apozol, Juchipila Valley.

Valley (Cerro Tepisuazco, Jalpa, and Apozol zone), through the Altos region (López et al. 1994), east to León, Guanajuato (López and Ramos 1992), north through the Encarnación de Díaz region (Jalisco and Aguascalientes), up to the Villa García region in eastern Zacatecas, and south to the Atemajac Valley (Schöndube and Galván 1978). This ceramic type has also been found as an intrusive in the Sayula Basin (Noyola 1994:79, Figure 4). The Juchipila negative annular base bowl is an elite ware, contemporary with the Tepozan negative ware (see Figure 10.8) of the La Quemada complex to the north. The two types share some iconographic design elements, but this distinctive annular base bowl has not been identified in the Malpaso Valley as yet. The distribution of the annular based negative painted bowls (see Figures 10.19a and b and 10.20) can be taken as evidence of an important interaction sphere linking these contiguous regions, which can be tentatively identified as the Altos-Juchipila subsphere (see Figure 10.13).[13]

Fragments of molded facial sections of effigy vessels constitute another diagnostic element of the Juchipila Valley. These have been found at San Aparicio in the Altos region (Jiménez 1989:14, Figure 2, 1995:Figure 1B; Williams 1974:28), in the Atemajac Valley (Schöndube and Galván 1978; Schöndube 1983), and from the sites of Cerritos Colorados and Atoyac in the Sayula Basin (Noyola 1994:62–63, Figures 2 and 3; Ramirez Urrea 1997).[14]

The Epi-Classic architectural components of Cerro Tepisuazco have produced a wide variety of pseudocloisonné vessels, as well as shell ornaments, greenstones, and turquoise. As mentioned above, one specific variety of pseudocloisonné decorated vessel found in Tepisuazco has been found previously in La Quemada and Totoate.

In 1991, the authors identified an intrusive circular Guachimonton complex in the Cerro Tepisuazco site, where the predominant architectural pattern is the rectangular plaza-pyramid complex. This has since been verified by Phil Weigand (Weigand et al. 1999). The presence of the rectangular plaza architecture with the circular architecture also occurs in Totoate (Kelley 1971) and is discussed below. At present the chronology of this particular important structure can only be inferred. The presence of Gavilan Polychrome, an Amapa ceramic type (Meighan 1976), in Tepisuazco would seemingly correlate to the dating of the circular complex.

The Postclassic occupation of the Juchipila Valley is limited and known only from historical descriptions. The Contact period occupants of the region are reported to be Caxcan, who in 1541 participated in the famous Mixton war. Unfortunately, the archaeology of this group is unknown.

Figure 10.18. Negative polychrome tripod molcajete with mammiform supports, Juchipila Valley.

From the data available at present, it is very clear that the Juchipila Valley was an integral part of west Mexico through its Preclassic and Classic periods.

THE VALPARAISO-BOLAÑOS VALLEY

Totoate is a very large site occupying a clearly defensible position on the top of a high mesa above the narrow canyon through which the Río Mezquital-Bolaños flows. There is a complex assortment of courts, platforms, boulders with petroglyphs, and other features but, most significantly, there is a large circular masonry walled court with platforms and rooms attached to it and a circular tower in which Hrdlicka found cremation burials with paint cloisonné pottery accompaniments. This structure is startlingly similar to the "great sanctuaries" or large kivas of the American Southwest. Across the canyon from Totoate, on Cerro Prieto, are other ruins with similar circular courts with attached platforms. In both ruins the ceramic complex does not at all resemble that of Alta Vista or La Quemada. Here is a new and different cultural complex, placed in a key position between the Alta Vista phase of the Chalchihuites Culture and the Mesoamerican cultures of Jalisco to the south (Kelley et al. 1961:28)

Long ago, Kelley (personal communication) recognized the importance of the Valparaiso area; that it was a

natural junction, where north-south and east-west trade and contact routes crossed along this section of the Mesoamerican frontier. The La Florida complex is located at the hub of a series of important surrounding complexes. It is approximately equidistant from the Chalchihuites area, Sain Alto, Cerro de las Viboras, the upper Bolaños area, the Malpaso Valley, and the Juchipila Valley. Its placement is strongly suggestive of a major role in cultural and trade contacts along the frontier. (Weigand 1978b:113)

The Valparaiso-Bolaños Valley is located in western Zacatecas and north-central Jalisco. The Río Bolaños is 320 km long, flowing from the north to its confluence with the Río Santiago in the south. A major tributary to the Bolaños is the Río Colotlán, which enters the valley from the east and is formed by the union of the Río Jerez and the Río Tlaltenango. The Valparaiso Valley contains the headwaters of the Río Bolaños, which flows into the Río Santiago between the Magdalena Basin of Jalisco and the Ixtlán del Río region of Nayarit. The valley is relatively narrow for most of its course and is deeply cut in some areas. The river is flanked by mountain ranges exceeding 2,500 m in elevation. They include the Sierra los Huicholes on the west and east and the intervening upland that separates the Bolaños Valley from the Jerez Valley and the Tlaltenango Valley. Environmental differences from north to south are pronounced, including a transition from semiarid, hot climate with some thorn scrub and nopal forest in the north to a wetter, slightly cooler climate, which in the valley bottom includes subtropical scrub.

Current knowledge of the Prehispanic period of the Bolaños area is almost entirely due to the work of María Teresa Cabrero and her students. In the early 1980s, extensive survey of the Valparaiso Valley, including excavations at the site of La Florida, was undertaken by Cabrero as part of the Cañada de Bolaños Project (Cabrero 1989; Jaramillo 1984). Cabrero's work in the valley defined the northernmost distribution of the circular architectural pattern described for the core area of the Teuchitlán tradition of highland Jalisco (Weigand 1985, this volume).

Based on the work at La Florida, a regional Bolaños culture was defined. During the first five centuries A.D., there was a movement of sedentary agricultural populations out of the Lake Magdalena region of Jalisco into the Bolaños Valley. These settlers brought with them the practice of shaft tomb burial and circular patio architecture characteristic of the Teuchitlán tradition (Cabrero

Figure 10.19. Juchipila Valley ceramics. *Top row,* Atoyac (Sayula correlate) Black Incised wares. *Middle row: a,* negative paint olla sherd; *b,* negative plain annular base bowl sherd; *c,* early Gavilan Polychrome sherd (intrusive). *Bottom row:* Heads from Type I figurines.

1989, 1994; Weigand 1985). In the Valparaiso region, extremely large shaft tombs, circular architecture, and two diagnostic ceramic types, an orange-on-cream and a distinctive negative ware, have been identified. Chronological placement by Cabrero of Bolaños Valley sites and their associated artifacts was based initially on architectural and ceramic indices. In the absence of absolute dates and other data, a preliminary chronology spanning two broad periods has been proposed: Period I (200 B.C.–A.D. 700) and Period II (A.D. 700–1100; Cabrero 1989, 1992). The transition between Period I and Period II is marked by a strong shift in the architectural pattern of circular plazas and shaft tombs to rectangular patios or courts and burial in mounds, pits, and *tumbas de camara.*

Ceramic correlations with other regions during the later phase suggest chronological overlaps with the Alta Vista and Las Joyas phases of the Chalchihuites area, Early Chametla in Sinaloa, and Ixtlán del Río in Nayarit (Cabrero 1989:345–346; Gifford 1950; Kelley and Winters 1960). This confirmed a previous observation by Kelley on the long occupation of the Bolaños Valley based on his limited excavations in Totoate (1971:769–770).

From the vantage of the Valparaiso Valley, Cabrero proposed:

The economy of the Bolaños culture had to be tied directly to those of the Chalchihuites, Malpaso, and the Magdalena Lake Basin regions. With Chalchihuites there is evidence of similar ceramic types and the pos-

Figure 10.20. Negative paint polychrome annular base bowl, Juchipila Valley.

sible exploitation of greenstone. With Malpaso there is also a similarity in some ceramic types, and with the Magdalena Lake Basin there is a similarity in architectural patterns and the sharing of the shaft tomb tradition. With respect to its three neighbors, the Bolaños culture must have played a secondary role within the pan-regional exchange system and may have been dependent on one of these neighboring cultures during certain times. (Cabrero 1989:324–325)[15]

Since the early 1990s, work in the middle Bolaños Valley in the sites of El Piñón and Pochotitán has produced a series of sealed shaft tombs (Cabrero 1998; Cabrero and López 1998; López 1994). The El Piñón shaft tomb figurines and ceramics, radiocarbon dated from the second to the fifth centuries A.D., reflect the regional character of the Bolaños culture, one that is distinct from that of the contemporary Huitzilapa shaft tombs from the Teuchitlán core area (Ramos and López 1996). The Pochotitán circular architectural complex has been radiocarbon dated to A.D. 135 (Cabrero 1998:288), and the Huitzilapa circular complex "A" produced two dates: A.D. 160 (cal. A.D. 96–248) and A.D. 290 (cal. A.D. 160–415). Cabrero's most recent field season at El Piñón, in 1998, yielded shaft tomb–related circular architecture on a lower level of a hill of the same name (Cabrero, personal communication 1998). This circular complex has been dated to ca. A.D. 50. Interestingly, both the Pochotitán and El Piñón dates are much too early to be part of the Teuchitlán expansion (Teuchitlán I).

In the first detailed discussion of the chronological development of the Teuchitlán tradition, Weigand (1985:70) described the chronometric dates for the Classic period of this tradition as "few (and far from the lakes)." In fact, he used dates from Kelley's (1971a) work in Totoate in northernmost Jalisco, where a small and obviously derivative circular complex, first explored by Ales Hrdlicka (1903), was dated to ca. A.D. 200–700. Apparently based on these dates, Weigand proposed the Teuchitlán I phase, ca. A.D. 400–700, which was characterized by the expansion of the tradition into peripheral regions, most notably the Bolaños Valley.

Interestingly, the Totoate site itself has presented numerous chronological puzzles for nearly a century. The Kelleys' (1971:770–774) excavations focused on two structures, Structure 1 and Structure 2, the latter of which had previously been excavated by Hrdlicka in 1898 and 1902. The Kelleys undertook trench excavations in Structure 1 and outlined a "nearly square court" platform compound that contained a central square altar. Outside the northeast corner of Structure 1, the remains of an earlier platform were found. The four radiocarbon dates from Totoate come from excavations in Structure 1: two come from the fill of the earlier platform remains (B.C. 51 ± 259 and B.C. 82 ± 194), and two come from contexts from above the floor in the patio. Of the latter two, one was from a burial found in front of the northern platform (A.D. 460 ± 95) and the other was taken from a trash deposit on the patio floor (A.D. 505 ± 95). These latter dates from Structure 1 are what Kelley considered markers for the main occupation of the site (Kelley 1971:771–772).

If we combine the notes and papers of Hrdlicka and the Kelleys, the chronological relationship of Structures 1 and 2 can be pieced together. In a personal communication in 1997, Kelley pointed out that Structure 2 was physically linked by a wall to the early platform situated below Structure 1. This strongly suggests that Structure 2, the circular patio, was constructed at an earlier period. Artifact material found by Hrdlicka suggests otherwise, however.

This presents a paradox that Kelley (1971) recognized. Hrdlicka's excavation at Totoate in 1898 and 1902 revealed later period artifacts found in association with the cremated remains of more than fifty people in three rooms in Structure 2. These include not only the famous pseudocloisonné bowls but charred textile fragments, shell and pyrite artifacts, obsidian, and a human effigy stone ax. Kelley's 1963 re-excavation in Structure 2, which targeted the same area, revealed almost nothing resembling Hrdlicka's finds.

Unfortunately for Kelley, this paradox could not have been resolved without returning to the original Hrdlicka notes on the Totoate excavations located in the National Anthropological Archives in Washington, D.C. Careful scrutiny reveals two errors in Hrdlicka's 1903 publication. The less significant error is the orientation of Hrdlicka's trenches in the central altar of Structure 2, which are depicted at about 90 degrees off the actual. Though important, this error is nearly inconsequential given Hrdlicka's more substantial mistake or the inadvertent reversal of the description of Mound A and Mound D in his publication. The central altar in Structure 2 is labeled on Hrdlicka's published map as Mound A, yet the actual description of the central altar corresponds in the text to the description of Mound D. Alternatively, the description of Mound A corresponds to Mound D on the 1903 map. This lateral mound is located on the west side of the patio. It was here that Hrdlicka found his cremations and exotic artifacts. Consequently, and based on Hrdlicka's publication, Kelley never actually reexcavated this portion of the site.

This answers the question why Kelley's results did not resemble Hrdlicka's. Nevertheless, the chronological question remains concerning late materials in the earlier Structure 2. One possibility is that the cremations and associated artifacts are intrusive. This is a likely explanation, since introduction of human mass burials into partially abandoned sites is not an uncommon occurrence in north-central frontier Mesoamerica (e.g., Abbott Kelley 1978; Nelson et al. 1992; Pickering 1985). In fact, Cabrero suggests that there may have been a regular transformation of earlier circular patios in the Bolaños into necropoli (Cabrero 1989:283–285). Resolution of the Totoate paradox reinforces Cabrero's and her colleagues' more recent work. For the site itself, it seems clear that the occupation of Structure 2 probably predates A.D. 500 or 450 and may be as old as the first decade of the Christian era.

The ceramics from Totoate, therefore, span several occupations and as many as nine or ten centuries. A recent examination of the ceramics recovered from Kelley's excavations in Structure 1 resulted in the identification of a number of important diagnostic ceramic types. Bolaños red and black-on-buff negative tripod bowls and simple bowls predominate.[16] Early intrusive types include Chinesco Black-on-white and Gavilan Polychrome. The Tlaltenango Black Incised;[17] Villanueva, Coyotes, and El Salto Incised (Malpaso Valley); Suchil Red-on-brown and Refugio Red-on-brown (Suchil branch of the Chalchihuites); and brown and black incised plaques (Malpaso varieties), one Amapa (Type 2-C) spindle whorl, and one Cerrito de García (Type f) figurine are evidence of an occupation in the site through the entire Classic period into the early Postclassic.

When assessing the evidence for the early chronology of Structure 2 in Totoate and the later chronology for the square patio compound of Structure 1, together with the radiocarbon dates from the Pochotitán, El Piñón (Bolaños), and Huitzilapa (core) circular complexes, one must reconsider the actual dates of the Teuchitlán expansion. The expansion of the Teuchitlán tradition in Teuchitlán I appears to have occurred between ca. 50 B.C. and A.D. 400, and not the proposed A.D. 400–700. This would require a major revision of Weigand's (see this volume) current dating of the Ahualulco phase, the main phase of the Teuchitlán tradition, and that of both the Teuchitlán I and II phases. This revision is more consistent with the chronology of the west Mexican shaft tomb tradition in highland Jalisco, which seems generally to extend from ca. 200 B.C. to A.D. 350/400 (Cabrero 1998; Long 1966; Ramos and López 1996; Valdez 1994, 1996).

In the Bolaños Valley, the transition from circular architecture to the square patio-altar compound like that of Totoate and rectangular platform architecture like that of El Piñón probably occurred between ca. A.D. 400 and 500. This transition may be indicative of increased interaction with its northern and eastern neighbors from the Chalchihuites, Malpaso, and Juchipila regions, with which Bolaños shared the copa-olla pseudocloisonné ceremonial complex between ca. A.D. 600 and 900 (Holien 1977).[18]

SUMMARY

The goal of this chapter has been to highlight what is known of the archaeology of southern Zacatecas. It should be clear that there is a great deal yet to discover and learn of the archaeology of this vast area. Recent research in La Quemada has provided a somewhat clearer understanding of the site's chronology (Jiménez 1989, 1997, 1998; Lelgemann 1992, 1999; Nelson 1997), thus allowing us to eliminate much previous speculation regarding the temporal placement of the site's occupation. First and foremost, the Malpaso Valley (La Quemada) should be seen as one of several continuous regional developments that extend from the Suchil branch of Chalchihuites culture to the northwest, to the Juchipila Valley and the Altos to the south and southeast, to the partially contemporary Bolaños culture.

One thing that appears to distinguish the cultures of the northern periphery from the rest of Mesoamerica is the rapid and complex formative stage through which these societies passed (Kelley 1989a). By A.D. 500, most, if not all, of the cultures discussed were simultaneously becoming more socially, politically, and economically complex. These developments peaked between A.D. 650 and 800, with both La Quemada and the Suchil branch of the Chalchihuites cultures peaking simultaneously. It seems the Prehispanic sedentary societies in Zacatecas started relatively late and reached complexity rapidly.

A key question yet to be resolved pertains to the initial developments at large sites such as La Quemada, Alta Vista, and Cerro Moctehuma. Was the social and political complexity seen at these sites between A.D. 400 and 500 the result of isolated, in situ evolution, or did these sites evolve simultaneously as a result of interregional interaction and a response to external stimuli? The resolution of this question is important if we are to understand Middle Classic period cultural dynamics of the region, especially in reference to macroregional, core-periphery models.

As of now, it seems clear that both the Chalchihuites and the Malpaso cultures evolved out of a common simple agricultural village horizon. As the Chalchihuites culture developed specialized economic activities characteristic of a true periphery setting, it may have stimulated the need for the development of a geographic intermediary to link Chalchihuites to major exchange networks to the south and southeast and to the west Mexican core. La Quemada may have obtained that role, serving as a major administrative/redistribution center (middleman) in the exchange of the area's many resources.

A previous examination (Jiménez 1992b) of this area has noted that peer-polity interaction (Renfrew and Cherry 1986) seems pertinent among the major sites within the "northern sphere," defined by a series of shared or overlapping ceramic complexes, shared architectural styles, and iconography. At present, the distribution of the Type I figurine, pseudocloisonné ceramics, and the plaza-altar-pyramid complex during the Epi-Classic suggests the importance of symbolic entrainment among these polities. It is possible to model a number of elite interregional exchange networks, via a series of down-the-line exchanges, which crisscrossed the northwest frontier in practically all directions through interregional interaction spheres.

Recent advances in our understanding of obsidian utilization tend to confirm these observations (Darling 1998; Milhauser 1999). Obsidian utilization manifests two patterns of raw material acquisition and distribution: local acquisition and trade, and long-distance exchange of prismatic blades from sources to the south. The local pattern features use of poor- to medium-quality sources of raw material found in the highland regions' neighboring lowland valley agricultural zones. Up to five source areas consisting of multiple sources and volcanic flows have been documented, including the Llano Grande source in Durango, the Huitzila–La Lobera source area on the Zacatecas-Jalisco border, and Nochistlan on the eastern side of the Sierra de Morones bordering the Altos region of Jalisco. Two other source areas, the Chapalagana-Colorado and the Valparaiso-Bolaños, are believed to exist based on chemical composition of artifacts, although these have not been located on the ground (Darling 1998).

Local obsidian exploitation is straightforward in the north-central frontier. Since most available sources are of roughly the same quality, with the exception of the low-quality Nochistlan material, particular regions tended to use the nearest available source. Supply zones around these sources are readily distinguished and tend to vary in size according to their geographic location, accessibility, and the relative proximity of an alternate source. In general, zones of supply do not exceed a radius of 125 km from the source, and the relative frequency at archaeological sites of raw material from sources exhibits a decline with distance. Supply zones denote regular source exploitation by a population through direct access means.

Distribution of raw materials outside supply zones, through some form of exchange, did take place at the regional level and indicates potential relationships between peer polities in the Malpaso, Bolaños, Juchipila, and Tlaltenango valleys (Figure 10.21). The Chalchihuites zone relied on the Llano Grande source for raw material, with the exception of populations in the Río Colorado branch, which shared a source area with the Sierra del Nayar and perhaps the northern Valparaiso-Bolaños.

Obsidian exchange patterns replicate ceramic distributional patterns and point toward a greater unity of exchanged wares throughout the Malpaso, Juchipila, Tlaltenango, and Bolaños regions, particularly after the retraction of the Teuchitlán tradition, before A.D. 600. Greater interconnectivity locally, described as peer-polity interaction, may have been further enhanced by trade and movement of exotics.

In this way, the second pattern of obsidian distribu-

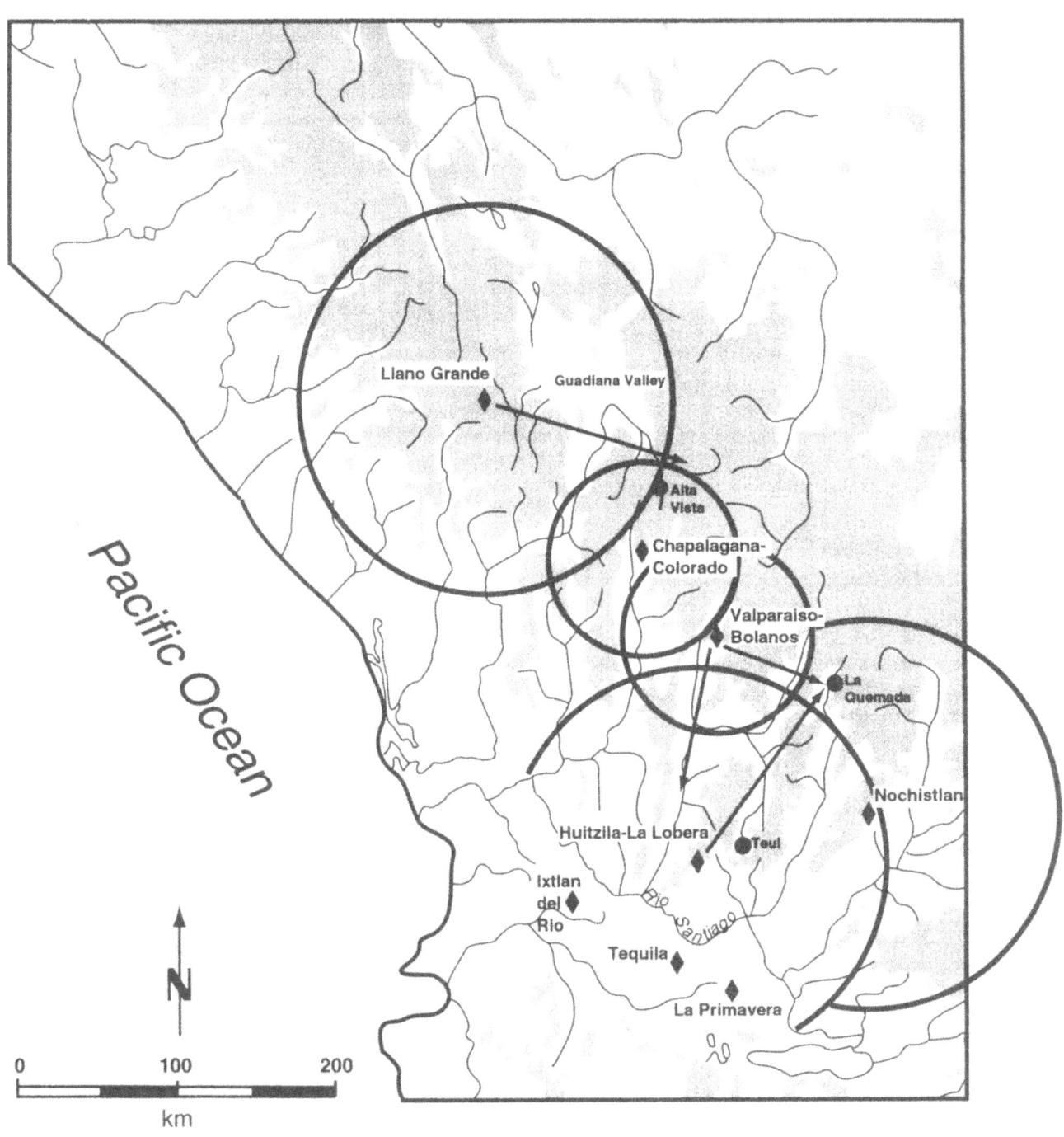

Figure 10.21. Distribution networks of obsidian raw material in the north-central frontier of Mesoamerica. Circles indicate supply zones around known and proposed source areas. Arrows indicate probable exchange of material to regions outside supply zones.

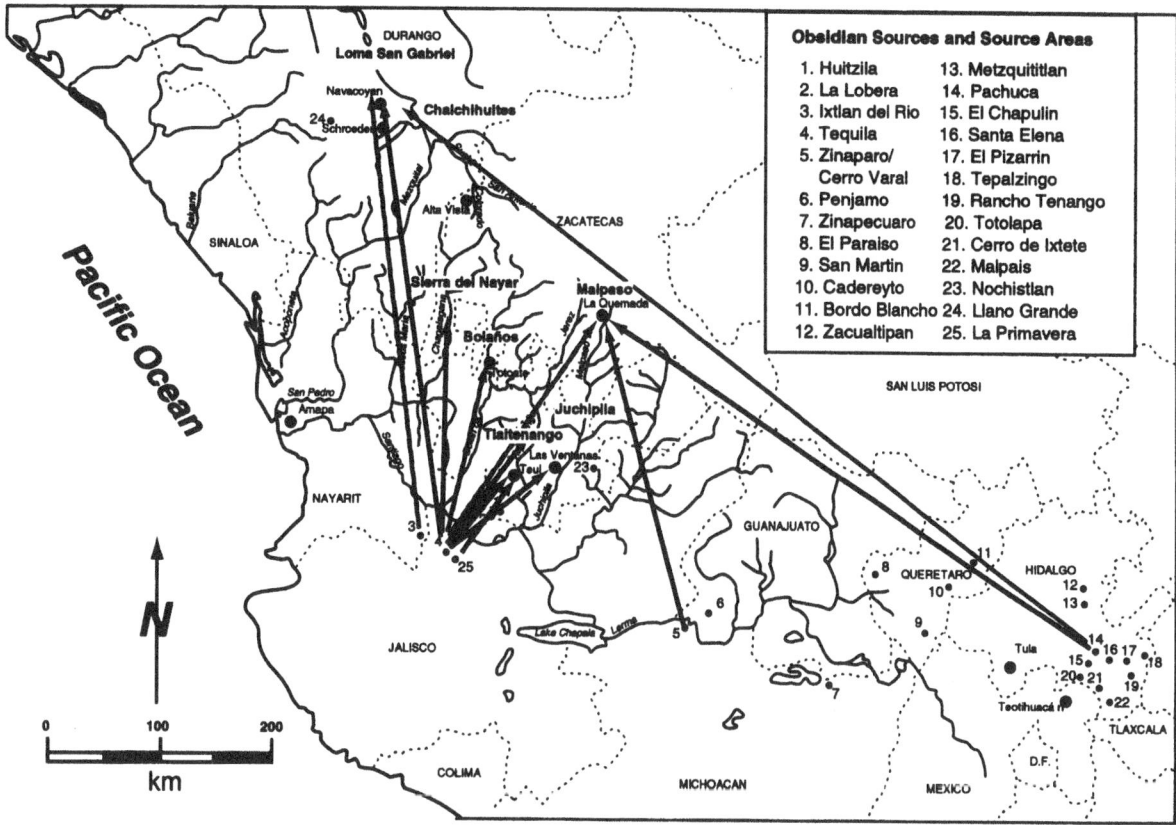

Figure 10.22. Distribution of prismatic blades from raw material sources in the north-central mesoamerican frontier based on compositional analysis.

tion, or the exchange of finished prismatic blades, points to probable routes of exchange between emergent polities with cultural systems located to the south. Evidence of prismatic blade production in the north-central frontier is absent. Compositional analysis of prismatic blades demonstrates two primary blade source areas: Pachuca in Hidalgo and sources associated with the Sierra la Primavera and the Tequila Volcano in Jalisco. A third source that supplied the Malpaso Valley is Cerro Varal in Michoacán. The occurrence of prismatic blades is limited to sites with formal architecture, and the blades generally appear in very small quantities (Figure 10.22).

These two patterns illustrate that distributional overlaps characterized as spheres in both ceramics and local obsidian point toward some form of peer-polity interaction between the north-central frontier and west Mexico that emerged with the retraction of the Teuchitlán system. The patterns of long-distance elite exchange suggest continued participation of the north in the larger west Mexican and mesoamerican worlds after the decline of both Teuchitlán and Teotihuacán.

Portable exotics such as obsidian blades occur in the north-central frontier, but one does not find central mesoamerican ceramics. After A.D. 600, with the exception of ceramic trade from the West Coast into the Bolaños-Tlaltenango and Guadiana-Chalchihuites valleys, the archaeological ceramic complex of the north-central frontier is all its own but clearly mesoamerican in derivation.

Local interaction has been defined as overlapping artifact distributions indicative of peer-polity interaction. This is a useful perspective since it argues, on the one hand, that the southern valleys of Zacatecas were not dependent colonies budding off central mesoamerican states, and, on the other hand, that they were not entirely closed systems either.

When we consider the cultural dynamics of the north-central frontier of Mesoamerica, the regional spheres that overlap with the boundaries of the Epi-Classic "northern sphere" should be contemplated as important resource zones. To the northwest, at around ca. A.D. 600, the Alta Vista phase occupation of the Suchil branch of Chalchihuites has begun at the same time as "southwestern" turquoise appears in Chalchihuites and Malpaso. Meanwhile, at the same time to the southeast of the northern sphere, obsidian from northern Michoacán and Pachuca regions appears in La Quemada. The ties to the Jalisco-Colima sphere have obvious implications for salt production in the Sayula Basin (Liot 1996, 1998), whereas the ties to Bolaños strongly suggest the movement of shell and cotton from the region of Amapa/Pacific coast and obsidian from highland Jalisco.

In most areas of Mesoamerica, outside the Valley of Mexico, the Epi-Classic was a period of regional apogee during which interregional interaction seems to have been at its most intense. Events in the northwest frontier were clearly an expression and in part a result of Epi-Classic developments in other areas of Mesoamerica.

In 1974, in one of his most stimulating articles, J. Charles Kelley (1974:23–24) proposed the existence of an interaction sphere for pseudocloisonné ceramics corresponding to many of the regions contemplated in this chapter. He concluded: "Other such interaction spheres may be identifiable in Northwestern Mesoamerica and clearly the more obvious traits that mark their unity as spheres will be supplemented by others when further investigations are made.... Working out the patterns, distributions, affiliations, operations, and functions of such interaction spheres promises to be a rewarding task for future investigations."

NOTES

1. At the time of this writing, excavations in the Malpaso Valley were concentrated in three areas within the site of La Quemada, primarily in contexts associated with its apogee and terminal phase architecture. Achim Lelgemann conducted excavations in the Citadel in the extreme northern precinct of La Quemada (Lelgemann 1997, 1999). Ben Nelson excavated on the western slope of the site on and around terrace 18 (Nelson 1993, 1997; Nelson et al. 1992) and is in the process of excavating the site of Pilarillos. Jiménez excavated in the southern ceremonial precinct in the Hall of Columns, the ball court, the votive pyramid plaza, and at the base of the Cuartel (Jiménez 1990, 1992a, 1998). In an effort to document earlier occupations at the site, test excavations in the deep fill of the terraces are planned. Likewise, extremely little excavation has been carried out in smaller sites that abound in the valley. This is in sharp contrast to the Chalchihuites region, where numerous village sites were tested before excavations began at Alta Vista.

2. The importance of the Loma San Gabriel culture lies in its relations with the preceramic and early ceramic groups of northern Mexico. Although the northern frontier has often been seen as a hard frontier, characterized by sedentary vs. nomadic populations (Armillas 1969), Loma clearly manifests the complexity of frontier dynamics. It seems to be an intermediate semisedentary or sedentary society whose role in northwestern Mexican prehistory is often overlooked. Loma groups seem to have been present throughout the long history of the north, developing out of the late Archaic period groups of the area and surviving almost into Historic times.

Loma peoples may have played a critical role in the regional economies of northwestern Mexico. For example, in view of the distribution of Loma as currently known (Foster 1985, 1995a) and the presence of southwestern turquoise in Chalchihuites, Malpaso, and Nayar contexts during the Epi-Classic period, Loma may have played a part in any process that moved items such as turquoise southward. Loma constitutes one of the most important directions for future study in the region. Although Loma-like ceramics have been reported in the Malpaso Valley, the extent and nature of such an early ceramic period is not understood.

3. Although unaware of Beatriz Braniff's (1972) previous Morales-Canutillo correlate, both Betty Bell (1974) and Glen Williams (1974) have noted a relationship between the early Altos ceramics and the Chalchihuites Canutillo phase wares. Clearly, the "initial wave" of early mesoamerican village occupation in the north had something to do with the Guanajuato/ Bajío and Altos and Juchipila regions. It is also very important to understand that the pseudocloisonné ceramic vessel published by Bell (1974) in association with her Cerro Encantado excavations is actually from a private collection from the area. The Cerro Encantado materials, including the Type I figurines described by Williams (1974) from the site, suggest an occupation from ca. A.D. 100–900.

4. A tentative ceramic typology exists for the Malpaso Valley and is in process of finalization through the collaboration of J. Andy Darling, Achim Lelgemann, Vince Schiavitti, Ben Nelson, and Peter Jiménez Betts. The descriptions of the incised-engraved wares are based, in part, on those proposed by Charles Trombold (1985, 1986).

5. The presence of Villanueva and Coyotes incised ceramics in the excavations of Structure 1 in Totoate and the two radiocarbon dates of A.D. 460 and A.D. 505 (Kelley 1971:771) that Kelley associates with the main occupation of Totoate correlate with the chronology for the Malpaso complex.

It should be noted that in the Malpaso Valley no regional variety of interior incised-engraved ware has been identified. At this point it seems diagnostic only of the Chalchihuites (Canutillo) area. As of 1998, dating this complex is limited to ceramic correlation and one radiocarbon date of A.D. 540 ± 80 from Nelson's (1997) excavations of a small hearth found directly over bedrock in the fill of terrace 18. Future work at the site will undoubtedly identify construction periods, the earliest beginning at around A.D. 450–500. It is therefore likely that the Malpaso complex, by correlation, can be dated earlier, but for the present we will retain a conservative estimation of its dating.

6. Radiocarbon dates from three burned beams found directly over the floor and under baked roof fragments in the Hall of Columns seem to mark the peak of construction at La Quemada. These dates are A.D. 870 to 990 (Beta–74016, 1-sigma calibration); A.D. 680 to 800 (Beta–74018, 1-sigma calibration); and A.D. 670 to 780 (Beta–74019, 1-sigma calibration).

Midden 170, associated with the Cuartel, produced four radiocarbon dates for the main corpus of ceramics of this complex: A.D. 770–890 (Beta–74021, 1-sigma calibration); A.D. 800 to 960 (Beta–74022, 1-sigma calibration); A.D. 720 to 740 (Beta–74023, 1-sigma calibration), and A.D. 760 to 880 (Jiménez 1997). Radiocarbon dates for the Malpaso outlier MV–138 range from A.D. 450 to A.D. 975 (Trombold 1990:Figure 4).

7. In the Malpaso Valley, the champleve technique was limited to the pseudocloisonné ceramics and was not developed as that seen in the Michilia ceramic type of the Chalchihuites area. There are general similarities between the incised-engraved types of the La Quemada complex and Chalchihuites engraved types (rim tabs, compound silhouette, leg forms, and some cross-hatching technique). As with the earlier incised-engraved wares of the Malpaso complex, however, the La Quemada complex incised-engraved wares are distinguishable by their austere execution and simple design patterns. Zoomorphic designs are not as common as among the Chalchihuites Michilia and Vesuvio ceramic types.

The generic relationship that exists between the incised-engraved wares of Chalchihuites and Malpaso Valley incised-engraved wares is not paralleled in the red-on-cream or the red-on-brown wares. In the Malpaso Valley, these wares never attain the fine painted line or the iconographic complexity of the Chalchihuites wares (Gualterio Red-on-cream and Suchil Red-on-brown). The two regions in question do share a wide-necked olla type known in the Malpaso Valley as El Sabino Red-on-brown (wide line paint). As noted, the red-on-cream and red-on-brown ceramics of the Malpaso Valley (La Quemada complex) have a very distinctive regional character with the red-on-cream ollas and bowls (Amboso type) sharing only general elements with the later Mercado ware of Chalchihuites.

The Tepozan negative painted polychrome ceramics of the Malpaso Valley represent a break with all previous ceramic types in the region. Seen in this ware for the first time is a wide variety of shapes and design elements manifesting a high level of technical and artistic skill. The iconography is rich and varied. The sudden appearance of this type suggests an increase in interaction southward with the neighboring Juchipila and Altos region, where negative painted wares appear from late Formative times (Bell 1974; Jiménez 1988). Notably, the Tepozan wares share some iconographic elements with the contemporary Michilia incised-engraved, as well as the quarter layout of Suchil Red-on-brown, of the Chalchihuites area. Localized styled representations, however, such as coyote, feline, and eagle, which were previously absent, suddenly appear in this type. This type is an elite ware, as is pseudocloisonné. An important variant within the Tepozan negative type is the tripod mammiform support bowl (Batres 1903; Lelgemann 1992:Figure 20a; Nelson 1993:Figure 10.6, Trombold Collection from the 1974 investigations), which has a correlative distribution (regional variant) to the Juchipila (Jiménez 1988) and Atemajac valleys (Galván 1976:lam. 11-G) to the south. In the Atemajac Valley, they form part of the Ixtepete–El Grillo complex (A.D. 600–900). This is the only variant within the Tepozan negative type that has any direct external correlate. The Tepozan ware per se has not yet been identified outside the Malpaso Valley.

8. Holien (1977:Figure 22) shows and describes a very distinctive decorative layout of a pseudocloisonné bowl from Totoate. Fragments with this unique design have been found in midden 170 at La Quemada and also at the site of Cerro del Tepesuazco in Jalpa in the northern Juchipila Valley.

9. In November 1997, Ma. Teresa Cabrero provided Jiménez the opportunity to study her ceramic collections for the Bolaños area. We were able to identify intrusive ceramic types from various areas. I greatly appreciate her collaboration and assistance. Cabrero is currently undertaking a more detailed analysis of middle Bolaños region ceramics.

10. For the descriptions of the Type I figurines throughout this area, see Braniff 1990, 1992a; Galván 1976; Jiménez 1988, 1995; Nelson 1993; Saenz 1966; Sánchez Correa 1995; Trombold 1985; Williams 1974. Otto Schöndube (personal communication 1994) found the Type I figurines associated with Cerrito de García type figurines and Ixtepete–El Grillo complex ceramics at Juanacatlán, Jalisco. Although they were initially assigned to the Epi-Classic (Jiménez 1989), a later revision of the El Cóporo, Guanajuato, ceramic sequence (blanco levantado and thin orange ceramics) by Braniff (1990) suggested that Type I figurines were more likely associated with the Middle Classic period (Jiménez 1992b). In a later discussion of El Cóporo ceramic types, Braniff (1992a) included Valle San Luis Polychrome in what we now can consider a Cóporo phase context (mixed fill between floors) that corresponds to the Epi-Classic period. Thus, the Type I figurine from El Cóporo appears to retain its Epi-Classic (A.D. 600/650–850) association and is contemporaneous with other Type I figurines from the general region.

11. A series of hearths from the banquette of the plaza of the votive pyramid at La Quemada produced two radiocarbon dates: A.D. 1000 to 1040 (Beta–74024, 1-sigma calibration) and A.D. 910 to 920 and A.D. 950 to 1020 (Beta–74025, 1-sigma calibration). Armillas's work in the Cuartel also produced a number of late, post–A.D. 900 dates from the southern section of La Quemada (see Trombold 1990:Figure 4). Current excavations in the Citadel, in the extreme northern end of the site, have produced some similarly late radiocarbon dates from fire pits in the Ciudadela (Lelgemann 1999). To date, no Toltec artifacts have been identified in the Malpaso Valley.

12. The present synthesis on Juchipila is based on analysis of the Sescosse collection (Kelley 1971), which consists of ceramic materials salvaged from the Juchipila Valley when Sr. Sescosse served as INAH's delegate in Zacatecas. The collection comes from a series of contexts from the Río Apozol floodplain in and around the sites of Mesa de la Purísima and la Tirisia (Jiménez 1989, 1995).

The José Muro Ríos collection from the Apozol zone is from the site of Loma del Tecalli and from the Jalpa Museum, which exhibits collections from the Cerro del Indio and Cerro Tepisuazco. Other ceramic data from this region come from recent INAH salvage work in the town of Juchipila and surface collections from the monumental site of Las Ventanas. The present excavation of the ceremonial site of Cerro Tepisuazco above the Jalpa floodplain by Jiménez and García Uranga is, to date, the primary source of information for the Classic period occupation in the valley.

13. The geographical distribution of the Altos annular-based negative painted polychrome bowl is for the most part centered on the Río Verde, which probably hints of its importance as an Epi-Classic communication artery. Most of the "Altos" sphere occurs within the limits of the southern section (south of the Malpaso Valley) of the "northern sphere" (i.e., Type I figurine). An eastern extension of the Altos sphere protrudes into the region of Cerritos de Raya near León, Guanajuato (Ramos and López 1992), although Type I figurines have not yet been identified there. Its northernmost extension is into the La Montesa and Villa García regions, to the east of the Malpaso Valley. It also extends through the northern Juchipila Valley to the Jalapa region (the Cerro Tepesuazco site) and south through the Juchipila Valley to the Tepatitlán region. As mentioned above, this ceramic type is intrusive in the Sayula Basin, as is the Type I figurine (Noyola 1994:79; Otto Schöndube and Susana Ramírez Urrea, personal communication 1994).

To the northeast, centered in the San Luis Potosí Valley, Valle San Luis Polychrome (Crespo 1991; Braniff 1992a) appears to be another key horizon marker for the Epi-Classic. Intrusive in the Malpaso Valley, this ceramic type is seen in high frequencies in the Cerritos, Zacatecas (Braniff 1992a), La Montesa, and Villa García regions, 90 km east of the Malpaso Valley. The La Montesa region seems to mark a transitional zone where three major spheres for the Epi-Classic and their diagnostic elements—the Type I figurine, the annular based Altos type bowls, and Valle San Luis Polychrome—come together. Valle San Luis Polychrome is intrusive in El Cóporo (Braniff 1992a), the La Gavia region of northwest Guanajuato (Sánchez Correa 1995), and El Cerrito de Rayas, Guanajuato (Ramos and López 1992). These areas make up what appears to be the western edge of the Altos sphere. Here Valle San Luis Polychrome is found in association with the Type I figurine. Valle San Luis Polychrome seems to be an important ceramic sphere, which in its westernmost extension (La Montesa) seems to overlap into the northern sphere. In the extreme southeast portion of this zone, it is found intrusive in the El Cerrito, Querétaro, region of the Bajío (Crespo 1991). To the south, it is intrusive in the Río Verde region of San Luis Potosí (Michelet 1984).

In the southeastern margins of the northern sphere, in the Altos-Juchipila subsphere, in archaeological contexts at La Gavia, Guanajuato (Sánchez Correa 1995), and in the Sierra de Comanja, Guanajuato (Ramos and López 1992), the Epi-Classic is defined by the presence of the Garita Incised and Cantinas Red-on-cream, major markers of the central Bajío region (Castañeda et al. 1998). These markers also extend to the Cuitzeo zone in Michoacán. This overlap of ceramic types is important and may have implications for studying the exchange of obsidian in the region.

14. The identification of the regional variant of the Atoyac incised bowls from the Juchipila Valley was first made by Jean Guffroy in 1996 and was subsequently confirmed by Susana Ramírez, Luís Gómez Gastélum, and Javier Reveles, all members of the Proyecto Arqueologico de Sayula. The Jalpa Museum has examples of Cerrito de García figurines reported to be from the site of Cerro de Tepisuazco in the Juchipila Valley. Others are from the José Muro collection from the Apozol zone, an association confirmed by Ramírez Urrea, Gómez Gastélum, and Reveles. For a description of the Cerrito de García figurine (Type f), see Gómez Gastélum and de la Torre Ruiz 1996:141–142, and for a discussion of their distribution, see Ramírez Urrea 1997. In the Sayula Basin these figurines have been found at Cerritos Colorados, Casita, and El Aguacatito; in the Atemajac Valley at El Ixtepete (Saenz 1966); and on the Pacific coast at Playa del Tesoro, Colima (Beltrán 1991). For examples of the effigy ollas, see Jiménez 1989, 1995; Lumholtz 1902; Noyola 1994; Schöndube 1983; Jiménez and Williams 1974.

15. Translated by Jiménez.

16. The Bolaños negative painted ceramics can be distinguished from all other negative types in the area because of their wide line (buff) decoration and characteristic orange-red paint.

17. The incised wares of the Tlaltenango Valley are distinguishable by a deep, wide incision.

18. The work by Cabrero and López (1998) in El Piñón has identified two phases of occupation at the site. The early circular complex and shaft tombs are found on the lower section of the hill, and the Epi-Classic rectangular architectural component is located higher on the hill. Excavation in the Epi-Classic architectural complex has resulted in the recovery of the diagnostic ceramics for this period in the Bolaños region, four types (three ceramic and one plaque type) of which have been identified in La Quemada phase contexts at La Quemada.

CHAPTER ELEVEN

THE ARCHAEOASTRONOMICAL SYSTEM IN THE RÍO COLORADO CHALCHIHUITES POLITY, ZACATECAS

An Interpretation of the Chapín 1 Pecked Cross-Circle

J. CHARLES KELLEY AND ELLEN ABBOTT KELLEY

THE CEREMONIAL CENTER of Alta Vista, Chalchihuites (Figure 11.1), is located in the Río Colorado Valley in western Zacatecas at 23°28.8' north latitude and 103°56.7' west longitude, only 0°2.3' north of the present Tropic of Cancer (Aveni et al. 1982:316). The site is situated on the apex and eastern slope of a minor ridge on the outwash plain of the mountains that bound the Río Colorado (a branch of the Río Suchil) on the west, at an elevation of over 2,260 m. Today cultivated fields surround the site, and in 1971 the site itself was cultivated, with lush cornfields interrupted by thick stands of tree-sized prickly pear, grasses, and scattered *huisachi* trees. Horse-rider trails and country roads, most of them following the course of prehistoric roadways, converge on the site. On the north and on the south, especially, major arroyos isolate it effectively; to the east the fields slant steeply downward, bypassing the large Alta Vista mining group on their left.

Alta Vista, in keeping with its name, commands a broad view of the Río Chalchihuites Valley, where cultivated lands of red-colored soils rise steeply on the east to the town of Chalchihuites and its great spring, the Spanish mine of La Esmeralda, and the mountains that form a horizon calendar beyond. Unlike the craggy hill site of La Quemada, Alta Vista does not stand out aggressively on its low ridge.

THE ALTA VISTA POLITY

Alta Vista did not exist as an isolated ceremonial center. The upper Río Colorado/Suchil drainage, at least, appears to have been an organized cultural system, or polity, during the full Nucleation period,[1] with related site components, including the ceremonial center of Alta Vista, fortified hilltop astronomical observation sites on the north and south, many hamlets ("*ranchos*") scattered along the Río Colorado (Chalchihuites) and its tributaries, and numerous mining groups.[2] During the previous Village Formative period, Canutillo phase villages were widespread in the entire Río Suchil drainage and apparently in the upper Río Chapalagana drainage as well.

The site of Alta Vista had no natural defenses, but some seven kilometers to the south the site of Cerro el Chapín occupies a high fortified butte, as does Cerro Pedragoso to the northeast. Chapín and Pedragoso on their apexes could have functioned both as astronomical observation points and as strongholds defending the ceremonial center and the many villages and hamlets surrounding it.

Alta Vista is the major ceremonial center of the Chalchihuites cultural tradition. On the basis of 51 radiocarbon determinations, we believe the site was occupied from ca. A.D. 400/450 until ca. A.D. 900/925. The

Figure 11.1. The ceremonial center of Alta Vista, Chalchihuites, Zacatecas. Courtesy of Alejandro Peschard F.

Chalchihuites cultural tradition, in the Río Suchil area of Zacatecas and Durango, is thought to have existed from ca. A.D. 200/300 through A.D. 950/1000. There is reason to believe that the site itself was established by an astronomically oriented group from the mesoamerican core, probably Teotihuacán, searching for the place where there was only one zenith passage of the sun, the Tropic of Cancer.

Early excavation of parts of the nucleus of the site was made by archaeologist Manuel Gámio in 1908 (Gámio 1910). Archaeologists from the Southern Illinois University at Carbondale carried out excavations at Alta Vista in 1971, 1974, and 1975–76, after a previous decade of excavations in village sites in the area. Excavations were resumed at the site under our direction in 1991–93, under the auspices of INAH and the state of Zacatecas, in collaboration with Zacatecas state archaeologist Peter Jiménez Betts and INAH archaeologist Baudelina García U. Excavations at Alta Vista are ongoing under the direction of archaeologist García U.

THE HORIZON CALENDAR AND THE ARCHAEOASTRONOMICAL ARRAY

Observations made during fieldwork by the Southern Illinois University at Carbondale at Alta Vista in the 1970s clearly demonstrated that the Sierra de Chalchihuites (part of the Sierra Prieta) formed an eastern horizon calendar, neatly bracketing the solstices as seen from Alta Vista. When the structure named the Labyrinth, or Observatory (Figure 11.2), was excavated there during the 1975–76 season, it was observed that the equinox sunrise over the small isolated peak of Picacho Pelón in the horizon calendar, viewed from the Labyrinth, sent light rays into that structure, illuminating the Temple of the Suns. On the summer solstice, the single zenith passage of the sun in the Labyrinth was displayed when the included gnomon cast no shadows at noon. It was noted also that the site was situated virtually on the Tropic of Cancer and that survey stakes plastered into the walls of the building indicated that its location and layout had been planned carefully.

The aid and advice of archaeoastronomer Anthony Aveni was sought; after he visited the site, he confirmed previous observations and verified both the existence of the horizon calendar and the fact that original constructions at Alta Vista had their diagonals oriented to the cardinal directions, apparently a unique orientation in Mesoamerica (Aveni et al. 1982).

At the suggestion of Aveni, Kelley and associates observed the summer solstice sunrise from the high fortified site of Cerro el Chapín. Observed from one of the two large pecked cross-circle petroglyphs on the eastern edge of Chapín (Chapín 1), the sun was seen to rise directly behind the same Picacho Pelón, confirming a prediction made by Aveni. Later Aveni returned to Chapín on the summer solstice and confirmed this sighting (Aveni et al. 1982).

Still later we viewed the winter solstice sunrise from the high fortified site of Cerro Pedragoso, located north of Alta Vista, and observed that at that time the sun rose over the same Picacho Pelón (Figure 11.3). Thus, it was determined that Alta Vista was the planned center of a three-site archaeoastronomical complex, anchored on the pecked cross-circles on Chapín. These pecked cross-circles indicate a significant relation of the local system with Teotihuacán, where they occur in considerable numbers (Aveni 1988; Aveni and Hartung 1985; Aveni et al. 1978; Millon 1973).

Figure 11.2. The Labyrinth Observatory at Alta Vista. Note the free-standing gnomon at the end of the feature.

THE CROSS-CIRCLE PETROGLYPHS

The studies of Aveni and others have contributed greatly to knowledge of the now famous pecked cross-circle petroglyphs. These were formed by pecking small circular pits into rock outcrops or into plastered building floors. Here reference is made only to double circles of peck marks crossed by lines of pecked marks dividing the circle into four quadrants. Other petroglyphs depicted as squares, with "wings" at the corners, almost certainly were playing boards for the games of *quince* or *patoli*.

Although the petroglyphs differ from place to place, there are certain elements that are widely shared. The division of the figures into quadrants undoubtedly represents the four world quarters, the fourfold division of *trecenas* (13-day ritual periods of the calendar) under the four year-bearers (*tlalpilli*), and the fourfold astronomical division of the year formed by the equinoxes and the solstices, and is a constant element.[3] In many cases the arms of the cross each form a 10–4–4 ratio (the number 18), if the pits at their intersections with the circles are not counted. The central pit probably represents zero; it may also represent a world center or place of emergence and in some instances the sun. Counts of the pits often include numbers familiar in mesoamerican calendric calculations, including the uniquely mesoamerican 260 ritual day count, about which Caso (1971:333) notes, "The calendar is one of the basic traits of Mesoamerican culture and is not found outside Mesoamerica."[4]

There is general agreement that the petroglyphs functioned in some way as calendars. In some instances they appear to represent a sort of surveying benchmark as well, serving to orient the observer and to provide planning data. Because of the interrelation of the calendar and astronomical observations, the petroglyphs are also thought to represent recording devices for astronomical observations.

The hypothesis here advanced is that these figures are (1) individual mnemonic devices for esoteric, calendric, ritualistic data, in effect, numerical "anagrams." It has been suggested that the calculations were made by placing pebbles in the holes (Worthy and Dickens, Jr. 1983). (2) The figures may have been used for prognostications, demonstrations, or predictions of astronomical calendrical events, and perhaps as heuristic devices for novices. (3) They may be regarded as individualized substitutions for actual codices, encoded by their makers, who alone, together with assistants or novices, can decipher them, and, as such, are records of calendric and astronomical events.[5] (4) They may have been created and maintained over long periods of time by religious societies dedicated to keeping count of the days, the *veintenas* (20-day "months"), the *trecenas* (13-day ritual periods), and the calendar rounds (52-year "centuries"); and to making the routine astronomical observations necessary for keeping the calendar updated and corrected.

These petroglyphs have been found in large numbers at Teotihuacán and its environs, including the state of Mexico, at Uaxactun (3 examples; Smith 1950); at a site near Purepero in Michoacán (Aveni and Hartung 1985); the two examples from Cerro el Chapín (Aveni et al. 1982:324–326; Castañeda, in Amadór 1892:235; Gámio 1910:477), one, the Tuitan circle, from the

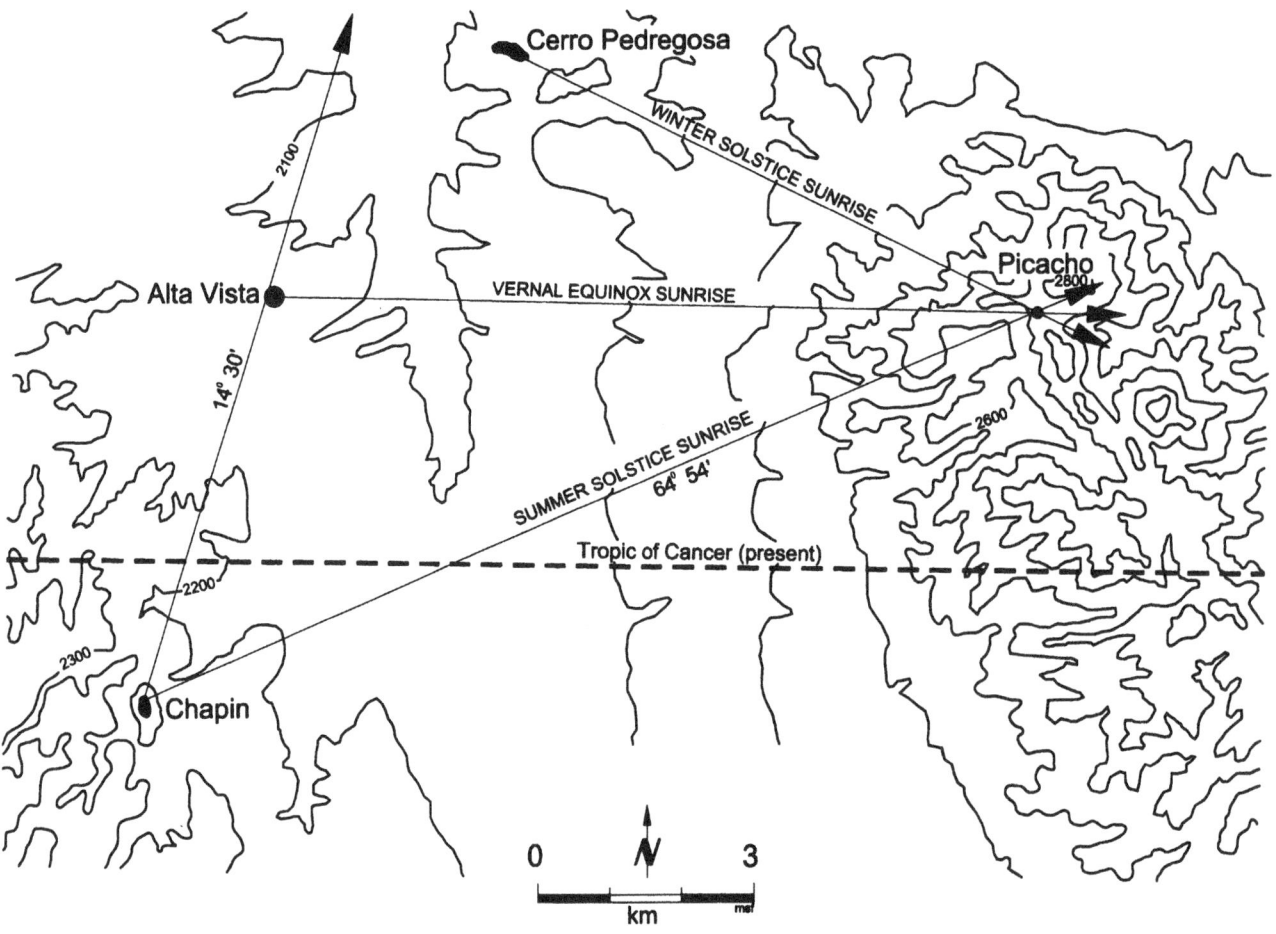

Figure 11.3. The Chalchihuites astronomical array.

malpais area southeast of the city of Durango (Aveni et al. 1982:329); and others. Notably, as already mentioned, a building called the Labyrinth, or Observatory, at the Alta Vista site apparently was constructed to observe the equinox sunrise, the single zenith passage of the sun, and probably other solar and stellar events.

THE CERRO EL CHAPÍN CROSS-CIRCLE PETROGLYPHS

The Cerro el Chapín pecked cross-circles lie about 7 km from Alta Vista, and the latter site is approximately 14°30' east of north from Chapín (measured on the Centenal map), which is very close to "Teotihuacán North" (15°30'; Millon 1973:37). In the Alta Vista field notes from the 1971 excavations, there is a notation of an alidade back-shot to the center of Chapín from the pyramid at Alta Vista, recorded as 15°45' west of south.

It was known that Alta Vista was located directly west of Picacho Pelón, with the walls of major structures carefully staked out. Why that specific point on the mesa west of Picacho had been selected was not clear at first. But if the 14°30' east of north location of Alta Vista (or 15°45'?) is not just a remarkable coincidence, this datum must indicate that the entire archaeoastronomical complex was planned from and based on Cerro el Chapín and that the hypothesis of a Teotihuacán–Alta Vista relationship is further supported.

The Cerro el Chapín examples, especially Chapín 1, have been studied intensively.[6] The numerology of Chapín 1 includes observable or inferential numbers of 0, 1(?), 2, 4, 5, 9, 10, 13, 18, 20, 25, 26, 28, 36, 45, 46, 50, 52, 72 (73 with zero counted as one), 100, 104; the total number of pits is 260, plus the putative zero central point, which may on occasion have served as the number 1. Two extra larger pits were placed in opposed quadrants; quadrants basically were oriented northeast,

Figure 11.4. The Chapín 1 pecked cross petroglyph.

northwest, southwest, and southeast (Figures 11.4 and 11.5).

Aveni (1988:469) has advised that researchers should not look at these depictions solely through Western eyes. Nevertheless, almost all researchers have regarded the intersecting crossed lines as a unitary element, plus the double circle of pits as a second unitary item. This probably is, at least partially, erroneous; they appear to be unified parts of the whole.

The hypothesis proposed here is that each concentric circle served to record calendric day counts (including the five "bad days" of the *nemontemi*), the outer circle recording the days of the *veintenas,* or 20-day months, and the inner circle recording the days of the *trecenas,* or 13-day ritual periods; and that the 10–4–4 (18) cross line pits functioned to record the 18 *veintenas* of the solar year. To the creator, the petroglyph must have been a patterned array of numbers to be encoded according to his needs, accounting for the diversity in numbers and other features in such depictions elsewhere.

The total count of pits in the outside circle, including those at the intersections of the cross arms, is 104. This certainly represents two full calendar rounds of 52 solar (vague) years of 365 days. Furthermore, Carlson (1991:212) states that the number 104, at least in Maya astronomy, was a factor in creating a Great Venus cycle (65 × 584 [approximate Venus cycle] = 104 × 365 = 146 × 260 = 37,960 days). The four 10–4–4 (18) cross arms total 72, and adding to it the zero point serving as the number 1 brings the count to 73, the number of ritual years in the calendar round. Additionally, Carlson notes that 73 × 8 = 584; the average synodic period of Venus equals 583.92 days.

There may be further support for the Venus connection in the iconography of Chalchihuites ceramics. Several recovered vessels of the type Suchil Red-on-brown have interior quadrate designs produced by intersecting "serpent bands"; two of the opposed quadrants are filled with geometric line figures. The other two opposed quadrants are filled with life forms. Common is a *cipactli*-like figure (Figure 11.6a) with a multipointed star on each side. Braniff (1995), in an intuitive discussion of these *chimeras,* notes that the claws are those of a bird and the bifurcated tongue is that of a serpent; hence this is a caiman-serpent-bird (Figure 11.6b and c). Jiménez (1995:Figure 8c) notes a similar combination of elements (tiger, serpent, and bird) in a sherd of Vesuvio Red-Filled Engraved from Alta Vista and comments on the similarity of this design to a Teotihuacán mural illustrated by Sejourné (1957:196). The "stars" shown also are probably Venus symbols, and they may represent the planet in its morning and evening star aspects.[7] At the small Chalchihuites site of Potrero del Calichal, a burial (no. 34) was accompanied by an exceptional example of such a Suchil plate or shallow bowl (catalog no. PC 636). The interior is decorated in the customary four quadrants, formed by the crossed bands with apparent serpent markings and a double concentric circle pattern, plus one central dot (place of emergence, world center, sipapu, or sun symbol?) at their central intersection (Figure 11.7). Two opposed quadrants are filled with parallel bands of geometric motifs (double straight lines, negative squiggly lines, double positive squiggly lines). The other two opposed quadrants are each occupied by an anthropomorphic robed figure that may represent a priest holding in his right hand a vertical rod ending in a salver on which rests a severed dripping human heart. The figures each have two overlapping heads, eyes, and plumed headdresses. One of these heads is shown as hatched, the other solid, perhaps representing duality—life and death.

In these two panels, the interior bordering lines each have 14 attached figures, which may represent the five pointed half-stars of Teotihuacán[8] thought to represent Venus symbols (Carlson 1993) at Teotihuacán, Cacaxtla, and elsewhere. The number 28 (14 × 2), as noted, is a significant number in mesoamerican calendrics, representing an approximation of a lunar cycle and a cipher

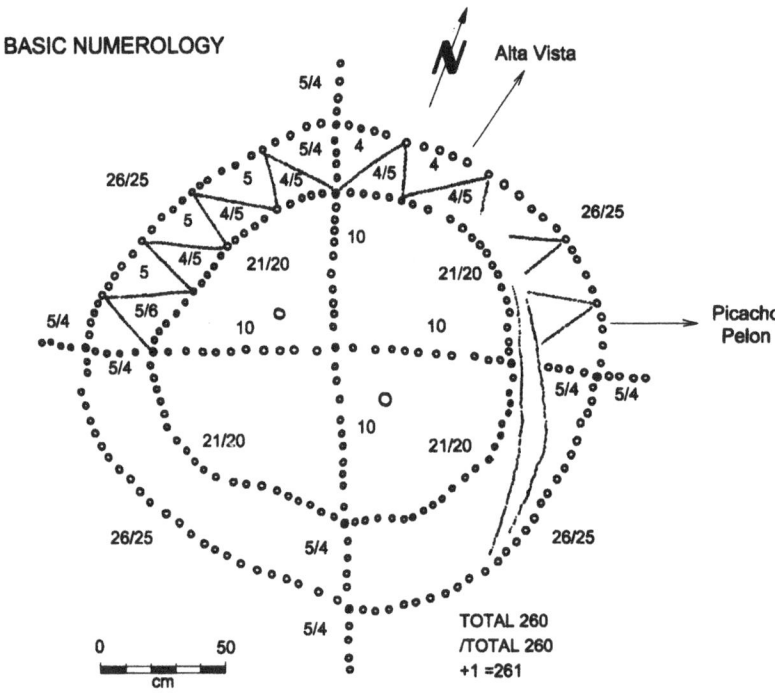

Figure 11.5. The basic numerology of the Chapín 1 pecked cross.

in the calculation of a solar year of 364 days (13 × 28). It is also the number of columns of the second construction phase in the Hall of Columns at Alta Vista. The entire complex illustration may well represent a Venus-related human sacrifice (Carlson 1991) like those at Teotihuacán and Cacaxtla.

That calendrical and astronomical data were not only manipulated but recorded in Chapín 1 seems certain, but the recording system requires analysis. Worthy and Dickens, Jr. (1983), apparently using Chapín 1 as their example, have demonstrated that a series of operations carried out by placing and removing pebbles in the pits in a specific sequence using only the pits in the cross, plus the two paired larger pits, could produce the number of days of the 365-day solar year. That the technique of using pebbles or other items placed in various pits could be used in calculations seems probable, but it does not solve the problem of recording days and various multiples thereof.

It is suggested that an astronomical priesthood, or specific shamans, charged with maintenance of the calendar could have kept a count of the days of the solar and/or ritual year by placing pebbles (or beans, as in the *patoli* game) in the pits, day by day, until solar and ritual year counts were completed. Alternately, pigments in various colors may have been the recording units, perhaps used with wooden pegs. It would have been necessary that such items remain in place for long periods of time, perhaps by gluing with pitch or through careful routine maintenance. Individual years could have been recorded by count markers on the pecked cross-circles and also by placing a ritual arrow in a container, as done elsewhere in Mesoamerica and in one instance at Alta Vista.[9]

As noted above, intensive analysis of the Chapín 1 petroglyph has indicated that it was a remarkably well engineered computing device. It had the potential for calculating and recording at least two full calendar rounds, using only numbers and calculations (verifiable yearly by observation of the summer solstice or zenith sun passage), without using glyphs for the names of days and "months," which would have been common knowledge of the observers.

There remains the question how the successive calendar rounds were recorded, if indeed they were. Caso (1971:335; also Lizardi Ramos 1959:1:233–234) notes that the Mexico City area has produced serpent heads marked with a series of bars and dots, apparently recording an eighth New Fire Ceremony, presumably the final one held in A.D. 1507. Caso believed the eight taken

Figure 11.6. Representations of caiman-like figures. *a,* Representation of Tezcatlipoca with a *cipactli*-like figure; *b–c,* representations of caiman monster on Chalchihuites Suchil Red-on-brown pottery.

Figure 11.7. A Suchil Red-on-brown bowl from the site of Potrero del Calichal with a possible representation of a robed priest.

together covered the Aztec period, dating back to A.D. 1116 (52 × 8).

In Chapín 1, a series of open incised triangles pointing to pits on the exterior and connecting the two circles at intervals of five pits, with exceptions, may represent recordings of New Fire Ceremonies held at the end of each calendar round of 52 years and incorporating the five unnamed days (*nemontemi*) of the 360 + 5-day year. There are eight of these triangles, beginning at the eastern "spoke" and moving progressively counterclockwise, putatively representing calendar rounds and New Fire Ceremonies. If so, eight New Fire Ceremonies would represent 8 × 52 years (416 years), plus any extra beginning or terminal years.

Earlier, the eight major periods of massive plastering of the ceremonial nucleus of Alta Vista—Structure 2—had been tentatively identified as marking the beginnings of calendar rounds (Abbott Kelley 1978), because of the mesoamerican custom of refurbishing old temples or constructing new ones after each New Fire Ceremony. This datum would correspond to the use of the triangles in Chapín 1, with the implication that the latter was established coincidentally with very early construction at Alta Vista, radiocarbon dated at A.D. 410 (330–490; Beta 73994; uncorrected; calibrated by Beta at 1 sigma A.D. 430–620), or even earlier. Nicholson (1971:409) notes, with reference to mesoamerican migrations: "The erection of a shrine for the patron deity usually constituted the first official act of settlement of a new community."

The pecked cross-circle petroglyphs (Chapín 1 and 2) located on the eastern edge of Cerro el Chapín cannot be dated archaeologically, inasmuch as the associated ruins appear to range through the entire gamut of the Suchil branch phases of the Chalchihuites cultural tradition, together with one structure apparently representative of the putatively earlier Loma San Gabriel culture (Foster 1985, 1995a; Kelley 1971). The discovery of a pair of these markers at Teotihuacán, one carved in a plaster floor, led Millon to believe they were used to lay out the east-west axis of the city grid (Millon 1973:Figures 57a and b); no precise dates were given, but probably they date at least to the Early or Late Tlamimilolpa phase, A.D. 250–350 (Rattray 1991:5–6) or earlier. At Uaxactun, examples occur carved in plastered floors dated calendrically to Tzakol I at ca. A.D. 357–445 (A. L. Smith 1950:Figure 151, and plans of Structure A–5, Vault Ic–f). Robert E. Smith (1955:3) dated the Tzakol period to A.D. 278–593. Chapín 2 may indeed have been created with a New Fire Ceremony around A.D. 400, but Chapín 1 appears to be later.

The Chapín 2 pecked cross-circle petroglyph has not been studied in detail. It is smaller than Chapín 1 and is not well preserved. It may represent the first actual appearance of Teotihuacán astronomer-priests in the Alta Vista area, whereas the fully developed Chapín 1 petroglyph was pecked and made operational with the construction of the Hall of Columns and its great forecourt at ca. A.D. 400/450. It is also possible that Chapín 1 was carved with the arrival of the contingent that constructed the Teotihuacán-style Apartment Compound and the Labyrinth at Alta Vista around A.D. 500/550. Which, if either, of these possibilities is correct cannot be verified with known data. Notably, the first three of the triangles of Chapín 1 putatively representing New Fire or calendar-round dates were depicted incomplete. It is possible, therefore, that these represent remembered calendar-round occurrences that took place while Chapín 2 was in use but where there apparently was no recording of such dates. In any event, the complexity of Chapín 2, and its direct association with visible astronomical phenomena, indicates that its format, like that of later Chapín 1, was based on long-term actual observations, which must have been recorded in some way.

THE MODEL

The basic question we faced was, How can one proceed in order to interpret or "decode" such a complex artifact? "The facts do not speak for themselves; they must be cross-examined" (Kluckhohn 1940:42 [statement attributed to Talcott Parsons]). Because the creators and users could never be present to explicate the "code," it seemed clear that experimentation was the only possible procedure. A variety of models must be developed until (and if) one could be found that when applied would appropriately use all data and produce a workable mesoamerican calendar.

Certain clues are available, however. If the pits of the outer circle numbered 104, each of the cross arms would then have 18 pits, plus the central "zero" point. The number 18 suggests a recording of the 18 months of the year. The "Calendar Wheel," as pictured in Sahagún (Book 7, Anderson and Dibble 1953, Illustrations, 20, and descriptive text, attributed to Paso y Troncoso 1898, 1905–1906), resembles a modified version of the pecked cross-circles. It is depicted as a circular device made up of 13 concentric circular bands (14 lines) divided by directional cross arms into four named quarters, with a circular center design.

The text indicates that actually four spirals are represented instead of the concentric bands. Each of the cross arms bears numbers 1–13. The associated text reads in part:

> The table ... is the year count, and it is a most ancient thing. ... It proceedeth in this way: they begin with the east, which is where the reeds are ... and say One Reed. And thence they go to the north, where the flint is, and they say Two Flint Knife. Then they go to the west where the house is and they say Three House. Then they go to the north [sic; south], which is where the rabbit is, and they say Four Rabbit. Then they turn to the east and say Five Reed. And thus they go, making four revolutions, until they reach thirteen, so that they end where they began. And then they return to one, saying One Flint Knife. And in this way, making revolutions, they assign thirteen years to each of the characters, or to each of the four quarters of the world. And the fifty-two years are completed, which is a bundle of years, when ... the new fire is made. ... Then they again count as at the beginning.

In this example there is a clear generic relation to the Chapín cross-circles but a great number of differences. Just as the Mexica no longer used the bar and dot for numbers as in Teotihuacán, Maya, and others (Caso 1971:335; Marcus 1992:96), and as Teotihuacán did not use the Maya Long Count, so the Chapín calendars focus on the 18 20-day months of the year rather than on the 13-day periods (*trecenas*) featured in the Mexica calendar. The count of 18 *veintenas* plus the 5 days of *nemontemi* is ancient and important because it correlates with the astronomical year, whereas the 260 days of *trecenas* is an esoteric mesoamerican count that relates to the astronomical year only by complex calendrical calculations. Both are essential elements of the mesoamerican calendar and must be incorporated in any model that may explicate the Chapín 1 calendar. Notably, the Mexica calendar, as described by Sahagún, may have been used for prognostications and as a mnemonic device, but it could not have been used for actual recording of calendric counts. This is also the case with the various calendars illustrated by Aveni (1980:155, Figure 57).

The literature is remarkably lacking in descriptions of actual recording devices, with the exception of the ethnographic Chamula wooden calendar board (Aveni 1980:43–44, Figure 14; Gossen 1974; Marshack 1974:Figures 1–4). The latter had a count of days marked on wood with charcoal, recording 18 specially indicated months of 20 days, plus one set of 5 days, totaling 365 days. The female shaman who owned it reportedly marked it every morning; other shamans in the village kept similar records on wood. The charcoal markings had been erased and marked over again many times, and the board reportedly was more than one hundred years old. Marshack (1974:264) noted: "The Chamula board is cumulative and notational. It is possible, therefore, that the essential pattern, breakdown and count might have been symbolized in permanent form on stone. However, I know of no such published artifact." According to Aveni (1980:43, referring to Lincoln 1942), the Ixil people in Guatemala were using a 260-day calendar in the 1940s, kept by one shaman and correlated with the 365-day calendar by another shaman specializing in the 20-day months.[10] Perhaps the Chapín 1 petroglyph supplies the archaeological artifact that Marshack speculated should exist.

In developing a satisfactory model, various options had to be considered. If the outer circle represented a count of the days of the month, including the extra 5 days of the *nemontemi*, where should the count begin, and should it proceed clockwise or counterclockwise? There are 26 pits within each quarter of the outer circle, but the 20 of the month and a 5-day addition numbered only 25. What was the 26th pit used for in the count? Should the 20-day count run from 1 to 20 or from 0 to 19?

If the inner circle was used for the 13-day count, did it begin at the same point as the 20-day count and proceed in the same direction? Did its count range from 1 to 13, or from 2 to 14? If the 18 pits of the cross arms represented a device for keeping count of the months, did the count begin in the center or at the end of the arms? Did each quarter represent one year, and if so, did the count proceed continuously within that quarter until all 18 months had been recorded on the cross arm? What was the use of the two larger pits present in opposed quadrants? If the total count of the outer ring (104) represented two 52-year "centuries," how was one "century" recorded? Why did the arms of the cross point not directly to the cardinal points but to another set of azimuths? What was the significance of the other azimuths? Was the Chapín–Alta Vista calendar identical to any other known calendar, or did it represent an altered version, an innovation? In the latter case, why and when was the change made?

The answers to these questions would determine the structure of the model, and hence, all questions must be answered. Because much of the archaeological evidence indicated a possible Teotihuacán origin for Alta Vista, available sparse data for the Teotihuacán calendrical system should be used in developing the model. Otherwise, general data regarding the many diverse mesoamerican calendars should be used. Finally, only repeated trial-and-error experiments could possibly determine the structure of the model. This was a daunting task, and in fact much work over a period of two years was required to produce the hypothetical model presented below.

In the accompanying illustrations, an attempt has been made to show what the actual operation of Chapín 1 may have been. Several different experimental efforts were made to produce a working calendar, but only the one shown here actually worked. The choice was made to begin the day count at the intersection of the eastern cross arm with the circles, because of its proximity to the summer solstice viewpoint (zenith passage of the sun as seen in the Labyrinth at Alta Vista), plus the belief that the initial count should begin at the intersection of a cross arm, where the triangles begin.

Also, Aveni and others (1982) noted regarding this cross arm: "The eastern axis (center to east) of the Chapín 1 petroglyph points toward azimuth 74°32′.... Are these axial deviations deliberate? In the last case the sun rises in the indicated direction on May 1 and August 15, a pair of dates curiously close to the zenith passage dates at Copan" (Aveni et al. 1982:325). Millon (1993:35 n. 7) states that a sight line directed from the mouth of the sacred cave beneath the Pyramid of the Sun reached a spot on the western horizon on April 29

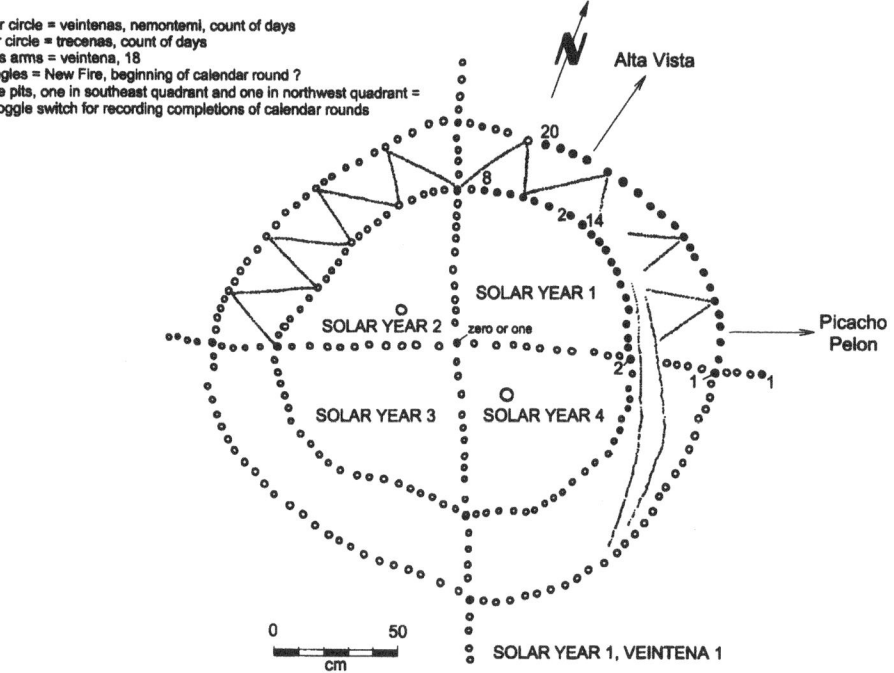

Figure 11.8. The Chapín 1 petroglyph with Solar Year 1, *Veintena* 1 represented.

and August 12—the latter date celebrating the legendary date "when time began" (August 11, 12, or 13). These dates are sufficiently close, as Aveni and others (1982) noted with particular interest, to those of the Chapín sunrise dates (see discussion of Millon below). This provided the emphasis to use the eastern cross arm of Chapín 1 as a starting point (Figure 11.8). Day number 1 was chosen to begin the 20-day count of the first *veintena*, and counting continued counterclockwise, following the direction of the count in the Codex Fejervary Mayer (Burland 1950),[11] until the count of 20 was reached, assuming that the count was 1 to 20 and not 0 to 19 (as may have been the case earlier at Teotihuacán).

The next choice was what number to use to begin the *trecena* count. The decision was made to begin it with 2, at the pit corresponding to 1 on the *veintena* pit, and count first to 14, because Edmonson (1988:241) identifies this as the Teotihuacán count. Again, it seems probable that Teotihuacanos established Alta Vista after discovering the place (Alta Vista and Chapín) where, probably to their amazement, there was only one zenith passage of the sun—the Tropic of Cancer.

The *trecena* count was continued counterclockwise until the number 14 was reached; then the count was begun again at 2 and continued to the pit corresponding to 20 on the *veintena* circle, completing the first cycle (Figure 11.9). This then was recorded as 1 on the corresponding cross arm, beginning at the outer end, although it could just as well have begun at the inner pit. This action was repeated until the *veintena* count on the cross arm reached 18, completing the first solar year of 365 days, including 28 *trecenas*, 20 *veintenas*, and 5 days of *nemontemi* (in pits available on the outer circle; Figure 11.10). If Edmonson (1988:242) is correct in his suggested choice, the first *veintena* day at Teotihuacán and Chapín–Alta Vista may have been one Alligator (Cipactli), as in the later Mexica calendar (Caso 1971:Figure 1, Table 6; Edmonson 1988:Figure 4). Notably, what appears to be the Cipactli is the life form consistently depicted on the exterior encircling decorative band of the early Michilia Red-Filled Engraved pottery of the Teotihuacán analog Apartment Compound (Structure 3) at Alta Vista. Therefore, year one, *veintena* one, *trecena* one should have begun with one Cipactli, two Tochtli (Rabbit). Year two should have begun with one Cipactli, two Acatl (Reed); year three with one Cipactli, two Tecpatl (Flint); year four with one Cipactli, two Calli (House). Tochtli, Acatl, Tecpatl, and Calli were all Year Bearers and occurred in that order (Caso 1971:347, Table 6). To continue with this procedure, the count was then shifted to the second quadrant (year two), until 18 pits were recorded on its cross arm (Figure 11.11). This procedure was continued until all four quadrants were completed. At that time the remaining vacant pit on each circle could have been filled, bringing the *nemontemi* count to six rather than five (Figure 11.12), thus making a needed leap-year correction, inasmuch as the length of the tropical or solar year is 365.2422 days, not 365 days. Addition of an extra day every four years, as indicated in the model, brings the count very close to the actual year length. Nevertheless, general expert opinion seems to rule out this possibility (Edmonson 1988:116). Actually, the question of leap-year calendrical corrections seems to be controversial. Caso (1971:348) states that no leap-year correction was made in the mesoamerican calendar. Berlin (1951:159), however, using ethnographic data and early manuscript material for the Tzotzil Indians of Chiapas, who retain much of ancient Maya practices, stated: "Comparing the [calendrical] data, one sees at once that they have remained the same in all details through a period of at least 250 years. It is therefore evident that the Indians must have adopted a system of leap-years." Edmonson (1988:116) gives a different explanation:

> The shortfall of .2422 days per vague year will cause the summer solstice to occur later and later in the native calendar with the passage of time. A leap-year correction analogous to the Julian calendar could easily accommodate this by advancing the date of the New Year by 1 day every 4 years or 20 days every 80 days. The Middle American calendars do almost exactly the opposite. Recognizing that the 1,508 years of the solar era actually make up only 1,507 real (tropical) years of 365.2422 days, they set out to erase the extra year by subtracting one 20-day month every 83 years. . . [but] the invention of the Kaminaljuyu calendar rendered this series obsolete.

He further commented, regarding the new leap-year correction, that a change from a summer solstice to a spring equinox initial naming of the year (p. 118) would solve the problem: "The adoption of initial naming of the year at Kaminaljuyu implies awareness of a solar era of exactly 29 calendar rounds (550,420 days), which is astronomically correct. . . . In the context of its derivation from a terminally named calendar, . . . and of the numerological elegance and simplicity of its internal organization, however, the Kaminaljuyu calendar provides clear evidence that it was consciously designed to measure the solar era as well as the year. And it did so with stunning accuracy."

But the Chapín 1 "calendar" clearly seems to have been based on the observation of the summer solstice, which means that it differed from the Kaminaljuyu calendar. Edmonson (1988:124) identifies the Teotihuacán calendar as a spring-era calendar with initial naming. Accordingly, if Cerro el Chapín and Alta Vista represent a Teotihuacán presence, as now believed, the Chapín 1 "calendar" is a new one, with a summer solstice orientation. The reason for such an innovation is obvious. Because of the location of these sites on the Tropic of Cancer, astronomical attention was fixed on the summer solstice, where the single zenith passage of the sun occurs.

Because of the clear view that observers on Cerro el Chapín had of the summer solstice sunrise over Picacho Pelón, it is possible that a delay of one day every four years in its appearance would be observable and call for a one-day addition to the year, as proposed in the model. And if a one-day delay was not observable, continuous recording certainly would make the delay obvious after X number of days, allowing the change to be incorporated in the structure of the recording device. A graffito in the Labyrinth at Alta Vista apparently depicts a person facing Picacho Pelón and observing it with the aid of a vertical pole equipped at the top with specialized features. This recalls the "devices for seeing" held by several gods (including Tezcatlipoca) in the codices (Aveni et al. 1982:322–324, Figures 3a and b). If such a device was used at Alta Vista/Chapín, astronomical observations may have been relatively accurate and delays in the appearance of the solstice sunrise more precisely observed.

Whatever the case, in Chapín 1 the potential for making a direct fourth-year leap-year correction existed. The only other possibility that occurs to us is that the planners felt it necessary to add another pit to complete the full 73 *trecena* count needed to record the 52-year cycle; perhaps, as noted above, this correction capacity represents a Chapín and Alta Vista innovation. If indeed the time of the fourth-year (or X-year) solstice sunrise over Picacho was delayed, observers on Chapín could not have ignored the fact that the event then was one day (or X days) slow, requiring an extra one-day (or X-day) correction. Again, the implication is that many years of actual observation had occurred before the petroglyph was pecked into place.

At the end of the four-year cycle, all markers would have been removed and the procedure begun again from

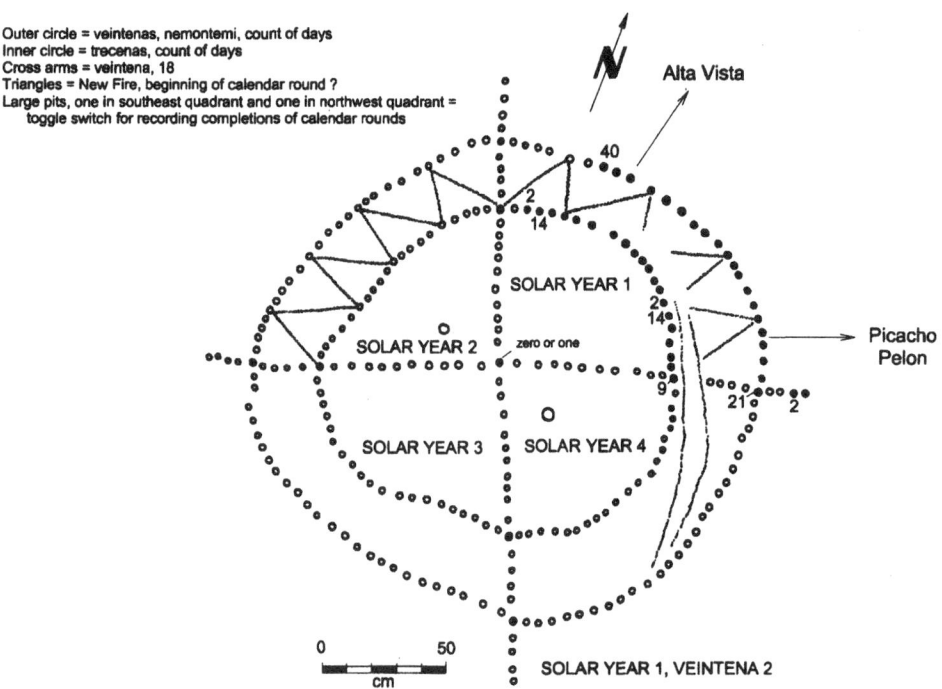

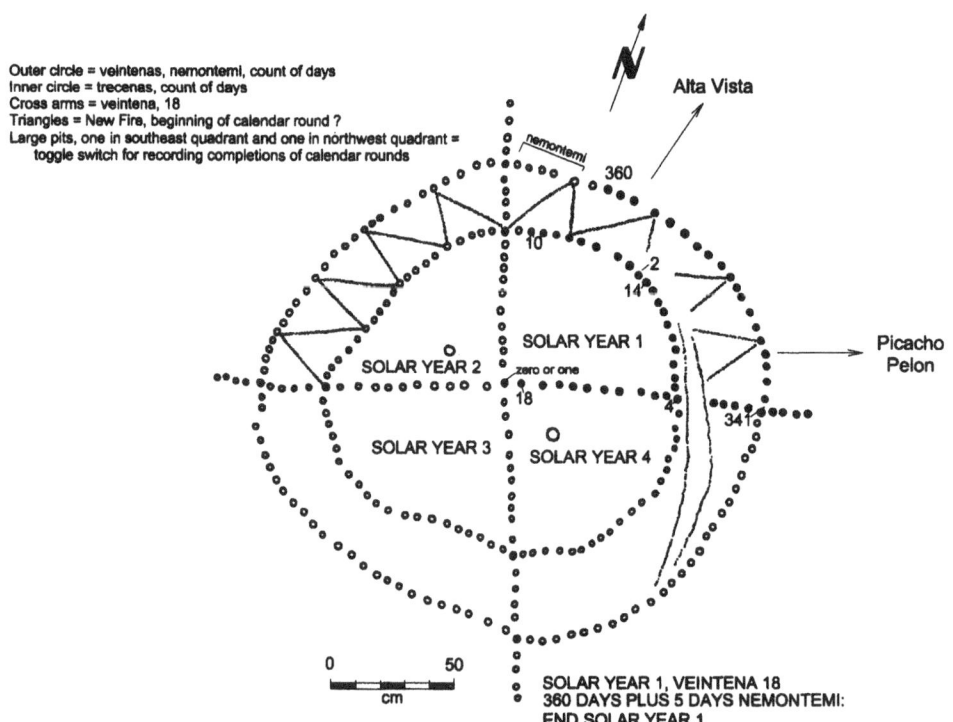

Figure 11.9 (above). The Chapín 1 petroglyph with Solar Year 1, *Veintena* 2 represented.

Figure 11.10. The Chapín 1 petroglyph, 360 days plus 5 days *nemontemi*; end of Solar Year 1, *Veintena* 18.

THE CHAPÍN I PECKED CROSS-CIRCLE

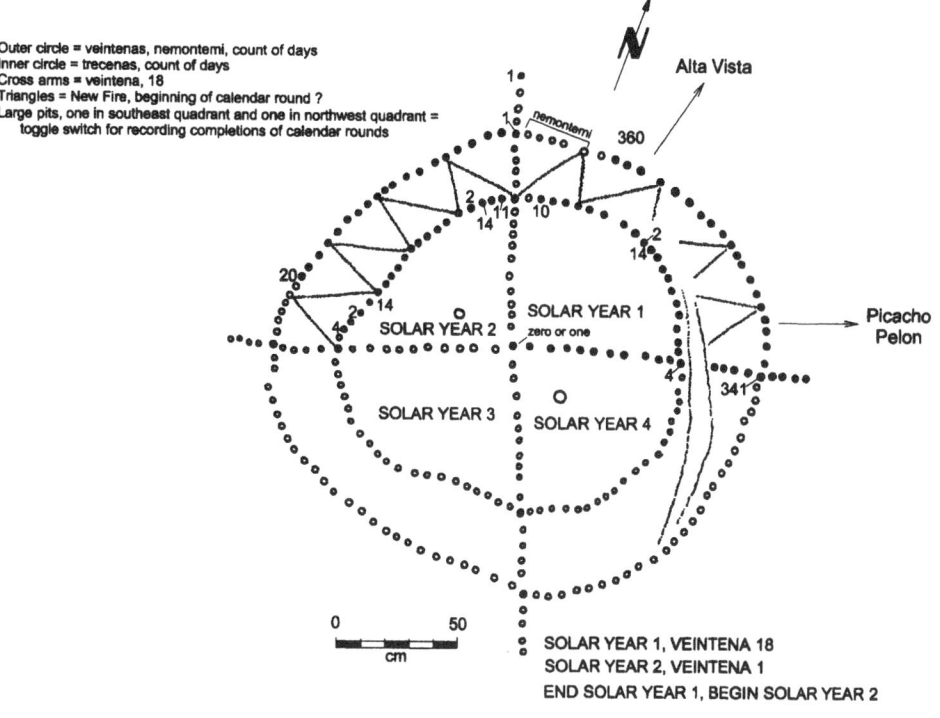

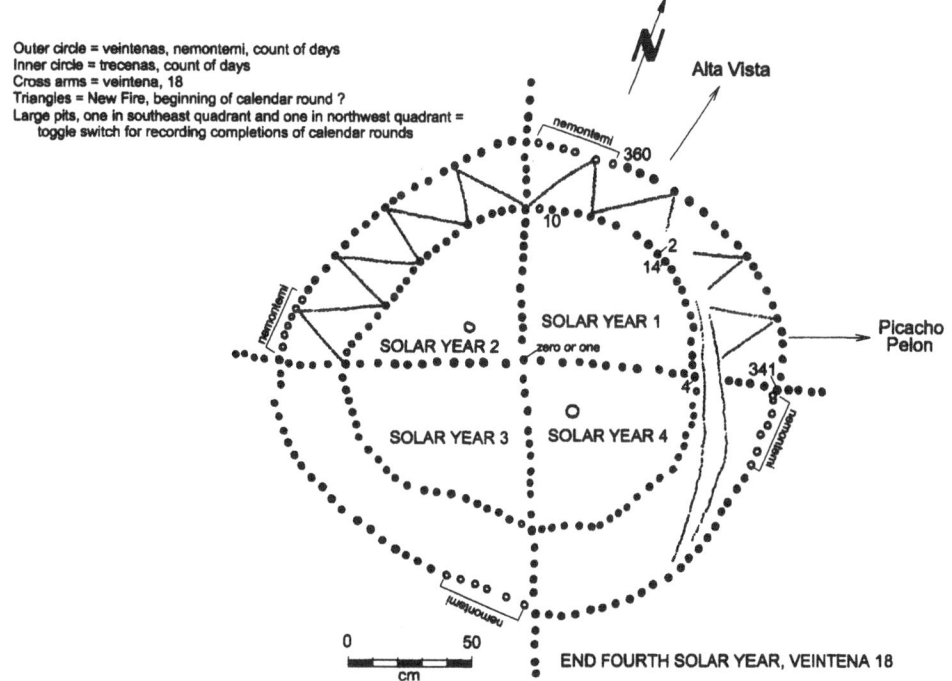

Figure 11.11 (above). The Chapín 1 petroglyph, end of Solar Year 1, beginning of Solar Year 2.

Figure 11.12. The Chapín 1 petroglyph, end of Solar Year 4, Veintena 18 (calendar corrected for leap year by adding an extra *nemontemi* day?).

the *veintena* and *trecena* dates reached at that point. When 52 *veintenas* and 73 *trecenas* (72 years recorded on the four 18 pit cross arms, plus the center pit used as a one) had been counted (including the *nemontemi* days), the first calendar round could be recorded by marking one of the two large pits and placing the first angled marker. The entire process could have been repeated until the second calendar round had been marked by filling the second large circular pit and fulfilling the double 52-year count recorded on the outer circle. Theoretically, the process could have been continued indefinitely, using the two large pits as a sort of toggle switch.

In the use of Mexica day names and other data, the assumption is that these were the ones used also in earlier calendars, but Marcus (1992:95–96) warns that this is erroneous, inasmuch as many variations of the calendar existed. The mesoamerican calendar is quite complex and not one easily interpreted by non-epigraphers such as ourselves. The interpretation given here may or may not be correct, although the internal evidence (it works!) suggests that it does have some validity. But there is no assurance that those who created this remarkable calendar used it as presented in the experimental model discussed here. In any event, the present interpretation very probably has not included all the potential usages of this marvelously engineered calendrical and astronomical device.

Finally, it does not seem possible that such a complex and data-filled device was invented or produced by the simple local villagers of the Canutillo phase; rather, its complexity provides additional evidence for the presence of mesoamerican priest-astronomers, possibly Teotihuacanos, in the area at that time. The discovery that in the Chapín–Alta Vista area the sun apparently died and was reborn to begin a second trip to the south must have been a remarkable one. It seems probable that the summer solstice sunrise seen from Chapín (zenith passage at Alta Vista) must have been used to inaugurate a new calendar round, even if this meant changing the contemporary Teotihuacán calendar to create a new one. Was this, by any chance, the real creation of the Fifth Sun?

DISCUSSION

What purpose can be served by development of a model such as the one presented above? We believe that as a working model it suggests how one cross-circle petroglyph may have functioned. The model should be checked rigorously by experienced epigraphers for errors that would invalidate it. If it represents a Chalchihuites innovation, however, they should not discard it simply because it differs from other known calendars. It appears that if this was a new calendar, it had no noticeable effect on other known calendars; that is, it had no known lineal descendants. This is explainable because Alta Vista itself was apparently destroyed by conquest, accompanied by burning and a massacre, in the late ninth century A.D., and was reoccupied only briefly by the assailants.

We regard each circle-cross petroglyph as a unique production. Using the methods we have employed here for creating a model, other researchers could carefully examine in detail other cross-circle petroglyphs (or "plasterglyphs") to determine if somewhat similar calendrical models can be developed. If this attempt proved feasible, it would offer support for the model presented here. We also plan to study other cross-circle petroglyphs using similar methods.

NOTES

1. The new cultural sequence for the Chalchihuites culture in the Suchil area includes an early Village Formative period, followed by a Nucleation period, and ending with a Terminal period. Only the Canutillo ceramic phase has been identified for the first period; for the Nucleation period, the Alta Vista ceramic phase is divided into an early Atrium subphase and a later Florescent subphase. The subsequent Terminal period is characterized by the Calichal and Ayala ceramic phases.

2. Some researchers have viewed the Chalchihuites aboriginal mines as the prime mover in the region's development (Schiavetti 1995; Weigand 1968, 1982). There now appears to be little supporting evidence for this view. The obvious large scale of the mining operation is impressive, but viewing it as more or less a seasonal activity spread over some five centuries reduces its importance considerably. Failure to identify specific products of the mines elsewhere suggests that the mining activity was carried on primarily for local consumption.

3. The concept of a fourfold division of the world is widespread. For example, the Navajo Indians conceptualize their world in such a quartered view, with world mountains bounding the four directions. This worldview is expressed in the sand paintings that their "chanters" (shamans) make during spe-

cific ceremonials (see Griffin-Pierce 1992 for elaboration and illustration of this theme). The contemporary surveyors' compass is another example of the use of the quartered directional format. If only this concept were involved, there would be little significance to the petroglyphs.

4. Brad Schafer (1996:2) has warned that credulous archaeologists often erroneously ascribe astronomical significance to numbers they find on rocks or ceramics. Here we are concerned with several numbers that are known to have astronomical/calendrical significance in various mesoamerican cultures.

5. There is strong evidence that, when actual codices were unavailable, astronomer-priests retained the requisite body of ritual and astronomical data in their memories. Devices such as the cross-circle petroglyphs would serve as powerful mnemonic aids for retaining and using this mass of remembered data.

6. The drawing of the Chapín 1 petroglyph used here was made originally by J. Charles Kelley, aided by Michael Foster and Kevin Kelley. A heavy sheet of plastic was placed over the petroglyph and anchored in place. Each pecked pit was recorded by drawing a red circle on the plastic and by punching a hole in the pit center. All lines were marked, including cracks in the rock, and north was indicated on the drawing using a Brunton compass. Through the assistance of Anthony Aveni, this life-size drawing was reduced to page size by Horst Hartung.

7. We are indebted to John Carlson for calling this possibility to our attention. Also, we wish to thank Anthony Aveni for reading this chapter in manuscript and indicating the need for clarification of some items.

8. These figures are depicted in miniature, and not all of them are five-pointed. The artist seems to have had this representation in mind, however.

9. In the northwest entrance of Structure 4 at Alta Vista, fragments of a red and white painted cylinder, made of adobe, were found. This cylinder had formerly stood upright like a "barber pole" in the entryway. On its interior there was a cast of a bundle of canes or arrows tied together by encircling cords at intervals. This artifact almost certainly represented the "bundle of the years" closed at the end of each calendar round, with the enclosed arrows representing individual years of the 52-year count. The number of canes or arrows in this particular bundle could not be ascertained because the perishable items had long ago disappeared and the end sections of the bundle were not found.

10. If a Chamula-like board marking off the 20 days of each of 18 months, plus the 5 days of the *nemontemi*, was kept by one shaman, and another shaman kept a similar board marking off the 13 ritual days of the 260-day count plus the *nemontemi,* placing them together side by side in proper coordination would produce an arrangement like that of the two concentric circles of Chapín 1. But the circular nature of the Chapín circle enabled a perpetual recording system. And the Chamula-type recording boards lacked the cross arms that made possible the recording of each 20-day month in the Chapín petroglyph, as well as other data. But the relationship in techniques is clearly represented. When the Chamula-type board was filled, the charcoal marker lines were erased and the count began again, just as in the Chapín 1 petroglyph, where the pit markers must have been erased or removed when the four-year cycle there was completed.

11. Note in the discussions above that in the Sahagún calendar as described, the movement was counterclockwise, as in our model.

CHAPTER TWELVE

THE ARCHAEOLOGY OF DURANGO

MICHAEL S. FOSTER

IN MANY RESPECTS the modern state of Durango is as much a geopolitical and ecological frontier in modern Mexico as the region was prehistorically in Mesoamerica. As in the past, Durango's rural nature and low population density contrast with the bustling cities of central Mexico. Culturally, politically, and socially, it is a transitional zone. It could be argued that the people of Durango lack the cosmopolitan air of the city dwellers, that they are politically less bound by the central authority in "el Capital," that they are more self-sufficient than their brethren in the city, and that they are closer to the land.

The Sierra Madre Occidental, an impressive range of mountains and canyons, dominates western and central Durango from the Chihuahua border in the north to the Zacatecas and Jalisco borders in the south. To the west, the Sierra drops sharply to the Pacific coastal plain, and to the east, it gives way to a series of smaller ranges, foothills, and valleys, some of which contain remnants of Pleistocene lakes. The eastern part of the state includes the western fringes of the Mesa del Norte, dominated by the Chihuahuan Desert. Altitude moderates the climate, and the desert gradually gives way to oak-covered foothills that, in turn, give way to the pine forests of the Sierra.

Archaeological research in Durango, which has been extremely limited, has focused on the ceramic period.

The first accounts of Durango archaeology appear in the late 1500s and early 1600s as the Spanish colonized the region in the quest of wealth and souls. Some of the more detailed references of ruins in the region occur in the Anuas of 1604 and 1612 (see Pérez de Ribas 1645 and Alegre 1841). In the late 1800s, Lumholtz (1902) visited the area in search of the southernmost limit of the "cliff dwellers" of the American Southwest. Guillemin Tarayre (1867) reported extensively on prehistoric ruins in northwest Mexico, including Durango (providing a map of the site of Santa Ana near Zape), as part of a mineralogical survey of the region. Hewett (1936) visited northern Durango in 1906 and only briefly reported on the archaeology of the area. It was not until Mason (1937) and Brand (1939) visited the area in 1936 that more substantial accounts of the region's prehistory appear. Mason searched for evidence of early humans (Paleoindian and Archaic); Brand focused his efforts on the geography, natural history, and archaeology of the Zape area in a study of the northernmost expression of mesoamerican culture. Both noted the presence of the "Chalchihuites–La Quemada" cultural pattern, and Brand (1939) recorded the presence of Aztatlán ceramics from coastal west Mexico (Sauer and Brand 1932).

In the 1950s, J. Charles Kelley (1956, 1971) began working in Durango. His interest also was in the

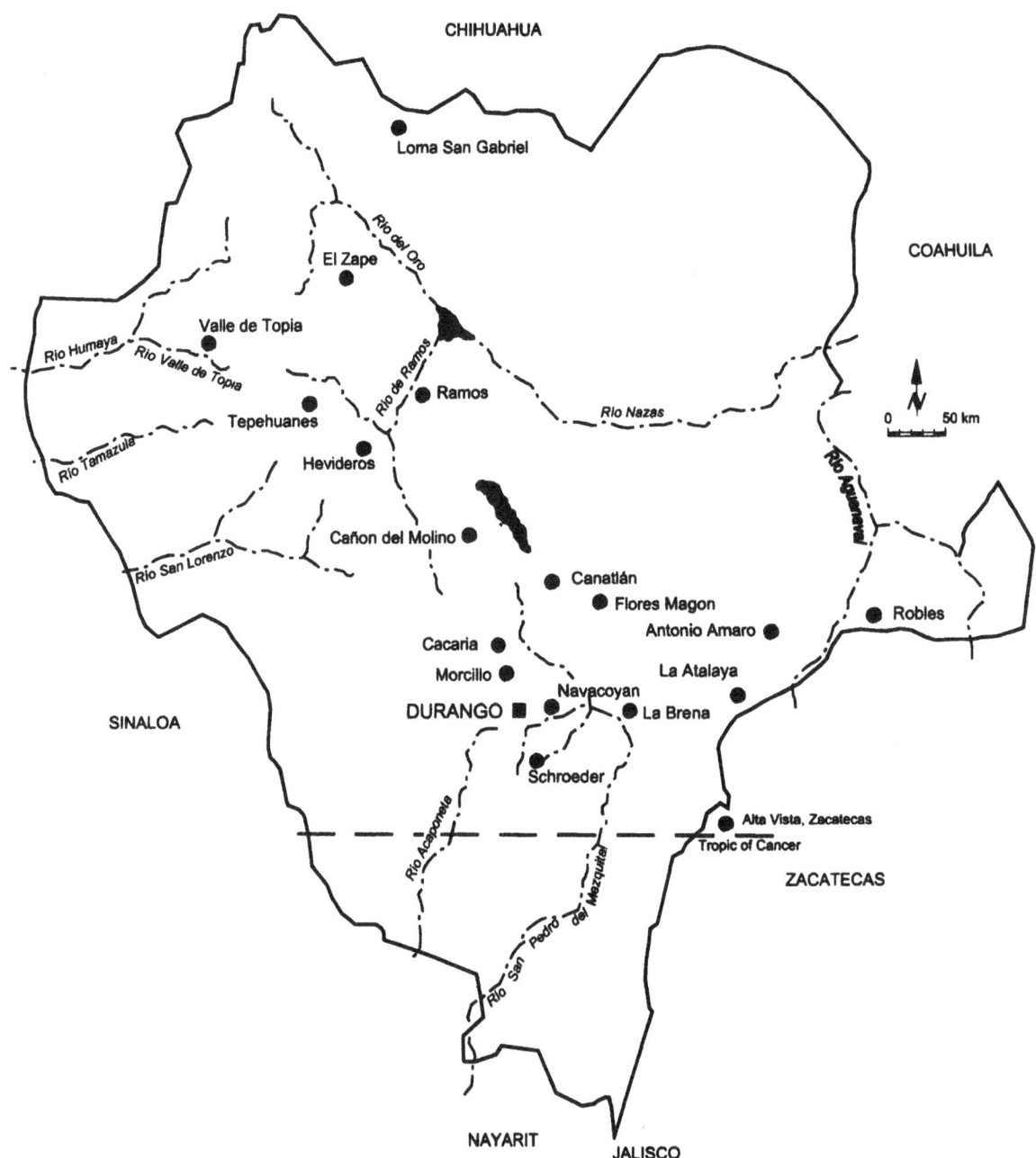

Figure 12.1. Archaeological sites and areas of Durango.

mesoamerican culture(s) of the area and the dynamics of the northwestern mesoamerican frontier. He conducted a series of reconnaissance surveys and limited excavations along the eastern foothills of the Sierra Madre from Zape and Villa Ocampo in the north to the vicinity of the city of Durango in the south. Of particular note are the excavations at the Schroeder site (Kelley 1971, 1990a; Kelley and Winters 1960; see Figure 12.1). The Weicker site (Foster 1986a; Kelley and Shakelford 1954), La Manga, and Santa Ana near Zape were also partially excavated. The work near Villa Ocampo resulted in the identification of what was to become the type site for the Loma San Gabriel culture (Kelley 1956:132–133).

In the late 1950s, Richard Brooks (1971) conducted a survey of south-central and southern Chihuahua and northern Durango. Limited excavations were carried out at several cave and open sites near Zape. The cave sites produced quantities of macrobotanical and human remains (Brooks and Brooks 1978; Brooks et al. 1962; Foster 1984). Howard (1957) and Lister and Howard (1955) provided the first detailed descriptions of Chalchihuites materials from sites near the city of Durango, including Navacoyan. Although looting destroyed Navacoyan, J. Charles Kelley documented much of its ceramic assemblage before it was lost to the scientific world. In the mid–1970s, I conducted a reconnaissance survey of portions of Durango as part of dissertation research (Foster 1978, 1985). Ramírez M. (1988) published a brief overview of previous anthropological and archaeological research in Durango as part of a volume on northwest Mexico (García Mora 1988). More recently, avocational archaeologists Ganot R., Peschard F., and Lazalde have described a number of sites from across Durango. Their most important contribution has been the study of a collection of material looted from the site of Cañón del Molino (Ganot R. and Peschard F. 1995, 1997; Lazalde 1987). Within the last several years, the Instituto Nacional de Antropología e Historia (INAH) sponsored a limited stabilization and excavation project at the Schroeder site (La Ferrería; Guevara Sánchez 1994), and some work has been carried out at the site of Hervideros (Hers 1993b).

In Durango, perhaps as much as in any place in northwest Mexico, the lack of broad-scale archaeological surveys and intensive excavations has resulted in an extremely limited knowledge of the area's prehistory. Nevertheless, sufficient information is available to provide a general reconstruction of a portion of it. This chapter summarizes Durango's culture history, describes sites, discusses pan-regional interaction, and offers some thoughts on the direction of future research.

PALEOINDIAN AND ARCHAIC PERIODS

The earliest inhabitants of Durango are poorly understood. A single Clovis-like projectile point (Figure 12.2) is reported from near the city of Durango (Kelley 1953b; Lorenzo 1953), and Spence (1971) reports an early point fragment from the Río Florido in northern Durango. Pleistocene faunal remains have been recovered from Durango, but none are associated with cultural material.

Kelley (1953b, 1989b) recorded a small Archaic site, Los Caracoles, exposed in the bank of an arroyo on the northwest side of Laguna Santiaguillo. Several stone-lined hearths, charcoal, and lithic artifacts were noted.

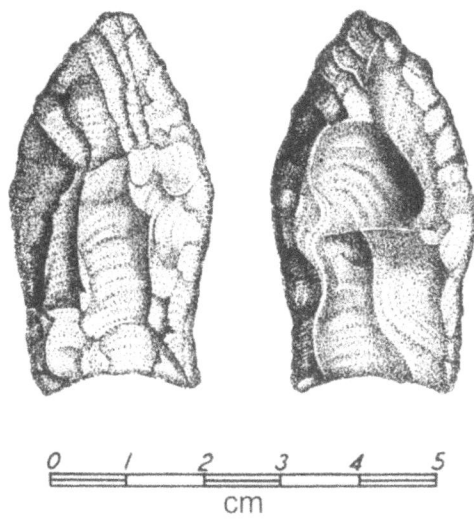

Figure 12.2. Fluted point from Durango.

The artifacts were similar to Cochise materials from the American Southwest. Other chipped stone artifacts, one-hand shaped and unshaped manos, and several basin-shaped metates were recovered from the site's surface. Similar remains were also recovered from the Laguna Medina site on the eastern shore of an artificial lake south of Laguna Santiaguillo. Obsidian-hydration dates from the site cluster between 224 B.C. and A.D. 122 (Meighan 1978). Kelley (1989b) recorded other Archaic period sites, including one, the Río Mesquital, near the El Saltito waterfall that had a varnished basalt chopper and fire-cracked rock reminiscent of Malpais and San Dieguito materials from the Sierra Pinicate area of northern Sonora (Hayden 1976).

Archaic remains of central and southern Durango are assigned to the Los Caracoles complex (Spence 1971). These materials appear related to the San Pedro stage of the Cochise culture in the American Southwest and to materials from Chihuahua (Marrs 1949). The Los Caracoles complex artifact assemblage includes a variety of side scrapers, plane scrapers, and choppers and lenticular, triangular, and corner-notched projectile points. Two other late Archaic complexes, the Las Nieves and Santa Marta, may be derived from the Los Caracoles complex (Spence 1971).

Silva and Hester (1973) report a preceramic site, the Robles site, on a tributary of the Río Aguanaval in extreme eastern Durango. Catan, Desmuke, Lerma, Shumla, Ellis, Ensor, Yarbrough, Scallorn, and Figueroa projectile point types were present. Numerous serrated, triangular, corner-notched, basally notched, and stemmed projectile points, bifaces, and some flake material were also found. The projectile point styles indicate the site may date from as early as 8000 B.C. to the late prehistoric period. Other preceramic sites, petroglyph sites, and rockshelters are reported in the area.

Lazalde (1992) has recently published a catalog of projectile point types from surface contexts around Durango. Several Paleoindian points and many Archaic type points with affinities to southwestern, Texas, Chihuahua, and Coahuila point types are represented.

A concerted effort is needed to address the nature and extent of early human occupation of the Durango area. The few Paleoindian points found suggest the area was occupied at the end of the Pleistocene or early Holocene. The Archaic remains are related to those found in adjacent areas of northern Mexico and the American Southwest. Although little can be said regarding settlement and mobility, most of the sites recorded or observed appear to be small campsites. Many Los Caracoles point and tool types carry over into the ceramic period Loma San Gabriel and Chalchihuites cultures.

CERAMIC PERIOD

The ceramic period in Durango is better documented than the earlier Paleoindian and Archaic periods, and most of what is known stems directly from the work of J. Charles Kelley and his students. Kelley's (1971, 1990a) work along the eastern flanks of the Sierra Madre resulted in the definition of two major ceramic period cultures, the Loma San Gabriel and the Guadiana branch of the Chalchihuites.

Loma San Gabriel

The Loma San Gabriel (Loma) culture of Durango and western Zacatecas was defined after several seasons of reconnaissance surveys and limited excavations in the Zape area and near Villa Ocampo in northern Durango (Kelley 1956:130–133). Loma sites often occur on the tops of isolated hills or on elevated settings with arable land and water below. The sites are generally small and consist of small, rectangular structures defined by rows of vertically placed stone slabs. A plainware and a redware that sometimes occurs in a fugitive form dominate the ceramics from these sites. Kelley (1956) noted that the "elaborate masonry structures, pyramids, legged vessels, cloisonné ware, and other items of Mexican culture" were not associated with Loma and suggested that it was not a mesoamerican culture.

Loma material culture is simple, and it is believed that most items were produced at the household level for local use. The ceramic assemblage (Foster 1980, 1981, 1985, 1995a) is dominated by Loma Plain, a fairly coarse type that ranges in color from buff to orange to brown. Loma Plain vessels range from vase-like to large ollas with flaring or recurvate rims. Small, unrestricted, and slightly restricted bowls, including composite types, also occur. Most Loma vessels are ollas of various sizes thought to have been used in food preparation and storage. Bowls occur infrequently, and items such as comales, plates, and ladles have not been identified (Foster 1980, 1981, 1985). In the Durango area, Chalchihuites influence in Loma ceramics can be seen in the form of incised, tripod, and handled wares.

Variants of Loma Plain include Loma Textured, a brushed or textured ware; Loma Red, a red-slipped type with surface colors that range from a badly weathered matte red to a moderately well polished red to a fugitive red slip; and rarely, Loma White, a type either slipped white or made from an unslipped white paste. Another common type is Chico Red-on-brown. It generally exhibits a less coarse paste than Loma Plain. Bowl exteriors and interiors are fairly well scraped and smoothed. The slip ranges from a reddish brown to brown with red designs that occur as bands or curved lines on the exterior and along the rims and interiors of bowls or, in one case, as a horned serpent on the interior of a bowl (Kelley 1971:800). Overall surface condition of this type is quite variable.

The ground stone assemblage includes basin metates, one-hand manos, pestles, small stone balls, abrading stones, three-quarter- and full-grooved axes, and mauls. Projectile points, bifaces, knives, and a variety of scraper types made from local rhyolites, cherts, and some obsidians make up the chipped stone assemblage. Most of the tools appear to be derived from the Los Caracoles complex, although several tool types—handled endscrapers and curved and disk knives—may have Chalchihuites origins (Spence 1971). Other Loma artifact types include spindle whorls, perforated and unperforated sherd disks, worked sherds, beads, figurine fragments, and shell beads.

Loma sites are primarily hamlets and small villages that usually lack any significant organization of structures. Cobble and slab stone house foundations, ranging from about 2 m by 2 m to 5 m by 6 m, are scattered across sites in any open, level area. Single and contiguous rooms are primarily square or rectangular, although occasionally circular foundations 2 to 3 m in diameter are found. It is assumed that these foundations supported wattle-and-daub or jacal superstructures. At some sites, site structure is more formal with rooms or blocks of rooms organized around small plazas.

Occasionally, house foundations are found within compound walls as if they were defining household units (Foster 1986a). In other instances, compounds were constructed from fairly large boulders and may have served as defensive structures (e.g., the Loma San Gabriel site). Small-scale terracing is found at some sites. Its function is unclear, however; the terracing does not appear to be associated with either large-scale agriculture or habitation.

Other feature types include small, piled, cobble stone altars and large, paved, slightly raised, rectangular foundations that may represent some form of communal structure. Larger truncated platform mounds have also been recorded on Loma sites. In general, Loma sites in the Chalchihuites core area of western Zacatecas more frequently exhibit somewhat more formalized site structure.

As previously noted, Loma sites are commonly found on elevated points of land such as mesa tops or benches above arable land and water, suggesting that defense may have sometimes been a consideration. In addition to the open sites, many rockshelters and caves (cliff dwellings) were occupied (Brand 1939; Brooks and Brooks 1978; Brooks et al. 1985; Lazalde 1984).

Loma peoples appear to have subsisted on a mix of agriculture and hunting and gathering (Brooks et al. 1962; Foster 1984). A variety of corn, beans, and squash was grown and supplemented by gathered wild plant foods such as agave, cacti, yucca, nuts, seeds, and berries. Hunted animals included fish, rabbits, squirrels, rodents, deer, and possibly mountain sheep. Wild foodstuffs were probably relied on more intensively during seasonal shortages of stored foods or during times of environmental stress when agricultural produce was limited.

No chronometrically defined phase sequence has been established for Loma, although Lazalde (1987) has divided Loma culture history into three broad periods: Period I, Pre-Chalchihuites (50/100 B.C. to A.D. 600); Period II, Chalchihuites (A.D. 600 to 1450); and Period III, Tepehuan (A.D. 1450 to the Historic period). This scheme, however, has not been generally employed.

Loma appears to have developed out of the local Archaic culture(s) sometime before A.D. 1, possibly as early as 300 B.C. Evidence from western Zacatecas (Abbott Kelley 1976) indicates that Loma people were living a well-developed settled village way of life at the time of the earliest mesoamerican (Canutillo phase) developments in the area (A.D. 100–300). The Loma culture seems to have coexisted with the Chalchihuites culture as it developed and occupied western Zacatecas and Durango until its collapse around the A.D. 1400s (Foster 1995b; Kelley 1971, 1985a). Riley and Winters (1963) suggest direct continuity between the late Chalchihuites and Loma San Gabriel and the historic Tepehuan peoples of the area. More recently, Willett (1997), although apparently unaware of the Riley and Winters argument, has suggested that the Southern Tepehuan *xiotalh* ceremony may have its roots in the Guadiana Chalchihuites.

Kelley (1971) and Foster (1985) argue that Loma represents a simple frontier, nonmesoamerican adaptation lacking social and economic complexity and that it co-occupied western Zacatecas and Durango with the mesoamerican Chalchihuites culture. Furthermore, they suggest that some form of Loma existed from the end of the Archaic period to the early Protohistoric period (see Riley and Winters 1963). As some additional data have accumulated and the nature of Loma has been more fully discussed, it now appears Kelley and Foster have oversimplified Loma cultural history and development. In part, the Kelley and Foster view was grounded in what appears to be the temporal continuity and wide distribution of the Loma ceramic tradition (Foster 1981). Any refinement or reevaluation of the Loma tradition as defined by Kelley and Foster has been limited because of the lack of new, systematically collected data.

Despite major gaps in data and areal coverage and the need for new information, the following tentative summary of Loma prehistory is offered. As previously stated, it appears that Loma developed out of the local Archaic as the initial ceramic, sedentary culture of the area. It may be that in the first few centuries A.D. some Loma populations were incorporated into the mesoamerican cultural tradition, resulting in the appearance of the Canutillo phase. The best example of this comes from Gualtario Abajo (Abbott Kelley 1976) in western Zacatecas. Many Loma sherds from the site exhibit incising and other traits manifested in Canutillo phase ceramics. These are either imitations of Canutillo types or prototypes of Canutillo types. It appears that in the Río Colorado Valley, and possibly the Río Suchil Valley, of western Zacatecas the Late Formative period Canutillo-Vesuvio phase continuum was truncated by the Alta Vista phase. The Alta Vista phase represents the apex of Chalchihuites cultural development. Kelley (1985a) suggests it represents an intrusion into the area and that Canutillo-Vesuvio populations of western Zacatecas were absorbed into the Chalchihuites culture. At the same time, other Loma populations were pushed to the adjacent foothills of the Sierra Madre. Here they maintained their lifestyle while interacting with Chalchihuites populations. Farther north in Durango, Loma populations appear to have had little contact with the Chalchihuites culture until A.D. 800 to 1000, when a Chalchihuites influx occurred as the Chalchihuites tradition was collapsing in western Zacatecas (Kelley 1990a, 1990b). Little is known of Loma or Chalchihuites occupations of western Zacatecas after A.D. 1000.

The Chalchihuites intrusion into Durango appears to have caused the displacement of some local Loma peoples (Kelley 1971). In some places such as Cañón del Molino (Ganot R. and Peschard F. 1995), however, there may have been significant acculturation of either Loma peoples into Chalchihuites groups or Chalchihuites peoples into Loma groups. Additionally, data from the Río Ramos area in eastern Durango (Brooks 1978) suggest that local non-Chalchihuites cultures (Loma San Gabriel) became more sociopolitically complex than earlier believed. The Río Ramos area has produced small ceremonial sites that, based on material culture, appear to be Loma. It seems that there was some significant local variability in what has been called Loma, although it is still poorly understood.

Furthermore, as time passes, the differences between Loma and Chalchihuites appear to break down. Many sites have what appear to be Chalchihuites and Loma ceramic assemblages present. Over time, the paste of Chalchihuites ceramics generally becomes indistinguishable from that of Loma ceramics, although the exterior of the vessel is decorated in Chalchihuites style. This is seen as evidence of a blending of the cultures.

The picture becomes more complicated during the Río Tunal, Calera, and Molino phases, A.D. 1150/1200 to 1400/1450. During this time, West Coast cultures strongly influence the Guadiana Chalchihuites. New design elements appear in Chalchihuites ceramics as the area is incorporated into the Aztatlán Mercantile System (Kelley 1986a, 1990a; see Kelley this volume). Chalchihuites ceramics clearly reflect a change in that cultural tradition. In fact, it can be argued that the Guadiana Chalchihuites no longer can be called Chalchihuites. The expanded influence of the West Coast and other areas of northwest Mexico and the fusion of the Loma and Chalchihuites cultures appear to have resulted in the emergence of a new cultural tradition, one that may have eventually given rise to the Tepehuan (Riley and Winters 1963; Willett 1997).

Recently, the concepts of the Chalchihuites and Loma cultures as posed by Kelley (1971) and Foster (1985) have been criticized (Hers 1988, 1989a, 1989b). Hers lumps the ceramic period cultures (Chalchihuites, La Quemada, Río Bolaños, and Loma) in northern Jalisco, central and western Zacatecas, and Durango as a pre-1940s characterization of the "Chalchihuites culture." This homogenization of northwest Mexican archaeology serves only to substantiate largely antiquated and diffusionist arguments regarding the relationship of certain archaeological traits found in central and northern frontier Mesoamerica while ignoring the obvious and considerable variation present in the archeological record. Hers provides no archaeological data to support her characterization, and implicit in her arguments is an apparent lack of understanding of some of the most basic principles of archaeological method and theory. It is argued here that Loma is clearly a separate, identifiable cultural manifestation in the archaeological record of the region. As noted elsewhere (Foster 1995a), Hers appears not to recognize the apparent continuity between Loma and the earlier local Archaic tradition (Foster 1985; Spence 1971); the obvious differences between the Loma and Chalchihuites chipped stone tools (Spence 1971); the significant differences between Loma and Chalchihuites ceramics, especially early in the Chalchihuites sequence (Loma ceramic types are not simply the domestic wares of the Chalchihuites culture; Foster 1981, 1985; Kelley 1971; Kelley and Abbott Kelley 1971); that although both the Loma and Chalchihuites cultures used cobble stone and slab stone in construction, there are clear differences in construction techniques and in the types of structures and features built; the significant differences in intrasite organization of features and in overall settlement patterns; and that despite claims to the contrary (e.g., Cruz 1994:45–46), there are many examples of Loma sites in both Durango and Zacatecas that lack any evidence of Chalchihuites contact. Furthermore, Hers (1989b) and Cruz (1994) do not appear to understand the principles of intrusive artifacts and archaeological context. Additionally, recent studies into the procurement and use of obsidian in Zacatecas and Durango have shown that although Loma and Chalchihuites peoples in Durango exploited local obsidian sources, their patterns of procurement and use are quite distinctive (Darling 1993b, 1998). Also, Darling notes that obsidians from Jalisco and central Mexico occur in Chalchihuites sites but not in Loma sites, indicating that the Guadiana Chalchihuites were participating in an exchange system (Aztatlán) that apparently excluded Loma.

In summary, there are significant differences between Loma and Chalchihuites material cultures, site structure, settlement patterns, levels of sociopolitical integration, ceremonialism, and regional and pan-regional interaction. Loma seems to be the western Zacatecas and Durango manifestation of a broader plainware-brownware tradition that tied the early ceramic period cultures of northwest Mexico and the American Southwest to one another (Foster 1982, 1986b, 1989, 1991, 1995a; Kelley 1966; Kelley and Abbott Kelley 1975). To say the least, there is yet a great deal to be learned about the nature and role of Loma in the history of northwest Mesoamerica.

Other Nonmesoamerican Cultural Complexes

Spence (1978) has described three other nonmesoamerican complexes, the Chivas (A.D. 660–950), Baole (A.D. 600–650), and Madroños (A.D. 650–950), in Durango. Data were derived from sites near Las Animas, west-northwest of the city of Durango. These complexes also appear to have developed out of the local Archaic culture. The Chivas complex chipped stone assemblage is quite similar to that of Loma, but Chivas ceramics differ from Loma ceramics, most notably in including a blackware not found in Loma contexts.

The poorly understood Baole complex may be a more localized development. Its ceramic assemblage includes redwares that increase in frequency through time and a blackware that decreases in frequency through time. The Madroños complex material culture is very similar to Loma's and may represent the spread of Loma along the eastern foothills of the Sierra Madre. The significance of these complexes is not understood, but their presence shows the variability of cultural developments in Durango.

Guadiana Branch Chalchihuites Culture

The reason for and timing of the expansion of the Chalchihuites culture into Durango from the western Zacatecas core area are matters to be resolved. The expansion is believed to coincide with the decline and collapse of the Suchil Chalchihuites in western Zacatecas. The earliest Guadiana Chalchihuites phase, the Ayala phase, is virtually identical to the Calichal phase at Alta Vista, and the subsequent Las Joyas phase parallels the Retoño phase at Alta Vista. Kelley (1971, 1985a) has argued that the Durango phases are outgrowths of the western Zacatecas phases.

There is some evidence, such as at the Schroeder site, to suggest that the movement of Chalchihuites peoples into Durango dislocated some Loma populations (Kelley 1990a, 1991), but there does not appear to be any evidence of a military conquest of the area. Whether the Chalchihuites expansion was the result of the movement of disenfranchised Suchil elites or peasantry or whether it was the result of an attempt to stabilize or compensate for the apparent decline of the Chalchihuites in western Zacatecas remains to be determined. Whatever the case, after A.D. 1000, the Chalchihuites tradition seems to have disappeared in western Zacatecas.

Dating the Guadiana Chalchihuites Sequence

The Guadiana Chalchihuites sequence was originally divided into four phases—the Ayala, Las Joyas, Río Tunal, and Calera—dating from A.D. 550 to 1350 (Kelley 1971). Kelley (1985a) subsequently revised the dating of the Chalchihuites sequence based on a series of radiocarbon dates from Alta Vista. In this study, the Guadiana sequence dates were placed from ca. A.D. 875 to 1400+, and a tentative fifth phase, the Molino phase, was added. In discussing the revised chronology (Figure 12.3), Kelley posed three alternative positions regarding the dating of the Guadiana sequence: (1) abandon the previous dates for the Guadiana branch, which required accepting the revised Suchil series and modifying the Guadiana dates to make them more recent; (2) accept the previous Guadiana sequence but carefully reanalyze dates and associated ceramic assemblages and discard the new Suchil dates in favor of the old Suchil sequence; or (3) accept the dates from both branches, which would make the two sequences partly contemporary. At the heart of Kelley's interpretation is how the Suchil and Guadiana sequences relate to each other. Kelley believed the Guadiana sequence developed out of and was mostly later than the Suchil sequence. The Guadiana sequence, as initially defined and dated, was based on the stratigraphic ceramic sequence and several radiocarbon determinations from the Schroeder site (Kelley and Abbott Kelley 1971).

In his reassessment, Kelley discarded the Schroeder site radiocarbon dates and a single date from La Atalaya. Most of the Guadiana branch radiocarbon dates (which

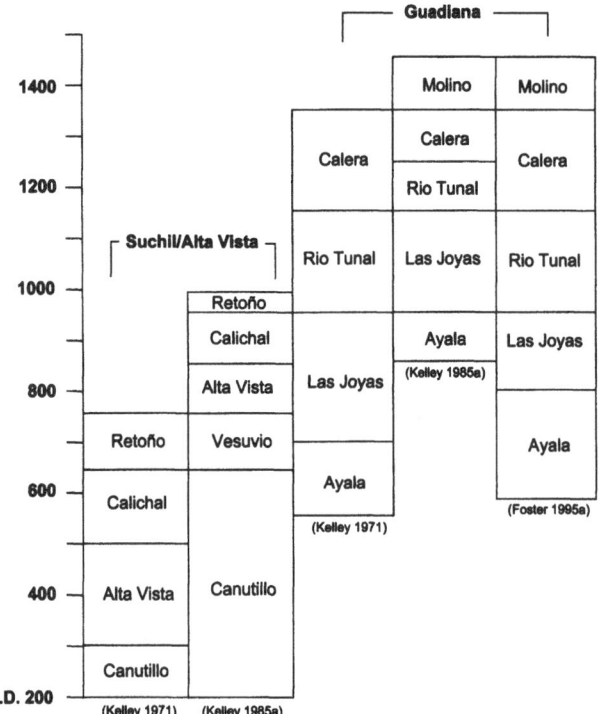

Figure 12.3. Chalchihuites phase sequences.

were uncorrected) are associated with Ayala and Las Joyas phase ceramics. Several Schroeder dates, 664 B.C. and A.D. 419 and 506, are early and are probably associated with an earlier Loma component. Five other dates range from A.D. 661 to 751, and a sixth date is A.D. 819. Kelley (1985a:271) notes that two dates, A.D. 751 and 819, are associated with a more or less equal mix of Ayala and Las Joyas phase ceramics. Using these dates, Kelley set the temporal boundary of the Ayala and Las Joyas phases at A.D. 850. The corrected dates (see Foster 1995b) suggest that a date of A.D. 750 to 800 may be more appropriate, however.

When, then, does the Ayala phase begin? Three dates, A.D. 663, 683, and 697, cluster. The A.D. 663 date is associated with pure Ayala phase ceramics, and the A.D. 683 date is associated with a mix of Ayala and Las Joyas phase ceramics. Thus, it is possible to infer an even earlier end to the Ayala phase than the A.D. 800 date suggested above. It appears the Ayala phase was established by the mid A.D. 600s. The A.D. 697 date lacks association with diagnostic artifacts, and it is assigned to the Ayala phase based on the date itself.

Although Kelley discarded it, the date A.D. 751 from La Atalaya is important. It is associated with Ayala phase ceramics, and, like the Schroeder dates, it indicates that the Ayala phase was well established by the mid A.D. 700s. Its corrected range further indicates that the date is likely no older than A.D. 600. This, and the stratigraphic position of the material from which the date was derived, suggests an Ayala phase occupation of the site that began before the mid A.D. 700s, perhaps the late A.D. 600s or early A.D. 700s. Here it is suggested the Ayala phase is best dated between the mid A.D. 600s and the early A.D. 800s. This is essentially the same conclusion reached by Kelley (1985a) in his discussion of alternative 2.

The dating of the remainder of the Guadiana sequence is even more problematic. Only a single radiocarbon date, A.D. 1215, from an ambiguous context at the Schroeder site, is available. Although Kelley (1985a) tentatively assigned it to the late Río Tunal phase, under both his old and new sequences, it is a Calera phase date. It is of no use in resolving the dating of the Guadiana sequence.

One method of partially resolving the dating of the Guadiana sequence is to turn to the West Coast. Kelley and Winters's (1960) revision of West Coast sequences was based on data from the Schroeder site. This revision stood untested until excavations at Amapa (Grosscup 1964, 1976; Meighan 1976) and Peñitas (Bordaz 1964). The coastal sequences were also reevaluated in light of radiocarbon dates from west Mexico (Long and Taylor 1966), and the Kelley and Winters scheme was generally supported. More recently, data from the Marismas Nacionales have provided some additional support for their temporal scheme (Foster 1995b).

Based on the dating of the Baluarte phase (Chametla) and Ayala phase, Kelley and Winters inferred early and continued contact between the West Coast and the Durango uplands. Grosscup (1976:243) suggests that the contact did not occur until near the end of the Baluarte and Amapa phases, when people moved to higher land. At the time, Grosscup had no explanation for the abandonment of low coastal areas. There is evidence to suggest a submergence of portions of the coast beginning about A.D. 700 (the end of the Amapa and Baluarte phases; Connally 1984a). If a migration of coastal peoples did occur, this might explain the influx of coastal trade goods into Durango around A.D. 700.

It appears the Ayala phase was established before the initiation of contact between the coast and the highlands, and it appears to have continued after contact was established. Therefore, Kelley's (1971) initial date of A.D. 700 for the end of the Ayala phase seems to be too early, and his (Kelley 1985a) revised end date of A.D. 950 may be too late. Therefore, based on the ^{14}C dates, ties to the Chametla area, and Chametla's temporal relationship to Amapa, the dating of the Ayala phase to between the early A.D. 600s and the early A.D. 800s appears to be supported.

The West Coast data also offer some help at the other end of the sequence. Grosscup (1976) notes some direct similarities between the Amapa and Durango ceramic assemblages. In particular, he notes similarities between Santiago White-on-red (Amapa) and Nayar White-on-red (Chalchihuites) and suggests rough contemporaneity between the Ixcuintla and Santiago phases of Amapa and the Calera phase in Durango. The Ixcuintla phase is dated from A.D. 1150 to 1375, and the Santiago phase is dated A.D. 1375 to the mid-1400s. The Calera phase is suggested to begin about A.D. 1150 and extend to perhaps the early A.D. 1400s.

Dating the intermediate phases of the Guadiana sequence is primarily a matter of speculation based on ties to the West Coast. The Las Joyas phase appears to begin ca. A.D. 800 and last to A.D. 950, whereas the Río Tunal phase dates remain as originally suggested, A.D. 950–1150. The newly proposed Molino phase would begin ca. A.D. 1400 and last possibly to contact.

Correlation of the Suchil and Guadiana Branch Sequences

When Kelley's (1985) revised dates for the Guadiana sequence are rejected in favor of a slightly modified version of his original sequence, a potential dilemma arises regarding the dating of the Suchil–Alta Vista sequence. Kelley (1971, 1985a) has argued the Guadiana branch developed out of the Suchil branch, a position that seems supported by ceramic evidence (Kelley and Abbott Kelley 1971). Kelley and Abbott Kelley argue that the Mercado (and Amaro) Red-on-cream of the Calichal phase is also the initial Ayala phase ceramic type. Suchil Red-on-brown and Michilia Red-Filled Engraved of the Alta Vista phase are rare in Durango. In other words, Mercado and Amaro appear in the Guadiana area with no local ancestral forms, and if Kelley's new dates for the Suchil branch and old dates for the Guadiana branch are accepted, the Suchil branch could not have given rise to the Guadiana branch as we now understand it. Therefore, it is suggested here that the Ayala and Las Joyas phases are contemporaneous, at least in part, with the Calichal and Retoño phases.

The Guadiana Sequence

The Guadiana Chalchihuites sequence is based almost solely on the work done at the Schroeder site (Kelley 1971, 1990).

AYALA PHASE (A.D. 600/650–800)

The Ayala phase is defined by the presence of Mercado and Amaro Red-on-cream (Figure 12.4) ceramic types (Abbott 1960; Kelley and Abbott Kelley 1971). Today the Kelleys (personal communication 1990) no longer consider the differences between the two types significant. Amaro Red-on-cream appears as bowls with decorated interiors, whereas Mercado Red-on-cream comes in a greater variety of vessel forms with decoration limited to the exterior of vessels. Both are commonly decorated with geometric and life-form elements. Amaro interiors are often halved or quartered with life forms or geometric designs within the panels. Mercado life forms usually occur in panels on the sides of vessels below the rim, and Mercado tripod vessels commonly have rim tabs on them.

It is during the Ayala phase that there is the first evidence of Chalchihuites contact with West Coast cultures. Baluarte phase ceramics from the Chametla area are found and include Early and Middle Chametla Polychrome, Middle Chametla Polychrome Engraved, Chametla Black-band Engraved, Chametla Red-rim ware and Red Rim Utility ware, Chametla Scalloped Rim, Marbelized Interior ware, and Mano Colorado ware (Kelly 1938). Other West Coast materials found include figurines (White-Filleted), spindle whorls, and a variety of small items (Kelley and Winters 1960).

A new pottery type, Refugio Red-on-brown (Kelley and Abbott Kelley 1971), is introduced at the end of the Ayala phase. It is poorly made and appears to emerge as the last gasp of the Suchil Chalchihuites in western Zacatecas (Kelley 1990a). Refugio Red-on-brown appears to evolve quickly into Neveria Red-on-brown, a type that becomes the diagnostic ceramic type of the Las Joyas phase.

LAS JOYAS PHASE (A.D. 800/850–950)

Neveria Red-on-brown (Kelley and Abbott Kelley 1971) commonly appears as basket-handled vessels (Figure 12.5). The handles are, in most cases, representations of double-headed serpents grasping opposing sides of the vessel in their mouths. The handles are decorated with various symbols, including the Venus symbol, the cross of Quetzalcoatl, eagles, anthropomorphs, and serpents. Vessel exteriors are decorated with probable representations of the Earth Monster, Xolotl, and animals such as dogs, coyotes, and squirrels.

The Las Joyas phase also marks the appearance of another interesting ceramic type, Lolandis Red-Rim

Figure 12.4. Ayala phase ceramics. *a–d*, Mercado Red-on-cream; *e–f*, Amaro Red-on-cream.

(Kelley and Abbott Kelley 1971). Although this type had its origins on the West Coast, it was produced in quantity in Durango (Kelley 1990a). This, and a significant increase of West Coast influence in the Durango uplands at this time, has led Kelley (1990a) to suggest a migration of West Coast peoples or, at a minimum, the migration of some West Coast potters into the uplands. It is also possible, however, that with the importation of Lolandis Red-rimmed into Durango, it became so popular that it was quickly and commonly imitated. In fact, the abundance of Lolandis Red-rimmed in the uplands has led some working on the West Coast to speculate about the possibility of its being an upland innovation.

Chametla and Amapa ceramics, smoking pipes, copper ornaments, raw shell and shell ornaments, spindle whorls, and pyrite mirrors also appear in Las Joyas phase contexts. Among the ceramic types identified are Aztatlán Ware, Cerro Izabel Incised, and Aguaruto Exterior Incised.

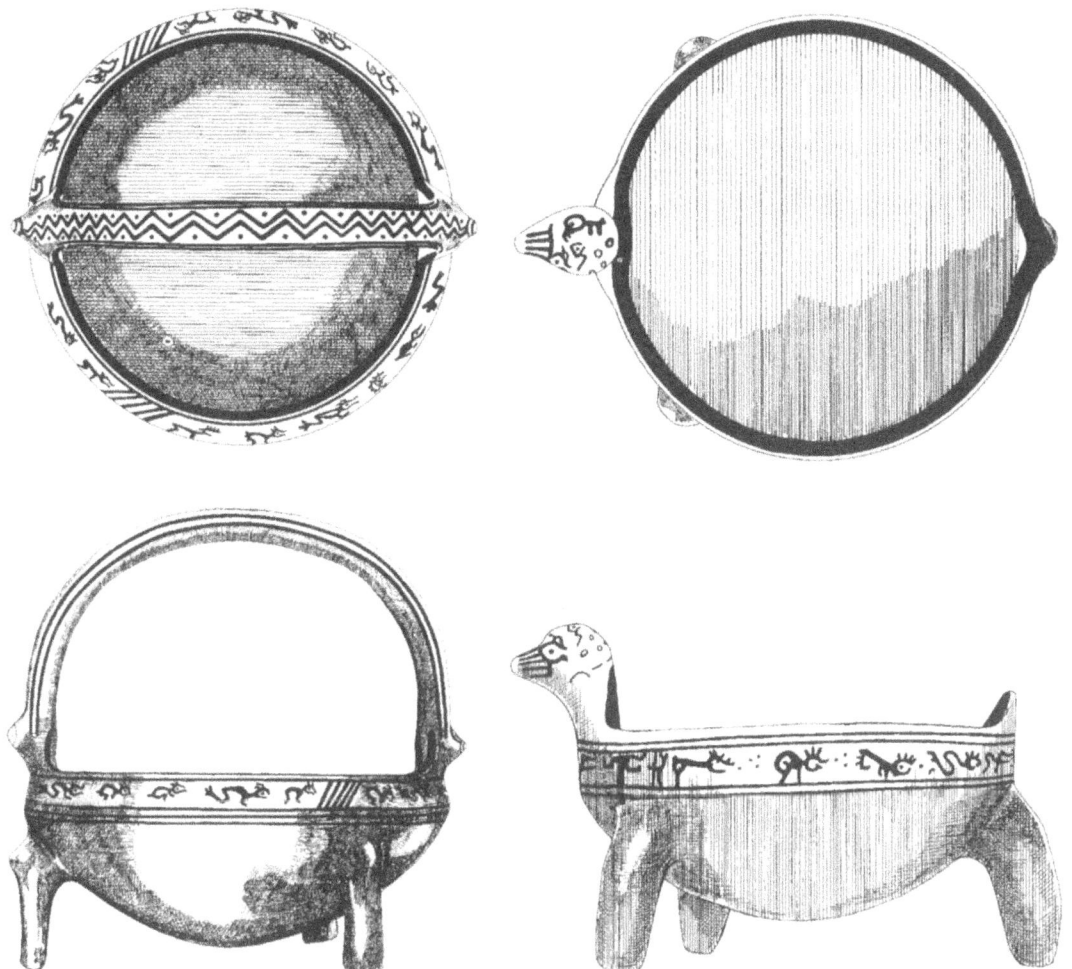

Figure 12.5. Neveria Red-on-brown (Las Joyas phase).

The northwest Mexican uplands are clearly integrated into the Aztatlán Mercantile System at this time.

A utility ware, El Campo Buff, is introduced. In addition to the plainwares, polished red and black wares, some of which occur as effigy vessels, are present. Also introduced for the first time are molcajetes (Morcillo Molcajetes), which occur most frequently as small tripod vessels.

Río Tunal Phase (a.d. 950–1150)

During the Río Tunal phase, the Guadiana Chalchihuites reached its maximum geographic extent. Río Tunal phase components have been identified as far north as the Zape area and to the northeast in the Villa Ocampo area. In the Guadiana Valley, the Río Tunal and subsequent Calera phases are represented by a scattered occupation (Kelley 1971).

The diagnostic ceramic type for the Río Tunal phase, Otinapa Red-on-white (Figure 12.6), is decorated in a deep red on a cream to chalky-white slip (Kelley and Abbott Kelley 1971). Decorative elements are geometric and rectilinear and occur almost exclusively on the exterior of vessels in "bold, exuberant, and large" execution (Kelley 1971:796). The most common vessel forms are ollas, smaller globular jars with straight or slightly flaring necks, and large bowls that often have composite shapes. Basket-handled Neveria type vessels decorated in the Otinapa style sometimes occur. Morcillo Molcajetes are common, and a new ceramic type, Canatlán Red-band, is introduced. Canatlán Red-band vessels come in a variety of forms from large ollas to small, shallow bowls.

Stone pestles and paint palettes occur with a variety of other material culture. Guasave and Sinaloa polychromes are found, as are smoking pipes and cop-

Figure 12.6. Otinapa Red-on-white (Río Tunal phase).

per. Their presence indicates continued interaction in the Aztatlán Mercantile System.

CALERA PHASE (A.D. 1150–1350/1400)

The Calera phase is poorly understood and represented. It was best expressed in central and southern Durango, and at the Schroeder site it represents either an ephemeral terminal occupation or perhaps a limited late reoccupation of the site. Many new traits were introduced into the area and greatly influence local culture(s). In fact, it can be argued that nearly all vestigial traits of the Chalchihuites ceramic tradition have been extensively modified or have disappeared by this time.

The diagnostic pottery type of the Calera phase is Nayar White-on-red (Figure 12.7; Kelley and Abbott Kelley 1971; Peithman 1961). The upper two-thirds to three-quarters of the vessels are slipped in a bright red that is decorated with a thick white paint that flakes off easily. Decorative elements tend to be rather large and are haphazardly placed around the vessel's body. Nested triangles and circles, panels divided into quarters, and checkerboard-like designs are common.

A new ceramic type, Madero Fluted (Figure 12.7), appears and with Nayar White-on-red and Canatlán Red-band makes up the diagnostic Calera phase ceramic assemblage. Other items thought to be associated with the Calera phase are smoking pipes and collar-button spindle whorls.

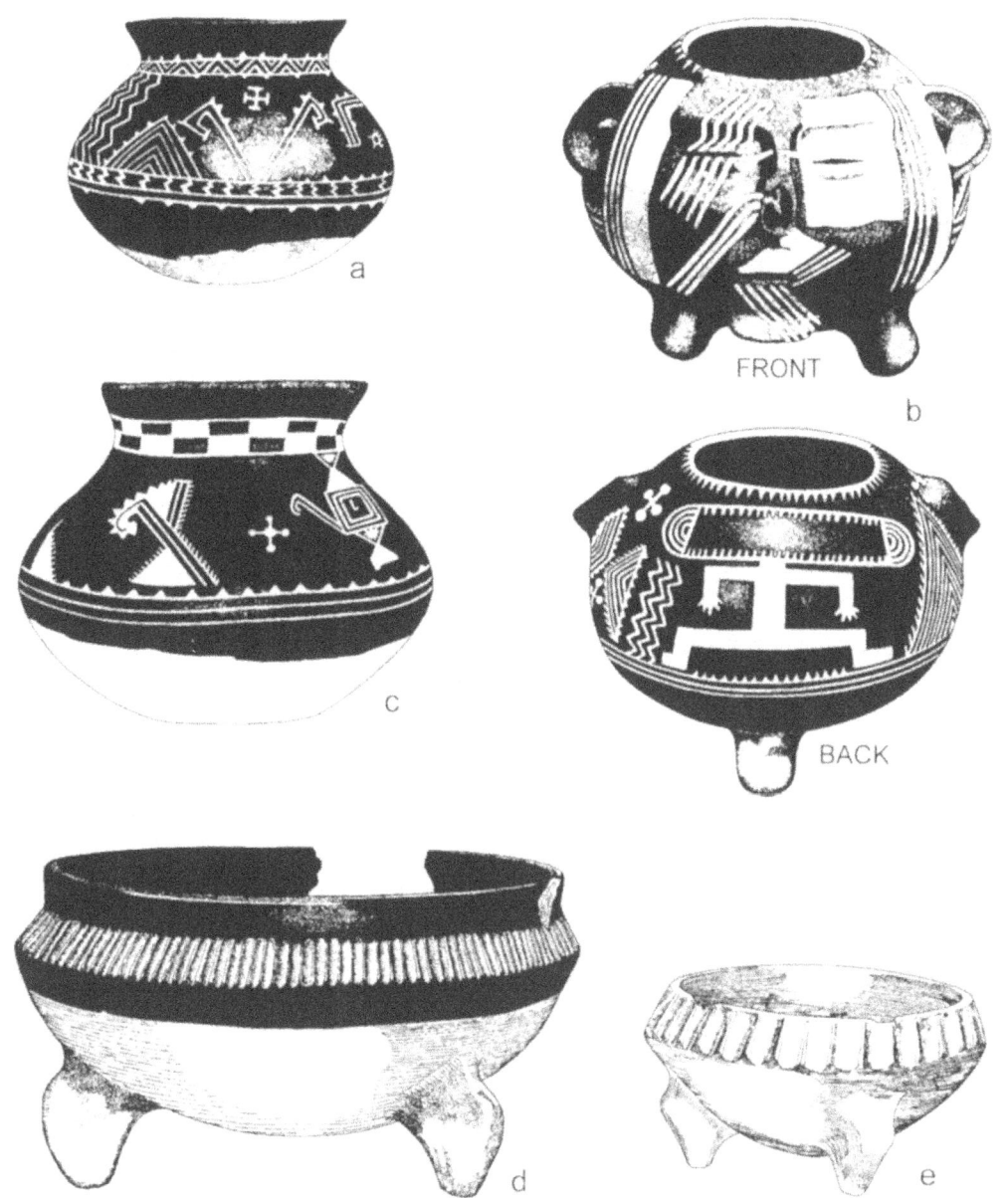

Figure 12.7. Calera phase ceramics. *a–c*, Nayar White-on-red; *d–e*, Madero Fluted.

MOLINO PHASE (A.D. 1350–1400+)

Based on a collection of material from the site of Cañón del Molino (Ganot R. and Peschard F. 1995, 1997; Kelley 1986a), Kelley (1985a) proposed a fifth phase for the Guadiana Chalchihuites sequence, the Molino phase. Aztatlán materials are common at the site, and the late ceramic assemblage is clearly a mix of Chalchihuites and West Coast ceramic traits. Molino Red-on-cream (Figure 12.8), a well-made and polished ware, exhibits vessel forms adapted from West Coast types and decorative elements that combine Chalchihuites and West Coast styles (Ganot R. and Peschard F. 1995:Figure 8.6, 1997). The significance of the Molino phase in regional prehistory has yet to be defined, however.

PREHISTORIC TO HISTORIC TRANSITION

At the time of Spanish contact, the Tepehuan occupied most the area that was once the homeland of the Loma San Gabriel and Chalchihuites cultures. Riley and Win-

Durango (Foster 1994). Ethnohistorically, the area comprised the territories of the Acaxee and the Xixime, both members of the Cahitan language group. At contact, the Acaxee lived in scattered villages in the uplands and foothills of western Durango and Sinaloa and practiced dry land farming. They were actively engaged in warfare and were known to take trophy heads and cannibalize their captives (Beals 1932, 1933).

SITES

Despite the limited scale of research in Durango, the small number of sites investigated have produced significant insights into regional prehistory. Numerous sites occur in the vicinity of the city of Durango, including the most extensively investigated site in Durango, the Schroeder site (Kelley 1971, 1990a). Masonry structures are scattered across two hills and an intervening saddle overlooking the Río Tunal. House platforms, a small pyramid and associated sunken courtyards, a small open-ended ball court, and a pyramid are present. The site's occupation extends from the Ayala phase into the Calera phase (ca. A.D. 600–1350), with the heaviest occupation during the Ayala and Las Joyas phases. An early Loma component was also identified. The site is a large habitation site with public architecture and space, lacking the architectural scale, complexity, and intrasite organization of major Suchil branch sites in Zacatecas. Also found were intrusive West Coast ceramics, spindle whorls, and copper (Kelley and Winters 1960). INAH recently sponsored limited work at the Schroeder site (Guevara Sánchez 1994). It is important to note that the prehistoric mines reported by Guevara Sánchez are actually historic tin mines that were being worked at the time of Kelley's excavations.

While excavations were being carried out at the Schroeder site, the small site of La Manga, about 2 km away, was tested (Jay 1957). The site is scattered across a hilltop and down onto a terrace overlooking the Río Tunal. Several small paved platforms constructed from rectangular stones and extending about 30 cm above ground level were excavated. Some small plazas partially surrounded by low walls were also present.

Loma ceramic types dominated the ceramic assemblage. Less than 2 percent of the ceramics were Chalchihuites types (Refugio Red-on-brown, Mercado Red-on-cream, and Otinapa Red-on-white). It is also noteworthy that other contemporaneous Chalchihuites types were not represented (Jay 1957). A single West

Figure 12.8. Molino Red-on-cream (Molino phase). Courtesy of Tom Herrschaft.

ters (1963) have suggested a direct prehistoric to historic continuum of peoples in the area, noting a series of specific traits in Tepehuan material culture, including pipes, terraced incense burners, and certain ceramic traits, that appear to be derived from prehistoric times. Early Tepehuan ceramics included tripod and handled vessels reminiscent of Chalchihuites ceramic types. More recently, Willett (1997) has suggested that the Southern Tepehuan *xiotalh* ceremonies have their roots in Guadiana Chalchihuites.

Little is known of the prehistory of the western

Coast sherd, a probable Chametla type, was recovered along with pottery disks, manos, metates, projectile points, a handled end-scraper, several cores, hammerstones, full- and three-quarter-grooved axes, a maul, and some obsidian flakes.

Another site on the Río Tunal east of the city of Durango is Navacoyan. Looting in the early 1950s destroyed most of the site, and what is known of it comes from a large surface collection (Howard 1957) and Kelley's (1971) analysis of a collection of the looted ceramics. The site appears to have contained many burials with associated funerary objects. Ceramic types reported include El Conejo Red-filled Engraved, Amaro Red-on-cream, Mercado Red-on-cream, Otinapa Red-on-white, Nayar White-on-red, and Canatlán Red-band along with molcajetes, redwares, and plainwares. Navacoyan also produced West Coast ceramic types, Tuxpan Incised and Mangos Engraved, associated with the Amapa and Ixcuintla phases. The occupation of the site appears to date primarily to the Río Tunal and Calera phases.

A series of small sites was recorded by Kelley and the University of Chicago west of the city of Durango. One, the Weicker site (Foster 1986a; Kelley and Shakelford 1954), was partially excavated. Two compounds defined by low cobble walls (Figure 12.9), each containing three small one- and two-room structures, were exposed. The two-room structures consisted of one room with a compacted dirt floor and one with a paved stone floor. The compounds measured nearly 5 m by 10 m and slightly more than 6 m by 12 m. The individual rooms averaged about 2 m square. Small clay-lined hearths occurred between several of the rooms within the compounds.

The Weicker site ceramic assemblage consisted of Loma plainwares and several sherds of Canatlán Redband. Two Chalchihuites style spindle whorls, apparent trade items, were also recovered and suggest a Calera phase association (A.D. 1150–1400) for the site. Basin metates, handstones, gouges, end-scrapers, a whetstone, and several projectile point types were also recovered. The site is thought to represent a late, Loma hamlet occupied by several extended families. A third, unexcavated compound is also present at the site. The site may be typical of many late Loma sites scattered in the uplands of the Sierra.

La Atalaya, near Villa Union, was tested in 1962 (Kelley 1963). The site is on a low knoll near the Río Poanas. A large room containing three columns (a fourth was probably destroyed when a concrete cross was placed at the site) was excavated. The columns were made of rubble set in and plastered over with adobe. Cultural fill in this part of the site was nearly 3 m deep, and a portion of a masonry wall representing an earlier occupation was exposed in the fill below the columns.

Most of the ceramic types were Ayala phase, Amaro and Mercado Red-on-cream. Earlier types included Canutillo Engraved, El Conejo Red-filled Engraved, Suchil Red-on-brown, and Vesuvio Red-filled Engraved. Later types include Refugio Red-on-brown, some Neveria Red-on-brown, Morcillo Molcajete, Madero Fluted, and Nayar White-on-red. Several sherds of Middle Chametla Polychrome, Vista Paint Cloisonné, and Negative Paint ware were found along with figurines, sherd disks, a ceramic trumpet in the form of a conch shell, shell beads, bone awls and pendants, and a variety of chipped and ground stone tools. The occupation of the site seems to have spanned the Guadiana sequence and is of particular interest because of the pre–Ayala phase Chalchihuites materials present.

Cliff dwellings are also known from the southern and western margins of Durango (Lazalde 1984, 1987). One of the best preserved is La Cueva de Maguey. The cave is about 45 m wide, 15 m deep, and 5 m high. The structures were made from wattle and daub, several two-story structures are present, a small room block abuts the back wall of the cave, and several isolated free-standing structures occur. Doorways are rectangular or rectangular with rounded arches. Materials found at the site include corncobs, manos, metates, sherds, and several bowls. Ceramic types identified include Nayar Red-on-white, Canatlán Red-band, and Madero Fluted.

A smaller, partially destroyed cliff dwelling, Cerro Blanco, is reported near the town of Mesquital (Lazalde 1984, 1987). One habitation structure occurred in each of two adjacent overhangs. Another cliff dwelling was investigated as part of a survey in the Municipio of Canatlán, northeast of the city of Durango (Martinez 1981). The Cueva de San Pablo contained several habitation rooms, some of which had attached smaller storage features and granaries. The walls of these structures were made from adobe and masonry. Investigation of the site was limited to seven test pits and surface collections. Ceramic types identified include a Chivas complex blackware, El Campo Buff, Chalchihuites plain and red wares, Canatlán Red Banded, Amaro Red-on-cream, Mercado Red-on-cream, Suchil Red-on-brown, a bichrome similar to Chico Red-on-brown, Loma Plain, Chico Red-on-brown, Loma Textured, and Loma White.

Of particular note are the remains of agave fiber cordage and mats, including three cotton possible tumpline

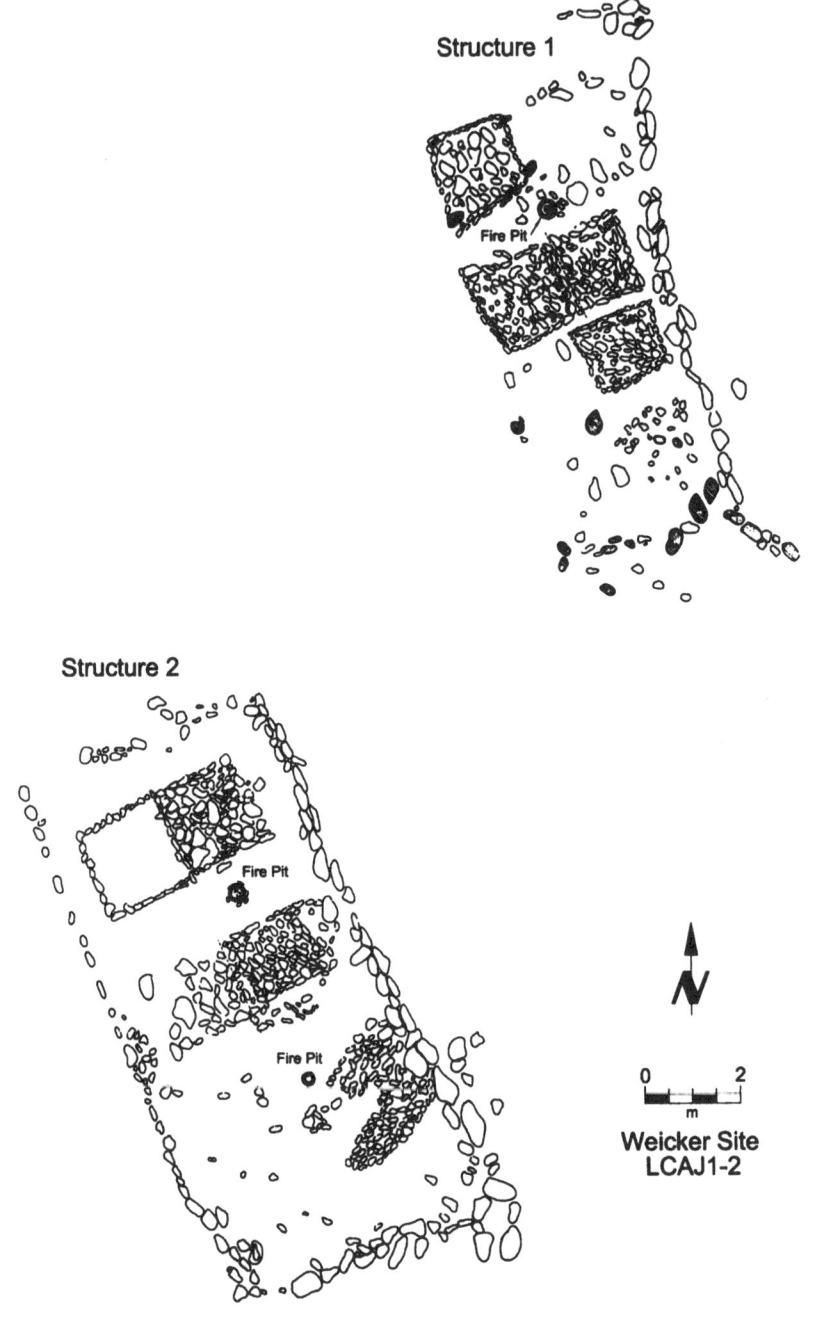

Figure 12.9. The Weicker site compounds.

headbands (Figure 12.10). These were colored in yellows, greens, and blues. Anthropomorphs are represented on one, and on another are figures similar to the alligator monster depicted on Suchil Red-on-brown vessels (Kelley and Abbott Kelley 1971:Plates 19 and 22). The design on the third specimen appears to be geometric. The ceramic types present suggest a date of occupation for the site from A.D. 600 to A.D. 1150 or later.

A number of sites in central Durango are of note, including Cañón de Molino, Hervideros, and Carcaria. Cañón del Molino (Molino) is known by the work of avocational archaeologists Jaime Ganot R., Alejandro Peschard F., and Jesus Lazalde. The most comprehensive description of Molino is that of Ganot R. and Peschard F. (1995, 1997). The site itself consists of two elements. Part of the site is located at the foot of a flu-

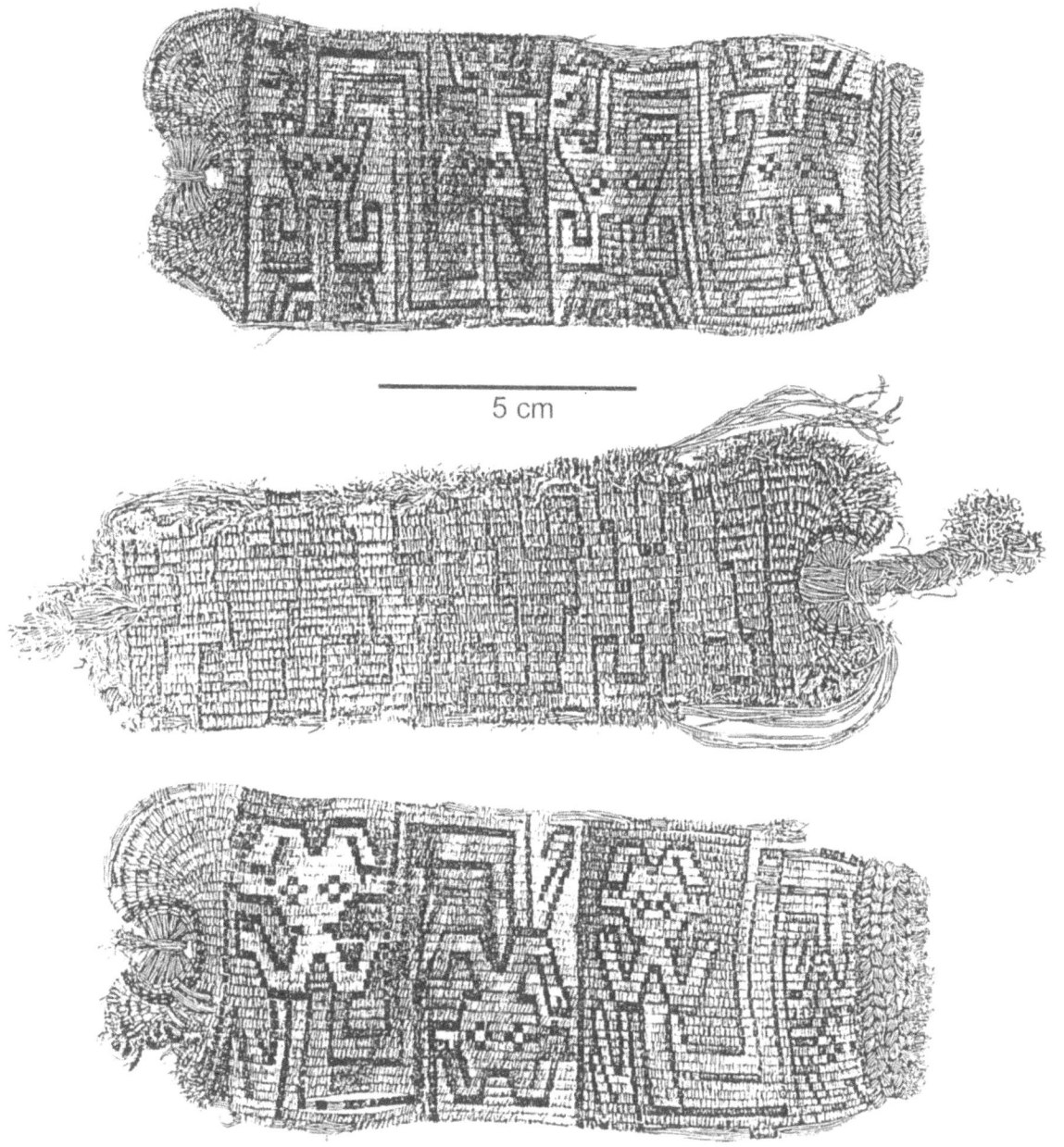

Figure 12.10. Possible tumpline headbands from Cueva de San Pablo.

vial terrace on the northern side of the Río Guatimape. Partially buried cobble stone foundations forming rectangular rooms are scattered along the terrace. The other portion of the site is located atop a hill 200 m directly above the lower part of the site. Some artificial terracing, courtyards, small mounds (altars), and house foundations are present. Because of the presence of circular structures of coarse slab stone masonry along the southern edge of the site, in contrast to the other structures at the site, which are of cobble stone masonry, Ganot R. and Peschard F. suggest that two different occupations are represented.

The Molino ceramic assemblage is an interesting mix of Loma, Chalchihuites, and West Coast types. Las Joyas, Río Tunal, and Calera phase types are represented. As previously noted, El Molino Red-on-cream, the diagnostic type of the Molino phase (Kelley 1986a), is a combination of Chalchihuites and West Coast design elements on vessel forms adopted from the West Coast. Also, many Loma vessels take the form of Chalchihuites types, such as Neveria basket-handled vessels and tripod forms with rim tabs such as those found on Mercado Red-on-cream vessels.

West Coast pottery and other artifacts were found at Molino. Guasave Red-on-buff, Lolandis Red-rimmed, Iguanas Polychrome, Tuxpan Engraved, Mangos Engraved, Santiago Red-on-orange, and Culiacán Polychrome are represented. Smoking pipes, like the Cocoyolitos types from Chametla and those described for Tacuichamona (Sauer and Brand 1932), were also present along with copper bells, a Tlaloc effigy, a copper turtle and other pendants, a crescent pectoral, a seal, rings, bracelets, chains, and needles. Projectile points, stone sculptures and palettes, small carved stone ornaments, a carved stone incense burner, and shell pendants, beads, a carved pectoral, and bracelets were also found, as were rectangular notched sherds, possible fishing net weights, small stone discoids, metates, stone molcajetes, pestles, three-quarter-grooved axes, and hammerstones.

Most of the artifacts recovered apparently came from burials. Burial types include inhumations and secondary burials in large plain or decorated ollas. Thirty-seven skulls were recovered, 34 of which exhibit some degree of tabular-erect cranial deformation (Figure 12.11; Peschard F. 1970, 1983). This is particularly interesting in that cranial deformation was rare in the uplands of northwest Mexico but common on the West Coast. One individual exhibited type A–3 tooth mutilation (Romero Molina 1986). The presence of these individuals, the abundance of West Coast items, and the significant influence of West Coast culture(s) on the Molinoans have led Kelley (1986a) to suggest the presence of a trading enclave or actual migration of West Coast peoples to Molino.

Hervideros is a large site on a hill overlooking the Río Nazas. The opposite ends of the hill are elevated. Cobble stone foundations surrounding plazas are scattered across the top and down the upper slopes of the hill, and a ball court is present (Hers 1989b). Chalchihuites ceramics, including some Michilia Red-filled Engraved, are reported along with Culiacán Polychrome and some red-on-brown types similar to those from Guasave (Kelley 1971; Mason 1937). Loma ceramics are common, and some occur in the form of Chalchihuites types. Other artifacts reported include copper, figurines, shell or bone beads, obsidian debitage, stone axes, and conical and biconical ceramic spindle whorls. Recent work at Hervideros (Hers 1993a) has done nothing to expand current understanding of the site.

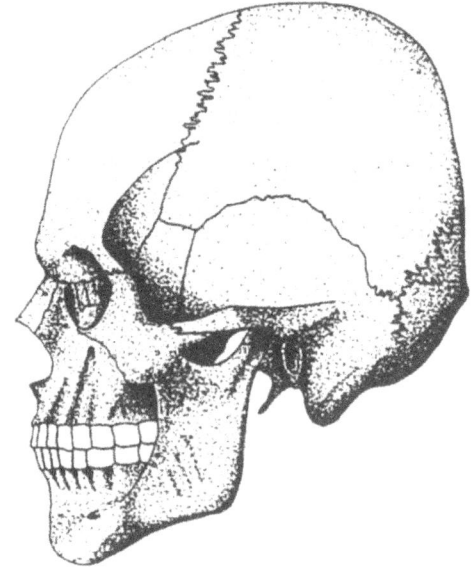

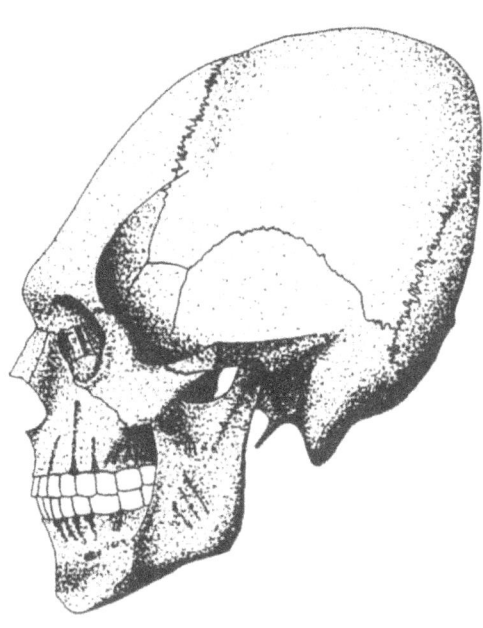

Figure 12.11. Examples of tabular erect (tabular erect, plano occipital/plano lamdica, and tabular erect, oblique) cranial deformation. Courtesy of Alejandro Peschard F.

Several sites, besides the Schroeder site and Hervideros, have small, open-ended ball courts (Kelley 1991). The playing alleys of the known Durango courts are delineated by low banquettes made from slab and cobble stones. The Schroeder site's court, Structure 6, was 4 m wide, 10 m long, and paved with caliche, and its long axis was oriented slightly to the northwest. The alley contained quantities of Loma Plain sherds. It is not known if it is a Loma court or if it is actually associated with the Chalchihuites occupation of the site.

Los Castillos, southwest of the city of Durango, has two ball courts. The alley of Court A, oriented slightly to the northeast, measures 4.5 m wide and 12.7 m long. Court B, oriented slightly to the northwest, is 4.57 m wide and 16.8 m long. Both Loma and Chalchihuites ceramics and architecture are present on the site. Cacaria, near Nicolas Bravo, also contains a small, open-ended ball court that measures 5.25 m wide and 15 m long and is oriented slightly northeast. Mason (1937; Kelley 1991) recorded two ball courts near Los Fresnos about 120 km northwest of the city of Durango. Both are similar to those already described. Data on them are limited, but the alley of one measures over 4 m wide and 15.5 m long. As Kelley (1991; Sauer 1932) notes, this area, on a branch of the Río San Lorenzo, was an early route from the coast into the Durango highlands. One of Nuño de Guzmán's expeditions traversed the Río San Lorenzo in 1531–32.

Numerous sites are reported from the Zape area, the two largest being Santa Ana (Guillemin Tarayre 1867) and Cerro de la Cruz. Santa Ana is on a low hill southwest of the pueblo of Zape. Test excavations at the site revealed low platform mounds, associated plazas, and masonry foundations (Kelley 1971). A central court measuring approximately 15 m by 20 m is surrounded by mounds. Loma Plain dominates the ceramic assemblage, which includes some redwares, Canatlán Redband, and several sherds of Otinapa Red-on-white. Ceramic pipes, spindle whorls, manos, metates, axes, projectile points (side-notched, lenticular, stemmed, and triangular), bifaces, obsidian, shell, and copper are reported as well. No West Coast polychromes have yet been reported for the site, which is thought to date between A.D. 950 and the mid A.D. 1300s.

Cerro de la Cruz is on a large, isolated hill overlooking Zape. The hill is accessible only from its northern slope. Below the crest of the hill is a series of large boulder alignments, the function of which is unclear. They do not appear to be associated with either agriculture or habitation. It is possible they were part of a defensive system or some other type of system designed to limit or control access to the site. Once beyond the stone alignments, a succession of isolated house foundations occurs. These include both circular and rectangular foundations constructed from cobbles and vertical stone slabs that are often tied to bedrock outcrops or large boulders that appear to have functioned as parts of the structures' foundations and walls. Atop the crest of the hill is a large bedrock outcrop modified into a large platform. This appears to be the primary ceremonial feature at the site. Along the southern edge of the hilltop is a level terrace that appears to have been a habitation zone. A concentration of cultural debris, including burnt daub and a series of bedrock mortars, is present on this terrace.

The elevated position of Cerro de la Cruz and the presence of the possible fortification of the only access to the site suggest it is a defensive site. Cerro de la Cruz may be the major site in the area, but little can be said about its role in the area's prehistory. Dating of this site is problematic. The only diagnostic artifact reported for the site is a Loma copy of an El Conejo Red-filled Engraved, suggesting an Ayala phase association.

Another site has been reported in Zape at the foot of Cerro de la Cruz (Ganot R. and Peschard F. 1990; Lazalde 1987). The construction of a house resulted in the recovery of an Ixcuintla Polychrome vessel, a type diagnostic of the Ixcuintla phase at Amapa (A.D. 1100–1300).

North of Zape on the Río Sestin is the site of La Cueva de los Muertos Chiquitos, the most intensively studied site in the area (Brooks and Brooks 1978; Brooks et al. 1962; Foster 1984). Excavations there identified structural remains, macrobotanical remains, complete remains of 16 individuals, and fragmentary remains of others. The structural remains consisted of two puddled adobe floors under which burials had been placed. It is not clear if these floors were put in place to seal the burials or if they are an artifact of an occupation. Below Floor A were the remains of six children. It has been suggested that they died at about the same time and were buried simultaneously; their deaths were perhaps the result of an epidemic. Their bodies, wrapped in petates and cloth, were placed on the bedrock floor of the cave in an arching line. One child's head was placed on a pillow, and an offering of bundled wood, roasted corn, and beans was placed with it. Burial offerings were associated with several other individuals under Floor A and included a turquoise mosaic, shell pendants and beads, wooden pendants, and a cloth belt. The fragmentary remains of an adult were also present.

The remains of eight children and one adult were found under Floor B. Many fragmentary remains were also recovered. The ages of the children ranged from 0–3 months to one year. One child was buried in an olla, and the others were wrapped in petates or cloth or both.

Quantities of sherd material, including Loma Plain, Loma Red, Loma Textured, and Chico Red-on-brown, were also recovered. Several undescribed types, including red-on-buffs, reds, blacks, and what appears to be

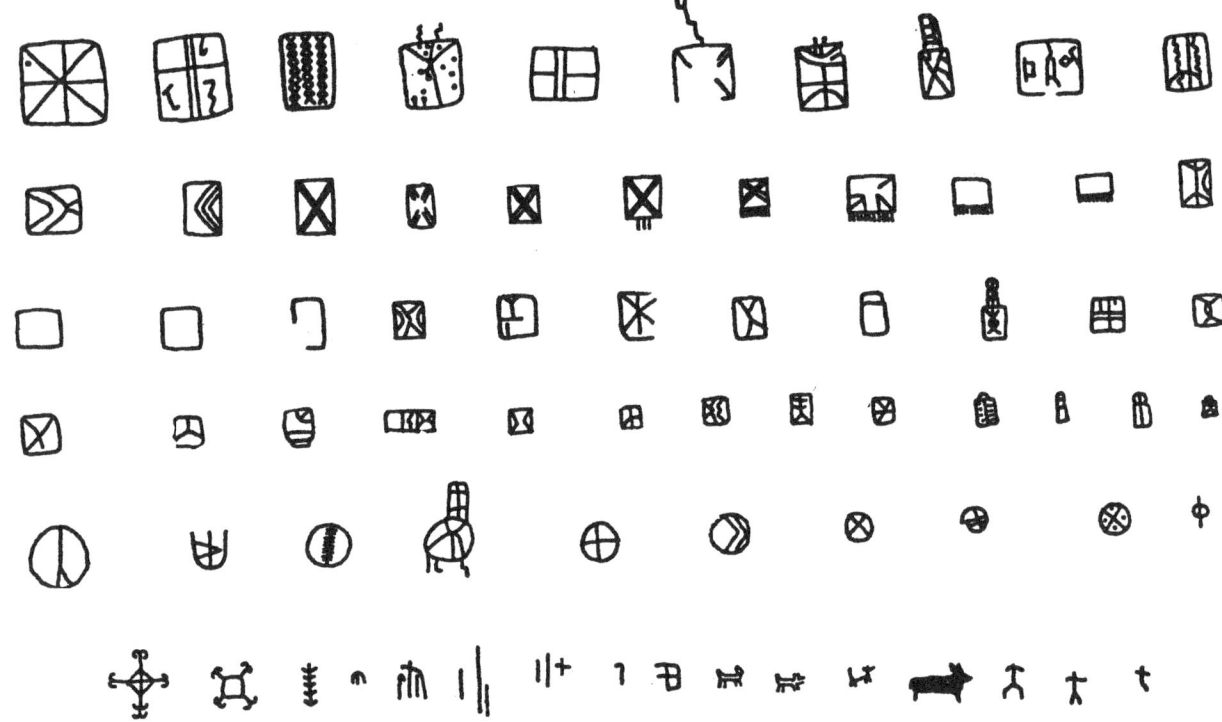

Figure 12.12. Petroglyphs from the Zape observatory. Courtesy of Jamie Ganot R. and Alejandro Peschard F.

red-on-black ceramics, were also present, along with a three-legged wooden stool.

The macrobotanical remains recovered include both domesticated and wild species such as cucurbits, agave, yucca, cacti, piñon nuts, walnuts, composites, mushrooms, three types of beans including a Carib lima, five types of corn, and possibly cotton. Faunal remains include coyotes, jackrabbits, squirrels, mice, rats, deer, and mountain sheep.

The stratigraphic position of the two floors suggests they were constructed at different times. A radiocarbon date of A.D. 682, corrected, was obtained for the site. Additionally, a sherd of Otinapa Red-on-white (Río Tunal phase) suggests a date of A.D. 950 to 1150 for some occupation of the site.

La Cueva de Dos Puertos, just north of Muertos Chiquitos, produced a partially mummified skull that exhibited tabular oblique cranial deformation. Based on comparative and distributional studies of this type of deformation, Brooks and Brooks (1980) suggest that he was a long-distance trader from a region other than Zape.

Another site of interest near the caves is a petroglyph site associated with a possible observatory (Ganot R. and Peschard F. 1997; Lazalde 1987; Peschard F. et al. 1984).

The glyphs depicted do not appear to be part of a coherent glyph panel, although they are clearly mesoamerican in origin; they are both rectangular and circular (Figure 12.12). Some are divided into quarters and may represent the four world quarters or calendrical symbols. Others have crossed bands that represent celestial elements such as the sun, eclipses, and clouds or rain. The glyphs are associated with two natural, free-standing stone columns that, with the western horizon, may have been used to observe equinox and solstice events. Using an Aztec analog, Joyce Marcus (personal communication 1990) suggested that these petroglyphs might mark ethnic boundaries or places of special ceremonial activities.

Other sites in the Zape area are similar to those previously described. Cerro de los Tepehuanes, south of Zape, has stone foundations on it, but no plazas or platforms are readily identifiable. The mesas to the east and north of Zape are also reported to have sites with stone foundations on them (Brooks 1971). In the valleys west and southwest of Zape, several isolated circular foundations, possible field houses for agricultural activities, have been identified.

Several sites are reported near Villa Ocampo on the Río Florido, the most notable being Loma San Gabriel,

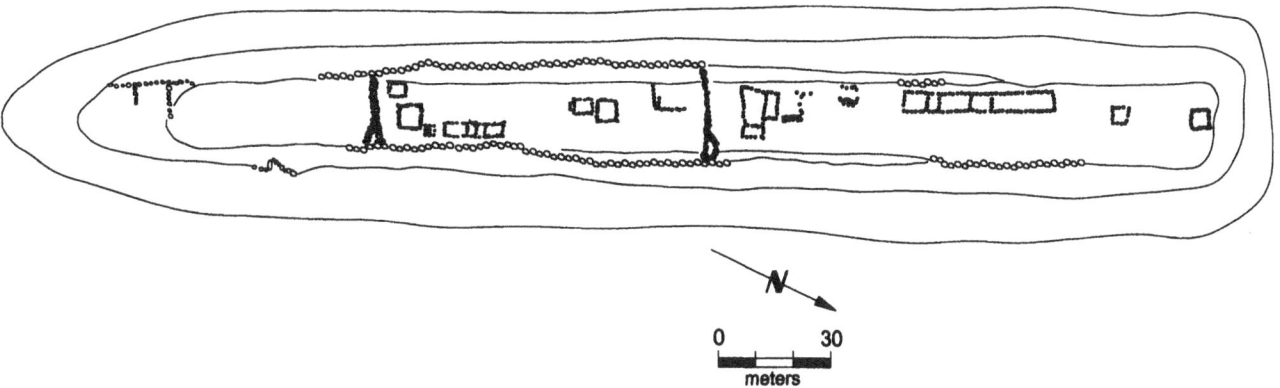

Figure 12.13. The Loma San Gabriel site.

the type site for the Loma culture (Brooks 1978; Foster 1978; Kelley 1956, 1971). Situated atop an isolated north-south oriented mesa, the site consists of a series of rectangular and square stone foundations (Figure 12.13). More than 20 rooms are present, including several larger, possible special-use or communal structures. Many rooms are contiguous, and a small altar is found at the north end of the site. Structures in the central portion of the site are enclosed in a compound with rock walls about a meter in height. The compound's crosswalls incorporate circular rooms. It is not known whether the compound represents socially restricted space or if it is a defensive feature.

Sherds, mainly Loma Plain, and debitage are scattered on the slopes below the site. Several small side-notched projectile points, metate and mano fragments, and bedrock mortars were also noted, along with a sherd of Otinapa Red-on-white. A date of the mid A.D. 1300s is suggested for the site.

The mesa on which the Loma San Gabriel site is located, together with an adjacent mesa, form a *boquilla*, or narrow pass, through which the Río Florido flowed until being dammed in the early 1980s. On the lower terraces of the hill across from the Loma San Gabriel site were several other sites. One consisted of several round stone foundations, and the other consisted of both round and square stone foundations. These were destroyed by dam construction. Although little is known of the extent of the prehistoric occupation of the area, it was probably sizable.

The Río Ramos area (Brooks 1971, 1978; Foster 1978) of east-central Durango is interesting in that it exhibits little evidence of Chalchihuites contact or influence. A cluster of sites occurs at the confluence of the Ríos Ramos and Escobedo and near the pueblo of Ramos. This area may represent a fairly pure Loma enclave. Loma Plain ceramics dominate the ceramic assemblages at the sites recorded. A single sherd of Vesuvio Red-filled Engraved was recorded at the site of Espia.

The site of El Cerro de Creston de los Indios, located along a cliff edge overlooking the Río Ramos, is of particular note. The central portion of the site is enclosed by a low rock wall with two round rooms about 1.5 m in diameter built into it. Square and rectangular rock foundations dominate the site's architecture, although several round rooms are present. Near the center of the site is a small platform mound surrounded by a series of rooms. These features clearly form some sort of ceremonial or elite complex. Many house foundations also occur outside the walled portion of the site. The walled area may represent an elite or ceremonial precinct within the site or perhaps some type of defensive compound. Besides some Loma Plain ceramics, artifacts at this site include debitage, manos, and many trough metate fragments. It is interesting that if this is a Loma site, it appears to represent a level of sociopolitical organization not commonly associated with Loma.

Two other sites, El Cerro Canyon and Cerro de los Corralitos de los Indios, also exhibit fairly formal site structures with contiguous rooms bordering a platform or plaza-like area (Brooks 1971). Elsewhere in the Río Ramos area, sites exhibit less formal intrasite organization with structures more randomly dispersed across sites. Both contiguous and isolated rectangular or circular rooms occur. Site locations include isolated hills and mesas and hillsides. Artifact assemblages include plainwares, debitage, and ground stone fragments.

The material culture on the Río Ramos sites suggests they are Loma. Several sites, however, exhibit a greater degree of architectural complexity and organization than is generally known for Loma sites. It is possible the Río Ramos area represents a region where Loma evolved to a higher level of sociopolitical organization, perhaps because the area was relatively independent of Chalchihuites influence. Moreover, these sites may represent a cultural manifestation other than Loma. It is also important to note that although some Río Ramos sites are fairly complex, they do not, as Brooks (1978) suggests, attain the architectural massiveness or complexity of the Chalchihuites sites in central and southern Durango such as the Schroeder site.

The Topia area of extreme northwestern Durango is poorly known archaeologically but nevertheless is of particular interest. Following branches of the Río Culiacán, the Spanish reached the highlands through this area. Kelley (1986a), noting the importance of the Topia area in prehistoric interaction between the West Coast and the Durango highlands, has referred to it as a "gateway."

DISCUSSION

Archaeological research has documented a long and complex human history for the Durango region. Nevertheless, despite a basic understanding of the region's prehistory, there are many significant gaps in our current knowledge of the area's past. Vast portions of Durango remain unknown archaeologically, and many issues regarding the timing and nature of prehistoric human use and occupation of the area cannot be addressed with the data available at present. Also, our current understanding of both the Loma San Gabriel and Guadiana Chalchihuites occupations of Durango is limited. Without additional work, including both broad-scale systematic, intensive survey and excavations, our knowledge of the region's prehistory will remain incomplete.

With the expansion of the Chalchihuites culture into the Loma homeland along the eastern foothills of the Sierra Madre beginning in the Ayala and Las Joyas phases, the region fell within the traditionally defined maximum extent of Mesoamerica. By the A.D. 1300s, if we associate the distribution of Chalchihuites (and West Coast) ceramics with the maximum extent of Mesoamerica, the frontier reached as far north as the Zape area.

The expansion of the Chalchihuites tradition into Durango clearly influenced the developmental trajectory of the local Loma culture. As discussed earlier, the reasons for this expansion remain points of speculation. Regardless, the Chalchihuites established a widespread presence along the eastern foothill zone of the Sierra Madre. If Chalchihuites peoples actually moved into Durango, it appears that the expansion was a peaceful one. This is not to say that warfare, in the form of territorial conquest, territorial defense, or ceremonial capturing of slaves or sacrificial victims, did not occur or was not part of the Chalchihuites culture (or, perhaps, the Loma culture).

Ayala and Las Joyas phase ceramics indicate that these phases were direct developments out of the western Zacatecas sequence (Kelley 1971; Kelley and Abbott Kelley 1971). Subsequent Chalchihuites cultural development in Durango, however, was clearly influenced by contact with West Coast cultures. Significant changes occur in the Chalchihuites decorated ceramic assemblage during the Río Tunal and Calera phases, resulting in the loss of many design elements and other attributes that defined the Chalchihuites culture. These changes are significant enough to raise the question whether the Chalchihuites culture is an identifiable entity in the archaeological record after the early A.D. 1000s. Is this change significant enough to define a new late prehistoric and protohistoric cultural tradition for the area or do we simply recognize the fact that the late Chalchihuites of Durango looks different from the early Chalchihuites of western Zacatecas? Whatever the case, it appears that by the end of the Río Tunal phase a transition had occurred, one that apparently represents an amalgamation of the Chalchihuites and Loma traditions as influenced by interaction with West Coast cultures.

Another topic requiring further study is the relationship of the highland Durango cultures with those of the coastal Pacific lowlands. Kelley (see this volume) has documented the existence of a widespread exchange network, the Aztatlán Mercantile System, linked to (but not necessarily directed by) exchange networks in central Mexico. This mercantile system is an outgrowth of the Aztatlán tradition of highland and coastal west Mexico (see Mountjoy this volume). This is clear evidence that the Aztatlán tradition penetrated and influenced the cultures of highland Durango. The presence of West Coast ceramics, design elements on local ceramics, and the physical remains of what may have been West Coast migrants or traders are all strong indications of a West Coast presence in the Durango highlands. Nevertheless, many questions remain. Are we dealing with a formal, directed exchange network involving long-distance traders, down-the-line exchange, prestige exchange, or variations of these possibilities? It is likely that no single mechanism was in place and that exchange between the West Coast cultures was complex and dynamic.

What were West Coast and Chalchihuites people exchanging? To date, no Chalchihuites ceramic types are reported from the West Coast. It is likely that the elaborate polychromes of the West Coast cultures were themselves items of trade. They were probably high-value items, as were the copper, shell, obsidian, smoking pipes, and other items traded into the highlands. Kelley (1986a) has suggested that other coastal resources such as dried shellfish and shrimp were traded as well. He further proposes that various plant and animal products from the mountains, foothills, and adjacent desert may have been sought after by West Coast peoples.

Another critical issue focuses on Chalchihuites and Loma chronology. No chronometrically based temporal framework has been established for Loma. What is known is based primarily on ceramic and projectile point cross-dating. Some obsidian-hydration determinations are available (Spence 1978), but until an independent hydration rate is established for the highlands, obsidian dating will remain problematic. Chronometric data for the Chalchihuites sequence are limited as well. The defining and refining chronologies for both the Chalchihuites and Loma sequences are a paramount and fundamental issue for future research in the area.

Loma San Gabriel is probably best thought of as a local culture that is part of a bigger plain and red-on-brown ware tradition that was widespread throughout northwest Mexico. Loma or Loma-like ceramics are present in the Malpaso Valley of south-central Zacatecas and along the eastern foothills of the Sierra Madre from western Zacatecas to the Río Conchos in southern Chihuahua. Loma ceramics show strong affinities to Plainware period types in the Casas Grandes zone of Chihuahua, to types of the Río Sonora culture of eastern Sonora, and to early Mogollon types of southern New Mexico and southeastern Arizona (Foster 1982, 1986b, 1995a). Before Loma can be fully understood, it is necessary to develop a better knowledge of the spatial and temporal variability in what is being called Loma archaeology. Do we call the plainware manifestations of the Malpaso Valley Loma, is the Río Ramos area part of the Loma culture, and what of the variability represented by local complexes such as the Chivas, Baole, and Madroños (Spence 1978)? As previously argued, Loma is seen as a separate archaeological manifestation from the Chalchihuites. What is being called Loma, although it appears to lack the complexity and sophistication of the Chalchihuites culture, should not be ignored (Hers 1989a, 1989b).

The eastern foothills of the Sierra Madre are seen as a major corridor for the spread of agricultural and ceramic technology into the American Southwest. The work in the Zape area (Brooks et al. 1962; Cutler 1978; Foster 1984) shows that a variety of cultigens was being grown in northern Durango by the A.D. 700s. Research that addresses the appearance and adoption of cultigens in northwest Mexico is needed, as is the study of its impact on the development of sedentarism. Did cultigens spread from a west Mexican hearth or from central Mexico or from both? What were the processes involved, and did they parallel those elsewhere in Mexico (Stark 1981)? What was the role of local cultures in the spread of agricultural technology to the American Southwest? These are basic and important questions yet to be addressed.

On the other end, the transition to history is another topic to be investigated. Riley and Winters's (1963; Willett 1997) suggestion that there is continuity between the late Chalchihuites and Loma and the historic Tepehuan populations of Durango is of particular interest. Since much of Durango is fairly undeveloped, many of the sites that date to the late prehistoric and early historic periods may be relatively undisturbed. Such sites may afford a unique opportunity to document the transition to history and the early historic period of the area archaeologically.

Finally, the archaeology of Durango offers its students the opportunity to investigate many significant anthropological questions. Frontier dynamics, the interaction between simple and more complex societies, and the consequences of culture contact and interaction are but a few of the many broader topics that can be examined.

ACKNOWLEDGMENTS

I thank J. Charles and Ellen Kelley for permission to use Sandra Rife's illustrations of Chalchihuites pottery and their generous help and support over the years. J. Charles is greatly missed. I would also like to thank Peter Jiménez, Baudelina García Urnaga, Jamie Ganot R., Alejandro Peschard F., Jesus Lazalde, and Raul Toledo Faris for their varied assistance. Special thanks are owed Andrew Darling for his comments on this effort. Jane Bradley and Shirley Gorenstein also provided helpful comments.

CHAPTER THIRTEEN

RECENT ADVANCES IN CHIHUAHUAN ARCHAEOLOGY

RONNA JANE BRADLEY

CHIHUAHUA, the largest state in Mexico, encompassing 247,087 km², was known to the Spanish as Nueva Vizcaya (Figure 13.1). Marked by the United States–Mexico border to the north, the Río Grande to the east, and high mountains on the south and west, Chihuahua has two principal physiographic provinces, the Sierra Madre Occidental and the Basins and Ranges (Brand 1936, 1937; Schmidt 1973, 1992). The basin and range country is dotted with numerous seasonal lakes that fill with the runoff from the eastern slopes of the Sierra Madre.

The vast majority of prehistoric inhabitants occupied northwestern Chihuahua in the vicinity of Casas Grandes, where three distinct river valleys drain from south to north (Di Peso 1966:4). The Casas Grandes Valley, the dominant and most fertile valley, lies parallel to and nearest the mountains. The Santa María Valley, about 50 km to the east, is smaller with less surface water and bottomland. The Río del Carmen Valley is 45 km east of the Santa María. These valleys drain into shallow lakes: Laguna Guzmán, Laguna de Santa María, and Laguna de Patos. Archaeological sites occur with great frequency along the Río Casas Grandes, gradually decrease in number along the Río Santa María, and continue to diminish along the Río del Carmen (Di Peso 1966:4).

The Sierra Madre occupies a large portion of western Chihuahua, where the diverse topography creates a variety of environmental zones that host numerous plant and animal species. The steep slopes of the high Sierra and low barrancas provide a natural seasonal diversity of plants and animals, accessible through vertical movement of populations. Some of the barranca floors have the highest mean temperatures in the state and the lowest elevations. The lowest mean annual temperatures and the highest elevations in Chihuahua occur in the Sierra (Schmidt 1973:17).

The diversity of plant and animal resources attracted prehistoric and modern aboriginal populations. The Tarahumara, who have occupied the Sierra for centuries, exhibit a variety of adaptive strategies that demonstrate the versatility of vertical relief and seasonal movement (Bennett and Zingg 1935).

Several different vegetation zones are found in Chihuahua. The upper elevations of the Sierra Madre Occidental are characterized by a conifer forest biotic community (Pase and Brown 1982), and a woodland community (Brown 1982a) occupies the lower elevations where the forest gives way. Grasslands (Brown 1982b) and semidesert grasslands (Brown 1982c) cover extensive portions of the state. Semidesert grassland occupies the lower elevations, where it contacts the Chihuahuan desertscrub community (Brown 1982d).

The plant communities provide habitat for a variety of faunal species, from small desert-dwelling reptiles and

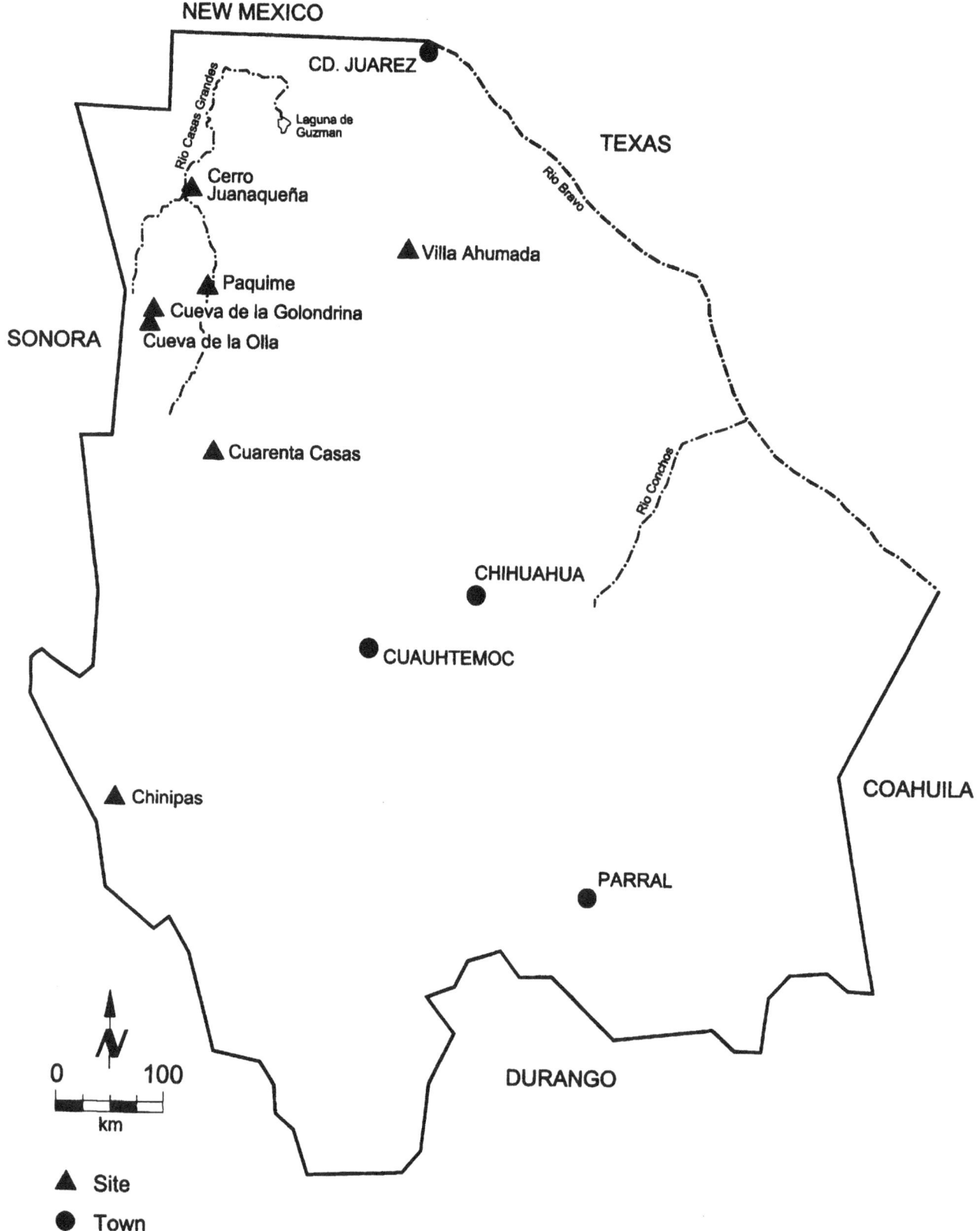

Figure 13.1. Major sites in Chihuahua.

mammals to large mammals in the woodland and forest zones. Rivers attract riparian flora and accompanying fauna and stretch across the arid countryside. Before the advent of sedentary agriculturists, hunters and gatherers occupied large portions of Chihuahua, where seasonal (and vertical) movement provided year-round resources. Although their existence is not well documented, mobile groups probably persisted into the late prehistoric period and coexisted with agriculturists who occupied the river valleys and uplands.

EARLY ARCHAEOLOGICAL INVESTIGATION AND INTERPRETATION

Alvar Núñez Cabeza de Vaca was among the first Europeans to visit Chihuahua, between 1534 and 1536. Obregón probably provided the first written account of archaeological remains in Chihuahua, however, with his description of General Francisco de Ibarra's 1564–65 expedition into the area (Hammond and Rey 1928). The abandoned ruins of Paquimé were encountered by the expedition, which found ruins scattered over a distance of eight leagues up and down the river valley from Paquimé. The nomadic groups that occupied the area at the time of the Spanish entrada described the former inhabitants as enemies of groups on the west side of the Sierra who fled five jornadas to the north after they were defeated in war.

Jesuit missionaries infiltrated Chihuahua in the 1620s, and Franciscan missionaries entered during the 1660s (A. F. Bandelier 1892; Bannon 1955). The Pueblo Revolt of 1680 stimulated Spanish settlement of the northern Sierra river valleys, causing revolts among the Janos, Sumas, and other indigenous groups that occupied the Casas Grandes area. The entry of the Apaches into the area during the late seventeenth century virtually closed the region for more than two hundred years (Di Peso 1966:11) and led to the establishment of presidios at places such as Janos by the early to mid–1700s (Griffen 1988a, 1988b).

In the 1800s, travelers, explorers, and military scouts provided brief accounts of archaeological remains in Chihuahua (Bartlett 1965; Bourke 1886; Escudero 1834; García Conde 1842, 1849; Guillemin-Tarayre 1867, 1869; Hardy 1829). Bartlett (1965) described the ruins of Casas Grandes in 1852 and noted similarities with other ruins along the Gila and Salt drainages in Arizona. He indicated that in the 1850s artifacts were being looted from ruins and sold across Chihuahua.

Bourke (1886) visited Chihuahua as part of General George Crook's expedition into the Sierra Madre in search of Chiricahua Apaches in the 1880s. He noted the abundance of ruins in the Sierra between Chihuahua and Sonora, describing masonry walls, structures, and check dams. The trails followed by the expedition across the Sierra likely dated back to prehistoric times.

The first anthropologist to visit the region was Adolph F. Bandelier (1892), who traveled into Sonora, crossed the Sierra Madre, and arrived in Chihuahua in 1885. Bandelier recorded numerous villages and trincheras and described the plain and decorated pottery of the region. Crossing the Sierra near the Río Bavispe, he noted many cobble alignments or check dams associated with ruins. He described distinct changes in the ceramics, from low-quality plainwares of Sonora to thin-walled, polished, and painted pottery characteristic of the Casas Grandes area. He visited a number of cliff dwellings and other sites, noting that the highest concentration of sites was on the west side of the Casas Grandes Valley just north of Paquimé. One of the first to produce a map of Paquimé, Bandelier defined mounds, a canal, two reservoirs, a raised canal or road in the bottomland below the ruin, and the main room blocks with four to five stories. In addition to quantities of ceramics, ground stone, shell, axes, cotton cloth, and turquoise, he discussed a large meteorite that had been taken from the site (Bandelier 1892; Guillemin-Tarayre 1867, 1869; Tassin 1902). Remnants of the early pothunters' tunnels were later discovered during the excavation of Paquimé (Di Peso 1966:11).

Following Bandelier, a number of explorers visited Chihuahua (Blackiston 1905, 1906a, 1906b, 1906c, 1908, 1909; Lumholtz 1902; Schwatka 1893). Frederick Schwatka (1893) described ruins in the Corralitos, Piedras Verdes, and Tapecitos valleys, including canals, check dams, and fortified hilltop sites with roads.

Some of the most important documentation of northern Mexico was that of Lumholtz (1902). He recorded a number of sites, excavated in the Cave Valley area near the Piedras Verdes drainage, and excavated near San Diego in the Casas Grandes Valley. His travels in the Sierra near Nacori Chico provided evidence for old trails, numerous ruins, and fortresses. Lumholtz's writings stimulated interest in the Sierra Madre and Casas Grandes areas and remain an important contribution today.

A. H. Blackiston (1905, 1906a, 1906b, 1909) conducted limited excavations at some sites in Cave Valley. He also identified numerous trincheras, which he thought were defensive in nature, and discussed large stone circles with what appeared to be slag adjacent to them. The features were thought by Blackiston to be copper smelters. Recent work in the Casas Grandes area indicates that large stone circles were roasting pits (Minnis, personal communication 1997).

During the early 1900s, explorers and archaeologists maintained an interest in Chihuahua. Edgar Hewett (1908) made several excursions in an attempt to define the extent of the Casas Grandes culture. With an interest in the origin and migration myths of the Aztecs, Hewett (1923:50) suggested that the inland basin of northern Chihuahua might be the "Vale of Aztlán."

Hewett's work attracted the attention of A. V. Kidder, who conducted fieldwork in 1916 in the Babicora area and in Garabato Canyon (Kidder 1939). He included the northern Sierra in the Southwest culture area and extended the Casas Grandes culture area into eastern Sonora and southwestern New Mexico (Kidder 1924). In an analysis of 190 vessels from the Peabody Museum, he noted general similarities between the Casas Grandes and Mimbres ceramic traditions and, based on the presence of Gila Polychrome, suggested that the Casas Grandes culture was contemporaneous with the Postclassic Hohokam (Kidder 1916).

Mexican archaeologists also conducted work in Chihuahua during the early 1900s. Noguera (1926, 1930) reported the results of a survey in the Casas Grandes area. He described Paquimé and the adobe architecture and ceramics of the area. Marquina (1928) discussed comparisons of Casas Grandes architecture, and Robles's study of the archaeology of the Casas Grandes area followed in 1929. Amsden (1928) completed a reconnaissance of the Bavispe Valley and of the Yaqui and Río Sonora drainages of Sonora, where he defined both peripheral Casas Grandes and Río de Sonora culture sites. The late 1930s saw the publication of an archaeological atlas of Mexico (Marquina 1939) that included many of the Chihuahuan sites.

One of the earliest excavation projects in Chihuahua was initiated by Carey (1931, 1954, 1955) in the Babicora and Corralitos areas. After an extensive study of museum collections, he conducted surface collections and excavation at several sites in the region. Carey was able to establish a ceramic chronology and found evidence of two occupations in the Babicora area. The upper level contained Chihuahuan polychromes, and an earlier occupation contained black-on-red ware. His excavations in the Corralitos area did not result in as much information because the sites had been highly disturbed by pothunting. Nevertheless, Carey's investigations produced stratigraphic evidence for changes from early predominance of plainwares and bichromes to later dominance of polychromes. As pointed out by J. H. Kelley and others (1999), unlike some of his contemporaries, such as Brand (1933, 1935, 1943b), Carey (as well as Amsden) viewed the remains from central Chihuahua as a separate culture rather than a periphery of or corridor to the Casas Grandes area.

Additional work in the Casas Grandes periphery was conducted in 1933 with the excavation by Kidder and the Cosgroves of the Pendleton Ruin in southern New Mexico (Kidder et al. 1949, 1974). The site contained approximately 100 contiguous rooms organized around plazas and represented a brief Animas phase occupation dating in the A.D. 1300s. The ceramic types at Pendleton indicated that the Animas phase, previously thought to succeed the Ramos phase, was instead a contemporaneous northern expression of the Ramos phase.

During the late 1920s and 1930s, several extensive surveys of northwestern Mexico and portions of the Southwest were conducted. Sauer and Brand (1930, 1931) completed a reconnaissance survey of parts of Sonora and southeastern Arizona. Chihuahuan ceramics dominated the ceramic assemblage on sites as far south as the Sahuaripa Valley, south of the Río Yaqui, and west as far as Fronteras. Chihuahuan ceramics also occurred in small quantities on some sites in the Trincheras area. Also, Brand (1935) detailed pottery types in northwestern Chihuahua, indicating that the most intense and widespread occupation of the area occurred during the late Pueblo III to Pueblo IV times. An additional publication grew out of his 1933 thesis concerning the historical geography of northwestern Chihuahua (Brand 1943b). It remains one of the most complete descriptions of the archaeology of Chihuahua, with a discussion of sites by drainage. Brand was interested in defining the extent of the culture temporally and spatially and determining affiliations with surrounding areas. He suggested that the northern Sierra cultures originated in the river valleys and moved into the highlands to escape pressure from nomadic groups moving in from the east. He later conducted an additional survey in the Zape area in Durango in an attempt to investigate relationships between the Casas Grandes culture and Mesoamerica (Brand 1939). Approximately five hundred sites in the northern Sierra were recorded by Brand and his students during this time.

Sayles (1936a, 1936b) recorded more than two hundred additional sites during a 1933 reconnaissance survey of Chihuahua oriented toward tracing the southeastern extension of the Hohokam culture (Sayles 1936a, 1936b). The survey, which included some stratigraphic testing, identified a variety of site types, architectural patterns, and artifacts. Sayles proposed a Mogollon-affiliated early occupation defined as the Medanos phase; followed by the Babicora phase, evident in cliff dwellings; the Ramos phase, evident at Paquimé; the Animas phase, representing the establishment of larger pueblos; the Carretas phase, representing a breakdown of the large pueblos; the Conchos phase of Spanish contact; and the Lipan phase, marking the Apache infusion (Di Peso 1966). Fueled by Sayles's findings, Gladwin (Sayles 1936b) proposed that the cultures originated in the highlands and later moved to the eastern valleys. In addition, he stressed the importance of Mimbres influences during the Babicora phase and the Salado migration into Chihuahua during the Ramos phase.

In 1936, Brand directed reconnaissance and excavations at sites in the Carretas drainage, yielding data on Culberson Ruin and Joyce Well (Osborne and Hayes 1938). Investigation of cliff dwellings in the Garabato drainage and testing of the Aqua Zarca and La Morita sites northwest of Casas Grandes in the Carretas drainage were also carried out (Lister 1939, 1946). Ceramics from the cliff dwellings and the Carretas area were similar, indicating they were occupied during the Ramos phase.

The intensity of work seen during the early portion of the twentieth century slowed during the 1940s through the early 1950s. Some work continued in the Sierra, with Zingg's (1940) excavations of cave sites in southern Chihuahua. Lister's (1953, 1958) work continued in the Cave Valley area, resulting in the definition of three primary occupational phases: (1) pre–A.D. 900, a preceramic culture with corn and stone tools, (2) a tenth-century A.D. Mogollon-like culture, and (3) multistoried cliff houses with Mogollon-like affinities whose occupants later migrated into the eastern river valleys and were absorbed into Puebloan culture. During this period, J. Charles Kelley (1966) suggested that there should be a reexamination of the dominant culture for possible mesoamerican origins.

These early investigations raised a number of issues and provided structure for subsequent research. One of the most important questions addressed by early research, and one that remains a central theme today, has to do with the origins of the Casas Grandes population and whether it was a product of indigenous growth or movement of groups into the area or both. Lister's (1958) work provided a good start by yielding excavated data on cave sites, but little research on early occupations of the basins and river valleys was completed. W. W. Taylor's work, discussed in the next section, followed up on earlier investigations and provides a basic understanding of the early inhabitants of northeastern Chihuahua.

Another issue focuses on the contemporaneity of Paquimé with other sites in the region. Research (Hill 1992; Pearson and Sánchez M. 1990) has continued to concentrate on gaining a better understanding of temporal issues through additional studies of tree rings and ceramic cross-dating.

In addition, investigation of the true nature and extent of the Chihuahuan culture remains a central focus of research today. In the spirit of early scholars such as Brand and Sayles, research in outlying areas and questions regarding specific aspects of the Paquimé system have continued to be of interest. Another significant issue concerns the role of Mesoamerica and the Southwest in the development of Chihuahuan culture and the impact of Casas Grandes on other culture areas. These problem domains, most of which were raised by early research, are still important points of discussion.

MODERN ARCHAEOLOGICAL INVESTIGATION IN CHIHUAHUA

Charles C. Di Peso (1974; Di Peso et al. 1974) began his excavation of the large site of Paquimé in the late 1950s. Several years of long field seasons and millions of artifacts later, the most intensive archaeological investigation ever conducted in Chihuahua yielded a wealth of information. The interpretation of the data sparked debate among archaeologists in the Southwest and Mesoamerica and has resulted in a continued interest in the area and, more recently, the accumulation of additional data from archaeological projects oriented toward addressing some of the issues. Before the completion of the Joint Casas Grandes Expedition (JCGE), Di Peso (1966) published an overview of the archaeology and ethnohistory of the northern Sierra Madre region and of his work at Paquimé. The Casas Grandes report was completed in the mid–1970s, and since that time new projects and publications have ensued. Most research has centered on the late prehistoric period and the Casas Grandes phenomenon; ultimately, there needs to be a concerted effort toward the investigation of earlier materials. The next section reviews the corpus of modern archaeological investigation in the area and discusses current models proposed by various researchers.

The Joint Casas Grandes Expedition and the Advent of the Pochteca Model

The JCGE operated in Chihuahua from 1958 through 1961 under the cooperative efforts of the Amerind Foundation and the Instituto Nacional de Antropología e Historia (INAH) (Di Peso 1966:16). The project focused on excavating the western portion of the large site of Paquimé (Chih:D:9:1), exposing numerous structures and other architectural features (Figures 13.2, 13.3, and 13.4) as well as artifacts. Four smaller sites in the area were also partially excavated, including the Convento site (Chih:D:9:2), Reyes Site No. 1 (Chih:D:9:13), and Reyes Site No. 2 (Chih:D:9:14), which provided information on the earlier Viejo period. Two sites from the Tres Ríos area, La Casa Fimbres (Chih:G:2:1) and Casa de Robles Site 2 (Chih:G:2:3), yielded information from the Tardío period.

The results of the excavations at Paquimé are presented in three volumes (Di Peso 1974), along with five volumes that contain detailed summaries of the data (Di Peso et al. 1974). Various additional summaries of the Paquimé excavations and the Casas Grandes region are available (Contreras 1986; Di Peso 1966; Foster 1990, 1992; Márquez-Alameda 1990, ed. 1992; Minnis and Whalen 1991; Phillips 1989, 1990a, 1991), as well as critiques of Di Peso's perspectives and interpretations (McGuire 1980, 1993; Minnis 1984, 1988, 1989; Reyman 1995; Woosley and Ravesloot 1993). In addition, two recent overviews provide some of the background of Di Peso's ideas (McGuire 1993; Riley 1993).

The excavations at Paquimé produced an enormous amount of data. Between the 1960s and 1974, Di Peso's ideas evolved, and a series of articles reflects those changes. Initially, Di Peso (1966, 1968a, 1968b) described in general terms the architecture, artifacts, temporal scheme, and other interpretations from the excavations at Paquimé. This sequence of articles introduced the idea of foreign influence from Mesoamerica and the pochteca concept. Later he developed ideas on the importance of irrigation for the large population base around Casas Grandes (Di Peso 1971a, 1971b).

Di Peso (1974) defined six periods of occupation in the Casas Grandes region: Preceramic (?–A.D. 1), Plainware (A.D. 1–700), Viejo (A.D. 700–1060), Medio (A.D. 1060–1340), Tardío (A.D. 1340–1660), and Españoles (A.D. 1660–1821). Early developments are similar to those in other parts of the Southwest, with evidence for Paleoindian followed by Archaic occupation of the region. The Plainware period marks the beginning of sedentary villages, similar to adaptations in other portions of the Mogollon area. Foster (1982, 1986b) and Kelley (1966) discuss similarities between the Loma San Gabriel sites in southern Chihuahua and the developmental Mogollon as well as other areas in northwest Mexico (Foster 1995b). Early sites in the Casas Grandes area also exhibit similarities to the early Mogollon. The Viejo period is represented by several cave sites in the mountains and valley pithouse villages (Di Peso 1974:1; Lister 1958). During the latter part of the Viejo period, adobe-walled surface structures came into use. The Medio period reflects a time of significant population growth and cultural development. In addition to Paquimé, large sites were constructed throughout portions of Chihuahua along major river and drainage systems, and cliff dwellings were occupied in the upland areas. Whereas the earlier periods represent indigenous population development, drastic changes in population growth and material culture in the Medio period were attributed to outside influence from mesoamerican polities (Di Peso 1974:Vol. 2). The Medio period was divided into three phases: Buena Fé, Paquimé, and Diablo. Buena Fé phase architecture included a group of single-story structures placed in contiguous fashion around enclosed courtyards and compounds. During the Paquimé phase, widespread rebuilding efforts were initiated that produced large, multistory residential complexes and extensive public architecture. The number of rooms increased threefold from the Buena Fé phase (342 rooms) to the Paquimé phase (over 1,596 rooms). The dwellings were serviced by drainage ditches, a reservoir, and a small canal or acequia that brought water from a spring located over 2 km to the northwest. Estimates indicate that more than 2,200 individuals occupied the site during its zenith. The degeneration and eventual destruction of Paquimé occurred during the Diablo phase. The Tardío period reflects a drastic decline in the population and eventual protohistoric occupation of the area by mobile hunter-gatherers. The Españoles period represents a historic occupation of the region (Di Peso 1974:Vol. 3).

Out of the JCGE project came issues related to the origin of the Casas Grandes or the Chihuahuan culture and the chronology of development. Di Peso's original dating scheme, based on dendrochronological samples that were not cutting dates (Scott 1966), raised questions concerning the early nature of the developments and the early occurrence of Salado polychromes at the site. Additional questions regarding the complexity of social organization and the nature of production at the site of Paquimé and the surrounding region were raised.

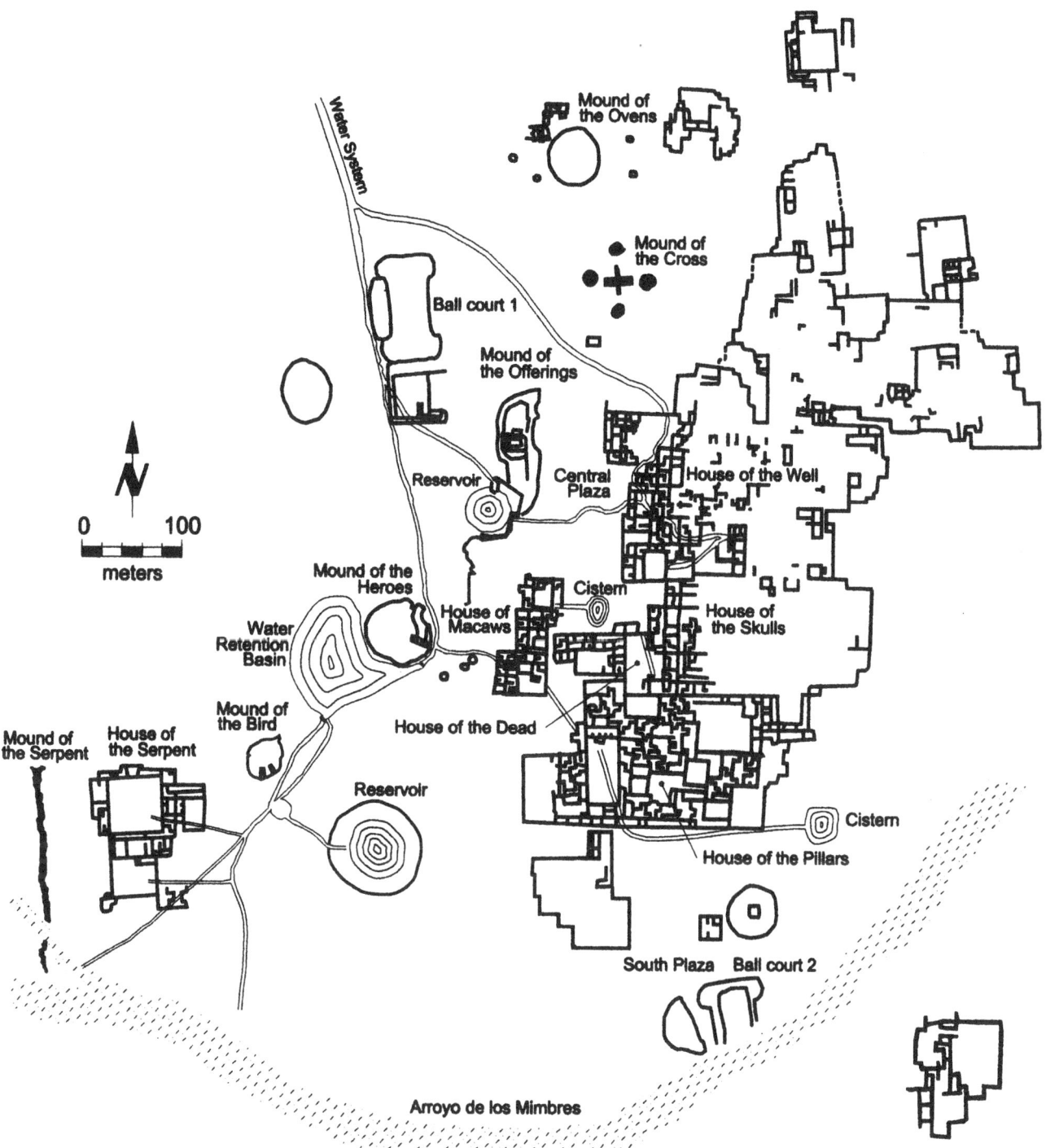

Figure 13.2. Site map of Paquimé (Guevara Sánchez 1985).

Figure 13.3. View from the House of the Well to the main plaza at Paquimé.

Moreover, issues concerning the regional system were introduced, including the degree of cohesiveness of sites in the region and the extent of the Casas Grandes influence. Finally, Di Peso's (1974) suggestions regarding the importance of trade and mesoamerican influence at Paquimé were among the most controversial issues raised. Following Ferdon's (1955) earlier discussion of pochteca in the Southwest, Di Peso dubbed Paquimé a mesoamerican outpost occupied by pochteca traders. The following sections outline some of the subsequent research that has stemmed from the original excavations of Paquimé and other sites in the Casas Grandes area.

Indigenous Growth and the Development of the Chihuahua Culture

Most of the work done in Chihuahua has focused on the late prehistoric period, and little is known about earlier occupations. The fact that few Paleoindian and Archaic sites have been recorded in northwest Chihuahua is related to the limited amount of systematic survey conducted in the region. Most projects, including the recent ones, have relied on reconnaissance strategies to locate sites, and those that are most easily discernible are the Medio house mounds.

A Clovis point and a Folsom point fragment have been reported (Aveleyra 1961; Di Peso 1965). Some of the most extensive Archaic remains reported are from southeastern Chihuahua (Marrs 1949). Marrs describes a variety of projectile points and other lithic tools from surface sites. His term "Paleo-Indian" is used to describe both Paleoindian and Archaic projectile points. The Archaic styles exhibit affinities to materials from Ventana Cave and the Playa or San Dieguito complex, spanning the time from 8600 B.C. to A.D. 1. Marrs focused on the development of a chronological history and the simi-

Figure 13.4. Macaw nesting boxes at Paquimé.

larities between artifacts from southeastern Chihuahua and the American Southwest.

Sites that date to the Archaic period are known from excavations conducted by Lister (1958) in cave dwellings in the Sierra Madre. Since that time, only a limited number of projects have been initiated in the area, and few have focused on early manifestations. Much of what is known about the early inhabitants of Chihuahua has been derived from studies in adjacent areas, such as Coahuila, Nuevo León (Epstein 1969), Tamaulipas (Taylor 1966), and southern New Mexico (Beckett and MacNeish 1994; MacNeish 1992, 1993; MacNeish and Beckett 1987; Márquez-Alameda 1992).

Taylor (1966:60) described the state of knowledge of the Archaic on the northeastern frontier of Mesoamerica: "Ethnographic evidence being nil and archival materials few and faulty, the archaeological record is little better." Three complexes have been defined in Coahuila and far eastern Chihuahua. Evidence for the Ciénegas complex was derived from three cave sites in the Cuatro Ciénegas Basin in central Coahuila and features typical early Archaic artifacts such as wood, fiber sandals, and various other biotic and stone materials. The Coahuila complex is a widespread manifestation that extends from the Río Grande to the northern edges of the Laguna District and from the Sierra Madre Oriental to the Coahuila-Chihuahua border. It was long lived, with radiocarbon dates that range from 7600 B.C. to A.D. 185 (Taylor 1966:63). There is evidence for considerable change through time in settlement patterns, degree of mobility, and artifact forms. The early Coahuila period reflects relatively sedentary and localized adaptations of "tethered nomadism" that gave way to increased mobility during the middle period. Finally, the late Coahuila and early Jora periods represent a time of increased cultural integration and adaptive strategies that

Taylor (1966:65) likens to "ranging nomadism." The Jora complex is a late Archaic manifestation representing a reconstitution and reintegration of culture in the Coahuila area. El Paso Brown ceramics, associated with the Jornada Mogollon, are found on some Jora sites, indicating possible external influences from the La Junta de los Ríos area (Taylor 1966:83).

More recently, the Bolsón de Mapimí, in the far southeast corner of Chihuahua, has been the focus of investigation of Archaic-like adaptations that include a persistence of hunter-gatherer lifeways (González 1985, 1992). Base camps, limited activity sites, and overnight camps have been recorded.

A sequence for the Archaic period in Chihuahua has recently been defined based on excavations from rockshelters in southern New Mexico and west Texas (Beckett and MacNeish 1994; MacNeish 1992, 1993; MacNeish and Beckett 1987). The Gardner Springs phase represents the earliest Archaic occupation of the area, dating from 6000 to 4300 B.C. Diagnostic artifacts include Bajada, Jay, Río Grande, and Abasolo projectile point styles. The Keystone phase dates from 4000 to 2000 B.C. and is distinguished by a transitional Bat Cave style projectile point, as well as Amargosa, Pelona, and Shumla styles. The Fresnal phase dates from 2500 to 900 B.C. and is characterized by Chiricahua, Agustín, La Cueva, Maljamar, San José, and Fresnal point styles, among others. The Hueco phase, marked by Hueco, Armijo, San Pedro, and Hatch point styles, dates from 900 B.C. to A.D. 200. Farther east, where the Chihuahuan border meets the Big Bend area of Texas, Mallouf (1992) described the Archaic as extending from about 6500 B.C. to A.D. 900.

Recent work by the Proyecto Arqueológico de Chihuahua (PAC) from 1990 to 1996 has yielded surprisingly little evidence for Archaic occupation in southern Chihuahua (J. H. Kelley et al. 1999). Although a number of Archaic style projectile points were recorded during the course of the project, none could be tied to specific dates (Jane H. Kelley, personal communication 1995). Most of the sites recorded by the PAC date to the Medio and Viejo periods (Di Peso 1974).

Ongoing research by John Roney has increased our understanding of late Archaic occupations in northern Chihuahua and has the potential to contribute greatly to our understanding of the Archaic occupations of the area. Roney (1996a) has documented a series of cerros de trincheras along the Río Casas Grandes that appear to be major residential complexes occupied between 1000 B.C. and A.D. 500. Characterized by a massive complex of walls, terraces, stone circles, and other features, they are situated on the summits and slopes of hills. Approximately twelve sites are known in western Chihuahua (Roney 1996a). Three sites, Cerro Juanaqueña, Cerro los Torres, and Cerro Vidal, have been mapped and documented. The largest, Cerro Juanaqueña (Gerald 1990), covers about 8 ha. The walls and terraces on the sites were used to retain soil and form level areas. A rich artifact assemblage includes lithic debitage, hammerstones, cores, preforms, bifaces, and projectile points. Several hundred basin metates ground into boulders are present, along with one-hand manos and several slab metates. Initially, dating of the sites was problematic, but the virtual absence of pottery (six and seven sherds on two sites) and the presence of quantities of late Archaic projectile point forms indicated late Archaic occupations dating between 1000 B.C. and A.D. 500 (Roney 1996b). The labor-intensive nature of the features and the fact that they appear primarily agricultural has led Roney (1996b) to speculate that the sites are agricultural. Furthermore, he suggests that the trincheras may have served as fortifications. Since most of the trincheras are located along river systems, he speculates that they represent defensible residences placed along prime riverine areas to ensure control of farmland subject to competition during a period of burgeoning agriculture. These cerros de trincheras are among the first sites in Chihuahua that illustrate extensive architectural construction and cooperative labor efforts during the Archaic period.

Hard and Roney (1998) have recently reported the results of additional research at Cerro Juanaqueña. The site exhibits over 8 km of terrace walls that form 468 terraces and 100 rock rings. The terraces appear to have been constructed in order to create level surfaces for residential occupation. Postholes and burned clay daub have been uncovered, along with rich deposits of ashy soil, animal bone, corn, squash, and wild plant remains. Numerous Late Archaic projectile points, slab and basin metates, and large quantities of chipped stone debris indicate a substantial aggregated occupation. Cerro Juanaqueña casts doubts on traditional models that depict Late Archaic groups as mobile hunter-gatherers who lived in small, dispersed groups. On the contrary, this site, with radiocarbon dates from corn that cluster around 3,000 years B.P., provides evidence for early aggregation of groups into sedentary villages and much more complex variability in adaptive strategies than has previously been recognized for that time period.

The limited number of excavations and systematic surveys, the ephemeral and often buried nature of Archaic sites, and the fact that archaeologists have focused on the Medio period sites have led to the persistence of a paucity of data on the Archaic and on early Formative period cultural developments. Research currently under way holds the promise of adding greatly to knowledge of Archaic adaptations in Chihuahua.

In an overview of the prehistory of Chihuahua and Sonora, Phillips (1989) discussed the ceramic period prehistory of Chihuahua in six areas: southern, central, northeast, southeast, southwest, and northwest. Extreme southern Chihuahua exhibits materials from Loma San Gabriel, which in western Zacatecas and Durango is characterized by small hamlets and villages; plain, red, white, and red-on-brown ceramics; and surface habitation rooms (Foster 1978, 1982, 1985, 1986a; Kelley 1956, 1971). Aside from the expansion of the Chalchihuites culture into Loma San Gabriel territory around A.D. 200, there is little change within this Mogollon-like occupation, which may have spanned a 1,200- to 1,600-year sequence (Foster 1986a:9). Until recently, the archaeology of central Chihuahua had seen only limited reconnaissance survey (Sayles 1936a), but in the mid-1990s the PAC survey recorded a number of sites around a series of basins with remains distinct from Chihuahuan culture sites (J. H. Kelley et al. 1999). Sites are characterized as hamlets of pit structures or jacals, with agriculture, undecorated pottery, and occupation dates that range from A.D. 800 to 1225. Northeast Chihuahua, southern New Mexico, and west Texas were home to the Jornada Mogollon (Lehmer 1948). Nomadic exploitation of the area occurred throughout prehistory, with sedentary occupation along the Río Bravo in the vicinity of Big Bend. Southeast Chihuahua contains an extension of the Jornada Mogollon into the Río Bravo and the Río Conchos areas, reflecting late prehistoric and protohistoric occupations (Kelley 1985b, 1986b, 1992; Mallouf 1987, 1992). Additionally, some of the base camps and limited-activity sites in the Bolsón de Mapimí are ceramic period limited-use sites (González 1985, 1992). Most appear to represent temporary seasonal use of the region.

Mallouf (1985, 1987, 1992) has documented an occupation of eastern Chihuahua by late prehistoric to protohistoric nomadic groups of the Cielo complex who constructed circular stone structures and lived primarily by hunting. Conchos groups, nomadic hunters with a variety of material culture, are documented for the area (Guevara Sánchez 1991). Southwest Chihuahua contains cliff dwellings in the Sierra Madre, burial caves, and open sites. Plainwares as well as decorated ceramics reminiscent of those from Casas Grandes are present (Phillips 1989). Northwest Chihuahua is where the bulk of archaeological research has been conducted, and the focus of that work has been on the Casas Grandes occupation. The remainder of this overview discusses that research.

Chronology of Cultural Developments: Refinements in Dating

One of the greatest points of contention to arise from the Casas Grandes excavations was the dating of the Paquimé sequence. Di Peso's (1974) original scheme is based on noncutting dates from beams recovered during excavation. The beams had been trimmed, eliminating the outer rings and sapwood. Using specimens from Paquimé, the Laboratory of Tree-Ring Research (Scott 1966) developed a 500-year-long floating chronology. This was eventually matched with indices from Flagstaff and the Río Grande, providing a tree-ring index for northwest Mexico. Six hundred samples from cliff dwellings and open sites yielded 86 dates, none of which were cutting dates.

A number of scholars have criticized Di Peso's (1974; Di Peso et al. 1974:Vol. 4) use of the tree-ring dates and the early beginning dates for Gila Polychrome (Braniff 1986; Carlson 1982; Doyel 1976:12–13; LeBlanc 1980, 1986; Lekson 1984; Wilcox 1986b; Wilcox and Shenk 1977:64–68).

A revision of the dates has recently been proposed based on a reevaluation of the dendro specimens (Dean and Ravesloot 1993; Ravesloot et al. 1995). The Robinson-Ahlstrom (1980) regression equation was used to derive projected felling dates by estimating the number of sapwood rings from the number of heartwood rings, yielding a conservative estimate of the true cutting dates. This technique was used successfully in the Río Grande Valley of New Mexico. The 45 estimated felling dates range from A.D. 1161 to 1419. Five date to the late A.D. 1100s, one in the early A.D. 1400s, and the remainder in the thirteenth and fourteenth centuries. Most important, the reevaluation indicates that the occupation of the units (that yielded dates) postdated A.D. 1200; building activity was concentrated in the thirteenth and fourteenth centuries; the site was inhabited in the fifteenth century; and some construction or repair may have occurred as late as the A.D. 1470s (Dean and Ravesloot 1993:93; Ravesloot et al. 1995). Based on this revision, the occupation is approximately 100 to 150 years more recent than previously thought, making it coeval with the Western Pueblo and other late southwestern developments and postdating the Classic Mimbres and Chacoan florescence.

The reevaluation of the Paquimé dates has also raised questions concerning the phases defined by Di Peso (1974). The revision reveals problems in the Buena Fé to Paquimé sequence, with overlapping date ranges that suggest a single unit rather than sequential phases (Dean and Ravesloot 1993:96). The three noncutting dates used to date the beginning of the Buena Fé phase occur in rooms that yielded other samples with much later dates, bringing into question the validity of the Buena Fé designation. Moreover, the later placement of the Buena Fé and Paquimé phases leaves a gap between the termination of the Perros Bravos phase and the beginning of the Buena Fé phase. Dean and Ravesloot (1993:98) suggest that the Perros Bravos phase is also later than originally defined, with a termination date of A.D. 1150 to 1200. Finally, the revisions result in a considerable shortening of the length of the Diablo phase of the Medio period and the Robles phase of the Diablo period, bringing the occupation and abandonment of the site much closer to the Spanish entrada. Phillips (1989:383, 1990b; Phillips and Carpenter 1999) has questioned the existence of a Robles phase, suggesting that the sites assigned to the Robles are actually Medio period sites.

Also, recent research in the Sierra has yielded dendrochronological samples from cliff dwellings (Pearson and Sánchez M. 1990). Four sites south of Casas Grandes were investigated and mapped, and core samples were taken. These sites have architectural styles similar to those of other cliff dwellings such as Cuarenta Casas and Cave Valley (Guevara Sánchez 1984, 1986, 1988; Guevara Sánchez and Phillips 1992; Lister 1958), and preliminary data indicate that the sites are contemporaneous with the Medio period.

In addition, analysis of ceramics from the El Zurdo site in the Babicora Basin has contributed to a refinement of the ceramic sequences in the area. El Zurdo was recorded by the PAC survey, and portions were subsequently excavated (Hill 1992). A minimum of two components are represented at El Zurdo, a Viejo period occupation with pit structures, and a later Medio period component with multistoried surface structures. Data indicate an increase in the frequencies of plainwares and a decrease in textured wares from the Viejo to the Medio period. Similarly, there is an increase in the frequencies of painted wares during the Medio period and a decrease in the frequencies of blackwares. This stands in contrast to Paquimé, where blackwares increase through time.

The Casas Grandes System: Extent, Social Complexity, and Nature of Production

While some scholars have been concerned with temporal issues, others have attempted to address questions related to the nature and extent of the Casas Grandes phenomenon, its social complexity, and the scale of production of the regional system (Bradley 1986, 1987, 1993, 1996a, 1996b, 1999; Braniff 1986; Breitburg 1993; Contreras 1986; Cruz 1997; Cruz and Maxwell 1999; DeAtley 1980; DeAtley and Findlow 1982; Doolittle 1993; Douglas 1992, 1995; Guevara Sánchez 1986; J. H. Kelley et al. 1999; Leubben et al. 1986; Minnis 1984, 1988, 1989; Minnis and Whalen 1989, 1991; Minnis et al. 1993; Pailes and Reff 1985; Pearson and Sánchez M. 1990; Ravesloot 1988; Whalen and Minnis 1996a, 1996b, 1999; Woosley and Olinger 1993). Approaching the issues from various perspectives and using different methods, these researchers have made some progress in our understanding of the nature and extent of the Casas Grandes system.

ORGANIZATION OF AGRICULTURAL PRODUCTION

One of the issues regarding agricultural production at Paquimé is based in Di Peso's arguments for an integrated food production system using sophisticated agricultural strategies. His interpretations of an expansive, integrated system of terraces and canal irrigation controlled by the Paquimé elite have been questioned, and recently scholars have begun to investigate the area more thoroughly, looking for agricultural features, canals, and other evidence for intensive agriculture.

Herold (1965) reported on an intensive study of trincheras in the Río Gavilán and Río Piedras Verdes areas, where trincheras, check dams, linear borders, terraces, and riverside trincheras were recorded. Trincheras are distributed primarily in the northern part of the Sierra, although some appear as far south as Creel (Howard and Griffiths 1966). They tend to be concentrated around habitation sites, and more appear on the western side of the continental divide than on the eastern side, indicating that they were associated not only with the Paquimé agricultural system but with other systems as well.

Leubben and others (1986) worked Elvino Whetten Pueblo near the Río Gavilán, an area that contained many agricultural trincheras and field houses. Arguing against Di Peso (1974), they suggest that the trincheras in the Sierra are unevenly distributed and not part of a cohesive system. Furthermore, this particular terrace system is in an adjacent drainage, the Río Bavispe, not in the Río Casas Grandes drainage. They argue that the features result from a need to create deep soil in the shallow and rocky soils of the mesa tops and slopes.

Schmidt and Gerald (1988) found that water-control devices in the Sierra Madre are associated with soil parent material and the seasonal distribution of precipitation. The features in the northern and western extremes of the Sierra are associated with andesite surface rock that weathers quickly and produces fertile soil. The Sonoran side of the range has more even moisture distribution than the Chihuahuan side, resulting in more favorable conditions for habitation and farming sites. In opposition to Di Peso's (1974) position that the water-control devices were constructed by corvée labor for erosion control to protect the bottomlands of the Casas Grandes Valley, Schmidt and Gerald (1988) contend that the features were built to increase the agricultural productivity of the slopes, probably as a result of population pressure.

A study of the terrace soils and adjacent streamside alluvium along the Río Gavilán indicates that more water was available for plant growth in the terraced soils than in unterraced areas (Herold and Miller 1995). The terraces attract extra water from runoff of rain and snowmelt, permitting increased levels of crop production. Herold and Miller (1995:150) point out that the terrace systems that receive small amounts of runoff (linear borders and sideslope terraces) require minimal levels of maintenance (indicated by the fact that they have survived 800 years), whereas cross-channel terraces are more easily destroyed by runoff and need constant maintenance.

Doolittle (1993) has checked for canals and other agricultural features in the Casas Grandes area and admitted that although evidence is sparse, floodplain canal irrigation was very important at Paquimé. He questioned the origin of the canal features as mesoamerican, however, arguing instead that they may have been derived from southwestern sources. Doolittle (1993; as well as Bandelier 1892) suggested that the system at Casas Grandes was morphologically and technologically similar to Hohokam systems. Earlier work (Doolittle 1990) has shown that the valley-bottom canals at Casas Grandes are in a class by themselves. No other canals as large, or in as systematic and complex arrangement, occurred anywhere else in Mexico prehistorically (Doolittle 1993:143). Doolittle's ideas may hold merit: it is logical that techniques for dealing with arid environments emerge in those environments; nevertheless, several contradictions in his work have been discussed by J. Charles Kelley (1993:233–234). Moreover, Doolittle argued for a highly complex system of canals and other agricultural features at Paquimé but criticized Di Peso (1974) for overstating the degree of integration and complexity of the agricultural systems in the Casas Grandes Valley.

Most recently, J. H. Kelley and others (1999) report findings from the Babicora area, noting the paucity of water-control features in west-central Chihuahua as compared with the Casas Grandes Valley. Those identified were near El Zurdo. This is an interesting contrast to the Casas Grandes area and may be related to temporal and population density factors. Many of the sites in the Babicora area predate Paquimé. Research has shown that there is an increase in the use of intensive agricultural techniques such as terraces, mulch gardens, and canals/acequias during late prehistory that is associated with population growth and aggregation (Anscheutz 1995; Lang 1995; Maxwell 1995).

Canal irrigation exemplifies agricultural intensification, but it is by no means the only indication of sophisticated farming strategies. Moreover, canal irrigation is limited to valley bottoms and may be no more labor-intensive than expansive terrace systems. Throughout the Southwest, research documents the use of a variety of techniques for the intensification of agricultural production, most of which involve the artificial manipulation of soil and water in specific areas (Anscheutz 1995; Fish 1995; Maxwell 1995). As previously discussed, after the initial labor investment in construction of large terrace systems, some linear borders and terraces require little ongoing maintenance, whereas others that crosscut active arroyos require constant upkeep. Therefore, the use of stone to enhance the soil depth and increase moisture retention is as sophisticated as channeling water to crops via canals and must be taken into consideration when evaluating the intensity of agricultural production in the region.

NATURE AND EXTENT OF THE CASAS GRANDES SYSTEM AND REGIONAL RELATIONSHIPS

Other scholars have sought to define the extent of the Casas Grandes culture. Some projects were conducted during and just after the completion of the Paquimé excavations and before the publication of their results. Others are more recent and integrate Di Peso's data (Di Peso et al. 1974), building on interpretations that came out of the JCGE.

Investigating outlying areas, Lambert and Ambler (1961) excavated cave sites in Hidalgo County in southern New Mexico that contained Chihuahuan ceramics and yielded evidence of short-term use. A second project involved excavation of two Animas phase sites, Clanton Draw and Box Canyon (McCluney 1962), that exhibited Chihuahuan wares in small proportions. Finally, a third related project resulted in the excavation of Joyce Well, another Animas phase pueblo, one with unusually high proportions of Ramos and El Paso polychromes (McCluney 1963). The Ramos polychromes were apparently locally produced. Joyce Well is a slightly unusual Animas phase representation because of its high proportion of intrusive Chihuahuan and El Paso ceramics. Recent obsidian-hydration dates from a cluster of specimens fall between A.D. 1147 and 1325 (Carpenter 1985), slightly earlier than the average of corrected radiocarbon dates (A.D. 1390).

Other small projects have resulted in brief reports. Fritz (1969) reports the results of a surface collection from the Rancho El Espia site near Janos. Quantities of shell beads and almost nine hundred obsidian arrow points were recovered. A variety of other small sites have also been located in northern Chihuahua with Casas Grandes materials present (Phelps 1964). Curtis Schaafsma (1979) provided an overview linking the El Paso phase of the Jornada Mogollon and the Casas Grandes phenomenon. Similar connections are evident from rock art styles (P. Schaafsma 1980).

Work in southern New Mexico is pertinent to the archaeology of Chihuahua, including research in the Mimbres area (LeBlanc 1976, 1977; LeBlanc and Nelson 1976; LeBlanc and Whalen 1980; Ravesloot 1979) and in the Animas Valley (DeAtley 1980; DeAtley and Findlow 1982; Findlow and Bolognese 1982; Findlow and DeAtley 1976, 1978). Much of the Mimbres work resulted in models that connected the rise of Casas Grandes to the collapse of the Classic Mimbres and the full integration of later Animas and Black Mountain phase populations into the Casas Grandes system. LeBlanc (1980) argued that the Animas, Black Mountain, and El Paso phases were regional variants of the Casas Grandes culture. Alternatively, Ravesloot (1979) proposed that Animas populations were not fully integrated into the Casas Grandes system but involved loose-knit interaction in which ritual and exotic goods were exchanged in a fashion similar to that of the Tewa.

The Animas Valley project resulted in basic settlement pattern studies and definition of site types (Findlow and DeAtley 1976, 1978) and catchment systems (Findlow 1979). Findlow and Bolognese (1982) examined fall-off patterns of obsidian from a source in the area but have been criticized because the source was not localized and because of the statistical techniques used (Douglas 1995:246). DeAtley (1980) and DeAtley and Findlow (1982) dealt with the Animas phase and Ramos style ceramics from sites in southern New Mexico with the premise that similarities in design styles reflect interaction and communication. DeAtley found stylistic elements similar to those from Casas Grandes but combined in different ways, reflecting a weak network of interaction on the northern Casas Grandes frontier (DeAtley 1980). Problems with DeAtley's approach have been noted by Douglas (1995:247), who criticized sampling sizes, statistics, and methodology.

Some of the most important research in Chihuahua has involved the continued investigation of cave sites in the Sierra Madre (Guevara Sánchez 1984, 1986, 1988; Pearson and Sánchez M. 1990). Despite early work by Lister (1958) in Cave Valley, our understanding of the relationships between the mountain dwellers and the valley occupants is relatively poor. Data from ceramics indicate the occupations are contemporaneous, however, and it is hoped the acquisition of additional dendrochronological specimens will increase our understanding of the temporal relationship of the two groups. Shell, amassed in the millions at Paquimé, appears to have been moved across the mountain zones from the Gulf of California, along routes that were likely still used when the Spanish and later explorers entered the area (Bourke 1886; Hammond and Rey 1928). Other goods such as macaws may have traveled along the same routes, along with groups who introduced copper technology, hand drums, and other items with ritualistic value from west and northwest Mexico (Bradley 1996a; Kelley 1993, this volume). The exotics from Paquimé indicate that the Casas Grandes population had a primary orientation toward the mountains, along well-traversed routes within the Sierra. Future research may indicate that regional ties were stronger with groups in the mountainous zones than with outlying sites along the river valleys. A current project excavating rockshelters in the Sierra of southern Chihuahua, directed by S. Lewenstein of the Universidad de Puebla, will likely contribute data to this issue (Lewenstein, personal communication 1995).

Research in the valleys south and east of Casas Grandes indicates there was some interaction in the area between Casas Grandes and the Río Santa María (Minnis and Whalen 1991; Minnis et al. 1993; Whalen and

Minnis 1996a, 1996b), and the Babicora Basin (J. H. Kelley et al. 1996; J. H. Kelley et al. 1999). It does not appear to have been intense, however. Kelley and others (1999) have located sites in the northern portion of their PAC study area that date to the same general period as Paquimé and other sites in the Casas Grandes area, but few late sites are present in the southern PAC area. Their research has shown that the intensity of occupation throughout the Santa María and Babicora areas was high during the Viejo period. The high population level suggests to them that the "seedbed" of Chihuahuan culture was very large and that the southern areas were active participants in the cultural developments that culminated in the Casas Grandes phenomenon.

Research led by the INAH–Centro Chihuahua and archaeologists from the University of New Mexico and the Museum of New Mexico is currently under way. Work is being conducted at two large sites, the Galeana site on the Río Santa María and Villa Ahumada along the Río el Carmen (Maxwell and Cruz 1999; Robert Leonard, personal communication 1997). Thus far, limited excavation has yielded some interesting results. The Galeana site is one of the largest along the Río Santa María, with deep deposits and the potential to yield important information relative to the Casas Grandes regional system (Robert Leonard, personal communication 1997). Four radiocarbon dates from Villa Ahumada have yielded dates within the thirteenth century, and two dates from disturbed contexts fall in the fifteenth to seventeenth centuries (Maxwell and Cruz 1999). Archaeomagnetic dates also indicate a thirteenth-century occupation. Villa Ahumada exhibits a mix of Chihuahuan and El Paso phase Jornada Mogollon ceramics. Researchers do not consider it a part of the Casas Grandes political system; rather, it appears that the Casas Grandes system boundaries lie to the west.

Studying Ramos Polychromes using X-ray fluorescence, Woosley and Olinger (1993) suggest that Ramos ceramics were produced at Casas Grandes and distributed outward. Beyond a distance of 70 to 80 km, however, the frequency of Ramos drops off dramatically and there appears to have been localized production of the style. Characteristic of the Ramos Polychrome from Casas Grandes is the standardization of forms, sizes, surface treatment, and design elements, suggesting an emphasis on select symbols and styles, and shared beliefs (Woosley and Olinger 1993:124–125). The implications for production of the Ramos ceramics are that they were manufactured by specialists for local to regional consumption (less than approximately 80 km distant) on a relatively large scale by producers who shared clay and temper sources as well as stylistic values and beliefs.

In an earlier investigation of specialization at Paquimé, Minnis (1988) defined four examples of specialized production: shell ornaments, macaws, turkeys, and agave resources. He based his assignments on the amount and distribution of the materials, the scale and formalization of their production facilities, and the degree of centralization within Casas Grandes itself.

Contrary to the anthropological and archaeological literature, in which specialists are associated with specific hierarchical levels of sociopolitical organization, specialization in subsistence economies is associated with demand for goods and not necessarily with political organization. For instance, modern-day Mata Ortiz in Chihuahua has become an intensive production area for ceramics, with marketplaces that extend throughout the world. The potters who produce the wares are not governed by high levels of sociopolitical organization; rather, they are driven by the market for the commodities. In addition, although they are specialists in ceramic production, they also tend to subsistence-level tasks such as ranching and farming. Therefore, when we think about ceramic production, specialization, and sociopolitical organization, we must critically examine the various aspects to avoid suggesting a degree of social organization that is not valid.

In addition to ceramics, research has centered on a variety of other goods, including macaws, shell, agave, and turkeys. The role of Paquimé in the region has been investigated by scholars concerned with the level of social organization and its relation to production and the role of elites within the society. Minnis (1984) looked at the distribution of macaws, turquoise, copper, and shell from the northeast periphery of Paquimé within the Mimbres, Animas, and Black Mountain Mogollon areas. He saw little evidence of an integrated regional system dominated by Casas Grandes. His arguments were based on the fact that exports are found in small quantities at most sites. Also, Minnis (1984) refuted Di Peso's (1974) ideas about Paquimé's being a trading center. He argued that other than shell ornaments (which approached almost four million), none of the materials occurred in unusually large quantities as might be expected. These arguments were made in spite of the fact that the 14.6 kg of copper, 2.1 kg of turquoise, and 344 scarlet macaws greatly exceed those found on virtually all other sites in the Southwest.

In a later analysis of intrasite and regional organization at Casas Grandes, Minnis (1989) looked at architecture, water distribution systems, and intrasite distribution of wealth items and found that although economic specialization in shell and macaws may have occurred, its scale is unclear. Minnis (1989) projected a 130-km limit on regional interaction and suggested that although there was a certain mesoamerican character about the site of Paquimé, there was minimal evidence for intense interaction with Mesoamerica. In a critique of the world-systems models that have been proposed for the area (Di Peso 1983; Plog et al. 1982; Pailes and Reff 1985; Whitecotton and Pailes 1986), Minnis (1989) suggested an alternative model, the peer-polity concept (Renfrew and Cherry 1986). The peer-polity approach operates under the assumption that cultural change occurred among polities with similar levels of sociopolitical organization and strong interactive relationships and that changes occurred across regions at about the same time without a single locus of innovation. The problem with this model is that Paquimé appears to have been the primate center of the entire region, with a series of secondary or smaller sites in the immediate area, followed by tertiary sites and those representing marginal participation in regional activities. There is no evidence for polities of comparable size and complexity in the Casas Grandes area.

Chihuahua has recently been the focus of two large projects (Whalen and Minnis 1999). Fieldwork conducted as the Reconocimiento Regional de Paquimé (RRP), directed by Minnis and Whalen, has yielded data from the northwestern part of Chihuahua surrounding Casas Grandes (Minnis and Whalen 1989, 1991; Whalen and Minnis 1999). The PAC was conducted southeast of Paquimé in an area between Laguna Bustillos and the Babicora Basin (J. H. Kelley and Stewart 1991, 1992; J. H. Kelley et al. 1999). Reconnaissance survey, systematic survey, and limited excavation have produced a great deal of data on sites within the Chihuahuan region. The RRP project has documented site structure and artifacts on sites in the immediate Casas Grandes area, the Carretas and San Pedro areas to the northwest of Paquimé, and the Santa María drainage to the southeast. Eighty-seven sites were recorded during the 1989 field season (Minnis et al. 1993). The survey provided evidence for macaw-keeping on several sites in the Casas Grandes area, most within a 30-km radius of Paquimé. Data from the PAC survey, which located 120 sites between Laguna Bustillos and the Babicora Basin, also indicate that macaws were kept at sites in west-central Chihuahua (J. H. Kelley et al. 1999; Minnis et al. 1993). These investigators suggest there is evidence for tight control of macaw production within Casas Grandes's sphere of strongest influence (30-km radius), whereas in west-central Chihuahua macaw production may have been more autonomous (Minnis et al. 1993).

Whalen and Minnis (1996a) have used ball courts found by the PAC and other projects (Naylor 1995) to address political centralization in the Casas Grandes region. Fifteen ball courts have been recorded in outlying sites in northwestern Chihuahua and two additional courts in southern New Mexico. In addition, four are reported from surveys in Sonora (Braniff 1988, 1992b; Doolittle 1988). Several different types of courts are represented, including I-shaped, T-shaped, and simple open courts. None resembles the elliptical features in the Hohokam area (Whalen and Minnis 1996a). All appear to date to the Medio period, A.D. 1200–1450, and the majority occur on sites near Paquimé. Based on studies from Mesoamerica, where ball courts were common in systems that were fragmented into competing units and lacked strong centralized control (Santley et al. 1991), Whalen and Minnis (1996a) argue for a similar scenario in the Casas Grandes area. They suggest that, like mesoamerican courts, ball courts in the Casas Grandes region served as stages for factional or personal competitions. Since they occur most abundantly within about a day's walk of Paquimé, there is an indication of a relatively high level of factional rivalry and low level of political centralization among the elites of the core zone (Whalen and Minnis 1996a). In essence, Whalen and Minnis view Paquimé as a midlevel complex society (see Earle 1991; Upham 1991) in which emergent elites lacked the coercive power that characterized many established societies in Mesoamerica during the Classic and Postclassic periods. Midlevel complex societies are characterized by widespread factional competition and by alliances achieved through the exchange of prestige goods.

Prestige models for the Casas Grandes area have been discussed by a number of investigators (Bradley 1986, 1987, 1993, 1996a, 1996b, 1999; McGuire 1986; Stark 1986). Whalen and Minnis (1996b) have incorporated a prestige model at a local and regional level to discuss the context of production in the Casas Grandes area. Artifacts recorded during the 1989 RRP survey from sites in the Casas Grandes, Santa María, San Pedro, and Carretas clusters are used to address questions of interaction or regional cohesion within the survey area. Mean frequencies of ceramic types indicate stronger similarities between the Casas Grandes and San Pedro clusters than the other units. They also examined the distribution of macaw cages and found they were limited to sites within a 30-km radius of Paquimé. In addition, Whalen and Minnis (1996b) examined the presence or absence of shell on sites and found patterns consistent with the polychrome pottery distribution frequencies. In actuality, marine shell is very scarce to nonexistent on most of the sites in the Casas Grandes region (Bradley 1996a). Marine shell was represented by only 16 pieces, whereas the remaining are primarily minute fragments of freshwater shells that occur naturally in the soils along some of the drainages. The position that marine shell was used as a major prestige item within the region is not yet substantiated by the data; if one looks beyond the region to distant areas, however, shell constituted part of a prestige exchange network extending far into what is now Arizona and New Mexico (Bradley 1996a, 1996b).

Casas Grandes as a Trading Center: Long-Distance Interaction and Exchange

Any model of Mesoamerican-Southwestern relations must be built on an adequate data base for both areas. (Kelley 1993:229)

This section reviews some of the progress that has been made in the investigation of long-distance interaction and exchange in the Casas Grandes area since the excavation of Paquimé. In addition, some of the models and approaches that have emerged from this research are discussed (see Bradley 1996a). Excellent overviews of these models have also been presented by Ferdon (1995), McGuire (1993), Riley (1993), and Wilcox (1986b).

The controversies raised over the pochteca model permeated southwestern archaeology during the 1970s and 1980s, forging new approaches and causing archaeologists to embrace new models for understanding relationships in the Southwest. J. Charles Kelley (1986a, 1993, 1995, this volume) has proposed an alternative to the pochteca concept in his discussion of trocadores of the Aztatlán tradition and the goods they distributed. Backed by a thorough review of the literature, Kelley's model envisions extensive long-distance trade along coastal and inland routes by itinerant traders or vanguard merchants who moved copper bells, pyrite mosaic plaques, shells, turquoise, macaws, feathers, cotton, and a variety of other subsistence items throughout northwest Mesoamerica and the Southwest. More recently, Foster (1999) has argued, using Kelley's Aztatlán mercantile model, that the Medio period florescence was the direct result of incorporation of local Casas Grandes leadership into the Aztatlán sphere of influence. Going a bit further, Schaafsma (1997) has suggested that the people of Paquimé were related to or derived from people on the West Coast of Mexico.

One of the most popular models in use is the world-systems model. This approach (Wallerstein 1974, 1979) has been used in a variety of ways to describe relationships within and between Mesoamerica and the Southwest (Blanton et al. 1981:245–250; Di Peso 1983; Pailes and Whitecotton 1979, 1995; Peregrine and Feinman 1996; Plog et al. 1982; Upham 1982, 1986; Weigand 1982; Whitecotton and Pailes 1986; Wilcox 1986a). One variation defines strong interdependencies between the core (Mesoamerica) and peripheral areas (Southwest; Pailes and Whitecotton 1979; Weigand 1982; Whitecotton and Pailes 1986), whereas others favor the heuristic approach of a core-periphery structure and holistic world-system concept (Plog et al. 1982; Upham 1982:6, 1986; Wilcox 1986b:30–36). Several very different explanatory trajectories have been created under the auspices of one model. Because of the generalities adopted with the world-systems concept, isolationist and imperialist polemic divisions are found within very different constructs classified as world-systems models. The world-systems approach provides a useful framework for viewing macroregional relationships, but innate within the model are concepts of economic dependence and political domination similar to those espoused by the original pochteca model.

Unlike other traditional positions, social interaction models, such as prestige and peer polity, are political economic models that recognize the importance of social interaction and the allocation and movement of goods in social control and political manipulation (Brown et al. 1990; Brumfiel and Earle 1987; Renfrew and Cherry 1986; Renfrew and Shennan 1982). Certain types of exchange serve as instruments of political activity, wherein there is competition for a limited supply of luxury goods necessary to discharge social obligations (Ekholm 1977; Friedman and Rowlands 1977:132–143).

The peer-polity concept has been used as an alternative to the world-systems model for portions of northwest Mexico and the Southwest (Minnis 1989). Peer-polity philosophy involves interaction between autonomous sociopolitical units, producing neighboring polities of comparable scale and organization. Interchange could involve a range of goods and information, imitation and emulation, competition, and warfare

(Renfrew and Cherry 1986). Within a peer-polity structure, transformations in material culture and social organization might occur at about the same time but would not be expected to stem from a single locus of innovation. Unlike the pochteca and world-systems concepts, the peer-polity model assumes that the polities involved are autonomous. The general nature of the peer-polity model provides a structural framework from which more specific expectations can be initiated, with the recognition of several different types of interactive and integrative processes that may affect cultural development. Noteworthy criticism of the peer-polity approach points out that it should not be used as an isolationist alternative to the world-systems view, obscuring the importance of long-distance relationships (McGuire et al. 1994:242).

As an alternative to models that specify political domination or are nonspecific in their structure, prestige exchange focuses on the social context of exchange. In a prestige-goods economy, individuals may obtain power and prominence by controlling access to goods obtainable through external exchange (McGuire 1986:251). Like the peer-polity position, the prestige exchange concept assumes initially that the societies involved are autonomous units but bound by gift exchange. Select individuals with elevated status (elites) maintain power and prestige through access to rare resources and restricted knowledge. The subjugal relationships between elites and their subordinates are dependent on the ideology and the social meaning applied to goods, not the use of force.

Important to prestige exchange economies are the social and ideological relationships established and promoted by the exchange of goods and information. Accompanying luxury items are religious ideologies, social behavioral standards, and secret and public knowledge. The interaction promotes not only the distribution of goods, ideas, religious beliefs, and knowledge over large areas but also solidarity within a network that has the potential also to be highly unstable. Alliances based on exchange of goods and information provide a buffering mechanism against an erratic and harsh environment, a way of obtaining mates, solidarity against enemies, and other insurances against threatening situations (Lightfoot 1981; Lightfoot and Feinman 1982; Upham 1982). At the same time, the alliances formed within a prestige exchange network are subject to many uncertainties associated with social organizational, political, and environmental problems, as well as influences from outside the network which can have disastrous effects on relationships within the system.

Recent examination of shell ornament exchange networks within the Southwest used a prestige exchange model (Bradley 1993, 1996a, 1996b, 1999). Stylistic and chemical analysis of shell ornaments from sites in the Hohokam, Sinagua, Western Pueblo, Anasazi, and Mogollon areas produced patterns that indicate the presence of two major exchange networks within the Southwest, one associated with the movement of Casas Grandes shell and another tied to Hohokam networks (Bradley 1996a, 1996b, 1999). The Western Pueblo, Mogollon, and late Anasazi sites appear to be involved in the Casas Grandes network, and there is a correlation with sites involved in the Kachina or Southwestern Cult (Adams 1991; Crown 1994). Sites with Casas Grandes shell often have macaws and other goods associated with ritual. Casas Grandes appears to have been the focal point for the development of the Fourmile (Pinedale) style, an attribute associated with the origin of the Kachina Cult (Adams 1991:100). Furthermore, similarities in stylistic motifs between Chihuahuan polychromes and Salado polychromes associated with the Southwestern Cult demonstrate interaction between Casas Grandes and the Salado area (Crown 1994).

In addition to networks north, the Paquimé inhabitants demonstrate ties to northwest Mexico. Shell ornaments from the coast of Jalisco and Nayarit were recovered, along with copper technology, scarlet macaws, ceramic hand drums of west Mexican design (locally made), spindle whorls, and ceramics from Jalisco, Nayarit, and Durango.

A recent study of 622 copper bells in the Southwest and northwest Mexico incorporates a prestige concept and refutes the idea that Paquimé was the source for copper bells in the Southwest (Vargas 1995). West Mexico is the suggested source for the bells, which exhibit the full range of variability. Vargas (1995) found early styles to occur on sites in the Hohokam, Flagstaff, Chaco Canyon, and Mimbres Valley, with the greatest quantities and diversity in the Hohokam. Later styles occur in the Hohokam and Salado region, Sinagua, and Paquimé.

The prestige exchange concept permits examination of systems at various scales and does not imply equal access to exotic goods for all sites. That is, in a prestige economy we would not expect steady fall-off in numbers of items with distance from the site; therefore, some areas are in between, where low-level or little exchange takes place. As Douglas (1987, 1990, 1992, 1995) has pointed out from his studies in the Animas Valley, exchange relations subsume complex patterns of social negotiations, alternative exchange relations, and different technical skills that are all mediated by differing transaction costs. He argues that exchange should be considered from a dynamic perspective, considering transaction costs of regional exchange and the effects of subsistence and settlement on exchange systems. Prestige exchange involves fragile relationships subject to many perturbations (Bradley 1996a). A consideration of the dynamic nature of the system is crucial.

Although Casas Grandes was an active participant in exchange with the Southwest and northwest Mexico, the longevity of those trade relationships is not well understood. Enormous quantities of ceramics, shell, turquoise, copper, minerals, and other items were buried under debris after the site was abandoned. Questions remain as to whether the exchange network was functioning at its height by the time the site was destroyed or whether the inhabitants were preparing for large-scale exchange. Di Peso argues that Paquimé witnessed years of decline and finally catastrophic attack, at which time the site was burned (Di Peso 1974:2:320). Burned walls and beams, unburied human bodies, broken altar stones and figures, and breeding turkeys and macaws left to die in their pens are among the evidence for a catastrophic attack. Although warfare may have ultimately led to the demise of Paquimé, it is also believed to have been an ongoing, integral part of Casas Grandes society, as indicated by the presence of trophy skulls and objects of human bone (Ravesloot and Spoerl 1989). Similarly, Whalen and Minnis (1996a) suggest that the ball courts represent factional competition among elites within the Casas Grandes area.

Di Peso's (1974:2:320) estimate of an A.D. 1340 catastrophic end of Paquimé is approximately 100 to 150 years early, based on recent reevaluation of the tree-ring dates (Dean and Ravesloot 1993; Ravesloot et al. 1995). The new dates place the abandonment as late as A.D. 1500, much closer to the Spanish entrada (Dean and Ravesloot 1993:98). This revision suggests only two to three generations between site abandonment and the arrival of the Spanish, making it easier to accept some of the early Spanish annals of the area based on indigenous oral historical accounts.

SUMMARY AND DISCUSSION

Despite recent and ongoing research, few new working models have been formulated, and even fewer tested. Di Peso's pochteca model reigned amid critique and criticism for many years; more recently, researchers have proposed alternatives such as the world-system (Di Peso 1983; Pailes and Whitecotton 1995; Plog et al. 1982; Wilcox 1986b), prestige (Bradley 1993, 1996a, 1996b), and peer-polity models (Minnis 1988) and critiques of the regional system approach (Douglas 1995). There are difficulties with formulating testable models, and data make up one of the most vital components. Before the recent surveys conducted in Chihuahua, data at the regional level were not available. With the advances made we can begin to better understand the role of Casas Grandes within the region and clarify long-distance relationships. Clearly, Paquimé was involved in extensive complex relationships with distant polities, and more work needs to be done before we can adequately understand those relationships.

This overview of Chihuahuan archaeology has provided brief reference to the torrent of progress currently being made toward understanding prehistoric occupation of the region. Our knowledge of Chihuahuan archaeology over the past forty years has greatly advanced since Di Peso first began excavations at Paquimé. Yet many issues regarding the region's prehistory remain unanswered: the nature and extent of Paleoindian and Archaic occupations, the development of the indigenous population base, the establishment of large sites and their role in the region, intra- and interregional relationships, pan-regional ties to Mesoamerica and the Southwest, and the demise of the Casas Grandes system are but a few of the topics to be more fully explored.

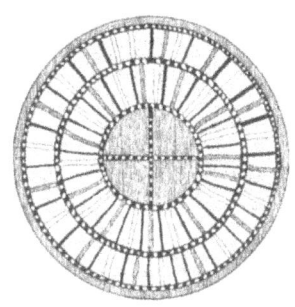

CHAPTER FOURTEEN

THE ARCHAEOLOGICAL TRADITIONS OF SONORA

MARÍA ELISA VILLALPANDO

IN THE EARLY 1500s, Captain Diego de Guzmán established a Spanish presence on the Pacific northwest coast of Mexico after a violent conquest of its indigenous peoples. Small villages of Spaniards and Indians brought from Michoacán and central Mexico were formed into the colonial provinces of Chiametla and Culiacán. These provinces were dependents or tributaries of Nueva Galica. It is curious that the Spanish, despite many expeditions like those of Diego de Guzmán, Vázquez de Coronado, and Francisco de Ibarra, did not advance farther north. Although the Spanish penetrated what is now Sonora, they did not settle there. Was there a cultural or ecological boundary that deterred Spanish colonization of this region?

Part of the answer to this question lies in the archaeological record of the area. It is important to understand, however, that archaeological research in northwest Mexico, including Sonora, is still in an initial descriptive stage. Many issues regarding the basic culture history of the region remain unresolved. Vast areas of northwest Mexico have seen little if any archaeological investigation. Nevertheless, what has been done has resulted in a general understanding of the region's prehistory, and it is clear that the area was occupied for thousands of years before the arrival of Columbus. Furthermore, the archaeological cultures of Sonora were not mesoamerican, and they evolved independently of Mesoamerica. That is to say, they were distinctive in character from their contemporaries in the mesoamerican heartland. They were also different from their counterparts in much of the American Southwest, and it is suggested here that rather than being part of the Greater Southwest, the region is best viewed as the northwestern hinterlands of Mesoamerica, the Northwest.

For this discussion of Sonoran prehistory, the region is broken into two general geophysical or ecological zones that, in turn, reflect two broad cultural systems. These are the lowlands, the desert and plains of the western coastal plain of Sonora (the Sonoran Desert), and the uplands, the mountains and valleys (basin and range country) of the northern Sierra Madre Occidental (Figure 14.1). The archaeological traditions of the lowlands include the Trincheras, Central Coast, and Huatabampo cultures. The uplands archaeological traditions include the Río Sonora and Casas Grandes cultures. Although the Prehispanic cultural traditions of these two geophysical zones interacted and were similar in some ways, they were also quite different from one another.

A knowledge of Prehispanic traditions of northwest Mexico, their local developments and internal relationships, is important not only because they are different from those of Mesoamerica but also because the Spanish colonial system was built on and partially overlapped the prehistoric cultures found there. Although it appears

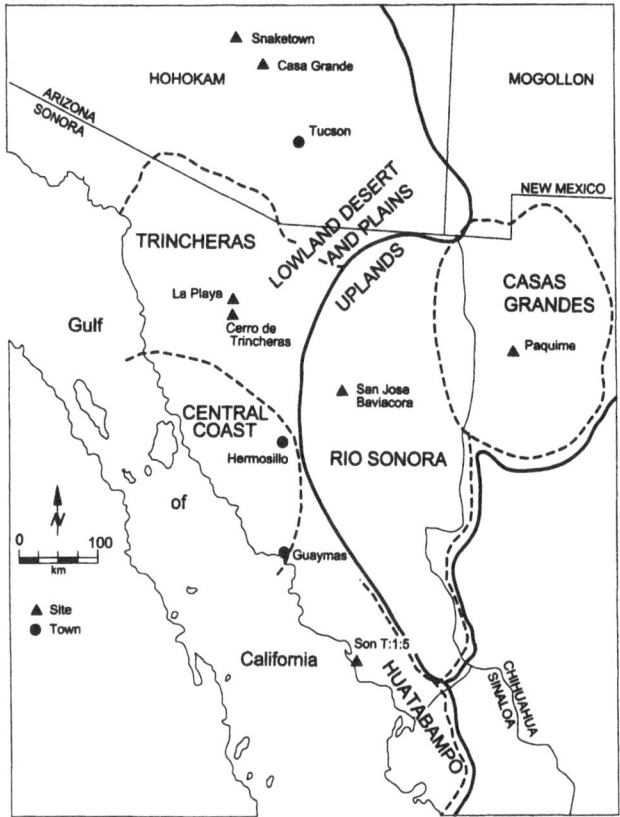

Figure 14.1. Archaeological sites, traditions, and ecological boundaries of Sonora.

the archaeological cultures of the area can be grouped into two general geocultural systems, the Spanish did not seem to recognize this. Likewise, those who describe the northwestern mission system generally do not note differences among the native communities of the region.

Before discussing the culture history and dynamics of prehistoric Sonora, it is important to identify the broad characteristics of the cultures of the region and what distinguishes them and their setting in this portion of the Northwest from Mesoamerica. Braniff (1985, 1992b) provides a summary of the main traits that differentiate core Mesoamerica from its northwestern frontier and hinterlands.[1] Cultivation techniques in the arid Northwest were different from those in the mesoamerican core. In the Northwest, dry farming was uncertain and irrigation appears early. Subsistence was based on the basic triad of maize, beans, and squash along with a strong dependence on wild resources. This pattern generally persisted into the Spanish Colonial period.[2]

Population densities were lower in the Northwest than in most regions of Mesoamerica,[3] and settlements were organized differently. There were no true cities, although a settlement hierarchy appears to have existed in some areas. Settlement types ranged from clustered villages to dispersed rancherías. With the exception of a few larger sites, settlements were not widely dispersed and were found mainly along the rivers or near other water sources. By the end of the Prehispanic period, larger sites were abandoned as populations moved to smaller and more dispersed settlements. Most of the sites in the Northwest hinterlands lack the systematic intrasite layout of mesoamerican sites or even those found to the south in Sinaloa. Northwestern societies generally lacked the hierarchical sociopolitical organization found in most of Mesoamerica, and it is likely most sociopolitical decisions were based on consensus (McGuire et al. 1994). It has also been suggested that some areas were organized into "statelets" (Doolittle 1988; Riley 1987, 1990).

The geographic variability and the perceived limits of the resources available played an important role in how the cultures of northern Sinaloa and Sonora differed from those found south of the Tropic of Cancer.[4] Except for the higher peaks, the region north of the Río Fuerte is covered with xerophytic vegetation. This area is made up of desert plains, basins, and river valleys with mountain ranges to the east. Despite its apparent harshness, the Sonoran Desert has been described as a truly rich area for gathering because of the multiseasonal abundance, diversity, and the storability of its plant foods (Felger and Moser 1985). Perhaps the most limiting element for the development of agricultural traditions in this region was the lack of a dependable water supply.

PREHISPANIC CULTURAL SYSTEMS OF THE DESERT AND PLAINS LOWLANDS

During the Paleoindian period and until the late Archaic period, subsistence in the lowlands was based exclusively on hunting and gathering. Around 400 B.C. to A.D. 200, groups of people began to cultivate some crops in the river valleys of the Northwest. The favorable environment allowed a substantial degree of sedentism and the early adoption of agriculture. Additionally, the exceptionally plentiful resources supported sedentary lifestyles among groups that hunted and gathered. Northwestern hunters and gatherers foraged for resources such as mesquite beans from riverine zones, permitting extended residence at Late Archaic sites (e.g., Fish et al. 1992:14–15).

The adoption of agriculture and sedentism led to a transformation of settlement patterns and the sociopolitical differentiation of space as communities acquired their own territories. In the centuries before the Spanish conquest (A.D. 1100 to ca. 1350), this region was occupied by fairly complex societies with economies that were involved in well-developed exchange relations for a variety of items. It appears certain that after the adoption of agriculture by the sedentary populations of the Trincheras tradition, other riverine groups in the lowlands also adopted it. Early dates for maize agriculture are also associated with the Huatabampo lowland tradition, but the nomadic peoples of the lowland Central Coast tradition never adopted agriculture.

Trincheras Tradition

Along the Altar, Magdalena, and Concepción drainages in the lower Sonoran Desert, farming and ceramic-producing communities developed after ca. A.D. 750. Known archaeologically as the Trincheras tradition, these communities were dispersed along the northernmost coast and coastal plain of the Gulf of California. These agricultural communities practiced irrigation early but were socially and economically less sophisticated than their Hohokam neighbors to the north. Nevertheless, the Trincheras tradition was an important component in the exchange networks of Hohokam communities of the Gila and Salt valleys in southern and central Arizona.

Trincheras tradition communities had almost exclusive access to a very special item, shell from the Gulf of California. In fact, shell exploitation and exchange appears to have been a primary economic activity associated with this tradition. Pelecypods and gastropods from the Gulf of California and the middle Pacific coast enabled the Trincheras, Huatabampo, and Central Coast traditions to play a significant role in the regional exchange networks.

McGuire and Villalpando (1993) have reported on Trincheras tradition sites from the Altar Valley, where the initial Trincheras occupation is the Atil phase. It is defined by the appearance of two plainware ceramic types and a fine-lined specular type, Trincheras Purple-on-red. Trincheras ceramics are commonly found as intrusive ceramics in Santa Cruz and Sacatón phase contexts in the Phoenix Basin. Much like the Hohokam, early Trincheras peoples lived in shallow pithouse villages located along the floodplains of river valleys. Although they practiced cremation, few other aspects of their material culture and cultural pattern are similar to those of the Hohokam.

The subsequent Altar phase (A.D. 800–1300) is characterized by an increase in the number, size, and variety of sites. In the Altar Valley, sites were more numerous during the Altar phase than at any other time. Ceramic types associated with this phase include a plainware, Trincheras Purple-on-red nonspecular, Trincheras Purple-on-brown, Altar Polychrome, and Nogales Polychrome. The first cerros de trincheras were occupied,[5] and pithouse villages were established in the floodplain. Associated with some sites were structures called *corrales* (Figure 14.2), which are thought not to be habitation features.[6] The dramatic increase in the number and types of sites suggests an increase in size and differentiation of the population at the sites.

The succeeding Realito phase (A.D. 1300–1450) is marked by a decrease in the overall number and variety of sites, but there is an incremental increase in site size. Realito phase habitation sites differ in important ways from the earlier Altar phase sites. There is a shift in their location from the floodplain to terraces. These sites had low, indistinct, oval mounds up to 1.5 m in height. In contrast to the trend found in habitation sites, cerros de trincheras sites are smaller in size and artifact density on them is lower. Interpretations based on surface collections in the Altar Valley suggest that the cerros de trincheras of the Altar phase were abandoned and new ones built in the Realito phase.

The Altar and the Realito phases are the only phases in which there is evidence of long-distance exchange in the Altar Valley. Substantial evidence for shell jewelry manufacture and shell trade has been found. Because of the abundance of shell remains, both unworked shell and the by-products of shell manufacturing, early studies of La Playa suggested that the site was a center for the production of shell jewelry (Johnson 1960, 1963, 1966; Woodward 1936).

La Playa is an impressive site covering about 12 km^2 (Figure 14.3). The Río Boquillas cuts through the site. Several thousand roasting pits of various sizes and at least 18 large earthen mounds covered with fire-cracked rock are scattered across the site. Upward of 200 to 400 human burials are exposed at the site's surface or in the face of the arroyos that cut through the site. Tightly flexed inhumations are the most common form of burial present, along with semiflexed inhumations and numerous cremations. Dog burials are also common. Recent work at La Playa (Carpenter et al. 1997; Sánchez et al. 1997) has resulted in the identification of substantial Middle and Late Archaic components that show evidence of early agriculture. Six radiocarbon dates from La Playa indicate the use of *Zea mays*, mesquite, and cheno-am as early as 400 B.C. (Sánchez et al. 1997). The site may have been occupied as late as the eighteenth century.

Figure 14.2. A corral site, SON:F:2:50, in the Altar Valley.

Another important shell-production locality was the site of Cerro de Trincheras, the primary center of the Trincheras tradition (Villalpando 1997). The high percentage of shell debris on the surface and a high density of associated specialized polished stone artifacts thought to be connected with shell jewelry production support this conclusion. A variety of species, including *Olivella, Nassarius, Columbell, Thais, Conus,* and *Glycymeris,* were made into whole shell beads, engraved rings and bracelets, and zoomorphic pendants. Manufacturing techniques appear different from those of neighboring areas to the north and east (Casas Grandes), suggesting a regional sphere of production.

The site of Cerro de Trincheras, located in the Río Magdalena Valley, has been the focus of recent research (McGuire and Villalpando 1995, 1997, 1998; Villalpando 1997). Cerro de Trincheras is a large, isolated volcanic hill rising over 160 m above the surrounding plain. The hill covers an area of over 90 ha. More than 900 terraces (trincheras) occur at the site, mainly on the north side of the hill (Figure 14.4). Most are 15 to 30 m in length and rise from 10 cm to more than 3 m in height. Some extend for more than 100 m in length.

Portions of 21 terraces were excavated. Fifteen houses, 26 rock rooms, and 118 other features were identified. The floors of the houses were not well defined, and the hearths present were informal. Two interesting features that were probably special-use features, La Cancha and El Caracol, were also excavated.

Artifactual material, the bulk of it ceramic sherds, was abundant at the site. The majority of ceramics were plainware, and decorated types were rare. The most common decorated types were Casas Grandes types and include Ramos, Babicora, and Carretas polychromes. A few decorated Trincheras types—Trincheras Purple, Purple-on-brown, Purple-on-red, and Nogales Polychrome—were also recovered, as were a few Hohokam and other southwestern types (Gallaga 1997). In general, intrusive ceramic types make up only a very small percentage of the ceramic assemblage. As noted earlier, shell jewelry production appears to have been a major activity at the site. The Trincheras people probably obtained shell and perhaps

Figure 14.3. La Playa.

finished jewelry through exchange with peoples of the Central Coast tradition (Villalpando 1997). Interaction and exchange with cultures to the east and north appear to have been fairly restricted. The site is thought to date to between A.D. 1300 and 1450, the El Realito phase or Phase 4 (McGuire and Villalpando 1995, 1996, 1997). Also during this time, the geographical extent of the Trincheras culture contracted.

It has been pointed out that the Trincheras tradition was not a homogeneous phenomenon, and contemporaneous sites often existed at different development levels (e.g., Bowen 1972; Braniff 1985:187). Outside the Trincheras core area, the settlement organization and the ceramics assemblages from sites do not necessarily parallel those from sites of the Altar Valley sequence.

In the Altar Valley, there seems to be a marked and dramatic change in the settlement pattern from the Altar phase to the Santa Teresa phase (A.D. 1450–1690). The number and variety of sites decline precipitously, and they are smaller and less complex. The scale of occupation appears to have declined to the level seen in the earlier Atil phase. The material culture of these sites greatly resembles late Prehispanic assemblages from southern Arizona.

When the Spaniards arrived in the area occupied by prehistoric Trincheras and Hohokam communities, they named it the Pimeria Alta. Most Prehispanic sites of the region were in ruins, although a few major settlements were still inhabited. During this time, settlements of the Sopa O'Odham were established. Some were subsequently abandoned and periodically reoccupied. This continued until the missionaries congregated the Sopa O'Odham into the native Christian communities of the late seventeenth century.

Huatabampo Tradition

South of the Trincheras area lies the homeland of the Huatabampo tradition. It is known from archaeological research conducted in the 1930s and more recently

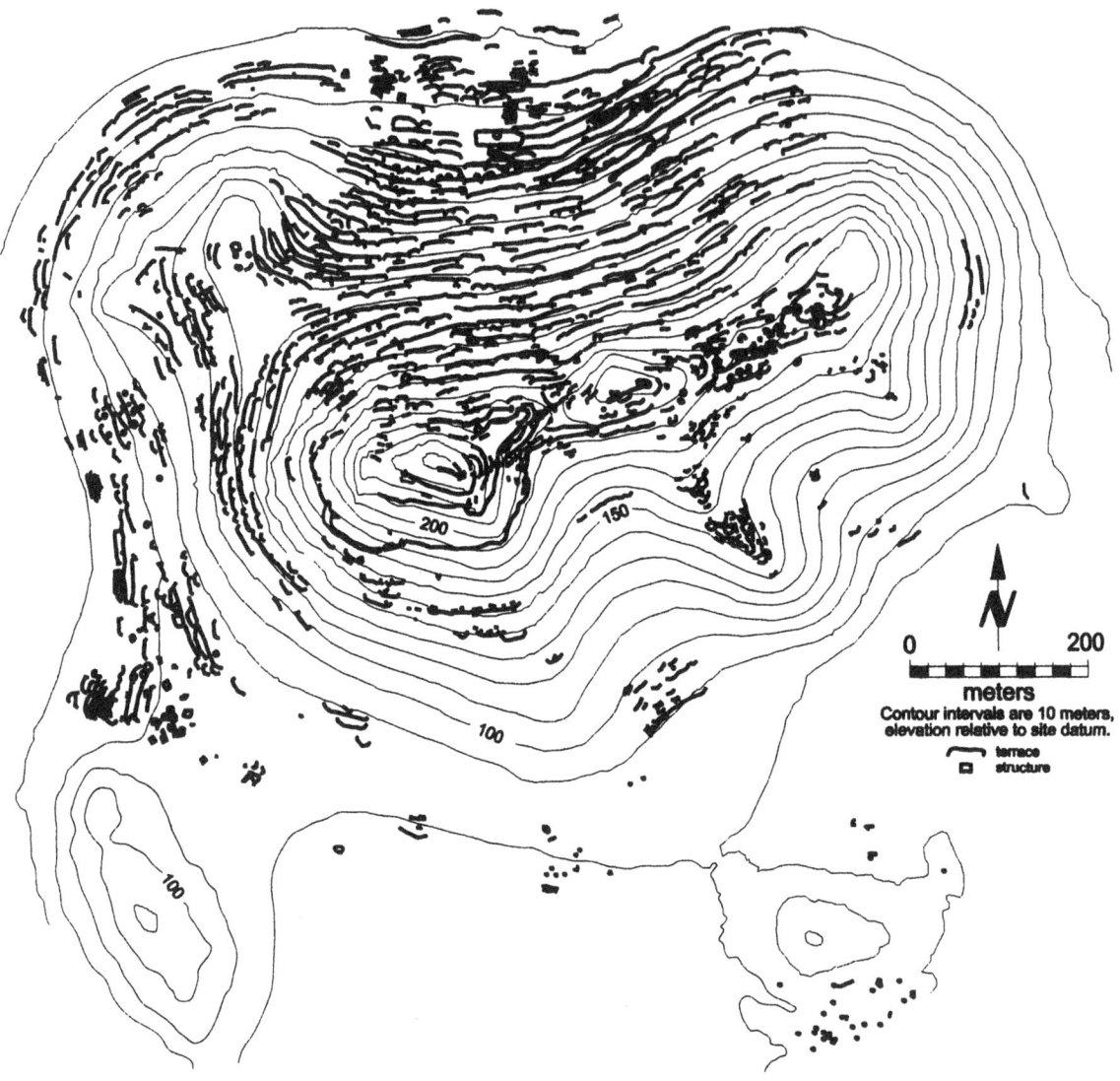

Figure 14.4. Cerro de Trincheras. Courtesy of James P. Holmlund; © Geo-Map, Inc. 1999, Tucson, Arizona.

in the 1980s (Alvarez Palma 1981, 1982, 1985, 1991a, 1991b; Ekholm 1942). Alvarez Palma's excavations at several Huatabampo sites (e.g., Son T:1:15) have recovered some mesoamerican items such as prismatic blades, and there is a mixing of some west Mexican mesoamerican traits with some Hohokam traits in a local development. Some of the best examples of this mixing are figurines that appear to blend the styles of Chametla (Kelly 1938) with those of the Hohokam (Figure 14.5). The associated materials show that this tradition played an important role as a boundary between the northernmost expression of some mesoamerican or, more accurately, western mesoamerican traditions and the cultural traditions that developed to the north.

The nature of preceramic period settlement in the Huatabampo area is unknown. Some of the extensive shell middens along the coast could predate the ceramic period. Huatabampo settlement patterns are somewhat better understood. Several large sites have been found along lagoons, estuaries, and major rivers. Huatabampo peoples appear to have located their villages to maximize access to marine, riverine, and hill slope resources. Around 200 B.C., maize and beans were cultivated, but hunting, fishing, shellfishing, and the gathering of wild plants appear to have been equally important in the subsistence economy. The regional settlement pattern shows a high concentration of sites in association with paleolagoons, where Huatabampo peoples could obtain

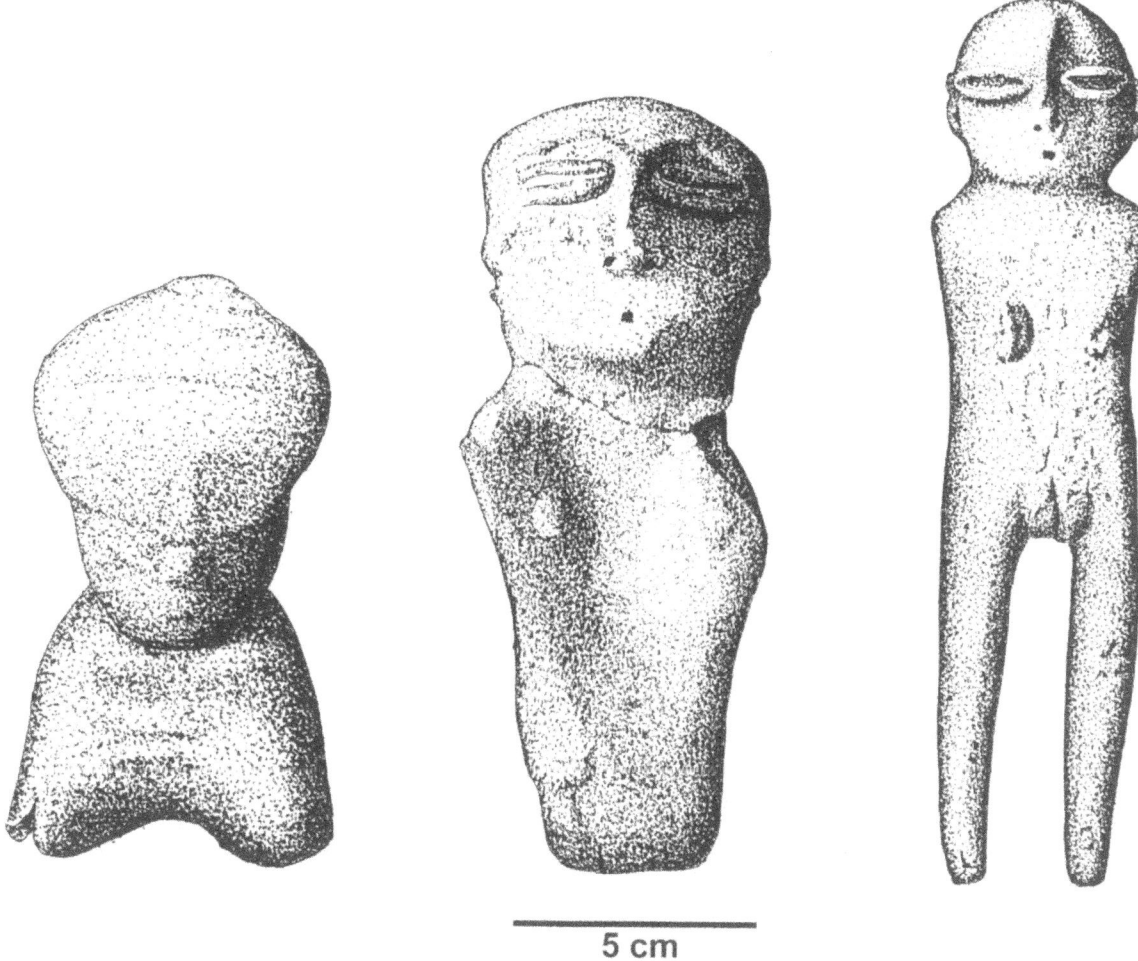

Figure 14.5. Figurines from Huatabampo. Courtesy of Tom Herrschaft.

wild resources and practice runoff agriculture. It has been pointed out that during prehistoric times environmental conditions would have been different from those of today. The climate would have been less severe, and even though the vegetation was similar to that of the present, its distribution would have been wider and denser (Alvarez Palma 1991a).

The Huatabampo settlement pattern is characterized by dispersed villages with houses constructed from perishable materials and possibly adobe or lath and mud (*bajareque*). Settlements were located in the Río Mayo and Río Fuerte valleys, on the coastal plain, and up into the low sierra.[7] The villages consisted of scattered noncontiguous dwellings and included communal spaces, trash mounds, and cemeteries with inhumations containing offerings. Dog burials are also found.

Huatabampo pottery is distinctive. It is a hard unpainted redware with complex shapes that resembles Amapa (Meighan 1976) and Capacha (Kelly 1980) pottery. Except for vessel shape, Huatabampo pottery generally resembles other Sonoran redwares. There is also extensive evidence of shell jewelry manufacture. The communities in this area had an extended role in the intraregional exchange networks. They probably exchanged raw shell with Río Sonora and Casas Grandes Viejo period communities in the uplands. Techniques for manufacturing bracelets were similar to those of the Trincheras tradition and unlike those of the Casas Grandes and Hohokam traditions. Huatabampo communities probably obtained turquoise and figurines in exchange with communities to the north and ceramics and occasionally obsidian blades from their mesoamerican neighbors to the south. Despite the fact that little is known of the Huatabampo tradition's level of regional integration, clear evidence exists for exchange with groups to the north, south, and east.

A phase sequence has not yet been defined for the Huatabampo tradition, and the current understanding of its sociopolitical and economic development is limited. Huatabampo people seem to have achieved a level of social integration similar to that reached at the end of the Atil phase of the Trincheras tradition. Around A.D. 700 to 750, when farming conditions were favorable, internal developments and regional dynamics led to an increase in the number of Huatabampo sites. Archaeological evidence suggests Huatabampo peoples were essentially egalitarian in terms of production and consumption, although there is some indication of an incipient level of social differentiation within the society itself.

The Huatabampo tradition appears to end at around A.D. 1000, a time that marks the close of supraregional integration in the general area. The causes of this change are unknown. One possibility is rapid environmental degradation that affected subsistence resources. There seems to have been an abandonment of coastal sites and trade routes as well. Some people seem to have relocated to the north, while others appear to have moved south, joining groups along the West Coast.

Huatabampo ceramics appear in the earliest levels of the Guasave sequence, which ends in the fifteenth century.[8] The Guasave tradition is culturally intermediate between west Mexico and the Southwest.

Cahitan speakers were living in the region when the Spaniards invaded it. The early *Relaciones* spoke of scattered rancherías on the southern side of the Río Mayo. Most of the larger Prehispanic sites were abandoned, and local Mayo groups did not appear to be participating in any regional exchange networks. The Mayo were clearly different from the Yaquis to the north and the dozen other ethnic groups surrounding them.

After some centuries of a considerable population increase and differentiation in the lowland communities, their complex settlements (sometimes with elaborate communal or ceremonial structures) were abandoned. As an adaptation to a changing physical and perhaps social environment, villages became smaller and subsistence activities shifted to a stronger dependence on the gathering of wild resources.[9]

Central Coast Tradition

Prehistorically, nomadic populations also occupied the desert coastal lowlands of Sonora. These peoples are sometimes referred to as the prehistoric Seri and were known in Spanish colonial times as the Heris, Seres, or Seris. The central coastal area has few sources of potable water, and almost no native plants are suitable for cultivation. Until the end of the nineteenth century, hunting, fishing, and gathering were the only subsistence activities possible.

The nomadic groups of the Central Coast tradition are included in this discussion because of the important role they played in the intraregional exchange networks of the region. They had access to one of the most valuable of all Prehispanic items in the region, shell. Because of their adaptation to marine environments, it has also been suggested that they played a role in regional salt procurement and exchange.

Numerous coastal and inland sites in the area exhibit clear evidence of Paleoindian and Archaic occupations. Artifacts, especially Clovis points, from these periods come mostly from private collections. The Central Coast tradition itself begins at or before A.D. 700 with the introduction of Tiburón Plain pottery (Figure 14.6). Tiburón Plain is common on central coast sites and is an exceedingly thin and hard ceramic type that is also known as "eggshell pottery" (Bowen 1969). The Central Coast peoples most commonly manufactured seed jars, or *tecomates*, that were probably used for the transportation and storage of water. Tiburón Plain persists to at least A.D. 1700, when these nomadic peoples began manufacturing modern Seri pottery, a ware that was not as thin and hard. Horse manure was used for temper (Bowen and Moser 1968). It is likely that Central Coast peoples acquired ceramic technology from their northern neighbors.

The social and economic complexity of the coastal groups did not change notably over time. In socioeconomic terms they are best described as a mobile band society. They moved seasonally over large areas, taking advantage of a variety of wild resources, and they developed specialized technologies for the gathering and processing of mesquite beans and other tree legumes, agave, and marine grasses. During severe droughts they may have obtained maize from their neighbors.

Central Coast bands depended heavily on marine resources, as shown by the presence of dense shell middens along the Gulf Coast. Habitation structures were made from perishable materials, and it appears that one island group used caves for habitation. They practiced inhumation and sometimes buried the dead in shell middens.

Some Central Coast peoples maintained strong ties to Trincheras communities. The Arroyo Bacoachi may have served the main trade route for shell procurement.

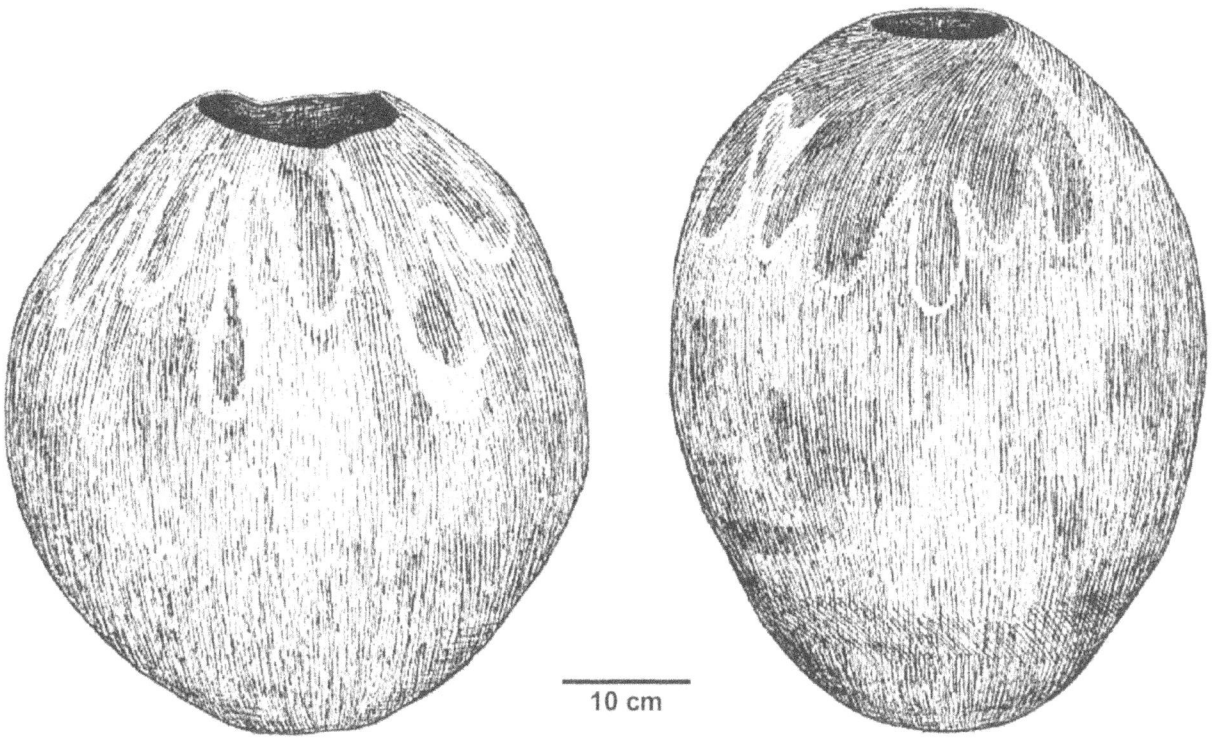

Figure 14.6. Seri Tiburón Plain tecomates.

Trincheras polychrome is present at many Central Coast sites and is sometimes the only intrusive ceramic type found. The shell jewelry produced by the Central Coast peoples was not as elaborate as that made by Trincheras or Huatabampo peoples.

As previously stated, it is important to recognize the presence of the Central Coast tradition in the prehistory of the Sonoran lowlands because of the role its peoples played in regional exchange networks. Clearly, they did not achieve the same level of social and economic complexity as either the Trincheras or Huatabampo traditions. Prehistoric intraregional exchange networks in the area were broken by the Spanish colonial system, and Central Coast groups were never again part of a larger interaction sphere. In historical times, Seri communities engaged in exchange with local farmers, obtaining grains that contributed to their subsistence needs.[10]

PREHISPANIC CULTURAL SYSTEMS OF THE UPLANDS OF CENTRAL AND EASTERN SONORA

The uplands of central and eastern Sonora make up the second geophysical system occupied by the Prehispanic cultures of the region. This zone consists of the northern Sierra Madre Occidental and adjacent basin and range county. The major characteristics of the upland archaeological traditions clearly separate them from those of the lowland desert plains.

Río Sonora Tradition

Río Sonora sites are found in the mountains and valleys east of the Sierra Madre Occidental from near the international border to northern Sinaloa, and west from the Río San Miguel to the present state of Chihuahua. The Moctezuma and Sahuaripa river valleys also contain sites belonging to this tradition. The Río Sonora Valley is the most intensively studied area within the boundaries of the Río Sonora tradition. One site, San José Baviácora, is particularly well known (Dirst 1979; Pailes 1980).

Although there is little evidence for it and no systematic effort has been made to identify an Archaic occupation, it is assumed such an occupation precedes the ceramic period of the area (Pailes 1984:331). Evidence for the initial Early phase comes from just one site. Its setting is different from sites of subsequent phases, suggesting that Early phase settlement patterns may be different from those of later times. The site contained an abundance of ceramics and lithics, but no house remains were identified (Pailes 1973, 1984).

The following Middle phase (Pailes 1973, 1984) is dated from A.D. 1000 to 1150 or 1200. Doolittle (1988) refers to this time as Period 1 (A.D. 1080 to 1200), following Amsden (1928). The phase begins with the appearance of pithouses (houses-in-pits) and textured red-on-brown ceramics. As in the archaeological traditions mentioned above, Middle phase people developed an agricultural base while remaining strongly dependent on hunting and gathering. The settlement pattern was one of habitation sites on the slopes and ridges overlooking the floodplain of the main river valleys. There is an early and a late style of pithouse, and the latter was probably associated with storage facilities.

During the next stage, the Late phase or Period 2 (A.D. 1200 to early 1300), the use of pithouses decreased and rectangular surface structures appeared. One-room structures were most common, but larger sites often have dwellings of two to five rooms. The number and size of sites increased, and they gradually became more complex. Textured pottery continued to be made, but some new stylistic innovations were introduced. The presence of Chihuahuan polychromes increased as well.

San José Baviácora, the major site of the Middle phase, continued growing during the Late phase, and two other large sites appeared. Public architecture was in the form of rectangular ball courts and elongated platforms. The trincheras sites of the Río Sonora Valley date to this phase, but the character of the sites and associated material suggests a separate tradition. These sites may represent a population expansion into the valley (Pailes 1984:314).

In the Late phase (see Doolittle 1988), probably during the fourteenth and fifteenth centuries, farming activities became more complex with the use of elaborate soil-retention and irrigation techniques. At the end of the fifteenth century, Río Sonora communities were cultivating a tepary bean, cotton, and two annual crops of maize (Doolittle 1988).

Two major centers with associated dependent nucleated villages have been recorded in the Río Sonora Valley. Based on the analysis of settlement pattern data and estimated population densities, some researchers have characterized the Río Sonora tradition as having been organized into "statelets" (Braniff 1991b; Doolittle 1984, 1988; Pailes 1990; Riley 1987). McGuire and Villalpando (1989) have questioned the idea of statelets, however. The suggestion that statelets existed is based on the assumption that most houses at these sites were contemporaneous. It is argued here that contemporaneity is difficult to determine and that therefore the estimated population densities based on this assumption may be flawed.[11] McGuire and Villalpando also question the conclusion that the Río Sonora Valley was the center of the most complex socioeconomic developments in this northern zone. Even if we accept the archaeological interpretations, it is important to note that the remains in the Río Sonora Valley are not particularly large, elaborate, or numerous when compared with other northwest Mexican sites.

There is ample evidence of the exchange of pottery, shell, and copper bells, possibly for or by the elites who controlled the valleys. The presence of a high percentage of Chihuahuan polychromes and other data prompted Pailes (1978, 1984:319–325) to propose a model of Casas Grandes immigration in the Río Sonora Valley. He suggests the immigration was stimulated by the mercantile activities of Casas Grandes during the Río Sonora Middle phase. The existence of a possible entrepot at the site of Fronteras could partially explain Casas Grandes's decline as Fronteras began to develop its own trading networks. It is clear that during the centuries before Spanish colonization, the Río Sonora tradition was closely linked to events east of the Sierra Madre. In contrast to the view held in Colonial times, the Sierra Madre was not considered a physical boundary in Prehispanic times.

The Río Sonora people shared some general cultural traits with their lowland counterparts, despite the fact that the two groups occupied significantly different ecological and geophysical provinces. Both areas produced societies that were hierarchically organized around some form of elites, both acquired and exchanged goods in regional and pan-regional exchange networks, and in both areas agriculture supplemented with hunting and collecting provided the main subsistence base.

In southern Sonora, the Río Sonora tradition is expressed in another phase sequence (Pailes 1973, 1976). The Los Camotes and San Bernardo phases appear to be associated with the expansion of the Río Sonora culture into southern Sonora. Two other phases, the Batacosa and Cuchujaqui, appear to be local developments of southern Sonora and northern Sinaloa.

Some authors (e.g., Braniff 1985) believe the historic Opata are the direct descendants of the Casas Grandes and Río Sonora peoples. They suggest that there is a continuum in the occupation of the area between the Late phase and early historic times. This is based, in part, on early Spanish accounts that contain references to "kingdoms," "provinces," and "cities" in the area. Although these designations have raised questions as to the nature of the prehistoric and protohistoric populations in the region, they clearly indicate that a substantial population was present in the region. Within a few years after the Spanish invasion, however, the evidence for such populations, if they did exist, was gone and the surviving native populations of the region were reduced to the same low level of social complexity found throughout most of northern Mexico at that time (e.g., Reff 1991).

Casas Grandes Tradition

The major cultural tradition of the Sonoran uplands was the Casas Grandes tradition (Di Peso 1974). Most often, the Casas Grandes tradition is associated with Prehispanic Chihuahua, as if the border between modern Sonora and Chihuahua had always existed. Nevertheless, the Casas Grandes tradition is seen as one of the most important cultural developments in the Northwest, not only because of its suggested connection with Mesoamerica but because it represents the highest level of economic and social development north of the mesoamerican frontier (see Bradley this volume).

Some have suggested that the Río Sonora tradition was a manifestation of the Casas Grandes tradition, except that it was located on the western side of the Sierra Madre rather than on the eastern side. Here, however, it is argued that significant differences separated the two traditions.

There is evidence of preceramic occupation on both flanks of the Sierra Madre Occidental and the Chihuahuan Desert. The Viejo period, A.D. 600–1150, of the Casas Grandes region (Di Peso 1974) was a manifestation of the Mogollon tradition found in New Mexico and Arizona. People lived in round and later in square pithouses, and some of the larger villages had communal structures that were larger than domestic structures. Viejo period peoples produced textured and red painted brownware pottery.

During the Medio period, A.D. 1150–1450 (Ravesloot et al. 1995), the site of Paquimé and the Casas Grandes tradition reached their peak. Paquimé was clearly the primary center of the Casas Grandes tradition. Its construction was well planned, and it consisted of a central multistoried residential core and a ceremonial precinct. Around A.D. 1300, the need for more cultivable land and a water supply led to the development of an extensive system of soil containment (terracing) to maximize agricultural production and prevent water erosion along the eastern flanks of the Sierra Madre. Hundreds of small villages were established on the hill slopes above major rivers. An extensive canal system provided water for irrigation and domestic use at Paquimé. The Casas Grandians' abundant food supply was supplemented with a variety of wild resources obtained by hunting and gathering. They also practiced aviaculture, raising macaws that provided birds and feathers for exchange and ceremonial activities (Di Peso 1974; Minnis et al. 1993).

Casas Grandes controlled a hinterland that included all of northwest Chihuahua, and its influence extended into western Sonora, New Mexico, and west Texas. Casas Grandes ceramics have been found at Cerro de Trincheras in the Altar Valley, at Huatabampo sites, and in association with offertories and cremations at sites in the Alto Bavispe and Fronteras river valleys (Braniff 1985, 1986). The Alto Bavispe and Fronteras river valleys are considered part of the Río Sonora tradition, and more work is needed in order to assess their relationship with the Casas Grandes core area.

Paquimé's socioeconomic and political complexity has led some authors (e.g., Di Peso 1974) to suggest that pochteca built the site as a trading outpost for the shipment of northwestern items to the mesoamerican heartland. Nevertheless, some recent studies question both the mesoamerican origin of the site and its status as a trading center.[12]

Based on an analysis of the burials at Paquimé, it was suggested that Medio period society at Paquimé was hierarchically organized (Ravesloot 1988). It is suggested here that an important factor in the development of the Medio period was warfare, used by the elite to maintain control over outlying communities (see also Ravesloot and Spoerl 1989). This strong social pressure could explain the influence of the Casas Grandes tradition over adjacent areas as well as its eventual collapse.

SUMMARY

The main difference between the lowland and upland cultural systems can be found in the levels of sociopolitical complexity they achieved. Other traits or adaptations that differentiate them include cultivation techniques: in the lowlands, the use of irrigation was more extensive. Large irrigation canals several kilometers in length were built off major rivers to irrigate large areas of arable land. In the uplands, agricultural intensification focused on the development of terraces to contain cultivable land and maximize the use of runoff rainfall. Although agriculture provided the majority of the food supply in both areas, the gathering of wild food resources contributed heavily to the subsistence base.

Differences can be seen in the types of architecture found in the two areas as well. In the early period, pithouses were used in both the uplands and lowlands. In the thirteenth and fourteenth centuries, there was a shift to surface structures in the uplands, some of them (as at Paquimé) quite elaborate. In the lowlands, pithouses continued as the common form of habitation feature. As for ceramics, in the lowlands coiled and paddle-and-anvil manufacturing techniques were dominant. Shells were sometimes used to scrape the interior of a vessel and thin it. In the uplands, coiling was the most common form of ceramic production, there was a great variety of polychromes and zoomorphic vessels (effigies), and the unpainted wares often had a "brushed" or textured surface. The manufacture of shell jewelry was more sophisticated in the uplands, at Casas Grandes (Bradley 1996a), than in the lowlands, where a variety of techniques from the very simple materials of the Central Coast and Trincheras traditions to the more elaborate techniques of the Hohokam are found.

It is generally agreed that climatic changes in the middle fifteenth century resulted in the increased desertization of Sonora and much of the Northwest in general. This probably explains the drastic decrease in the number and size of the sites and why many of the Prehispanic peoples of the region reverted to a less complex social organization and lifeway.

When the Spanish entered the area, they found something quite different from what they had known in Mesoamerica. By that time, the boundary that had separated the lowland and upland cultures had broken down, and these regions lacked the social or economic centralization that once identified them. Although the groups that occupied the region at contact appeared to be in the process of expanding their territories, the lack of cultural cohesion in the area eventually stopped the Spanish colonial advance until the introduction of the mission system. The mission system established a centralized authority that restructured the dispersed ethnic communities into a unique colonial system. The provinces of Sonora, Sinaloa, and Ostimuri were established, with the Sierra Madre forming the eastern boundary of these colonial domains. These provinces eventually became the modern states of Sonora and Sinaloa. By the end of the Colonial period, the Spanish had advanced no farther than the Tucson Basin. It took the Spanish nearly three centuries to spread across this vast region, one they never completely controlled.

NOTES

1. Braniff (1985:77–99), from the perspective of world-system theory, proposed that two clearly different northwestern regional systems existed during the Protohistoric period. She suggests the boundary between the Pima and the Opata occurred at the Río San Miguel.

2. Early Spanish chroniclers noted that local indigenous populations growing corn, beans, and squash relied heavily on wild plants to supplement their diets. Cacti produced edible tunas or fruits, pods from trees such as mesquite were ground for flour, and agave produced not only wine, honey, and vinegar but also fiber and needles for sewing (Pérez de Rivas 1985:1:34).

3. Some estimations put the highest population densities in the Río Sonora Valley in 1519 at 2.3 people per square kilometer, whereas at the same time a general average for Mesoamerica was 10–12 people per square kilometer. The highest estimate for the central highlands was 75–112.5 people per square kilometer (Braniff 1985:83).

4. The decisions of both individuals and groups regarding the location of activities and the use of land are not made in a vacuum, being strongly influenced by the total environment within which the decision maker operates. Location itself forms an important part of this total environment, and the locational environment or spatial context of a decision maker derives both from the physical and human characteristics of the location itself and from the characteristics of its surrounding space (Chapman 1979:11–12).

5. *Cerros de trincheras* are the terraced hillside sites from which the tradition derives its name.

6. Nonhabitation structures are square or rectangular in shape, generally larger than 5 x 10 m, with stone walls higher than 1 m. There has been no systematic study of such features, and little is known of their distribution within sites.

7. Based on stylistic and technological elements and the distribution of sites, the core area of the Huatabampo culture appears to be the alluvial plain of the Río Fuerte to the Río Mayo. The maximum southern limit, however, based on the excavations by Ekholm (1942), may be the Guasave area. The northern limit could be the Río Yaqui (Alvarez Palma 1991b:46–47).

8. The Huatabampo chronometric dates suggest the cultural sequence ends at A.D. 950. At the site of Guasave, the

Huatabampo tradition precedes the Aztatlán phase (A.D. 1000–1450; Alvarez Palma 1991a:47; see also Carpenter 1997).

9. The houses of the local indigenous peoples were organized in rancherías or villages not very distant from one another, about two or three leagues apart. They were located on or near arable land (Pérez de Rivas 1985:1:33).

10. As the crops were harvested, the Seris would enter the villages of their friends and exchange fish for corn and other agricultural produce (Pérez de Rivas 1985:1:35).

11. "A total of 224 houses from 65 settlements were identified for the Early phase occupation in the Río Sonora Valley. Using 6.1 persons per house, and assuming that all houses were occupied, a population of approximately 1,400 people is estimated for the valley. Relic house foundations from the Late phase totaled 1,289 from 162 settlements . . . nearly 7,900 people for the Late phase" (Doolittle 1988:52–53).

12. McGuire (1993:35) states, discussing the views of several southwestern archaeologists contemporary with Di Peso: "These archaeologists did not feel that items from Mesoamerica were common enough in the Gran Chichimeca to bear out Di Peso's theory. They asserted that the Mesoamerican items, rites, motifs, styles, and beliefs in the Gran Chichimeca could have come via more casual contacts. These individuals agreed that Paquimé was a major trade center but viewed it as mainly a local development." See also McGuire 1980 and Minnis 1988.

CHAPTER FIFTEEN

FROM TZINTZUNTZAN TO PAQUIMÉ

Peers or Peripheries in Greater Mesoamerica?

MICHAEL W. SPENCE

CENTRALISMO IN MESOAMERICA

THIS BOOK is the latest in a growing series of edited works devoted to the archaeology of west or northwest Mexico or both (Bell, ed. 1974; Boehm de Lameiras and Weigand 1992; Dahlgren and Soto de Arechavaleta 1995; Foster and Weigand 1985; Mathien and McGuire 1986; Reyman 1995; Riley and Hedrick 1978; Woosley and Ravesloot 1993). The introduction to this volume by Gorenstein and Foster echoes a long-standing complaint, voiced in many of the earlier collections, that the findings of archaeologists working in these regions have not received the attention they deserve. Mesoamericanists instead have remained focused on the better-known (at least so far) and often more spectacular remains of the central highlands, the Gulf Coast, and the Maya region (Weigand 1992a). In effect, many of the regions considered in the present volume have been excluded from Mesoamerica or relegated to the status of peripheries that benefited from but did not contribute to the development of mesoamerican civilization.

Nevertheless, it must be admitted that many of the earlier archaeologists working in this vast area have implicitly colluded in this *centralismo* by suggesting that these regions became "mesoamericanized" only in the later stages of their culture histories. Others have endorsed the primary role of the "heartland" by proposing world-system and core-periphery models to explain the movement of goods and ideas between central Mexico and the West and Northwest. Although these models have been challenged (e.g., Stark 1986), they have created a perspective that has become deeply embedded in the archaeological literature. Even this volume, although it includes several chapters contesting this view, implicitly adopts it through its attempt to cover some thirteen states of Mexico, from Michoacán to Chihuahua. After all, what coherence could such a vast area have, apart from its apparently marginal location when viewed from the rather smug perspective of central Mexico?

As Gorenstein and Foster point out, however, Mesoamerica is by no means the clearly defined entity we have assumed it to be. Despite numerous attempts to pin it down, the most recent being a concerted examination of the topic at the 1989 XIX Mesa Redonda of the Sociedad Mexicana de Antropología, Mesoamerica remains elusive in its defining criteria and its extent, both of which have changed over time (Braniff 1974; Contreras R. 1990). Much of this uncertainty is due to the work of investigators in the West and Northwest, whose findings have undermined our earlier, rather simplistic notions of Mesoamerica. The field has been opened to alternative perspectives, always a healthy development (Nalda 1990). As Braniff (1995:202; this volume) has emphasized, we can now entertain the idea that cultural practices and elements moved into, not just out from, the "core" (see also Hers 1989a), and that even the frontier between settled mesoamericans and the more nomadic Chichimecs to the north was a porous and fluctuating zone of peaceful contact and exchange rather than the rigid and confrontational border assumed by many earlier scholars.

Despite the growth of these new perspectives, breaking the old habits of thought will not be easy. They are locked in the archaeological language of the debate. Even among those who see no imbalance in the interactions between the societies of central Mexico and those of the West and Northwest, terms such as "periphery" are still used to characterize the latter regions. We must explicitly question whether the mesoamerican "core" is really a core, and so by extension whether its "periphery" is really a periphery. Stark (1986:272) is careful to use the term "periphery" in a purely geographic sense, avoiding any implication of structural or economic inequality. In fact, she questions the existence of any such imbalance. We must follow that example and avoid a priori assumptions about the degree to which any one region dominates or even demographically outweighs another. As part of this approach, we should keep in mind that it is people, not regions, that interact. As Stark (1986:282) notes, the materials and messages transmitted between interacting elites may be quite different from those communicated by entrepreneurially oriented merchants.

THE ROLE OF TEOTIHUACÁN

Teotihuacán has frequently been invoked to explain cultural developments in other parts of Mesoamerica. In some cases there is good reason for this. In Kaminaljuyu, for example, Teotihuacán influences and even the actual presence of Teotihuacanos is signaled by talud-tablero architecture and a variety of goods produced in or distributed through Teotihuacán (Kidder et al. 1974; Sanders and Michels 1977; Spence 1996). Similar enclaves, or at least clear evidence of interaction with Teotihuacán, appear at a variety of other sites in Guatemala, Belize, and Veracruz (Spence 1996). In west and northwest Mexico, however, evidence of Teotihuacán contact is "spotty" (Aronson 1996:167). Although some Teotihuacán goods appear in Michoacán, the Bajío, and Jalisco, few sites are involved and the quantities of imported goods are limited (Pollard, this volume; Braniff, this volume; Weigand 1992b).

In demographic terms there is no doubt that Teotihuacán was indeed huge, with a population estimated at some 125,000 (Millon 1992). Whether this size created a large consumer demand for goods from the West and Northwest is quite another matter. The population of the Basin of Mexico in the Middle Classic period (ca. A.D. 200–650) may have been only about 230,000, the bulk of it packed into the city (Sanders et al. 1979). Beyond Teotihuacán, the population was dispersed widely in hamlets, villages, and some smaller centers.

This population distribution suggests that any significant consumer demand would have been concentrated in the city itself. There, however, the demand for goods was considerable. Except perhaps for the last century of its existence, prestige and luxury goods circulated widely in the city, rather than being restricted to a small elite (Sempowski 1994:252, 263–264). Nevertheless, this demand was oriented largely toward the south and east, regions that show evidence of direct and at times intense interaction with Teotihuacán.

Goods from the West and Northwest, in contrast, appear only sparsely in Teotihuacán sites. Some have adopted Kolb's (1987:20, 81) suggestion that the quantities of Pacific *Spondylus calcifer* found at Maquixco el Bajo, a site near the west edge of Teotihuacán, were imported from west Mexico. This species, however, is widely distributed along the Pacific coast, from Sonora to Ecuador (Kolb 1987:20). It may equally well have reached Teotihuacán through its links with Kaminaljuyu and Balberta (Kidder et al. 1974; Bové et al. 1993). Phil Weigand has said that some sherds from the Maquixco el Bajo excavations may be from Jalisco, Nayarit, and Zacatecas (including the Chalchihuites culture), but no details have been provided (Kolb 1987:82–83). On the other hand, some ceramic vessels and figurines from Michoacán have been found at a site near the west edge of Teotihuacán and may represent an enclave of Michoacanos in the city (Sergio Gómez Chávez, personal communication 1993).

Most models that suggest that substantial interaction with the West or Northwest was developed before our chronologies were refined. Thus, it was suggested that Alta Vista was founded by migrating elites related to, if not from, Teotihuacán, and that the materials taken from the extensive Chalchihuites mines went largely to supply Teotihuacán with pigments, green stone, and other goods (Aveni et al. 1982; Kelley 1983b; Weigand 1982). In effect, the post-Canutillo phase Suchil Chalchihuites culture developed as the result of a Teotihuacán colonization effort, intended to secure a steady supply of desired materials for the city.

Archaeologists are now moving away from this position. It is becoming clear that the Chalchihuites mines are primarily Epi-Classic in date and that their extent can be adequately explained by small-scale exploitation over the course of some centuries to supply regional consumers (Kelley and Kelley, this volume; Schiavitti 1995). Also, although Alta Vista may have been founded about A.D. 450, it reached its peak in the ninth century (Foster 1995b:85; Kelley 1990b). The idea of an ongoing relationship between Teotihuacán and Alta Vista is further weakened by the absence of Teotihuacán items in Alta Vista and the virtual absence of Chalchihuites artifacts in Teotihuacán (see also Hers 1989a:50, 188). The one possible exception to the latter is a rim sherd from Maquixco el Bajo that Weigand says "appears to be from the Chalchihuites area during the Classic" (Kolb 1987:82–83).

Nevertheless, there is one striking parallel that must be explained: the Cerro el Chapín 1 pecked cross-circle (Aveni et al. 1982; Kelley and Kelley, this volume). Although widely distributed in Mesoamerica (one even appears 130 km to the north, in Durango; Aveni et al. 1982:319, 331), these features are clearly concentrated around Teotihuacán and associated sites (Aveni 1989). There is no doubt that the Chapín 1 example closely matches those found in central Mexico. Still, it remains possible that it was made by people who had learned the science from some region closer to hand than Teotihuacán (Cowgill 1997:134). Folan et al. (1987) located another example at Cerrito de la Campana, a Teotihuacán-related site in the Temascalzingo area, in the state of Mexico near the Río Lerma and the Michoacán border. Perhaps, as intervening areas are more thoroughly explored, other examples will be found.

Weigand (1992b) proposed a different sort of effect that Teotihuacán may have had in the West. He suggested that the distinctive Teuchitlán tradition of Jalisco may have evolved in part as a local response to pressure from Teotihuacán or allied groups in the Atemajac Valley, as a form of indigenous resistance. Again, the theory encounters chronological difficulties. The cultural expression in the Atemajac Valley that Weigand refers to, the El Grillo phase, is actually Epi-Classic, ca. A.D. 600–1000 (Beekman 1996a; Schöndube B. and Galván V. 1978). By the time this phase was developing, Teotihuacán had either already collapsed or was withdrawing from its former position of dominance in Mesoamerica. The presence of occasional Thin Orange sherds in some earlier Teuchitlán tradition sites indicates some link to Teotihuacán, but there is no evidence that Teotihuacán's presence was immediate enough to provoke the sort of response Weigand has suggested.

The realization that many of the cultures and sites in the West and Northwest were Epi-Classic, combined with the earlier date (A.D. 650) now suggested for the collapse of Teotihuacán (Cowgill 1996, 1997), has generated a new set of theories about the nature of Teotihuacán's impact on those regions. It seems that the correspondence in time between the disintegration of Teotihuacán and the development of vigorous new polities to the west and northwest cannot be entirely coincidental (Nelson 1997). One feature in particular requires explanation: the appearance of talud-tablero architecture in a number of apparently Epi-Classic sites in Michoacán and Jalisco. This architectural form has often been considered a hallmark of the Teotihuacán state, though some have cautioned that its association with Teotihuacán is not as tight as has been assumed (Laporte 1987).

There are several possible explanations for the wide distribution of the talud-tablero in Epi-Classic Mesoamerica. For one, it may represent a special phenomenon, the invocation through architectural imagery of the power of a great civilization that had already passed into legend (Spence 1996:343). This would be a particularly plausible explanation for those regions where Teotihuacán had played a major role in local affairs during the preceding Middle Classic period; some Epi-Classic echo of its past importance would not be surprising. The post–A.D. 600 talud-tablero structures in the Maya region, like 5D-43 of Tikal, may be cases in point.

Another possibility is that the Epi-Classic examples of talud-tablero no longer bear any reference at all to Teotihuacán. Variants of this facade may simply have become a generalized architectural symbol for the state or the public realm, or even just an attractive way to decorate a building. In this sense, it might be expected virtually anywhere in Mesoamerica, regardless of the area's prior relationship with Teotihuacán. This explanation would fit with the network strategy that Blanton and others (1996) believe dominated political systems in the Epi-Classic period; talud-tablero architecture would have become an "international style."

The third possibility is that talud-tablero architecture was introduced by refugees from Teotihuacán (Pollard, this volume). Most of those leaving Teotihuacán during its decline could have been accommodated easily enough elsewhere in the Basin of Mexico, which was not heavily populated then. Some may have moved into the Valley of Toluca, which shows a population expansion at about that time (Sugiura Y. 1996). Refugees would probably have moved to areas that were familiar to them or already occupied by people with whom they had some prior relationship (Sugiura Y. 1996:248–249). This would certainly have been true of the Valley of Toluca, where populations with Teotihuacán-style pottery and talud-tablero architecture were established in the Middle Classic (Díaz O. 1993). And it is possible that some refugees would have traveled even farther afield. Teotihuacán's collapse involved internal conflict and violence against the ruling element of the city (Millon 1988), so fleeing elites may have wished to put a considerable distance between themselves and their former subjects.

It is difficult to say which of these possibilities applies to the sites in west Mexico with talud-tablero architecture. Some of them are in Michoacán, but their dates are not firmly established. Loma de Santa María may be a Middle Classic period site (Trejo de la Rosa 1979; Manzanilla López 1988). Tres Cerritos is more difficult to place. The tomb with multiple burial chambers built into the talud-tablero structure there is not a Teotihuacán feature (Macías Goytia and Vackimes Serret 1988). Tingambato, dated to the Epi-Classic (Pollard, this volume), also has talud-tablero architecture associated with a tomb, this one containing at least 50 individuals (Lagunas R. 1987). At least some of the Michoacán sites with talud-tablero architecture, then, are probably Epi-Classic sites occupied by people with a decidedly non-Teotihuacán mortuary program. They may represent the first scenario outlined above, an indigenous population that continued the use of talud-tablero because of its reference to a now mythical Teotihuacán, but the presence of an earlier Middle Classic occupation closely linked to Teotihuacán has still to be demonstrated.

The Epi-Classic talud-tablero expressions in the Atemajac Valley, on the other hand, may have been constructed by elite refugees from Teotihuacán. Although the pottery is generally quite different from that of Teotihuacán, the mortuary practices of the El Grillo phase are unlike those of the preceding Tabachines shaft tomb culture and show some features present also in Teotihuacán: individual burial, emphasis on the seated and flexed positions, and the frequent inclusion of miniature vessels (Aronson 1996:167; see also Cabrero G. 1995:69). Nevertheless, one would have to explain why fleeing elites would move so far, to an area with no earlier Teotihuacán presence, and why local people would have suffered their intrusion. It should be noted that such an intrusion would have been a major event in local political history. The appearance of foreign patterns in public architecture indicates the foreign control of local labor, implying the subordination of local authority to the newcomers (Sanders and Price 1968:166–167). Could a group of refugee Teotihuacanos have really accomplished this? Although the El Grillo phase may represent such a case, the evidence as it stands is not convincing.

It seems that we have a lot more thinking, and digging, to do on this topic. It would help if we had a better understanding of the archaeology of the intervening areas (Aronson 1996:167) and a more precise chronology of developments in the Atemajac Valley. For that matter, more precision in the chronology of Teotihuacán itself would be useful. There were apparently episodes of internal conflict and political revision before the final collapse, and some of them may have had some limited effect on the societies to the west (Cowgill 1997:155). Also, the scope of investigation should be expanded to include osteological data. Comparisons of skeletal series from Teotihuacán with those of west Mexico may shed light on the question of population movements.

There is also a structural perspective on central and west Mexico relationships. Stark (1986:284) and Nelson (1993; see also Blanton et al. 1996:10) have suggested that the collapse of Teotihuacán may have freed "peripheral" polities to develop their own potential. More recently, however, Nelson (1997:89) has rejected this idea, at least with respect to La Quemada, because it presumes a prior Middle Classic phase of Teotihuacán domination in the area, a phase for which there is no evidence. Still, as Nelson notes, there is the troubling coincidence of "core" collapse and "periphery" growth (1997:107).

Blanton and others (1996) have proposed another possible mechanism. They say that mesoamerican history shows a continuing oscillation between what they call "corporate" and "network" strategies of governance. With the collapse of Teotihuacán, a corporate state, network strategies became the dominant pattern in the Epi-Classic. Blanton and others (1996:10) say that these may always be present in the peripheries of corporate states. It might be suggested, however, that the factional conflicts of the Teotihuacán collapse (Millon 1988) created a situation in which militarism and competition for power inevitably dominated post-Teotihuacán central Mexico politics. Leaders who adopted network strategies engaged in intense competition, relying on inter-elite exchange systems, alliances, and politically advantageous marriages to enhance their authority. Prestige goods and knowledge, including religious concepts and iconographic expressions, moved over large areas. Network strategies are inherently expansive, as leaders develop exchange ties and relationships far afield in order to obtain the exotic goods and knowledge necessary to maintain their positions at home.

This could explain the wide circulation of goods and ideas, such as pseudocloisonné and talud-tablero architecture, in the Epi-Classic period. These became elements of an "international style" that developed with the burgeoning communication and exchange networks characteristic of the Epi-Classic polities. Though Teotihuacán may have been the original source of inspiration for some of these elements, in the Epi-Classic they would have taken on new meanings, ones responsive to the political imperatives of the time.

If interpretations of some skeletal concentrations at Alta Vista, Cerro del Huistle, and La Quemada as the display of conquered enemies are correct, military conflict must have played a significant role in the competition among Epi-Classic elites (Abbott Kelley 1978; Hers 1989a; Pickering 1985). Some caution is required here, however (Faulhaber 1960:140–142). Thorough osteological analyses of the skeletal material, coupled with careful attention to context, are necessary. The Cerro del Huistle discovery indicates some sort of *tzompantli,* which in Late Postclassic central Mexico would have been used for the display of enemies' heads (Hers 1989a:89–91). This function also seems plausible for the Cerro del Huistle case, where the heads, mostly of adult males, were apparently pierced and suspended while still fleshed. Nevertheless, some further confirmation, such as evidence of biologically diverse origins or a high incidence of perimortem trauma, would be welcome. Some displays of skeletal elements or body parts or both seem to have involved ancestors and kin rather than enemies (Nelson et al. 1992). The public curation of ancestral bones would not be unexpected in political systems based on a network strategy, since the "patrimonial rhetoric" deployed to support political status in such systems often includes reference to descent (Blanton et al. 1996:5).

THE AZTATLÁN COMPLEX

The Aztatlán complex, the expression of the Mixteca-Puebla sphere in the West and Northwest, may have developed as early as A.D. 800–900 (Kelley, this volume; Mountjoy 1990). Kelley (this volume) places its peak in Late Aztatlán, which he equates with Aztec I in the Basin of Mexico and, based partially on the chronology of Sanders et al. (1979), dates to A.D. 1150–1350/1400. Recent work in the Basin of Mexico and at Cholula, however, suggests that Aztec I and the Mixteca-Puebla style were certainly present in those areas by A.D. 1000, and perhaps earlier (Cowgill 1996; Lind 1994; McCafferty 1994; Parsons et al. 1996). Thus, the early dates suggested for Aztatlán by Kelley (this volume) and Mountjoy (1990, this volume) may not be far off the mark. If so, the Aztatlán complex would represent an Early Postclassic (A.D. 900–1250) phenomenon that developed hard on the heels of the Epi-Classic expressions discussed above.

The varieties and quantities of materials circulating in the Early Postclassic period may have been greater than in the Epi-Classic. Copper items, turquoise, prismatic blades of fine west Mexico obsidians, elaborate polychrome ceramics, and even some Plumbate pottery were among the goods involved (Ganot R. and Peschard F. 1995; Kelley, this volume; Weigand and Spence 1982). Blanton and others (1996:10) cite this system as an example of the network strategy and identify the Mixteca-Puebla ceramics as an "international style" (see also Pohl and Byland 1994). As before, elites were collecting prestige goods and knowledge from near and far to support their claims in the competition for regional power. The inclusion of knowledge, both mundane and exotic, and the necessity of appeal to supernatural authority in these competitions led to a set of mutually understood ideological concepts and a common symbolic grammar (Braniff 1995; Kelley, this volume; Pohl and Byland 1994).

Although this seems to be a plausible model of the developments in Postclassic west and northwest Mexico, it must still be thoroughly tested. One important question concerns the mechanism for the circulation of these concepts and goods. Kelley (this volume) suggests the *trocador,* the mobile merchant, as a principal agent of transmission. These merchants could not have been purely entrepreneurial. As Stark (1986:282) has pointed out, commercially driven traders would not have been likely to communicate, let alone instill, the concepts and information necessary for effective participation in broader ideological and iconographic systems. To accomplish that, the mobile merchants must have been agents or members of the interacting elites. This does not deny an entrepreneurial motivation, but it qualifies it.

In her discussion of the iconography, Braniff (1995:182) has cautioned that the meanings associated with a symbol can change with time and context. This raises the question of the degree to which this "international style" actually represents a single, widespread system of belief and ritual, as opposed to a set of loosely structured and regionally reinterpreted symbols. If vessels bearing complex Mixteca-Puebla iconographic motifs were widely circulated, their presence far from their source of manufacture could not be taken necessarily to mean local understanding and acceptance of the message encoded in the images. They could simply have been reinterpreted in local terms. On the other hand, if these elaborate motifs had been faithfully reproduced on local pottery, it would imply something more. Reinterpretation in terms of local concepts and beliefs would be expected to result in some selection and alteration of the images, their recasting in a locally intelligible format. In the absence of evidence for such reinterpretation, one could suggest that the formal body of beliefs expressed in the images had been transmitted intact and was largely accepted by the recipients.

Thus, we must determine just how international this "international style" really is. Technical analyses of the pottery, employing petrographic and trace element methods, will play a crucial role in this effort. They have proved to be very informative about Mixteca-Puebla ceramics in central Mexico (Neff et al. 1994) but to date have been applied to only a few western and northwestern cases (Strazicich 1996; Woosley and Olinger 1993). If manufacturing centers and distribution spheres can be identified and associated with iconographic systems, we will understand a great deal more about the Aztatlán network and its sociopolitical foundations.

In sum, the idea of a large and economically integrated central Mexico population exerting a major impact on the development of western and northwestern societies is a figment of archaeological imagination. In the Middle Classic period, Teotihuacán's acquisitive gaze was turned more to the east and south. Some adjacent peoples to the west and north were certainly interacting with Teotihuacanos, but the nature of this interaction is not clear and most of the region was unaffected. With the collapse of Teotihuacán, central Mexico splintered into a number of vigorously competing smaller polities that would have been even less able to dominate those of the West and Northwest in any respect (political, economic, or religious), although paradoxically the circulation of goods and ideas among all these societies may have increased substantially at this time.

This situation persisted through the Epi-Classic and Early Postclassic periods. Interaction among the regions was clearly occurring, but it was probably on a relatively equal footing and often screened through intervening polities and agents. It is only with the ascendancy of the Triple Alliance (A.D. 1428–1520) in the Late Postclassic period that central Mexico may have become integrated and populous enough to effect some limited restructuring of economic practices and institutions in the West and Northwest.

FUTURE DIRECTIONS

Archaeologists have become increasingly aware that *centralismo,* though it may explain the imbalance in wealth and power between center and periphery in Mexico today, is not a tenable characterization of past interactions. This growing realization is reflected in the trend away from world-system and core-periphery models, and the focus on explanatory concepts that assume a more equitable balance among interacting polities. Kelley's (1986a, this volume) *trocador* model, the peer-polity model discussed by Jiménez Betts and Darling (this volume; see also Renfrew 1986), and the network strategy concept of Blanton and others (1996) are cases in point. Regrettably, though, the terminology and even some of the assumptions from our brief flirtation with core-periphery theory linger on. These must be explicitly recognized and tested if we are to make any further progress.

Nevertheless, it may still be helpful to look to the archaeology of the mesoamerican "heartland" for some suggestions for the future directions of research in the west and northwest. For example, syntheses in the West and Northwest (including this volume) have typically covered a great deal of territory, spatially, chronologically, and topically. This is necessary in the earlier stages of investigation, when regions have to be defined and an initial chronology developed, but the absence of tighter focus can eventually stall progress. Syntheses of such broad geographic scope are usually constrained topically to some degree, dealing only with certain time periods (e.g., Diehl and Berlo 1989) or subjects (e.g., Chase and Chase 1992; Nicholson and Quiñones Keber 1994). Some similar efforts are now appearing in the archaeological literature of west and northwest Mexico (Cabrero G. 1995; Hosler 1994).

As always, more fieldwork is also needed. In some areas, broad survey coupled with test excavation is still necessary. Foster (this volume) has shown that this is the case for Durango, where our understanding of the archaeological resources is still in its infancy. Jane Kelley and Joe Stewart (1991, 1992) have only recently completed an extensive survey of west-central Chihuahua.

In other regions, a different approach is needed. The Teuchitlán tradition, for example, is known largely through surface reconnaissance. The very limited subsurface data come almost entirely from monitoring the activities and finds of looters (Beekman 1996b:136; Weigand 1985:52, 70). Some of our information on the Aztatlán complex also comes from looted graves (Ganot R. and Peschard F. 1995). It is now time for intensive excavation, especially in view of the accumulating damage caused by looters and development (Mountjoy 1995d). This will not only provide far more detailed and reliable evidence but will also relieve us of some of the troubling ethical problems that come of dealing with looted data. As any thoughtful perusal of Alison Wylie's (1996) excellent discussion of the subject shows, there are major moral and practical difficulties involved in even casual and distanced use of looted evidence. In the long run, we are probably just creating a greater threat to archaeological resources for an incommensurate return of data.

The course of future investigations, then, should include concentrated examinations of key sites and areas. The long-term investigation of the Suchil branch of the Chalchihuites culture by the Kelleys is a fine example of what is needed (Abbott Kelley 1978; Kelley 1983b, 1990b). The work of Nelson and his students (Nelson et al. 1992; Strazicich 1996) and of Jiménez Betts (this volume) at La Quemada, coupled with Trombold's (1985, 1991) study of the site's broader Malpaso Valley context, is another case in point.

In addition, technical analyses designed to identify the sources and circulation spheres of particular archaeological materials will be crucial. Samples of adequate size from archaeologically defined proveniences are essential for such studies. Looted materials should not even be considered, given the inherent uncertainties about their contexts. Excellent recent analyses along these lines have dealt with obsidian (Trombold et al. 1993), turquoise (Weigand and Harbottle 1992), metals (Hosler 1994), and ceramics (Strazicich 1996; Woosley and Olinger 1993).

Ultimately, I am suggesting that we follow the course J. Charles Kelley laid out for us with his own work: broad survey to gain some idea of the distribution of archaeological resources in a region, followed by intensive excavations at key sites with analysis and publication of the data and the application of the results to questions of broader anthropological interest. Along the way, time should be set aside for the sort of very detailed analysis of a particular data set that is best exemplified by the Kelleys' (this volume) remarkable reconstruction of the use of the Cerro del Chapín cross-circle. As Kelley knew, the grand sweep and the minutiae are equally important in understanding the past. To date, archaeology in west and northwest Mexico has perhaps concentrated a bit too much on the grand sweep.

Fortunately, there is a large pool of dedicated and competent scholars, many of them represented in this volume, working in the archaeology of west and northwest Mexico. They are well aware of the potential of this vast region to enrich, even revolutionize, our understanding of Mesoamerica. It is difficult to imagine a satisfactory account of mesoamerican history that does not include some of their stories: the great Tarascan state, which brought the Aztec war machine to a grinding halt in the west (Pollard 1993); the long Teuchitlán tradition, with its unique circular architecture, and the sociopolitical implications of that architecture (Weigand 1990a, 1996); and the Chalchihuites culture, with its extensive mines, complex architecture, and enigmatic mortuary displays (Abbott Kelley 1978; Kelley 1983b, 1990b). There is not much time to waste, however. As the pace of development and looting quickens (Mountjoy 1995d), we may once again find that the archaeology of central Mexico is showing us the way of the future. In this case, it is not a happy prospect (Parsons 1989).

REFERENCES

ABBREVIATIONS

CEMCA   Centre d'Etudes Mexicaines et Centramericaines
ENAH   Escuela Nacional de Antropología e Historia
INAH   Instituto Nacional de Antropología e Historia
HBMI   *Handbook of Middle American Indians*
MNA   Museo Nacional de Antropología
ORSTOM   Instituto de Investigación Científica para el Desarrollo en Cooperación
SAA   Society for American Archaeology
SEP   Secretaría de Educación Pública
SMA   Sociedad Mexicana de Antropología
UNAM   Universidad Nacional Autónoma de México

Abbott, E.
1960   *An Analysis of Mercado Red-on-Cream: A Diagnostic Ceramic Grouping of the Ayala Phase of the Chalchihuites Culture.* Unpublished Master's thesis, Department of Anthropology, Southern Illinois University, Carbondale.

Abbott Kelley, E.
1976   Gualterio Abajo: An Early Mesoamerican Settlement on the Northwestern Frontier. In *Las fronteras de Mesoamérica,* vol. 1, pp. 41–50. XIV Reunión de la Mesa Redonda, SMA, México, D.F.
1978   The Temple of the Skulls at Alta Vista, Chalchihuites. In *Across the Chichimec Sea: Papers in Honor of J. Charles Kelley,* edited by C. L. Riley and B. C. Hedrick, pp. 102–126. Southern Illinois University Press, Carbondale.

Abbott Kelley, E., and J. C. Kelley
1980   Sipapu and Pyramid Too: The Temple of the Crypt at Alta Vista, Chalchihuites. *Transactions of the Illinois State Academy of Science* 73:62–79. Springfield.

Acosta, J. R.
1939   Exploraciones arqueológicas realizadas en el estado de Michoacán durante los años de 1937 y 1938. *Revista Mexicana de Estudios Antropológicos* 3(2):85–99.

Adams, E. C.
1991   *The Origin and Development of the Pueblo Katsina Cult.* University of Arizona Press, Tucson.

Alcaraz L., L.
1991   Intentaban vender las piezas arqueológical. *Vallarta Opina* 12(4,732):1, 4. Puerto Vallarta, Jalisco.

Alegre, F. X.
1841   *Historia de la Compañía de Jesús en Nueva España.* 3 vols. México, D.F.

Algaze, G.
1993   Expansionary Dynamics of Some Early Pristine States. *American Anthropologist* 95:304–333.

Allen, B. L., and G. G. Connally
1977   Soil and Soil Stratigraphic Units of the West Mexican Coastal Plain (Abstract). *Geographical Society of America Abstracts with Programs* 9. Boulder.

Alvarez Palma, A. M.
1981   Machomoncobe, un sitio arqueológico en el área de Huatabampo. In *Memorias del VI Simposio de Historia de Sonora,* pp. 1–17. IIH-UNISON, Hermosillo.
1982   Archaeological Investigations at Huatabampo. In *Mogollon Archaeology: Proceedings of the 1980 Mogollon Conference,* edited by P. H. Beckett and K. Silverbird, pp. 239–250. Acoma Books, Ramona, California.

1985 Sociedades agrícolas. In *Historia general de Sonora (período prehistórico y prehispánico)*, vol. 1. Gobierno del Estado de Sonora, Hermosillo.

1991a Huatabampo: Consideraciones sobre una aldea agrícola prehispánica en el sur de Sonora. *Noroeste México* 9:9–93. Centro Regional Sonora, INAH, Hermosillo.

1991b La arqueología de las planicies del sur de Sonora y norte de Sinaloa. In *El noroeste de México: Sus culturas étnicas*. MNA, México, D.F.

Alvarez Palma, A. M., and M. E. Villalpando

1980 Investigaciones arqueológicas en el area de Huatabampo. In *Memorias del V Simposio de Historia de Sonora*. IIH-UNISON, Hermosillo.

Amadór, E.

1892 *Bosquejo histórico de Zacatecas*. Zacatecas.

Amsden, M.

1928 Archaeological Reconnaissance in Sonora. *Southwest Museum Papers* 1. Southwest Museum, Los Angeles.

Anawalt, Patricia R.

1998 They Came to Trade Exquisite Things: Ancient Mexican-Ecuadorian Contacts. In *Ancient West Mexico: Art and Archaeology of the Unknown Past*, edited by R. Townsend, pp. 233–249. Art Institute of Chicago and Thames and Hudson, London.

Anderson, A. J. O., and C. E. Dibble (translators and editors)

1953 *Florentine Codex: General History of the Things of New Spain, Book 7—The Sun, Moon, and Stars, and the Binding of the Years. Fray Bernardino de Sahagún.* Monographs of the School of American Research, no. 14, part 8. Santa Fe.

Anscheutz, K. F.

1995 Saving a Rainy Day: The Integration of Diverse Agricultural Technologies to Harvest and Conserve Water in the Lower Río Chama Valley, New Mexico. In *Soil, Water, Biology, and Belief in Prehistoric and Traditional Southwestern Agriculture*, edited by H. W. Toll, pp. 25–39. New Mexico Archaeological Council Special Publication 2. C & M Press, Denver.

Arensberg, C.

1968 The Urban in Cross-Cultural Perspective. In *Urban Life: Readings in Urban Anthropology*, edited by G. Gmelch and W. P. Zenner, pp. 37–47. St. Martin's Press, New York.

Armillas, P.

1964a Northern Mesoamerica. In *Prehistoric Man in the New World*, edited by J. D. Jennings and E. Norbeck, pp. 291–330. University of Chicago Press, Chicago.

1964b Condiciones ambientales y movimientos de pueblos en la frontera septentrional de México. In *Homenaje a Fernando Márquez-Miranda*, pp. 62–82. Publicaciones del Seminario de Estudios Americanistas y Seminario de Antropología Americana, Universidades de Madrid y Sevilla, Madrid.

1969 The Arid Frontier of Mexican Civilization. *Transactions of the New York Academy of Sciences*, ser. 2, 31(6):694–704. New York Academy of Sciences, New York.

Arnauld, M. C.

1987 Asentamientos lacustres prehispánicos en la ciénega de Zacapu: Problemas arqueológicos y sedimentológicos. Paper presented at El Hombre y los Lagos en el Centro y Occidente de México, CEMCA, México, D.F.

Arnauld, M. C., P. Carot, and M. F. Fauvet Berthelot

1988 Asentamientos lacustres en la ciénega de Zacapu, Michoacán (Preclásico-Postclásico). In *Primera Reunión sobre las Sociedades Prehispánicas en el Centro Occidente de México, Memoria*, edited by R. Brambila and A. M. Crespo, pp. 165–175. Cuaderno de Trabajo 1, Centro Regional de Querétaro, INAH, México.

1993 Arqueología de las lomas en la cuenca lacustre de Zacapu, Michoacán, México. *Collection Etudes Mesoaméricaines* 11–13, *Cuadernos de Estudios Michoacanos* 5. CEMCA, México, D.F.

Arnauld, M. C., and B. Faugere-Kalfon

1998 Evolución de la ocupación humana en el centro-norte de Michoacán (Proyecto Michoacán, CEMCA) y la emergencia del estado Tarasco. In *Génesis, culturas y espacios en Michoacán*, edited by V. Darras, pp. 13–34. CEMCA, México.

Aronson, M. A.

1993 *Technological Change: West Mexican Mortuary Ceramics*. Unpublished Ph.D. dissertation, Department of Materials Science and Engineering, University of Arizona, Tucson.

1996 Technological Change: Ceramic Mortuary Technology in the Valley of Atemajac from the Late Formative to the Classic Periods. *Ancient Mesoamerica* 7:163–168.

Ashmore, W. A. (editor)

1981 *Lowland Maya Settlement Patterns*. School of American Research, Santa Fe, and University of New Mexico Press, Albuquerque.

Aveleyra Arroyo de Anda, L.

1961 El primer hallazgo Folsom en territorio mexicano y su relación con el complejo de puntas acanaladas in Norteamérica. In *Homenaje a Pablo Martinez del Río, XXV Aniversario de la Primera Edició de los Origines Americanos*, pp. 31–48. INAH, México, D.F.

Aveleyra Arroyo de Anda, L., L. M. Maldonado Koerdell, and P. Martínez del Río

1956 *Cueva de la Candelaria*, vol. 1. Memorias del INAH, no. 5. México, D.F.

Aveni, A. F.

1980 *Skywatchers of Ancient Mexico*. University of Texas Press, Austin.

1988 The Thom Paradigm in the Americas. In *Records in Stone*, edited by C. Ruggles, pp. 442–472. Cambridge University Press, Cambridge.

1989 Pecked Cross Petroglyphs at Xihuingo. *Archaeoastronomy* 14:S73–S115.

Aveni, A. F., and H. Hartung

1985 Las cruces punteados en Mesoamérica: Version actualizada. In *Cuadernos de arquitectura mesoamericana* 4:3–13. UNAM, División de Estudios de Posgrado, Facultád de Architectura, México, D.F.

Aveni, A. F., H. Hartung, and B. Buckingham

1978 The Pecked Cross Symbol in Ancient Mesoamerica. *Science* 2:202–267.

Aveni, A. F., H. Hartung, and J. C. Kelley

1982 Alta Vista (Chalchihuites): Astronomical Implications of a Mesoamerican Ceremonial Outpost at the Tropic of Cancer. *American Antiquity* 47:316–335.

Bandelier, A. F.
1892 *Final Report of Investigations among the Indians of the Southwestern United States Carried on Mainly in the Years from 1880 to 1885*. Papers of the Archaeological Institute of America, American Series 4. Cambridge University Press, New York.

Bandelier, F. R.
1932 *A History of Ancient Mexico*. Fisk University Press, Nashville.

Bannon, J. F.
1955 *The Mission Frontier in Sonora, 1620–1687*. U.S. Catholic Historical Society Monograph Series, no. 26. New York.

Barnett, H. G.
1953 *Innovation: The Basis of Cultural Change*. McGraw-Hill, New York.

Bartlett, J. R.
1965 [1854] *Personal Narrative of Explorations and Incidents in Texas, New Mexico, California, Sonora, and Chihuahua, Connected with the United States and Mexican Boundary Commission during the Years 1850, 51, 52, and 53*. 2 vols. Río Grande Press, Chicago.

Batres, L.
1903 *Visita a los monumentos arqueológicos de "La Quemada," Zacatecas*. Imprenta de la Viuda de Francisco Díaz de León, México, D.F.

Baus de Czitrom, C.
1989 Panorama de datos del Formative en Colima y regiones cercanas. *El Preclásico o Formativo: Avances y perspectivas*, edited by M. Carmona M., pp. 27–38. INAH and MNA, México, D.F.

Beals, R. L.
1932 *The Comparative Ethnology of Northern Mexico before 1750*. Ibero-Americana, no. 2. University of California Press, Berkeley.
1933 *The Acaxee*. Ibero-Americana, no. 6. University of California Press, Berkeley.

Beaumont, P.
1932 *Crónica de Michoacán (1776–1780)*. Archivo General de la Nación, 17–19, México, D.F.

Beckett, P. H., and R. S. MacNeish
1994 The Archaic Chihuahua Tradition of South-Central New Mexico and Chihuahua, Mexico. In *Archaic Hunter-Gatherer Archaeology in the American Southwest*, edited by B. J. Vierra, pp. 335–337. Eastern New Mexico University Contributions in Anthropology, vol. 13, no. 1. Eastern New Mexico University, Portales.

Beekman, C. S.
1996a *The Long-Term Evolution of a Political Boundary: Archaeological Research in Jalisco, Mexico*. 2 vols. Unpublished Ph.D. dissertation, Department of Anthropology, Vanderbilt University.
1996b Political Boundaries and Political Structure: The Limits of the Teuchitlán Tradition. *Ancient Mesoamerica* 7:135–147.

Bell, B. B.
1971 Archaeology of Nayarit, Jalisco, and Colima. In *Archaeology of Northern Mesoamerica, Part 2*, edited by G. F. Ekholm and I. Bernal, pp. 694–753. HBMI, vol. 10, R. Wauchope, general editor. University of Texas Press, Austin.
1972 Archaeological Excavations in Jalisco, Mexico. *Science* 175:1238–1239.
1974 Excavations at El Cerro Encantado, Jalisco. In *The Archaeology of West Mexico*, edited by B. B. Bell, pp. 147–167. Sociedad de Estudios Avanzados del Occidente de México. Ajijic, Jalisco.

Bell, B. B. (editor)
1974 *The Archaeology of West Mexico*. Sociedad de Estudios Avanzados del Occidente de México. Ajijic, Jalisco.

Beltrán, U.
1982 *Tarascan State and Society in Prehispanic Times: An Ethnohistorical Inquiry*. Unpublished Ph.D. dissertation, Department of History, University of Chicago, Chicago.
1986 Estado y sociedad Tarascos. In *La sociedad indígena en el centro y occidente de México*, edited by P. Carrasco, pp. 45–62. El Colegio de Michoacán, Zamora.

Beltrán M., J. C.
1991 *Los concheros del Puerto de Salagua (Playa del Tesoro)*, vol. 1. Tesis Profesional, ENAH, INAH, México, D.F.

Bennett, W. C., and R. M. Zingg
1935 *The Tarahumara: An Indian Tribe of Northern Mexico*. University of Chicago Press, Chicago.

Bennyhoff, J. A.
1966 Chronology and Periodization: Continuity and Change in the Teotihuacán Ceramic Tradition. In *Teotihuacán, onceavamesa redonda: El valle de Teotihuacán y su contorno*, pp. 19–29. SMA, México, D.F.

Berger, R., R. E. Taylor, and W. F. Libby
1966 Radiocarbon Content of Marine Shells from the California and Mexican West Coast. *Science* 153:864–866.

Berlin, H.
1951 The Calendar of the Tzotzil Indians. In *The Civilization of Ancient America*, edited by Sol Tax, pp. 155–161. International Congress of the Americanists, Chicago.

Blackiston, A. H.
1905 Cliff Dwellings of Northern Mexico. *Records of the Past* 4:355–361.
1906a Casas Grandian Outposts. *Records of the Past* 5:142–147.
1906b Cliff Ruins of Cave Valley, Northern Mexico. *Records of the Past* 5:5–11.
1906c Ruins of the Cerro de Montezuma. *American Anthropologist* 8:256–261.
1908 Ruins of the Tenaja and the Río San Pedro. *Records of the Past* 7:282–290.
1909 Recently Discovered Cliff Dwellings of the Sierra Madre. *Records of the Past* 8:20–32.

Blanton, R. E., G. Feinman, S. Kowalewski, and P. Peregrine
1996 A Dual-Processual Theory for the Evolution of Mesoamerican Civilization. *Current Anthropology* 37:1–14.

Blanton, R. E., S. A. Kowalewski, G. M. Feinman, and J. Appel
1981 *Ancient Mesoamerica: A Comparison of Change in Three Regions.* Cambridge University Press, Cambridge.

Boehm de Lameiras, B., and P. C. Weigand (editors)
1992 *Origen y desarrollo de la civilización en el occidente de México.* El Colegio de Michoacán, Zamora.

Bordaz, J.
1964 *Precolumbian Ceramic Kilns at Peñitas, a Postclassic Site in Coastal Nayarit, Mexico.* Unpublished Ph.D. dissertation, Department of Anthropology, Columbia University, New York.

Bourke, J. G.
1886 *An Apache Campaign in the Sierra Madre.* Charles Scribner's Sons, New York.

Bové, F. J., S. Medrano B., B. Lou P., and B. Arroyo L. (editors)
1993 *El Proyecto Balberta: La transición entre el Formativo Terminal y el Clásico temprano en la costa Pacífica Guatemala.* University of Pittsburgh, Latin American Archaeology Publications, and the Asociación Tikal, Guatemala.

Bowen, T.
1969 *Seri Prehistory: The Archeology of the Central Coast of Sonora, Mexico.* Anthropological Papers, no. 27. University of Arizona Press, Tucson.
1972 *A Survey and Re-evaluation of the Trincheras Culture, Sonora, Mexico.* Ms. on file, Centro Regional de Sonora, Hermosillo.

Bowen, T., and E. Moser
1968 Seri Pottery. *The Kiva* 31(1):14-36.

Bradley, R. J.
1986 Shell Species and Exchange: A Brief Review of Shell at Casas Grandes and Its Role in Exchange on the Northwest Frontier of Mesoamerica. Paper presented at the 51st Annual Meeting of the SAA, New Orleans.
1987 Marine Shell Ornament Production at Casas Grandes, Chihuahua: The Role of Shell in Exchange Systems in Northwest Mexico and the Southwest. Paper presented at the 52nd Annual Meeting of the SAA, Toronto.
1993 Marine Shell Exchange in Northwest Mexico and the Southwest. In *The American Southwest and Mesoamerica: Systems of Prehistoric Exchange,* edited by J. E. Ericson and T. G. Baugh, pp. 121-151. Plenum Press, New York.
1996a *The Role of Casas Grandes in Prehistoric Shell Exchange Networks within the Southwest.* Unpublished Ph.D. dissertation, Department of Anthropology, Arizona State University, Tempe.
1996b Networks of Shell Ornament Exchange: A Critical Assessment of Prestige Economies in the North American Southwest. Paper presented at the 1996 Southwest Symposium, Tempe.
1999 Shell Exchange within the Southwest: The Casas Grandes Interaction Sphere. In *The Casas Grandes World,* edited by C. F. Schaafsma and C. L. Riley, pp. 213-228. University of Utah Press, Salt Lake City.

Brand, D. D.
1933 The Historical Geography of Northwestern Chihuahua. Unpublished Ph.D. dissertation, Department of Geography, University of California, Berkeley.
1935 The Distribution of Pottery Types in Northwest Mexico. *American Anthropologist* 37:287-305.
1936 *Notes to Accompany a Vegetation Map of Northwest Mexico.* University of New Mexico Bulletin, Biological Series, vol. 4, no. 4.
1937 *The Natural Landscape of Northwestern Chihuahua.* University of New Mexico Bulletin, Geological Series, vol. 5, no. 2.
1939 Notes on the Geography and Archaeology of Zape, Durango. In *So Live the Works of Men: Seventieth Anniversary Volume Honoring Edgar Lee Hewett,* edited by D. D. Brand and F. E. Harvey, pp. 75-105. University of New Mexico Press, Albuquerque.
1943a The Chihuahua Culture Area. *New Mexican Anthropologist* 6-7:115-158.
1943b An Historical Sketch of Geography and Anthropology in the Tarascan Region. *New Mexico Anthropologist* 6-7(2):37-108.
1958 *Coastal Study of Southwest Mexico, Part II.* Department of Geography, University of Texas, Austin.
1980 A Persistent Myth in the Ethnohistory of Western Mexico. *Tlalocan* 7:419-436.

Braniff C., B.
1965 Investigaciones arqueológicas en Guanajuato, México, 1965: Consideraciones preliminares. Ms. on file, MNA, México, D.F.
1972 Sequencias arqueológicas en Guanajuato y la cuenca de México: Intento de correlación. In *Teotihuacán,* XI Mesa Redonda, SMA, 2:273-323. México, D.F.
1974 Oscilación de la frontera septentrional mesoamericana. In *The Archaeology of West Mexico,* edited by B. B. Bell, pp. 40-50. Sociedad de Estudios Avanzados del Occidente de México, Ajijic, Jalisco.
1975a The West Mexican Tradition and the Southwestern United States. *The Kiva* 41:215-222.
1975b Arqueología del norte de México. In *Los pueblos y señoríos teocráticos: El período de las ciudades urbanas,* pp. 217-272. Panorama Histórico y Cultural 7. INAH, México, D.F.
1985 *La frontera protohistórica Pima-Opata en Sonora, México: Proposiciones arqueológicas preliminares.* 3 vols. Instituto de Investigaciones Antropológicas, UNAM. México, D.F.
1986 Ojo de Agua, Sonora, and Casas Grandes, Chihuahua: A Suggested Chronology. In *Ripples in the Chichimec Sea: New Considerations of Southwestern-Mesoamerican Interactions,* edited by F. J. Mathien and R. H. McGuire, pp. 70-80. Southern Illinois University Press, Carbondale.
1988 A propósito de el ulama en el norte de México. *Arqueología* 3:47-94. Dirección de Monumentos Prehispánicos, INAH, México, D.F.
1989a Oscilación de la frontera mesoamericana: Un nuevo ensayo. *Arqueología* 1:99-114.
1989b El Formative en el norte de México. In *El Preclásico o Formativo: Avances y perspectivas,* edited by M. Carmona Macias, pp. 443-460. MNA, INAH. México, D.F.

1990 Comentarios—Avances y perspectivas sobre la región del norte de México y su desarrollo en los siglos XI al XII. In *Mesoamerica y norte de México, siglo IX-XII: Seminario de Arqueología "Wigberto Jiménez Moreno,"* edited by F. Sodi Miranda, pp. 655-656. INAH, México, D.F.

1991a La serrana sonorense. *El noroeste de México: Sus culturas étnicas.* MNA, México, D.F.

1991b La estratigrafía de Morales, Guanajuato: La cerámica. Informe, Subdirección de Estudios Arqueológicos. INAH, México, D.F.

1992a *La estratigrafía arqueológica de Villa de Reyes, San Luis Potosí.* Colección Científica, INAH. México, D.F.

1992b *La frontera protohistórica Pimaopata en Sonora, México: Proposiciones arqueológicas preliminares,* vols. 1-3. Colección Científica, Serie Arqueología. INAH, México, D.F.

1995 Diseños tradicionales mesoamericanos y norteños: Ensayo de interpretación. In *Arqueología del norte y del occidente de México: Homenaje al Doctor J. Charles Kelley,* edited by B. Dahlgren y Ma. D. Soto de Archavaleta, pp. 181-209. Instituto de Investigaciones Antropológicas, UNAM, México, D.F.

1998 *Morales, Guanajuato, y la tradición Chupícuaro.* Colección Científica, Serie Arqueología. INAH, México, D.F.

Bravo Ugarte, J.
1962 *Historia sucinta de Michoacán.* Vol. 1, *Michoacán: El estado tarasco.* Editorial Jús, México, D.F.

Bray, W.
1989 Fine Metal Jewelry from Southern Mexico. In *Homenaje a J. L. Lorenzo,* edited by L. Mirambell, pp. 243-275. Serie Prehistoria, no. 188, INAH, México, D.F.

Breitburg, E.
1993 The Evolution of Turkey Domestication in the Greater Southwest and Mesoamerica. In *Culture and Contact: Charles C. Di Peso's Gran Chichimeca,* edited by A. I. Woosley and J. C. Ravesloot, pp. 153-172. University of New Mexico Press, Albuquerque.

Brooks, R. H.
1971 *Lithic Traditions in Northwestern Mexico, Paleo-Indian to Chalchihuites.* Unpublished Ph.D. dissertation, Department of Anthropology, University of Colorado, Boulder.

1978 A Loma San Gabriel/Chalchihuites Cultural Manifestation in the Río Ramos Region, Durango, Mexico. In *Across the Chichimec Sea: Papers in Honor of J. Charles Kelley,* edited by C. L. Riley and B. C. Hedrick, pp. 83-95. Southern Illinois University Press, Carbondale.

Brooks, R. H., M. S. Foster, and S. T. Brooks
1985 Observed Mortuary Practices from La Cueva de los Muertos Chiquitos, near Zape Chico, Durango, Mexico. Paper presented at the 50th Annual Meeting of the SAA. Denver.

Brooks, R. H., L. Kaplan, H. C. Cutler, and T. W. Whitaker
1962 Plant Material from a Cave on the Río Zape, Durango, Mexico. *American Antiquity* 27:356-369.

Brooks, S. T., and R. H. Brooks
1978 Paleoepidemiology as a Possible Interpretation of Multiple Child Burials near Zape Chico, Durango, Mexico. In *Across the Chichimec Sea: Papers in Honor of J. Charles Kelley,* edited by C. L. Riley and B. C. Hedrick, pp. 96-101. Southern Illinois University Press, Carbondale.

1980 Cranial Deformation: Possible Evidence of Pochteca Trading Movements. *Transactions of the Illinois State Academy of Science* 72:4:1-12. Springfield.

Brown, D. E.
1982a Madrean Evergreen Woodland. *Desert Plants* 4(1-4):59-65.
1982b Plains and Great Basin Grasslands. *Desert Plants* 4:(1-4):115-121.
1982c Semidesert Grassland. *Desert Plants* 4:(1-4):123-131.
1982d Chihuahuan Desertscrub. *Desert Plants* 4:(1-4):169-179.

Brown, J. A., R. A. Kerber, and H. D. Winters
1990 Trade and the Evolution of Exchange Relations at the Beginning of the Mississippian Period. In *The Mississippian Emergence,* edited by B. D. Smith, pp. 251-280. Smithsonian Institution Press, Washington, D.C.

Brown, R. B.
1985 A Synopsis of the Archaeology of the Central Portion of the Northern Frontier of Mesoamerica. In *The Archaeology of West and Northwest Mesoamerica,* edited by M. S. Foster and P. C. Weigand, pp. 219-236. Westview Press, Boulder.

Brumfiel, E., and T. Earle
1987 *Specialization, Exchange, and Complex Societies.* Cambridge University Press, Cambridge.

Bunzel, R.
1959 *Chichicastenango.* University of Washington Press, Seattle.

Burland, C. A.
1950 *The Four Directions of Time.* Page 1 of Codex Fejerary Mayer. Reproduced in serigraph by Louie Ewino. Santa Fe, New Mexico.

Brush, C. F.
1965 Pox Pottery: Earliest Identified Mexican Ceramic. *Science* 149:3680:194-195.

Butterwick, C.
1993 Architectural Figures and Archaeology of West Mexico. Ms. on file, Denver Museum of Natural History.

Cabrera Castro, R.
1986 El desarrollo cultural prehispánico del Bajo Río Balsas. In *Arqueología y etnohistoria del estado de Guerrero,* pp. 119-151. INAH y Gobierno del Estado de Guerrero.

1987 Tzintzuntzan: Décima temporada de excavaciones. *Homenaje a Román Piña Chan,* pp. 531-565. Serie Antropología 79. Instituto de Investigaciones Antropológicas, UNAM, México, D.F.

Cabrero G., M. T.
1989 *Civilización en el norte de México: Arqueología de la Cañada del Río Bolaños.* Serie Antropología 103. Instituto de Investigaciones Antropológicas, UNAM, México, D.F.

1992 La cultura Bolaños como respuesta a una tendencia expansiva. In *Origen y desarrollo de la civilización en el occidente de México,* edited by B. Boehm de L. and P. C. Weigand, pp. 339–358. El Colegio de Michoacán, Zamora.

1994 Las costumbres funerarias de la cultura de Bolaños y su relación con la tradición de tumbas de tiro del occidente de México. In *Arqueología del occidente de México,* edited by E. Williams and R. Novella, pp. 61–92. El Colegio de Michoacán, Zamora.

1995 *La muerte en el occidente del México prehispánico.* UNAM, México, D.F.

1998 Algunas consideraciones de carácter socioeconómicas de la "Cultura de Bolaños." In *El occidente de México: Arqueología, historia y medio ambiente: Perspectivas regionales,* edited by R. Avila, J. P. Emphoux, L. Gastélum, S. Ramírez, O. Schöndube, and F. Valdez, pp. 287–294. ORSTOM, Universidad de Guadalajara, Guadalajara.

Cabrero G., M. T., and C. López

1998 Las tumbas de tiro de El Piñón, el Cañón de Bolaños. *Latin American Antiquity* 9:328–341.

Cárdenas, E.

1998 *El Bajío en el Protoclásico (300 dC): Análisis regional y organización política.* Tesis, El Colegio de Michoacán, Zamora.

Carey, H. A.

1931 An Analysis of Northwestern Chihuahua Culture. *American Anthropologist* 33:325–374.

1954 Grant No. 1597 (1953): The Ancient Indian Culture Centering in the Casas Grandes Valley, Northwestern Chihuahua, Mexico. *Yearbook of the American Philosophical Society,* pp. 313–316.

1955 Grant No. 177: The Casas Grandes Culture, Chihuahua, Mexico. *Yearbook of the American Philosophical Society,* pp. 314–316.

Carlson, J. B.

1991 *Venus Regulated Warfare and Ritual Sacrifice in Mesoamerica: Teotihuacán and Cacaxtla.* Technical Publication no. 7. Center for Archaeoastronomy, University of Maryland, College Park.

1993 Rise and Fall of the City of the Gods. *Archaeology:* 46:6:58–69.

Carlson, R. L.

1982 The Polychrome Complexes. In *Southwestern Ceramics: A Comparative Review,* edited by A. H. Schroeder, pp. 201–234. *Arizona Archaeologist* 15. Arizona Archaeological Society, Phoenix.

Carot, P.

1990 La originalidad de Loma Alta, sitio protoclásico de la Ciénega de Zacapu. In *La época Clásica: Nuevos hallazgos, nuevas ideas,* edited by A. Cardos de Mendez, pp. 293–306. MNA and INAH, México, D.F.

1992 La cerámica protoclásica del sitio de Loma Alta, municipio de Zacapu, Michoacán: Nuevos datos. In *Origen y desarrollo de la civilización en el occidente de México,* edited by B. Boehm de L. and P. C. Weigand, pp. 69–101. El Colegio de Michoacán, Zamora.

Carot, P., M. F. Fauvet Berthelot, L. Barba, K. Link, A. Ortiz, and A. Hesse

1998 La arquitectura de Loma Alta, Zacapu, Michoacán. In *El occidente de México: Arqueología, historia y medio ambiente: Perspectivas regionales,* edited by R. Avila, J. P. Emphoux, L. Gastélum, S. Ramirez, O. Schöndube B., and F. Faldez, pp. 345–361. ORSTOM, Universidad de Guadalajara, Guadalajara.

Carpenter, J. P.

1985 The Obsidian Hydration Dating of the Joyce Well Site. Report on file, Laboratory of Anthropology, Museum of New Mexico, Santa Fe.

1996 *El ombligo en la labor: Differentiation, Interaction, and Integration in Prehispanic Sinaloa, Mexico.* Unpublished Ph.D. dissertation, Department of Anthropology, University of Arizona, Tucson.

1997 Passing through the Netherworld: New Insights from the American Museum of Natural History's Sonora-Sinaloa Archaeological Project (1937–1940). In *Prehistory of the Borderlands: Recent Research in the Archaeology of Northern Mexico and the Southern Southwest,* edited by J. P. Carpenter and G. Sanchez, pp. 113–127. Arizona State Museum, University of Arizona, Tucson.

Carpenter, J. P., G. Sánchez, and M. E. Villalpando

1997 Rescate arqueológico La Playa (SON:F:10:3), municipio de Trincheras, Sonora. Informe al Consejo de Arqueología, INAH, México, D.F.

Carrasco, P.

1986 Economía política en el reino Tarasco. In *La sociedad indígena en el centro y occidente de México,* edited by P. Carrasco, pp. 63–102. El Colego de Michoacán, Zamora.

Caso, A.

1930 Informe preliminar de las exploraciones realizadas en Michoacán. *Anales del Museo Nacional de Arqueología, Historia y Etnografía* 6:446–452.

1943 The Calendar of the Tarascans. *American Antiquity* 9:11–20.

1967 *Los calendarios prehispánicos.* UNAM, México, D.F.

1971 Calendrical Systems of Central Mexico. In *Archaeology of Northern Mesoamerica,* part 1, edited by G. F. Ekholm and I. Bernal, pp. 333–348. HBMI, vol. 10, R. Wauchope, general editor. University of Texas Press, Austin.

Castañeda, C., B. Cervantes, A. M. Crespo, and L. M. Flores

1989 Poblamiento prehispánico en el centro norte de la frontera mesoamericana. *Antropología* 28:34–43.

Castañeda, C., L. M. Flores, A. M. Crespo, J. A. Contreras, T. Durán, and J. C. Saint-Charles

1988 Interpretación de la historia del asentamiento en Guanajuato. In *Primera Reunión sobre las Sociedades Prehispánicas en el Centro Occidente de México,* edited by R. Brambila and A. M. Crespo, pp. 331–356. INAH, México, D.F.

Castañeda, R. A.

1892 Las ruinas indígenas de Chalchihuites. In *Bosquejo histórico de Zacatecas,* edited by E. Amadór, pp. 231–238. Zacatecas, Zacatecas.

Castillo T., N.

1968 *Algunas técnicas decorativas de la cerámica arqueológica de México.* Seire Investigaciones 16. INAH, México, D.F.

Castro-Leal, M.
1986 *Tzintzuntzan, capital de los Tarascos*. Gobierno del Estado de Michoacán, Morelia.

Castro-Leal, M., and L. Ochoa
1975 El Ixtepete como un ejemplo de desarrollo cultural en el occidente de México. *Anales del Instituto Nacional de Antropología e Historia*, Época 7a, 5:121–154.

Cattaneo, C.
1956 (1845) *Scritti economici*, vol. 3. Edited by Alberto Bertolini, pp. 3–30. Florence.

Cervantes, B., A. M. Crespo, and L. M. Flores
1981 Tunal grande frontera de equilibrio para Mesoamérica. *Fronteras* 13:257–266.
1989 Tunal grande frontera de equilibrio para Mesoamérica. *Fronteras*, Arqueología Especial 13:257–266. Teruel.

Chadwick, R.
1971 Archaeological Synthesis of Michoacán and Adjacent Regions. In *Archaeology of Northern Mesoamerica*, vol. 11, part 2, edited by G. F. Ekholm and I. Bernal, pp. 657–693. HBMI, R. Wauchope, general editor. University of Texas Press, Austin.

Chapman, K.
1979 *People, Pattern, and Process: An Introduction to Human Geography*. Edward Arnold, London.

Chase, D. Z., and A. F. Chase
1992 *Mesoamerican Elites: An Archaeological Assessment*. University of Oklahoma Press, Norman.

Chi, C.
1963 [1936] *Key Economic Areas in Chinese History, as Revealed in the Development of Public Works for Water-Control*. Reprint. Paragon, New York.

Clavijero, F. J.
1974 *Historia antigua de México*. Cuarta Edición, Colección "Sepan Cuantos" 29. Editorial Porrúa, México, D.F.

Cobean, R. H.
1978 *The Pre-Aztec Ceramics of Tula, Hidalgo, Mexico*. Unpublished Ph.D. dissertation, Department of Anthropology, Harvard University, Cambridge.
1990 *La cerámica de Tula, Hidalgo*. Colección Científica, Estudios sobre Tula 2. INAH, México, D.F.

Connally, G. G.
1974 A Soil Stratigraphic Model for the Age and Origin of the West Mexican Coastal Plain. In *The Marismas Nacionales of Mexico: Report on Continuing Investigations of the Archaeology and Related Natural Science Studies*. West Mexican Prehistory, part 8, pp. 5–20. State University of New York at Buffalo.
1977 The West Mexican Coastal Plain: Physiographic Definition (Abstract). *Geological Society of America Abstracts with Programs*, vol. 5, Boulder.
1984a Soil Stratigraphy and Inferred Tectonic History of the West Mexican Coastal Plain. In *Neotectonics and Sea Level Variations in the Gulf of California*, edited by V. Malpica-Cruz, S. Celis-Gutiérrez, J. Guerrero-García, and L. Otrlieb, pp. 56–73. Hermosillo.
1984b Age and Origin of the Teacapan Peninsula and Surrounding Areas of the Marismas Nacionales, West Mexico. Manuscript.

Contreras, E.
1986 *Paquimé, zona arqueológica de Casas Grandes, Chihuahua*. Centro Regional de Chihuahua, INAH, Chihuahua.

Contreras R., J. A.
1987 *La presencia tarasca en el estado de Guanajuato: Fluctuación de fronteras*. Tesis para Licenciatura, Universidad Veracruzana, Xalapa.
1990 Río Lerma, frontera norte mesoamericana? *Revista Mexicana de Estudios Antropológicos* 36:147–162.

Coon, C. S.
1950 *A Reader in General Anthropology*. Henry Holt, New York.

Corona Núñez, J.
1950 Informe referente al descubrimiento y exploración en San Juan de Abajo, perteneciente al municipio de Compostela. Report on file, Archivo del INAH, Departamento de Monumentos Prehispánicos, México, D.F.
1955 *Tumba de El Arenal, Etzatlán, Jalisco*. Informes no. 3. INAH, México, D.F.
1957 *Mitología tarasca*. Fondo de Cultura Económica, México, D.F.
1958 *Exploración en las ruinas del Teul de González Ortega, Zacatecas*. Informe, Archivo Técnico del INAH, Zacatecas.
1972 Los Teotihuacanos en el occidente de México. In *Teotihuacán*. XI Mesa Redonda, SMA, 2:253–256. México, D.F.

Cottrell, D. J.
1973 Some Geomorphological Aspects of the Marismas Nacionales. In *The Marismas Nacionales of Mexico: Report on Continuing Investigations of the Archaeology and Related Natural Science Studies*. West Mexican Prehistory, part 6. Department of Geology, State University of New York at Buffalo.

Covarrubias, M.
1957 *Indian Art of Mexico and Central America*. Alfred A. Knopf, New York.
1961 Notas para la estudio de la arqueología de la costa de Jalisco. *Eco* 7:4–7.

Cowgill, G.
1996 Discussion. *Ancient Mesoamerica* 7:325–331.
1997 State and Society at Teotihuacán, Mexico. *Annual Review of Anthropology* 26:129–161.

Crabtree, R.
1961 Two Urn Burials from Santa Cruz, Nayarit. Ms. on file, Department of Anthropology, University of California, Los Angeles.

Crane, H. R., and J. B. Griffin
1958a University of Michigan Radiocarbon Dates II. *Science* 127:1098–1105.
1958b University of Michigan Radiocarbon Dates III. *Science* 128:117–123.

Crespo, A. M.
1976 *Villa de Reyes, San Luis Potosí*. Colección Científica, no. 24. INAH, México, D.F.
1986a La cerámica blanco levantado en la secuencia de El Cerrito, Querétaro. Paper presented at the Reunion sobre Cerámicas Prehispánicas en el Centro Occidente de México, Morelia.

1986b Elementos cerámicos en asentamientos toltecas de Guanajuato y Querétaro. Paper presented at el Homenaje al Doctor J. Charles Kelley, Zacatecas.

1991 El recinto ceremonial de El Cerrito. In *Querétaro prehispanico*, edited by A. M. Crespo and R. Brambila, pp. 163–223. Colección Científica. INAH, México, D.F.

Crespo, A. M., and R. Brambila (editors)
1991 *Querétaro prehispánico*. Colleción Científica. INAH, México, D.F.

Crown, P. L.
1994 *Ceramics and Ideology: Salado Polychrome Pottery.* University of New Mexico Press, Albuquerque.

Cruz, C. L.
1994 *Modelo de un sistema de intercambio en el occidente de México durante el Clásico mesoamericano con énfasis en el Cañon de Bolaños, Jalisco y Zacatecas.* Tesis, Licenciado en Arqueología, ENAH, INAH. México, D.F.

Cruz A., R
1997 Recientes investigaciones arqueológicas en Villa Ahumada, Chihuahua. In *Prehistory of the Borderlands: Recent Research in the Archaeology of Northern Mexico and the Southern Southwest*, edited by J. Carpenter and G. Sánchez, pp. 1–9. Arizona State Museum Archaeological Series, no. 186. Arizona State Museum, University of Arizona, Tucson.

Cruz A., R., and T. D. Maxwell
1999 The Villa Ahumada Site: Archaeological Investigations East of Paquimé. In *The Casas Grandes World*, edited by C. F. Schaafsma and C. L. Riley, pp. 43–53. University of Utah Press, Salt Lake City.

Culbert, T. P.
1977 Early Maya Development at Tikal, Guatemala. In *The Origins of Maya Civilization*, edited by R. Adams, pp. 27–43. School of American Research, Santa Fe, and the University of New Mexico Press, Albuquerque.

Culbert, T. P., and D. S. Rice (editors)
1990 *Precolumbian Population History in the Maya Lowlands.* University of New Mexico Press, Albuquerque.

Curtin, P. D.
1986 *Cross-Cultural Trade in World History.* Cambridge University Press, Cambridge.

Cutler, H. C.
1978 Corn from Seven Durango (Mexico) Caves. In *Across the Chichimec Sea: Papers in Honor of J. Charles Kelley*, edited by C. L. Riley and B. C. Hedrick, pp. 186–189. Southern Illinois University Press, Carbondale.

Dahlgren, B., and Ma. D. Soto de Arechavaleta (editors)
1995 *Arqueología del norte y del occidente de México: Homenaje al Doctor J. Charles Kelley.* Instituto de Investigaciones Antropológicas, UNAM, México, D.F.

Darling, J. A.
1990 Informe de la primera temporada del Proyecto Arqueológico del Valley de Tlaltenango, Zacatecas. Report on file, Archivo Técnico de INAH, Zacatecas.
1993a Obsidian Sources in the Valle de Tlaltenango, Zacatecas. Paper presented at the symposium Perspectivas sobre la Arqueología de la Periferia Septentrional de Mesoamérica, Zacatecas.
1993b Notes on Obsidian Sources of the Southern Sierra Madre Occidental. *Ancient Mesoamerica* 4:245–253.
1998 *Obsidian Distribution and Exchange in the North-Central Frontier of Mesoamerica.* Unpublished Ph.D. dissertation, Department of Anthropology, University of Michigan, Ann Arbor.

Darras, V.
1994 Las actividades de talla en los talleres de obsidiana del conjunto Zináparo-Prieto, Michoacán. In *Arqueología del occidente de México: Nuevas aportaciones*, edited by E. Williams and R. Novella, pp. 139–158. El Colegio de Michoacán, Zamora.
1998 La obsidiana en la *Relación de Michoacán* y en la realidad arqueológica: Del símbolo al uso del uso de un símbolo. In *Génesis, culturas y espacios en Michoacán*, by V. Darras, pp. 61–88. CEMCA, México, D.F.

Davies, N.
1987 *The Aztec Empire: The Toltec Resurgence.* University of Oklahoma Press, Norman.

Day, J. S.
1994 Central Mexican Imagery in Greater Nicoya. In *Mixteca-Puebla: Discoveries and Research in Mesoamerican Art and Archaeology*, edited by H. B. Nicholson and E. Quiñones Keber, pp. 235–248. Labyrinthos Press, Culver City, California.

Dean, J. S., and J. C. Ravesloot
1993 The Chronology of Cultural Interaction in the Gran Chichimeca. In *Culture and Contact: Charles C. Di Peso's Gran Chichimeca*, edited by A. I. Woosley and J. C. Ravesloot, pp. 83–103. University of New Mexico Press, Albuquerque.

DeAtley, S. P.
1980 *Regional Integration of Animas Phase Settlements on the Northern Casas Grandes Frontier.* Unpublished Ph.D. dissertation, Department of Anthropology, University of California, Los Angeles.

DeAtley, S. P., and F. J. Findlow
1982 Regional Integration of the Northern Casas Grandes Frontier. In *Mogollon Archaeology: Proceedings of the 1980 Mogollon Conference*, edited by P. H. Beckett and K. Silverbird, pp. 263–277. Acoma Books, Ramona, California.

Delgado, D.
1969 *Arquitectura funeraria precolombina en el estado de Jalisco.* Unpublished Master's thesis, Department of Anthropology, University of California, Los Angeles.

Díaz del Castillo, B.
1956 [1632] *The Discovery and Conquest of Mexico, 1517–1521*, edited by I. A. Leonard. Farrar, Straus, and Cudahy, New York.

Díaz O., C.
1987 *El occidente de México.* García Valadéz, Editores, México, D.F.
1993 Ocoyoacac: Un sitio con influencia teotihuacana en el valle de Toluca. Paper presented at the Taller de Discusión de la Cronología de Teotihuacán. Centro de Estudios Teotihuacanos, Teotihuacán, México, D.F.

Diehl, R. A. (editor)
1974 *Studies of Ancient Tollan: A Report of the University of Missouri Tula Archaeological Project.* University of Missouri Monographs in Anthropology 1. Columbia.

Diehl, R. A., and J. C. Berlo (editors)
1989 *Mesoamerica after the Decline of Teotihuacán, A.D. 700–900.* Dumbarton Oaks, Washington, D.C.

Diehl, R. A., R. Lomes, and J. T. Wynn
1974 Toltec Trade with Central America: New Light and Evidence. *Archaeology* 27:182–187.

Di Peso, C. C.
1965 The Clovis Fluted Point from the Timmy Site, Northwest Chihuahua, Mexico. *The Kiva* 31:83–87.
1966 Archaeology and Ethnohistory of the Northern Sierra. In *Archaeological Frontiers and External Connections,* edited by G. F. Ekholm and G. R. Willey, pp. 3–25. HBMI, vol. 4, R. Wauchope, general editor. University of Texas Press, Austin.
1968a Casas Grandes and the Gran Chichimeca. *El Palacio* 75:4:45–61.
1968b Casas Grandes: A Fallen Trading Center of the Gran Chichimeca. *Masterkey* 42:20–37.
1971a Casas Grandes Water Control System. *Cochise Quarterly* 1:7–11.
1971b Use and Abuse of Southwestern Rivers: The Pueblo Dweller. In *Hydrology and Water Resources in Arizona and the Southwest: American Water Resources Association, Arizona Section, and Arizona Academy of Science, Hydrology Section, Meetings, 1971, Proceedings,* vol. 1, pp. 381–396.
1974 *Casas Grandes: A Fallen Trading Center of the Gran Chichimeca,* vols. 1–3. Amerind Foundation Publications, Dragoon, Arizona, and Northland Press, Flagstaff, Arizona.
1983 The Northern Sector of the Mesoamerican World System. In *Forgotten Places and Things: Archaeological Perspectives on American History,* edited by A. E. Ward, pp. 11–21. Contributions to Anthropological Studies 3. Center for Anthropological Research, Albuquerque.

Di Peso, C. C., J. B. Rinaldo, and G. J. Fenner
1974 *Casas Grandes: A Fallen Trading Center of the Gran Chichimeca,* vols. 4–8. Amerind Foundation Publications, Dragoon, Arizona, and Northland Press, Flagstaff, Arizona.

Dirst, V. A.
1979 *A Prehistoric Frontier in Sonora.* Unpublished Ph.D. dissertation, Department of Anthropology, University of Arizona, Tucson.

Doolittle, W. E.
1984 Settlements and the Development of "Statelets" in Sonora, Mexico. *Journal of Field Archaeology* 11:13–24.
1988 *Pre-Hispanic Occupance in the Valley of Sonora, Mexico: Archaeological Confirmations of Early Spanish Reports.* Anthropological Papers, no. 48. University of Arizona Press, Tucson.
1990 *Canal Irrigation in Prehistoric Mexico: The Sequence of Technological Change.* University of Texas Press, Austin.
1993 Canal Irrigation at Casas Grandes: A Technological and Developmental Assessment of Its Origins. In *Culture and Contact: Charles C. Di Peso's Gran Chichimeca,* edited by A. I. Woosley and J. C. Ravesloot, pp. 133–151. University of New Mexico Press, Albuquerque.

Douglas, J. E.
1987 Late Prehistoric Archaeological Remains in the San Bernardino Valley, Southeastern Arizona. *The Kiva* 53:35–52.
1990 *Regional Interaction in the Northern Sierra: An Analysis Based on the Late Prehistoric Occupation of the San Bernardino Valley, Southeastern Arizona.* Unpublished Ph.D. dissertation, Department of Anthropology, University of Arizona, Tucson.
1992 Distant Sources, Local Contexts: Interpreting Nonlocal Ceramics at Paquimé (Casas Grandes), Chihuahua. *Journal of Anthropological Research* 48:1–24.
1995 Autonomy and Regional Systems in the Late Prehistoric Southern Southwest. *American Antiquity* 60:240–257.

Doyel, D. E.
1976 Salado Cultural Development in the Tonto Basin and Globe-Miami Areas, Central Arizona. *The Kiva* 42:5–16.

Drennan, R. D.
1984a Long-Distance Transport Costs in Pre-Hispanic Mesoamerica. *American Anthropologist* 88:105–112.
1984b Long-Distance Movement of Goods in the Mesoamerican Formative and Classic. *American Antiquity* 49:27–43.

Earle, T. (editor)
1991 *Chiefdoms: Power, Economy, and Ideology.* Cambridge University Press, New York.

Edmonson, M. S.
1988 *The Book of the Year: Middle American Calendrical Systems.* University of Utah Press, Salt Lake City.

Ekholm, G. F.
1940 The Archaeology of Northern and Western Mexico. In *The Maya and Their Neighbors,* pp. 307–320. D. Appleton-Century, New York.
1942 *Excavations at Guasave, Sinaloa, Mexico.* Anthropological Papers of the American Museum of Natural History, 38(2). New York.

Ekholm, K.
1977 External Exchange and the Transformation of Central African Social Systems. In *The Evolution of Social Systems,* edited by J. Friedman and M. J. Rowlands, pp. 115–136. Duckworth, London.

Epstein, J. F.
1969 *The San Isidro Site: An Early Man Campsite in Nuevo León, Mexico.* Anthropology Series, no. 7. Department of Anthropology, University of Texas, Austin.

Escudero, J.
1834 *Noticias estadísticas del estado de Chihuahua.* México, D.F.

Estrada Balmori, E.
1945 La decoración en la cerámica de Chupícuaro. *Revista Mexicana de Estudios Antropológicos* 7(1, 2, 3):103–112. SMA, México, D.F.

Estrada Balmori, E., and R. Piña Chan
1948 Complejo funerario en Chupícuaro. In *El occidente de México: Cuarta Reunión de Mesa Redonda*, pp. 40–41. SMA, México, D.F.

Fahmel Beyer, B.
1981 *Dos vajillas toltecas de comercio: Tohil Plumbate y Fine Orange*. Tesis Profesional, ENAH, INAH, México, D.F.
1988 *Mesoamérica tolteca: Sus cerámicas de comercio principales*. Serie Antropológica 95. Instituto de Investigaciones Antropológicas, UNAM, México, D.F.

Faulhaber, J.
1960 Breve análisis osteológico de los restos humanos de La Quemada, Zacatecas. *Anales del Instituto Nacional de Antropología e Historia* 12:131–149.

Felger, Richard S., and Mary Beck Moser
1985 *People of the Desert and Sea*. University of Arizona Press, Tucson.

Ferdon, E. N., Jr.
1955 *A Trial Survey of Mexican-Southwestern Architectural Parallels*. School of American Research Monographs, no. 21. Santa Fe.
1995 The Early Setting. In *The Gran Chichimeca: Essays on the Archaeology and Ethnohistory of Northern Mesoamerica*, edited by J. E. Reyman, pp. 8–12. Avebury Press, Brookfield, Vermont.

Findlow, F. J.
1979 A Catchment Analysis of Certain Prehistoric Settlements in Southwestern New Mexico. *Journal of New World Archeology* 3:1–15.

Findlow, F. J., and M. Bolognese
1982 Regional Modeling of Obsidian Procurement in the American Southwest. In *Contexts for Prehistoric Exchange*, edited by J. E. Ericson and T. K. Earle, pp. 53–81. Academic Press, New York.

Findlow, F. J., and S. P. DeAtley
1976 Prehistoric Land Use Patterns in the Animas Valley: A First Approximation. *Anthropology UCLA* 6:1–57.
1978 An Ecological Analysis of Animas Phase Assemblages in Southwestern New Mexico. *Journal of New World Archeology* 2:6–18.

Fischer, C. S.
1976 *The Urban Experience*. Harcourt, Brace, and Jovanovich, New York.

Fish, S. K.
1995 Mixed Agricultural Technologies in Southern Arizona and Their Implications. In *Soil, Water, Biology, and Belief in Prehistoric and Traditional Southwestern Agriculture*, edited by H. W. Toll, pp. 101–116. New Mexico Archaeological Council Special Publication 2. C & M Press, Denver.

Fish, S. K., P. R. Fish, and J. H. Madsen
1992 *The Marana Community in the Hohokam World*. Anthropological Papers, no. 56. University of Arizona Press, Tucson.

Fisher, C., H. P. Pollard, and C. Federick
1998 Landscape Change and Socio-Political Development within the Lake Pátzcuaro Basin. Paper presented at the 63rd Annual Meeting of the SAA, Seattle.

Florance, C. A.
1985 Recent Work in the Chupícuaro Region. In *The Archaeology of West and Northwest Mesoamerica*, edited by M. S. Foster and P. C. Weigand, pp. 9–45. Westview Press, Boulder.
1989 *A Survey and Analysis of Late and Terminal Preclassic Settlement along the Lerma River in Southeastern Guanajuato, Mexico*. Unpublished Ph.D. dissertation, Department of Anthropology, Columbia University, New York.
1993 The Preclassic in Southeastern Guanajuato and Observations on the Relationships with the Basin of Mexico and West Mexico. Paper presented at Perspectivas sobre la Arqueología de la Periferia Septentrional de Mesoamérica, Zacatecas.

Flores de Aguirrezabal, Ma. D., and C. A. Quijada López
1980 Distribución de objetos de metal en el occidente de México. In *Rutas de intercambio en Mesoamérica y norte de México* 2:83–88. XVI Mesa Redonda, SMA, México, D.F.

Folan, W., L. Folan, and A. Ruiz P.
1987 La iconografía de Huamango, municipio de Acambay, estado de México: Un centro regional otomí de los siglos IX a XIII. In *Homenaje a Roman Piña Chan*, edited by B. Dahlgren, C. Navarrete, L. Ochoa, M. del C. Serra Puche and Y. Sugiura, pp. 411–453. UNAM, México, D.F.

Folan, W., E. Kintz, and L. Fletcher
1983 *Coba: A Classic Maya Metropolis*. Academic Press, New York.

Ford, James
1969 *A Comparison of Formative Cultures in the Americas*. Smithsonian Institution Press, Washington, D.C.

Foster, M. S.
1978 *Loma San Gabriel: A Prehistoric Culture of Northwest Mexico*. Unpublished Ph.D. dissertation, Department of Anthropology, University of Colorado, Boulder.
1980 Loma San Gabriel: Una cultura del noroeste de Mesoamérica. In *Rutas de intercambio en Mesoamérica y norte de México*, vol. 2, pp. 175–182. XVI Mesa Redonda, SMA, Saltillo, Coahuila.
1981 Loma San Gabriel Ceramics. PANTOC 1:17–36. Universidad Autónoma de Guadalajara.
1982 The Loma San Gabriel-Mogollon Continuum. In *Mogollon Archaeology: Proceedings of the 1980 Mogollon Conference*, edited by P. H. Beckett and K. Silverbird, pp. 251–261. Acoma Books, Ramona, California.
1984 Loma San Gabriel Subsistence Patterns: A Preliminary Discussion. *Anthropology* 8:1:13–30.
1985 The Loma San Gabriel Occupation of Zacatecas and Durango, Mexico. In *The Archaeology of West and Northwest Mesoamerica*, edited by M. S. Foster and P. C. Weigand, pp. 327–351. Westview Press, Boulder.
1986a The Weicker Site: A Loma San Gabriel Hamlet in Durango, Mexico. *Journal of Field Archaeology* 13:7–20.
1986b The Mesoamerican Connection: A View from the South. In *Ripples in the Chichimec Sea: New Considerations of Southwestern-Mesoamerican Interactions*, edited by F. J. Mathien and R. H. McGuire, pp. 55–69. Southern Illinois University Press, Carbondale.

1989 El Preclásico en el noroeste de Mesoamérica: Perspectivas. In *El Preclásico o Formativo: Avances y perspectivas: Seminario de Arqueología "Dr. Roman Piña Chan,"* edited by M. Carmona Macias, pp. 425–442. INAH, México, D.F.

1990 Casas Grandes as a Mesoamerican Center and Culture. In *Actas del Primer Congreso de Historia Regional Comparada 1989,* edited by A. Márquez-Alameda, pp. 33–39. Universidad Autónoma de Ciudad Juárez, Juárez.

1991 The Early Ceramic Period in Northwest Mexico: An Overview. In *Mogollon V,* edited by Patrick H. Beckett, pp. 155–165. COAS Publishing and Research, Las Cruces, New Mexico.

1992 Arqueología del valle de Casas Grandes: Sitio Paquimé. In *Historia general de Chihuahua I: Geología, geografía y arqueología,* edited by A. Márquez-Alameda, pp. 229–282. Universidad Autónoma de Ciudad Juárez y Gobierno del Estado de Chihuahua, Chihuahua.

1993 Lowland-Highland Exchange in Western Mesoamerica: West Coast Ceramics in the Highlands of Northwest Mexico. Paper presented at the Seminario de Arqueología, Perspectivas sobre la Arqueología Septentrional de Mesoamérica, Zacatecas.

1994 The Metates Mine Project: A Report on a Reconnaissance Survey of the Project Area and Related Background Information. Report prepared for Western Cultural Resource Management, Boulder.

1995a The Chalchihuites Chronological Sequences: A View from the West Coast of Mexico. In *Arqueología del norte y del occidente de México: Homenaje al Doctor J. Charles Kelley,* edited by B. Dahlgren and Ma. D. Soto de Arechavaleta, pp. 67–92. Instituto de Investigaciones Antropológicas, UNAM, México, D.F.

1995b The Loma San Gabriel Culture and Its Suggested Relationships to Other Early Plainware Cultures of Northwest Mesoamerica. In *The Gran Chichimeca: Essays on the Archaeology and Ethnohistory of Northern Mesoamerica,* edited by J. E. Reyman, pp. 179–207. Avebury Press, Brookfield, Vermont.

1999 The Aztatlán Tradition of West and Northwest Mexico and Casas Grandes: Speculations on the Medio Period Florescence. In *The Casas Grandes World,* edited by C. F. Schaafsma and C. L. Riley, pp. 149–163. University of Utah Press, Salt Lake City.

Foster, M. S., and P. C. Weigand (editors)
1985 *Archaeology of West and Northwest Mexico.* Westview Press, Boulder.

Freddolino, M. K.
1973 *An Investigation into the "Pre-Tarascan" Cultures of Zacapu, Michoacán, Mexico.* Unpublished Ph.D. dissertation, Department of Anthropology, Yale University, New Haven.

Freidel, D. A.
1979 Culture Areas and Interaction Spheres: Contrasting Approaches to the Emergence of Civilization in the Maya Lowlands. *American Antiquity* 44:36–54.

Friedman, J., and M. J. Rowlands
1977 *The Evolution of Social Systems.* Duckworth, London.

Frierman, Jay D. (editor)
1969 *The Natalie Wood Collection of Pre-Columbian Ceramics from Chupícuaro, Guanajuato, Mexico.* Occasional Papers of the Museum and Laboratories of Ethnic Arts and Technology, no. 1. University of California, Los Angeles.

Fritz, G. L.
1969 Investigations at the Rancho el Espia Site, Northwestern Chihuahua. *Transactions of the Fifth Archaeological Symposium for Southeastern New Mexico and Western Texas,* pp. 51–63. El Llano Archaeological Society, Portales, New Mexico.

Fry, R. E. (editor)
1979 *Models and Methods in Regional Exchange.* SAA Papers, no. 1.

Furst, P. T.
1966 *Shaft Tombs, Shell Trumpets, and Shamanism: A Cultural-Historical Approach to Problems in West Mexican Archaeology.* Unpublished Ph.D. dissertation, Department of Anthropology, University of California, Los Angeles.

1974 Some Problems in the Interpretation of West Mexican Tomb Art. In *The Archaeology of West Mexico,* edited by B. B. Bell, pp. 132–146. Sociedad de Estudios Avanzados del Occidente de México, Ajijic, Jalisco.

1999 Shamanic, Symbolism, Transformation, and Deities in West Mexican Funerary Art. *Ancient West Mexico: Art and Archaeology of the Unknown Past,* edited by R. Townsend, pp. 169–190. Art Institute of Chicago and Thames and Hudson, London.

Gali, R.
1946 Arqueología de Tzintzuntzan. *Anales del Museo Michoacano* 2(4):50–62.

Gallaga M., E.
1997 *Análisis de la cerámica policroma del sitio Cerro de Trincheras, Sonora, México.* Tesis, ENAH, INAH, México, D.F.

Galván, J.
1976 *Rescate arqueológico en el fraccionamiento tabachines, Zapopan, Jalisco.* Cuadernos de los Centros 28. Dirección de los Centros Regionales, INAH, México, D.F.

1991 *Las tumbas de tiro del valle de Atemejac, Jalisco.* Colección Científica, Serie Arqueología 239. INAH, México, D.F.

Gámio, M.
1910 Los monumentos arqueológicos de las inmediaciones de Chalchihuites, Zacatecas. *Anales del Museo Nacional de Arqueología, Historia y Etnología* 2:469–492. Museo Nacional de Arqueología, Historia e Etnología, México, D.F.

Ganot R., J., and A. Peschard F.
1990 El Postclásico temprano en el estado de Durango. In *Mesoamérica y norte de México, siglo IX–XII,* edited by F. S. Miranda, pp. 401–416. INAH and MNA, México, D.F.

1995 The Archaeological Site of El Cañón del Molino, Durango, Mexico. In *The Gran Chichimeca: Essays on the Archaeology and Ethnohistory of Northern Mesoamerica,* edited by J. E. Reyman, pp. 146–178. Avebury Press, Brookfield, Vermont.

REFERENCES

1997 *Aztatlán: Apuntes para la historia y arqueología de Durango*. Secretaría de Educación, Cultura y Desporte. Gobierno del Estado de Durango.

Ganot R., J., J. F. Lazalde, and A. A. Peschard F.
1983 Relación prehispánica entre las culturas del noroeste de México y el sitio El Cañón del Molino en el estado de Durango. Paper presented at the XVIII Mesa Redonda of the SMA, Taxco.

García A., A.
1976 Estratificación social entre los Tarascos prehispánicos. In *Estratificación social en la Mesoamérica prehispánica*, edited by P. Carrasco and J. Broda, pp. 221–214. Centro de Investigaciones Superiores, INAH, México, D.F.

García C., P.
1842 *Ensayo estadístico sobre el estado de Chihuahua*. Chihuahua.
1849 *El album mexicana*. México, D.F.

García Cook, A., and F. Rodríguez
1975 Excavaciones arqueológicas en Gualupita las Dalias, Puebla. *Communicaciones, Proyecto Puebla-Tlaxcala* 12:1–8. Fundación Alemana para Investigación Científica, Puebla.

García M., C. (editor)
1988 *La antropología en el norte de México*. Colección Biblioteca del INAH. INAH, México, D.F.

Geertz, C.
1973 *The Interpretations of Cultures*. Basic Books, New York.

Gerald, R. E.
1990 Report on a University of Texas at El Paso Mini-Grant to Investigate Prehistoric Fortifications in a Primitive State in the Casas Grandes Area of Chihuahua. *The Artifact* 28(3):59–64.

Gifford, E. W.
1950 *Surface Archaeology of Ixtlán del Río, Nayarit*. University of California Publications in American Archaeology and Ethnology, 43:183–302. University of California Press, Berkeley.

Gill, G. W.
1971 *The Prehistoric Inhabitants of Northern Coastal Nayarit: Skeletal Analysis and Description of Burials*. Unpublished Ph.D. dissertation, Department of Anthropology, University of Kansas, Lawrence.
1985 Cultural Implications of Artificially Modified Human Remains from Northwestern Mexico. In *The Archaeology of West and Northwest Mesoamerica*, edited by M. S. Foster and P. C. Weigand, pp. 193–215. Westview Press, Boulder.

Gladwin, H. S., E. B. Haury, E. B. Sayles, and N. Gladwin
1938 *Excavations at Snaketown: Material Culture*. Gila Pueblo Medallion Papers, no. 25. Gila Pueblo, Globe, Arizona.

Glaascock, M., R. S. Herrera, and H. Neff
1997 Hydration and Source Analysis of Obsidian from Excavated Archaeological Contexts in the Municipality of Puerto Vallarta, Mexico. *Report from the Research Reactor Center*. University of Missouri, Columbia.

Glassow, M. A.
1967 The Ceramics of Huistla, a West Mexican Site in the Municipality of Etzatlán, Jalisco. *American Antiquity* 32:64–83.

Gómez Gastélum, L., and R. A. de la Torre Ruiz
1996 Figurillas "Cerrito de García" de la cuenca de Sayula, Jalisco. *Estudios del Hombre* 3:127–150. Universidad de Guadalajara, Guadalajara.

González, L. A.
1985 The Bolsón de Mapimí Archaeological Project. In *The Archaeology of West and Northwest Mesoamerica*, edited by M. S. Foster and P. C. Weigand, pp. 383–391. Westview Press, Boulder.
1992 La población prehispánica Cazadora-Recolectora y el desierto de Chihuahua. In *Historia general de Chihuahua I: Geología, geografía y arqueología*, edited by A. Márquez-Alameda, pp. 163–185. Universidad Autónoma de Ciudad Juárez and Gobierno del Estado de Chihuahua, Chihuahua.

González Crespo, N.
1979 *Patrón de asentamientos prehispánicos en la parte central del Bajo Balsas: Un ensayo metodológico*. Departamento de Prehistoria, Colección Científica 73. INAH, México, D.F.

Gorenstein, S.
1985 *Acambaro on the Tarascan-Aztec Frontier*. Vanderbilt University Publications in Anthropology, no. 32. Nashville.

Gorenstein, S., and H. Perlstein Pollard
1983 *The Tarascan Civilization: A Late Prehispanic Cultural System*. Vanderbilt University Publications in Anthropology, no. 28. Nashville.
1991 Xanhari: Protohistoric Tarascan Routes. In *Ancient Road Networks and Settlement Hierarchies in the New World*, edited by C. D. Trombold, pp. 169–185. Cambridge University Press, Cambridge.

Gossen, G. H.
1974 A Chamula Calendar Board. In *Mesoamerican Archaeology: New Approaches*, edited by N. Hammond, pp. 217–253. Duckworth, London.

Gottman, J.
1964 De la ville d'aujourd'hui à la ville de demain: La transition vers la ville nouvelle. *Prospective* 11:171–180. Paris.

Graham, J. A. (editor)
1966 *Ancient Mesoamerica*. Peek Publications, Palo Alto, California.

Graham, M. M.
1989 Tomb of Life: The Symbolism of Seashells in the Pre-Columbian Art of West Mexico. Report on file, El Colegio de Michoacán.

Greengo, R. E., and C. W. Meighan
1976 Additional Perspective on the Capacha Complex of Western Mexico. *Journal of New World Archaeology* 1:5:15–23.

Griffen, W. B.
1988a *Apaches at War and Peace: The Janos Presidio, 1750–1858*. University of New Mexico Press, Albuquerque.
1988b *Utmost Good Faith: Patterns of Apache-Mexican Hostilities in Northern Chihuahua Border Warfare, 1821–1848*. University of New Mexico Press, Albuquerque.

Griffin-Pierce, T.
1992 *Earth Is My Mother, Sky Is My Father: Space, Time, and Astronomy in Navajo Sandpainting.* University of New Mexico Press, Albuquerque.

Grinberg, D. M. K. de
1988 Relaciones metalúrgias en América prehispánica: III—Tecnologias metalúrgicas tarascas. Paper presented at the 46th International Congress of Americanists, Amsterdam.

Grosscup, G.
1964 *The Ceramics of West Mexico.* Unpublished Ph.D. dissertation, Department of Anthropology, University of California at Los Angeles.
1976 The Ceramic Sequence at Amapa. In *The Archaeology of Amapa, Nayarit,* edited by C. W. Meighan, pp. 208–272. Monumenta Archaeologica, 2. Institute of Archaeology, University of California at Los Angeles.

Guevara L., G.
1981 *Reporte de la zona arqueológica de Chacalilla, municipio de San Blas, Nayarit.* Cuadernos de los Centros Regionales: Occidente, no. 1. INAH, México, D.F.

Guevara Sánchez, A.
1984 *Las Cuarenta Casas: Un sitio arqueológico del estado de Chihuahua.* Cuadernos de Trabajo, 27. Departamento de Prehistoria, INAH, México, D.F.
1985 *Apuntes para la arqueología de Chihuahua.* Cuaderno de Trabajo, 1. Centro Regional de Chihuahua, INAH.
1986 *Arqueología del área de las Cuarenta Casas, Chihuahua.* Colección Científica, no. 151. INAH, México, D.F.
1988 *Arqueología del valle de las Cuevas, Chihuahua: Reconocimientos.* Cuadernos de Trabajo, 5. Dirección de Monumentos Prehispánicos, INAH, México, D.F.
1991 Algunos aspectos de la aculturación de los grupos conchos del centro del estado de Chihuahua. In *Actas del Segundo Congreso Historia Regional Comparada 1990.* Universidad Autónoma de Ciudad Juárez, Juárez.
1994 *Sitio arqueológico de la Ferrería, Durango: Trabajos de 1993.* Colección Durango. Gobiernor del Estado de Durango, Secretaría de Educación, Cultura y Deporte, Dirección de Asunto Culturales, Durango.

Guevara Sánchez, A., and D. A. Phillips, Jr.
1992 Arqueología de la Sierra Madre Occidental en Chihuahua. In *Historia general de Chihuahua I: Geología, geografía y arqueología,* edited by A. Márquez-Alameda, pp. 187–213. Universidad Autónoma de Ciudad Juárez and Gobierno del Estado de Chihuahua, Chihuahua.

Guillemin-Tarayre, E.
1867 Notes archéologiques et ethnographiques: Vestiges laissés par les migrations américaines dans le nord du Mexique. *Commission Scientifique de Mexique* 3:341–470. Paris.
1869 *Exploration minéralogique des régions mexicaines.* Paris.

Hammond, G. P., and A. Rey (translators, editors, and annotators)
1928 *Obregón's History of Sixteenth Century Explorations in Western America Entitled: Chronicle, Commentary, or Relation of the Ancient and Modern Discoveries in New Spain, New Mexico, and Mexico, 1584.* Wetzel, Los Angeles.

Handlin, O., and J. Burchard (editors)
1963 *The Historian and the City.* MIT Press, Cambridge.

Harbottle, G.
1975 Activation Analysis Study of Ceramics from the Capacha (Colima) and Opeño (Michoacán) Phases of West Mexico. *American Antiquity* 40:453–458.

Harbottle, G., and P. C. Weigand
1992 Turquoise in Pre-Columbian America. *Scientific American* 266(2):78–85.

Hard, R. J., and J. R. Roney
1998 A Massive Terraced Village Complex in Chihuahua, Mexico, 3000 Years before Present. *Science* 279:1661–1664.

Hardy, R. W. H.
1829 *Travels in the Interior of Mexico.* London.

Hassig, R.
1985 *Trade, Tribute, and Transportation.* University of Oklahoma Press, Norman.
1988 *Aztec Warfare: Imperial Expansion and Political Control.* University of Oklahoma Press, Norman.

Haury, E. W.
1976 *The Hohokam: Desert Farmers and Craftsmen.* University of Arizona Press, Tucson.

Hayden, J. D.
1976 Pre-altithermal Archaeology in the Sierra Pinacate, Sonora, Mexico. *American Antiquity* 41:3:274–289.

Healan, D. M.
1992 Proyecto arqueológico en la región de Zinapécuaro, Michoacán: Análisis de materiales. *Boletín del Consejo de Arqueología, 1991,* pp. 147–148. INAH, México, D.F.
1997 Prehispanic Quarrying in the Ucareo-Zinapécuaro Obsidian Area. *Ancient Mesoamerica* 8:77–100.

Healan, D. M. (editor)
1989 *Tula of the Toltecs: Excavations and Survey.* University of Iowa Press, Iowa City.

Heizer, R. F., and J. A. Bennyhoff
1972 Archaeological Investigation of Cuicuilco, Mexico, 1957. *National Geographic Society Research Reports, 1955–60,* pp. 93–104. Washington, D.C.

Helms, M. W.
1979 *Ancient Panama: Chiefs in Search of Power.* University of Texas Press, Austin.

Herold, L. C.
1965 *Trincheras and Physical Environment along the Río Gavilán, Chihuahua, Mexico.* Publications in Geography, Technical Paper 65(1). University of Denver, Denver.

Herold, L. C., and R. F. Miller
1995 Water Availability for Plant Growth in Precolumbian Terrace Soils, Chihuahua, Mexico. In *Soil, Water, Biology, and Belief in Prehistoric and Traditional Southwestern Agriculture,* edited by H. W. Toll, pp. 145–153. New Mexico Archaeological Council Special Publication 2. C & M Press, Denver.

Herrejón Peredo, C.
1978 La pugna entre Mexicas y Tarascos. *Cuadernos de*

Historia 1:11–47. Universidad Autónoma del Estado de México, Toluca, México.

Hers, M. A.
1988 Caracterización de la cultura chalchihuites. In *Primera Reunión sobre las Sociedades Prehispánicas en el Centro Occidente de México: Memoria,* edited by R. Brambila and A. M. Crespo, pp. 23–37. INAH, México, D.F.
1989a *Los Toltecas en tierras chichimecas.* Cuadernos de Historia del Arte, 35. Instituto de Investigaciones Estéticas, UNAM, México, D.F.
1989b Existió la cultura loma San Gabriel? El caso de Hervideros, Durango. *Anales del Instituto de Investigaciones Estéticas* 60:33–57.
1993a La Sierra del Nayar en el contexto del septentrión mesoamericano. Paper presented in Seminario de Arqueología, Perspectivas sobre la Arqueología de la Periferia Septentrional de Mesoamérica. INAH, Zacatecas, Zacatecas.
1993b Investigaciones arqueológicas en Hervideros, Durango: Primeros avances. *Transición* 13:4–12.

Hewett, E. L.
1908 *Les communautés anciennes dans le désert américain.* Librairie Kundig, Geneva.
1923 Anahuac and Aztlan: Retracing the Legendary Footsteps of the Aztecs. *Art and Archaeology* 16(1–2):35–50.
1936 *Ancient Life in Mexico and Central America.* Bobbs-Merrill, Indianapolis.

Hill, W. D.
1992 *Chronology of the El Zurdo Site, Chihuahua.* Unpublished Master's thesis, Department of Archaeology, University of Calgary, Calgary.

Hines, M. H., S. A. Tomka, and K. W. Kibler
1994 *Data Recovery Excavations at the Wind Canyon Site, 41HZ119, Hudspeth County, Texas.* Reports of Excavations, no. 99. Dewitt and Associates, Austin, Texas.

Hirth, K. G.
1978 Interregional Trade and the Formation of Prehistoric Gateway Communities. *American Antiquity* 43:35–45.

Hodder, I.
1980 Trade and Exchange: Definitions, Identification, and Function. In *Models and Methods in Regional Exchange,* edited by R. E. Fry, pp. 151–156. SAA Papers, no. 1.

Holien, T.
1977 *Mesoamerican Pseudo-Cloisonné and Other Decorative Investments.* Unpublished Ph.D. dissertation, Department of Anthropology, Southern Illinois University, Carbondale.

Holien, T., and R. Pickering
1978 Analogues in a Chalchihuites Culture Sacrificial Burial. In *Middle Classic Mesoamerica, A.D. 400–700,* edited by E. Pasztory, pp. 145–157. Columbia University Press, New York.

Holmes, W. H.
1914 Area of American Culture Characterization Tentatively Outlined as an Aid in the Study of Antiquities. *American Anthropologist* 16:413–446.

Hosler, D. H.
1988a Ancient West Mexican Metallurgy: A Technological Chronology. *Journal of Field Archaeology* 15:191–217.
1988b Ancient West Mexican Metallurgy: South and Central American Origins and West Mexican Transformations. *American Anthropologist* 90:832–855.
1994 *The Sounds and Colors of Power: The Sacred Metallurgical Technology of Ancient West Mexico.* MIT Press, Cambridge.

Hosler, D., and A. Macfarlane
1996 Copper Sources, Metal Production, and Metals Trade in Late Postclassic Mesoamerica. *Science* 273:1819–1824.

Howard, A. M.
1957 Navacoyan: A Preliminary Survey. *Bulletin of the Texas Archaeological Society* 28:181–189.

Howard, W. A., and T. M. Griffiths
1966 *Trinchera Distribution in the Sierra Madre Occidental, Mexico.* Publications in Geography, Technical Paper 66(1). University of Denver, Denver.

Hrdlicka, A.
1903 The Region of the "Chichimecs," with Notes on the Tepecanos and the Ruin of La Quemada, Mexico. *American Anthropologist* 5:385–440.

Hubbs, C. L., and G. I. Roden
1964 Oceanography and Marine Life along the Pacific Coast. In *Natural Environment and Early Cultures,* edited by R. C. West, pp. 143–186. HBMI, vol. 1, R. Wauchope, general editor. University of Texas Press, Austin.

Hurtado Mendoza, F.
1986 *La religión prehispánica de los Purhépechas.* Un testimonio del Pueblo Tarasco, Morelia.

Hutchinson, G. E., R. Patrick, and E. Deevey
1956 Sediments of Lake Pátzcuaro, Michoacán, México. *Bulletin of the Geological Society of America* 67:1491–1504.

INEGI (Instituto Nacional de Estadística, Geografía e Informática)
1985 *Síntesis geográfica del estado de Michoacán.* INEGI, Secretaría de Programación y Presupuesto, México, D.F.

Jackson, J. B.
1984 *Discovering the Vernacular Landscape.* Yale University Press, New Haven.

Jaramillo Luque, R.
1984 *Patron de asentamiento en el valle de Valparaiso, Zacatecas.* Tesis de Licenciatura, ENAH, INAH, México, D.F.

Jay, P.
1957 *Archaeological Investigations at La Manga, Durango, Mexico.* Unpublished Master's thesis, Department of Anthropology, Southern Illinois University, Carbondale.

Jiménez B., P.
1988 Ciertas inferencias de la arqueología del sur de Zacatecas. In *Primera Reunión sobre las Sociedades Prehispánicas en el Centro Occidente de México: Memoria,* edited by R. Brambila and A. M. Crespo, pp. 39–50. Centro Regional de Querétaro, Cuaderno de Trabajo 1. INAH, México, D.F.
1989 Perspectivas sobre la arqueología de Zacatecas.

Arqueología 5:33–50. Dirección de Monumentos Prehispánicos, INAH, México, D.F.

1990 Proyecto La Quemada temporada, 1987–1988. *Boletín del Consejo de Arqueología,* pp. 67–70. INAH, México, D.F.

1992a Una red de interacción del noroeste de Mesoamérica: Una interpretación. In *Origen y desarrollo de la civilización en el occidente de México: Homenaje a Pedro Armillas y Angel Palerm,* edited by B. B. d. Lameiras and P. C. Weigand, pp. 177–204. El Colegio de Michoacán, Zamora.

1992b Proyecto La Quemada. *Boletín del Consejo de Arqueología, 1991,* pp. 149–153. INAH, México, D.F.

1995 Algunas observaciones sobre la dinámica cultural de la arqueología de Zacatecas. In *Arqueología del norte y del occidente de México: Homenaje al Doctor J. Charles Kelley,* edited by B. Dahlgren and Ma. D. Soto de Arechavaleta, pp. 35–66. Instituto de Investigaciones Antropológicas, UNAM, México, D.F.

1997 Avances recientes in la arqueología del valle de Malpaso (La Quemada). Paper presented in the IV Coloquio Bosch-Gimpera. Instituto Investigaciones Antropológicas, UNAM, México, D.F.

1998 Areas de interacción del noroeste mesoamericano. In *Memoria, VI Coloquio de Occidentalistas,* edited by R. Avila, J. Emphoux, L. Gastélum, S. Ramírez, O. Schöndube, and F. Valdez, pp. 295–303. ORSTOM, Universidad de Guadalajara, CEMCA, UNAM, Guadalajara.

Johnson, A. E.

1960 *The Place of the Trincheras Culture of Northern Sonora in Southwestern Archaeology.* Unpublished Master's thesis, Department of Anthropology, University of Arizona, Tucson.

1963 The Trincheras Culture of Northern Sonora. *American Antiquity* 29:174–186.

1966 Archaeology of Sonora, Mexico. In *Archaeological Frontiers and External Connections,* edited by G. F. Ekholm and G. R. Willey, pp. 26–37. HBMI, vol. 4, R. Wauchope, general editor. University of Texas Press, Austin.

Keen, A. M.

1958 *Sea Shells of Tropical West America.* Stanford University Press, Stanford.

Kelley, J. C.

1952a The Historic Indian Pueblos of La Junta de los Rios. *New Mexico Historical Review* 27:257–295.

1952b Factors Involved in the Abandonment of Certain Peripheral Southwestern Settlements. *American Anthropologist* 54:355–387.

1953a The Historic Indian Pueblos of La Junta de los Rios. *New Mexico Historical Review* 28:21–51.

1953b Report of Reconnaissance and Excavation in Durango and Southern Chihuahua, Mexico. In *Yearbook of the American Philosophical Society,* pp. 172–176.

1955 Juan Sabeata and Diffusion in Aboriginal Texas. *American Anthropologist* 57:981–995.

1956 Settlement Patterns in North-Central Mexico. In *Prehistoric Settlement Patterns in the New World,* edited by G. R. Willey, pp. 128–139. Viking Fund Publications in Anthropology, no. 23. New York.

1963 *Northern Frontier of Mesoamerica.* First Annual Report: August 5, 1961–August 15, 1962. Report submitted to the National Science Foundation, Washington, D.C.

1966 Mesoamerica and the Southwestern United States. In *Archaeological Frontiers and External Connections,* edited by G. F. Ekholm and G. R. Willey, pp. 95–110. HBMI, vol. 4, R. Wauchope, general editor. University of Texas Press, Austin.

1971 Archaeology of the Northern Frontier: Zacatecas and Durango. In *Archaeology of Northern Mesoamerica, Part 2,* edited by G. F. Ekholm and I. Bernal, pp. 768–801. HBMI, vol. 11, R. Wauchope, general editor. University of Texas Press, Austin.

1974 Speculations on the Culture History of Northwestern Mexico. In *The Archaeology of West Mexico,* edited by B. B. Bell, pp. 19–39. Sociedad de Estudios Avanzados del Occidente de México, Ajijic, Jalisco.

1983a Hypothetical Functioning of the Major Postclassic Trade System of West and Northwest Mexico. Paper presented at the XVIII Mesa Redonda of the SMA, Taxco.

1983b *El centro ceremonial en la cultura de Chalchihuites.* Instituto de Investigaciones Antropológicas, Secretaría Ejecutiva del Consejo de Estudios de Posgrado, UNAM, México, D.F.

1985a The Chronology of the Chalchihuites Culture. In *The Archaeology of West and Northwest Mesoamerica,* edited by M. S. Foster and P. C. Weigand, pp. 269–287. Westview Press, Boulder.

1985b A Review of the Archaeological Sequence at La Junta de los Rios. In *Proceedings of the Third Jornada Mogollon Conference,* edited by M. S. Foster and T. C. O'Laughlin. *The Artifact* 23(1–2):149–159.

1986a The Mobile Merchants of Molino. In *Ripples in the Chichimec Sea: New Considerations of Southwestern-Mesoamerican Interactions,* edited by F. J. Mathien and R. H. McGuire, pp. 81–105. Southern Illinois University Press, Carbondale.

1986b *Jumano and Patarabueye: Relations at La Junta de los Rios.* Anthropological Papers, Museum of Anthropology, University of Michigan, no. 77. Ann Arbor.

1989a The Retarded Formative of the Northwest Frontier of Mesoamerica. In *El Preclásico o Formativo: Avances y perspectivas: Seminario de Arqueología "Dr. Roman Piña Chan,"* edited by M. Carmona Macias, pp. 405–423. INAH, México, D.F.

1989b A Brief Commentary on the Archaic Horizon in Western Durango and Zacatecas, Mexico. Ms. on file, Centro Regional Zacatecas, INAH.

1990a The Early Post-Classic in Northern Zacatecas and Durango: IX to XII Centuries. In *Mesoamérica y norte de México, siglos IX–XII,* edited by F. Sodi Miranda, pp. 487–519. SMA-INAH, México, D.F.

1990b The Classic Epoch in the Chalchihuites Culture of the State of Zacatecas. In *La época Clásica: Nuevos hallazgos, nuevas ideas,* edited by A. Cardos de Mendez, pp. 11–14. MNA and INAH, México, D.F.

1991 The Known Ballcourts of Durango and Zacatecas. In *The Mesoamerican Ballgame,* edited by V. L. Scar-

borough and D. R. Wilcox, pp. 87–101. University of Arizona Press, Tucson.
1992 La cuenca del Río Conchos: Historia, arqueología y significado. In *Historia general de Chihuahua I: Geología, geografía y arqueología,* edited by A. Márquez-Alameda, pp. 131–136. Universidad Autónoma de Ciudad Juárez and Gobierno del Estado de Chihuahua, Chihuahua.
1993 Zenith Passage: The View from Chalchihuites. In *Culture and Contact: Charles C. Di Peso's Gran Chichimeca,* edited by A. I. Woosley and J. C. Ravesloot, pp. 227–250. University of New Mexico Press, Albuquerque.
1995 Trade Goods, Traders, and Status in Northwestern Greater Mesoamerica. In *The Gran Chichimeca: Essays on the Archaeology and Ethnohistory of Northern Mesoamerica,* edited by J. E. Reyman, pp. 102–145. Avebury Press, Brookfield, Vermont.

Kelley, J. C., and E. Abbott Kelley
1966 The Cultural Sequence on the North Central Frontier of Mesoamerica. *Actas y Memorias del XXXVI Congreso Internacional de Americanistas* 1:325–344.
1971 *An Introduction to the Ceramics of the Chalchihuites Culture of Zacatecas and Durango, Mexico, Part 1: The Decorated Wares.* Mesoamerican Studies, no. 5. Research Records of the University Museum, Southern Illinois University, Carbondale.
1975 An Alternative Hypothesis for the Explanation of Anasazi Culture History. In *Collected Papers in Honor of Florence Hawley Ellis,* edited by T. R. Frisbie, pp. 178–223. Papers of the Archaeological Society of New Mexico, no. 2. Hooper Publishing, Norman, Oklahoma.

Kelley, J. C., and W. J. Shackelford
1954 Preliminary Notes on the Weicker Site, Durango. *El Palacio* 61:145–150.

Kelley, J. C., W. W. Taylor, and P. Armillas
1961 Archaeological and Ecological Investigation of the North Central Frontier of Mesoamerica and the Relationships of the Cultures of Central Mesoamerica, the Gran Chichimeca, and the American Southwest. Research proposal submitted to the National Science Foundation. Southern Illinois University, Carbondale.

Kelley, J. C., and H. D. Winters
1960 A Revision of the Archaeological Sequence in Sinaloa, Mexico. *American Antiquity* 25:547–561.

Kelley, J. H., L. C. Neff, and A. C. MacWilliams
1996 Report of the 1996 Field Season, Proyecto Arqueológico Chihuahua. Report submitted to INAH.

Kelley, J. H., and J. D. Stewart
1991 Proyecto Arqueológico Chihuahua. *Boletín del Consejo de Arqueología, 1990.* INAH, México, D.F.
1992 Proyecto Arqueológico Chihuahua, temporada de 1991. *Boletín del Consejo de Arqueología, 1991.* INAH, México, D.F.

Kelley, J. H., J. D. Stewart, A. C. MacWilliams, and L. C. Neff
1999 A West Central Chihuahuan Perspective on Chihuahuan Culture. In *The Casas Grandes World,* edited by C. F. Schaafsma and C. L. Riley, pp. 63–78. University of Utah Press, Salt Lake City.

Kelly, I.
1938 *Excavations at Chametla, Sinaloa.* Ibero-Americana 14. University of California Press, Berkeley.
1939 An Archaeological Reconnaissance of the West Coast: Nayarit to Michoacán. *XXVII Congreso Internacional de Americanistas* 1:74–77. México, D.F.
1945a *Excavations at Culiacán, Sinaloa.* Ibero-Americana 25. University of California Press, Berkeley.
1945b *The Archaeology of the Autlan-Tuxcacuesco Area of Jalisco, Part I.* Ibero-Americana 26. University of California Press, Berkeley.
1947 *Excavations at Apatzingan, Michoacan.* Viking Fund Publications in Anthropology, no. 7. New York.
1949 *The Archaeology of the Autlan-Tuxcacuesco Area of Jalisco, II: The Tuxcacuesco-Zapotitlan Zone.* Ibero-Americana 27. University of California Press, Berkeley.
1974 Stirrup Pots from Colima: Some Implications. In *The Archaeology of West Mexico,* edited by B. B. Bell, pp. 206–211. Sociedad de Estudios Avanzados del Occidente de México, Ajijic, Jalisco.
1980 *Ceramic Sequence in Colima: Capacha, an Early Phase.* Anthropological Papers of the University of Arizona, no. 37. University of Arizona Press, Tucson.

Kelly, I., and B. Braniff
1966 Una relación cerámica entre Occidente y la Mesa Central. *Boletín del INAH* 23:26–27. México, D.F.

Kidder, A. V.
1916 The Pottery of the Casas Grandes District, Chihuahua. In *Holmes Anniversary Volume: Anthropological Essays,* pp. 253–268. Washington, D.C.
1924 *An Introduction to Southwestern Archaeology: With a Preliminary Account of the Excavations at Pecos.* Phillips Academy, Department of Archaeology, Southwestern Expedition Papers, no. 1.
1939 Notes on the Archaeology of the Babicora District, Chihuahua. In *So Live the Works of Men: Seventieth Anniversary Volume Honoring Edgar Lee Hewett,* edited by D. D. Brand and F. E. Harvey, pp. 221–230. University of New Mexico Press, Albuquerque.

Kidder, A. V., H. S. Cosgrove, and C. B. Cosgrove
1949 *The Pendleton Ruin, Hidalgo County, New Mexico.* Contributions to American Anthropology and History, no. 50. Carnegie Institution of Washington, Publication 585. Washington, D.C.

Kidder, A. V., J. D. Jennings, and E. M. Shook
1977 *Excavations at Kaminaljuyu, Guatemala.* Pennsylvania State University Press, University Park. Originally published 1946, Carnegie Institution of Washington, Washington, D.C.

Kirchhoff, P.
1943 Mesoamérica: Sus límites geográficas, composición étnica y caracteres culturales. *Acta Americana* 1:92–107.

Kluckhohn, C.
1940 The Conceptual Structure in Middle American Studies. In *The Maya and Their Neighbors,* pp. 41–51. D. Appleton-Century, New York.

Kolb, C.
1987 *Marine Shell Trade and Classic Teotihuacán, Mexico.* BAR International Series 364. Oxford.

Koll, R. B.
1982 Archaeological Reports: Shores of Lake Chapala, Jalisco, Mexico. PANTOC 4:19–32.

Lagunas R., Z.
1987 *Análisis de los restos oseos humanos procedentes de la tumba núm. 1 de Tingambato, Michoacán.* Avances en Antropología Física, 3. INAH, México, D.F.

Lambert, M. F., and J. R. Ambler
1961 *A Survey and Excavation of Caves in Hidalgo County, New Mexico.* Monograph no. 25. School of American Research, Santa Fe.

Lang, R. W.
1995 The Fields of San Marcos: Agriculture at a Great Town of the Galisteo Basin, Northern New Mexico. In *Soil, Water, Biology, and Belief in Prehistoric and Traditional Southwestern Agriculture,* edited by H. W. Toll, pp. 41–76. New Mexico Archaeological Council Special Publication 2. C & M Press, Denver.

Laporte, J. P.
1987 El "talud-tablero" en Tikal, Petén: Nuevos datos. In *Homenaje a Roman Piña Chan,* edited by B. Dahlgren, C. Navarrete, L. Ochoa, M. del C. Serra Puche, and Y. Sugiura, pp. 265–316. UNAM, México, D.F.

Lazalde, J. F.
1984 Patrones de asentamiento tipo "Cliff Dwellers" en el norte de México (Durango). PANTOC 7:89–108.
1987 *Durango indígena.* Privately printed. Durango.
1992 Puntas de proyectil, catálogo. Museo Regional Universidad de Juárez del Estado de Durango, Durango.

Lázaro de Arregui, D.
1946 *Descripción de la Nueva Galicia.* Sevilla.

LeBlanc, S. A.
1976 Mimbres Archeological Center: Preliminary Report of the Second Season of Excavation, 1975. *Journal of New World Archaeology* 1(6):1–23.
1977 The 1976 Field Season of the Mimbres Foundation in Southwestern New Mexico. *Journal of New World Archaeology* 2(2):1–24.
1980 The Dating of Casas Grandes. *American Antiquity* 45:799–806.
1986 Aspects of Southwestern Prehistory, A.D. 900–1400. In *Ripples in the Chichimec Sea: New Considerations of Southwestern-Mesoamerican Interactions,* edited by F. J. Mathien and R. H. McGuire, pp. 105–134. Southern Illinois University Press, Carbondale.

LeBlanc, S. A., and B. A. Nelson
1976 The Question of Salado in Southwestern New Mexico. *The Kiva* 42(1):71–79.

LeBlanc, S. A., and M. E. Whalen
1980 *An Archeological Synthesis of South-Central and Southwestern New Mexico.* Report on file, Bureau of Land Management, Las Cruces, New Mexico.

Lehmer, D. J.
1948 *The Jornada Branch of the Mogollon.* University of Arizona Bulletin 19(2), Social Science Bulletin 17. Tucson.

Lekson, S. H.
1984 Dating Casas Grandes. *The Kiva* 50:55–60.

Lelgemann, A.
1992 The Chronology of La Quemada, Zacatecas, and the Classic Occupation of the Northwestern Periphery of Mesoamerica. Unpublished Master's thesis, Free University of Berlin.
1997 Orientaciones astronómicas y el sistema de medida en La Quemada, Zacatecas, México. *Indiana* 14:99–125. Berlin.
1999 *Die Zitaddelle von La Quemada.* Unpublished Ph.D. dissertation, Free University of Berlin.

León, N.
1888a Calendario de los Tarascos. *Anales del Museo Michoacano,* 1:33–42. Morelia.
1888b Las yácatas de Tzintzuntzan. *Anales del Museo Michoacano* 1:65–70. Morelia.
1979 [1903] *Los Tarascos.* Museo Nacional, México, D.F. Reprint. Editorial Inovación, México, D.F.

Leubben, R. A., J. G. Andelson, and L. C. Herold
1986 Elvina Whetten Pueblo and Its Relationship to Terraces and Nearby Small Structures, Chihuahua, Mexico. *The Kiva* 51:165–187.

Lightfoot, K. G.
1981 *Prehistoric Political Development in the Little Colorado Region, East-Central Arizona.* Unpublished Ph.D. dissertation, Department of Anthropology, Arizona State University, Tempe.

Lightfoot, K. G., and G. Feinman
1982 Social Differentiation and Leadership Development in Early Pithouse Villages in the Mogollon Region of the American Southwest. *American Antiquity* 47:64–86.

Lincoln, J. S.
1942 *The Maya Calendar of the Ixil of Guatemala.* Carnegie Institution of Washington, Publication 528, Contribution 38. Washington, D.C.

Lind, M. D.
1994 Cholula and Mixteca Polychromes: Two Mixteca-Puebla Regional Sub-Styles. In *Mixteca-Puebla: Discoveries and Research in Mesoamerican Art and Archaeology,* edited by H. B. Nicholson and E. Quiñones Keber, pp. 71–99. Labyrinthos Press, Culver City, California.

Liot, C.
1996 Reflexiones teóricas sobre las ténicas de producción de sal, en los sitios de la cuenca de Sayula. In *Estudios del Hombre 3,* edited by O. Schöndube and F. Valdez, pp. 151–162. Universidad de Guadalajara.
1998 La sal de Sayula: Cronología y papel en la organización del poblamiento prehispánico. In *Memoria: VI Coloquio de Occidentalistas,* edited by R. Avila, J. Emphoux, L. Gastélum, S. Ramírez, O. Schöndube, and F. Valdez, pp. 135–156. ORSTOM, Universidad de Guadalajara, CEMCA, UNAM, Guadalajara.

Lister, R. H.
1939 *A Report on the Excavations Made at Agua Zarca and La Morita in Chihuahua.* University of New Mexico, Research Graduate School, vol. 3, no. 1. Albuquerque.
1946 Survey of Archaeological Remains in Northwestern Chihuahua. *Southwestern Journal of Anthropology* 2:433–453.
1949 *Excavations at Cojumatlan, Michoacan, Mexico.* University of New Mexico Publications in Anthropology, no. 5. Albuquerque.

1953 Excavations in Cave Valley, Chihuahua, Mexico: A Preliminary Note. *American Antiquity* 19:166–169.

1958 *Archaeological Excavations in the Northern Sierra Madre Occidental, Chihuahua and Sonora, Mexico.* University of Colorado Studies, Series in Anthropology, no. 7. Boulder.

Lister, R. H., and A. M. Howard

1955 The Chalchihuites Culture of Northwest Mexico. *American Antiquity* 21:122–129.

Litvak King, J.

1968 Excavaciones de rescate en la presa de la villita. *Boletín del* INAH 31:28–30.

Lizardi R., C.

1959 El calendario maya-mexicano. In *Esplendor del México antiguo*, vol. 1, edited by R. Noriega, C. Cook de Leonard, and J. R. Moctezuma, pp. 221–242. Centro Investigaciones Antropológicas, México, D.F.

Long, S. V.

1966 *Archaeology of the Municipio of Etzatlán, Jalisco.* Unpublished Ph.D. dissertation, Department of Anthropology, University of California at Los Angeles.

Long, S. V., and R. E. Taylor

1966 Chronology of a West Mexican Shaft-Tomb. *Nature* 212:651–652.

Long, S. V., and M. V. V. Wire

1966 *Excavations at Barra de Navidad, Jalisco.* Antropológica no. 18. Instituto Caribe de Antropología y Sociología, Caracas.

López, C., and Ma. T. Cabrero

1995 Las tumbas de tiro del piñón en el Cañón del Bolaños, Jalisco. Paper presented at the 61st Annual Meeting of the SAA, New Orleans.

López A., A.

1975 El fundamento mágico-religioso del poder. *Estudios de Cultura Nahuatl* 12:197–240.

López C., C.

1994 *Modelo de un sistema de intercambio en el occidente de México durante el Clásico mesoamericano con énfasis en el Cañón de Bolaños, Jalisco y Zacatecas.* Tesis, ENAH, INAH, México, D.F.

López Mestas Camberos, L., and J. Ramos de la Vega

1992 *Investigaciones arqueológicas en la sierra de Comanja-Guanajuato.* Tesis, Universidad Autónoma de Guadalajara/ENAH, México, D.F.

1995 Tumba de tiro en Huitzilapa, Jalisco. *Arqueología Mexicana* 2:7:59–61.

1998 Excavating the Tomb at Huitzilapa. In *Ancient West Mexico: Art and Archaeology of the Unknown Past*, edited by R. F. Townsend, pp. 53–70. Art Institute of Chicago.

López Mestas Camberos, L., J. Ramos de la Vega, and C. Santos R.

1994 Sitios y materials: Avances del proyecto arqueológico altos de Jalisco. In *Contribuciones al arqueología y ethnohistoria del occidente de México*, edited by E. Williams, pp. 279–296. El Colegio de Michoacán, Zamora.

López-Portillo y Weber, J.

1935 *La conquista de la Nueva Galicia.* Talleres Gráficos de la Nación, México, D.F.

Lorenzo, J. L.

1953 A Fluted Point from Durango, Mexico. *American Antiquity* 18:394–395.

Lumholtz, C.

1902 *Unknown Mexico.* 2 vols. Charles Scribner's Sons, New York.

Lumholtz, C., and A. Hrdlicka

1898 Marked Human Bones from a Prehistoric Tarasco Burial Place in the State of Michoacan, Mexico. *Bulletin, American Museum of Natural History* 10:61–79.

Macías Goytia, A.

1988 La arqueología en Michoacán. In *La antropología en México: Panorama histórico*, 13, edited by M. Mejía Sánchez, pp. 89–132. Colección Biblioteca, INAH, México, D.F.

1989 Los entierros de un centro ceremonial tarasco. In *Estudios de antropología biológica*, Serie Antropológica 100, pp. 531–559. UNAM, México, D.F.

1990 *Huandacareo: Lugar de juicios, tribunal.* Colección Científica, 222, INAH, México, D.F.

1992 Investigación arqueológica: Avances en Cuitzeo. *Boletín del Consejo de Arqueología, 1991*, pp. 176–180. INAH, México, D.F.

Macías Goytia, A., and K. Vackimes Serret

1988 Tres Cerritos, Cuitzeo, Michoacán. In *Primera Reunión sobre las Sociedades Prehispánicas en el Centro Occidente de México, Memoria*, pp. 161–164. INAH, México, D.F.

1990 Proyecto cuenca de Cuitzeo. *Boletín del Consejo de Arqueología, 1989*, pp. 71–81. INAH, México, D.F.

MacNeish, R. S.

1948 *Prehistoric Relationships between the Cultures of the Southeastern U.S. and Mexico in Light of an Archaeological Survey of the State of Tamaulipas.* Unpublished Ph.D. dissertation, Department of Anthropology, University of Chicago.

1958 *Preliminary Archaeological Investigations in the Sierra de Tamaulipas, Mexico.* Transactions of the American Philosophical Society 48:part 6.

1992 Fases del arcaico tradición Chihuahua: Síntesis. In *Historia general de Chihuahua I: Geología, geografía y arqueología*, edited by A. Márquez-Alameda, pp. 121–136. Universidad Autónoma de Ciudad Juárez y Gobierno del Estado de Chihuahua, Chihuahua.

1993 *Preliminary Investigations of the Archaic in the Region of Las Cruces, New Mexico.* Historic and Natural Resources Report no. 9. Cultural Resources Management Program, Directorate of Environment, Fort Bliss, Texas.

MacNeish, R. S., and P. H. Beckett

1987 *The Archaic Chihuahua Tradition.* COAS Monograph no. 7. Las Cruces, New Mexico.

Maldonado C., R.

1980 *Ofrendas asociadas a entierros del Infiernillo en el Balsas.* Colección Científica, INAH, México, D.F.

Mallouf, R. J.

1985 *A Synthesis of Eastern Trans-Pecos Prehistory.* Unpublished Master's thesis, Department of Anthropology, University of Texas, Austin.

1987 *Las Haciendas: A Cairn-Burial Assemblage from Northeastern Chihuahua, Mexico.* Texas Historical Commission, Office of the State Archaeologist, Report 35. Austin.

1992 La prehistoria del noroeste de Chihuahua: Complejo cielo y distrito La Junta. In *Historia general de Chihuahua I: Geología, geografía y arqueología,* edited by A. Márquez-Alameda, pp. 137–162. Universidad Autónoma de Ciudad Juárez and Gobierno del Estado de Chihuahua, Chihuahua.

Malo Z., M.
1972 Noticia del San Miguel prehispánico: En de la Maza, Francisco. In *San Miguel de Allende.* Frente de Afirmación Hispanista A.C., México, D.F.

Manzanilla López, R.
1988 Salvamento arqueológico en Loma de Santa María, Morelia, Michoacán. In *Primera Reunión sobre las Sociedades Prehispánicas en el Centro Occidente de México: Memoria,* pp. 151–159. Centro Regional de Querétaro, INAH, México.

Manzanilla López, R., and J. A. Talavera G.
1988 Informe de los trabajos de salvamento e investigación arqueológica en la población de Mochicahui, municipio de Fuerte, estado de Sinaloa. Report on file, Dirección de Antropología Física, Departamento de Salvamento Arqueología, INAH. México, D.F.

Marcus, J.
1992 *Mesoamerican Writing Systems: Propaganda, Myth, and History in Four Ancient Civilizations.* Princeton University Press, Princeton.

Mariano de Torres, F.
1965 *Crónica de la sancta provincia de Xalisco.* Instituto Jalisciense de Antropología e Historia, Guadalajara.

Márquez-Alameda, A.
1990 Hacia una síntesis de la arqueología del noroeste de México. In *Actas del Primer Congreso de Historia Regional Comparada 1989,* pp. 23–32. Universidad Autónoma de Ciudad Juárez, Juárez.

1992 Sobre los pobladores más antiguos del actual estado de Chihuahua. In *Historia general de Chihuahua I: Geología, geografía y arqueología,* edited by A. Márquez-Alameda, pp. 105–120. Universidad Autónoma de Ciudad Juárez and Gobierno del Estado de Chihuahua, Chihuahua.

Márquez-Alameda, A. (editor)
1992 *Historia general de Chihuahua I: Geología, geografía y arqueología.* Universidad Autónoma de Ciudad Juárez and Gobierno del Estado de Chihuahua, Chihuahua.

Marquina, I.
1928 Estudio arquitectónico comparativo de los monumentos arqueológicos de México. *Contributions of Mexico to the 23rd International Congress of the Americas,* pp. 1–86.

1939 Atlas arqueológico de la República Mexicana. *Instituto Panamericana Geografía y Historia,* Pub. 41.

Marrs, G. J.
1949 *Problems Arising from the Surface Occurrence of Archaeological Material in Southeastern Chihuahua, Mexico.* Unpublished Master's thesis, Department of Anthropology, University of New Mexico, Albuquerque.

Marshack, A.
1974 The Chamula Calendar Board: An Internal and Comparative Analysis. In *Mesoamerican Archaeology: New Approaches,* edited by N. Hammond, pp. 255–270. University of Texas Press, Austin.

Martínez, B., and L. F. Nieto
1987 *Distribución de asentamientos prehispánicos en la porción central del Río Laja.* Tesis Colectiva, ENAH, INAH, México, D.F.

Martínez M., M. G.
1981 *Recorrido arqueológico en el municipio de Canatlán, Durango: Proyecto de rescate a cueva de San Pablo Canatlán, Durango.* Informe, Centro Regional Norte-Centro, INAH, Torreón.

Mason, J. A.
1937 Late Archaeological Sites in Durango, Mexico, from Chalchihuites to Zape. In *Twenty-Fifth Anniversary Studies, Publications of the Philadelphia Anthropological Society,* 1:117–126. Philadelphia.

Mastache, A. G., and R. H. Cobean
1989 The Coyotalatelco Culture and the Origins of the Toltec State. In *Mesoamerica after the Decline of Teotihuacán, A.D. 700–900,* edited by R. A. Diehl and J. C. Berlo, pp. 49–67. Dumbarton Oaks, Washington D.C.

Mathien, F. J., and R. H. McGuire (editors)
1986 *Ripples in the Chichimec Sea: New Considerations of Southwestern-Mesoamerican Interactions.* Southern Illinois University Press, Carbondale.

Matson, F. (editor)
1965 *Ceramics and Man.* Aldine, Chicago.

Maxwell, T. D.
1995 A Comparative Study of Prehistoric Farming Strategies. In *Soil, Water, Biology, and Belief in Prehistoric and Traditional Southwestern Agriculture,* edited by H. W. Toll, pp. 3–12. New Mexico Archaeological Council, Special Publication 2. C & M Press, Denver.

McBride, H. W.
1969 The Extent of the Chupicuaro Tradition. In *The Natalie Wood Collection of Pre-Columbian Ceramics from Chupicuaro, Guanajuato, Mexico,* edited by J. D. Frierman, pp. 33–49. Occasional Papers of the Museum and Laboratories of Ethnic Arts and Technology, no. 1. University of California, Los Angeles.

1974 *Formative Ceramics and Prehistoric Settlement Patterns in the Cuauhtitlan Region, Mexico.* Unpublished Ph.D. dissertation, Department of Anthropology, University of California, Los Angeles.

McCafferty, G. G.
1994 The Mixteca-Puebla Stylistic Tradition at Early Postclassic Cholula. In *Mixteca-Puebla: Discoveries and Research in Mesoamerican Art and Archaeology,* edited by H. B. Nicholson and E. Quiñones Keber, pp. 53–77. Labyrinthos Press, Culver City, California.

McCluney, E. B.
1962 *Clanton Draw and Box Canyon.* Monograph no. 26. School of American Research, Santa Fe.

1963 The Excavation of the Joyce Well Site, Hidalgo County,

New Mexico. Ms. on file, Museum of New Mexico, Laboratory of Anthropology, Santa Fe.

McCosh, R., H. P. Pollard, and A. Hirshan
1997 Prehispanic Settlement and Chronology in the Lake Pátzcuaro Basin: The Urichu, Xarácuaro, and Pareo Polities. Paper presented at the 62nd Annual Meeting of the SAA, Chicago.

McGuire, R. H.
1980 The Mesoamerican Connection in the Southwest. *The Kiva* 46(1–2):3–38.
1986 Economies and Modes of Production in the Prehistoric Southwestern Periphery. In *Ripples in the Chichimec Sea: New Considerations of Southwestern-Mesoamerican Interactions,* edited by F. J. Mathien and R. H. McGuire, pp. 243–269. Southern Illinois University Press, Carbondale.
1993 Charles Di Peso and the Mesoamerican Connection. In *Culture and Contact: Charles C. Di Peso's Gran Chichimeca,* edited by A. I. Woosley and J. C. Ravesloot, pp. 23–38. University of New Mexico Press, Albuquerque.

McGuire, R. H., E. C. Adams, B. A. Nelson, and K. Spielman
1994 Drawing the Southwest to Scale: Perspectives on Macroregional Relations. In *Themes in Southwest Prehistory,* edited by G. J. Gumerman, pp. 239–265. School of American Research Press, Santa Fe.

McGuire, R. H., and A. Valdo Howard
1987 The Structure and Organization of Hohokam Shell Exchange. *The Kiva* 52:113–146.

McGuire, R. H., and M. E. Villalpando
1989 Prehistory and the Making of History in Sonora. In *Columbian Consequences,* edited by D. H. Thomas, pp. 213–228. Smithsonian Institution Press, Washington, D.C.
1993 *An Archaeological Survey of the Altar Valley, Sonora, Mexico.* Arizona State Museum Archaeological Series, no. 184. Arizona State Museum, University of Arizona, Tucson.
1995 Excavaciónes arqueológicas en Cerro de Trincheras: Informe de la temporada de excavaciones, 1995. Report submitted to the Consejo de Arqueología, INAH. Centro INAH Sonora, Hermosillo.
1996 Cerro de Trincheras: A Terraced Village in the Magdalena Valley, Sonora, Mexico. Paper presented at the 61st Annual Meeting of the SAA, New Orleans.
1997 Cerro de Trincheras, un sitio arqueológico en el noroeste de Sonora. *Arqueología* 17:49–62. Coordinación Nacional de Arqueología del INAH, México, D.F.
1998 Cerro de Trincheras: A Prehispanic Terraced Town in Sonora, Mexico. *Archaeology in Tucson* 12(1). Newsletter of the Center for Desert Archaeology, Tucson.

Meighan, C. W.
1969 Cultural Similarities between Western Mexico and Andean Regions. In *Precolumbian Contact within Nuclear America,* edited by J. C. Kelley and C. L. Riley, pp. 11–25. Mesoamerican Studies, Series '69M4A, Research Records of the University Museum. Southern Illinois University, Carbondale.
1971 Archaeology of Sinaloa. In *Archaeology of Northern Mesoamerica,* part 2, edited by G. F. Ekholm and I. Bernal, pp. 754–767. HBMI, vol. 11, R. Wauchope, general editor. University of Texas Press, Austin.
1972 *Archaeology of the Morett Site, Colima.* University of California Publications in Anthropology, vol. 7. University of California Press, Berkeley.
1978 Application of Obsidian Dating to West Mexican Archaeological Problems. In *Across the Chichimec Sea: Papers in Honor of J. Charles Kelley,* edited by C. L. Riley and B. C. Hedrick, pp. 83–95. Southern Illinois University Press, Carbondale.

Meighan, C. W. (editor)
1976 *The Archaeology of Amapa Nayarit.* Monumenta Archaeologica, 2. The Institute of Archaeology, University of California at Los Angeles.

Meighan, C. W., and L. J. Foote
1968 *Excavations at Tizapan el Alto, Jalisco.* Latin American Studies, vol. 11. University of California, Los Angeles.

Metcalfe, S., R. B. Brown, and S. P. Harrison
1987 Late Holocene Human Impact on Lake Basins in Central Mexico. *XII I.N.Q.U.A.* Ottawa.

Metcalfe, S. E., and S. P. Harrison
1983 *Preliminary Reconstructions of Late Quaternary Environmental Change as Recorded by Lake Margin Deposits in the Basin of Zacapu, Michoacán.* Tropical Paleoenvironments Research Group, School of Geography, Oxford University.

Michelet, D.
1984 *Río Verde, San Luis Potosí, Mexique.* Collection Etudes Mesoaméricaines 9. CEMCA, México, D.F.
1986 Informe preliminar general del Proyecto Arqueológico Michoacán, México. CEMCA, México, D.F.
1988a *La ceramique de Projet Michoacán.* CEMCA, México, D.F.
1988b Apuntes para el análisis de las migraciones en el México prehispánico. In *Movimientos de población en el occidente de México,* edited by T. Calvo and G. López, pp. 13–24. CEMCA and El Colegio de Michoacán, México, D.F.
1989 La parte centro-norte de Michoacán. In *Historia general de Michoacán,* vol. 1, edited by E. Florescano, pp. 155–168. Gobierno del Estado Michoacán, Morelia.
1990 El centro-norte de Michoacán en el Clásico: Algunas reflexiones. In *La época Clásica: Nuevos hallazgos, nuevas ideas,* edited by A. Cardos de Méndez, pp. 279–291. MNA and INAH, México, D.F.
1994 *Río Verde, San Luis Potosí (Mexique).* Collection Etudes Mesoaméricaines 9. CEMCA, México.
1995 La zona occidental en el Postclásico. In *Historia antigua de México: Vol. 3, El horizonte Postclásico y algunos aspectos intelectuales de las culturas mesoamericanas,* edited by L. Manzanilla and L. López Lujan, pp. 153–188. INAH, UNAM, and Grupo Editorial Miguel Angel Porrúa, México, D.F.
1996 Gente del golfo tierra adentro? Algunas observaciones acerca de la región de Río Verde, S.L.P. In *Cuadernos de Arquitectura Mesoamericana* 8:80–83. Facultad de Arquitectura, UNAM, México, D.F.

Michelet, D. (editor)
1992 *El Proyecto Michoacán, 1983–1987: Medio ambiente e introducción a los trabajos arqueológicos.* Collection Etudes Mesoaméricaines 11–12/Cuadernos de Estudios Michoacanos 4. CEMCA, México, D.F.

Michelet, D., M. C. Arnauld, and M.-F. Fauvet Berthelot
1989 El Proyecto del CEMCA en Michoacán. Etapa I: Un balance. *Trace* 16:70–87. CEMCA, México, D.F.

Michelet, D., G. Migeon, and G. Pereira
1995 Informe de los trabajos de campo realizados en el Malpaís de Zacapu (Octubre–Noviembre de 1994). CEMCA, México, D.F.

Milhauser, J. K.
1999 *Ritual, Social, and Economic Dimensions of Obsidian Use in the Malpaso Valley, Zacatecas, Mexico, A.D. 500–900.* Unpublished Master's thesis, Department of Anthropology, Arizona State University, Tempe.

Millon, R.
1973 *Urbanization at Teotihuacan, Mexico: The Teotihuacan Map: Text.* University of Texas Press, Austin.
1981 Teotihuacan: City, State, and Civilization. In *Supplement to the HBMI,* edited by V. R. Bircker and J. A. Sabloff, pp. 198–243. University of Texas Press, Austin.
1988 The Last Years of Teotihuacan Dominance. In *The Collapse of Ancient States and Civilizations,* edited by N. Yoffee and G. Cowgill, pp. 102–164. University of Arizona Press, Tucson.
1992 Teotihuacan Studies: From 1950 to 1990 and Beyond. In *Art, Ideology, and the City of Teotihuacan,* edited by J. C. Berlo, pp. 339–429. Dumbarton Oaks, Washington, D.C.
1993 The Place Where Time Began: An Archaeologist's Interpretation of What Happened in Teotihuacan History. In *Teotihuacan: Art from the City of the Gods,* edited by K. Berrin and E. Pasztory, pp. 16–43. Thames and Hudson, New York.

Millon, R., B. Drewitt, and G. Cowgill
1973 *Urbanization at Teotihuacan, Mexico.* University of Texas Press, Austin.

Minnis, P. E.
1984 Peeking under the Tortilla Curtain: Regional Interaction and Integration on the Northern Periphery of Casas Grandes. *American Archaeology* 4:181–193.
1988 Four Examples of Specialized Production at Casas Grandes, Northwestern Chihuahua. *The Kiva* 53:181–194.
1989 The Casas Grandes Polity in the International Four Corners. In *The Sociopolitical Structure of Prehistoric Southwestern Societies,* edited by S. Upham, K. G. Lightfoot, and R. A. Jewett, pp. 269–305. Westview Press, Boulder.

Minnis, P. E., and M. E. Whalen
1989 El sistema regional de Casas Grandes. *Boletín del Consejo de Arqueología* 1:86–90. México, D.F.
1991 El sistema regional de Casas Grandes. In *Actas del Segundo Congreso Historia Regional Comparada 1990,* edited by A. Márquez-Alameda, pp. 45–55. Universidad Autónoma de Ciudad Juárez, Chihuahua.

Minnis, P. E., M. E. Whalen, J. H. Kelley, and J. D. Stewart
1993 Prehistoric Macaw Breeding in the North American Southwest. *American Antiquity* 58:270–276.

Moedano, H.
1941 Estudio preliminar de la cerámica de Tzintzuntzan: Temporada III. *Revista Mexicana de Estudios Antropológicos* 5:21–42.
1946 La cerámica de Zinapécuaro, Michoacán. *Anales del Museo Michoacano* 2:439–449.

Moguel Cos, M. A.
1987 *Trabajos de salvamento arqueológico en las cuencas de Cuitzeo, Pátzcuaro y Zirahuén: Un intento de interpretación cultural.* Tesis, ENAH, INAH, México, D.F.

Mountjoy, J. B.
1969 On the Origin of West Mexican Metallurgy. In *Precolumbian Contact within Nuclear America,* edited by J. C. Kelley and C. L. Riley, pp. 26–42. Mesoamerican Studies, Series '69M4A, Research Records of the University Museum. Southern Illinois University, Carbondale.
1970a *Prehispanic Culture History and Cultural Contact on the Southern Coast of Nayarit, Mexico.* Unpublished Ph.D. dissertation, Department of Anthropology, Southern Illinois University, Carbondale.
1970b La sucesión cultural en San Blas. *Boletín del INAH* 39:41–48. México, D.F.
1974a San Blas Complex Ecology. In *The Archaeology of West Mexico,* edited by B. B. Bell, pp. 106–119. Sociedad de Estudios Avanzados del Occidente de México, Ajijic, Jalisco.
1974b Some Hypotheses Regarding the Petroglyphs of West Mexico. *Mesoamerican Studies,* no. 9, Research Records of the University Museum. Southern Illinois University, Carbondale.
1978 Tercera temporada del Proyecto Tomatlán de Salvamento Arqueológico. Report on file, Departamento de Salvamento Arqueológico, INAH, México, D.F.
1982a *El Proyecto Tomatlán de Salvamento Arqueológico.* Colección Científica Arqueología, no. 122. INAH, México, D.F.
1982b An Interpretation of the Pictographs at La Peña Pintada (Jalisco, Mexico). *American Antiquity* 47:110–126.
1983a Nuevos hallazgos sobre la habitación formativo medio en San Blas, Nayarit. Paper presented at the XVIII Mesa Redonda of the SMA, Taxco.
1983b Investigaciones arqueológicas en la cuenca del Río Tomatlán, Jalisco, 1975–1977. *PANTOC* 5:21–50. Universidad Autónoma de Guadalajara.
1984 Significado de dos documentos del siglo XVII en la interpretación de petroglifos encontrados en la cuenca del Río Tomatlán, Jalisco. *Investigaciones Recientes en el Area Maya* 4:487–494. SMA, México, D.F.
1987a Antiquity, Interpretation, and Stylistic Evolution of Petroglyphs in West Mexico. *American Antiquity* 52:210–211.
1987b *El Proyecto Tomatlán de Salvamento Arqueológico: El arte repestre.* Coleccíon Científica, no. 163. INAH, México, D.F.
1988 Proyecto Arqueológico Valle de Banderas: Primera

temporada (1987). Report on file, Departamento de Arqueología, INAH, México, D.F.

1989a Algunas observaciones sobre el desarrollo del Preclásico en la llanura costera del occidente. In *El Preclásico o Formativo: Avances y perspectivas,* edited by M. Carmona Macias, pp. 11–26. INAH, MNA, México, D.F.

1989b Proyecto Arqueológico Valle de Banderas: Segunda temporada (1988). Report on file, Departamento de Arqueología, INAH, México, D.F.

1990 El desarrollo de la cultura Aztatlán visto de su frontera suroeste. In *Mesoamerica y norte de México, siglos IX–XII,* edited by F. Sodi Miranda, pp. 541–564. INAH, México, D.F.

1991a La tercera temporada del Proyecto Valle de Banderas (1990). Report on file, Departamento de Arqueología, INAH, México, D.F.

1991b The Analysis of Preclassic Figurines Excavated from the Site of La Pintada in the Central Coastal Plain of Jalisco, Mexico. In *The New World Figurine Project,* vol. 1, edited by T. Stocker, pp. 85–97. Research Press, Provo, Utah.

1991c West Mexican Stelae from Jalisco and Nayarit. *Ancient Mesoamerica* 2:21–33.

1992 Rescate arqueológica en el sitio de La Pedrera. Report on file, Departamento de Arqueología, INAH, México, D.F.

1993a Prehispanic Cultural Development along the Southern Coast of West Mexico. Paper presented at the Semenario de Arqueología, Perspectivas sobre la Arqueología de la Periferia Septentrional de Mesoamérica, Zacatecas.

1993b Cuarta (1992) temporada del Proyecto Arqueológico Valle de Banderas. Report on file, Departamento de Arqueología, INAH, México, D.F.

1993c El pasado prehispánico del municipio de Puerto Vallarta. In *Una aproximación a Puerto Vallarta,* edited by J. Olveda, pp. 23–40. México, D.F.

1995a La sexta (1994) temporada del Proyecto Arqueológico Valle de Banderas. Report on file, Departamento de Arqueología, INAH, México, D.F.

1995b Some Important Resources for Prehispanic Cultures of West Mexico. In *The Gran Chichimeca: Essays on the Archaeology and Ethnohistory of Northern Mesoamerica,* edited by J. E. Reyman, pp. 61–87. Avebury Press, London.

1995c Análisis cronológico de la cerámica del Formativo, excavada en el sitio de La Pintada, Jalisco. In *Archaeología del norte y del occidente de Mexico: Homenaje al Doctor J. Charles Kelley,* edited by B. Dahlgren and Ma. de los D. Soto de Arechavaleta, pp. 115–130. UNAM, México, D.F.

1995d Propuestas para el futuro de la arqueología en el occidente de México. *Revista Mexicana de Estudios Antropológicos* 41:73–81.

1996a Cálculos de la población prehispánica en la cuenca del Río Tomatlán. *In Estudios del Hombre 3,* edited by O. Schöndube and F. Valdez, pp. 173–194. Universidad de Guadalajara, Guadalajara.

1996b El valle de Banderas como zona fronteriza durante el Preclásico Tardío. Paper presented at the IV Coloquio de Occidentalistas, Guadalajara.

1997 Esculturas antropomórfas de la costa del occidente de México. Paper presented at the 49th International Congress of Americanists, Quito, Ecuador.

1998a The Evolution of Complex Societies in West Mexico: A Comparative Perspective. In *Pre-Columbian Contact within Nuclear America,* edited by J. C. Kelley and C. L. Riley, pp. 251–265. Southern Illinois University Museum, Carbondale.

1998b El valle de Banderas como zona fronteriza durante el Preclásico Tardío. In *El occidente de México: Arqueología, historia y medio ambiente,* pp. 255–263. Universidad de Guadalajara and Instituto Francés de Investigación Científica para el Desarrollo en Cooperación, Guadalajara.

1998c Arqueología costera el occidente de México: Qué? Cuando? Como? y Porque? In *Antropología e historia del occidente de México: XXIV Mesa Redonda de la Sociedad Mexicana de Antropología* 1:427–451. México, D.F.

Mountjoy, J. B., B. S. Aburto, L. Barba, and S. Gutiérrez
1983 Late Postclassic Commerce in the Tomatlán River Valley, Jalisco: Clay Mining and Analysis of Fine Paste Pottery. In *Mining and Mining Techniques in Ancient Mesoamerica,* edited by P. C. Weigand and G. Gwynne. *Anthropology* 6:1–2:189–198. State University of New York at Stony Brook.

Mountjoy, J. B., and C. Claassen
1989 Seasonality and Diet of Middle Formative People on the Central Coast of Nayarit, Mexico. Paper presented at the 88th Annual Meeting of the American Anthropological Association, Washington, D.C.

Mountjoy, J. B., and D. Peterson
1973 *Man and the Land at Prehispanic Cholula.* Publications in Anthropology, no. 4. Vanderbilt University, Nashville.

Mountjoy, J. B., and M. K. Sandford
1995 Costumbres mortuorias durante el Preclásico Tardío/Clásico temprano en el valle de Banderas, costa del occidente de Méxcio. Paper presented at the 2nd International Conference on Mummies, Cartagena, Colombia.

Mountjoy, J. B., and J. P. Smith
1985 An Archaeological Patolli from Tomatlán, Jalisco, Mexico. In *Contributions to the Archaeology and Ethnology of Greater Mesoamerica,* edited by W. Folan, pp. 240–262. Southern Illinois University Press, Carbondale.

Mountjoy, J., R. E. Taylor, and L. Feldman
1972 Matanchén Complex: New Radiocarbon Dates on Early Coastal Adaptation in West Mexico. *Science* 175:1242–1243.

Mountjoy, J. B., and L. Torres M.
1985 The Production and Use of Prehispanic Metal Artifacts in the Central Coastal Area of Jalisco, Mexico. In *The Archaeology of West and Northwest Mesoamerica,* edited by M. S. Foster and P. C. Weigand, pp. 133–152. Westview Press, Boulder.

Mota y Escobar, D. A. de la
1940 *Descripción geográfica de los reinos de Nueva Galicia, Nueva Vizcaya y Nuevo León.* Editorial Pedro Robredo, México, D.F.

Mozillo, E.
1990 Proyecto Las Ventanas. *Boletín del Consejo de Arqueología*, pp. 91–96. INAH, México, D.F.

Muller, E. F.
1948 Cerámica de la cuenca del Río Lerma. In *El occidente de México*, pp. 50–54. Cuarta Reunión de Mesa Redonda, México, D.F.

Muller, F.
1979 *Estudio tipológico provisional de la cerámica del Balsas Medio.* Colección Científica, no. 78. INAH, México, D.F.
1990 *La cerámica de Cuicuilco B: Un rescate arqueológico.* Colección Científica, no. 186. INAH, México, D.F.

Muller, F., and C. Lizardi Ramos
1959 La Pirámide 6 de Huapalcalco, Hidalgo, México. *Cuadernos Americanos* 33:146–157.

Mumford, L.
1938 *The Culture of Cities.* Harcourt, Brace, New York.
1961 *The City in History: Its Origins, Its Transformations, and Its Prospects.* Harcourt, Brace and World, New York.

Nalda, E.
1975 *UA San Juan de Río.* Tesis, ENAH, INAH, México, D.F.
1990 Que es lo que define *Mesoamérica?* In *La validez teórica del concepto mesoamérica: XIX Mesa Redonda de la SMA*, pp. 11–20. Colección Científica, no. 198. INAH, México, D.F.

Naylor, T. H.
1995 Casas Grandes Outlier Ballcourts in Northwest Chihuahua. In *The Gran Chichimeca: Essays on the Archaeology and Ethnohistory of Northern Mesoamerica*, edited by J. E. Reyman, pp. 224–239. Avebury Press, Brookfield, Vermont.

Neff, H., R. Bishop, E. Sisson, M. Glaascock, and P. Sisson
1994 Neutron Activation Analysis of Late Postclassic Polychrome Pottery from Central Mexico. In *Mixteca-Puebla: Discoveries and Research in Mesoamerican Art and Archaeology*, edited by H. B. Nicholson and E. Quiñones Keber, pp. 117–141. Labyrinthos, Culver City, California.

Neiderberger, C.
1976 *Zohapilco: Cinco milenos de ocupación humana en un sitio lacustre de la cuenca de México.* Colección Científica, no. 30. INAH, México, D.F.
1987 Paleopaysages et archéologie pre-urbaine de Bassin de México. *Collection Etudes Mesoaméricaines*, pp. 1–11. Centre d'Etudes Mexicaines et Centraméricaines, México, D.F.

Nelson, B. A.
1990 Observaciones acerca de la presencia tolteca en La Quemada, Zacatecas. In *Mesoamerica y norte de México, siglos IX–XII*, edited by F. Sodi Miranda, pp. 521–539. INAH, México, D.F.
1993 Outposts of Mesoamerican Empire and Architectural Patterning at La Quemada, Zacatecas. In *Culture and Contact: Charles C. Di Peso's Gran Chichimeca*, edited by A. I. Woosley and J. C. Ravesloot, pp. 173–189. University of New Mexico Press, Albuquerque.
1997 Chronology and Stratigraphy at La Quemada, Zacatecas, Mexico. *Journal of Field Archaeology* 24:85–109. Boston University.

Nelson, B. A., J. A. Darling, and D. A. Kice
1992 Mortuary Practices and Social Order at La Quemada, Zacatecas, Mexico. *Latin American Antiquity* 3:298–315.

Nicholson, H. B.
1960 The Mixteca-Puebla Concept in Mesoamerican Archaeology: A Reexamination. In *Men and Cultures: Selected Papers from the Fifth International Congress of Anthropological and Ethnological Sciences, Philadelphia, September 1–9, 1956*, edited by F. C. Wallace, pp. 612–617. University of Pennsylvania, Philadelphia.
1971 Religion in Pre-Hispanic Central Mexico. In *Archaeology of Northern Mesoamerica*, part 1, edited by G. F. Ekholm and I. Bernal, pp. 395–446. HBMI vol. 10, R. Wauchope, general editor. University of Texas Press, Austin.
1982 The Mixteca Puebla Concept Revisited. In *The Art and Iconography of Late Post-Classic Central Mexico*, edited by E. H. Boone, pp. 227–249. Dumbarton Oaks, Washington, D.C.

Nicholson, H. B., and C. W. Meighan
1974 The UCLA Department of Anthropology Program in West Mexican Archaeology-Ethnohistory, 1956–1970. In *The Archaeology of West Mexico*, edited by B. B. Bell, pp. 6–18. Sociedad de Estudios Avanzados del Occidente de México, Ajijic, Jalisco.

Nicholson, H. B., and E. Quiñones Keber (editors)
1994 *Mixteca-Puebla: Discoveries and Research in Mesoamerican Art and Archaeology.* Labyrinthos Press, Culver City, California.

Nicholson, H. B., and J. Smith
1962 Interrelationships of New World Cultures, Project A: Central and South Pacific Coast, West Mexico, Preliminary Report, 1960 Season. *Katunob* 3:3:5–8.

Noguera, E.
1926 *Ruinas arqueológicas de Casas Grandes.* Publicaciones SEP 2(14). México, D.F.
1930 *Ruinas arqueológicas del norte de México, Casas Grandes (Chihuahua), La Quemada, Chalchihuites (Zacatecas).* Publicaciones SEP, pp. 5–27. Talleres Gráficos de la Nación, México, D.F.
1931 Exploraciones arqueológicas en las regiones de Zamora y Pátzcuaro, estado de Michoacán. *Anales del Museo Nacional de México* 4(1):88–104.
1942 Exploraciones en El Opeño, Michoacán. *XXVII Congreso Internacional de Americanistas* 1:574–201. México, D.F.
1944 Exploraciones en Jiquilpan. *Anales del Museo Michoacano* 3:37–52. Morelia.
1948 Estado actual de los conocimientos acerca de la arqueología del noroeste de Michoacán. In *El occidente de México*, Cuarta Mesa Redonda, SMA.
1954 *La cerámica arqueológica de Cholula.* Editorial Guarania, México, D.F.
1965 *La cerámica arqueológica de Mesoamérica.* Instituto

de Investigaciones Históricas, Primera Serie, no. 86. UNAM, México, D.F.

Novela, Roberto, and Ma. A. Moguel Cos
1998 Zona constera del norte de Michoacán: Resumen de los trabajos de campo de la primera temporada. In *Génesis, culturas y espacios en Michoacán*, edited by V. Darras, pp. 113–139. Centre Francis d'Etudes Mexicaines et Centraméricaines, México, D.F.

Noyola, A.
1994 Análisis preliminar de la cerámica del fraccionamiento San Juan, Atoyac, Jalisco. In *Contribuciones a la arqueología y etnohistoria del occidente de México*, edited by E. Williams, pp. 55–92. El Colegio de Michoacán, Zamora.

Obregón, B. D.
1924 *Historia de los descubrimientos antiguos y modernos de la Nueva España, escrita por el Conquistador Baltazár de Obregón, 1584*. SEP, México, D.F.

Odena, G. L.
1990 La composición étnica en el Postclásico y la cuestión chichimeca. In *Mesoamérica y norte de México, siglo IX–XII*, edited by F. Sodi M., pp. 451–458. MNA and INAH, México, D.F.

O'Hara, S., F. A. Street-Perrott, and T. P. Burt
1993 Accelerated Soil Erosion around a Mexican Highland Lake Caused by Prehispanic Agriculture. *Nature* 362:48–51.

Ohnersorgen, M. A., and M. D. Varien
1996 Formal Architecture and Settlement Organization in Ancient West Mexico. *Ancient Mesoamerica* 7:103–120.

Olguin, E. M.
1993 Objetos arqueológicos de concha depositados en la Casa de la Cultura del municipio de Santiago Papsquiaro, Durango. *Transición* 13:23–27.

Oliveros, J. A.
1974 Nuevas exploraciones en El Opeño, Michoacán. In *The Archaeology of West Mexico*, edited by B. B. Bell, pp. 182–201. Sociedad de Estudio Avanzados del Occidente de México, Ajijic, Jalisco.
1975 Arqueología del estado de Michoacán. In *Los pueblos y señoríos teocráticos: México, panorama histórico y cultural*, 7:207–214. INAH, México, D.F.
1989 Las tumbas mas antiguas de Michoacán. In *Historia general de Michoacán: Vol. 1, Epoca prehispánica*, edited by M. Castro-Leal, pp. 123–134. Instituto Michoacano de Cultura, Morelia.
1992 El Valle Zamora-Jacona: Un proyecto arqueológico en Michoacán. In *Origen y desarrollo de la civilización en el occidente de México*, edited by B. Boehm de L. and P. C. Weigand, pp. 239–249. El Colegio de Michoacán, Zamora.

Oliveros, J. A., and M. de los Ríos Paredes
1993 La cronología de El Opeño, Michoacán: Nuevos fechamientos por radio-carbon. *Arqueología* 9–10:45–48.

Osborne, D., and A. Hayes
1938 Some Archaeological Notes from Southern Hidalgo County, New Mexico. *New Mexico Anthropologist* 3:21–23.

Othón de Menhdizábal, M.
1946 *Obras completas*, vol. 2. Talleres Gráficos de la Nación, México, D.F.

Pailes, R.
1973 *An Archaeological Reconnaissance of Southern Sonora and Reconsiderations of the Río Sonora Culture*. Unpublished Ph.D. Dissertation, Department of Anthropology, Southern Illinois University, Carbondale.
1976 Relaciones culturales prehistóricas en el noroeste de Sonora. In *Sonora: Antropología del desierto*, edited by B. Braniff and R. S. Felger, pp. 134–143. Coleccíon Científica, no. 27. INAH, México, D.F.
1978 The Río Sonora Culture in Prehistoric Trade Systems. In *Across the Chichimec Sea: Papers in Honor of J. Charles Kelley*, edited by C. L. Riley and B. C. Hendrick, pp. 134–143. Southern Illinois University, Carbondale.
1980 The Upper Río Sonora Valley in Prehistoric Trade. In *New Frontiers in the Archaeology and Ethnohistory of the Greater Southwest*, edited by C. L. Riley and B. Hedrick, pp. 20–39. *Transactions of the Illinois State Academy of Science* 72(4). Springfield.
1984 Agricultural Development and Trade in the Río Sonora. In *Prehistoric Agricultural Strategies in the Southwest*, edited by S. K. Fish and P. R. Fish, pp. 309–326. Anthropological Research Papers, no. 33. Arizona State University, Tempe.
1990 Elite Formation and Interregional Exchanges in Peripheries. In *Perspectives in Southwestern Prehistory*, edited by P. Minnis and C. Redman, pp. 213–228. Westview Press, Boulder.

Pailes, R. A., and D. T. Reff
1985 Colonial Exchange Systems and the Decline of Paquimé. In *The Archaeology of West and Northwest Mesoamerica*, edited by M. S. Foster and P. C. Weigand, pp. 353–363. Westview Press, Boulder.

Pailes, R. A., and J. W. Whitecotton
1979 The Greater Southwest and Mesoamerican World System: An Exploratory Model of Frontier Relationships. In *The Frontier: Comparative Studies*, vol. 2, edited by W. W. Savage, Jr., and S. I. Thompson, pp. 105–121. University of Oklahoma Press, Norman.
1995 The Frontiers of Mesoamerica: Northern and Southern. In *The Gran Chichimeca: Essays on the Archaeology and Ethnohistory of Northern Mesoamerica*, edited by J. E. Reyman, pp. 13–45. Avebury Press, Brookfield, Vermont.

Paredes, C. S.
1976 *El tributo indígena en la región del lago de Pátzuaro, siglo XIV*. Tesis de Licenciatura, UNAH, INAH, México, D.F.
1979 El sistema tributario prehispánico entre los Tarascos. Manuscript.

Parsons, J. R.
1976 Settlement and Population History of the Basin of Mexico. In *The Valley of Mexico: Studies in Pre-Hispanic Ecology and Society*, edited by E. R. Wolf, pp. 69–100. School of American Research, Santa Fe, and University of New Mexico Press, Albuquerque.
1989 Arqueología regional en la cuenca de México: Una

estrategia para la investigación futura. *Anales de Antropología* 26:157–257.

Parsons, J. R., E. Brumfiel, and M. Hodge
1996 Developmental Implications of Earlier Dates for Early Aztec in the Basin of Mexico. *Ancient Mesoamerica* 7:217–230.

Pase, C. P., and D. E. Brown
1982 Rocky Mountain (Petran) and Madrean Montane Conifer Forests. *Desert Plants* 4(1–4):43–48.

Paso y Troncoso, F. del
1898 *Codíce del Palais Bourbon de Paris*. Florence, Italy.
1905–6 *Papeles de Nueva España*. Segunda Seri, Geografía y Estadistica. 6 vols. Madrid.

Pearson, D., and F. Sánchez Martínez
1990 Casas-Acantilado in Chihuahua: Nueva evidencia en la Sierra Madre Occidental. *Arqueología* 4:41–58.

Peithman, R. I.
1961 *Culture History and Significance of Nayar White-on-Red*. Unpublished Master's thesis, Department of Anthropology, Southern Illinois University, Carbondale.

Peñafiel, A.
1890 *Monumentos del arte mexicano antiguo*. Berlin.

Pendergast, D. M.
1962a Metal Artifacts in Prehispanic Mesoamerica. *American Antiquity* 27:520–545.
1962b Metal Artifacts from Amapa, Nayarit, Mexico. *American Antiquity* 27:370–379.

Peregrine, P. N., and G. M. Feinman
1996 *Pre-columbian World Systems*. Monographs in World Archaeology, no. 26. Prehistory Press, Madison.

Pereira, G.
1996 Nuevos hallazgos funerarios en Loma Alta, Zacapu, Michoacán. In *Las cuencas del occidente de México: Epoca prehispánica*, edited by E. Williams and P. C. Weigand, pp. 105–129. ORSTOM, CEMCA. El Colegio de Michoacán, Zamora.
1997 Informe sobre el estudio tafonómico y bio-cultural de los restos humanos de Tingambato, Michoacán. Ms. on file, Dirección de Antropología Física, INAH, México, D.F.

Pérez de Ribas, A.
1645 *Historia de los triunfos de Nuestra Santa Fé, en las misiones de la provincia de Nueva España*. Madrid.
1985 *Páginas para la historia de Sonora: Triunfos de Nuestra Santa Fé*. 2 vols. Gobierno del Estado de Sonora, Hermosillo.

Peschard F., A. A.
1970 *Estudio morfológico de la deformación craneana artificial en el estado de Durango*. Universidad Juárez del Estado de Durango, Tesis Recepcional, Escuela de Medicina, Durango.
1983 Restos oseos del Cañón del Molino, Durango. Paper presented at the XVIII Mesa Redonda of the SMA, Taxco.

Peschard F., A. A., J. Ganot, and J. Lazalde
1984 Petroglifos de El Zape, Durango: Un calendario solar en el norte de México. Paper presented at Symposia de Arqueoastronomía y Ethnoastronomía, Ciudad Universitaria, UNAM, México, D.F.

Pétrequin, P. (editor)
1994 *8000 años de la cuenca de Zacapu*. Collection Etudes Mesoaméricaines II–14, Cuadernos de Estudios Michoacanos 6. CEMCA, México, D.F.

Phelps, A. L.
1964 *Cultural Analysis of Prehistoric Indian Sites of Northern Chihuahua, Mexico*. El Paso Archaeological Society Special Report 2.

Phillips, D. A.
1989 Prehistory of Chihuahua and Sonora, Mexico. *Journal of World Prehistory* 3:373–401.
1990a Areas arqueológicas de Chihuahua. In *Actas del Primer Congreso de Historia Regional Comparada 1989*, edited by A. Márquez-Alameda, pp. 11–21. Universidad Autónoma de Ciudad Juárez, Juárez.
1990b A Re-evaluation of the Robles Phase of the Casas Grandes Culture, Northwest Chihuahua. Paper presented at the 55th SAA Annual Meeting, Las Vegas, Nevada.
1991 Arqueología de la Sierra Madre Occidental en Chihuahua. In *Actas del Segundo Congreso de Historia Regional Comparada 1990*, edited by A. Márquez-Alameda, pp. 80–87. Universidad Autónoma de Ciudad Juárez, Juárez.

Phillips, D. A., and J. P. Carpenter
1999 The Robles Phase of the Casas Grandes Culture. In *The Casas Grandes World*, edited by C. F. Schaafsma and C. L. Riley, pp. 84–92. University of Utah Press, Salt Lake City.

Pickering, R. B.
1985 Human Osteological Remains from Alta Vista, Zacatecas: An Analysis of the Isolated Bone. In *The Archaeology of West and Northwest Mesoamerica*, edited by M. S. Foster and P. C. Weigand, pp. 289–325. Westview Press, Boulder.

Pickering, R. B., and Ma. T. Cabrero
1998 Mortuary Practices in the Shaft-Tomb Region. In *Ancient West Mexico: Art and Archaeology of the Unknown Past*, edited by R. Townsend, pp. 71–87. Art Institute of Chicago and Thames and Hudson, London.

Piña Chan, R.
1977 *Bitacora: Centro regional de México-Michoacán*. SEP-INAH, México, D.F.

Piña Chan, R., and K. Oí
1982 *Exploraciones arqueológicas en Tingambato, Michoacán*. INAH, México, D.F.

Plog, F., S. Upham, and P. C. Weigand
1982 A Perspective on Mogollon-Mesoamerican Interaction. In *Mogollon Archaeology: Proceedings of the 1980 Mogollon Conference*, edited by P. H. Beckett and K. Silverbird, pp. 227–238. Acoma Books, Ramona, California.

Pohl, J., and B. Byland
1994 The Mixteca-Puebla Style and Early Postclassic Socio-Political Interaction. In *Mixteca-Puebla: Discoveries and Research in Mesoamerican Art and Archaeology*, edited by H. B. Nicholson and E. Quiñones Keber, pp. 189–199. Labyrinthos, Culver City, California.

Polaco, O. J., and T. Alvarez
1978 *Informe de los restos procedentes de Tomatlán, Jalisco*. Laboratorio de Paleozoología, INAH, México, D.F.

Pollard, H. P.
1972 *Prehispanic Urbanism at Tzintzuntzan, Michoacán*. Unpublished Ph.D. dissertation, Department of Anthropology, Columbia University, New York.
1977 An Analysis of Urban Zoning and Planning in Prehispanic Tzintzuntzan. *Proceedings: American Philosophical Society* 121:46–69.
1979 Paleoecology of the Lake Pátzcuaro Basin: Implications for the Development of the Tarascan State. Paper presented at the 43rd International Congress of Americanists, Vancouver.
1980 Central Places and Cities: A Consideration of the Protohistoric Tarascan State. *American Antiquity* 45:677–696.
1982a Ecological Variation and Economic Exchange in the Tarascan State. *American Ethnologist* 9:250–268.
1982b Water and Politics: Paleoecology and the Centralization of the Tarascan State. Paper presented at the 44th International Congress of Americanists, Manchester, England.
1983 La cuenca del lago de Pátzcuaro: Población y recursos durante el período prehispánico y comienzas del hispánico, 1500–1550. *Revista de la Universidad* 2:22–23, Nueva Epoca. Universidad Michoacana, Morelia.
1987 The Political Economy of Prehispanic Tarascan Metallurgy. *American Antiquity* 52:741–752.
1988 Irechequa Tzintzuntzan: Variation on a Mesoamerican Theme. Paper presented at the 46th International Congress of Americanists, Amsterdam.
1991 The Construction of Ideology in the Emergence of the Prehispanic Tarascan State. *Ancient Mesoamerica* 2:167–179.
1992 Proyecto Urichu, desarrollo del estado Tarasco. *Boletín del Consejo de Arqueología, 1991*, pp. 222–224. INAH, México, D.F.
1993 *Tariacuri's Legacy: The Prehispanic Tarascan State*. University of Oklahoma Press, Norman.
1994a Ethnicity and Political Control in a Complex Society: The Tarascan State of Prehispanic Mexico. In *Factional Competition and Political Development in the New World*, edited by E. Brumfiel and J. W. Fox, pp. 79–88. Cambridge University Press, Cambridge.
1994b Merchant Colonies, Semi-Mesoamericans, and the Study of Cultural Contact: A Comment on Anawalt (1992). *Latin American Antiquity* 4:383–385.
1995 Estudio del surgimiento del estado Tarasco: Investigaciones recientes. In *Arqueología del occidente y norte de México*, pp. 29–63, edited by E. Williams and P. C. Weigand. El Colegio de Michoacán, Zamora.
1996 La transformación de elites regionales en Michoacán central. In *Las cuencas del occidente de México: Epoca prehispánica*, edited by E. Williams and P. C. Weigand, pp. 131–156. ORSTOM, El Colegio de Michoacán, CEMCA, México, D.F.

Pollard, H. P., M. Glaascock, and M. Rizo
1999 Preliminary Analysis of Obsidian Sources from the Lake Pátzcuaro Basin: The Urichu, Xarácuaro, and Pareo Polities. Paper presented at the 21st Annual Meeting of the Midwest Mesoamericanists, Michigan State University, East Lansing.

Pollard, H. P., and S. Gorenstein
1980 Agrarian Potential, Population, and the Tarascan State. *Science* 209:274–277.

Pollard, H. P., and T. A. Vogel
1994a Late Postclassic Imperial Expansion and Economic Exchange within the Tarascan Domain. In *Economies and Politics in the Aztec Realm*, edited by M. Smith and M. Hodge, pp. 447–470. Institute for Mesoamerican Studies. University of Texas Press, Austin.
1994b Implicaciones políticas y económicas del intercambio de obsidiana dentro del estado Tarasco. In *Arqueología del occidente de México nuevas aportaciones*, edited by E. Williams and R. Novella, pp. 159–182. El Colegio de Michoacán, Zamora.

Porter, M.
1948 Pottery Found at Chupícuaro, Guanajuato. In *El occidente de México, Cuarta Reunion de Mesa Redonda*, pp. 42–47. SMA, México, D.F.
1956 *Excavations at Chupícuaro, Guanajuato, Mexico*. Transactions of the American Philosophical Society 46:515–637. Philadelphia.

Porter de Moedano, M.
1945 Estudio de la cerámica: La estratigrafía. *Revista Mexicana de Estudios Antropológicos* 7(1, 2, 3):91–101. SMA, México, D.F.

Ramírez M., A.
1988 La antropología en Durango. In *La antropología en México: Panorama histórico: 12. La antropología en el norte de México*, edited by C. García Mora, pp. 309–344. Colección Biblioteca del INAH, México, D.F.

Ramírez Urrea, S.
1997 El papel interregional de la cuenca de Sayula, Jalisco, en el Epiclásico y Postclásico temprano: Observaciones preliminares. Paper presented at the IV Coloquio Bosch-Gimpera, Guadalajara, Jalisco.

Ramos de la Vega, J., and M. L. López Mestas Camberos
1992 *Investigaciones arqueológicas en la Sierra de Comanja, Guanajuato*. Tesis de Licenciatura Inédita, Escuela Nacional de Antropología/Universidad Autónoma de Guadalajara.
1994 El sitio de Huitzilapa y su tumba de tiro bóveda. Paper presented at the West Mexico Shaft Tomb Symposium, Denver Museum of Natural History.
1995 Datos preliminares sobe el descubrimiento de una tumba de tiro en el sitio de Huitzilapa, Jalisco. *Ancient Mesoamerica* 7:121–134.
1996 Arqueología de la Sierra de Comanja-Guanajuato. In *Tiempo y territorio en arqueología: El centro-norte de México*, edited by A. M. Crespo and C. Viramontes, pp. 93–113. INAH, México, D.F.
1998 Investigaciones arqueológicas en Huitzilapa, Jalisco. In *El occidente de México: Arqueología, historia y medio ambiente: Perspectivas regionales*, edited by R. Avila, J. P. Emphoux, L. Gastélum, S. Ramírez, O. Schöndube, and F. Valdez, pp. 157–166. Universidad de Guadalajara, ORSTOM, Guadalajara.

Ramos de la Vega, J., M. L. López Mestas Camberos, and R. B. Pickering

1996 La tumba de tiro de Huitzilapa, Jalisco. Paper presented at the IV Coloquio de Occidentalistas, Guadalajara.

Rattray, E. C.
1991 Fechamientos de radiocarbono en Teotihuacán. *Arqueología*, pp. 3–18. Revista de la Dirección de Arqueología del Instituto Nacional de Antropología e Historia, Segunda Epoca. México, D.F.

Ravesloot, J. C.
1979 *The Animas Phase: Post-Classic Mimbres Occupation of the Mimbres Valley, New Mexico*. Unpublished Master's thesis, Department of Anthropology, Southern Illinois University, Carbondale.
1988 *Mortuary Practices and Social Differentiation at Casas Grandes, Chihuahua, Mexico*. Anthropological Papers of the University of Arizona, no. 49. University of Arizona Press, Tucson.

Ravesloot, J. C., J. S. Dean, and M. S. Foster
1995 A New Perspective on the Casas Grandes Tree-Ring Dates. In *The Gran Chichimeca: Essays on the Archaeology and Ethnohistory of Northern Mesoamerica*, edited by J. E. Reyman, pp. 240–251. Avebury Press, Brookfield, Vermont.

Ravesloot, J. C., and P. M. Spoerl
1989 The Role of Warfare in the Development of Status Hierarchies at Casas Grandes, Chihuahua, Mexico. In *Cultures in Conflict: Current Archaeological Perspectives*, edited by D. C. Tkazak and B. C. Vivian, pp. 130–137. Proceedings of the 20th Annual Chacmool Conference, Archaeological Association of the University of Calgary, Calgary.

Reff, D. T.
1991 *Disease, Depopulation, and Culture Change in Northwestern New Spain, 1518–1764*. University of Utah Press, Salt Lake City.

Regino T., A.
1991 Hallan en San Vicente, Nayarit: 17 piezas arqueológicas. *Vallarta Opina*, pp. 1 and 4. Puerto Vallarta.

Relación de Michoacán (1541)
1956 *Relación de las ceremonias y ritos y población y gobierno de Michoacán*. Reproducción facsimilar del Ms IV de El Escorial, Madrid. Aguilar Publicistas, Madrid.
1980 *La relación de Michoacán*. Versión paleográfica, separación de textos, ordenación coloquil, estudio preliminar y notas de F. Miranda. Estudios Michoacanos V. Fimax, Morelia, Michoacán.

Relaciones Geográficas (1579–81)
1985 *Relaciones y memorias de la provincia de Michoacán, 1579–1581*. A. Ochoa S. and G. Sánchez D., editors. Universidad Michoacana, Ayuntamiento de Morelia, Morelia.
1987 *Relaciones geográficas del siglo XVI: Michoacán*. Edición de René Acuña, Instituto de Investigaciones Antropológicas, Serie Antropológica, 74. UNAM, México, D.F.

Renfrew, C.
1986 Introduction. In *Peer Polity Interaction and Socio-Political Change*, edited by C. Renfrew and J. Cherry, pp. 1–18. Cambridge University Press, Cambridge.

Renfrew, C., and J. Cherry (editors)
1986 *Peer Polity Interaction and Socio-Political Change*. Cambridge University Press, Cambridge.

Renfrew, C., and S. Shennan
1982 *Ranking, Resource, and Exchange: Aspects of the Archaeology of Early European Society*. Cambridge University Press, New York.

Reyman, J. E. (editor)
1995 *The Gran Chichimeca: Essays on the Archaeology and Ethnohistory of Northern Mesoamerica*. Avebury Press, Brookfield, Vermont.

Riley, C. L.
1987 *The Frontier People: The Greater Southwest in the Protohistoric Period*. University of New Mexico Press, Albuquerque.
1990 A View from the Protohistoric. In *Perspectives on Southwestern Prehistory*, edited by P. Minnis and C. Redman, pp. 228–238. Westview Press, Boulder.
1993 Charles C. Di Peso: An Intellectual Biography. In *Culture and Contact: Charles C. Di Peso's Gran Chichimeca*, edited by A. I. Woosley and J. C. Ravesloot, pp. 11–22. University of New Mexico Press, Albuquerque.

Riley, C. L., and B. C. Hedrick (editors)
1978 *Across the Chichimec Sea: Papers in Honor of J. Charles Kelley*. Southern Illinois University Press, Carbondale.

Riley, C. L., and H. D. Winters
1963 The Prehistoric Tepehuan of Northern Mexico. *Southwestern Journal of Anthropology* 19:177–185.

Robinson, W. J., and R. V. N. Ahlstrom
1980 A Re-evaluation of Using Heartwood to Estimate Sapwood. Report submitted to the Taylor Museum, Colorado Springs Fine Arts Center, Colorado Springs.

Robles, C.
1929 *La región arqueológica de Casas Grandes*. México, D.F.

Rodríguez, F.
1983 *Outillaje lithique de chasseurs-collecteurs du nord de Mexique*. Collection Etudes Mesoaméricaines II-6. CEMCA. Editions Recherche sur les Civilizations, Paris.
1985 *Les Chichimeques*. Collection Etudes Mesoaméricaines I-12. CEMCA. México, D.F.

Romero Molina, J.
1986 *Catálogo de la colección de dientes mutilados prehispánicos. IV*. Colección Fuentes. INAH, México, D.F.

Roney, J. R.
1996a Late Archaic Cerros de Trincheras in Northwestern Chihuahua. Paper presented at the 61st Annual Meeting of the SAA, New Orleans.
1996b Cerro Juanquena: A Late Archaic Cerro de Trincheras in Northwestern Chihuahua. Paper presented at the Conference on the Archaic Prehistory of the North American Southwest, Albuquerque.

Roskamp, H.
1998 *La historiografía indígena de Michoacán: El lienzo de Jucutácato y los títulos de Carapan*. Research School CNWS, Leiden University, Leiden.

Rousseau, X.
1990 *Comentarios al Coloquio de Occidentalistas*. Laboratorio de Antropología, Universidad de Guadalajara.

Rubín de la Borbolla, D. F.
1939 Antropología Tzintzuntzan-Ihuatzio: Temporadas I y

II. *Revista Mexicana de Estudios Antropológicas* 3:99–121.
1941 Exploraciones arqueológicas en Michoacán: Tzintzuntzan temporada III. *Revista Mexicana de Estudios Antropológicas* 5:5–20.
1944 Orfebrería tarasca. *Cuadernos Americanos* 3:125–138.

Rzedowski, J.
1978 *Vegetación de México*. Editorial Limusa, México, D.F.

Sáenz, C. A.
1966 Cabecitas y figurillas de barro del Ixtépete, Jalisco. *Boletín del Instituto Nacional de Antropología e Historia* 24:47–49. INAH, México, D.F.

Sahagún, B. de (1569)
1950–69 *Florentine Codex: General History of the Things of New Spain*. A. Anderson and C. Dibble, translators. University of Utah Press, Salt Lake City, and School of American Research, Santa Fe.

Saint-Charles, J. C.
1990 *Cerámicas arqueológicas del Bajío: Un estudio metodológico*. Tesis de Licenciatura, Universidad Veracruzana, Jalapa.
1991 *Cerro de la Cruz, San Juan del Río, Querétaro: Informe de análisis de materiales*. Centro de Estudios e Investigaciones Antropológicas, Universidad Autónoma de Querétaro. Informe al Consejo de Arqueología, INAH, México, D.F.

Saint-Charles, J. C., and M. Arguelles
1991 Cerro de la Cruz: Persistencia de un centro ceremonial. In *Querétaro prehispánico*, edited by A. M. Crespo and R. Brambila, pp. 57–97. Colección Científica. INAH, México, D.F.

Sánchez, G., J. P. Carpenter, and M. E. Villalpando
1997 Proyecto La Playa: Five Thousand Years of Occupation in the Boquillas Valley, Sonora, Mexico. Paper presented at the 61st Annual Meeting of the SAA, New Orleans.

Sánchez Correa, S. A.
1995 La Gavia, Guanajuato: Aproximación al desarrolla cultural de una porción del Bajío noroccidental. Unpublished Master's thesis, ENAH, INAH, México, D.F.

Sánchez Correa, S., and E. Marmolejo Morales
1990 Algunas apreciaciones sobre el Clásico en el Bajío Central, Guanajuato. In *La época Clásica: Nuevos hallazgos, nuevas ideas: Seminario de Arqueología*, edited by A. Cardos de Méndez, pp. 267–278. MNA and INAH, México, D.F.

Sanders, W. T., and J. Michels (editors)
1977 *Kaminaljuyu and Teotihuacán: Prehistoric Culture Contact*. Pennsylvania State University Press, University Park.

Sanders, W. T., J. R. Parsons, and R. S. Santley
1979 *The Basin of Mexico: Ecological Processes in the Evolution of a Civilization*. Academic Press, New York.

Sanders, W. T., and B. J. Price
1968 *Mesoamerica: The Evolution of a Civilization*. Random House, New York.

Santley, R. S., M. J. Berman, and R. T. Alexander
1991 The Politicization of the Mesoamerican Ballgame and Its Implications for the Interpretation of the Distribution of Ballcourts in Central Mexico. In *The Mesoamerican Ballgame*, edited by V. Scarborough and D. R. Wilcox, pp. 3–24. University of Arizona Press, Tucson.

Sauer, C. O.
1932 *The Road to Cibola*. Ibero-Americana 3. University of California Press, Berkeley.
1948 *Colima of New Spain in the Sixteenth Century*. Ibero-Americana 29. University of California Press, Berkeley.

Sauer, C. O., and D. D. Brand
1930 Pueblo Sites in Southeastern Arizona. *University of California Publications in Geography* 3:415–458.
1931 Prehistoric Settlements of Sonora with Special Reference to Cerro de Trincheras. *University of California Publications in Geography* 5:67–148.
1932 *Aztatlan: Prehistoric Mexican Frontier on the Pacific Coast*. Ibero-Americana 5. University of California Press, Berkeley.

Sayles, E. B.
1936a *An Archaeological Survey of Chihuahua, Mexico*. Medallion Papers, no. 22. Gila Pueblo, Globe, Arizona.
1936b *Some Southwestern Pottery Types, Series V*. Medallion Papers, no. 21. Gila Pueblo, Globe, Arizona.

Schaafsma, C. F.
1979 The El Paso Phase and Its Relationship to the Casas Grandes Phenomenon. In *Jornada Mogollon Archaeology: Proceedings of the First Jornada Conference*, edited by P. Beckett and R. Wiseman, pp. 383–388. COAS Publishing, Las Cruces, New Mexico.
1997 Ethnohistoric Groups in the Casas Grandes Region, circa A.D. 1500–1700. In *Layers of Time: Papers in Honor of Robert H. Weber*, edited by M. S. Duran and D. T. Kirkpatrick, pp. 85–98. Archaeological Society of New Mexico, no. 23. Albuquerque.

Schaafsma, P.
1980 *Indian Rock Art of the Southwest*. School of American Research, Santa Fe, and University of New Mexico Press, Albuquerque.

Schafer, B.
1996 Numerology. *Archaeoastronomy and Ethnoastronomy News*, p. 2. Center for Archaeoastronomy, College Park, Maryland.

Schiavitti, V. W.
1995 *Organization of the Prehispanic Suchil Mining District of Chalchihuites, Mexico, A.D. 400–950*. Unpublished Ph.D. dissertation, Department of Anthropology, State University of New York at Buffalo.

Schmidt, R. H., Jr.
1973 *A Geographical Survey of Chihuahua*. Southwestern Studies Monograph no. 37. University of Texas at El Paso. Texas Western Press, El Paso.
1992 Chihuahua, tierra de contrastes geográficos. In *Historia general de Chihuahua I: Geología, geografía y arqueología*, edited by A. Márquez-Alameda, pp. 47–101. Universidad Autónoma de Ciudad Juárez and Gobierno del Estado de Chihuahua, Chihuahua.

Schmidt, R. H., Jr., and R. E. Gerald
1988 The Distribution of Conservation-Type Water-Control Systems in the Semi-Arid Northern Sierra Madre Occidental. *The Kiva* 53:165–179.

Schneider, J.
1977 Was there a Pre-Capitalist World-System? *Peasant Studies* 6:20–29.

Schöndube B., O.
1980 Epoca prehispánica. In *Historia de Jalisco: Vol. 1, Desde los tiempos prehistóricos hasta fines del siglo XVII*, edited by J. M. Muriá, pp. 113–257. Unidad Editorial del Gobierno de Jalisco, Guadalajara.
1983 Hallazgos en el hospital de Belén. PANTOC 5:51–68. Universidad Autónoma de Guadalajara, Guadalajara, Jalisco.
1987 El occidente de México: Algunas de sus características y problemas. In *Homenaje a Román Piña Chan*, pp. 403–410. Instituto de Investigaciones Antropológicas, Serie Antropológica, 79. UNAM, México, D.F.
1998 Identification of Plants and Animals on Colima Style Ceramics. Paper presented at the West Mexico Shaft Tomb Symposium, Denver Museum of Natural History, Denver.

Schöndube B., O., and L. J. Galván V.
1978 Salvage Archaeology at El Grillo-Tabachines, Zapopán, Jalisco, Mexico. In *Across the Chichimec Sea: Papers in Honor of J. Charles Kelley*, edited by C. L. Riley and B. C. Hedrick, pp. 144–164. Southern Illinois University Press, Carbondale.

Schortman, E. M., and P. A. Urban
1987 Modeling Interregional Interaction in Prehistory. In *Archaeological Advances in Method and Theory*, vol. 11, edited by M. B. Schiffer, pp. 37–95. Academic Press, New York.
1992 *Resources, Power, and Interregional Interaction*. Plenum Press, New York.

Schwatka, F.
1893 *In the Land of Cave and Cliff Dwellers*. Cassell, New York.

Scott, P. K.
1978 The Marismas Nacionales: An Historical View of the Conquest and Early Post-Conquest Periods. Manuscript.

Scott, S. D.
1966 *Dendrochronology in Mexico*. Papers of the Laboratory of Tree-Ring Research, no. 2. University of Arizona Press, Tucson.
1974 Archaeology and the Estuary: Researching Prehistory and Paleoecology in the Marismas Nacionales, Sinaloa and Nayarit, Mexico. In *The Archaeology of West Mexico*, edited by B. B. Bell, pp. 51–56. Sociedad de Estudio Avanzados del Occidente de México, Ajijic, Jalisco.
1985 Core versus Marginal Mesoamerica: A Coastal West Mexican Perspective. In *The Archaeology of West and Northwest Mesoamerica*, edited by M. S. Foster and P. C. Weigand, pp. 181–192. Westview Press, Boulder.

Sejourné, L.
1957 *Pensamiento y religión en el México antiguo*. Fondo de Cultura Económica, México, D.F.
1970 Arqueología del valle de México, 1. *Culhuacán*. México, D.F.

Seler, E.
1908 *Gesammelte Abhandlungen zur Amerikanischen Sprach und Altertumskunde*, vol. 3. Behrend, Berlin.
1960 Die Ruinen von La Quemada im Staate Zacatecas [1908]. In *Gesammelte Abhandlungen zur Amerikanischen Sprach und Altertumskunde*, vol. 3, pp. 545–559. Akademische Drucksund Verlagsanstalt, Graz, Austria.

Sempowski, M.
1994 Mortuary Practices at Teotihuacán. In *Mortuary Practices and Skeletal Remains at Teotihuacán*, by M. Sempowski and M. W. Spence, pp. 1–311. University of Utah Press, Salt Lake City.

Sepúlveda y H., M. T.
1988 *La medicina entre los Purépecha prehispánicos*. Serie Antropológica, 94. UNAM, México, D.F.

Shenkel, J. R.
1971 *Cultural Adaptation to the Mollusk: A Methodological Survey of Shell Mound Archaeology and a Consideration of the Shell Mounds of the Marismas Nacionales, Mexico*. Unpublished Ph.D. dissertation, Department of Anthropology, State University of New York at Buffalo.
1974 Quantitative Analysis and Population Estimates of the Shell Mounds of the Marismas Nacionales, Sinaloa and Nayarit, Mexico. In *The Archaeology of West Mexico*, edited by B. B. Bell, pp. 51–56. Sociedad de Estudio Avanzados del Occidente de México, Ajijic, Jalisco.
1978 Shell Mounds of the Marismas Nacionales. Manuscript.

Silva, J. P., and T. R. Hester
1973 Archaeological Materials from a Nonceramic Site in Eastern Durango, Mexico. In *Contributions of the University of California Archaeological Research Facility*, pp. 149–165. University of California, Department of Anthropology, Berkeley.

Sirkin, L.
1978 The Marismas Nacionales: Palynological Studies. Manuscript.

Smith, A. L.
1950 *Uaxactún, Guatemala: Excavations of 1931–1937*. Carnegie Institution of Washington, Publication 588. Washington, D.C.

Smith, M. E.
1996 *The Aztecs*. Blackwell, Oxford.

Smith, M. E., and C. M. Heath-Smith
1980 Waves of Influence in Postclassic Mesoamerica? A Critique of the Mixteca-Puebla Concept. *Anthropology* 4:15–50.

Smith, R. E.
1955 *Ceramic Sequence at Uaxactún, Guatemala*, vol. 1. Publication no. 20, Middle American Research Institute. Tulane University, New Orleans.

Snarskis, M.
1985 Ceramic Analysis (Appendix III). In *Acambaro: Frontier Settlement on the Tarascan-Aztec Border*, by S. Gorenstein, pp. 207–296. Publications in Anthropology, no. 32. Vanderbilt University, Nashville.

Snedaker, S. C.
1971 The Calón Shell Mound: An Ecological Anachronism.

In *Archaeological Reconnaissance and Excavations in the Marismas Nacionales: Sinaloa and Nayarit, Mexico. West Mexican Prehistory*, part 5. Department of Anthropology, State University of New York at Buffalo.

Sociedad Mexicana de Antropología
1947 *El occidente de México*. SMA, México, D.F.

Solórzano, F.
1980 Prehistoria. *Historia de Jalisco* 1:71–110. Gobierno del Estado de Jalisco, Guadalajara.

Soto de Arechavaleta, Ma. de D.
1982 *Análisis de la tecnología de producción de taller de obsidiana de Guachimonton, Teuchitlán, Jalisco*. Tesis, ENAH, México, D.F.

Spence, M. W.
1971 *Some Lithic Assemblages of Western Zacatecas and Durango, Mexico*. Mesoamerican Studies, no. 8. Research Records of the University Museum, Southern Illinois University, Carbondale.
1978 A Cultural Sequence from the Sierra Madre of Durango, Mexico. In *Across the Chichimec Sea: Papers in Honor of J. Charles Kelley*, edited by C. L. Riley and B. C. Hedrick, pp. 165–189. Southern Illinois University Press, Carbondale.
1996 A Comparative Analysis of Ethnic Enclaves. In *Arqueología mesoamericana: Homenaje a William T. Sanders I*, edited by A. Mastache, J. R. Parsons, R. Santley, and M. del C. Serra Puche, pp. 333–353. INAH, México, D.F.

Stark, B. L.
1981 The Rise of Sedentary Life. In *Archaeology*, Supplement 1, edited by V. R. Bricker, pp. 345–372. *HBMI*, Supplement 1, J. A. Sabloff, volume editor. University of Texas Press, Austin.
1986 Perspectives on the Peripheries of Mesoamerica. In *Ripples in the Chichimec Sea: New Considerations of Southwestern-Mesoamerican Interactions*, edited by F. J. Mathien and R. H. McGuire, pp. 270–290. Southern Illinois University Press, Carbondale.

Steward, J.
1955 *Theory of Culture Change*. University of Illinois Press, Urbana.

Stocker, T.
1983 *Clay Figurines from Tula, Hidalgo, Mexico*. Unpublished Ph.D. dissertation, Department of Anthropology, University of Illinois, Urbana.

Strazicich, N. M.
1995 *Prehispanic Pottery Production in the Chalchihuites and La Quemada Regions of Zacatecas, Mexico*. Unpublished Ph.D. Dissertation, Department of Anthropology, State University of New York at Buffalo.
1996 Neutron Activation Analysis of Pottery and Clays from the Chalchihuites Region of Northern Mexico. Paper presented at the Archaeometry Conference, State University of New York, Buffalo.

Street-Perrott, F. A., R. A. Perrott, and D. Harkness
1989 Anthropogenic Soil Erosion around Lake Pátzcuaro, Michoacán, during the Preclassic and Late Postclassic-Hispanic Period. *American Antiquity* 54:759–765.

Stuart, G.
1992 Better Loams and Gardens: The Archaeological Potential of Palynological Research on Chinampas Highland Lake Areas of Jalisco, Mexico. Report on file, Department of Anthropology, Arizona State University, Tempe.

Sugiura Y., Y.
1996 El Epiclásico y el problema del Coyotlatelco vistos desde el valle de Toluca. In *Arqueología mesoamericana: Homenaje a William T. Sanders*, edited by A. Mastache, J. R. Parsons, R. Santley, and M. del C. Serra Puche, pp. 233–255. INAH, México, D.F.

Taladoire, E.
1989 Las canchas de juego de plota de Michoacán. *Trace* 16:88–99. CEMCA, México, D.F.

Tassin, W.
1902 The Casas Grandes Meteorite. *U.S. National Museum Proceedings* 5:69–74. Washington, D.C.

Taylor, R. E.
1987 *Radiocarbon Dating: An Archaeological Perspective*. Academic Press, New York.

Taylor, R. E., and R. Berger
1967 Radiocarbon Content of Marine Shells from the Pacific Coasts of Central and South America. *Science* 158:1180–1182.

Taylor, W. W.
1966 Archaic Cultures Adjacent to the Northeastern Frontiers of Mesoamerica. In *Archaeological Frontiers and External Connections*, edited by G. F. Ekholm and G. R. Willey, pp. 59–94. HBMI, vol. 4, R. Wauchope, general editor. University of Texas Press, Austin.

Tello, A.
1968 *Crónica miscelánea de la sancta provincia de Xalisco, Libro II*, vol. 1. Instituto Jalisciense de Antropología e Historia, Guadalajara.

Torquemada, Fray Juan de
1986 *Monarquia indiana*. 3 vols. 6th ed. Editorial Porrúa, México, D.F.

Trejo de la Rosa, L.
1979 Loma de Santa María, Morelia, Mich. In *Bitácora 1997: Centro Regional México-Michoacán*, edited by R. Piña Chan, pp. 24–27. INAH, México, D.F.

Trombold, C. D.
1976 Spatial Distribution, Functional Hierarchies, and Patterns of Interaction in Prehistoric Communities around La Quemada, Zacatecas, Mexico. In *Archaeological Frontiers: Papers on New World High Cultures in Honor of J. Charles Kelley*, edited by R. B. Pickering, pp. 149–182. Research Records, no. 4. University Museum Studies, Southern Illinois University, Carbondale.
1985 A Summary of the Archaeology in the La Quemada Region. In *The Archaeology of West and Northwest Mesoamerica*, edited by M. S. Foster and P. C. Weigand, pp. 237–267. Westview Press, Boulder.
1986 A Preliminary Guide to Incised/Engraved Ceramics and Their Site Distributions in the La Quemada Region, Zacatecas, Mexico. Report on file, INAH Centro Regional, Zacatecas.
1990 A Reconsideration of Chronology for the La Quemada

Portion of the Mesoamerican Frontier. *American Antiquity* 55:308–324.

1991 Causeways in the Context of Strategic Planning in the La Quemada Region. In *Ancient Road Networks and Settlement Hierarchies in the New World*, edited by C. D. Trombold, pp. 145–168. Cambridge University Press, New York.

Trombold, C. D., J. Luhr, T. Hasenaka, and M. Glaascock

1993 Chemical Characteristics of Obsidian from Archaeological Sites in Western Mexico and the Tequila Source Area: Implications for Regional and Pan-regional Interaction within the Northern Mesoamerican Periphery. *Ancient Mesoamerica* 4:255–270.

Turner II, C. G.

1993 Southwest Indians: Prehistory through Dentition. *National Geographic Research and Publication* 9:1:32–53.

Upham, S.

1982 *Politics and Power*. Academic Press, New York.

1986 Imperialists, Isolationists, World Systems, and Political Realities: Perspectives on Mesoamerican-Southwestern Interaction. In *Ripples in the Chichimec Sea: New Considerations of Southwestern-Mesoamerican Interactions*, edited by F. J. Mathien and R. H. McGuire, pp. 205–219. Southern Illinois University Press, Carbondale.

1991 *The Evolution of Political Systems: Sociopolitics in Small-Scale Sedentary Societies*. Cambridge University Press, New York.

Valdez, F.

1993a Las áreas domésticas en el sitio San Juan, Atoyac, Jalisco. In *Contribuciones a la arqueología y etnohistoria del occidente de México*, edited by E. Williams, pp. 23–53. El Colegio de Michoacán, Zamora.

1993b Variabilidad en los patrones de asentamiento en la cuenca de Sayula, Jalisco: Estudio arqueológico de la evolución en los usos del espacio rural. *Trace* 24:47–53.

1994 Tumbos de tiro en Usmajac (Jalisco): Hacia una reoritatción de la temática. *Trace* 25:96–111.

1996 Tiempo, espacio y cultura en la cuenca de Sayula. In *Estudios del Hombre 3*, edited by O. Schöndube and F. Valdez, pp. 15–36. Universidad de Guadalajara, Guadalajara.

Valdez, F., and C. Liot

1993 La cuenca de Sayula: Yacimientos de sal en la frontera oeste del estado Tarasco. In *El Michocán antiguo*, edited by B. Boehm de Lameiras, pp. 285–305. El Colegio de Michoacán, Zamora, and Gobierno del Estado de Michoacán.

Valdez, F., C. Liot, R. Acosta, and J. P. Emphoux

1996 The Sayula Basin: Lifeways and Salt Flats of Central Jalisco. *Ancient Mesoamerica* 7:171–186.

Vargas, V. D.

1995 *Copper Bell Trade Patterns in the Prehispanic U.S. Southwest and Northwest Mexico*. Arizona State Museum Archaeological Series, no. 187. University of Arizona, Tucson.

Velasco, M.

1990 El norte de Mesoamérica: Al Sierra Gorda. In *Mesoamérica y norte de México, siglos IX–XII*, edited by F. Sodi Miranda, pp. 459–466. MNA and INAH, México, D.F.

Villalpando, M. E.

1997 La tradición trincheras y los grupos costeros del desierto sonorense. In *Prehistory of the Borderlands: Recent Research in the Archaeology of Northern Mexico and the Southern Southwest*, edited by G. Sánchez and J. P. Carpenter, pp. 95–112. Arizona State Museum Archaeological Series, no. 186. University of Arizona, Tucson.

Villanueva G., G.

1979 Evidencias arqueozoológicas de explotación de recursos litorales en Tomatlán, Jalisco. *Boletín de INAH* 3:30:20–37. México, D.F.

Villanueva G., G., J. Manrique E., and L. López M.

1996 Especies marinas ofrendadas en la tumba de tiro de Huitzilapa. Paper presented at the IV Coloquio de Occidentalistas, Guadalajara.

Visitación

1937 Visitación que se hizo en la Conquista, donde fue por Capitán Francisco Cortéz, en Nuño de Guzmán contra Hernán Cortés, sobre los descubrimientos y conquistas de Jalisco y Tepic, 1531. *Boletín del Archivo General de la Nación* 8:4:556–572. México, D.F.

Vivó Escoto, J. A.

1964 Weather and Climate of Mexico and Central America. In *Natural Environment and Early Cultures*, edited by R. C. West, pp. 187–215. HBMI, vol. 1, R. Wauchope, general editor. University of Texas Press, Austin.

von Winning, H.

1956 Offerings from a Burial Mound in Coastal Nayarit. *Masterkey* 30:157–170.

1974 *The Shaft Tomb Figures of West Mexico*. Southwest Museum, Los Angeles.

von Winning, H., and O. Hammer

1972 *Anecdotal Sculpture in Ancient West Mexico*. Ethnic Arts Council, Natural History Museum of Los Angeles County.

Wallerstein, I.

1974 *The Modern World System I*. Academic Press, New York.

1979 *The Modern World System II*. Academic Press, New York.

Warren, J. B.

1985 *The Conquest of Michoacán*. University of Oklahoma Press, Norman.

1990 *Diccionario grande de la lengua de Michoacán*. [Sixteenth century.] Fimax Publicistas, Morelia, Michoacán.

Warren, J. B. (editor)

1977 *La conquista de Michoacán, 1521–1530*. Fimax Publicistas, Morelia, Michoacán.

Watts, W., and J. P. Bradbury

1982 Paleoecological Studies at Lake Patzcuaro on the West-Central Mexican Plateau and at Chalco in the Basin of Mexico. *Quaternary Research* 17:56–70.

Weaver, M. P.

1969 A Reappraisal of Chupicuaro. In *The Natalie Wood Collection of Pre-Columbian Ceramics from Chupicuaro, Guanajuato, Mexico*, edited by J. D. Frierman, pp. 3–15. University of California, Los Angeles.

1972 *The Aztecs, Maya, and Their Predecessors.* Seminar Press, New York.
1981 *The Aztecs, Maya, and Their Predecessors: Archaeology of Mesoamerica.* 2nd ed. Academic Press, New York.
1993 *The Aztecs, Maya, and Their Predecessors: Archaeology of Mesoamerica.* 3rd ed. Academic Press, New York.

Weigand, P. C.
1968 The Mines and Mining Techniques of the Chalchihuites Culture. *American Antiquity* 33:45–61.
1974 The Ahualulco Site and the Shaft-Tomb Complex of the Etzatlán Area. In *The Archaeology of West Mexico,* edited by B. B. Bell, pp. 120–131. Sociedad de Estudios Avanzados del Occidente de Mexico, Ajijic, Jalisco.
1975 Circular Ceremonial Structure Complexes in the Highlands of Western Mexico. In *Archaeological Frontiers: Papers on New World High Cultures in Honor of J. Charles Kelley,* edited by R. B. Pickering, pp. 183–227. Research Records, no. 4. University Museum Studies, Southern Illinois University, Carbondale.
1977 La prehistoria de Zacatecas: Una interpretación. In *Zacatecas: Anuario de historia I,* edited by Cuauhtémoc Esparza Sánchez, pp. 203–249. Universidad Autónoma de Zacatecas, Zacatecas.
1978a The Prehistory of Zacatecas: An Interpretation. Part I. *Anthropology* 2:67–87. State University of New York at Stony Brook.
1978b The Prehistory of Zacatecas: An Interpretation. Part II. *Anthropology* 2:103–117. State University of New York at Stony Brook.
1982 Mining and Mineral Trade in Prehistoric Zacatecas. In *Mining and Mining Techniques in Ancient Mesoamerica,* edited by P. C. Weigand and G. Gwynne, pp. 87–134. *Anthropology* 6, special issue. State University of New York at Stony Brook.
1985 Evidence for Complex Societies during the Western Mesoamerican Classic Period. In *The Archaeology of West and Northwest Mesoamerica,* edited by M. S. Foster and P. C. Weigand, pp. 47–91. Westview Press, Boulder.
1986 *Coyula.* Report submitted to the Centro Regional de Jalisco.
1988 Architecture and Settlement Patterns within the Western Mesoamerican Formative Tradition. In *El Preclásico o Formativo: Avances y perspectivas,* edited by M. Carmona, pp. 39–64. INAH, MNA, México, D.F.
1990a The Teuchitlán Tradition of Western Mesoamerica. In *La época Clásica: Nuevos hallazgos, nuevas ideas,* edited by A. Cardos de Méndez, pp. 25–54. MNA, INAH, México, D.F.
1990b Discontinuity: The Collapse of the Teuchitlán Tradition and the Early Postclassic Cultures of Western Mesoamerica. In *Mesoamérica y norte de México, siglos IX–XII,* edited by F. Sodi Miranda, pp. 215–222. INAH, México, D.F.
1991 The Western Mesoamerican Tlachco: A Two-Thousand-Year Perspective. In *The Mesoamerican Ballgame,* edited by V. L. Scarborough and D. R. Wilcox, pp. 73–86. University of Arizona Press, Tucson.
1992a Introducción. In *Origen y desarrollo de la civilización en el occidente de México,* edited by B. Boehm de L. and P. C. Weigand, pp. 13–26. El Colegio de Michoacán, Zamora.
1992b Central Mexico's Influences in Jalisco and Nayarit during the Classic Period. In *Resources, Power, and Interregional Interaction,* edited by E. Schortman and P. Urban, pp. 221–232. Plenum Press, New York.
1992c Ehecatl: Primer dios supremo del occidente? In *Origen y desarrollo de la civilización en el occidente de México,* edited by B. Boehm de L. and P. C. Weigand, pp. 205–237. El Colegio de Michoacán, Zamora.
1993a Evolución de una civilización prehispánica: Arqueología de Jalisco, Nayarit, y Zacatecas. El Colegio de Michoacán, Zamora.
1993b Large-Scale Hydraulic Works in Prehistoric Western Mesoamerica. In *Research in Economic Anthropology,* edited by V. L. Scarborough and B. Isaac, pp. 223–262. JAI Press, Greenwich.
1996 Teuchitlán Tradition of the Occidente of Mesoamerica. *Ancient Mesoamerica* 7:91–101.
1999 The Architecture of the Teuchitlán Tradition of Mexico's Occidente. In *Mesoamerican Architecture as a Cultural Symbol,* edited by J. K. Kowalski, pp. 87–109. Oxford University Press, Oxford.

Weigand, P. C., and C. S. Beekman
1998 The Teuchitlán Tradition: Rise of a State-like Society. In *Ancient West Mexico: Art and Archaeology of the Unknown Past,* edited by R. Townsend, pp. 35–51. Art Institute of Chicago and Thames and Hudson, London.

Weigand, P. C., and A. García de Weigand
1995 *Los orígenes de los Caxcanes.* Ensayos Jaliscienses. El Colegio de Jalisco, Zapopan.
1996 *Tenamaxtli y Guaxicar: Las raices profundas de la rebelión de Nueva Galicia.* El Colegio de Michoacán and Secretaría de Cultura de Jalisco, Zamora-Guadalajara.

Weigand, P. C., A. García de Weigand, and J. A. Darling
1999 El sitio arqueológico: "Cerro de Tepecuazco" (Jalpa, Zacatecas) y sus relaciones con la tradición de Teuchitlán. In *Tercer simposium: Los altos de Jalisco a fin de siglo,* edited by C. González Pérez, pp. 241–274. Sistema de Educación Media Superior, Universidad de Guadalajara, Jalisco.

Weigand, P. C., and G. Harbottle
1992 The Role of Turquoises in the Ancient Mesoamerican Trade Structure. In *The American Southwest and Mesoamerica: Systems of Prehistoric Exchange,* edited by T. G. Baugh and J. E. Ericson, pp. 159–177. Plenum Press, New York.

Weigand, P. C., and L. Neal
1989 Salt Procurement and Distribution in Ancient Western Mesoamerica. Manuscript.

Weigand, P. C., and M. W. Spence
1982 The Obsidian Mining Complex at La Joya, Jalisco. In *Mining and Mining Techniques in Ancient Mesoamerica,* edited by P. C. Weigand and G. Gwynne, pp. 175–188. *Anthropology* 6, special issue. State University of New York, Stony Brook.

West, M. S.
1964 *Tezoyuca: An Archaeological Excavation and Settlement Pattern Study of a Terminal Pre-classic Site and Its Implications in the Culture History of the Valley of Teotihuacán, Mexico.* Unpublished Master's thesis, Department of Sociology and Anthropology, Pennsylvania State University, University Park.
1965 Transition from Preclassic to Classic at Teotihuacán. *American Antiquity* 31:193-202.

West, R. C.
1964a The Natural Regions of Middle America. In *Natural Environment and Early Cultures,* edited by R. C. West, pp. 363-383. HBMI, vol. 1, R. Wauchope, general editor. University of Texas Press, Austin.
1964b Surface Configuration and Associated Geology of Middle America. In *Natural Environment and Early Cultures,* edited by R. C. West, pp. 33-83. HBMI, vol. 1, R. Wauchope, general editor. University of Texas Press, Austin.

Whalen, M. E., and P. E. Minnis
1996a Ball Courts and Political Centralization in the Casas Grandes Region. *American Antiquity* 61:732-746.
1996b The Context of Production in and around Paquimé, Chihuahua, Mexico. In *Interpreting Southwestern Diversity: Underlying Principles and Overarching Patterns,* edited by P. R. Fish and J. Reid, pp. 173-182. Arizona State University Anthropological Research Papers, no. 48. Arizona State University, Tempe.
1999 The Paquimé Regional System. In *The Casas Grandes World,* edited by C. F. Schaafsma and C. L. Riley, pp. 54-62. University of Utah Press, Salt Lake City.

Wheatley, P.
1971 *The Pivot of the Four Quarters.* Aldine, Chicago.

Whitecotton, J. W., and R. A. Pailes
1986 New World Precolumbian World Systems. In *Ripples in the Chichimec Sea: New Considerations of Southwestern-Mesoamerican Interactions,* edited by F. J. Mathien and R. H. McGuire, pp. 183-204. Southern Illinois University Press, Carbondale.

Wilcox, D. R.
1986a The Tepiman Connection: A Model of Mesoamerican-Southwestern Interaction. In *Ripples in the Chichimec Sea: New Considerations of Southwestern-Mesoamerican Interactions,* edited by F. J. Mathien and R. H. McGuire, pp. 135-154. Southern Illinois University Press, Carbondale.
1986b A Historical Analysis of the Problem of Southwestern-Mesoamerican Connections. In *Ripples in the Chichimec Sea: New Considerations of Southwestern-Mesoamerican Interactions,* edited by F. J. Mathien and R. H. McGuire, pp. 9-44. Southern Illinois University Press, Carbondale.

Wilcox, D. R., and L. O. Shenk
1977 *The Architecture of the Casa Grande and Its Interpretation.* Arizona State Museum Archaeological Series, no. 115. University of Arizona, Tucson.

Willett, E. R.
1997 The Dual Festival System of the Southern Tepehuan of Mexico. *Journal of the Southwest* 38:197-213.

Willey, G. R.
1966 *An Introduction to American Archaeology,* vol. 1. Prentice-Hall, Englewood Cliffs, New Jersey.

Willey, G. R., G. F. Ekholm, and R. F. Millon
1964 The Patterns of Farming Life and Civilization. In *Natural Environment and Early Cultures,* edited by R. C. West, pp. 446-498. HBMI, vol. 1, R. Wauchope, general editor. University of Texas Press, Austin.

Williams, E.
1992 *Las piedras sagradas: Esculturas prehispánicas del occidente de México.* El Colegio de Michoacán, Zamora.
1993 Historia de la arqueología en Michoacán. In *Il Coloquio Pedro Bosch-Gimpera,* edited by M. T. Cabrero G., pp. 195-236. Instituto de Investigaciones Antropológicas, UNAM, México, D.F.

Williams, G.
1974 External Influences and the Upper Río Verde Drainage Basin at Los Altos, West Mexico. In *Mesoamerican Archaeology: New Approaches,* edited by N. Hammond, pp. 21-48. University of Texas Press, Austin.

Wing, E. S.
1968 Preliminary Note on the Faunal Remains Excavated from Several Sites in Sinaloa and Nayarit, Mexico. In *Archaeological Reconnaissance and Excavations in the Marismas Nacionales, Sinaloa and Nayarit, Mexico,* pp. 150-152. West Mexican Prehistory, part 2. Department of Anthropology, State University of New York at Buffalo.

Wolf, E.
1959 *Sons of the Shaking Earth.* University of Chicago Press, Chicago.

Wolf, E. (editor)
1976 *The Valley of Mexico: Studies in Pre-Hispanic Ecology and Society.* School of American Research, Santa Fe, and University of New Mexico Press, Albuquerque.

Woodward, A.
1936 A Shell Bracelet Manufactory. *American Antiquity* 2:117-125.

Woosley, A. I., and A. J. McIntyre
1996 *Mimbres Mogollon Archaeology: Charles C. Di Peso's Excavations at Wind Mountain.* University of New Mexico Press, Albuquerque.

Woosley, A. I., and B. Olinger
1993 The Casas Grandes Ceramic Tradition: Production and Interregional Exchange of Ramos Polychrome. In *Culture and Contact: Charles C. Di Peso's Gran Chichimeca,* edited by A. I. Woosley and J. C. Ravesloot, pp. 105-131. University of New Mexico Press, Albuquerque.

Woosley, A. I., and J. C. Ravesloot (editors)
1993 *Culture and Contact: Charles C. Di Peso's Gran Chichimeca.* University of New Mexico Press, Albuquerque.

Worthy, M., and R. S. Dickens, Jr.
1983 The Mesoamerican Pecked Cross as a Calendrical Device. *American Antiquity* 48:573-576.

Wylie, A.
1996 Ethical Dilemmas in Archaeological Practice: Looting,

Repatriation, Stewardship, and the (Trans)formation of Disciplinary Identity. *Perspectives on Science* 4:154–194.

Zepeda, G.
1986 *El desarrollo de un nucleo poblacional asentado en la confluencia de los ríos Lerma y Guanajuato: Una apreciación.* Tesis, ENAH, INAH, México, D.F.

Zingg, R. M.
1940 *Report on Archaeology of Southern Chihuahua.* University of Denver Contributions, no. 3; Center for Latin American Studies, no. 1.

CONTRIBUTORS

Michael S. Foster
4505 E. Ute Street
Phoenix, Arizona 85044

Shirley Gorenstein
Rensselaer Polytechnic Institute
Professor Emerita
Troy, New York 12180-3590

Ronna Jane Bradley
University of New Mexico
Valencia Campus
251 B. Sichler Drive
Los Lunas, New Mexico 87031

Beatriz Braniff
Centro INAH Colima
Gabino Barrera No. 24
Col. Centro
Colima, CP 028000
Mexico

Cory Dale Breternitz
President
Center for Indigenous Studies in the
   Americas
1121 N. Second Street
Phoenix, Arizona 85004

J. Andrew Darling
Executive Director
Mexico-North Research Network
Col. Cuauhtemoc
16 de Septiembre 402
Chihuahua, Chihuahua
Mexico

Charles Florance
13 Belmonte Lane
Clifton Park, New York 12065

Peter Jiménez Betts
Instituto Nacional de Antropología
   e Historia
Centro Zacatecas
Ex-Colegio de San Luiz Ganzaga S/
   N
Lado Oriente
Plaza de Santo Domingo
Zacatecas, Zacatecas 9800
Mexico

Ellen Abbott Kelley
Adjunct Assistant Professor
Center for Big Bend Studies
Sul Ross State University
Alpine, Texas 79832

Joseph B. Mountjoy
Department of Anthropology
University of North Carolina at
   Greensboro
Greensboro, North Carolina 27412

Helen Perlstein Pollard
454 Baker Hall
Department of Anthropology
Michigan State University
East Lansing, Michigan 48824

Stuart D. Scott
Associate Professor Emeritus
Department of Anthropology
State University of New York at
   Buffalo
64339 E. Galveston Lane
Tucson, Arizona 85739

Michael W. Spence
Department of Anthropology
University of Western Ontario
London, Ontario N6A-5C2
Canada

María Elisa Villalpando
Instituto Nacional de Antropología
  e Historia
Centro Sonora
Jesús García Final y Pbro. José
  Esteban Sarmiento
Antigua Penitenciaria Colonial la
  Matanza
Apartado Postal 1664
Hermosillo, Sonora 83080
Mexico

Phil C. Weigand
Colegio de Michoacán
2320 North Kromer
Flagstaff, Arizona 86001

Participants and guests. Cultural Dynamics of Precolumbian West and Northwest Mexico

Back: Douglas Mitchell, Phil Weigand, Joseph Mountjoy, Jeffrey Dean, Ben Nelson, Peter Jiménez
Middle: Ma. de los Dolores Soto de Arechavaleta, Shirley Gorenstein, Stuart Scott, Michael Spence, Dorothy Hosler, Helen Pollard, Christine Robinson, Cory Dale Breternitz, Michael Foster
Front: Celia Weigand, Thomas O'Laughlin, Beatriz Braniff, J. Charles Kelley, María Elisa Villalpando, Baudelina Garcia U., Charles Florance

INDEX

Abbott Kelley, E., 16-17, 157
Acambaro, Guanajuato, 27, 37, 38, 39, 67
Acaxee, 210
Agua Zarca, Chihuahua, 225
Ahualulco, Jalisco, 50
Ajuno, Michoacán, 65
Alahuistlán, Guerrero, 71
Alta Vista, Zacatecas, 16-17, 143, 203; ceramics, 167; construction date, 187; Labyrinth or Observatory, 182, 184; La Quemada and, 163; photo of, 182; polity, 181-82; skeletal concentrations, 259; Teotihuacan and, 182, 256-57
Amapa, Nayarit, 129, 204; cenotaphs, 104; ceramics, 85, 100, 125, 126-28, 205; dating, 93; metal artifacts, 97, 139; Mixteca-Puebla traits at, 140, 149; occupation hiatus, 109; phase sequence, 110, 125, 149; shell and stone jewelry manufacture at, 97-98; site plan, 111; spindle whorls, 89, 96, 98; trade route, 142
Apatzingán, Michoacán, 93
Archaic: in Chihuahua, 228-31; in Durango, 199-200; in Jalisco, 45; in Michoacán, 61-62; in Teuchitlán region, 45; in West Mexico, 83-84
Architecture: burial mounds, 45-46; circular, 31-32, 40, 47, 52, 53, 55, 171, 173; hall of columns, 40, 163; house platform mounds, 110, 111; macaw nesting boxes, 229; platforms/platform mounds, 66, 93; talud-tablero, 63, 257-58; *yácatas,* 65, 67. *See also* Ball courts; Shaft tombs
Arensberg, C., 55
Arias, Nayarit, 100, 101, 104
Armillas, P., 5-6, 156, 157
Arocutin, Michoacán, 65

Arroyo Seco, Jalisco, 98
Aticama, Nayarit, 103
Atoyac, Jalisco, 170
Aveni, A. F., 182, 189
Aztatlán Mercantile System, 122, 218; antecedents, 142-44; Casas Grandes and, 237; cotton in, 96; early, 142, 144-46; late, 146-51; metallurgy and, 139
Aztatlán tradition/culture/complex: ceramics, 98, 111, 112, 139; dates, 96, 97, 142, 259; Derived, 142; distribution, 95-96; external relations, 99-100; sociopolitical organization and ritual, 98-99; subsistence and economy, 14-15, 96-98.
Aztecs, 71-76, 100
Aztec I, 140, 141, 147

Bajío, the, Guanajuato, 36, 37, 38, 39
Balberta, Guatemala, 256
ball courts: Aztatlán tradition, 98; in Casas Grandes region, 236; in Durango, 214-15; in Jalisco, 31; in Michoacán, 63; Teuchitlán tradition, 47, 55
Balsas/Mezcala culture, 62
Bandelier, A. F., 223
Barra de Navidad, Jalisco, 94, 101, 102
Basin of Mexico: ceramics in Guanajuato, 30, 31; chronology, 33; contact with Guanajuato, 28, 29; Tezoyuca phase, 29-30, 32, 37. *See also* specific site names
Bell, B. B., 178n3
Bennyhoff, J. A., 24, 37
Berlin, H., 191
Blackiston, A. H., 223-24
Blanton, R. E., 258

301

INDEX

Bolaños culture, 172, 174
Bolaños Valley, Zacatecas/Jalisco, 52, 171–74
Box Canyon, New Mexico, 234
Bradley, R. J., 18
Brand, D. D., 109, 111–12, 197, 224
Braniff C., B., 12–13, 23–24
Bunzel, R., 138

Cabrero G., M. T., 171, 172–73, 174
Cacaria, Durango, 215
Cacaxtla, Tlaxcala, 185, 186
Caiman monsters, 185, 187
Calendar: petroglyphs, 182, 183, 184–85, 186, 187–94, 195n10
Canal irrigation, 63, 233
Cañón del Molino, Durango, 150–51, 199, 202, 212–13; burials, 214; ceramics, 137, 146, 151, 209, 213–14; metal artifacts, 139, 147, 151
Capacha tradition/culture, 45, 62, 84–87
Carabin, Guanajuato, 36
Carey, H. A., 224
Carpenter, J. P., 112, 122, 154n11
Casa de Robles Site 2, Chihuahua, 226
Casas Grandes: Interaction Sphere, 151–52; polity, 19; tradition/culture, 233–37, 251. *See also* Paquimé
Caso, A., 183, 186–87
Ceboruco Hill, Nayarit, 103
Celaya, Querétaro, 39
Central Coast tradition, 248–49
Ceramic forms: annular base bowl, 127, 167, 169–70, 172, 173; basket-handled, 205, 207, 208; Chupícuaro, 23, 29; conch shell, 125; griddle, 94; Guasave, 150; incense burner, 98, 104; molcajete, 93, 94, 102, 111, 207; musical instruments, 94; squash, 89, 91; "stool," 93; tecomate, 85, 248, 249; tripod bowls, 39, 116, 117, 118, 120, 121, 125, 146, 169, 206, 207, 209. *See also* Figurines
Ceramic production: of Ramos Polychrome, 235
Ceramic types/wares: Aguaruto Exterior Incised, 146, 206; Aguaruto Incised, 120, 122, 144, 146, 147; Aguaruto Polychrome, 122, 144, 147; Alamitos Engraved, 122; Altar Polychrome, 243; Amaro Red-on-cream, 205, 206, 211; Amole Polychrome, 150; Atoyac Black Incised, 172; Aztatlán Polychrome, 112, 117, 146; Aztatlán Red-on-buff, 97; Aztatlán Ware, 144, 146, 147, 149, 206; Babicora Polychrome, 244; black and red, 22; black and red-on-brown, 26; black-banded, 112, 113, 122; black incised, 164; black-on-buff, 103, 112, 144; black-on-buff incised, 95; black polychrome, 22, 24, 25, 27; black-smudged, 120; blackware, 22; Blanco Levantado, 39, 40, 42; Bolaños wide-line negative, 146; Botadero Black-on-buff, 126; brown-on-red, 22; brown polychrome, 22, 24, 25, 27; Canatlán Red-band, 207, 208, 211, 215; Canutillo black incised-engraved, 157, 159, 162, 178n5, 179n7; Canutillo Engraved, 211; Carretas Polychrome, 244; Cerritos Engraved, 126; Cerritos Polychrome, 126; Cerro Isabel Engraved, 118, 119, 122, 146; Cerro Izabal, 144; Cerro Izabel Incised, 206; Chametla Black-band Engraved, 205; Chametla Engraved, 115; Chametla Plain, 115; Chametla Polychrome, 111–12, 114, 115; Chametla Red-rim, 205; Chametla Scalloped Rim, 205; Chico Red-on-brown, 200, 211, 215; Chihuahuan polychromes, 238, 250; Chinesco Black-on-white, 174; Chupícuaro polychrome, 37; Cocoyolitos Polychrome, 112; Cocoyotla Black-on-natural, 141, 147; Cojumatlán Polychrome, 147; Cojumatlán Polychrome Incised, 147; Coyotes Incised, 174; cream slipped, 91; Culhuacán Black-on-orange, 141, 147; Culhuacán Polychrome, 141, 147, 214; Culiacán Polychrome, 111, 214; Early Aztatlán, 146; Early Chametla Polychrome, 41, 122, 205; Early Chinesco, 146; Early Culiacán Polychrome, 122, 123; El Campo Buff, 206, 211; El Conejo Red-filled Engraved, 210, 211, 215; El Dorado Incised, 120; El Molino Red-on-cream, 213; El Paso Brown, 230; El Paso Polychrome, 152, 234; El Salto Incised, 174; El Taste Polychrome, 112, 116; El Taste Red-bordered, 112, 116; El Taste Rough, 112; El Taste Satin, 112; Fine Orange, 140, 150; fluted, 111; Garita, 39; Gavilán Polychrome, 146, 170, 172, 174; Gila Polychrome, 224, 231; Guasave Polychrome, 121; Guasave Red-on-buff, 146, 214; Huistla Polychrome, 149; Iguanas Polychrome, 96, 127, 214; Iguanas-Roblitos polychrome, 56; incised-engraved blackware, 39; Ixcuintla Polychrome, 127, 215; Jerezano White-on-red, 164; Lolandis Red-Rim, 144, 146, 205–6, 214; Loma Plain, 200, 211, 215, 217; Loma Red, 200, 215; Loma Textured, 200, 211, 215; Loma White, 200, 211; Madero Fluted, 208, 209, 211; Malpaso incised-engraved, 160, 162, 164; Mangos Engraved, 128, 211, 214; Mangos Polychrome, 128; Mano Colorado, 205; Marbelized Interior, 205; Mazatlán Polychrome, 111, 112, 116; Mercado Red-on-cream, 146, 205, 206, 211, 214; Mercado ware, 179n7; Michilia Engraved, 39; Michilia Red-Filled Engraved, 205, 214; Middle Chametla Polychrome, 205, 211; Middle Chametla Polychrome Engraved, 205; Middle-Late Culiacán Polychrome, 124; Mixtlán polychromes, 37; Molino Red-on-cream, 209, 210; Momax Deep Incised Red-Filled, 146; Morales incised, 160; Morales Polychrome, 39; Morales Red-on-buff, 38; Morcillo Molcajete, 207, 211; Morones Black-on-purple, 164; Murquia incised-engraved, 163; Naranja a Brochazos, 42; Navolato Polychrome, 122, 144; Nayar Red-on-white, 211; Nayar White-on-red, 205, 208, 209, 211; negative painted, 167, 168, 169–70, 172, 173, 180n13, 211; negative polychromes, 53–54, 64; Neveria Red-on-brown, 146, 205, 207, 211; Nogales Polychrome, 243, 244; Oconahua Red-on-white, 48, 49; orange and black-on-buff, 103; orange and black-on-cream, 57; orange-on-buff, 39; Otinapa Red-on-white, 207, 208, 211, 215, 217; Peñitas Engraved, 128; Plumbate, 42, 100, 142, 259; polished black, 111, 144; polished red, 144; pseudocloisonné, 40, 41, 52, 53, 56, 170, 173, 178, 179n7–8; Pseudo Paint-Cloisonné, 146; punctated, 84, 85; Quisillo Incised-engraved, 162; Ramos Polychrome, 151–52, 234, 235, 244; red-and-black, 103; red-and-white-on-buff incised, 95; red-on-brown, 26, 93, 146, 164, 166, 167; red-on-buff, 22, 39, 93, 94, 95, 144, 167; red-on-buff incised, 95; red-on-cream, 64, 91; red-on-

orange, 93, 94; red-on-white, 164, 165, 167; red-rimmed, 112, 122; red-rimmed red-on-buff incised, 111; redware, 22; Refugio Red-on-brown, 146, 174, 205, 211; rose/purple painted, 85; Salado polychromes, 238; Santiago Engraved, 128; Santiago Red-on-orange, 214; Santiago White-on-red, 205; Sentispac Buff, 128; shadow-stripped, 39; Sierra Brown-on-white, 164; Sinaloa Polychrome, 119, 140, 150; Soyale Red-on-cream, 166; Suchil Red-on-brown, 146, 165, 174, 179n7, 185, 205, 211; Tarascan polychrome, 69; Tepozan negative paint, 163–64, 165, 179n7; Teuchitlán Red-on-cream, 48, 52; Thin Orange, 39–40, 50, 62, 63, 257; Tiburón Plain, 248, 249; Tlaltenango Black Incised, 174; Tohil Plumbate, 140; Trincheras Purple, 244; Trincheras Purple-on-brown, 243, 244; Trincheras Purple-on-red, 243, 244; Tuitlán incised-engraved, 163; Tuxpan Engraved, 126, 214; Tuxpan Incised, 211; Tuxpan Red-on-orange, 126; Valle San Luis Polychrome, 41, 164, 180n13; Vesuvio Red-Filled Engraved, 185, 211, 217; Villanueva Incised-engraved, 162, 174; Vista Paint Cloisonné, 164, 166, 167, 211; white-on-red, 37; white-on-red polychrome, 167; Zaquil Black, 39; zoned incised, 84, 85

Cerrito de la Campana, Mexico, 257
Cerritos Colorados, Jalisco, 170
Cerro Blanco, Durango, 211
Cerro de la Cruz, Durango, 215
Cerro de la Cruz, Querétaro, 38
Cerro del Huistle, Jalisco, 259
Cerro de los Corralitos de los Indios, Durango, 217
Cerro de los Monos, Jalisco, 47, 48
Cerro de los Tepehuanes, Durango, 216
Cerro de Moctehuma, Chihuahua, 156
Cerro de Trincheras, Sonora, 244–45, 246, 251
Cerro el Chapín, Zacatecas, 181: calendrical petroglyphs, 17, 182, 183, 184–85, 186, 187–94, 195n10, 257
Cerro el Chivo, Guanajuato, 24
Cerro Encantado, Jalisco, 39, 41, 47–48, 168, 170, 178n3
Cerro Hervideros, Durango, 139
Cerro Juanaqueña, Chihuahua, 230
Cerro Pedragoso, Zacatecas, 181, 182
Cerro Prieto, Michoacán, 78, 79
Cerro Tepisuazco, Zacatecas, 169, 170
Cerro Varal obsidian source, Michoacán, 79, 177
Chacalilla, Nayarit, 95, 98
Chacmool, 69
Chalchihuites culture: Bolaños Valley and, 172–73; expansion into Durango of, 17, 143, 218; Guadiana, 17–18, 202, 203, 204, 205–9; history of study of, 155, 156, 157, 159; La Quemada and, 155–56, 157, 163–64; Loma San Gabriel culture and, 201–3, 218, 219; map of, 156; mining operations, 52, 194n2, 256–57; Suchil, 194n1, 203, 204, 205
Chametla, Sinaloa, 149; ceramics, 112, 113–16, 144; figurines, 133; as gateway community, 143, 144; phase sequence, 110, 111; pipes, 214
Charahuen, Michoacán, 65
Chehuayo, Michoacán, 62
Chicomostoc, 160

Chihuahua: environment, 221, 223; history of research in, 223–25; map, 222; modern investigations in, 225–26, 228–31; Paleoindian and Archaic periods in, 228–31. See also Casas Grandes; specific site names
Cholula, Puebla, 125, 140, 141, 147
Chumbícuaro culture, 62
Chupícuaro, Guanajuato, 22, 24, 25–27, 29
Chupícuaro culture, 8–9; in Bajío, 37; ceramics, 23, 37, 38; Chupícuaro phase, 25, 27, 29, 31, 32, 37, 38; Cuicuilco and, 11, 31, 33, 37–38; Early Chupícuaro phase, 9, 11, 25, 27, 28, 29, 32; history of research on, 21–24; map of area, 22; in Michoacán, 62; Mixtlán phase, 27–28, 32; Teuchitlán tradition and, 50; trade, 142; San Felipe phase, 28–29
Clanton Draw, New Mexico, 234
Classic period: collapse, 56, 57; landscape, 54–55; in Michoacán, 62–64; Teuchitlán tradition, 49–55
Cojumatlán, Michoacán, 139, 147
Convento, Chihuahua, 226
Copper: Casas Grandes and, 238; at Cojumatlán, 147; at Guasave, 150; in Michoacán, 64, 74–75; in Teuchitlán area, 57; in West Mexico, 97, 139, 147
Copujo, Michoacán, 78, 79
Cotton, 96, 102, 139
Coyula, Jalisco, 57
Craft specialization: in Tuxcacuesco tradition, 90
Cranial deformation, 214
Cruz Negra, Michoacán, 78, 79
Cuarenta, Jalisco, 40
Cuarenta Casas, Chihuahua, 232
Cueva de San Pablo, Durango, 211–12, 213
Cuicuilco, Mexico DF, 11, 30, 31, 32–33, 37–38
Cuitzeo, Michoacán, 39. See also Tres Cerritos
Culberson Ruin, New Mexico, 225
Culhuacán, Mexico, 140, 141, 146, 147
Culiacán (Culhuacán), Sinaloa, 150; ceramics, 123–25, 149; in historic period, 139; metal artifacts, 139; Mixteca-Puebla traits at, 140; phase sequence, 110, 122; site plan, 111
Curicaueri, 64

Darling, J. A., 16
DeAtley, S. P., 234
Dental mutilation, 63, 86, 149, 214
Díaz del Castillo, B., 141
Di Peso, C. C., 18, 146, 151, 225–26, 228, 232–33, 239
Doolittle, W. E., 233, 253n11
Durango: Chalchihuites culture in, 201–9; history of research in, 197–99; Loma San Gabriel culture in, 200–203; map of, 198; Paleoindian/Archaic in, 199–200; prehistoric to historic transition in, 209–10; problems needing investigation in, 218–19; sites of, 210–18. See also specific site names

Earth Monster, 98, 205
Ecuador, 64
Edmonson, M. S., 191
Ekholm, G. F., 112, 140

INDEX

El Alacrán, Nayarit, 88
El Arenal, Jalisco, 47, 48
El Calón, Sinaloa, 109, 129–33, 134
El Canton, Jalisco, 100
El Cerrito, Querétaro, 36, 39, 42
El Cerro Canyon, Durango, 217
El Cerro de Creston de los Indios, Durango, 217
El Ciruelo, Jalisco, 106
El Cóporo, Guanajuato, 40, 41, 179n10
El Grillo, Jalisco, 56, 57
El Infiernillo, Michoacán, 62
El Molino, Jalisco, 51
El Opeño, Michoacán, 45, 62, 84, 87
El Otero, Michoacán, 63
El Piñón, Jalisco, 165, 169, 173, 174, 180n18
El Ranchito, Jalisco, 105
El Reparito, Nayarit, 88, 89–90, 92
El Vergel, Zacatecas, 41
Elvino Whetten Pueblo, Chihuahua, 232
El Zape, Durango, 139, 216
El Zurdo, Chihuahua, 232
Epi-Classic period: in Malpaso Valley, 163, 178; in Teuchitlán area, 56, 57
Espia, Durango, 217
Etzatlán, Jalisco, 141
Exchange systems: Aztec-Tarascan, 72–75; Casas Grandes, 235, 237–39; coastal, 64; La Quemada, 175; Tarascan-West Mexico, 76–77. *See also* Aztatlán Mercantile System; Obsidian; Trade routes

Faunal remains: in Durango, 216; on northwest coast, 125, 134
Figurines (ceramic): architecture in, 47; Aztatlán tradition, 98; Capacha tradition, 87; Cerrito de García, 169; at Chametla, 133; Chametla White Filleted, 144; Chimalhuacán-like, 30, 31; Chupícuaro, 22, 23, 27, 29; cornudo (horned), 168, 169, 170; at El Calón, 132–33; El Taste slab, 112; flat or slab, 46; Hohokam, 41; Huatabampo tradition, 246, 247; La Quemada complex (Type I), 165–66, 167, 172, 179n10; Mazapa, 42; Mazapan style, 96, 98, 99, 100, 142; Nayarit style, 91; orange-on-cream, 172; rattle, 89; Red-on-Buff tradition, 94; Shaft Tomb tradition, 90, 91; Tula-Mazapan style, 56; Tuxcacuesco tradition, 88, 91–92; Type I, 41; *volador* style, 53; in western Jalisco, 46–47; White-Filleted, 205
Figurines (stone), 105
Floral remains: in Durango, 216; on northwest coast, 131–32
Florance, C. A., 8–9, 11
Foote, L. J., 147, 149
Formative period: at Marismas Nacionales, 132–33, 134; in western Jalisco, 45–49
Foster, M. S., 15, 17–18, 201
Fronteras, Sonora, 250

Galeana, Chihuahua, 235
Gerald, R. E., 233
Gill, G. W., 149
Glassow, M. A., 149

Grosscup, G., 149, 204, 205
Gualtario Abajo, Zacatecas, 201
Guanajuato: chronological sequence, 40. *See also* specific site names
Guasave, Sinaloa, 111; Carpenter on, 154n11; ceramics, 97, 112, 117–21, 150; dating of, 112, 140; Huatabampo tradition at, 252–53n8; metal artifacts, 139, 150; Mixteca-Puebla traits at, 140, 150; phase sequence, 110; restudy of, 112, 122

Hassig, R., 141
Hers, M. A., 159, 202
Hervideros, Durango, 199, 214
Hodder, I., 141, 146
Hohokam: ceramic designs, 39; figurines, 41; shell trade, 238; Trincheras tradition and, 243
Hosler, D. H., 64
Hrdlicka, A., 173–74
Huatabampo, Sonora, 41, 247
Huatabampo tradition, 245–48, 252–53n7–8
Huaxteca, 40
Huichol, 90
Huistla, Jalisco, 149
Huitzila-La Lobera obsidian source, Zacatecas-Jalisco, 175
Huitzilapa, Jalisco, 48, 88, 90, 174

Ihuatzio, Michoacán, 56, 69
Ixtapa, Jalisco: Aztatlán tradition at, 95, 96, 98; ceramics, 84, 88, 95, 98; dating of, 88, 96; figurines, 87, 99, 100; Mixtlán complex at, 28; platform mounds, 93; Post-Aztatlán traditions at, 100, 104, 105; stelae, 96, 99, 105
Ixtepete, 57
Ixtlán del Río, Nayarit, 57, 95, 106

Jackson, J. B., 54
Jalisco: environment, 43, 45; map, 44; phase sequence in, 28–29. *See also* specific site names
Jiménez B., P., 16
Joyce Well, New Mexico, 225, 234
Juchipila Valley, Zacatecas, 167; ceramics, 164, 168, 169–70, 171, 172, 173, 180n14

Kachina Cult, 238
Kaminaljuyu, Guatemala, 191, 256
Kelley, Ellen, 16–17
Kelley, J. C.: on Aztatlán culture, 139; on Aztatlán Mercantile System, 15–16, 218, 219; on Cerro Chapín, 16–17; on Guadiana Chalchihuites, 203–4, 205; on interaction spheres in northwestern Mesoamerica, 178; on Juchipila Valley, 167; on La Quemada, 155, 156–57, 159; on Loma San Gabriel culture, 201; on Totoate, 171; work at Culiacán, 122; work in Durango, 197–98
Kelly, I., 122, 133
Kidder, A. V., 224
Kirchhoff, P., 4

La Atalaya, Durango, 203, 204, 211
La Casa Fimbres, Chihuahua, 226

INDEX

La Cueva de Dos Puertos, Durango, 216
La Cueva de los Muertos Chiquitos, Durango, 215–16
La Cueva de Maguey, Durango, 211
La Florida, Zacatecas, 52, 162, 171
La Gloria, Guanajuato, 40
Laguna Medina, Durango, 199
La Joya obsidian source, Jalisco, 97
Lamanai, Belize, 74
La Manga, Durango, 198, 210
La Mesa del Temascal, Jalisco, 102, 103
La Morita, Chihuahua, 225
La Paila Cave, Coahuila, 42
La Pedrera, Nayarit, 85, 86, 88, 91, 97
La Pintada, Nayarit, 89, 90, 91, 92
La Playa, Sonora, 243, 245
La Quemada, Zacatecas, 16, 258; ceramics, 163–64, 165, 166; Chalchihuites and, 155–56, 157, 163–64; dating of, 163, 178–79n5–6, 179n11; end of occupation, 166–67; figurines, 165–66, 167; Kelley on, 155, 156–57; map of, 161; photo of, 162, 163; previous interpretations of, 160; recent excavations at, 178n1; road system, 158; role in exchange systems, 175; skeletal concentrations, 259
Las Animas, Durango, 203
La Venta, Jalisco, 51, 56
Lister, R. H., 147, 225
Lithics: of Loma San Gabriel culture, 200; in Tunal Grande area, 41–42; in West Mexico, 86, 89, 93–94, 102. *See also* Obsidian
Llano Grande obsidian source, Durango, 51, 175
Lo Arado, Jalisco, 104
Loma Alta, Michoacán, 38, 62, 63
Loma Alta complex, 39
Loma de Santa María, Michoacán, 258
Loma San Gabriel, Durango, 216–17
Loma San Gabriel tradition/culture, 17, 160; ceramics, 200; Chalchihuites culture and, 201–3, 218, 219; role in regional economies of, 178n2; sites in Durango, 210–11, 214–15, 217–18; site types, 200–201
Los Caracoles, Durango, 199
Los Castillos, Durango, 215
Los Portales Cave, Michoacán, 61–62
Lumholtz, C., 137–38, 151, 223

Macaws, 229, 235, 236, 237
Malpaso complex/culture, 160, 162, 175
Malpaso Valley, Zacatecas: ceramics, 160, 179n7; environment, 159; Epi-Classic period in, 163. *See also* La Quemada
Maquixco el Bajo, Mexico, 256, 257
Marismas Nacionales, Sinaloa/Nayarit, 15; dates from, 140; environment, 107–9, 110; map of, 130; phase sequence, 110, 125, 129–33; skeletal remains, 149
Marrs, G. J., 228–29
Marshack, A., 189
Matanchén, Nayarit, 83, 84, 134
McBride, H. W., 24
McGuire, R. H., 250, 253n12
Meighan, C. W., 147, 149
Mesa de la Gloria, Jalisco, 52

Mesoamerica: definition of, 4–7; "core and "periphery" in, 255–56; Michoacán and, 69–70
Metallurgy. *See* Copper
Mexica, 188–89, 194
Mexico, central and northern: climatic types, 11; natural regions, 10; precipitation, 12
Michoacán: Classic period in, 62–64; cultural sequence in, 59, 61; map of, 60; migration into, 65; Paleoindian and Archaic in, 61–62; Postclassic period in, 64–65; Preclassic period in, 62; Protohistoric period in, 65–68; two versions of past of, 69. *See also* specific site names
Mimbres, 224, 225, 234
Mixcoatl, 35
Mixteca-Puebla culture/complex, 100, 142; Aztatlán Mercantile System and, 140–41; ceramics, 140, 147, 149, 150, 259–60; dating of, 140
Mixtlán complex, 28
Mogollon, 225, 226, 251; Jornada, 230, 231, 234
Monte Albán, Oaxaca, 147
Morales, Guanajuato, 38
Morales complex, 38–39, 160
Morett, Colima, 88, 89, 92, 93, 94
Mountjoy, J. B., 14–15, 134, 142

Nahuapa, Jalisco, 95, 96; Aztatlán tradition at, 97, 98, 99; Post-Aztatlán tradition at, 100, 103, 104
Nanautzin (Nanahuatl), 140
Navacoyan, Durango, 139, 146, 150, 199, 211
Nelson, B. A., 258
New Fire Ceremony, 186, 187, 188
Nicholson, H. B., 140, 187
Nochistlan obsidian source, Jalisco, 175
Noguera, E., 59

Obregón, B. de, 150
Obsidian: Aztatlán tradition, 97; exchange of Tarascan state, 73, 77–80; distribution on north-central frontier, 175–77; green, 73; northwest coast, 111; Post-Aztatlán traditions, 103; prismatic blades, 103, 177; Teuchitlán tradition, 49; workshops near Teuchitlán, 53. *See also* specific source name
Olinger, B., 152
Oliveros, J. A., 45
Otomi, 42
Oztoman, Guerrero, 71

Pachuca obsidian source, Hidalgo, 177
Pachuca-I obsidian source, Michoacán, 78, 79
Paleoindian: in Chihuahua, 228; in Durango, 199; in Michoacán, 61
Paquimé, Chihuahua, 18; abandonment of, 239; agricultural system, 232–33; Aztatlán Mercantile System and, 15–16; dating of, 231–32; Di Peso at, 225–26, 228; early investigations of, 223, 224, 225; map of, 227; photo of, 228, 229; teeth of inhabitants, 149; as trading center, 235, 237–39
Pareo, Michoacán, 65, 78, 79
Parsons, J. R., 141

Peer-polity interaction, 175, 177, 236, 237–38
Pendleton Ruin, New Mexico, 224
Peñitas, Nayarit, 110, 122, 125, 204
Penjamo-I obsidian source, Michoacán, 78, 79
Peralta A, Guanajuato, 40
Petroglyphs: Aztatlán tradition, 99; calendrical, 182, 183, 184–85, 186, 187–94, 195n10; Post-Aztatlán traditions, 104–5; Red-on-Buff tradition, 94; Shaft Tomb tradition, 92; at Zape observatory, 216
Peyote, 77
Pictographs, 105
Pipes, smoking, 139, 214
Pipiole, Jalisco, 51
Playa del Tesoro, Colima, 92, 93, 94, 95–96, 100
Pochotitán, Jalisco, 173, 174
Pochteca, 226, 228, 237
Pollard, H. P., 13–14
Porter, M. N. *See* Weaver, M. P.
Post-Aztatlán traditions, 100–106
Postclassic period: in Michoacán, 64–65; in Teuchitlán area, 57
Potrero del Calichal, 185, 187
Preclassic period: Late, 29–30, 32–33; in Michoacán, 62
Prestige exchange concept, 238–39
Protohistoric period: in Michoacán, 65–68
Puroaguita, Guanajuato, 24, 25, 27, 28, 29, 31

Querendaro, Michoacán, 63
Quetzalcoatl, 205
Quiñones Keber, E., 140

Rancho El Espia, Chihuahua, 234
Red-on-Buff tradition, 92–95
Relación de Michoacán, 65, 76, 77
Reyes Site No. 1–2, Michoacán, 226
Riley, C. L., 201
Río Mesquital, Durango, 199
Río Sonora tradition, 249–51
Rio Verde, San Luis Potosi, 40
Roads, 158
Robles, Durango, 199–200
Rock art. *See* Petroglyphs; Pictographs
Roney, J. R., 230

Sahagún, B. de, 75, 139, 188, 189
Salt, 53, 102–3
San Andrés, Jalisco, 48
San Aparicio, Zacatecas, 170
San Blas, Nayarit, 84, 85, 86, 88, 92
San Blas complex, 85, 87
San Gregorio, Michoacán, 147
San José Baviácora, Sonora, 249, 250
San Juan de Abajo, Nayarit, 104
San Juan de los Arcos, Jalisco, 48
San Pedro, Jalisco, 45
San Sebastian, Jalisco, 88
Santa Ana, Durango, 198, 215
Santa Cruz, Nayarit, 103
Santa Cruz de Barcenas, Jalisco, 56

Santa María, Michoacán, 62
Sta. María de las Navajas, Jalisco, 51
Sauer, C. O., 109, 111–12, 139
Sayles, E. B., 224–25
Schroeder, Durango, 122, 139, 198, 199, 210; ball court, 214–15; Calera phase at, 208; ceramics, 140, 146, 150; Chalchihuites occupation at, 143–44, 205; dates for, 203–4
Scott, S. D., 15
Sculpture, 69, 105. *See also* Stelae
Seri, 248
Serpentine, 103
Shaft tombs: in Bolaños Valley, 173; El Arenal phase, 47–48; El Opeño style, 45, 46, 47, 62; Red-on-Buff tradition, 94. *See also* Shaft Tomb tradition
Shaft Tomb tradition, 88–92, 168
Shell: Aztatlán tradition, 97; in Casas Grandes region, 237, 238; Central Coast tradition, 248; Red-on-Buff tradition, 94; in Sonora, 252; Trincheras tradition, 243, 244; Tuxcacuesco tradition, 90
Sierra la Primavera obsidian source, Jalisco, 177
Site 5, Guanajuato, 32
Site 9–10, Guanajuato, 30, 31
Site 11, Michoacán, 97
Site 42, Michoacán, 85, 86
Site 68, Michoacán, 97
SON:F:2:50, 244
Sonora: Casas Grandes tradition in, 251; Central Coast tradition in, 248–49; Huatabampo tradition in, 245–48; map of, 242; Mesoamerica and, 241, 242; population density in (1519), 252n3; Río Sonora tradition in, 249–51; Trincheras tradition in, 243–45. *See also* specific site names
Spindle whorls: Aztatlán tradition, 96, 98, 144; Chalchihuites, 208; Post-Aztatlán traditions, 102; Shaft Tomb tradition, 89–90
Spondylus, 106
Stelae: Aztatlán tradition, 99; Post-Aztatlán tradition, 100, 104, 105
Steward, J. H., 6–7

Tabachines, Jalisco, 47, 48, 88, 94
Tacuichamona, Sinaloa, 214
Tarascans/Tarascan state, 4, 14, 42; emergence of, 64; extent of, 59–61, 72, 73; kings of, 65, 66; mobile traders of, 137–38; obsidian exchange of, 73, 77–80; relations with Aztec, 71–76; relations with West Mexico, 76–77, 106; *yácatas* of, 65, 67
Taximaroa, Michoacán, 73, 75
Taylor, W. W., 229–30
Tebelchia, Jalisco, 102
Techaluta, Jalisco, 53, 57
Tenochtitlán, Mexico DF, 55
Teocaltiche, Jalisco, 88
Teotihuacán, Mexico, 32, 55; calendar system, 189–90, 191; ceramic conch shells, 125; ceramics in north-central Mexico, 39, 50; cross-circle petroglyphs, 182, 183, 188; influence in northwest-West Mexico, 256–59, 260; mask in Michoacán, 63; Venus symbols, 185, 186

INDEX

Tepehuaje, Jalisco, 56
Tepehuan, 210
Tequila Volcano obsidian source, Jalisco, 177
Teuchitlán, Jalisco, 51, 53, 54, 88
Teuchitlán tradition/region: Ahualulco phase, 50; ceramics, 53, 54; chronological sequence, 46; Chupícuaro culture and, 50; circular structures, 40, 47, 55; collapse of, 56, 57; correlation of cultural traits for, 49; dating of, 174; El Arenal phase, 46–49, 50, 51; El Opeño phase, 45; fortified sites, 51–52; landscape, 54–55; map, 44; population, 54; population implosion, 50, 52–53; Teuchitlán I phase, 50, 52; Teuchitlán II phase, 52, 56, 57; urbanization in, 55; in Valparaiso Valley, 171
Tezcatlipoca, 187
Tezoyuca, Mexico, 31
Tikal, Guatemala, 257
Tingambato, Michoacán, 63, 258
Tizapan el Alto, Jalisco, 139, 147
Tlaloc, 105, 214
Tlapacoya, Mexico, 132
Tlatilco, Mexico, 37
Tobacco, 139
Tocuaro, Michoacán, 65
Toltec, 36, 42, 100, 157
Tomatlán, Jalisco, 141
Totoate, Jalisco: ceramics, 146, 162, 164, 169, 170, 174; dating of, 52, 173, 178n5; Kelley's work at, 171, 172, 174
Trade routes, 138, 141. *See also* Aztatlán Mercantile System; Exchange systems
Tres Cerritos (Cuitzeo), Michoacán, 63, 67, 258
Trincheras, 230–33
Trincheras tradition, 243–45
Trombold, C. D., 157
Tula, Hidalgo, 36, 40, 56, 64, 79
Tunal Grande area, San Luis Potosí, 36, 41–42
Tuxcacuesco tradition, 88–92
Tzintzuntzan, Michoacán, 65–66, 67, 68, 77, 78

Uaxactun, Guatemala, 183, 188
Ucareo obsidian source, Michoacán, 73, 77, 78, 79
Urichu, Michoacán, 64, 65, 77, 78, 79

Valparaiso-Bolaños Valley, Zacatecas/Jalisco, 171–74
Varien, M. D., 54–55
Venus, 185
Villa Ahumada, Chihuahua, 235
Villa de Reyes, San Luis Potosí, 36, 40, 41, 42
Villalpando, M. E., 18–19, 250

Weaver, M. P., 6, 22–23
Weicker, Durango, 198, 211, 212
Weigand, P. C., 13, 28–29, 30, 31–32, 157, 171, 257
West Mexico: Archaic in, 83–84; copper in, 97, 139, 147; influence in Bajío region of, 40; map of, 9, 82, 108; research in, 8; relations with Tarascans of, 76–77, 106
Whalen, M. E., 236–37
Willey, G. R., 6
Wind Canyon, Texas, 152
Wind Mountain, New Mexico, 100, 146
Winters, H. D., 122, 139, 201, 204
Wolf, E., 5
World-systems model, 237

Xarácuaro, Michoacán, 65, 77, 78, 79
Xochipilli, 140
Xolotl, 205

Zacapu, Michoacán, 38, 64–65, 67
Zacatecas: chronological sequence, 40. *See also* specific site names
Zacatula, Guerrero, 72, 73
Zacualtipan, Michoacán, 78, 79
Zinaparo obsidian source, Michoacán, 64, 77, 78, 79
Zinapécuaro, Michoacán, 63, 77, 79
Zohapilco, Mexico, 132